D1030360

NATO ASI Series

Advanced Science Institutes Series

A series presenting the results of activities sponsored by the NATO Science Committee, which aims at the dissemination of advanced scientific and technological knowledge, with a view to strengthening links between scientific communities.

The Series is published by an international board of publishers in conjunction with the NATO Scientific Affairs Division.

A Life Sciences	Plenum Publishing Corporation
B Physics	London and New York
C Mathematical and Physical Sciences	Kluwer Academic Publishers
D Behavioural and Social Sciences	Dordrecht, Boston and London
E Applied Sciences	
F Computer and Systems Sciences	Springer-Verlag
G Ecological Sciences	Berlin Heidelberg New York Barcelona
H Cell Biology	Budapest Hong Kong London Milan
I Global Environmental Change	Paris Santa Clara Singapore Tokyo

Partnership Sub-Series

1. Disarmament Technologies	Kluwer Academic Publishers
2. Environment	Springer-Verlag / Kluwer Academic Publishers
3. High Technology	Kluwer Academic Publishers
4. Science and Technology Policy	Kluwer Academic Publishers
5. Computer Networking	Kluwer Academic Publishers

The Partnership Sub-Series incorporates activities undertaken in collaboration with NATO's Cooperation Partners, the countries of the CIS and Central and Eastern Europe, in Priority Areas of concern to those countries.

NATO-PCO Database

The electronic index to the NATO ASI Series provides full bibliographical references (with keywords and/or abstracts) to about 50 000 contributions from international scientists published in all sections of the NATO ASI Series. Access to the NATO-PCO Database is possible via the CD-ROM "NATO Science & Technology Disk" with user-friendly retrieval software in English, French and German (© WTV GmbH and DATAWARE Technologies Inc. 1992).

The CD-ROM can be ordered through any member of the Board of Publishers or through NATO-PCO, B-3090 Overijse, Belgium.

Series F: Computer and Systems Sciences, Vol. 164

Springer

Berlin
Heidelberg
New York
Barcelona
Budapest
Hong Kong
London
Milan
Paris
Singapore
Tokyo

Workflow Management Systems and Interoperability

Edited by

Asuman Doğaç

Software Research and Development Center
Department of Computer Engineering
Middle East Technical University
TR-06531 Ankara, Turkey

Leonid Kalinichenko

Russian Academy of Sciences
Institute for Problems of Informatics
Vavilov Street 30/6
Moscow, V-334, 117900 Russia

M. Tamer Özsu

Department of Computing Science
University of Alberta
Edmonton, Alberta, Canada T6G 2H1

Amit Sheth

Director, Distributed Information Systems Laboratories
Department of Computer Science
University of Georgia
415 Graduate Studies Research Center
Athens, GA 30602-7404, USA

Springer

Published in cooperation with NATO Scientific Affairs Division

Proceedings of the NATO Advanced Study Institute
on Workflow Management Systems (WFMS),
held in Istanbul, Turkey, August 12–21, 1997

Library of Congress Cataloging-in-Publication Data

Workflow management systems and interoperability / edited by Asuman
Dogac ... [et al.].
        p.   cm. -- (NATO ASI series. Series F, Computer and systems
sciences ; vol. 164)
    "Proceedings of the NATO Advanced Study Institute on Workflow
Management Systems (WFMS), held in Istanbul, Turkey, August 12-21,
1997"--T.p. verso.
    Includes bibliographical references and index.
    ISBN 3-540-64411-3 (alk. paper)
    1. Management information systems--Congresses. 2. Workflow-
-Management--Congresses. 3. Production management--Data processing-
-Congresses.   I. Dogac, Asuman, 1951-   . II. NATO Advanced Study
Institute on Workflow Management Systems (WFMS) (1997 : Istanbul,
Turkey) III. Series: NATO ASI series. Series F, Computer and
systems sciences ; no. 164.
T58.6.W67 1998
658.5'4--DC21   98-26399
                                                                   CIP

ACM Subject Classification (1998): H.4, J.6

ISBN 3-540-64411-3 Springer-Verlag Berlin Heidelberg New York

© Springer-Verlag Berlin Heidelberg 1998
Printed in Germany

Typesetting: Camera-ready by authors/editors
Printed on acid-free paper
SPIN: 10648795   45/3142 – 5 4 3 2 1 0

Preface

Workflow management systems (WFMS) are enjoying increasing popularity due to their ability to coordinate and streamline complex organizational processes within organizations of all sizes. Organizational processes are descriptions of an organization's activities engineered to fulfill its mission such as completing a business contract or satisfying a specific customer request. Gaining control of these processes allows an organization to reengineer and improve each process or adapt them to changing requirements. The goal of WFMSs is to manage these organizational processes and coordinate their execution.

The high degree of interest in WFMSs was demonstrated in the first half of the 1990s by a significant increase in the number of commercial products (once estimated to about 250) and the estimated market size (in combined product sales and services) of about \$2 billion in 1996. Ensuing maturity is demonstrated by consolidations during the last year. Ranging from mere e-mail based calendar tools and flow charting tools to very sophisticated integrated development environments for distributed enterprise-wide applications and systems to support programming in the large, these products are finding an eager market and opening up important research and development opportunities. In spite of their early success in the market place, however, the current generation of systems can benefit from further research and development, especially for increasingly complex and mission-critical applications.

Key deficiencies in current products include complexity in managing (installing, using, and maintain) them, limited resilience to failures and limited support for automatic recovery, lack of truly distributed architecture where the system components including the workflow engine is distributed (with resulting limitations on scalability), and lack of adequate support for the highly heterogeneous application environments where they are being deployed. Furthermore, these systems generally come up short in satisfying user expectations in areas such as data consistency, flexible worklist management and history tracking, supporting mobile users, and providing advanced security mechanisms.

A NATO Advanced Study Institute was organized to review and discuss the current state of the art and recent developments in workflow systems, in Istanbul, Turkey, during August 12–21, 1997. The ASI was organized around four major themes as follows: The first part of the ASI introduced workflow systems, presented the current state of the art as well as of the products, standards, and research. Integration of workflow systems with collaboration tools, scalable and dynamic coordination systems, and transactional support for cooperative applications were also discussed in this part. The second part of the ASI introduced the interoperability problem and presented an in-depth treatment of the subject focusing on workflow systems.

Since workflow management systems unavoidably involve heterogeneous information resources, one of the major problems they face is interoperability. In this respect a presentation provided the fundamentals of OMG's Object Management Architecture and CORBA. Interoperability in large-scale distributed information delivery systems and semantic interoperation issues along with workflow reuse were also addressed. The third part of the ASI focused on using workflows through the Internet. Today, the public Internet and corporate intranets have become the ubiquitous communication infrastructure for developing and deploying distributed services on top of heterogeneous computing platforms. In this part of the ASI, Internet-based workflow systems were presented and the opportunities provided by Internet/intranet technologies to enhance the capabilities of workflow systems were discussed. In the fourth part of the ASI some special issues, like security in workflow systems, reducing escalation costs in WFMS, and some recently developed workflow systems prototypes, were presented.

The institute brought together 80 attendees from many countries. There were 21 presentations and this book brings together the texts of these presentations. All of the papers have been edited extensively following the Institute.

We would like to express our gratitude to all the authors, who agreed to revise their contributions based on the discussions during the Institute. We would also like to mention the extraordinary work of the research assistants in Turkey, namely, Esin Gokkoca, Pinar Karagoz, Pinar Koksal, and Nesime Tatbul from the Software Research and Development Center of the Middle East Technical University in the local organization of the Institute. The final copy looks as nice as it does thanks to Pinar Koksal, Sena Arpinar, and Pinar Karagoz. Finally we would like to thank NATO, Middle East Technical University, and the Scientific and Technical Research Council of Turkey for their financial assistance.

April 1998

Asuman Doğaç
Leonid Kalinichenko
M. Tamer Özsu
Amit Sheth

Table of Contents

HP Workflow Research: Past, Present, and Future
Ming-Chien Shan, Jim Davis, Weimin Du, Ying Huang 92

Reducing Escalation-Related Costs in WFMSs
Euthimios Panagos, Michael Rabinovich 107

The Workflow Management System Panta Rhei
Johann Eder, Herbert Groiss, Walter Liebhart 129

**Enterprise-Wide Workflow Management
Based on State and Activity Charts**
Peter Muth, Dirk Wodtke, Jeanine Weissenfels, Gerhard Weikum,

Transactional Support for Cooperative Applications
Jürgen Wäsch, Karl Aberer, Erich J. Neuhold 304

Workflow Management: State of the Art Versus State of the Products

Ahmed Elmagarmid[1], Weimin Du[2]*

[1] Purdue University
   West Lafayette, IN 47907, USA
[2] Hewlett-Packard Labs.
   Palo Alto, CA 94304, USA

Abstract. It has been over ten years since the first workflow product was introduced. Despite the large number of workflow vendors and various research efforts all over the world, as well as the hype about the workflow market, workflow technology is still far from pervasive. This paper assesses the situation from a technical point of view, focusing on the development and enactment aspects of workflow processes. We discuss the current capabilities of workflow products, major issues that need to be addressed before workflow can be pervasive, as well as possible future trends and research that will help workflow succeed.

1. Introduction

1.1 Background

Computer technology has evolved to the extent that it is being used successfully in application domains such as banking, finance, and telecommunication. Such applications of computer technology have greatly increased productivity and provided better services. Despite their great success, these versions of computer applications have two major drawbacks.

First, they are monolithic in nature. All business policies and information accesses were originally hard-coded into the applications. These systems were difficult to maintain and enhance when business policies and data changed. The advance of database technology has successfully separated data accesses from the applications. As database applications, the applications are more adaptive to data changes. On the other hand, business policies are still hard-coded and any change requires modifying application code.

Second, they are isolated (i.e., stand-alone applications). The computer applications (especially those developed in old days) are usually designed and developed to work independently to solve specific problems. The advance of network and distributed computing technologies have made it possible for them to collaborate in primitive ways such as receiving and sending messages. There is, however, a great need to intergrate those isolated information and process islands at a higher level so that they can collaboratively provide business solutions that each individual application is unable to provide.

---

* The opinions presented in the chapter are those of the authors and do not represent those of Hewlett-Packard, Inc.

Workflow has been proposed to address the above problems of early computer applications. The basic idea behind the workflow technology is to separate business process and workflow management component from the existent applications to increase flexibility and maintainability. The major driving forces of workflow are two-fold: first is the need for business re-engineering whose main purpose is to increase productivity, reduce cost, and respond to the changing environment more quickly, and second is the the advent of technologies such as distributed computing, object technology, databases, etc. that facilitate open and reliable information exchange and collaboration across the organization.

The separation of business policies from applications makes (workflow-based) applications easier to maintain and enhance, because changes in procedures can be made using workflow tools without having to rewrite the application, as well as providing several other advantages. For example, as business procedures are automated, production can increase dramatically. A workflow system supports policy-driven allocation of resources and can therefore adapt dynamically to changing workloads. Since workflow processes can be understood by computers, it is also possible to develop workflow tools that track process executions and control process execution in more flexible ways. Another big advantage of workflow systems is that they simplify application development, not only because application components can be reused, but also because functions common to many applications such as recovery have already been provided by the underlying workflow management systems.

1.2 Workflow Systems

Workflow management is a diverse and rich technology and is now being applied to an ever increasing number of industries. Workflow is also a generic term which may refer to different things at different levels such as process modeling at the business process level, or process specification and enactment at the system level. In this paper, we discuss issues of process specification and enactment for various kinds of workflow systems (e.g., ad hoc, administrative, production, and collaborative workflow systems). The business perspective, such as issues of business re-engineering, process modeling, and BPR tools, will not be covered.

A workflow process, as defined in [WfMC 94b], is a coordinated (parallel and/or serial) set of process activities that are connected in order to achieve a common business goal. A process activity is defined as a logical step or description of a piece of work that contributes toward the accomplishment of a process. A process activity may be a manual process activity and/or an automated process activity. A workflow process is first specified using a process definition language and then executed by a workflow management system (WFMS). A WFMS is a system that completely defines, manages and executes workflow process through the execution of software whose order of execution is driven by a computer representation of the workflow process logic.

It has been over ten years since the first workflow product was introduced. There are now at least several dozens of workflow products available on the market with certain workflow capabilities. Workflow technology has been used in a wide range of application areas such as banking, finance, insurance, health care, telecommunication, manufacturing, and document management.

Despite all these efforts and its usefulness, workflow technology is far from pervasive in the business and industrial world. While there are many reasons for this, some major technical ones include

Infrastructure. Workflow systems are much more than just workflow engines that execute workflow processes. Successful execution of a workflow process requires proper support from the underlying infrastructure. For example, technologies such as distributed computing, object orientation, and security are necessary for the workflow engine to invoke external applications (especially legacy applications). Unfortunately, distributed computing and object technologies such as CORBA and ActiveX/DCOM have not been mature enough for real applications until recently.

Standards. The lack of standards has been one of the major obstacles to wide application of workflow technology. Unlike relational databases, each workflow vendor has its own workflow model, specification language, and API. Recent efforts by the Workflow Management Coalition (WfMC) have made significant progress, but there is still a long way to go.

Complexity. Workflow application development is a complex task involving more than simply specifying a process definition, itself a formidable task. Other and more difficult tasks include wrapping external applications to be invoked by the workflow engine, managing workflow resources, and setting up communication infrastructure. Unfortunately, current workflow systems provide little help for facilitating these tasks. Every major workflow applications require lengthy and intensive collaboration between the workflow vendors and the application developers.

Technology. Despite all the technical progress, workflow technology is still far from mature. For example, none of the existing workflow products or research prototypes can provide the same level of support as relational database management systems do for reliable and consistent process execution. It is true that many workflow applications do not need this level of support. But it is also important for the workflow management system to have the ability so that mission critical applications that are currently implemented using other technologies (e.g., database) can be re-engineered to use workflow.

There are other papers discussing the limitations of existing workflow products and outlining important research issues (see [A+ 97], [MAGK 95] and [VLP 95]). This paper focuses on technical solutions so that workflow will be more pervasive. We discuss both the current capabilities of workflow products and the major issues that need to be addressed before workflow can be successful in the market place.

2. Workflow Products

In this section, we first summarize the major features, enabling technologies, and successful applications of the current generation of workflow systems. We then describe a few industry trends that we believe are important to the next generation of workflow systems.

2.1 Current Status

Workflow systems have evolved at least three generations according to [MB 91]. The first generation of workflow systems are monolithic applications of a particular application area (e.g., image or document management). Second generation workflow systems factored out the workflow components but were still tightly coupled with the rest of the products. Third generation workflow systems have generic, open workflow engines which provide an infrastructure for robust production-oriented workflow. The workflow specification is given separately through a graphical user interface and is interpreted by the workflow engines. [VLP 95] has predicted a fourth generation of workflow systems that will be part of the middleware and will offer workflow services among other services.

2.1.1 Workflow Product Features. Workflow products of the early age (e.g., WorkFlo by FileNet) are image-based. The purpose of such systems is to automate and manage the flow of images, data, text, and other information throughout an organization. These systems are thus also data- or document-centric. The main function of a data-centric workflow process is to route the data (e.g., a design document) so that people can work on the data.

In recent years, most workflow vendors have either developed or relabeled their products as non image-based. Most of the workflow products are also process-centric (instead of data-centric) in the sense that workflow processes formalize and enforce business policies. On the other hand, there are still needs for data-centric workflow products and some vendors focus on that market segment.

In the following, we summarize major features of the current generation of workflow products that are non image-based and process-centric. Note that this is not a complete list and the listed features may also not be supported by all workflow products. Nevertheless, we believe that these features characterize the current generation of workflow products and are supported (at least partially) by most workflow products.

Graphical representation. Perhaps the most significant improvement of the current generation of workflow products over earlier generations is the ability to specify and represent workflow processes as graphical maps. In the map, major workflow steps, data and control flows, as well as other components of a workflow process are displayed graphically using icons and lines connecting icons. The idea is to provide an intelligible process view to non-programmers such as business analysts, re-engineering consultants, end-users and supervisors.

The workflow process map is now a standard component of all workflow products. But it differs significantly from vendor to vendor with respect to the information contained in the map and the way it is represented. For example, some products support only a single one-level map while others represent process maps hierarchically, i.e., that there is one main map which contains icons representing submaps. Some products manipulate workflow data explicitly on the map while others do not. The granularity of process maps is also different. For example, many products do not include specifics of the workflow activities. As noted in [S 95], process maps in most workflow products fail to describe the workflow process with sufficient clarity and completeness.

Architecture. Workflow systems, by nature, are distributed systems. Most workflow systems employ three tier client/server architecture and run on multiple platforms. There is a workflow engine which acts as a coordinator and stores meta information in the underline database. Other components of workflow systems such as the process monitor, the process starter, and the process controller are all clients of the engine. External applications that perform workflow tasks can be both geographically dispersed and on different platforms.

The workflow engines in most existing workflow systems are still centralized in the sense that the entire execution of a process is handled by a single workflow engine (or a cluster of engines that share the same data storage). It is possible in some workflow systems to start a subprocess at a different machine as a step of the containing process execution. But the subprocess execution and the containing process execution can be considered as separate process executions with little interaction except data passing at the beginning and end of the subprocess execution. No workflow systems can currently support reliable and consistent process execution collectively by more than one independent (share nothing) workflow engine.

Data model. In the WfMC workflow reference model, three kinds of workflow data have been identified: *process control data* that is manipulated by the workflow management system only; *process relevant data* that is used by both the application and workflow management system; and *application data* that is used by the workflow application only. The idea is to separate business policies (e.g., control flow and data used in flow control) from application details (e.g., data used to perform a task).

All workflow products have their data models but some of them are quite different from the WfMC model. For example, many workflow systems do not distinguish between process relevant data and application data. In these systems, workflow engines have accesses to all workflow data (including application data).

User model. A user model specifies each user's role and the role the user coordinate. The idea is to separate the concept of the logical role, which is the specification of capabilities needed to perform a task, and the concept of the physical resources, which have the capabilities to perform said task. Process designers specify roles for workflow tasks at design time. Similarly, specific resources that have the required capabilities will be assigned to the tasks at process execution time. The advantage is that the workflow process is not tied to specific resources which may change over the process lifetime.

There are still workflow products that do not distinguish between logical roles and physical resources. However, many workflow products do support this basic user model. Some even support a more complicated model that allows for the specification of a user's organization and manager, the function and processes that the user is authorized to use, and other features.

Rule capability. Almost all workflow products allow process executions that are more complicated than simple sequences. Complex flow control requires workflow products to have rule capability. Most workflow products have built-in rule engines. But the rule specification can be quite different. Some products provide script languages for rule specification while others have graphical rule editors that are easier to use.

Tools. One of the advantages of using workflow over monolithic applications is that workflow management systems include tools for process monitoring, tracking, and controlling. Most workflow products provide process development tools and some even provide animation and simulation tools.

2.1.2 Standards and Enabling Technologies. Standards and enabling technologies are important factors that must be addressed before workflow technology can be pervasive. In the past few years, significant progress has been made with respect to workflow related standards such as WfMC, MAPI-WF, and ODBC and enabling technologies such as email, CORBA, and ActiveX/DCOM.

WfMC standards. WfMC was founded in 1993 and is now considered the primary standard body for the workflow market. The standardization work of WfMC is centered around the *workflow reference model* (see Figure 1).

The reference model specifies a framework for workflow systems, identifying their characteristics, functions, and interfaces. The focus has been on

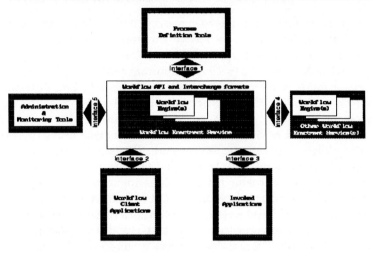

Fig. 1. WfMC workflow reference model

specifying the five APIs that surround the workflow engine. These APIs provide a standard means of communication between workflow engines and clients (including other workflow components such as process definition and monitoring tools). So far, WfMC has draft specifications for all APIs except interface 3. Most workflow vendors plan to support the WfMC APIs and some vendors have already demonstrated the WfMC APIs (e.g., for interface 2) working with their workflow engines.

Workflow interoperability and standards are vital as automation technology becomes more complex, and the Coalition's work in this industry is central to keeping up with the rapid progress. On the other hand, workflow standardization is still in its preliminary stage and has a long way to go.

MAPI workflow Framework. MAPI is a message API standard promoted by Microsoft and the MAPI workflow framework (MAPI-WF) is Microsoft's initiative to the WfMC. The idea is to combine the functionalities of workflow systems and the flexibility of messaging systems so that applications that span both messaging users and line-of-business applications can be deployed. It addresses the interoperability issue between messaging systems and workflow systems. In a message environment, a workflow request (e.g., of interface 4) can be packaged within some body part of a message. MAPI-WF provides a standard set of body parts and properties so that workflow packages can be delivered to and from the workflow engine. Workflow components (e.g., workflow engines, workflow applications, and workflow tools) that conform to MAPI-WF can communicate via messaging systems such as Microsoft Exchange.

Given the popularity of messaging systems and the influence of Microsoft, MAPI-WF will play an important role. Many workflow vendors have already expressed their intentions to support MAPI-WF in their workflow products. To the best of our knowledge, however, no vendors have actually demonstrated it in their products.

Enabling Technologies. The two most important enabling technologies for workflow systems in recent years are object technology and distributed computing technology. Unlike other software systems such as database management systems, by nature workflow systems are distributed and open. To perform a workflow task, the workflow engine needs to invoke remote workflow applications. Object and distributed computing technologies such as CORBA and ActiveX/DCOM are very useful in wrapping, managing, and invoking heterogeneous applications.

Several workflow products have used CORBA and ActiveX/DCOM as transport services to invoke remote applications. There is also research (see, e.g., [D+ 97]) investigating a CORBA-based workflow enactment system which supports a scalable software architecture, multi-database access, and an error detection and recovery framework.

2.2 Industry Trends

Workflow is a young rapidly changing area with existing workflow products evolving with new features and new products being introduced almost daily. It is still not clear what the next generation of workflow products will be. In the following subsections, we list some industry trends that are both important and general enough that they may be adopted by most workflow vendors. In the next section, we discuss some more advanced issues that are also important but are either not mature enough or general enough to that their adoption by workflow vendors in the near future is likely.

2.2.1 Open and Extensible Interfaces.

As mentioned, workflow systems are distributed and open by nature. The organizations that will use workflow systems already have computer networks, applications (e.g., spreadsheets), data (stored in files, databases, etc.), and other information. To be useful, a workflow management system must fit into the organization's existing computing environments.

Most existing workflow products include application programming interfaces. External applications can be integrated with the workflow system, and external data can be used for workflow process execution via, e.g., application data handlers. To be a really open workflow system, extensible interfaces needed for incorporating other existing resources and information that are needed in workflow process execution.

For example, events are one of the major means by which workflow processes interact with each other and with the external environment. A telecommunication network management process must be able to react to alarms generated by the managed telecommunication network and generate events to effect changes in the network. Although most workflow products still don't support events (especially external events that interact with external environments), some workflow systems do. Research projects that address this issue also exist.

Another example that requires extensible interfaces is the integration of existing corporate directories. Information about users and the corporate hierarchy is necessary for assigning resources to perform workflow tasks. Requiring users to register themselves to the workflow system as some products do is clearly not the best way. A more flexible method is to provide interfaces to integrate existing corporate directories into the workflow engine. This not only saves workflow application development time, but also makes later maintenance easier and avoids possible inconsistencies.

Some workflow products with extensible interfaces for integration of existing resource management systems already exist. In near future more products will incorporate the interface as this is a feature greatly appreciated by workflow application developers.

2.2.2 Process Development Environments. The development of workflow applications is generally difficult, due to their complexity. Current workflow products address this problem by providing graphical user interfaces for process design and management. GUI tools, however, only address one aspect of the problem which is relatively easy to deal with: specifying process templates. A harder problem is to integrate the workflow process with the computing environment. This is difficult because of the heterogeneity and complexity of the computing environments. To make things worse, most workflow vendors designed and marketed their products as generic tools trying to cover all application areas.

We believe that workflow will not become pervasive until the complexity of developing workflow applications can be significantly reduced. One way of doing that is to provide a good development environment. A good environment must be domain-specific to provide commonly used process templates, commonly used data forms, tools to wrap and manage commonly used applications, basic communication infrastructure, etc. Currently, there are special-purpose workflow products available on the market for specific domains. For example, Araxsys has products specifically targeting the healthcare market (see, e.g., [Arax 97]) and Ariba's products focus on operating resource management (see, e.g., [Ari 97]).

For the general-purpose workflow products, it is possible to develop special packages based on the general-purpose workflow engine. For example, FileNet has introduced VisualFlo/Payable for account payables. HP has introduced AdminFlow for business administration. Future such packages will be expected to cover application domains such as telecommunications, banking, and finance.

As mentioned before, an important aspect of a workflow process development environment is to wrap external applications to be used by workflow processes. The wrapped applications can be packaged into a library and then reused by workflow processes. Workflow process development can be further simplified if workflow activities can be reused. Workflow activities include more than just external applications to be invoked. Other information include: logical role specification that maps to the specific external application; data needed to perform the task; communication mechanisms; consistency and deadline specification, etc. Unfortunately, most workflow products do not support this level of reuse, as workflow activities contain process-specific information (e.g., position in the process) that cannot be reused. It is thus necessary to separate process-specific and process-independent parts of workflow activities. For example, HP's workflow product distinguishes between the two parts and allows the reuse of the process-independent parts of workflow activities. This allows a special-purpose workflow environment such as AdminFlow to be easily developed based on the general-purpose workflow engine.

2.2.3 Wide Area Workflow. The current generation of workflow products has been criticized for rigid process models, narrow application focus, and platform restrictions (see, e.g., [Delphi 97b]). These workflow products best service applications where business rules, process flows, and work participants are known in advance and rarely change. The advent of wide area networks and the World Wide Web has provided new opportunities for workflow. Most workflow vendors have provided web interfaces to their workflow products. There are also research projects trying to develop workflows on the web (see, e.g., [MPSK 97]).

As predicted in [Delphi 97b], one possible change for workflow technology is users' environments where workflow tasks are performed. Workflow users will have universal access available to them via open interfaces such as email, telephone, fax, pager, Web, and intranets/extranets to perform workflow tasks. The key is to separate workflow processes from the user environment so that changes on one side will not affect the other. The major difference between traditional and wide area workflows is that workflow users have control over what kind of information they receive and how they receive it. The advantage is faster response time and greater productivity by providing multiple access points to the same information and allowing users to use tools of their choice.

3. Workflow Research

Workflow is an active research area with research efforts occurring both in the academia and industry ([VLP 95] and [MAGK 95]). However, workflow research, especially that from academia, has made little impact on workflow products. There are two reasons for this situation. First, early workflow systems, having evolved from different areas such as office automation systems, job control systems, and document management systems, have struggled to define basic models, architectures, and functionalities, while workflow researchers, most with strong database backgrounds, have focused on introducing advanced database techniques to workflow systems. In addition to this, workflow vendors have not been very successful in applying workflow technology to applications that require advanced database features such as ACID transactions. Workflow researchers have also failed to develop techniques that are flexible enough for workflow systems.

Nevertheless, we believe that on-going research can address issues that are very important in making workflow pervasive. Our experience with customers shows that there are many workflow applications that require some level of transaction support. The requirements, however, are very different from those in database systems. As a result, not only do existing database techniques need to be adapted to fit into the workflow environment, but new techniques also need to be developed to address issues unique to workflow systems.

In the following section, we discuss some of the important research issues. We will emphasize differences between the database and workflow environments. Note that this is not a complete list of workflow research issues. The purpose here is to inspire research in these and other related areas.

3.1 Transactional Workflow

The concept of transactions was first introduced for database applications in [G 81]. A transaction is an execution unit with ACID properties: it maps a database from one consistent state to another (*consistency*); either all or none of its effects take place (*atomicity*); and the effects are made permanent once committed (*durability*). Multiple transactions may be executed concurrently, but the overall effect must be equivalent to some sequential execution (*isolation* or *serializability*).

Workflow models that support certain transactional properties have been viewed by many researchers as extensions to the relaxed transaction models (see, e.g., [SR 93], [CD 96], [GH 94], [TV 95b], [EL 95], [Ley 95], [Alo 96] and [KR 96]). It has been proven both possible and very useful to incorporate transactional semantics such as recovery, atomicity and isolation to ensure correct and reliable workflow executions (see, e.g., [J+ 96]). Database techniques have been adopted to provide transactional properties for workflow processes. For example, failure atomicity is ensured via both forward recovery (see, e.g., [EL 96]) and backward recovery (see, e.g., [Ley 95] and [DDSD 97]). Execution atomicity can also be ensured by specifying consistency units (or execution atomic units) of workflow processes and coordinating their executions to ensure M-serializability ([B+ 93], [RS 94] and [TV 95b]).

On the other hand, a workflow process is fundamentally different from a database transaction as discussed in [WS 97]. First, a workflow environment is more complicated than a database and involves heterogeneous and distributed components, as well as human interactions. Second, a workflow process is structurally more complex than a database transaction, and the execution of a process may establish quite complex control and data flow dependencies among the activities of the process. A workflow process specification may include conditional branching, concurrent execution of activities, loops, and other complex control structures.

Database recovery techniques such as logging have been successfully adopted in workflow systems. There are workflow products that support reliable workflow process executions. Ensuring atomic and consistent process execution, however, is still missing from workflow products and remains an open research issue. In this subsection, we discuss new issues in workflow compensation and concurrency control as the result of the above differences between the database and workflow environments.

3.1.1 Compensation.
Compensation has been used to simulate the transactional properties for long-running database applications that would be too expensive to be implemented as single ACID transactions (see, e.g., [GMS 87]). The idea was to implement such an application as a *saga* or sequence of ACID transactions so that resources needed only at a particular stage could be released after the corresponding transaction completes. Atomicity was simulated by compensating already completed transactions in reverse order.

In workflow systems, compensation is used to deal with process activity failures. When a process activity instance fails, the workflow management system is responsible for bringing the process execution to a designated *save point*, which is a previous execution step of the process. The save point represents an acceptable intermediate state of process execution and also a decision point where certain actions can be taken to fix the problem that caused the failure or choose an alternative execution path to avoid the problem. To roll back workflow process execution, compensation activities will be invoked to undo the effects of the completed activities.

Compensation is more complicated (and thus interesting) in workflow systems than in database systems for two reasons. First, compensation specification (i.e., when, what, and how to compensate) is more difficult, due to the complexity of workflow processes and activities. The compensation activity can be as complicated as (or even more complicated than) the original activity that needs to be compensated. Second, optimization of compensation processes (i.e., what activities don't need compensation) is important. Unlike database transactions which can be compensated and re-executed easily and efficiently, workflow compensation can be very costly. Therefore it is very important to avoid unnecessary compensation as much as possible.

Existing research on the issue has focused on the static specification of compensation scopes. For example, [Ley 95] discussed an enhancement to IBM FlowMark which allows the process designers to specify spheres of compensation to determine the scope and extent of compensation in case of activity failures. The failure of an activity may cause the compensation of just the failed activity, the entire containing sphere, or the containing sphere and other dependent spheres. A similar approach has also been proposed in

[CD 97] for hierarchical workflow processes. The compensation scope is determined in a bottom-up fashion: first to the designated save point in the transaction containing the failed activity, then to the designated save point of the higher level containing the transaction if the current level transaction can not handle the failure.

An interesting issue is how to make use of run time information in order to further avoid unnecessary compensation. As we mentioned, the purpose of compensation is to undo that which caused the failure so that the execution can resume. Thus, a workflow activity needs compensation if it contributes to the failure, and/or its re-execution is different from the original execution. Compensation scopes specify the activities that *might* affect the failed activities in some execution environments. However it is possible that an activity in a statically specified compensation scope did not contribute to a particular failure. For example, an activity a_1 affects a subsequent activity a_2 if another concurrent activity a_3 occurred before a_1. There is no need to compensate a_1 if a_2 failed before a_3 has started. This information, however, will only be available at run time. Identifying unnecessary compensation and avoiding it at run time is difficult because other nodes may be affected. But in many cases it is worth the effort because compensation and re-execution of workflow activities can be very expensive. [DDSD 97] presented some preliminary results along this line of research.

In general, we assume some kind of static relationship between the original execution and its compensation. For example, the same compensation strategy will be used for a workflow activity independent of the cause of failures. A compensation activity is defined for each activity or a group of activities that need compensation. This, however, may not be true in real life. There can be many different ways to recover a failed execution according to the cause of the failure, and the compensation process can be structurally independent of the original execution. Little research has been done in the area.

The most fundamental issue of compensation is, perhaps, the correct criteria for workflow process execution and compensation. In database systems, a compensation is correct if everything between the save point and the failure point is compensated and in the exact reverse order of the original execution. In workflow systems, we need a more relaxed criterion for optimization purposes. For example, the order requirement could be relaxed for compensations that are commutable. A good understanding of correct compensation is essential to efficient workflow compensation and may even be application-dependent.

3.1.2 Concurrency Control. Concurrency control is a classical technique in databases which ensures execution isolation of a transaction from other conflicting transactions. Although concurrency control has been considered either unnecessary or too costly for many workflow applications, it can be very important for some workflow applications where mission-critical operation requires a consistent view of the execution environment (see, e.g., [J$^+$ 96]).

The problem of concurrency control in workflow systems is, however, a little bit different from that in database systems. The purpose of concurrency control in database systems is to ensure execution isolation of database transactions which consist entirely of atomic read/write operations that are visible to the DBMS. In workflow systems, the WFMS ensures the execution isolation of workflow activities which consist of atomic read/write operations as well as external executions that are invisible to the WFMS. The WFMS is responsible for the consistency of the overall execution environment which includes both the internal database that is visible to the WFMS and the external systems which are invisible to the WFMS, as well as their cross consistency.

The fundamental issue of concurrency control in workflow systems is correctness criteria. Serializability, as used for database transactions, is too strict for most workflow applications. The main reason for this is that workflow activities are generally long-duration. It is unacceptable in many workflow applications to schedule conflicting activities sequentially as for read/write operations in database transactions. Relaxed correctness criteria (which might be application domain-specific) are essential in specifying and enforcing the correct workflow process executions. [KR 96] discussed some of the existing research on the subject.

Some existing research addresses the problem by specifying and enforcing data and execution dependencies among workflow activities (see, e.g., [Att 93], [TV 95a] and [GH 94]).
There is also research that adopts database techniques, but allows flexible specification of consistency requirements with respect to scope and granularity. For example, [TV 95a] allows for grouping a collection of workflow activities of a workflow process into a consistency unit and uses traditional concurrency control to ensure isolation of consistency units (in terms of serializability). Correct execution of activities inside a consistency unit is ensured by enforcing the proper data and execution dependencies.

3.2 Distributed Workflow Execution

Workflow systems are, by nature, are distributed systems. First, external applications that perform workflow tasks are often geographically dispersed. The workflow management system itself can also be distributed. The most common form of distributed WFMS is function distribution. In such a system, different workflow components that perform various workflow functions such as process definition, process execution, process monitoring, and resource assignment run at different sites. WFMS components interact with each other via messages or remote procedure calls. Another form of distribution is to perform a workflow function with multiple functionally equivalent WFMS components that share common storage (see, e.g., [KAGM 96]). For example, the execution of a workflow process can be collectively performed by several workflow engines sharing the same data storage for process definitions and execution states. Such a system provides better scalability and is resilient to workflow engine failure, but is still vulnerable to data storage failure.

The most difficult form of distribution is to have multiple independent WFMSs (sharing no common data storage) collectively execute a workflow process. In such a distributed system, each WFMS is itself a complete workflow system with its own engine and data storage. There is no centralized server keeping all the information about a process execution. Such a system may be preferred for performance or reliability reasons. The system is more efficient because workflow activities can be executed by the WFMSs that are close to the corresponding external applications (thus reducing communication cost between the WFMSs and applications) and because the WFMSs access process definitions and execution states locally (thus reducing communication cost between the WFMSs and the data storage). It is also more reliable because the failure of one or more WFMSs (including the corresponding data storage) does not stop workflow process executions. The overall system is functional as long as one of the WFMSs is still running.

There are two issues that are key when implementing such a distributed workflow system: data replication and execution coordination. Data replication is necessary to ensure reliable process execution. For example, the process execution can survive a single WFMS failure if the process definitions and execution states are replicated at more than one independent (e.g., primary and backup) WFMSs. Data replication (especially that of process execution states), however, can be very costly. Data replication can be provided by the WFMSs, or the underlying systems. The advantage of the workflow system level replication is flexibility. For example, workflow processes can be executed at different levels of reliability from no replication (efficient but vulnerable to single WFMS failure) to full replication (expensive but resilient to single WFMS failure).

Execution coordination is needed when more than one WFMS collectively execute a workflow process. For example, execution of a workflow activity by one WFMS may cause the entire process execution to be suspended, affecting all other WFMSs. The key is to transfer process information to a site when it is needed and in the right order. Static information such as process definitions can be replicated at all relevant sites, but run time information such as process instance states has to be transferred at run time from site to site. This can be done in two ways: by circulating all information pertaining to a process and its execution across different sites, or pre-compiling the process definition to determine at which sites the different activities are to be executed (see, e.g., [MAGK 95]). The advantage of the former approach is flexibility in the sense that the WFMS can choose to execute a workflow activity at any site according to the run time execution environment. The disadvantage is possible high communication cost, as the information package can be very large. The latter approach, on the contrary, can be efficiently implemented, because only relevant information is transferred to the site, but is inflexible. For example, if a workflow activity is pre-assigned to a site which is not accessible at the time, other sites cannot take over the execution as they do not have the information. Another problem with this approach is that most workflow products assign resources to a workflow activity at run time. The site that is pre-assigned to execute a workflow activity at process specification time can be far away from the resources (e.g., computer applications) to be invoked.

Concurrency control and compensation may also be complicated when the WFMS is distributed. For example, executions of conflicting activities at different sites have to be coordinated to ensure the consistency of the overall execution. Locking is generally not acceptable as workflow activities are often long running. Serializability, on the other hand, may not be needed for the execution. New correctness criteria and coordination algorithms need to be developed to ensure correct and efficient process execution.

3.3 Dynamic Workflow

One of the common assumptions made by most workflow research is the availability of pre-specified workflow definitions. Although there is research or even workflow products which allows for the modification of process definition at run time (see, e.g., [CCPP 96b]), it is still considered to be rare and costly.

Dynamic workflow systems are special workflow systems that have no pre-specified process specifications. They start with some initial activities. When an activity has completed, new activities will be selected according to the execution status and results of the current activity. In other words, the workflow is specified and executed at the same time, which is different from dynamic modifications of pre-specified workflow definitions.

Dynamic workflow systems are suitable for workflow applications where process specifications are frequently modified or cannot be pre-specified. For example, most product designs do not follow a strict process. They start with initial tasks (e.g., collecting requirements) and follow the general guidelines. Different tasks are performed in different orders according to the status of the design.

Dynamic workflow requires revisiting most of the research issues discussed before (as well as issues not mentioned in this paper). For example, specification of the consistency requirements will be different, due to the lack of the whole picture of the processes. For the same reason, coordination (especially in distributed environments) of activity executions would be difficult. There has been very little research regarding dynamic workflow. Recently, some research efforts have tried to implement dynamic workflow systems using mobile agents. But such efforts are still in their early stages and have not addressed the aforementioned issues.

4. Conclusions

As a solution to address many shortcomings of monolithic computer applications, workflow management systems have attracted interest from both industry and academia. While there is a high demand for workflow systems for all kinds of computer applications, workflow in general is far from pervasive. This paper tries to understand the situation from a technical point of view, focusing on the specification and enactment of workflow processes.

Based on our knowledge and experience, we believe that the following factors have all contributed to the current situation: (1) unavailability of proper infrastructure; (2) lack of standards; (3) complexity of workflow process development; and (4) immaturity of workflow technologies. Despite all the problems, great progress has been made in the last few years with respect to infrastructure, standards, and technologies. In this paper, we discuss both state of the products and state of the art of workflow management systems. The purpose of this paper is to inspire further research and development in some workflow areas that are important or essential to the pervasive of workflow systems.

Acknowledgements

We would like to thank Mary Loomis for her help and support in this writing and for her carefully reviewing the paper which greatly improves the quality and presentation. Thanks also to other members of the OpenPM team, Jim Davis, Ying Huang, and Ming-Chien Shan, for many fruitful discussions.

A Distributed Workflow and Product Data Management Application for the Construction of Large Scale Scientific Apparatus

R. McClatchey[1], J-M. Le Goff[2], N. Baker[1], W. Harris[1], Z. Kovacs[1]

[1] Dept. of Computing, Univ. West of England, Frenchay, Bristol BS16 1QY UK
   Phone: (+44) 1179 656261 ext. 3163 FAX: (44) 1179 763860
   Email: Richard.McClatchey@csm.uwe.ac.uk

[2] PPE/CMA Division, CERN, Geneva, 1211 Switzerland
   Phone: (+41) 22 767 6559 FAX: (+41) 22 767 8750
   Email: Jean-Marie.Le.Goff@cern.ch

Abstract. Recently there has been much discussion about workflow management for computer-based systems. Workflow management allows business managers to co-ordinate and schedule activities of organisations to optimise the flow of information or operations between the resources of the organisation. Scientific and engineering applications are also being viewed as potential areas in which the principles of workflow management can be applied. Scientific applications, however, present particular problems of workflow management. Not only do the workflow definitions change frequently [VWW96, ER95] but their refinement may only take place as a result of experimentation as the workflow process itself is followed. For these reasons and others commercial workflow management systems appear to be inadequate for the purposes of managing scientific workflow management applications.

The construction of large scale scientific and engineering systems necessitates the use of complex production management operations. The coordination of these operations can be difficult, particularly if the operations are distributed over many geographically separated institutes. In these environments there can be severe constraints both of time and budget so that controlled management of the inherent workflow processes becomes paramount. One example of this scientific development process is the construction of high precision scientific apparatus for high energy physics such as the Compact Muon Solenoid experiment [CMS95] (CMS) currently being undertaken for CERN, the European Centre for Particle Physics research. The construction of CMS is long scale (1998-2004), heavily constrained by resource availability and allocation and very state-of-the-art in nature. A research and development project, entitled CRISTAL (Cooperating Repositories and an Information System for Tracking Assembly Lifecycles) [LeG96], has been initiated to facilitate the management of the engineering data collected at each stage of production of CMS components. This paper reports on the aspects of scientific workflow management and product data management and the interface between the two which have been identified as being central to the assembly and production of the CMS detector.

1. Introduction

The Compact Muon Solenoid (CMS) high energy physics experiment [CMS95] will comprise several very large high resolution detectors for fundamental nuclear particles. Each detector will be constructed out of well over a million precision parts and will be produced and assembled during the next decade by specialised centres distributed world-wide. Each constituent part of each detector must be accurately measured and tested locally prior to its ultimate assembly and integration in the experimental area at CERN. Performance, resolution and other physical characteristics such as temperature dependence and radiation hardness will be carefully studied for each detector part. Much of the information collected during this phase will be needed not only to construct the detector, but for its calibration, to facilitate accurate simulation of its performance and to assist in its lifetime maintenance. During assembly, matching of detecting elements with electronics will be required to optimise physics performance, these tasks will be rather complex especially considering production is distributed world-wide.

The CRISTAL [LeG96] system is a prototype being developed in the first instance to monitor and control the production and assembly process of 110,000 lead tungstate ($PbWO_4$) mono-crystals, and their associated fast electronics, to be installed in the CMS Electromagnetic Calorimeter (ECAL). The software will be generic in design and hence reusable for other CMS detector groups. CRISTAL employs workflow and task management techniques to provide an infrastructure for work process tasks to cooperate and coordinate.

This paper discusses the distributed computing problems and design issues posed by this project. The overall software design architecture is described together with the main technological aspects of linking distributed object oriented databases via CORBA with WWW/Java-based query processing. The paper then concentrates on the design of the workflow management system of CRISTAL. The Petri-Net notation is described which is used to model the order of task (human and computer system) processing and synchronisation. These Petri-Net production schemes, are translated into executable code. Frequent rescheduling and/or redirection in the flow of work between production centres means that dynamic workflow schema evolution must be supported together with full event histories (i.e. audit trails of workflow activity). This paper discusses these distributed co-operation problems and the solutions adopted and concludes with experiences and insights gained so far in CRISTAL.

2. Background

The first phase of the CRISTAL project is concerned with the production and tracking of the $PbWO_4$ mono-crystals and their fast electronics to be installed in the CMS ECAL detector. Because of the number of crystals involved and the very high standard to which each must be grown there will be a number of Production Centres located in Russia, China, and the Czech Republic. Assembly of the crystals with their Avalanche Photo-Diodes (APDs) and associated electronics and mountings will take place in so called Regional

Centres located in Italy, UK, Russia and at CERN which will also act as the coordinator centre. The total time needed for the production of the crystals will be of the order of 5 to 6 years and will commence in 1998.

Each of the crystals will have their physical characteristics individually measured and recorded to facilitate calibration and to ensure consistency of the production process. Since the overall costs and timescales of crystal production must be strictly controlled, the efficiency of the production process is paramount. It therefore follows that quality control must be rigidly enforced at each step in the fabrication process.

The CRISTAL system must support the testing of detector parts, the archival of accumulated information, controlled access to data and the on-line control and monitoring of all Production and Regional Centres. The Crystal Detector is just one detector in the CMS experiment and the CMS experiment itself is just one of four to be used with the Large Hadron Collider (LHC) accelerator [LHC93]. A Product Data Management system (referred to at CERN as an Engineering Data Management System or EDMS) will be used to manage, store and control all the information relevant for the conception, construction and exploitation of the LHC accelerator and experiments during their whole life cycle estimated to be more than 20 years.

EDMS will define these systems in terms of product breakdown structures, assembly breakdown structures and manufacturing work breakdown structures. All the engineering drawings, blueprints, construction procedures, part definitions and part nominal values will be stored in EDMS. CRISTAL is consequently a production management and workflow management facility that controls and tracks parts through the manufacturing life cycle up to the final construction and assembly of the crystal detector. The relationship between CRISTAL and EDMS is shown in Figure 2.1.

The CRISTAL system must also provide the "as built" view to information stored during the manufacturing process and must be capable of providing rudimentary support for other views of the production data. Future groups and systems may well require a:

- Calibration Viewpoint. Where physicists will want to view and access part characteristic data for experiment calibration and event reconstruction purposes.
- Maintenance Viewpoint. Where engineers will refer to the production processes for assembly and disassembly procedures, update information collected through maintenance operations and design modifications throughout the experiments lifetime.
- Experiment Systems Management Viewpoint. Where the operations and management (so-called "slow control") system can view the part production history for configuration and fault management purposes.

In summary the CRISTAL project aims to implement a prototype distributed engineering information management and control system which will

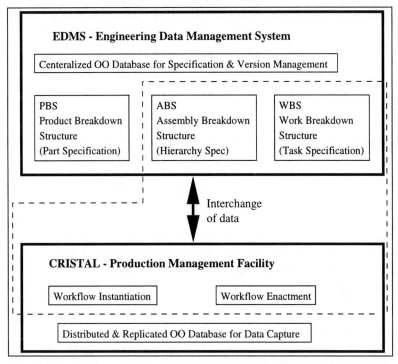

Fig. 1. The relationship between CRISTAL and EDMS (a PDM). (The dotted lines represent the limit of a typical workflow management system)

control the production process of the crystal detector and provide secure access to calibration and production data. The specific objectives are to:

- design and build a distributed information management system to control and monitor crystal production across all centres
- capture and store crystal calibration data during detector production
- provide detector construction with quality control and assembly optimization data
- integrate instruments used to characterise parts
- provide controlled, multi-user access to the production management system
- provide access to engineering and calibration data for CMS users

3. General Architecture and Design

Management information regarding the definition, configuration, version, performance and operational state of the distributed CRISTAL production line is stored in a central repository. This object based central repository also stores the definitions of all the parts that make up the detector together with the definitions of the instruments used to produce parts or take measurements of parts. It also stores descriptions of the life-cycle of each part (its production scheme) and descriptions of the tasks and activities performed on the part.

Each physical part is allocated a unique identifier (bar code) when it is produced. The unique identifier is used as a reference to an object description of the part in the central repository. The part object not only stores the current state and characteristics of the physical part but holds a reference to its current position in the production scheme and a reference to its possible future production flows. A part identifier is therefore used by a production operator to recall its life history and to provide navigational assistance as to the next possible sequence of tasks that could be executed.

This production scheme (or sequence of tasks) determines the order of tasks that can be applied to a part. Each type of part has a different production scheme. The human operator can trigger the execution of a task. The task execution script will run and (via the console) will prompt the operator to perform a number of manual operations, such as cleaning the part, or it may automatically trigger networked instruments to take measurements of the physical characteristics of the part. All the details of the task operations and the associated measurements and instruments involved are eventually stored in the central repository.

A part can be defined as a collection of parts, a necessary condition as the detector is gradually assembled. Over time the part and task definitions will evolve as a result of knowledge that emerges during detector testing and construction. A major critical design requirement is that the work flow management system of CRISTAL should follow and guide the environment instead of imposing constraints on the users. The analysis and design team has spent an exhaustive amount of time attempting to capture user requirements. These requirements have been published in a User Requirements Document which conforms to the PSS-05 Software Engineering Standards [ESA91] defined by the European Space Agency. The CRISTAL project follows this standard throughout the software life cycle.

The data handling and storage aspects of CRISTAL must be transparent to any of the users of the system irrespective of where they are located. Part, task, production scheme and system configuration data will be defined by the Coordinator at the CERN central site. The configuration and management of all the centres is controlled by the CERN central site. Once the production centres are registered and configured, parts will be produced and then shipped to further centres for testing and assembly.

Figure 3.1 illustrates the general organisation of a local centre. The Desktop Control Panel (DCP) is $Java^{TM}$ code which is executed from $Netscape^{TM}$ or a $Java^{TM}$ interpreter and provides the user interface to CRISTAL sessions for users. There is one session for each connected user. The session processes all queries and provides a viewpoint on the data according to the users role.

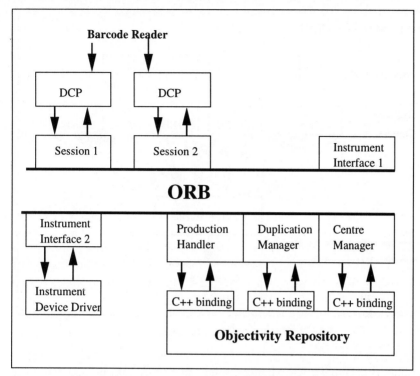

Fig. 2. The Local Centre Software Components

There are a number of local centre roles; Centre Supervisor, Operator and Information Systems Manager. By using a barcode reader on a part the Operators are guided via the DCP through the possible production task sequences that the part can take. All users can browse part characteristics and navigate through production schemes while Centre coordinators can modify local production schemes and tasks. The local production handler software component:

- manages local database access
- manages the production processing which includes:-
    optimising part information retrieval
    launching part production scheme
    instances launching workflow tasks
    updating part information
    updating part history
    enabling/disabling part
    production
- applies new version of the local production scheme

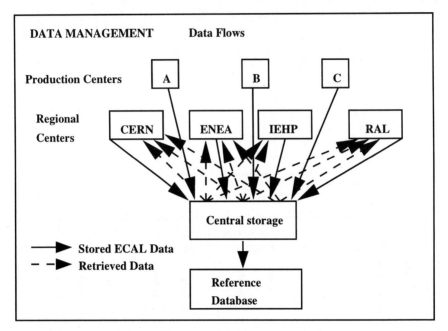

Fig. 3. The flow of data between Centres

- notifies the Duplication Manager when new part information has been stored

Each instrument in the Centre has an Instrument Interface through which it can receive measurement commands from the User via the Production Handler. The Instrument Interface communication protocol is ASCII based and is implemented either using CORBA or using a sockets interface driver depending on the instrument's computing capabilities. The measurements from the instrument are converted by the Instrument Interface from ASCII into an object based format that the Production Handler can use to store in the object Repository.

As the physical parts migrate across Europe and Asia through the production, testing and assembly life cycle so quick access will be required to the part objects which define the state of the part and hold references to its history and measured characteristics. The strategy being adopted is to only store those part objects in a Local Centre Repository which are directly related to physical parts held locally and to maintain a regularly updated centralised database at the CERN Central Centre. This data distribution strategy is detailed in the next section of this paper.

Figure 3.2 illustrates the data flows between centres. Eventually as the detector assembly nears completion the object based CERN central storage will become fully populated capturing the manufacturing and production process. Once the detector is up and running it is crucial for event recognition programs to have access to detector characteristics in order for nuclear physics event reconstruction and calibration to take place. This physical data collected during the detector assembly phase, a subset of the data contained in the central storage database, must be arranged and processed in order to populate the calibration database also known as the Reference Database.

4. Data Distribution Philosophy

The data handling and storage aspects of CRISTAL must be transparent to any users of CRISTAL wherever they are located. The main objective of the CRISTAL database system should be to provide maximum data availability with minimum local data storage. Part, task and production scheme data will be defined by the Coordinator at the central site (CERN) and captured in the central database. The Coordinator will determine when those definitions become active in the other centres and the CRISTAL software will distribute these definitions from the central site to outlying databases; thereafter the CRISTAL software will populate the new structures in those centres.

Data will be collected at each centre during the production/testing/ assembly lifecycle and will reside at the centre for as long as the part resides at that centre. Data collected locally will be duplicated in the central CRISTAL system for security, for access from other centres and to act as input to the final Reference Database (see figure 3.2.) An object duplication strategy is required in CRISTAL to provide transparent access to part definitions and characteristics across centres. Since the projected final amount of data in CRISTAL is of the order of 1 TeraByte, a fully replicated database approach with 10 centres (and therefore 10 TeraBytes of data) is not technically or economically feasible.

Dividing the database into autonomous *partitions*, each partition managing and controlling its own data and resources, allows concurrent access to information across the networks and reduces the impact of network failures. Availability of information, in the presence of failures, is achieved by replicating system resources such as hardware, software and data. This controlled replication eliminates any single point of failure in the distributed database. Data integrity is thereafter maintained through parallel synchronous updates. The Objectivity/Fault Tolerance^{TM} database option allows creation of a widely distributed database environment. Using this, the CRISTAL database is divided into autonomous groups, or partitions, which are distributed across multiple platforms with access provided by local or wide area networks. An autonomous partition can continue to work independently of the availability of other autonomous partitions. Furthermore the Objectivity/Data Replication^{TM} database option allows replication of the database across multiple partitions. This replication mechanism again relies on parallel synchronous updates.

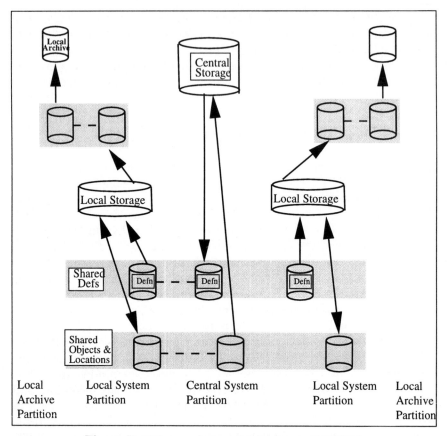

Fig. 4. Partitions and data distribution in CRISTAL

The CRISTAL database system has been built using Objectivity^{TM} and has the following set-up. Each local centre is equipped with two autonomous partitions. One partition holds the local data and definitions and the other holds the local archive database (see figure 4.1). The central system (at CERN) will have only one partition for the central database and associated definitions. The local centres store part information in the local base relevant for the parts currently located at that centre. If a part is to be shipped out to another centre for testing or assembly, the local archive base and the central database are updated to reflect new information and the part information is deleted from the local base. The central system's base always holds a complete record of all current part information.

Objects in the systems are named. The object name serves as the access point to the actual object and its OID. Given an object name, a mechanism is implemented which is responsible for mapping this object name to its OID and opening that object, regardless of where it resides in the system. To access an object in a multi-partition set-up, the partition, the database and the container of that object are required to open the object. To provide the appropriate handle, the class type is also needed. A hash table of locations is therefore maintained to hold the object name, its location and its class. A single database is dedicated to this hash table of data locations and this database is replicated across all the data partitions. Likewise, a hash table of locations is maintained within each centre and shared between the two autonomous partitions under that centre to facilitate archival. This archive hash table holds locations of objects stored in the archive base.

As parts are moved from one centre to another, the hash table of locations is updated to reflect the new location. This update is visible to all users as the hash table of locations is replicated across the local system partitions. The archive base and the archive hash table of locations are also updated. This scheme allows a user to query the location of all parts in the CRISTAL system irrespective of their location without having to maintain many duplicates of the same data at each centre.

5. Workflow Management in CRISTAL

A workflow management system (WFMS) [WFMC96, GHS95] is a system that completely defines, manages and executes workflows through the execution of software whose order of execution is driven by a computer representation of the workflow logic. Workflows are collections of human and machine based activities (tasks) that must be coordinated in order that groups of people can carry out their work. In CRISTAL it is the workflow system that "glues" together the different organisations, operators, processes, data and centres into a single coordinated managed production line. In general there are essentially two types of workflow that can be identified, coordination-based and production-based. coordination based workflows are evolving workflows defined to support knowledge workers and are suited to applications which involve developing a strategic plan and responding quickly to requests and most often use artificial intelligence techniques. Production-based workflow is a more structured, predefined process that is governed by policy and procedure. Areas in which this type of workflow is applicable is configuration management, purchase order processing, document routing and product life cycle management in systems manufacturing. From the viewpoint of the Coordinator, CRISTAL is a production-based workflow management system in that it keeps track of and coordinates the activity of the production of the crystal detector. From the physicists point of view the CRISTAL system stores and manages large volumes of scientific data and provides tools to search, retrieve and analyse it. Because of the scientific nature of the application CRISTAL has the following particular characteristics that distinguish it form other production work flow management systems:-

– once off production rather than a repetitive production line
– manages large quantities of complex structured physics data
– long production time scales with very long transactions
– workflow specifications will not be fully known even at production start
– workflow specifications will change during production
– very distributed system

The nature and construction of CMS means that not only will the result be just one product but that this product must be complete and correct at a fixed point in time. Because of the length of time and cost of the activities in the production and assembly of the parts the production process has been distributed across many centres in different countries. This reduces the central cost and increases the production through concurrency. However the production process must continue to run even when the connection to the CERN central system is lost. This means that we have had to design the workflow management engine to run at each local centre and to synchronise its activities with the central system when it can.

Although the detector can be considered a product, from a physicists point of view it is the building of an experiment. Therefore the measurements and data taken in the production process is crucial to the analysis of the results when the experiment is assembled and run. Traditional scientific applications that involve large amounts of data have focused on the database management side of the experimental data. It is the concentration on the management and coordination of the process and the context in which the scientific data is obtained that makes the CRISTAL system different from other workflow systems. The ideas used in CRISTAL appear to be similar to a newly emerging field of Scientific Workflow systems [WVM96].

6. Workflow System Design

The main components of a workflow management system are a workflow application programming interface and a workflow enactment service. In CRISTAL the workflow application programming interface as viewed through the Desktop Control Panel (DCP) allows Centre Supervisors in association with the CERN Centre Coordinator to specify workflows, specify ta sks and assign them to people and machines.

The specification tools used with this interface must allow the possible sequencing and precedence ordering of tasks to be described in order to fulfil the goals of the work process. The Centre Coordinator will define a nominal production scheme (or a sequence of tasks) which determines the order of tasks that must be applied to the parts. The Workflow Management Coalition (WfMC) [WFMC96], a standards body drawn from the community of Workflow Management System (WFMS) vendors, has begun to identify the primitives from which any WFMS should be built. The CRISTAL design has attempted where possible to adopt its recommendations. The WfMC architecture is fast becoming a defacto industrial standard so that future WfMC compliant WFMS products are likely to emerge and could later be incorporated via an API specification into CRISTAL. The WfMC have identified a set of six primitives with which to describe flows and hence construct a work flow specification. With these primitives it is possible to model any workflow that is likely to occur.

Figure 6.1 shows a partial production scheme for a part. Seven tasks are shown for the part. Some task are strictly sequential in nature (T3, T6 correlated tasks) and some are simple alternatives (T2, T3 AND-split) where order of task execution by operators is unimportant. In two cases the workflows are seen to join (AND-join). Because all flows used in this particular example are correlated and joined via ANDs then all tasks in the scheme must be executed. The four possible serialisable sequences of task execution (workflows) are shown in figure 6.1.

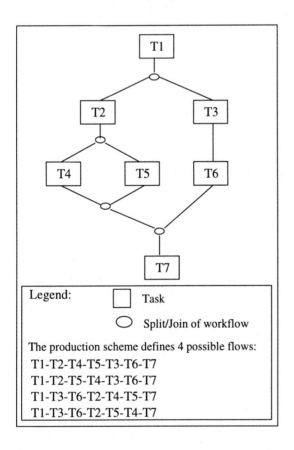

Legend:

☐ Task

◯ Split/Join of workflow

The production scheme defines 4 possible flows:
T1-T2-T4-T5-T3-T6-T7
T1-T2-T5-T4-T3-T6-T7
T1-T3-T6-T2-T4-T5-T7
T1-T3-T6-T2-T5-T4-T7

Fig. 5. Simplified Production Scheme for a Part

There are three other graphical workflow primitives in the WfMC scheme; OR-split, OR-join and Repeatable Task. It is envisaged that the first version of the whole distributed production scheme will be created at CERN by the Central Coordinator in co-operation with all the regional centres. This description of all the production flows for the parts will use the WfMC notation described above and will not use OR-splits and OR-joins. It is expected that the production schemes will evolve as production gets under way as discussed in the next section of this paper.

The workflow enactment service consists of an execution interface and an execution service provided by a workflow engine. The workflow engine is the component that executes the static workflow (production flow) descriptions which have been previously defined using a graphical tool and provides run time services capable of managing and these executing instances. The execution interface is provided by the common Desktop Control Panel (DCP). Centre Operators will be guided and prompted through this interface to perform correct sequences of procedures and measurement tasks on production parts. This interface will also allow the defined workflow model to be analysed and simulated. The notation of Petri nets [Pet77] appears to be an appropriate candidate for workflow execution mechanisms and was chosen in CRISTAL for the following reasons:-

- it is graphical and hence expressive but has formal semantics
- all of the six WfMC workflow primitives can be modelled using a Petri net
- has well known and documented analysis techniques for reachability and deadlock
- it has enhanced modelling features such as colour, time and hierarchy
- it is a possible future standard workflow work engine method

Petri net places model-causal relations, so that if a token appears in a place then the condition it represents will be true. Thus, for example, if one input place to a transition represents a crystal and a second input place represents an avalanche photo diode (APD) mounting then a token in each place models the condition "if crystal available an d APD mounting = true". Transitions model the tasks or activities to be performed so that, when fired, they launch messages to human operators, machines or software objects to perform the task. The task may well be composed of a number of subtasks the coordination of which may be modelled as an atomic transaction so may well have the states (executing, prepared to commit, committed, aborted). Failure of tasks is certainly a possibility in CRISTAL so when this occurs it will result in the tokens being put back to the input places. In this way the Petri net models a series of production task sequences ordered in time. The part then follows a route through the production scheme according to the firing rules [Egil97]. The workflow graphical descriptions as described by the CERN Coordinators are translated into a package of Java^{TM}[Java97] Petri net objects which represent the execution instance of the production scheme.

The design of the this Petri net specification execution service or work engine, has posed a number of problems some of which are:-

— one workflow engine service will not cope with the potentially large number of requests
— how to make the system scaleable as the number of parts and centres grows
— coping with distribution
— coping with dynamic change in workflow specification
— concurrency control problems between competing parts

The design approach taken in CRISTAL is to have a workflow engine for each part type. It is estimated that there will be about 300 types of parts and 500,000 parts altogether. When a part is produced or registered with the system its corresponding part object is associated with a workflow engine which is the execution instance of the workflow specification for that type of part. When an operator swipes a part barcode the object identifier is used to reference the parts own work engine stored as Java^{TM} byte code at the local centre. Because the work engine contains the current Petri net markings and hence current state of the part in the production flow, by swiping the part barcode the operator is informed of the possible next tasks that can be done on the part. Although the operator DCP interface shiws workflows and therefore does not resemble a Petri net, the action of selecting a task has the effect of firing a transition and hence executing the task.

There are a number choices to be made when implementing this part of the system. The work engine could be a Java^{TM} applet obtained from the local database which has a WWW interface (in early prototypes we used the O2^{TM} database with O2Web^{TM} rather than Objectivity^{TM}) and executed on the operator's Java^{TM} enabled browser. The main disadvantage with this approach is that the applet will not be able to access the local host file system or invoke local operating system commands because of Java^{TM} security mechanisms. If however the Java^{TM} work engine is stored and interpreted locally then these access restrictions do not apply. The disadvantages of just using Java^{TM} for the work engine is that it is limits the client server interaction with other distributed objects so in the current prototype we are using Orbix Web^{TM} from Iona Technologies [Iona97] which allows the client Java^{TM} applets to be downloaded to the DCP web browser. The Java^{TM} implemented work engines can then invoke remote CORBA [OMG92] objects using the location and access services of the local ORB.

Although some of the tasks are human based and can be directed to the user interface many tasks are machine based and require invocation of distributed objects on remote machine. An automated measuring instruments called ACCOS is an example. (This instrument, specially developed for CRISTAL, measures dimensions, light yield and transmission spectrum of crystals and can be instructed to start, stop and produce measurements through a networked object interface). Java^{TM} has the advantage that the work engine can run as an applet using a browser and the same browser can be used by the operator to view part data stored as images or documents thus allowing a common DCP for all users of the system. Another potential advantage of using Java^{TM} work engines is that being interpreted it is possible to make changes to the Petri net workflows without having to recompile parts of the system. Further design issues concerning dynamic change and object versions are discussed in the next section.

7. Coping with Dynamic Change

The main difficulty faced by the designers of the CRISTAL system is that of dynamic change to the definitions of the components that it manages. The hardware and software of the crystal detector is still very fluid in its design. It is one of the most complex CMS detectors and matters are made worse since its production process must be initiated early so that the CMS experiment can be assembled on time. It is envisaged that particularly in the early stage of production there will be many changes to the definitions of tasks and parts. If these definitions are kept statically in the database then problems of database dynamic schema evolution will result when definitions are changed and particularly when objects migrate from one centre to another. To circumvent the schema evolution problem we have introduced the concepts of meta-objects .

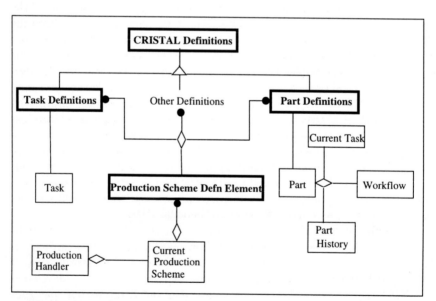

Fig. 6. CRISTAL Object Model Skeleton. (Meta-Objects are shown bold.)

Meta-objects are descriptions of the objects which are managed by the database. A subset of the CRISTAL object model detailing meta-objects shown is shown in figure 7.1. Meta-objects are customisable without affecting the underlying database schema. The concept of meta-objects comes directly from the ideas of reflection [PO94] that is the ability for a system to manage information about itself and to change aspects of the implementation of the system on an object-by-object basis.

The object framework of CRISTAL is a dynamic structure holding a description of itself which can be manipulated and configured whilst the system is running thus allowing incremental changes to be made. Within this framework all fundamental object classes are also are meta objects. In the current prototype these self descriptions have evolved in an ad hoc way without consideration of the descriptions being made available to other foreign systems which might in future wish to use CRISTAL. As discussed in the introduction the actual information required by CRISTAL in the future will depend very much on the viewpoint of the user and their role within CERN. If CRISTAL is to support a particular viewpoint such as Calibration, Maintenance or Experiment Systems Management a corresponding underlying object schema normalised to that viewpoint is required in order to successfully navigate through the schema and find relevant data.

Although the use of the meta-objects concept is powerful it will introduce added complications - for example, consider a production scheme change that has occurred part way through the manufacturing and assembly process. In this case some parts will have been produced and assembled according to one workflow whilst identical parts may have flowed though the same centres but been produced according to a different version of the workflow. Other identical part types may have been subjected to several version changes of the workflow whilst going through the production process. The change in workflow task sequence that comes about because of a workflow version change could have an affect on the production quality of the part. So not only are the measurements stored on the part, but also the task, its version and the corresponding workflow version needs to be stored.

Therefore each time a part is processed by a task a new task instance is created in the database to represent this activity. This object instance associated with the part holds the results of tasks and the conditions and versions under which they were carried out. In this way it is possible to maintain a complete audit trail or event history of all the workflow activity on all constituent parts.

8. Conclusions and Project Status

The CRISTAL project has already shown the viability and importance of adopting a dynamic object-oriented approach to the development of complex system software in a rapidly changing application environment and where many implementation choices need to be deferred. Since the project's inception a considerable amount of interest has been generated in meta-models and meta-object description languages [LV97]. Work is in progress within the OMG on the Meta Object Facility (MOF) [OMG96a] which is expected to manage all kinds of meta-models which are relevant to the OMG Architecture. Two of which are of particular significance to the CRISTAL project are the Manufacturing's Product Data Management Enablers [OMG96b] and Work Flow Facility [OMG97] meta-models. The second phase of the project aims to adopt this more open architectural approach in the hope that it will produce a more adaptable system capable of interoperating with future systems.

Through the use of the WfMC Terminology, the CRISTAL project has begun to demonstrate how workflow management functionality can be incorporated with product data management in order to provide support for scientific workflow applications. Future work in CRISTAL aims to provide the foundation for a general-purpose scientific workflow management system.

CRISTAL development was initiated in early 1996 at CERN and a prototype capture tool was developed using $O2^{TM}$ and WWW to allow existing aspects of ECAL construction to be incorporated in an object database. This prototype demonstrated the use of WWW with $O2^{TM}$ and allowed the capture of histograms holding such data as transmission spectra of crystals and can be viewed using a web browser by visiting http://hpcord02.cern.ch/cristal/main.html. The second phase of prototyping and technology evaluation was initiated in the summer of 1996 and development of this prototype is well under way and is based on the ECAL testing and construction programme in CMS. The OODBMS Objectivity^{TM} is being evaluated as a repository during this second phase of CRISTAL research and development.The project is following the ESA PSS-05 Software Engineering Standards. At the time of writing the final version of the User Requirements Document for the CRISTAL Prototype 2 system is complete and the Software Requirements Document almost complete. The object model is based on the Unified Method [BR95].

Acknowledgements

The authors take this opportunity to acknowledge the support of their home institutes. In particular the support of P Lecoq, J-L Faure and J-P Vialle is greatly appreciated. The help of A. Bazan, T Le Flour, S. Lieunard, D. Rousset, E. Leonardi, G. Barone and G. Organtini in creating the CRISTAL prototypes is especially recognised.

Workflow Applications to Research Agenda: Scalable and Dynamic Work Coordination and Collaboration Systems

Amit Sheth, Krys J. Kochut

Large Scale Distributed Information Systems Lab, Computer Science Department, The University of Georgia Athens, GA 30602-7404, USA

1. Introduction

A workflow is an activity involving the coordinated execution of multiple tasks performed by different processing entities [KS 95]. These tasks could be manual, or automated, either created specifically for the purpose of the workflow application being developed, or possibly already existing as legacy programs. A workflow process is an automated organizational process involving both human (manual) and automated tasks.

Workflow management is the automated coordination, control and communication of work as is required to satisfy workflow processes [S+ 96]. A Workflow Management System (WFMS) is a set of tools providing support for the necessary services of workflow creation (which includes process definition), workflow enactment, and administration and monitoring of workflow processes [WfMC 94b]. The developer of a workflow application relies on tools for the specification of the workflow process and the data it manipulates. The specification tools cooperate closely with the workflow repository service, which stores workflow definitions. The workflow process is based on a formalized workflow model that is used to capture data and control-flow between workflow tasks.

The workflow enactment service (including a workflow manager and the workflow runtime system) consists of execution-time components that provide the execution environment for the workflow process. A workflow runtime system is responsible for enforcing inter-task dependencies, task scheduling, workflow data management, and for ensuring a reliable execution environment. Administrative and monitoring tools are used for management of user and work group roles, defining policies (e.g., security, authentication), audit management, process monitoring, tracking, and reporting of data generated during workflow enactment.

Workflow technology has matured to some extent, and current products are able to support a range of applications. Nevertheless a majority of the workflow products are directed towards supporting ad-hoc or administrative workflows that serve as office automation types of applications, and primarily involve human tasks supported through forms-based interface. Support for more complex, production workflows is limited to more repetitive processes.

Many additional limitations remain, especially for supporting more demanding applications, more dynamic environments and for better support for human involvement in organizational activities. In this paper, we focus on two issues. The first issue relates to the challenges that could be addressed by evolving the current workflow technology. Two of the challenges to which we focus our attention in this paper are: (a) support for scalability, and (b) support for adaptable and dynamic workflows. Various other research challenges have also been recognized, and for some of them the research is further along.

The second issue we address in this paper is somewhat less well defined and longer term. It mainly relates to supporting a broader aspect of organizational activities. To support these, the workflow technology, owing to its emphasis on coordination, is only a part of the solution. Following the recent NSF workshop on Workflow and Process Automation in Information Systems [She 96], the report by a multidisciplinary group of researchers noted [S+ 96]:

> "Work Activity Coordination involves such multidisciplinary research and goes beyond the current thinking in contemporary workflow management and Business Process Reengineering (BPR). In particular, instead of perceiving problems in prototypical terms such as the information factory, white-collar work and bureaucracy, we believe that this limited point of view can be explained by a lack of synergy between organizational science, methodologies, and computer science. Multidisciplinary research projects, based on mutual respect and willingness to learn from another discipline, can help to create a thriving research community that builds upon the strengths of different disciplines, such as distributed systems, database management, software process management, software engineering, organizational sciences, and others."

Numerous multidisciplinary research issues, especially those relating to effective support for and providing satisfaction to humans as they participate in the organizational activities remain. At a technological level, two rapidly maturing technologies present special opportunities as they are complimentary to coordination focused workflow technology. One is the collaboration (and group work) technology, including video-conferencing and shared spaces, where the focus has been on synchronous communications and/or support for human intensive and ill defined (or ad-hoc) activities. The second is information management, including integrated access to the organization's (heterogeneous media) data or information assets. In this paper, we will only give some preliminary thoughts to the appealing research agenda of increasing integration of coordination (workflow), collaboration and information management technologies to support complex and fluid work activities in real-world organizations. At the technological level, Web, distributed object management (specifically CORBA), and Java allow us to interface and integrate disparate technologies with increasing ease.

The rest of this chapter is organized as follows. Section 2 provides a brief overview of the current workflow technology. In Section 3, we discuss short application scenarios that provide us motivation for research in scalability, adaptive and dynamic workflows, and combined support for coordination and collaboration. Section 4 contains an overview how our METEOR$_2$ workflow management system addresses the issues of scalability. Finally, Section 5. presents our early work on the architecture and design of a Workflow Coordination and Collaboration System to address the other two challenges of adaptable/dynamic workflows and integration of coordination and collaboration technologies. Conclusions are provided in Section 6.

2. Agenda for Current and Future Research

Workflow Management Systems today are being used to re-engineer, streamline, automate, and track organizational processes [JAD+94, GHS 95, F 95]. There has been a growing acceptance of workflow technology in numerous application domains such as telecommunications, software engineering, manufacturing, production, finance and banking, laboratory sciences, health care, shipping, and office automation. The current state-of-the-art in WFMSs is dictated by the commercial market [AS 96b]. Several hundred products that provide support for workflow management (in various degree) exist in the market today [S 95, F 95, GHS 95, SJo 96, AAEM 97]. These systems are primarily focused toward providing automation within the office environment with emphasis on coordinating human activities, and facilitating document routing, imaging, and reporting.

In the last few years, pervasive network connectivity, catalyzed by the explosive growth of the Internet has changed our computational landscape. Centralized, homogeneous, and desktop-oriented technologies have given way to more distributed, heterogeneous, and network-centric ones. This has raised challenging requirements for workflow technology in terms of being required to support large scale multi-system applications, involving both humans and legacy systems, in heterogeneous, autonomous and distributed (HAD) environments. Emerging and maturing infrastructure technologies for communication and distributed object management (e.g., CORBA/IIOP, DCOM/ActiveX, Java, Notes, and Web) have addressed many of these challenges, and are making it feasible to develop standards-based large scale, distributed application systems.

As a commercial technology, workflow technology has undoubtedly experienced significant success. This has lead to the desire for further research and development in the area for two directions. First, the requirements placed on some of these applications have tested the limits of the current workflow technology, highlighting the need for further research and development. Second, researchers and practitioners have identified new applications that could conceptually use this technology, but current workflow products, either do not address these emerging requirements, or do so very selectively.

Some of the apparent weaknesses that need to be addressed from the perspectives of database and distributed systems community researchers active in the workflow management area include limited support for heterogeneous and distributed computing infrastructures, lack of a clear theoretical basis, undefined correctness criteria, limited support for synchronization of concurrent workflows, lack of interoperability, minimal scalability and availability, and lack of reliability in the presence of failures and exceptions [B$^+$ 93, JNRS 93, GHS 95, AS 96b, KR 96b, LSV96, WS 96, WS 97, AAEM 97]. The issues of error handling and recovery [JNRS 93, A$^+$ 94, Ley 95, EL 96, WS 97, RSW 97, Wor 97], and of the role of transactions and transactional workflows [SR 93, GHS 95, TV 95a, KR 96b, LSV96, WS 97] recently have seen some attention, but will not be discussed further in this paper.

Researchers and practitioners in other relevant communities have correspondingly identified many other items that call for further research. The report for the multidisciplinary team from the NSF workshop identified the active research areas to include [S$^+$ 96]: Definition and Modeling; Representation, Language, and Meta-Modeling; Analysis, Testing, Verification and Evaluation; Simulation; Prototyping, Walk-through, and Performance Support; Administration, Staffing and Scheduling; Interoperation and Integration; Target Support Environment Generation; Monitoring and Measurement; Visualization; Enactment History Capture and Replay; Fault Detection, Error Handling or Repair; and Evolution, Continuous Improvement and Model Management.

3. Application Driven Motivation and Requirements

In this paper, we focus our attention on three of the many interesting challenges facing the workflow technology and requiring additional research. Where possible, we use application examples that have provided motivation and helped us understand some of these requirements. Discussions of workflow applications that are somewhat less relevant to our discussion, but are nevertheless interesting, appear in [JAD$^+$94, GHS 95, MC 96, S 95, DWS 96, SJo 96, SK$^+$ 96].

3.1 Scalability

Let us first discuss briefly three examples that point to different types of scalability needs. The first example is that of a somewhat traditional workflow application. It involves applying workflow and imaging technology in the Clark County Department of Business License for automating and streamlining the licensing system and to turn the department into a "paper-less environment"

[MC 96]. ActionWorkflow [Act 95] provided the workflow management infrastructure and Image X provided the imaging tools for this project.

Workflow requirements stemmed from the ineffectiveness of the previous system (which was primarily human-centered, paper based, and included an IBM ES 9000 mainframe program for information retrieval) to deal with the high demand for license renewals (approximately 72000 license renewals and applications annually). There was a need to automate the department and re-engineer business processes with emphasis on customer service. With a crude estimation of 250 working days, this gives around 290 instances of the workflow per day. While the 67 employees indicate the potential number of tasks involved in this workflow process, the number of tasks in the re-engineered process is unreported. The manual process for processing a request for general license that used to take 90-120 days took only 45 days after supporting a re-engineered process using the workflow and imaging technologies. While it seems that the current workflow products seem to support such medium scale applications, the question remains if the technology still imposes limitations that contributes to the 45 days period it still takes.

Service order processing, a telecommunications application, has been reported in [ANRS 92, GHS 95]. Unlike the previous example, operational system still does not use the modern workflow technology, and the workflow application was only written in prototypical form (compared to the commercial implementation in the previous application). It however gave a the following insights. The workflow involves interfacing with 15 to 25 legacy information systems (called Operation Support Systems). For special types of services such as a T1 line provisioning, a Bell company may only need to support tens of new workflow instances per day, while for more routine types of services such as POTS (Plain Old Telephone Service), thousands of new workflow instances would be generated. Because it takes several days in completing a service request, a WFMS may need to support tens of thousands of active workflow instances. In our views, three issues (and many other less important ones) that have hindered operationalization of workflow technology in this context are: administrative and managerial issues (mainly lack of management's understanding of the technology and its promise and the vested interests of those whose work could drastically change or be eliminated because of automation and reengineering afforded by the workflow technology), and concerns for robustness (including error handling and recovery) as any down time may not be acceptable and scalability (to support the high workloads).

Final application for our discussion in this area involves the use of workflows in a high-throughput mission-critical application system of tracking experimental data at the Center for Genome Research [BSR 96]. Workflow automation is used in the laboratory information systems setting to automate the handling of samples, testing, instrumentation, data capture, and tracking of event histories. The DBMS is primarily used in this project to control and track sample collection workflows.

The throughput of such experiments range in the order of approximately 15,000 transactions per day, with peak rates reaching 22.5 queries and updates per second [BSR 96]. To be effective in such high-throughput production environments, a lot is desired in terms of scalability, efficiency, and reliability of the underlying WFMS infrastructure and the processing entities or resources that perform the high frequency tasks. The authors address the requirements of the DBMS that forms one of the critical components of the WFMS, and discuss LabFlow-1, a database benchmark for high-throughput production WFMS. Some of the important requirements for the DBMS mentioned in [BSR 96] are:

- standard database features such as providing isolation, consistency, failure recovery, high-level query language and query-optimization;
- support for maintaining audit histories of the workflow activity (workflow tracking);
- ability to store complex-structured data; and
- ability to allow dynamic modification of the schema at run-time as the workflow itself is characterized by dynamism in terms of modification of flow of control and modification of tasks.

Two additional observations that are important with respect to the scalability in WFMSs are discussed next.

As a result of more automation and reengineering, number of instances of workflow that need to be managed would decrease. For example, if a workflow that used to take ten days will now take one day, than number of concurrent workflows to be managed for the same number of instances invoked will reduce by a factor of ten.

Perhaps the most important item related to the number of concurrent workflows is the tasks performed by humans. In general, a human performed (or manual) task would take significantly longer than a system performed (or automated) task and contribute to making the workflow instances long lived. Some of the human performed tasks could include the human involvement in error handling and recovery not handled automatically by the WFMS. Time it takes to complete some of the human performed tasks can also be unpredictable due to various reasons such as a decision making task involves consulting with someone else, the worker needs to attend to higher priority task or the worker goes on vacation. Some of the automated task can also take relatively long time, for example a task performed by a legacy system that uses a batch mode.

Now let us review some of the issues that are relevant to scalability from the perspective of a WFMS architecture.

The number of concurrent workflows, the number of instances of the workflows proceeded during a given period, and the average number of tasks in a workflow, all will have impact on the architectural issues.

Here is a non-exhaustive list of questions that would help us understand the scalability issues related to a WFMS:

- Do workflow modeling and design allow explicit allocation of tasks to different processing entities (that perform the tasks)? Do they allow specification of alternative processing entities? Does the design analysis tool help in analyzing these allocations?
- Is scheduling performed in a centralized manner or in a distributed manner?
- Are all relevant task managers (the processes on behalf of a WFMS that manage individual tasks) created as soon as the workflow instance starts, or only during some of the time (e.g., from the time its tasks has scheduling information to the time the task ends)?
- Do tasks of the same type share a task manager (i.e., do processes of WFMS components support multiple tasks, e.g., by using multi-threading)?
- What throughput limitations task managers impose? (As the task managers support more functionality, such as error handling and recovery, their size, complexity and I/O could increase by an order of magnitude or more).
- Does the WFMS support any form of load balancing, such as executing the tasks on alternative processing entities? Can it do so when alternatives are not explicitly specified in the design, either using run-time administrator or user intervention, or automatically?
- Can the processing entities or resources (e.g., DBMS in the third application above), which often predate the workflow applications and WFMSs, handle the load from workflow tasks (which may be new and in addition to other resource usage)? Do the operations from workflow tasks require synchronization?

In Section 4, we will discuss architectural and implementation decisions in an example WFMS that addresses many of these issues.

3.2 Adaptive and Dynamic Workflows

One of the most important of the demands evolving from new workflow applications is the ability of handling adaptable and dynamic workflows. Can a workflow (instance) and WFMS, through dynamic changes to its run-time environment, react and adapt to the rapid changes in process execution flow triggered by collaborative decision points, context-sensitive information updates, and other internal or external events? Some research issues in this area have been raised in the context of modeling and specification aspects appear in [HHSW 96] and the relevant issues involving organizational changes appear in [ER 95, H 95]. However, the literature that addresses some of the run-time system issues is scarce.

Let us discuss some of the requirements using two classes of applications found in healthcare and defense, respectively. Example healthcare clinical applications are discussed in [SK+ 96, HHSW 96].

The first example concerns the issue of *co-morbidity*, which often arises in the healthcare environment. Here, a lab procedure, for example, brings out previously unknown disease or condition, which also needs concurrent treatment along with the original disease or condition. A physician, after considering the lab results, may decide to initiate an ad-hoc workflow in order to perform additional tests in view of the new findings. Note that the changes or new additions cannot be made independently of the original workflow because they relate to the same person, and management of one disease may affect that of the other. Since the amount of possible combinations of procedures is extremely large, it is almost infeasible to create a fully defined, all encompassing workflow for handling all possible cases. Therefore, a WFMS capable of supporting highly dynamic, adaptable workflows needed.

As another example scenario, consider the following defense application. Assume that a plan formulation workflow is currently developing a plan to move 5,000 troops from one point to another in a hostile environment. Such a process requires a variety of tasks performed by or directed by humans and a set of automated tasks, with appropriate control and data dependencies and constraints among them. Now assume that the intelligence monitoring activity determined a higher level of threat and the number of required troops is increased to 10,000. It would be necessary to consider many alternatives in a decision making process, as well as interruptions and redirections of the plan formulation process being enacted, such as (a) can the current process be used to support planning for the new requirement, (b) how far the current process has progressed, (c) if it is in the early phases, can it be interrupted and modified so that when completed, new requirement can be met, (d) should the current process that will result in planning for 5,000 troops be completed and can another process to support planning of another 5,000 troops be started, with support for appropriate interactions between the new process with the previous one, or (e) should the current process be prematurely stopped and a new process to address the additional requirement of 5,000 troops be started?

There may be wide range of events or conditions to which the workflows and a WFMS may need to adapt to, including the reasons of exception handling and load balancing. Being able to adapt through dynamic changes to workflows can also be an approach to develop a more robust and scalable WFMS.

A non-exhaustive list of questions that would help us understand the support for adaptable and dynamic workflows is as follows:

- Which types of events does the workflow needs to adapt to? Examples include:
  - events resulting from execution of tasks
  - events from the changes in workflow specifications such as changes in persons or resources for a given role (e.g., due to change of work shift), or changes in the roles for given tasks (e.g., a new rule allowing a nurse practitioner to perform a task earlier requiring a physician to perform)

- events from WFMS and its components
- events from the infrastructure
- events from external events including those from processing entities and resources or any aspect of the computing environment including user interventions.

- What is the scope of the adaptation? Is the adaptation necessary for the workflow instance already in progress (i.e., is the workflow dynamic at the instance level)? Is the change applicable only to some of the active workflow instances or is it permanent for the workflow type? Will multiple versions of the same workflow type be managed and concurrently executed, and if so, which version should be used for the next invocation?
- How is the event conveyed to the WFMS (i.e., which protocols or APIs do monitoring agents or sentinels use to interact with the WFMS)?
- What are the ways in which a workflow may be dynamic (adding one or more tasks, adding additional conditions on or changing inter-task dependencies, adding new inter-task dependencies, creating a new version of a workflow type)?
- How do the changes interact or relate to on going instances of the workflows?
- How can you characterize a change to a workflow to be correct? Which criteria apply?
- Are the changes to a workflow introduced by a single task (an end-user or an automated task) or at the workflow administration level? Who should have the authority to introduce the changes and where?
- Since introducing changes dynamically may introduce logical errors to a workflow (or even a workflow type), what additional capabilities are needed in the area of error detection and recovery?

3.3 Integral Support for Collaboration

As noted earlier, work coordination, collaboration and information access are all key to providing a comprehensive support for organizational activities. Researchers in group-ware and organizational systems seem to have taken early steps in integrating the first two by adding coordination or workflow capabilities to group support systems. However, many distributed and information systems issues still need to be addressed. Recent progress in video-conferencing and web-based collaboration (application sharing and white boarding) has rapidly expanded the availability of collaboration systems, and provided better opportunity for merging these formerly distinct capabilities.

To fully appreciate the importance of dynamic, collaborative workflows, consider the following examples.

For the first application scenario, let us further extend upon our healthcare domain example. Suppose that in the process of a clinical workflow involving a primary physician, based on the available information, the physician decides to seek help of a consulting physician to determine the diagnosis. The collaboration process may involve synchronous communication through video-conferencing, application sharing and data sharing (e.g., through Microsoft's NetMeeting or Netscape's Collabra), or may place asynchronous consultation request whereby the patient data and a videotaped message is provided to the consulting physician to seek an off-line help. These types of scenarios are being supported in our CaTCH (Collaborative TeleConsulting for Healthcare) prototype system (see http://lsdis.cs.uga.edu for further information).

Next, let us consider defense applications. Plan development for a large military operation is a very complex process typically involving scores of military planners using a variety of software systems. A computerized system created to support such a planning process must be highly dynamic, capable of supporting a wide range of collaboration among planners attempting to solve various problems at different stages of the plan development.

Suppose the workflow users in maritime operations are informed of a sudden crisis and decision to react to the problem has been made at the higher level of command. The maritime user, using her map display, understands the impact of this decision and schedules a new task to immediately contain the effect of the problem. The coordination system overseeing planning workflows notices the change in the task mix being executed and automatically forwards a change notice to the planning system managing the air-campaign. The automated planning workflow system immediately starts a new process to identify alternatives and informs the corresponding workflow manager to start a task to involve a human planner.

The air operations workflow management system interrupts the human planner by changing the color of the air campaign that will be affected by this change in his map display. The planner notices the color change, and interacts with the automatic planning system. The automatic planning system displays the various alternatives as different color coded information on the map. The human planner (in cooperation with maritime operations) then initiates a new process involving a set of new tasks, some involving tasks supporting automated planning and some involving manual coordination tasks with the maritime planner. If needed, the two planners may interact through a collaboration component (including video-conferencing) that would also assist the interactions by providing appropriate contextual information.

The above scenario calls for launching a new process and modification to the existing processes. The new planning process may interrupt critical tasks in the maritime operations process plan or re-direct them in-order to deal with the crisis. It also involves creation of a set of recursively dependent processes that need to be coordinated at different levels of the coordination hierarchy. It would be desirable for the coordination system to manage the inter-dependent processes and assists the humans in understanding, interrupting, and redirecting them.

It is virtually impossible to fully account for all possible problems that might arise while coordinating the two independent planning workflows, as described above. Thus, the system must support other ways for seeking solutions. One possible way to achieve this is by "talking over", i.e. by conferencing between the appropriate commanders and planners.

Some of the question that need investigations are:

- How to uniformly model all objects (including resources) that represent coordination (tasks, sub-workflows, workflows) and collaboration (a video-conference session, white boarding, etc. with their time dimension)? How do you model dependencies for these two types of activities such as the following:
  - at some point in a workflow execution, a collaboration is started between humans and the workflow execution waits for the collaboration to end before it resumes, or
  - a collaboration activity designs a workflow and initiates it to watch how it is enacted
- In the above, is there a distinction between what constitutes coordination and what constitutes collaboration? What does it mean to lessen or remove that distinction in terms of a modeling paradigm?
- Can the result of a collaboration between humans be concretely and effectively captured to affect the coordination as appropriate (i.e., consistent with the decisions taken during the collaboration)?
- Is there a notion of correct execution that spans both these types of activities?
- When can you substitute a collaboration by a coordination (or vice-a-verse) and achieve perhaps better organizational effectiveness?
- How to model the collaboration that needs to be done at real time, as opposed to one that can be scheduled and deferred?

It seems that the level of technological integration is relatively easy, and some naive approaches may be adequate for certain applications. For example, we may simply treat collaboration as human tasks in a workflow design. However, some fundamental problems remain. What we believe is that on top of the *lower level* middleware supported by such technologies as Web, CORBA, database access APIs (ODBC, JDBC), etc. we will in the future have a *higher level* middleware, that provides the abstractions needed to seamlessly engage in coordination, collaboration, and information management activities. For brevity, we do not discuss the issues related to information management further.

4. METEOR₂ WFMS and its Support for Scalability

This section presents the current state-of-the-art in WFMS with the METE-OR₂ WFMS developed at the Large Scale Distributed Information Systems Lab., University of Georgia (LSDIS) as the example. An obvious reason for using this system as an example is that we know it well. Another important reason is compared to discussing a commercial product or a laboratory prototype is that although METEOR₂ is a result of a research project, it also represents a commercializable technology that is being tested by or used in three organizations (CHREF, NIST and Boeing) outside of the LSDIS, with more expected in near future. Also, METEOR₂ utilizes the modern infrastructure technologies (specifically, Web and CORBA) and can be viewed as an example of how current state-of-the-art WFMs cope with the demands placed on the workflow systems today.

METEOR₂ has been geared towards developing a multi-paradigm transactional WFMS capable of supporting large scale, mission critical, enterprise-wide and inter-enterprise workflow applications in HAD environments. METEOR₂ includes all of the necessary components to design, build, deploy, run, and monitor workflow applications. Some of its key features include:

- *Easy and quick application development*: This is critical for the system's acceptance and organization's productivity. METEOR₂ graphical workflow designer enables an easy, point-and-click creation of the workflow process, associated workflow data, and task details that map to actual user and application tasks. More importantly, the workflow design process is followed by a mostly automatic code generation of an executable workflow application. In particular, all WFMS related run-time code (for scheduling and error-handling/recovery to the extent supported) is automatically generated. Naturally some of the tasks may need to be developed by human involvement or may already exist (i.e., legacy system supported task).
- *Ease of use*: End users can continue to use their existing user interfaces or be supported through a Web browser enabled GUI that the system can automatically generate.
- *Support for heterogeneous tasks with transaction and legacy information system handling*: METEOR₂ model incorporates various task models have been defined to support integration of heterogeneous task types into the workflow model [KS 95, MSKW 96]. Task models include models for transactional, non-transactional, user and two-phase commit types of tasks. Ability to wrap legacy application and information systems is supported.
- *Support for distributed and heterogeneous computing environment*: Use of CORBA and Web-based environment support ability to develop distributed workflow applications running on heterogeneous computing environments.
- *Error handling and recovery*: These are integral to the METEOR₂ system with support for three-level object-oriented error handling and recovery

model, and the ability to automatically support handling of many types of exceptions [Wor 97].

- *Scalability*: METEOR$_2$ has been designed to handle workflow systems capable of carrying large loads. Specifically, we have considered a number of workflow applications described in the literature as ones challenging the capabilities of the WFMS systems available today.

Several enactment services have been designed and implemented based on various scheduling paradigms [MSKW 96]. These range from highly centralized ones to fully distributed implementations using CORBA and Web technologies (either exclusively, or in combination) as infrastructure for workflow enactment. Two distributed workflow enactment systems (ORBWork [KSM 97] and WEBWork [MPSK 97]) have been successfully used to support a comprehensive prototype of workflow applications, including the statewide immunization tracking workflow process involving multiple hospitals and healthcare providers [SK+ 96].

In the remainder of this section, we first present an overview of the METEOR$_2$ system. For the enactment service, we limit our attention to ORBWork. We also discuss scalability considerations in the context of ORBWork.

4.1 Workflow Design and Application Building in METEOR$_2$

The METEOR$_2$ graphical designer (MTDes) is used to develop a workflow application, in some cases leaving no extra work after a designed workflow is converted to a workflow application by the runtime code generator. MTDes has three components used to specify the entire map of the workflow, data objects manipulated by the workflow, as well as the details of task invocation, respectively. The task design component provides interfaces to external task development tools (e.g., Microsoft's FrontPage to design the interface of a user task, or a rapid application development tool). MTDes has the capability to model complex and varied tasks in a high-level conceptual and easy to use manner that shields the designer of the workflow from the underlying details of infrastructure or the runtime environment. It also aims at providing the user very few restrictions regarding the specification of the workflow. The designer assumes no particular implementation of the workflow runtime. Its independence from the runtime supports separating the specification aspects from the runtime.

MTDes has two design modes. The first mode, called *Process Modeler*, is aimed as a tool for the management of a typical enterprise. A workflow design may be initiated at the high, organizational level, without devoting any thought to the implementation details. This designer mode focuses on high-level specification issues without going into the procedural issues of the runtime. Thus the Process Modeler stresses the *what* of the process rather than the *how*.

The second mode, called *Workflow Builder*, assists in a GUI-supported development of a complete executable workflow application. The design specification created with the Process Modeler would be further refined in this mode. It is in this mode that we specify the entire map of the workflow including various tasks, task managers, and their interactions. This mode is intended for technical engineers or system analysts who would know the details of the underlying run time system and how the workflow application needs to be supported on it.

4.2 The Runtime Code Generator

The workflow specification created using MTDes is stored in an intermediate format called the Workflow Intermediate Language (WIL). The WIL format is similar in structure and semantics to the Workflow Process Definition Language (WPDL) of the Workflow Management Coalition and supports most aspects of our earlier intermediate languages, Workflow Specification Language (WFSL) and Task Specification Language (TSL) [KS 95]. A WIL specification includes all the predecessor-successor dependencies between the tasks as well as the data objects that are passed among the different tasks. It also includes definitions of the data objects, and the details of the task invocation details. Workflow definitions are stored in the workflow repository managed by the METEOR$_2$ repository service.

The functionality of MTDes has been tailored so that it allows for automatic code generation for a complete workflow application, except for some of the individual tasks participating in a workflow. It is not possible to generate code for all of the computer (automated) tasks, since the individual tasks must be provided later by task developers (or possibly already exist as legacy applications).

Each runtime (ORBWork and WEBWork) has a suitable code generator. The runtime code generators work either using the WIL specification file as input, or using the repository service directly. The code generator outputs code for task managers, including their scheduling components, task invocation code, data object access routines, and the recovery mechanism. The code generator also outputs the code necessary to maintain and manipulate data objects, created by the data designer. The details provided using the task designer mechanism is used to create the corresponding wrapper code for incorporating legacy applications with relative ease.

Details of MTDes and the WIL intermediate language are given in [Lin97, Zhe97].

4.3 METEOR$_2$ Runtime Support System

The METEOR$_2$ runtime architecture is centered around four major services: repository, enactment, monitoring, and error handling and recovery.

The METEOR$_2$ Repository Service is responsible for maintaining information about workflow definitions and associated workflow applications. The workflow designer, while using the graphical workflow design tool, communicates with the repository service and retrieves, updates, and stores workflow definitions. The designer is capable of browsing the contents of the repository and incorporating fragments (either sub-workflows or individual tasks) of already existing workflow definitions in the one being currently created. The repository service is also available to the enactment service (see below) and provides the necessary information about a workflow application to be started.

The METEOR$_2$ Enactment Service provides the necessary functionality for running workflow instances. The enactment service has two components responsible for activation of workflows and scheduling of tasks. The activation component allows the user to browse available workflow applications (using the repository service), select one of them, and then start a new workflow instance. The scheduling component of the enactment service is responsible for activating workflow tasks, once a workflow instance has been started. This part of the enactment service consists of the various task managers and their associated tasks, the user interfaces, the distributed error handling and recovery mechanisms, the scheduler (distributed among task managers) and the various monitoring components. As the web browser has become the preferred user interface tool, and has lead to Web-enabling of enterprise applications, we provide a browser-based interface for all end users to allow humans to participate seamlessly in workflows regardless of their location and (client) system platforms. Figure 1 shows some of the key modules of the METEOR$_2$ system and their interactions.

The METEOR$_2$ Monitoring Service fulfills the function of an overseeing entity. It monitors all of the currently active (enacted and not yet terminated) workflow instances. The monitoring service interacts with the enactment service. It is responsible for detection of various types of failures that cannot be detected within individual sub-components of the enactment service.

The METEOR$_2$ Recovery Service interacts with the enactment and monitoring services. It is utilized once a failure has been detected and one or several workflow instances must be restarted. Additional details for error handling and recovery can be found in [Wor 97]. The following sections describe the ORBWork enactment system and its associated recovery system.

4.4 The ORBWork Workflow Enactment System

As has been mentioned earlier, there is a host of different workflow management systems available in the commercial and the research arena. These systems vary widely from their design philosophy and methodology and hence in their implementation strategies. The METEOR$_2$ model does not assume any particular architecture of the workflow enactment system. We have, however, opted to have a fully distributed architecture of the enactment system. Even

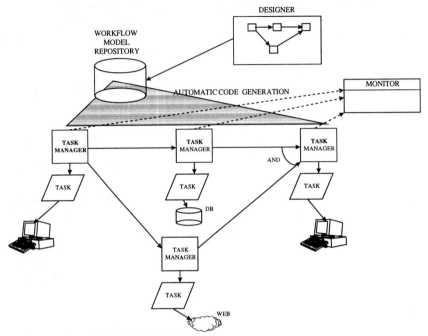

Fig. 1. The METEOR₂ Architecture

though this introduces additional overhead and complexities a distributed implementation entails, a fully distributed architecture offers significant advantages for providing a highly scalable workflow management system.

Right from the start, our philosophy has been to build a system where each and every module has sufficient independence to perform its job efficiently but, at the same time, is also responsible to some evaluation entities in the organization (which in our case would be a workflow monitor). Aside from scalability, another significant driving force in favor of the distributed architecture is the absence of a single point of failure. This also has a profound impact on error handling and recovery issues.

ORBWork relies on CORBA to supply the basic communication infrastructure. This was almost the natural choice once we decided on a distributed framework, since CORBA provides an infrastructure for facilitating development of reusable, portable and object-based software in a distributed and heterogeneous environment. Currently, ORBWork is built with the use of Orbix and associated products (including OrbixWeb, OTS, etc.) from Iona Technologies. (In our earlier prototype implementation, we had used Orbeline 2.0, now a Visigenic, Inc. product called VisiBroker for C++.)

All of the major components in ORBWork are implemented as CORBA objects. Also, it is common that tasks (or wrappers around existing legacy tasks) are also implemented as CORBA objects. As new CORBA services (in particular persistence and transaction) have become available in beta or product form (specifically from Iona), we have started to exploit them to reduce duplicating the corresponding functionality in the ORBWork implementation.

4.4.1 ORBWork's Distributed Scheduler and Task Manager Activation.

The METEOR scheduler plays a central role in the ORBWork enactment service. Each workflow task has an associated task manager. The task manager is activated by the METEOR scheduler, once the task's input dependency is satisfied. The task scheduler is also responsible for activating the successor task schedulers, if any.

METEOR$_2$ does not have a single entity responsible for scheduling activation of task managers. Instead, the scheduling information is distributed among the individual task schedulers. The control dependencies, as defined in the workflow designer, are represented in the workflow process definition. The workflow code generator reads the workflow definition (retrieved from the repository) and automatically creates the task schedulers for each individual task in the workflow.

Each task scheduler has the necessary information about its immediate predecessor and successor tasks, and thus it is capable of activating the successor task schedulers once the task it controls terminates. (Ongoing work involves adding the capability to update this information at any time to support dynamic workflows.) Each task scheduler is activated by a group of immediate predecessor task schedulers. Such an activation provides all of the necessary parameters (workflow instance id, input data object ids, etc.) to schedule the task execution.

In ORBWork, each individual task scheduler is implemented (in C++) as a CORBA object. One such object handles the scheduling responsibilities for all of the workflow instances that invoke the task controlled by the scheduler and hence this component is perpetual.

The task activation part handles the execution of the associated task. The task scheduler simply activates the associated task manager, also implemented as a CORBA object, to run the actual task. After the invoked task manager terminates, it informs its task scheduler that the task has terminated. The scheduler then proceeds with scheduling the successor tasks, as defined in the workflow.

Communication between two task schedulers as well as between a task scheduler and the associated task manager is implemented by IDL method calls. In particular, when a task scheduler wants to activate a successor task (in fact the task scheduler of the successor task), it binds to the CORBA object implementing the successor task scheduler and runs an appropriate IDL method to affect a transition.

METEOR$_2$ supports both automated tasks with no user involvement and human tasks involving participation of the end-users in a workflow application (e.g., to fill a form, validate data, carry out a task on a worklist, etc.).

Each user task has a template of an HTML form associated with it. Such a template is first automatically created by the workflow designer. Each template contains information regarding which data object attributes a particular user task should display in the form.

While the automatically generated template uses a relatively simple layout, a template may be (and most likely will be, for commercially deployed workflow applications) refined by using any commercially available HTML authoring tool (e.g., Microsoft's FrontPage). When a workflow instance reaches a user task, the task's template is instantiated to include the field values taken from the data objects manipulated by this workflow instance. Specifically, the task manager of the user task retrieves the associated HTML form template, accesses the data objects mentioned in the template and then creates an instance of the template using values from the data objects.

Through this mechanism, METEOR$_2$ separates the specification of data objects necessary for user tasks from their actual use at runtime. However, the data must be transferred between the "CORBA world" and the end-user domain, an HTML form. METEOR$_2$ uses Java applets (ORBWork's implementation uses Iona's OrbixWeb) to retrieve the form's data fields and directly invoke IDL operations on data objects to write the new field values (data objects are also implemented as CORBA objects; see below). The applet's code is generated automatically by the METEOR's code generator and attached to the end-user's HTML form.

4.4.2 Handling Workflow Data. All of the data that is transferred among tasks in a workflow is represented as a collection of CORBA objects. The data object naming scheme associates each object to its workflow instance.

The data objects are specified with the use of the workflow designer and incorporated into the resulting intermediate representation (and stored in the workflow repository). Then, the workflow code generator creates an appropriate IDL interface for each data object, as it generates code for the workflow definition.

Each data object supports the necessary functionality for providing its own persistence. This is implemented either with the use of an externally available persistent storage mechanism (for example an object-oriented database system) or by utilizing persistent object services offered by ORB.

4.5 Scalability of ORBWork

Scalability of the enactment system is one of the key requirements for workflow management systems today. We have leveraged the capabilities of the ORB object's location independence that allows us to place task schedulers, task managers, data objects, and even actual tasks on separate hosts. The scalability has been addressed in ORBWork in several ways:

– During the design process, the designer may indicate specific server nodes where a particular task should be performed. The task itself need not be located on the same server as the controlling task manager. A task placement can be determined at application installation time.

- Typically, completing a workflow instance is a long duration process. Keeping this in mind, we adopted the *late activation* policy for task managers, tasks, and data objects. No data objects are created until the workflow instance needs them. Similarly, task managers are not created until a workflow instance reaches a specific task. Thus, the number of active objects (or ORBWork components) is kept to a minimum.

- Communication between task schedulers (and task managers) is limited to method invocations that are "light-weight". Only data object references are transferred between task managers (no large amounts of data are ever exchanged). This approach is in contrast to that used by the INCA [BMR 96] model that passes process and workflow data between processing entities.

- Since ORBWork uses a fully distributed scheduler, there is no need for one, centrally managed scheduler. If necessary, each task scheduler may run on a separate host, allowing for the distribution of a potentially large load among many computers participating in a workflow. If the load carried by a single task scheduler is still too large, additional task schedulers may be added without much problem (a small amount of synchronization data must then be passed between task scheduler replicas). Each one would handle a portion of the overall number of workflow instances to be handled. A task scheduler supports multiple tasks instances corresponding to different workflow instances of the same type, reducing the number of CORBA objects needed for this purpose.

- The error handling and recovery framework for ORBWork (described in [Wor 97]) has also been defined in a scalable manner by using error class hierarchies, partitioning the recovery mechanism across local hosts, encapsulating and handling errors and failures as close to the point of origination as possible, and by minimizing the dependence on low-level operating system-specific functionality of the local processing entities.

5. New Challenges to Support Dynamic and Collaborative Work

Recently, there is increasing interest in developing adaptive workflows and dynamic WFMSs. Majority of current work address relevant issues at modeling and language levels [KS 95, ER 95, HHSW 96, JST97, H 97, R 97], with few efforts on implementations underway [MLB+ 97, Ta 97]. A particularly different approach to supporting adaptive workflow to react to the changes in local rules and other conditions is being developed using the notion of migrating workflows [CR 97]. Workflow Management Coalition (WfMC) targets specification and interoperability issues among current generation of products and do not yet support dynamic and flexible workflow processes. Related issues of integrating workflow or coordination technologies and collaboration technologies are investigated in [GAP 97, S97].

In this section, we will replace the term workflow by *work coordination and collaboration process* (WCC process, or simply *work process* when there is less chance for ambiguity). A WCC process implies support for *dynamic and collaborative* organizational activities. Developing systems that could support WCC processes stands out as one of the difficult new challenges in future evolution of the WFMSs. Such systems must be uniquely sensitive to a rapidly changing process execution triggered by collaborative decision points, context-sensitive information updates, and other external events. Its distributed, reliable design must also ensure the robustness and scalability expected of large-scale systems that support WCC processes. We term such systems as Work Coordination and Collaboration Systems (WCCS).

5.1 Work Coordination and Collaboration System

We now present a conceptual architecture for a WCCS which we have started to design and develop as a follow-up to our work on $METEOR_2$. We hope that this architecture can be used as a source of many challenging directions for the research agenda in the collaborative workflow systems of tomorrow.

Unlike existing workflow management technology, WCCS must support multiple, event-driven execution paths as an integral part of collaborative problem solving. The system must be able to determine the process flow (possibly in real time) as decision points are reached, since a more active and integrated information substrate (consisting of integrated databases, modern distributed computing infrastructure and middleware, and monitoring agents, as discussed later) is simultaneously pushing relevant updates to the appropriate WCC processes. As in traditional workflow managers, the entire WCC process is modeled as activities and tasks for the people and system components participating in accomplishing the work. System components can be of various types, including traditional compiled and interpreted programs, wrapped legacy code or its invocation, database transactions, scripts, or emerging network computing.

Overall, WCCS provides an automated infrastructure for collaboration both within any high-level process and for all the interactions and dependencies among them. Support tools can be invoked in a number of ways: automatically, as an embedded part of a particular activity; identified to a user as a tool that is potentially beneficial for a particular task at some specified point during the execution of a WCC process; or user-selectable, and available on an ad-hoc basis.

To support the collaborative process at the information level, users must have a suite of information processing tools, or utilities, upon which to draw. These utilities can assist users with the execution of a range of activities, including planning, scheduling, analysis, filtering, browsing, and integration.

Like the collaborative technologies, these utilities can be associated with a particular task or can provide a general purpose service.

The new approach involves agent-based technologies to encapsulate functions, such as metadata management, ontological-based search, brokering, mediation, and sentinel services all of which are required to carry out the higher level cognitive processes in the environment. Agents are also tailored according to organizational role of users, for example, emulating the rules of a chain of command and providing appropriate support for authorization.

5.2 WCCS Design

The key WCCS capabilities include:

- specification and support for *dynamic processes* that can change at run time automatically or with human input. Here, dynamic refers to: a) the ability of the run-time model of the execution engine to change course automatically to support a newly-specified next step in the work process execution, b) work processes with automated application tasks as well as user tasks involving human involvement with structured or unstructured collaboration among participants, c) concurrent execution of (sub)processes corresponding to interactions among different tasks;
- a high degree *process reuse*, using a repository for consistency of process ontology, resource ontology (including user-centered ontologies such as organizational roles, authorizations, user profiling, and other context required to create the appropriate views of information in a particular task), work process definitions, and detailed task specifications;
- collaboration, providing a variety of tools (voice, video, whiteboarding) supporting human interaction, both at the task level and the work coordination level;
- *adaptable* work processes, using monitoring agents (also called sentinels), or other appropriate agents, that react to changes in the relevant information resources, fuse the appropriate information, and notify the work coordination activities. Here, adaptable refers to the ability of the WCCS to monitor, interpret, and react to rapidly changing information sources;
- *visualization* of concurrently executing work processes as well as data manipulated by the work processes;
- *security*, including authentication, traditional subject-object as well as task-based access control, and the active modeling and management of authorizations, providing Web browsers enabled with Java as the user interface for system administration (not discussed in further in this paper).

Although the WCCS runtime will enable automation of significant portions of the work processes using application (automatic) tasks, there will be continued need for involvement of humans in the process. Thus, processes supported by WCCS will involve heterogeneous tasks, including both human and automated (programmed or system) tasks. The work performed by humans must be made easier and more productive. To this end, the tasks performed by humans in a work process can be enhanced with integrated collaboration support (including collaborative email, electronic discussion/whiteboarding, video/voice/data conferencing), and information/document search engine capable of accessing heterogeneous digital media (as in, for example, the Info-Harness system, see *http://lsdis.cs.uga.edu/infoharness*). The human collaboration will not be automatically managed or guided by the WCCS. However, WCCS will maintain an audit trail of the information processing and exchanges performed during a collaboration and enable such collaboration through appropriate Web-based tools.

The repository will contain process and information ontologies, and the tools to use them. It will consist of partial and complete designs and specifications of tasks, subprocesses and work processes. It will also support reuse of process components. An interesting feature it will support is the *plug-and-enactment* paradigm whereby process components in the repository can be used (through appropriate drag and drop support) on the visualization of a process being enacted to affect changes (such as interrupting, modifying, or redirecting) to the active processes. A unified WCCS user interface environment will support process design and development, browsing and querying of the repository, monitoring and tracking of processes being enacted by collaboration and enactment engine, and plug-and-enact interactions mentioned above.

Workflow process model supported by METEOR$_2$ is already quite comprehensive and sophisticated compared to contemporary WFMS products and WFMS research prototypes. It supports modeling of a hierarchical workflow process (with compound tasks), behavioral aspects of heterogeneous human-performed and application/system tasks (what can be observed, what can be controlled for a task execution by a given processing entity), inter-task dependencies (with control and data flow), specification of interfaces (involved in supporting legacy applications, client/server processing and distributed processing), run time environment and task assignments to various system components, error handling and recovery requirements, etc. Primary enhancement are needed in the areas of modeling collaboration and specification of dependencies or interactions among tasks that support coordination and collaboration. Some of these can be adapted from the work group or CSCW systems research.

5.3 WCCS Architecture

The overall architecture of WCCS to support adaptive, dynamic, and collaborative work processes is composed of a number of participating WCCS components. A key WCCS component is a Work Coordination and Collaboration Engine (WCCE). In addition to WCCE, each component contains a Work Coordination and Collaboration Agent (WCCA), which is responsible for coordination of inter-WCCS activities. WCCS also includes one or more

Monitoring Agents (MAs), whose task is to monitor any observable changes in the external environment and signal them to the involved WCCAs. External changes are recorded in the (logically) Integrated Heterogeneous Media Database (IHMDB). A schematic of the WCCS architecture is shown in Figure 2.

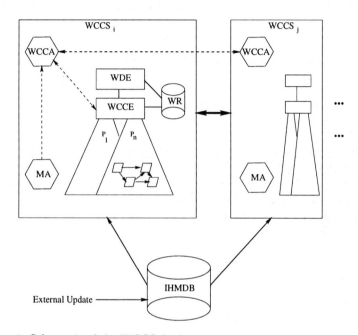

Fig. 2. Schematic of the WCCS Architecture

A WCCA oversees an associated WCCE. It can enact (possibly with a human involvement) a new work process instance and/or modify an already active one. A WCCA is also responsible for facilitating the inter-instance and inter-WCCS collaboration. In order to establish an inter-WCCS interaction, a WCCA receives a collaboration request from one of the tasks in a currently active instance. It then seeks out an appropriate peer WCCS and relays the request to the overseeing WCCA. Depending on the type of the request, the other WCCA may enlist an already active work process instance for participating in the requested collaboration, or enact a new instance.

The WCCS architecture also includes the Work Coordination and Collaboration Development Environment (WDE) and Work Coordination and Collaboration Repository (WR). To create the WDE component of the WCCS, we are planning to extend our current work to support the capability for multi-user design and a more dynamic and flexible model characterized above. Furthermore, WDE will have a tighter integration with WR and WCCE (as compared to the respective repository and run-time/enactment components of METEOR$_2$) to support the *plug-and-enactment* paradigm. WDE, like other components of WCCS will also utilize the Java-based technology supported by the latest network computing and distributed object management infrastructure.

All the WCCS sub-components come with Web-based graphical user interfaces as well as protocols for open interactions developed on top of latest industry standards.

5.4 Work Coordination and Collaboration Engine

WCCE provides a general framework for the enactment and management of highly dynamic, collaborative work processes. As in the current METEOR$_2$, the main component participating in the scheduling and task activation are task schedulers and task managers. Collectively, the core functionality of a task scheduler and task manager is implemented as a Universal Task Manager Server (UTMS). A UTMS may dynamically accept a task definition and then participate in a WCCS supported activity to which the accepted task definition belongs. Task definitions may be defined or modified statically, for example with the use of our WDE tool, or dynamically, during the lifetime of a work process instance.

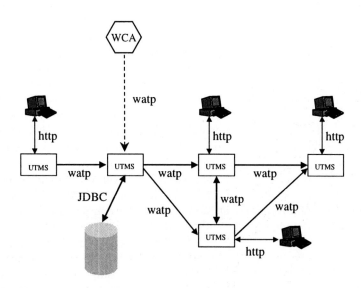

Fig. 3. Work Coordination and Collaboration Engine

A UTMS communicates with other UTMS's and WCCA using Work Activity Transport Protocol (WATP). An external process, such as a WCCA (or possibly a Work Activity Monitor, a part of WCCE) may create a new UTMS at a desired host. A WATP control message may be sent to the new (or already existing UTMS). Such a message may contain a task definition (or re-definition), task migration, or possibly task termination information.

Once a UTMS has been established as participating within a given work process, it takes part in scheduling its associated task, as subsequent work process instances reach this particular UTMS. The scheduling is achieved by sending WATP scheduling (transition) messages from a UTMS to its successors, according to the currently existing work process map.

In addition to handling WATP protocol, a UTMS is capable of handling the HyperText Transfer Protocol (HTTP) requests. Thus the end-users in work processes can communicate with any UTMS by means of a typical Web browser. As such, a UTMS may be regarded as a specialized HTTP server with limited functionality.

A UTMS manages a number of HTML pages and forms related to the task it controls, as well as forms dedicated to general administration functions. Instead of involving numerous CGI-scripts, a UTMS simply runs a process to fulfill a given request. That process may be executed in UTMS's own address space, as an independent thread, or possibly as a heavy-weight process. In addition, we envision that a UTMS may communicate with the outside world with the use of other well known protocols, such as ODBC, JDBC, or possibly SMTP. In that sense, a UTMS may be regarded as a *protocol translator*. Figure 3 shows how a WCCE may be realized using UTMSs.

A UTMS may be implemented in a variety of ways. However, we have chosen Java as it provides a portable, dynamic language. Because of Java's ability to dynamically load classes, implementation of dynamically loadable task definitions may be achieved quite easily. We plan to implement the WATP protocol on the CORBA/IIOP protocol.

6. Conclusions

Workflow technology has come a long way. Many routine (administrative) and ad-hoc processes found in an office environment can be supported by commercial products. Many organizations have achieved significant advantages using the workflow technology in terms of reduced paper work and faster flow of document-centric information (through electronic documentation and image flow systems), better quality (with more accurate information) of service to their customers (though faster access of electronic information, a side affect of some of the workflow automation), improvements through reengineering of processes, etc. As with the traditional 80-20 rule, 80% of simpler process can now be supported if there is enough will and resources on the part of an organization to use the workflow technology to achieve its advantages. Still perhaps 20% of processes– typically involving processes that can be described as more complex, evolving, mission-critical, and large-scale– cannot be supported by current generation of products. These processes also tend to be higher value (as may be indicated by the adjectives "complex" and "mission critical").

Of the many outstanding technical challenges, we chose to address three of the more important technical challenges in this paper: scalability of a WFMS, adaptability through dynamic workflows, and support for collaboration. Arguably, these challenges range from shorter term to longer term in a research agenda we envisage. For these three challenges, we gave example application scenarios to provide motivations and to discuss some of the key requirements and technical issues. For scalability, we used the METEOR$_2$ WFMS to discussed how a modern system can deal with many aspects of this challenge. For other two challenges, we outlined the research approach for our work in progress or planned in future, and even speculated on ways to approach the issues when we reached the limits of our current experience and understanding. Our most important message is that coordination (as supported by current generation of workflow technology), collaboration (as supported by CSCW and work group systems) and information management will increasingly come together to merge into a higher level form of middleware.

Acknowledgements

The METEOR team consists of Kemafor Anyanwu, Souvik Das, Yong Jiang, Krys Kochut (co-PI), Zonhwei Luo, John Miller (co-PI), Devanand Palaniswami, Kshitij Shah, Amit Sheth (PI), Devashish Worah, and Ke Zheng. Key past contributors include David Lin, Arun Murugan and Richard Wang. Special thanks for feedback from our industry partners who have tested and used METEOR$_2$ components at CHREF, SCRA, and NIST.

This research was partially done under a cooperative agreement between the National Institute of Standards and Technology Advanced Technology Program (under the HIIT contract, number 70NANB5H1011) and the Healthcare Open System and Trials, Inc. consortium. See URL: *http://www.-scra.org/hiit.html*. Additional partial support and donations are provided by Iona, Informix, I-Kinetics, Boeing, Hewlett-Packard Labs, Persistence, and others.

Design and Implementation of a Distributed Workflow Management System: METUFlow *

Asuman Dogac, Esin Gokkoca, Sena Arpinar, Pinar Koksal, Ibrahim Cingil,
Budak Arpinar, Nesime Tatbul, Pinar Karagoz, Ugur Halici, Mehmet Altinel

Software Research and Development Center
Department of Computer Engineering
Middle East Technical University (METU)
06531 Ankara Turkiye
asuman@srdc.metu.edu.tr

Abstract. Workflows are activities involving the coordinated execution of multiple tasks performed by different processing entities, mostly in distributed heterogeneous environments which are very common in enterprises of even moderate complexity. Centralized workflow systems fall short to meet the demands of such environments.

This paper describes the design and implementation of a distributed workflow management system, namely, METUFlow. The main contribution of this prototype is to provide a truly distributed execution environment, where the scheduler, the history manager and the worklist manager of the system are fully distributed giving rise to failure resiliency and increased performance.

1. Introduction

A workflow system can be defined as a collection of processing steps (also termed as tasks or activities) organized to accomplish some business process. A task may represent a manual operation by a human or a computerizable task to be invoked. Computerizable tasks may vary from legacy applications to programs to control instrumentation. In addition to the collection of tasks, a workflow defines the order of task invocation or condition(s) under which tasks must be invoked (i.e. control-flow) and data-flow between these tasks.

This paper describes the design and implementation of a workflow management system prototype, namely METUFlow. METUFlow handles the interoperability of applications on heterogeneous platform by using CORBA as the communication infrastructure. The distinguishing features of METUFlow are: a distributed scheduling mechanism with a distributed history and a distributed worklist management. In current commercial workflow systems, the workflow scheduler is a single centralized component. A distributed workflow scheduler, on the other hand, should contain several schedulers on different nodes of a network each executing parts of process instances. Such an architecture fits naturally to the distributed heterogeneous environments. Further

---
* This work is partially being supported by the Middle East Technical University, Project Number: AFP-97-07-02-08, by the Turkish State Planning Organization, Project Number: AFP-03-12DPT.95K120500, by the Scientific and Technical Research Council of Turkey, Project Number: EEEAG-Yazilim5 and by Sevgi Holding (Turkey).

advantages of such an architecture are failure resiliency and increased performance since a centralized scheduler is a potential bottleneck. In order to fully exploit the advantages brought by the distributed scheduling, METUFlow history management, workflow relevant data management and the worklist management are also handled in a distributed manner.

Data consistency can be violated by improper interleaving of concurrently executing workflows. Therefore, there should exist a mechanism to prevent such interleavings to ensure data consistency in workflow management systems (WFMS). In METUFLow, we introduce the concept of "sphere of isolation" for the correctness of concurrently executing workflows while increasing concurrency. Spheres of isolations are obtained by exploiting the available semantics in workflow specification.

METUFlow has a block structured specification language, namely METU-Flow Definition Language (MFDL). The advantages brought by this language can be summarized as follows:

- As noted in [S$^+$ 96], state-of-the-art workflow specification languages are unstructured and/or rule based. Unstructured specification languages make debugging/testing of complex workflow difficult and rule based languages become inefficient when they are used for specification of large and complex workflow processes. This is due to the large number of rules and overhead associated with rule invocation and management. MFDL prevents these disadvantages.
- A block structured language confines the intertask dependencies to a well formed structure which in turn proves extremely helpful in generating the guards of events for distributed scheduling of the workflow.
- A block not only clearly defines the data and control dependencies among tasks but also presents a well-defined recovery semantics, i.e., when a block aborts, the tasks that are to be compensated and the order in which they are to be compensated are already provided by the block semantics.

The paper is organized as follows: Section 2 describes the METUFlow Specification Language. In Section 3, we give the underlying mechanism of METUFlow scheduler. The architecture of METUFlow is provided in Section 4. In the sections that follow namely Section 5, 6, 7, 8 and 9, the details of the components of METUFlow, namely, scheduler, task handlers, worklist manager, history manager and transaction manager are explained. In Section 10, our concurrency control mechanism is described. Finally, the conclusions are provided in Section 11.

2. The Process Model and the METUFlow Definition Language: MFDL

In a workflow definition language, the tasks involved in a business process, the execution and data dependencies between these tasks are provided.

METUFlow Definition Language (MFDL) that we have designed has a graphical user interface developed through Java which allows defining a workflow by accessing METUFlow from any computer that has a Web browser. This feature of METUFlow makes it possible to support mobile users.

The WfMC have identified a set of six primitives with which to describe flows and hence construct a workflow specification [Hol 96]. With these primitives it is possible to model any workflow that is likely to occur. These primitives are: sequential, AND-split, AND-join, OR-split, OR-join and repeatable task. These primitives are all supported by MFDL through its block types. MFDL contains seven types of blocks, namely, serial, and_parallel, or_parallel, xor_parallel, contingency, conditional and iterative blocks. Of the above block types, serial block implements the sequential primitive. And_parallel block models the AND-split and AND-join primitives. AND-split, OR-join pair is modelled by or_parallel block. Conditional block corresponds to OR-split and OR-join primitives. Finally, repeatable task primitive is supported by the iterative block.

A workflow process is defined as a collection of blocks, tasks and subprocesses. A task is the simplest unit of execution. Processes and tasks have input and output parameters corresponding to workflow relevant data to communicate with other processes and tasks. The term *activity* is used to refer to a block, a task or a (sub)process. Blocks differ from tasks and processes in that they are conceptual activities which are used only to specify the ordering and the dependencies between activities.

The following definitions describe the semantics of the block types and compansation and undo activities where B stands for a block, A for an activity and T for a task.

Syntax 1 $B = (A_1; A_2; A_3; ....; A_n)$, where B is a serial block.

Definition 1 Start of a serial block B causes A_1 to start. Commitment of A_1 causes start of A_2 and commitment of A_2 causes start of A_3, and so on. Commitment of A_n causes commitment of B. If one of the activities aborts, the block aborts.

Syntax 2 $B = (A_1 \ \& \ A_2 \ \& \ ..... \ \& \ A_n)$, where B is an and_parallel block.

Definition 2 Start of an and_parallel block B causes start of all of the activities in the block in parallel. B commits only if all of the activities commit. If one of the activities aborts, the block aborts.

Syntax 3 $B = (A_1|A_2|.....|A_n)$, where B is an or_parallel block.

Definition 3 Start of an or_parallel block B causes start of all of the activities in the block in parallel. At least one of the activities should commit for B to commit but B can not commit until all of the activities terminate. B aborts if all the activities abort.

Syntax 4 $B = (A_1||A_2||.....||A_n)$, where B is an xor_parallel block.

Definition 4 Start of an xor_parallel block B causes start of all tasks in the block in parallel. B commits if one of the activities commits, and commitment of one activity causes the other activities in the block to abort. If all of the activities abort, the block aborts.

Syntax 5 B $= (A_1, A_2, ...A_n)$, where B is a contingency block.

Definition 5 Start of a contingency block B causes start of A_1. Abort of A_1 causes start of A_2 and abort of A_2 causes start of A_3, and so on. Commitment of any activity causes commitment of B. If the last activity A_n aborts, the block aborts.

Syntax 6 B $=$ (condition,A_1, A_2), where B is a conditional block.

Definition 6 Conditional block B has two activities and a condition. If the condition is true when B starts, then the first activity starts. Otherwise, the other activity starts. The commitment of the block is dependent on the commitment of the chosen activity. If the chosen activity aborts, then B aborts.

Syntax 7 B $=$ (condition;$A_1; A_2; .....; A_n$), where B is an iterative block.

Definition 7 The iterative block B is similar to serial block, but start of iterative block depends on the given condition as in a while loop and execution continues until either the condition becomes false or any of the activities aborts. If B starts and the condition is true, then A_1 starts and continues like serial block. If A_n commits, then the condition is reevaluated. If it is false, then B commits. If is true, then A_1 starts executing again. If one of the activities aborts at any one of the iterations, B aborts.

Syntax 8 A $= (A_c,$ AbortList$(A_c))$, where A_c is the compensation activity of A.

Definition 8 The compensation activity A_c of A starts if A has committed and any of the activities in AbortList(A_c) has aborted. AbortList is a list computed during compilation which contains the activities whose aborts necessitate the compensation of A. If both an activity and its subactivities have compensation, only the compensation of the activity is used. If only the subactivities have compensation, it is necessary to use compensations of the subactivities to compensate the whole activity.

Syntax 9 T $= T_u$, where T_u is the undo task of non-transactional task T.

Definition 9 The undo task T_u of T starts if T fails.

In addition to activities, there is an assignment statement in MFDL which accesses and updates the workflow relevant data.

The following is an example workflow defined in MFDL:

```
TRANS_ACTIVITY register_patient (OUT int patient_id);
TRANS_ACTIVITY delete_patient(IN int patient_id);
USER_ACTIVITY  examine_patient (IN int patient_id,
        OUT int blood_test_type_list[20],
        OUT int roentgen_list[20])
        PARTICIPANT DOCTOR;

USER_ACTIVITY  blood_exam (IN int patient_id,
        IN int  blood_test_type_list[20], OUT STRING result[20])
```

```
          PARTICIPANT LABORANT;
USER_ACTIVITY  roentgen (IN int patient_id,
        IN int roentgen_list[20], OUT STRING result[20])
        PARTICIPANT ROENTGENOLOGIST;
USER_ACTIVITY  check_result (IN int patient_id,
        IN  string result1[20], IN STRING result2[20])
        PARTICIPANT DOCTOR;
USER_ACTIVITY  cash_pay (IN int patient_id)
        PARTICIPANT TELLER;
USER_ACTIVITY  credit_pay (IN int patient_id)
        PARTICIPANT TELLER;
DEFINE_PROCESS check_up (IN int patient_id)
{
 ACTIVITY register_patient register;
 ACTIVITY delete_patient delete;
 ACTIVITY examine_patient examine;
 ACTIVITY blood_exam blood;
 ACTIVITY roentgen roent;
 ACTIVITY check_result check;
 ACTIVITY cash_pay cash;
 ACTIVITY credit_pay credit;

 var int patient_id;
 var STRING result1[20], result2[20];
 var int  blood_test_type_list[20], roentgen_list[20];

 IF (patient_id == 0)
     register(patient_id)
           COMPENSATED_BY delete(patient_id);
 examine(patient_id, blood_test_type_list,
         roentgen_list);
 AND_PARALLEL
 {
     blood(patient_id, blood_test_type_list, result1);
     WHILE (result2 == NULL)
           roent(patient_id, roentgen_list, result2);
 }
 check(patient_id, result1, result2);
 XOR_PARALLEL
 {
     cash(patient_id);
     credit(patient_id);
 }
}
```

This example is a simplified workflow of a check-up process carried out
in a hospital. First, a patient is registered to the hospital, if she/he has not
registered before. Then, she/he is examined by a doctor and according to the
doctor's decision, a blood test is made and roentgen is taken for the patient
in parallel. Since the patient need not wait for blood test to be finished in
order roentgen to be taken, these two tasks are executed in an and-parallel
block. Roentgen can be taken more than once, if the result is not clear. This

Table 1. Event Attributes

activity_types	start	abort/fail	commit/done
transactional	triggerable	immediate	normal
2PC_transactional	triggerable	normal,immediate	normal
non_transactional	triggerable	immediate	immediate
non_transactional with checkpoint	triggerable	immediate	immediate

is accomplished by an iterative block. After the results are checked by the doctor, the patient pays the receipt either in cash or by credit. These two tasks are placed in an xor_parallel block so that, cash and credit begins in parallel and commit of one causes the other to abort.

In METUFlow, there are five types of tasks. These are TRANSAC-TIONAL, NON_TRANSACTIONAL, NON_TRANSACTIONAL with CHE-CKPOINT, USER and 2PC_TRANSACTIONAL activities. USER activities are in fact NON_TRANSACTIONAL activities. They are specified separately in order to be used by the worklist manager which handles the user-involved activities. The states and transitions between these states for each of the activity types are demonstrated in Figure 1. The significant events in METU-Flow are start, commit and abort. The event attributes of these tasks are shown in Table 1. They are taken into account during guard generation. Normal events are delayable and rejectable (e.g. commit), inevitable events are delayable and nonrejectable, immediate events are nondelayable and nonrejectable (e.g. abort), and triggerable events are forcible (e.g. start).

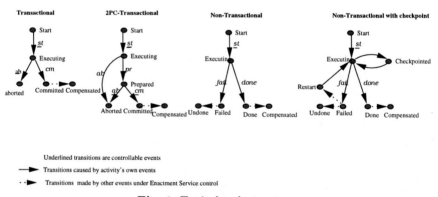

Fig. 1. Typical task structures

Note that the abort event of a 2PC_TRANSACTIONAL task after the coordinator has taken a decision is normal whereas it is immediate before the coordinator has taken a decision. Triggerable and normal events are controllable because they can be triggerred, rejected or delayed while immediate events are uncontrollable. We have chosen to include a second type of non-transactional activity, namely, NON-TRANSACTIONAL with CHECKPOINT, in our model by making the observation that certain non-transactional activities in real life, take checkpoints so that when a failure occurs, an application program rolls the activity back to the last successful checkpoint.

These activity types may have some attributes such as CRITICAL, NON_VITAL and CRITICAL_NON_VITAL. Critical activities can not be compensated and the failure of a non_vital activity is ignored [DHL 91, CD 96]. Besides these attributes, activities can also have some properties like retriable, compensable, and undoable. A retriable activity restarts execution depending on some condition when it fails. Compensation is used in undoing the visible effects of activities after they are committed. Effects of an undoable activity can be removed depending on some condition in case of failures. Some of these properties are special to specific activity types. Undo conditions are only defined for non-transactional tasks, because transactional tasks do not leave any effects when they abort. Only 2PC-transactional activities can be defined as critical. Note that the effects of critical activities are visible to the other activities in the workflow but the commitment of these activities are delayed till the successful termination of the workflow. An activity can be both critical and non_vital at the same time, but can not be critical and compensable.

In MFDL, activities in a process are declared using the reserved word ACTIVITY. This declaration allows the sharing of an activity definition among many workflow processes with possibly different attributes and properties for each instance.

3. Guard Generation for Distributed Scheduling

In this section, first the semantics of the block types are defined using ACTA formalism. We then show that the two dependencies provided in [Kle 91] are adequate to express the specified block semantics and result in simple guard expressions. Finally, a mechanism for guard construction is presented.

3.1 Semantics of the Block Types Using ACTA Formalism

We use the ACTA formalism [CR 91, CR 92] with slight modifications to express the semantics of block types[1] as follows:

Let t_i and t_j be two transactions.

– **Commit Dependency**(t_j CD t_i): if transaction t_i commits, then t_j commits.

---

[1] We treat fail/done event of non-transactional activities as abort/commit of transactional activities.

- **Commit-on-Abort Dependency**$(t_j$ CAD $t_i)$: if transaction t_i aborts, then t_j commits.
- **Abort Dependency**$(t_j$ AD $t_i)$: if transaction t_i aborts, then t_j aborts.
- **Abort-on-Commit Dependency**$(t_j$ ACD $t_i)$: if transaction t_i commits, then t_j aborts.
- **Begin Dependency**$(t_j$ BD $t_i)$: if transaction t_i begins executing, then t_j starts.
- **Begin-on-Commit Dependency**$(t_j$ BCD $t_i)$: if transaction t_i commits, then t_j begins executing.
- **Begin-on-Abort Dependency**$(t_j$ BAD $t_i)$: if transaction t_i aborts, then t_j begins executing.

Conditional dependencies are added to the ACTA formalism. These dependencies have an additional argument which is "condition". For example, a conditional begin dependency is expressed as BD(C). If condition C is true, then BD holds, else it does not hold.

Using the modified ACTA formalism, semantics of block types and compensation and undo activites can be restated as follows:

Semantics 1 $B = (A_1; A_2; A_3; .....; A_n)$, where B is a serial block.
- A_1 BD B
- A_{i+1} BCD A_i , $1 \leq i < n$
- B CD A_n
- B AD A_i ,$1 \leq i \leq n$

Semantics 2 $B = (A_1 \& A_2 \& ..... \& A_n)$, where B is an and_parallel block.
- A_i BD B ,$1 \leq i \leq n$
- B AD A_i ,$1 \leq i \leq n$
- $\forall i(B$ CD $A_i)$

Semantics 3 $B = (A_1 | A_2 | ..... | A_n)$, where B is an or_parallel block.
- A_i BD B ,$1 \leq i \leq n$
- $\exists i$ (B CD A_i) $\land$ $(\forall j((B$ CD $A_j)$ $\lor$ (B CAD $A_j)))$, $j \neq i$
- $\forall i(B$ AD $A_i)$

Semantics 4 $B = (A_1 || A_2 || ..... || A_n)$, where B is an xor_parallel block.
- A_i BD B ,$1 \leq i \leq n$
- $\exists i$ (B CD A_i) $\land$ $(\forall j(A_j$ ACD $A_i))$, $i \neq j$
- $\forall i(B$ AD $A_i)$

Semantics 5 $B = (A_1, A_2, ...A_n)$, where B is a contingency block.
- A_1 BD B
- A_{i+1} BAD A_i, $1 \leq i < n$
- B CD A_i, $1 \leq i \leq n$
- B AD A_n

Semantics 6 $B = (condition(C), A_1, A_2)$, where B is a conditional block.
- A_1 BD(C) B
- A_2 BD(¬C) B
- B CD(C) A_1

- B CD($\neg$C) A_2
- B AD(C) A_1
- B AD($\neg$C) A_2

Semantics 7 B = (condition(C);A_1; A_2; .....; A_n), where B is an iterative block.

- A_1 BD(C) B
- A_{i+1} BCD A_i, $1 \leq i < n$
- B CD($\neg$C) A_n
- B AD A_i

Semantics 8 A = (A_c, AbortList(A_c)), where A_c is the compensation activity of A.

- (A_c BCD A) $\wedge$ (A_c BAD AbortList(A_c))

Semantics 9 T = T_u, where T_u is the undo task of T.

- T_u BAD T

ACTA formalism specifies the transaction semantics of a model by presenting transaction relations with predefined dependencies. However, these dependencies are expressed at the abstract level and therefore the following two primitives [Kle 91, Att 93] are used to specify intertask dependencies as constraints on the occurrence and temporal order of events:

1. $e_1 \rightarrow e_2$: If e_1 occurs, then e_2 must also occur. There is no implied ordering on the occurrence of e_1 and e_2.
2. $e_1 < e_2$: If e_1 and e_2 both occur, then e_1 must preceed e_2.

The ACTA dependencies used in the specification of the block semantics are expressed in terms of these two primitives as follows:

- **Commit Dependency**(t_j CD t_i):
  ($Commit_{t_j} \rightarrow Commit_{t_i}$) $\wedge$ ($Commit_{t_i} < Commit_{t_j}$)
- **Commit-on-Abort Dependency**(t_j CAD t_i):
  ($Abort_{t_j} \rightarrow Commit_{t_i}$) $\wedge$ ($Commit_{t_i} < Abort_{t_j}$)
- **Abort Dependency**(t_j AD t_i):
  ($Abort_{t_j} \rightarrow Abort_{t_i}$) $\wedge$ ($Abort_{t_i} < Abort_{t_j}$)
- **Abort-on-Commit Dependency**(t_j ACD t_i):
  ($Abort_{t_j} \rightarrow Commit_{t_i}$) $\wedge$ ($Commit_{t_i} < Abort_{t_j}$)
- **Begin Dependency**(t_j BD t_i):
  ($Start_{t_j} \rightarrow Start_{t_i}$) $\wedge$ ($Start_{t_i} < Start_{t_j}$)
- **Begin-on-Commit Dependency**(t_j BCD t_i):
  ($Start_{t_j} \rightarrow Commit_{t_i}$) $\wedge$ ($Commit_{t_i} < Start_{t_j}$)
- **Begin-on-Abort Dependency**(t_j BAD t_i):
  ($Start_{t_j} \rightarrow Abort_{t_i}$) $\wedge$ ($Abort_{t_i} < Start_{t_j}$)

The guards of events corresponding to these two primitive dependencies are as follows [Att 93, S 96b]:

For the constraint $e < f$, which corresponds to the dependency $D_< = \bar{e} \vee \bar{f} \vee e \bullet f$, the guards are:

Table 2. Guards corresponding to the dependency set

dependency	e	f	$G(f)$	$G(e)$
A BD B	B_{st}	A_{st}	$\Box B_{st}$	TRUE
A BCD B	B_{cm}	A_{st}	$\Box B_{cm}$	TRUE
A BAD B	B_{ab}	A_{st}	$\Box B_{ab}$	TRUE
A CD B	B_{cm}	A_{cm}	$\Box B_{cm}$	TRUE
A CAD B	B_{ab}	A_{cm}	$\Box B_{ab}$	TRUE
A AD B	B_{ab}	A_{ab}	$\Box B_{ab}$	TRUE
A ACD B	B_{cm}	A_{ab}	$\Box B_{cm}$	TRUE

- $\mathcal{G}(e) = $ TRUE
- $\mathcal{G}(f) = \Diamond \bar{e} \vee \Box e$

Note that $\Box e$ means that e will always hold; $\Diamond e$ means that e will eventually hold (thus $\Box e$ entails $\Diamond e$). At runtime e can occur at any point in the history whereas f can occur only if e has occurred or it is guaranteed that $\bar{e}$ will occur.

For the constraint $f \to e$, which corresponds to the dependency $D_\to = \bar{f} \vee e$, the guards of events are:

- $\mathcal{G}(e) = $ TRUE
- $\mathcal{G}(f) = \Diamond e$

These guards state that e can occur at any time in the history; f can occur if e has happened or will happen.

3.2 Guard Construction Steps

We use the dependencies BD, BCD, BAD to compute start guards, AD, ACD to generate abort guards and CD, CAD to compute commit guards of activities [T 98]. Note that all of these dependencies are in the form of an expression which contains one subexpression with $\to$ primitive and the other with $<$ primitive with a conjunction in between them such as $(f \to e)$ $\wedge$ $(e < f)$. We present the construction of guards of events e and f for this dependency in the following [S 96b]:

$\mathcal{G}(e) = $ TRUE
$\mathcal{G}(f) = \mathcal{G}(D_\to, f) \wedge \mathcal{G}(D_<, f) = \Diamond e \wedge (\Diamond \bar{e} \vee \Box e) = (\Diamond e \wedge \Diamond \bar{e}) \vee (\Diamond e \wedge \Box e) = FALSE \vee (\Diamond e \wedge \Box e) = \Diamond e \wedge \Box e = \Box e$

Note that after simplification, the guard of f turned out to be $\Box e$. In other words, the occurrence of event f only requires event e to have already happened. This is an intuitively expected result since in our workflow specification, the occurrence of events only depends on the events already occurred with no references to the future events. This result facilitates the computation of the guards drastically. The guards of events of the dependency set corresponding to our workflow specification language are computed as presented in Table 2. Note that from this result, we conclude that if we want to compute the guard related to an activity A_1, we must consider only "A_1 ACTA_Dep A_2" type dependencies, not "A_2 ACTA_Dep A_1" type dependencies. The reason is that in the latter, the guard of any event related with A_1 is already TRUE from Table 2.

If we summarize, by starting with a block structured workflow specification language, we obtain a well defined set of dependencies, all in the form $(f \rightarrow e) \land (e < f)$. This produces very straightforward guards for events which in turn, makes it possible to compute the guards directly from the process definition with a simple algorithm. The complete guard generation process is outlined in Figure 2.

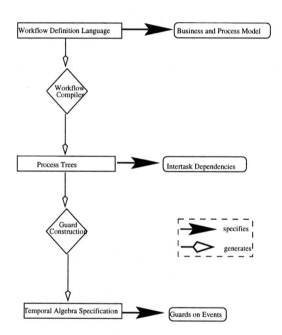

Fig. 2. Guard generation process

A process tree is generated from the workflow specification in MFDL. The process tree consists of nodes representing processes, blocks and tasks, and is used only during compilation time, execution being completely distributed. Each of the nodes is given a unique label to be referred in the execution phase. These activity labels make it possible for each task instance to have its own uniquely identified event symbols. This tree explicitly shows the dependencies between the activities of the workflow. In fact, with Table 2 at hand, it is possible to generate the guards of a process from its process tree. In the following we describe the guard construction process through an example.

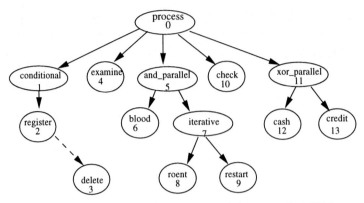

Fig. 3. Process tree of the example MFDL

In Figure 3, the process tree corresponding to MFDL example of Section 2 is given. The nodes shown in dashed lines are the compensation activities for the corresponding nodes.

Consider node 3 of Figure 3 which is a compensation task. Using Semantics 8:

$D_1 : 3$ BAD 0
$D_2 : 3$ BCD 2
$D : D_1 \wedge D_2$

Note that AbortList of 3 is $\{0\}$, because the compensation of 2 is needed only when 0 aborts. From Table 2,

$G(D_1, 3_{st}) = \Box 0_{ab}$
$G(D_2, 3_{st}) = \Box 2_{cm}$
$G(D, 3_{st}) = G(D_1, 3_{st}) \wedge G(D_2, 3_{st}) = \Box 0_{ab} \wedge \Box 2_{cm}.$

This guard states that task 3 should be started when process itself (node 0) is aborted while task 2 has committed.

In Figure 3, there is a restart node labeled as 9. This node is special to iterative block. Restart node is treated like the other children of the iterative node during execution. Its role is to prepare the block for the next iteration while the iteration condition is true. After restart node commits, the iteration condition is checked. If it is true, the next iteration starts. Otherwise, the iterative node commits, as stated in Semantics 7 (A_n corresponds to restart node). Note that this cyclic dependency in arbitrary tasks is handled in [S 96a] by resurrecting a guard under appropriate conditions. Ours is a practical implementation of this formal concept.

Table 3 shows the start, abort and commit guards for all the nodes of the example process tree given in Figure 3.

Table 3. Guards of the example workflow definition

label	start	start condition	abort	commit	commit condition
0	TRUE		$\square$ $1_{ab}\vee$ $\square$ $4_{ab}\vee$ $\square$ $5_{ab}\vee$ $\square$ $10_{ab}\vee$ $\square$ 11_{ab}	$\square 11_{cm}$	
1	$\square$ 0_{st}	patient_id $== 0$	$\square$ 2_{ab}	$\square$ 2_{cm}	
2	$\square$ 1_{st}		TRUE	TRUE	
3	$\square$ $0_{ab}\wedge$ $\square$ 2_{cm}		TRUE	TRUE	
4	$\square$ 1_{cm}		TRUE	TRUE	
5	$\square$ 4_{cm}		$\square 6_{ab}\vee$ $\square 7_{ab}$	$\square 6_{cm}\wedge$ $\square 7_{cm}$	
6	$\square 5_{st}$		TRUE	TRUE	
7	$\square 5_{st}$	result2 $==$ Null	$\square 8_{ab}\vee$ $\square 9_{ab}$	$\square 9_{cm}$	result2 $!=$ Null
8	$\square 7_{st}$		TRUE	TRUE	
9	$\square 8_{cm}$		TRUE	TRUE	
10	$\square 5_{cm}$		TRUE	TRUE	
11	$\square 10_{cm}$		$\square 12_{ab}\wedge$ $\square 13_{ab}$	$\square 12_{cm}\vee$ $\square 13_{cm}$	
12	$\square 11_{st}$		$\square 13_{cm}$	$\square 13_{ab}$	
13	$\square 11_{st}$		$\square 12_{cm}$	$\square 12_{ab}$	

It should be noted that in Table 3, some of the guards are set to TRUE right away. This is because either the occurrences of these events do not depend on the occurrence of any event or they are immediate events. Also note that, xor_parallel blocks identify a race condition without a need for preprocessing. For example, from Table 3, it is clear that abort of 12 is dependent on the commitment of 13 and commitment of 13 is dependent on the abort of 12. Obviously, this creates a deadlock situation. We implemented a modified 2 Phase Commitment protocol to handle this case (See Section 9.). When xor_parallel block starts, all of its immediate children are registered to the coordinator object belonging to this block. The coordinator keeps track of status of these children to ensure that only one of them commits. In this case, the abort and commit guards are not constructed any more for the child nodes.

4. METUFlow Architecture

A simplified architecture of METUFlow system is given in Figure 4. In METUFlow, first a workflow is specified using a graphical workflow specification tool which generates the textual workflow definition in MFDL as explained in Section 2. The core component of a workflow management system is the workflow scheduler which instantiates workflows according to the

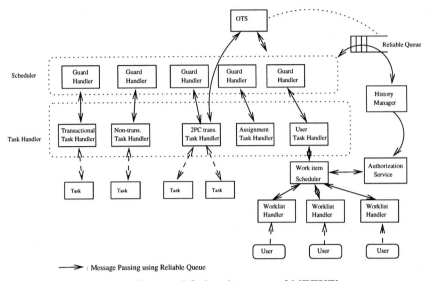

Fig. 4. The simplified architecture of METUFlow

workflow specification and controls correct execution of activities interacting with users via worklists and invoking applications as necessary. In METU-Flow, the functionality of the scheduler is distributed to a number of guard handlers which contain the guard expressions for the events of the activity instances as explained in Section 5. Also, there exists a task handler for each activity instance which acts as an interface between the activity instance and its guard handler. Details of task handling in METUFlow is discussed in Section 6. In a workflow management system, there are activities in which human interactions are necessary. In METUFlow, work item scheduler manages such interactions. It is responsible for progressing work requiring user attention and interacts with the scheduler through user task handler as shown in Figure 4. Work item scheduler uses the authorization service to determine the authorized roles and users. The detailed architecture of work item scheduler is provided in Section 7. History manager provides the mechanisms for storing and querying the history of both ongoing and past processes. It communicates with the scheduler through a reliable message queue to keep track of the execution of processes.

The communication infrastructure of METUFlow is CORBA but CORBA does not provide for reliable message passing, that is, when ORB crashes, all of the transient messages are lost. For this reason, we have implemented a reliable message passing mechanism which uses Object Transaction Service (OTS) based transaction manager (See Section 9.) to commit distributed transactions. Note that reliable message passing is necessary among all the components of METUFlow such as between guard handlers and task handlers as indicated in Figure 4.

5. Guard Handlers in METUFlow

After textual workflow definition is produced by MFDL, a process tree is generated using this textual definition as explained in Section 3.2. Three guard expressions for the significant events are generated for each node of the process tree. After the guards are constructed, an environment in which these guards are evaluated through the event occurrence messages they receive is created. Since METUFlow execution environment is distributed on the basis of activities, each activity should know when to start, abort or commit without consulting to a top-level central decision mechanism. For this purpose, a guard handler is associated with each activity instance which contains the guard expressions for the events of that activity instance [Gok 97]. Also, there exists a task handler for each activity instance which embodies a coarse description of the activity instance including only the states and transitions (i.e. events) that are significant for coordination. A guard handler provides the message flow between the activity's task handler and the other guard handlers in the system.

Each node in the process tree is implemented as a CORBA [SS 95, OMG 91] object with an interface for the guard handler to receive and send messages. Figure 5 shows the execution environment of objects of guard handler for the example check-up workflow. The reason for creating objects for each node rather than only for leaf nodes, which correspond to the actual tasks, is that carrying block semantics to the execution reduces the number of messages to be communicated. This is explained in the following example:

Assume that we have a process segment like:

```
serial {
        and_parallel {
            T1();
            T2();
            ...
            Tn();
        }
        and_parallel {
            T1();
            T2();
            ...
            Tn();
        }
}
```

Without a block abstraction during execution, the start guard of each activity in the second and_parallel block must contain the commit event of

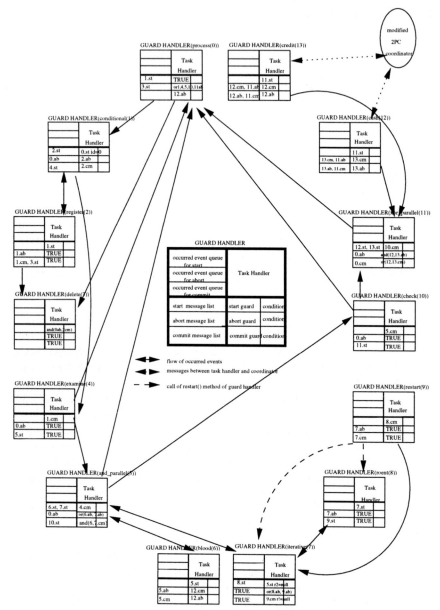

Fig. 5. Execution environment of objects of Guard Handler

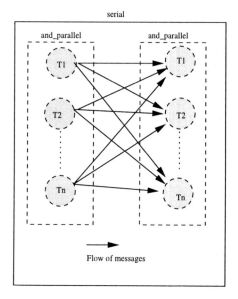

serial

Fig. 6. Environment of objects without block abstraction

each task of the first and_parallel block. Obviously this necessitates to communicate the commit event of each of the n tasks in the first and_parallel block to each of the n tasks in the second and_parallel block. Hence without a block abstraction, the number of messages to be communicated is n^2, as shown in Figure 6.

When block abstraction is used during execution as shown in Figure 7, the start guard of the second and_parallel block contains the commit event of the first and_parallel block. Thus the commit guard of the first and_parallel block contains the commit events of each of its n tasks; the start guards of each of the tasks in the second and_parallel block contain the start event of the second and_parallel block. For this case, the number of messages communicated reduces to $2n + 1$, as shown in Figure 7.

At compile time the guards are generated and stored locally with the related objects. The objects to which the messages from this object are to be communicated are also recorded. For example for task 3, since its start guard contains an abort event of the process, the abort_message_list of the process contains the object identifier of task 3 to indicate that the start guard of task 3 should be informed of the abort of the process. When an object receives an event to be consumed, it is placed in the occurred_events_queue of the related significant event of the object. Figure 5 explicitly shows the source and the destination of the messages.

A guard handler maintains the current guard for the significant events of the activity and manages communications. When a task handler is ready to make a transition, it attempts the corresponding event. Intuitively, an event can happen only when its guard evaluates to true. If the guard for the at-

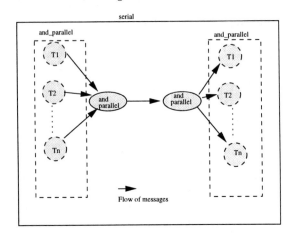

Fig. 7. Environment of objects with block abstraction

tempted event is true, it is allowed right away. If it is false, it is rejected. Otherwise, it is parked. Parking an event means defering its occurrence until its guard simplifies to true or false. When an event happens, messages announcing its occurrence are sent to the guard handlers of other related activities. Persistent queues are used to provide reliable message passing. When an event announcement arrives, the receiving guard handler simplifies its guard to incorporate this information. If the guard becomes true, then the appropriate parked event is enabled.

6. Task Handling in METUFlow

A task handler is created for each task instance. It acts as a bridge between the task and its guard handler. The guard handler sends the information necessary for the execution of the task, like the name of the task, parameters to the task handler and the task handler sends the information about the status of the task and changed values of the parameters to the guard handler. When a task starts, its status becomes *Executing*. If it can terminate successfully, then its status is changed to *Committed* or *Done* depending on whether it is a transactional or a non-transactional task. In case the task fails, its status becomes *Aborted* or *Failed*.

Task handler [K 98] is a CORBA object and has a generic interface which contains the following methods to communicate with its associated guard handler:

- **Init.** This method is used for passing initial data such as name of the task and initial parameters to the task handler.
- **Start.** This method is called by the guard handler when the start guard of the task evaluates to true. This causes the task handler to invoke the actual task.

The task handlers for each different type of task inherit from this interface and provide overloading of these methods and/or further methods as necessary as explained in the following:

- **Transactional task handler.** This type of task handler is coded for the transactional tasks. Even if a transactional task terminates successfully, its task handler should wait for the commit or abort message from the guard handler. Therefore, in addition to the common methods described above, this type of task handler provides two more methods, *Commit* and *Abort* to be called by the guard handler when a task is allowed to commit or abort respectively.

- **Non-transactional task handler.** This type of task handler handles tasks which are of type either non-transactional or non-transactional with checkpoint. The difference between non-transactional and non-transactional with checkpoint is that in the latter in case of a failure the application is rolled back to the latest checkpoint and not to the beginning. Since this does not affect the communication between the task and task handler, only one type of task handler is defined for both of them. Note that, non-transactional tasks terminate without waiting for any confirmation from the guard handler. They only inform the task handler about the status (*Done* or *Failed*).

- **Two phase commit task handler.** This type of task handler is required for two phase commit transactional tasks. The difference between this type of task and transactional tasks is that, the former provides an additional status message, namely *Prepared*. Thus, this type of task handler provides a method called *Prepare* to be called by the transaction manager.

- **User task handler.** This type of task handler is coded for the user tasks. User tasks are handled by work item scheduler and worklist handler (see Figure 4). The user task handler just stores the name of the task and the other necessary information to the repository from where the work item scheduler retrieves. The work item scheduler together with the worklist handlers informs the user about the tasks that she/he is responsible for and sends the status of the task to the user task handler (See Section 7.).

- **Assignment task handler.** This task handler does not cause any task to begin, but only a workflow relevant data assignment is done within the scope of a transaction.

In Workflow Reference Model of the Workflow Management Coalition [WfMC 94c], the task handlers are classified according to having local or remote access. This classification is due to the assumption that the scheduler is centralized. Since scheduling is handled in a distributed manner in METUFlow, there is no need for such a classification.

The tasks may define their status in a way that the task handler can not understand or the task may not understand the messages coming from the task handler. Therefore, it becomes essential to interfere the source code of existing tasks. If it is possible to make changes in the task, then additional calls are added to the code of the task to convert the status information and error messages so that task handler and task can understand each other. If this is not possible, then the existing task is encapsulated by a code which provides the required conversion.

```
register_patient()
{
  TaskExecuting();
  Connect_to_Database();

    /* This part of the code gets patient information from the user.
       A new patient_id is generated for this patient     */

  Insert_Into_Database(patient_info,status);
  if(status == True){
      ReadyToCommit();
      if( GetStatus() == Commit) {
      Commit();
      TaskCommitted();
      Return(patient_id);
      } else {

      Abort();
      TaskAborted();
      }
  } else {
      Abort();
      TaskAborted();
  }
}
```

Fig. 8. An Example Task Code

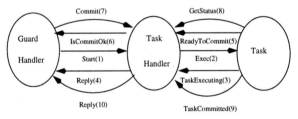

Fig. 9. Communication among Guard Handler, Task Handler and Task

In Figure 8, we provide the modified code of the transactional task, register_patient, taken from the example given in Section 2 to illustrate the first strategy. The calls which are written in boldface are added to the original code of the task. The meanings of these calls are as follows:

– **TaskExecuting()** informs the task handler that it has started executing.
– **ReadyToCommit()** informs the task handler that operation is terminated successfully.

- **TaskAborted()** informs the task handler that the final status is Abort.
- **TaskCommitted()** informs the task handler that the final status is Commit.
- **GetStatus()** checks the status message coming from the task handler.

The communication mechanism among guard handler, task handler and a task is provided in Figure 9. In the figure, the labels of the arrows show the message passing between the entities. The labels are numbered according to the order in which the calls are made and the figure describes the flow of messages for the scenario in which the task terminates successfully and its commit guard evaluates to true. When the start guard of the task evaluates to true, the guard handler of the task calls **Start** method of the task handler. This causes the task handler to start execution of the task. When the task starts executing, as the first operation, task handler is informed by calling **TaskExecuting** call. The status of the task is sent to the guard handler by the task handler in **Reply** method with the parameter *Executing*. Then the normal flow of the task begins. If patient information is written to the database successfully, the task handler is sent **ReadyToCommit** call. The task handler informs the guard handler that the task is ready to commit by calling its **IsCommitOk** method. If the commit guard of the task evaluates to true, the guard handler informs task handler about this situation by calling its **Commit** method. Otherwise, **Abort** method is called. Task checks whether the message sent is *Abort* or *Commit* by the **GetStatus** call. If task handler sends *Commit*, then task commits actually and claims the final state as *Commit*. In case of *Abort* message, task aborts and sends the final abort status. When final status is claimed by the task, the task handler informs the guard handler about the final status by calling **Reply** method again.

7. Worklist Management in METUFlow

The worklist manager is a software component which manages the interaction between workflow participants and the scheduler.

In METUFlow, the worklists are distributed, that is, a worklist at a site contains the work items to be accessed by the users at that site.

When a user activity is to be invoked by the scheduler, a user task handler created for this purpose stores the request (work item) into a request list within the scope of a transaction. Request list is a CORBA object and its implementation in a particular site depends on the persistent storage available in that site, that is, this CORBA object is implemented on a DBMS if it is available, otherwise it is implemented as a file. Worklist manager, as depicted in Figure 10 consists of two components. The first one, work item scheduler, decides on the assignment of work items to the worklists of the users in cooperation with the authorization service. The first version of the authorization

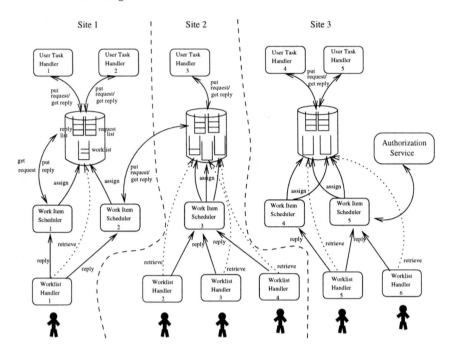

retrieve   :   retrives the worklist contents for the presentation to the user
put/get_request   puts (gets) a work item into (from) request list
put/get_reply   :   puts (gets) reply from the user into (from) reply list
reply   :   sends reply back (from worklist handler to work item scheduler)
assign   :   inserts work items into the worklists of the user

Fig. 10. Worklist Manager in METUFlow

service implemented contains the definitions of roles and their members, authorizations to execute tasks and constraints controlling the execution of
these authorizations. We plan to improve this service by involving periodic,
temporal, event based, distributed, constrained authorizations and authentication services. The work item scheduler is also responsible for putting
the reply back into the reply list, again, within the scope of a transaction.
That is, the reply list is a persistent CORBA object whose implementation
is realized through a DBMS or a file depending on the capabilities of the
site concerned. The second component, worklist handler is responsible for
retrieving work items to be presented to the user for processing.

A point to be noted over here is the following: CORBA provides location transparency, in other words the users need not be aware of the location of the objects to be created. However, CORBA does provide mechanisms to affect the object creation site although the specifics depends on the ORB at hand. First by default, an object is created at the local site if it is possible. Therefore, whenever there is a request to create a work item scheduler, it is created at the same site with the user task handler. In order to be able to create worklists at the same host with the involved user (or role), a list is kept which stores the association between the user-ids and host-ids. In METUFlow, lookup method of Orbix's locator class ([Iona 96]) is used for this purpose.

Finally, in order to provide access to the worklists through World-Wide-Web, we have chosen to implement them in Java which made it easier to connect to a CORBA compliant ORB, namely Orbix through OrbixWeb.

8. History Management in METUFlow

Workflow history management provides the mechanisms for storing and querying the history of both ongoing and past processes. This serves two purposes: First, during the execution of a workflow, the need may arise for looking up some piece of information in the process history, for example, to figure out who else has already been concerned with the workflow at what time in what role, and so on. This kind of information contributes to more transparency, flexibility and overall work quality. Second, aggregating and mining the histories of all workflows over a longer time period forms the basis for analyzing and assessing the efficiency, accuracy, and the timeliness of the enterprise's business processes. So, this information provides the feedback for continuous business processes re-engineering. Given that, much of the history information relates to the time dimension in that it refers to turnaround times, deadlines, delays, etc. over a long time horizon.

In consistence with its architecture, METUFlow history and workflow relevant data handling mechanism is based on CORBA. The history of each activity instance is implemented as a CORBA object. To exploit the advantages brought by the distributed execution of the workflow scheduler, history management should also be distributed. To make distributed history management possible, the persistent store in which the history information is kept, should also be distributed over the network.

The history of each activity instance is implemented as a CORBA object at the same site at which the activity object itself is invoked. If a DBMS is available at the concerned site, it is used as the persistent store, otherwise a binary file is used for this purpose. It is possible to have history objects created at the same site where they are activated to prevent the communication cost with the activity instance objects.

Each activity instance is responsible for its own history object and knows the object identifier of its parent activity instance. A child activity instance invokes a method to pass the object identifier of its own history object to its parent object. A parent activity instance object establishes the links between its own history object and its child's history object. Note that in the eventual history tree of the process instance obtained this way objects are linked through their object identifiers according to the process tree.

In summary, with a distributed history and workflow relevant data handling mechanism, availability and scalability aspects of the system are increased.

When it comes to querying history both for monitoring and for data mining purposes, having encapsulated these data as CORBA objects naturally yields to using the Query Service Specification of OMG.

The Query Service provides query operations on collection of objects. The Query Service can be used to return collections of objects that may be:

- selected from source collections based on whether their member objects satisfy a given predicate.
- produced by query evaluators based on the evaluation of a given predicate. These query evaluators may manage implicit collections of objects.

A Query Evaluator with temporal dimension is being developed for this purpose within the scope of the METUFlow project [Kok 97].

9. OTS Based Transaction Manager

In METUFlow, distributed transaction management is realized through a transaction manager that implements Object Transaction Service (OTS) Specification of OMG, OTS [OMG 95]. OTS specification describes a service that supports flat and nested transactions in a distributed heterogeneous environment. It defines interfaces that allow multiple, distributed objects to cooperate to provide atomicity of transactions. These interfaces enable the objects either to commit or to rollback all the changes together in the presence of failure.

Figure 11 illustrates the major components and the interfaces defined by OTS. In a typical scenario, a transactional client (transaction originator) creates a transaction obtaining a Control Object from a Factory provided by ORB. Transaction clients uses the Current pseudo-object to begin a transaction, which becomes associated with the transaction originator's thread. The Current interface defines operations that allow a client of OTS to begin and end transactions and to obtain information about the current transaction. A simplified version of Current interface is illustrated below:

```
interface Current {
  void begin();
```

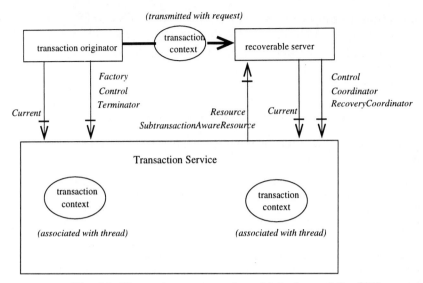

Fig. 11. The major components and interfaces of the OTS

```
void commit();
void rollback();
Status get_status();
string get_transaction_name();
   ...
}
```

ORB associates a Transaction Context with each Control object. A transaction context contains all the necessary information to control and to coordinate transactions. Transaction context is either explicitly passed as a parameter of the requests, or implicitly propagated by ORB, among the related transactional objects. The Control object is used in obtaining Terminator and Coordinator objects. Transactional client uses the Terminator to abort or to commit the transaction. Coordinator provides an interface for transactional objects to participate in two-phase-commit protocol. Transactional client sends requests to transactional objects. When a request is issued to a transactional object the transaction context associated with the invoking thread is automatically propagated to the thread executing the method of target object. A transactional object is the one that supports transaction primitives as defined by the standard. After the computations involved in the transaction have been completed, the transactional client uses the Current pseudo object to request that the changes be committed. OTS commits the transaction using 2PC protocol wherein a series of requests are issued to the registered resources. Thus, ORB provides the atomicity of distributed transactions.

In addition to the above usage of OTS, in METUFlow OTS implementation, a method is added to the Coordinator object to handle xor_parallel block which requires one and only one task to commit, for the commitment of the block.

10. Correctness Issues in METUFlow

Since workflows are long running activities, having the transactions to commit within the scope of a workflow instance is an accepted practice. Thus, the data modified by these transactions becomes accessible to the rest of the world which may cause inconsistencies. The problem is further complicated by the transactions that are compensated. Yet many scenarios in the operation of a workflow system require the preservation of data consistency of at least some data items.

It is possible to classify the data consistency problems involved into three categories:

1. Data inconsistency problems involving a single site,
2. Data inconsistency problems involving more than one site,
3. Data inconsistency problems due to compensation.

As an example to the problems of first category, consider an *Order Processing* workflow in a manufacturing enterprise. In the processing of the *Order Processing* workflow raw material stock is checked through a task to see whether there is enough raw material in the stock to process the order. If not, the missing raw materials are ordered from external vendors. Yet later in the process when the actual manufacturing is to start for this workflow instance there might not be enough raw material in the stock to process this order, because a concurrently running instance of the same or other workflows might have updated the stock. Of course, executing all these tasks within the scope of a transaction might have solved these problems but workflow systems are there to prevent the inefficiency of long running transactions.

An example to the data inconsistency problems involving more than one site is as follows: Consider the *Withdraw-Deposit* workflow of a bank involving two branches as shown in Figure 12. *Withdraw* task withdraws the given amount of money from an account at the first branch, and the *Deposit* adds this amount to another account at the second branch. To preserve data consistency, no other task accessing the same account in any of the involved branches should go in between these two tasks. For example, consider an *Audit* workflow which checks the balance of these accounts. If *Withdraw-Deposit* tasks and tasks of the *Audit* workflow are interleaved incorrectly as depicted in Figure 12, *Audit* misses the money being transferred between the two accounts.

As indicated in the literature [G 81, KLS 90], early exposure of uncommitted data is essential in the realm of long-duration and nested transactions such as workflows. Since the tasks of a workflow are the grain of interleaving, and intermediate results are exposed, undo operations can no longer use the before-images. In case of failures, compensating tasks may have to be used to semantically undo the effects of committed tasks. The third type of problem occurs when a committed task after disclosing its updates to the outside world is compensated. Tasks can be affected by the data disclosed by a previously committed task, in other words, their computations can be invalidated after the compensation of a task that they depend on.

In the following sections the solutions brought to these problems in METUFlow will be described.

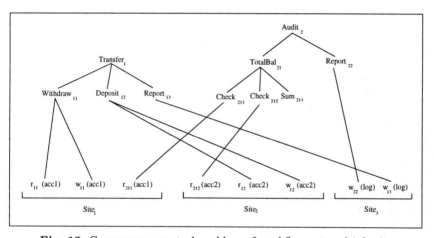

Fig. 12. Concurrency control problem of workflows at multiple sites

10.1 Concurrency Control in METUFlow

Data consistency can be violated by improper interleaving of concurrently executing workflows as discussed in the previous section. Also, such inconsistencies can occur due to improper interleaving of concurrently executing workflows and local transactions. Such interleavings must be prevented to ensure data consistency in WFMSs. In this section we introduce the "sphere of isolation" concept for the correctness of concurrently executing workflows. In achieving this goal we aim at increasing concurrency. Our starting point is to exploit the available semantics in workflow specification. How this semantic knowledge is extracted and usage of this knowledge to preserve data consistency are provided in the following.

10.1.1 Spheres of Isolation. We define a sphere of isolation to be the set of tasks that have data-flow and also serial control-flow dependencies among them. We claim that the workflow correctness can be provided by identifying the spheres of isolation in a workflow system automatically from the data and serial control-flow dependency information obtained from the workflow specification.

If at least one of the output parameters of a task is mapped to an input parameter of the second task, we say that there is a *data-flow dependency* between these two tasks. There is a *serial control-flow dependency* between two tasks, if one of them is *begin on commit dependent* on the other one (See Section 3.1), i.e., first task can begin only after the commitment of second task. Two tasks belong to same *sphere of isolation* (denoted as Π_i^j, which means j^{th} sphere of ith workflow) if there are *data-flow* and *serial control-flow dependency* between them. For example, the task checking raw material stock and stock update task in the manufacturing example belong to the same *sphere of isolation*. In our banking example depicted in Figure 12, $Withdraw_{11}$ and $Deposit_{12}$ tasks belong to the same *sphere of isolation*. Yet since there is no *data-flow dependency* between $Report_{13}$ and other two, $Report_{13}$ belongs to a different *sphere of isolation*. The complete list of *spheres of isolation* for Figure 12 is as follows: $\Pi_1^1 = \{Withdraw_{11}, Deposit_{12}\}$, $\Pi_1^2 = \{Report_{13}\}$, $\Pi_2^1 = \{Check_{211}, Check_{212}, Sum_{213}\}$, $\Pi_2^2 = \{Report_{22}\}$.

The point we want to make over here is the following: Since isolation of a whole workflow execution is unacceptable because of performance reasons, we want to discover smaller units of isolation. Since individual tasks of a workflow are isolated by local Resource Managers' concurrency controllers, our main concern is to observe data dependencies between these individual tasks and preserve these dependencies when required. Since we consider individual tasks as black boxes the only way of observing data dependencies between them is to check the *serial control-flow* and *data-flow dependencies* between them. Since these dependencies are available at design time, *spheres of isolation* can be determined automatically. Our notion of workflow correctness is based on the isolation of these spheres, i.e., if the tasks of a *sphere of isolation* execute at a single site, they are executed within the scope of a single transaction or if they execute at multiple sites their serialization order must be compatible at these sites. Note that, tasks which belong to different *spheres of isolation* may have incompatible serialization orders at multiple sites without violating the workflow correctness.

For example, since $Withdraw_{11}$ and $Deposit_{12}$ in Figure 12 belong to the same *sphere of isolation* their serialization order must be compatible at every site that they have executed, that is, $Site_1$ and $Site_2$. So, either $Withdraw_{11}$ must be serialized after $Check_{211}$ at $Site_1$ or $Deposit_{12}$ must be serialized before $Check_{212}$ at $Site_2$. Note that $Report$ tasks can be serialized in any order, since they do not affect the correct execution of other tasks. So, for example $Report_{13}$ should not necessarily have a consistent serialization order with $Wihdraw_{11}$ and $Deposit_{12}$ for the correctness.

10.1.2 A Correctness Theory for Workflows. A formal presentation of *sphere of isolation* and a correctness theory developed to express the ideas introduced in the previous section more precisely is given in [AAHD 97]. Note that the theory introduced in [AAHD 97] is motivated by the theoretical framework provided in [HAD 97] for nested transactions in multidatabases.

In this theory, an execution history of workflows is modelled by assuming an imaginary root (OMNI) for all submitted workflows. *Execution history of workflows* is a tree on tasks and → is a irreflexive and antisymmetric relation on the nodes of the tree. Actually, → is the ordering requirements on the leaf nodes due to execution order of conflicting data manipulation operations. Ordering imposed by leaf nodes are delegated to upper nodes in the hierarchy using the following axioms for any tasks t_i and t_j:

   i. transitivity: if $t_i \rightarrow t_j$ and $t_j \rightarrow t_k$ then $t_i \rightarrow t_k$

   ii. delegation: if $t_i \rightarrow t_j$ and

      a. if $parent(t_j) \notin ancestors(t_i)$ then $t_i \rightarrow parent(t_j)$

      b. if $parent(t_i) \notin ancestors(t_j)$ then $parent(t_i) \rightarrow t_j$. □

Within this theoretical framework, the correctness of a *sphere of isolation* can be checked and enforced by keeping its tasks under the same parent whereas unrelated parts of the workflow can be executed freely by making them the children of independent parents.

For example, consider the execution history in Figure 13 as a continuation of the example in Figure 12. *Spheres of isolation* are depicted within the dotted rectangles in the Figure 13. Parents of Π_1^1 and Π_1^2 are differentiated and a *virtual parent* for the elements of Π_1^2 is created and it is denoted as $Sphere_1^2$. Similarly, $Sphere_2^2$ is created for the elements of Π_2^2 and the parent of the tasks of Π_1^1 is renamed as $Sphere_1^1$ and the parent of the tasks of Π_2^1 is renamed as $Sphere_2^1$. Since $Withdraw_{11}$ and $Check_{211}$ have issued conflicting data manipulation operations on $acc1$ they are ordered as $Withdraw_{11} \rightarrow Check_{211}$ at $Site_1$. Also $Deposit_{12}$ and $Check_{212}$ are ordered as $Deposit_{12} \rightarrow Check_{212}$. Since, $Withdraw_{11}$ and $Check_{211}$ are ordered as $Withdraw_{11} \rightarrow Check_{211}$, $Withdraw_{11}$ and $Sphere_2^1$ (which is $parent(Check_{211})$) are ordered as $Withdraw_{11} \rightarrow Sphere_2^1$ (from Axiom ii.a above). Some of the delegated orderings are not shown in Figure 13 for the sake of simplicity. By applying the delegation axiom repeatedly, the following order is obtained between different *spheres of isolation*: $\{Sphere_1^1 \rightarrow Sphere_2^1, Sphere_2^2 \rightarrow Sphere_1^2\}$. This execution is serializable and correct from the application point of view. Observe that, since $Report_{13}$ belongs to a different *sphere of isolation* (Π_1^2), its inconsistent serialization order with $Withdraw_{11}$ and $Deposit_{12}$ does not affect the correct execution of the workflow.

10.1.3 Implementation Issues. As can be seen from the discussion presented above, the spheres of isolation in a workflow can be identified and we

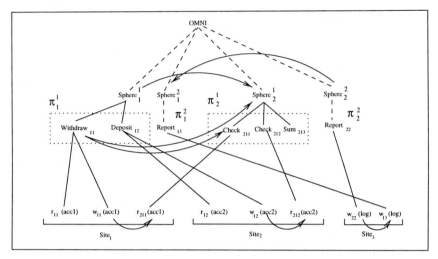

Fig. 13. Example Execution History

claim that correctness measures can be applied on the basis of spheres of isolation. In [AAHD 97] we present *Nested Tickets (NT)* technique to provide for the correctness of concurrently executing nested tasks of workflow systems, based on spheres of isolation. The main idea of *NT* technique is to give tickets to spheres and tasks. The *NT* technique makes the execution order of all tasks of a sphere of isolation to be consistent at all related sites. In other words, the consistency of serialization order of the tasks of a sphere of isolation is provided by guaranteeing them to be serialized in the order of their ticket numbers.

10.2 Future Considerations for Concurrency Control in METUFlow

Currently, we are in the process of developing a more efficient correctness notion for workflows exploiting workflow and task semantics in terms of semantic dependencies between tasks [A 97]. The concurrency control mechanism based on this semantic information will guarantee that only the task interleavings that preserve the correctness are allowed.

Another issue we are currently addressing is to bound the effects of compensation on the tasks that are affected by accessing data which is externalized by the compensated tasks [Arp 97]. Our primary goal is to analyze the implications of the compensation on the correctness of concurrent executions using task and workflow semantics and to provide correct executions with respect to compensation. We plan to present the user a mechanism with a flexibility of isolation levels that should be respected very much like the isolation levels of SQL-92. Hence critical tasks will have chance to choose not reading subject to compensation data.

11. Conclusions

Currently, the first prototype of METUFlow is operational. The system attempted to bring solutions to the following problems of the workflow systems:

1. Scalability and adaptability through distributed scheduling, history and worklist management.
2. Handling of invoked applications on distributed heterogenous environments through CORBA.
3. Supporting mobile users through the Java based Web interfaces.

With the future versions of METUFlow, we plan to attempt the following problems:

1. Deadlock and reachability analysis of workflow specifications [Cin 97].
2. Handling dynamic changes within workflow specification which boils down to changing guard expression of events dynamically in the system.
3. We also aim at an adaptable workflow system that will incorporate the functionality and therefore complexity only when it is actually needed. The notion of adaptability implies that the engine will run in different platforms ranging from a small set of PCs for minor administration tasks, to clusters of high end workstations connected through a wide area network for enterprise wide system.

HP Workflow Research:
Past, Present, and Future

Ming-Chien Shan, Jim Davis, Weimin Du, Ying Huang

Hewlett-Packard Labs., Palo Alto, CA 94304, USA
{shan, davis, du, yhuang}@hpl.hp.com

Abstract. Workflow research at HP Labs has evolved through three stages during the past four years. Our effort started with the enhancement of an existing HP workflow product – WorkManager. Then, based on customers' feedback, a new workflow prototype was developed to support the requirements of enterprise complex business process management. This formed the base for HPs second generation workflow product – AdminFlow. We are now exploring the third generation of workflow system that supports the Internet computing paradigm.

1. Introduction

The emergence of a truly global economics has immersed all businesses into an intensively competitive environment moving with accelerating rates of changes. Gradual improvements in productivity and enhancements in quality are no longer enough to maintain market leadership. The fast delivery of new products/services and the rapid modification of existing applications are key survival factors. These requirements have forced enterprises to look for new solutions, and workflow has emerged as one of the crucial technologies to meet these needs.

As the research arm for HP, we at HP Labs have engaged in workflow research since 1993. Our research effort has moved through three stages: advanced feature enhancement for HP's first generation workflow products; the development of a new workflow prototype to support the operation of enterprise level, mission critical business processes and the development of integrated business applications; and currently the investigation of the requirements for a workflow system supporting Internet-based business operations.

2. Stage 1: Advanced Feature Enhancements

In the early 1990s, HP rolled out several products to support collaborative computing, including WorkManager [HP 94] and SynerVision. Research activities at HP Labs were focused on how to consolidate these products into one product, i.e., how to design the model and function mappings between them. We also designed advanced features such as nested process, distributed process, and efficient rule engine to enhance WorkManager.

Like many other products on today's market, these products had their root in office automation and focused on document management capability with minimal support for task routing functions. These first generation workflow systems were intended mainly to automate document or forms flows among human workers in an organization [DES 97].

However, business process operations at the enterprise level are quite different from these in many crucial respects. First, there is a difference in scale and performance. The enterprise business processes may span many organizations within an enterprise and even across enterprises. Second, these first generation workflow systems typically used electronic mail for delivering tasks to human workers. Little support for automatic operation execution, monitoring workflows, enforcing consistency, or recovering from failure was provided. Third, the actual work supporting a step within an enterprise business process may be performed not only by humans, but also by computer software, or machines (e.g., instruments or robots). Hence, facility for acquiring, coordinating, invoking, and monitoring these resources are necessary.

As a matter of fact, the sales of these first generation workflow products stumbled in 1996 [Delphi 97b], due to the lack of features supporting enterprise-level business operations.

3. Stage 2: Enterprise Business Process Management System

Through comprehensive discussion with HPs world-wide customer partners engaged in business process re-engineering, we collected a solid set of enterprise business process management requirements and started the **OpenPM** project [Shan 96] in 1994 to design a new workflow system to meet these demands. The OpenPM prototype was completed in 1996 and forms the base for the HP **AdminFlow** product to be released in 1997. Because of these enterprise business operational features, AdminFlow won the "Best Collaborative Computing" product award at the 97 Electronic Messaging Association annual conference.

3.1 The Requirements

We highlight some key requirements for OpenPM prototype below:

− **Performance**
  The OpenPM engine needs to achieve a very high throughput. It should be able to provide a minimum dispatching capability of 12,000 activities per hour in steady state.
− **Scalability**
  The OpenPM engine should be scalable to support both small installations

with few and simple precesses as well as vast installations with many complex processes. A design goal was that on a HP Enterprise Business Server model H50, an OpenPM engine should support up to 1,000,000 active process instances. System capabilities should scale with the computational power available.

– **Distribution**

The OpenPM system should support configurations with multiple engine running on separate machines with remote sub-process execution capability.

– **Reliability**

The OpenPM engine should support 24x7 (8760 - 4) up-time, providing the underlying infrastructure, including database, backup strategy, network technology, and hardware, also supports 24x7 up-time.

– **Flexibility**

The OpenPM system should provide flexibilities in application interaction, database usage, and process enactment (e.g., ad-hoc routing, dynamic resource and priority assignment, transactional recovery and compensation, and mixed synchronous and asynchronous transports).

– **Usability**

The OpenPM system should provide open integration with third party tools for process design, and legacy system/application integration.

3.2 OpenPM Overview

The OpenPM prototype was designed as an open, enterprise capable, object-oriented workflow system to manage business activities supporting complex enterprise processes in a distributed heterogeneous computing environment. This middleware service that represents a substantial evolution from first generation workflow technologies.

Given the trend towards open systems and standards, a workflow system must coexist with and take advantage of standards-based commercial products for network communication, legacy application invocation, and system monitoring. In particular, the OMG's ORB, Microsoft DCOM, OSF's DCE, HP OpenView, and OSI X.400 technologies are expected to play an important role in the development of workflow systems. OpenPM provides a generic framework and a complete set of services for business process flow management, utilizing the above-mentioned standard technologies, and emphasizing performance, scalability, availability, and system robustness.

Basically, OpenPM provides:

– an open system adhering to CORBA-based communication infrastructure and providing WfMC standard interface,
– high performance due to optimized database access and commitment,
– effective management due to OpenView-based system management environment,

– a total solution for business re-engineering including a complete set of business application development tools.

The major research areas for OpenPM are:

– process flow model and language to support both computerizable and human activities,
– flow analysis and optimization,
– business rules and constraint management,
– failure and exception handling, including compensation activity management and distributed transaction manager coordination,
– resource assignment management to define and enforce the access constraints and organizational (e.g., role resolution) policies governing the assignment of resources to activities,
– process flow monitoring and dynamic change management,
– data consistency between OpenPM engine (internal) database and external information systems,
– high availability support,
– overall architecture of distributed process flow management system, including ORB, DCOM, DCE and E-mail technology deployment, and
– business application development toolkits.

3.2.1 OpenPM system. The overall architecture of OpenPM system is depicted in Figure 1. The core is the OpenPM engine, which supports five interfaces for *business process defining, business process execution, business process monitoring, resource & policy management,* and *business object management.*

A business process is specified via the process definition interface. An instance of the business process can be started, stopped, or intervened via the process execution interface. Status information for each process instance and configuration and load information for the entire system can be queried via the process monitoring interface. The resource and policy management interface is used at run-time to allocate execution resources to a task, according to the policies defined by the organization (including authorization and authentication) and the availability of the resources. The interaction with external world (e.g., the invocation of an application, the control of an instrument, or the delivery of a work order to a person's E-mail in-tray) is performed via the business object management interface.

3.2.2 OpenPM process model. A *business process* describes the sequencing, timing, dependency, data, physical agent allocation, business rule and organization policy enforcement requirements of business activities needed to enact work.

In OpenPM, a business process is represented as a directed graph comprising a set of nodes connected by arcs. There are two kinds of nodes: *work nodes* and *rule nodes*, as well as two kinds of arcs: *forward arcs* and *reset arcs.* A work node has at most one inward arc and one or more outward arcs. A rule node can have any number of inward and outward arcs.

Work Nodes represent activities to be performed external to the OpenPM engine. These activities include authorization, resource allocation, the execution of business objects, and the provision of input data for and output data from the business objects. Rule Nodes represent processing internal to the OpenPM engine. This processing includes decisions as to which nodes should execute next, the generation or reception of events, and simple data manipulation.

A work node is a place holder for a *process activity* that is a logical representation of a piece of work contributing toward the accomplishment of a process. A process activity is mapped to the invocation of an operation on *business objects* during the execution of the process. In a sense, a *process activity* represents the reusable aspects of a business activity, while *work node* is used to specify additional non-reusable aspects specific to this process.

Each *process activity* may represent a manual operation by a human or a computerizable task to execute legacy applications, access databases, control instrumentation, sense events in the external world, or even effect physical changes.

A process activity definition includes a *forward activity* with optional *compensation activity, cancel activity, resource management activity*, timeout/deadline information, and input/output data.

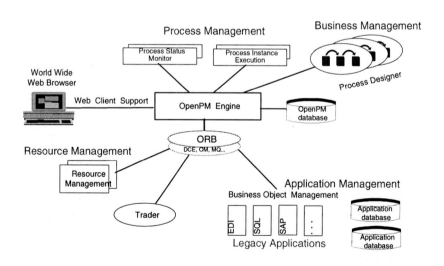

Fig. 1. OpenPM system architecture

Rule nodes are used to specify process flows that are more complex than a simple sequence. A rule language is used to program the rule node decision. When executed, a rule node determines which outward arc(s) to fire, based on the status passed along the inward arcs, the time at which each inward arcs are fired, and the process relevant data associated with the process instance.

Rule nodes are also used to support events. A rule node can raise events when conditions defined by the rules are met, and an event can activate rule nodes that have subscribed to the event.

Forward arcs represent the normal execution flow of process activities and form a directed acyclic graph. Successful completion of a node at the source end of a forward arc triggers the starting of the node at the destination end of the forward arc.

Reset arcs are used to support repetitions or explore alternatives in a business process. Reset arcs differ from forward arcs in that they reach backwards in the process graph.

Rule nodes are executed each time any inward arc fires. Work nodes have states of *initial* or *fired*. When the inward arc is fired on a work node in the initial state, the work node changes to fired state and performs its associated activity. When the inward arc is fired on a work node in the fired state, nothing is done.

A reset arc, together with the forward arcs between its destination and source, form loops. When traversed, a reset arc causes all nodes within these loops to be reset. Resetting a fired work node changes its state to *initial state* so that the node can be re-executed. Resetting an active work node cancels the current execution of the corresponding process activity and changes its state to *initial state*.

Associated with each business process, there is a *process data template* to be defined by the business process designer. The process data template is used by users to provide initial data for the creation of process instances. Based on the process data template and *read/write lists* of activities defined in a business process, at run-time, OpenPM will generate a *case packet* for each process instance to facilitate the data passing between activities and OpenPM engine.

An example of the process definition for SONET configuration management process is shown in Figure 3 in section 3.4.

3.2.3 OpenPM process execution. Figure 2 shows a simplified version of the component structure of OpenPM engine, which coordinates the overall execution flow of business processes. It functions as a highly reliable, log-based state machine. OpenPM engine interfaces with external environments through a uniform CORBA-based transport interface, independent of the actual physical dispatch of the requests.

The OpenPM engine launches business process instances in response to user requests. For each instance, OpenPM engine steps through the nodes according to the order specified in its business process definition. For work nodes, OpenPM engine will execute the associated process (forward) activity. For rule nodes, OpenPM engine will evaluate the rules and perform the rule actions when the rule conditions are met.

Each node transition will be durably logged to facilitate forward rolling of incompleted business processes at system restart time in the event of system failure or support activity compensation process in the case of business activity failure. In addition, OpenPM allows flexible specification of compensation scopes and actions [DDS 97] (e.g., compensation activity or cancel activity) to support various application needs.

In OpenPM, different versions of similar business processes are supported by the engine under the concept of *process group*. Users can designate a particular version as the default one, which will be used when no specific version is requested at business process instance creation time.

3.2.4 OpenPM business object. The OpenPM engine interacts with business activities supported by various kinds of implementations encountered in real life. These range from manual handling by human to automated application execution by computer. An infrastructure is needed to enable the effective management and invocation of these business activities.

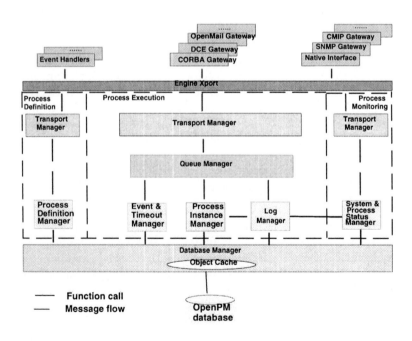

Fig. 2. OpenPM component structure

Distributed object technologies have become the primary infrastructure for enterprise-scale distributed computing. Among them, the OMG CORBA technology supports interoperability for application integration.

Based on CORBA technology, an OpenPM abstraction, called *business object*, will be built to encapsulate whatever the piece of work each process activity has to accomplish. The wrapping code will provide an IDL interface and the business objects are cataloged in OpenPM business object library.

Business object, as defined by OMG BOMSIG, is a representation of a thing active in the business domain, including its business name and definition, attributes, behavior, and constraints. It provides an uniform way to encapsulate legacy systems and applications, and a direct mapping, in understandable business terms, between the business model and the possibly sophisticated operational procedures of the business process system.

By representing these process activities in business objects, new business processes can be quickly created by assembling business objects to describe business processes. The business object library will also avoid the repetitive coding to tailor the business activity implementation into each individual business process.

3.2.5 OpenPM resource & policy management. A **resource** is a person, computer process, or machine that can be utilized to accomplish a task. A resource has a name and various attributes defining its characteristics (such as job code, skill set, organization unit, and availability). A **role** is a definition of a set of resources sharing some common characteristics. The introduction of roles provides a level of abstraction from the physical resource that performs the task.

A **policy** is a set of rules that determines how resources are related to tasks within a workflow system. One common use is for task assignment. Policies can be used to specify which resource or role is eligible or available to perform a task. Policies are also used to ensure proper authorization and authentication.

In OpenPM, the mapping between the business activity (i.e., task) specified in a business process and the business object (i.e., resource) to be invoked is resolved by the *Resource Manager* during run-time as part of the execution of the business activity. The Resource Manager also assumes the responsibility of life cycle management (i.e., creation, modification, and deletion) for resources.

OpenPM allows multiple resource managers to be used to resolve a single resource assignment request; each resolves the request at a different level within an organization[4].

At this point, we can characterize the overall OpenPM conceptual model of business process by four independent aspects. The OpenPM model:

- **functionally** defines what a process intends to achieve (via process definition specification),

- **behaviorially** describes how a process activity is conducted (via business object specification),
- **organizationally** determines who performs an activity (via role and policy specification), and
- **informationally** indicates which piece of data is consumed or produced by an activity (via process data template specification).

The separation of these four aspects for a business process maximizes the reusability and extensibility of business process applications since it allows changing one aspect of a business process application without having to change the others.

3.2.6 OpenPM worklist handler & application data handler. Two optional components, i.e., the *Worklist Handler* and the *Application Data Handler*, can be used in the OpenPM environment to facilitate the execution of business processes. Both components are designed to enhance the scalability of OpenPM systems.

The Worklist Handler supports both *engine-push* and *performer-pull* modes to provide more freedom of task assignment. The OpenPM uses *engine-push* to dispatch activities eligible to be performed. It supports high level of efficiency in the engine.

On the other hand, users often want to select from available work in a *performer-pull* mode. It supports:

- process activity performers to control the order in which they work on activities. They are able to see and select among the activities assigned to them,
- better response times and reduces the load on the Engine. Process activity performers interact with a Worklist Handler that may be in the same network vicinity as the process activity performer, and do not need to communicate with the Engine.
- the activity assignments to a group of performers that each carry out the same role. On completion of an activity, the performer claims the next outstanding activity from the common activity pool. This is useful for environments such as travel desks where it does not matter which travel consultant carries out an activity; the group simply shares the same activity pool (they are thus one resource from the Resource Manager's point of view).

In addition, the Worklist Handler supports the concept of *integration on demand*. Based on the task performer's profile, the Worklist Handler determines and launches a specific environment to an activity at run-time, rather than hard-wiring it into the process definitions.

The Application Data Handler supports the separation of *application specific data* and *process relevant data* to reduce the amount of data flow over the network. It also provides the preparation facility on application specific data to remove the burden on database access from activity performers.

3.2.7 OpenPM system and process management. OpenPM uses the Manager/Agent model [M 95] for system and process management. It provides the following functions:

− System Configuration.
  This function supports the engine configuration setting and engine alert message display,
− Operations Management.
  This function supports the engine startup/shutdown process and component registration,
− Performance Management.
  This function supports the display of the current value of engine heath parameters,
− Process Management.
  This function supports the status information for each individual business process instance.

To support these management functions, OpenPM engine maintains a comprehensive log of all events and provides a native interface as well as SNMP/CMIP gateways to facilitate integration with OpenView environments. Various formats and contents of the logged information can be customized to support the specific application needs.

3.2.8 OpenPM security. In today's business environments, security must be implemented enterprise-wide. OpenPM supports the following security features:

− authorization.
  The engine determines from the role information associated in the process definition whether a process activity performer or a system component carries out a particular operation. When a request is made to the engine, the Resource Manager checks the credentials of the requester against the security list. If they are not acceptable the request is rejected.
− authentication and encryption.
  The security service developed by OMG/OMA will provide for authentication and encryption. OpenPM plans to use this security service to prevent eavesdropping and forgery. The OpenPM infrastructure components will be able to identify each other and vouch for the credentials of end-user components.

3.3 OpenPM Application Development Facilities

In the "Industry Trends Scenario: Rethinking the IT Investment Paradigm" paper, dated March 28, 1997, Gartner Group defines strategic enterprise mutation as "the ability to rapidly modify enterprise business processes to meet changing market conditions".

To address this challenge, OpenPM separates the business relevant constructs of business processes, resource assignment, and task activities into independent layers. This allows corporations to develop strategic enterprise mutative solutions that can be modified on each layer independently so that business teams can focus on business processes, resources, and activities while IT teams can focus on the application/data management technologies.

Furthermore, we support the concept of *software factory*, which consists of a set of factories, tools, and methodologies collectively to support the *"Just in time"* business process application development lifecycle.

We developed the following factories, which are used to instantiate the different components as the building blocks for a business process application.

- business process factory.
  It consists of libraries of templates for various processes in different business domains.
- business object factory.
  It consists of libraries of skeletons for business objects to represent a resource, a process, an organization, or a policy. It also provides a way to make use of past investments in database systems, applications and computing platforms.
- common facility factory.
  It consists of libraries of routines providing interface glue to different communication infrastructures.

3.4 An Application Example

This section will describe the application of OpenPM system in a specific domain, that of SONET Configuration Management. This application was demonstrated at Telecom'95 Expo in Geneva.

The scenario demonstrated consists of the provisioning a new VC4/VC12 paths for customer which includes several different steps: search for a new route; negotiation of the Service Level Agreement (SLA) with the customer; configuration of this new path; and finally update of the SLA for this customer.

Searching for and configuring a new path in SONET are complex processes requiring a lot of interaction with the SONET MIB and network elements. This type of operation generates errors when performed manually by an operator as a set of individual uncorrelated activities.

In the demonstration, such complex operations are handled as business processes and automated by an OpenPM engine in an environment interacting with OpenView DM and Oracle DBMS applications.

Depending upon changing business needs, a customer may add or drop communication paths between certain end-points in his Private Virtual Network (PVN). In OpenPM, these services can be modeled as business processes to be executed by the service provider. Adding a new path may consist of the following activities and decision points:

1. Retrieve the customer's profile from the *customer* database for customer PVN specific information.
2. Locate the closest Add-Drop Multiplexes (ADMs) to the end-points, based on the information stored in the *SONET physical configuration* database.
3. Check whether fiber connections exist between the endpoints and the two end-ADMs.
4. If not, issue a request for an engineer to go onsite and physically connect the endpoints to the end-ADMs. After the establishment of the connection, the process will continue with step 5 and an independent subprocess will be initiated on the side to watch for resource changes.
5. Find valid routes between end-ADMs.
   This requires accessing to the *routing* table in SLA database to determine whether any valid routes exist between the two end-ADMs.
   Either a list of ADMs is returned identifying the ADMs that must be configured in order to realize the route, or "No Route Found" is returned. For a returned list of ADMs, this activity will then use the OpenView DM *Facility agent* to collect the port information stored in MIB and to determine the available ports between the ADMs that are fibered together and can be used to enable the path.
6. Check Network Element (NE) capabilities.
   For a ADM in the route, this activity uses the OpenView/DM *NE* agent to access the MIB information to determine whether a VC4 cross-connection can be set up in the ADM between the selected ports of the ADM.
   This activity has to be executed for each ADM in the route.
   Note that, during steps 5 and 6, if any additional resources become available, OpenPM will cancel any currently running activity and start the process over from step 5 in order to consider these newly available resources.
7. Get customer's approval of the selected configuration.
   Once a suitable path is identified, the customer will review the offer, including available date, charges, QoS, etc. Depending upon the business factors (e.g., cheapest service wanted), the customer may request a new search to be initiated, i.e., to loop back to step 5 to find another valid route.
8. Configure the selected route.
   This activity is responsible for setting up the cross-connections in each ADM via the invocation of the OpenView/DM NE agent, and updating the SLA database.

The OpenPM process definition supporting the above-mentioned SONET data path provisioning service is sketched in Figure 3.

4. Stage 3: Internet-Based Service Process Management System

Today, the world is undergoing rapid changes to move into the Internet age. The explosion in Internet business activities will raise the demand on business process management technologies to a new level.

Workflow systems, including OpenPM, were designed before the advent of the booming usage of Internet and were therefore based on the traditional client/server architecture. Such systems will not serve effectively for future even more dynamic and pervasive Internet-based business operations over various heterogeneous computing platforms. Examples of such operations include world-wide supply chain management, universal telecom service management, global banking service management, and mobile patience care service management.

These applications demand even higher degrees of scalability, flexibility, distribution, robustness, and heterogeneity support on the workflow system. The architecture of OpenPM, which separates the function, behavior, organization, and information aspects into independent components, provides a sound foundation towards this objective. However, there are new dimensions that need to be addressed.

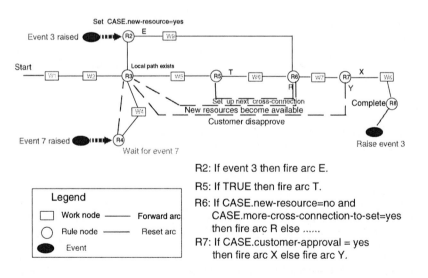

R2: If event 3 then fire arc E.

R5: If TRUE then fire arc T.

R6: If CASE.new-resource=no and
CASE.more-cross-connection-to-set=yes
then fire arc R else ......

R7: If CASE.customer-approval = yes
then fire arc X else fire arc Y.

Fig. 3. SONET path provisioning OpenPM process

True Internet applications are atomized - that is, composed of many discrete parts, any combination of which may be collected at run time, called upon to perform certain tasks, and then thrown away until needed again. Under this paradigm, the data – not necessarily the applications – are persistent.

In other words, the Internet computing paradigm requires the support of *dynamic software*. It may require no installation other than the Web-browser frontend, and a library containing a rich mixture of components downloadable from the Internet. All this late-binding and dynamic component assembly implies that the boundaries of future applications will change.

Therefore, we started a new project, called **FlowJet**, to explore the issues around using the **feature on demand** approach to support an open and flexible workflow system for the dynamic and mobile Internet business processes.

We plan to deploy FlowJet over all major computing platforms, ranging from mainframes, server workstations, single user desktop, and to mobile devices to information appliances.

4.1 FlowJet Overview

FlowJet is a modularized workflow management system targeted for both Internet/Intranet and traditional business process applications. FlowJet can be used for the following purposes:

- as an enterprise business process management system.
  In this mode, FlowJet runs as a main engine for the management of complex enterprise-wide business processes. This operational mode represents the full-fledged FlowJet server, which is usually executed at data center within an organization. The processes supported at this level are usually quite complex and are divided into subprocesses that will be executed either locally or remotely by other FlowJet full-fledged engine, personal business process manager, or web service manager.
- as a task agent of an FlowJet user.
  In this mode, FlowJet runs as a business object or Worklist Handler to other full-fledged FlowJet servers. The idea is for a particular FlowJet resource to perform tasks that are more complicated than single step activities.
- as a personal business process manager.
  In this mode, FlowJet runs as an independent workflow engine executing personal business processes. Users can define processes that make use of existing services available to them. The service can be a single local application encapsulated as a FlowJet business object, or a complex process to be executed at other full-fledged FlowJet servers.
- as a web service manager.

In this mode, FlowJet runs as part of a web server. It allows users to model their web activities as workflow processes. This can be viewed as a natural evolution of HTML and JavaScript. With FlowJet, users will be able to model and design their web pages as FlowJet processes. This is more powerful and flexible than HTML and JavaScript, and is also easier to use and maintain.

Reducing Escalation-Related Costs in WFMSs

Euthimios Panagos, Michael Rabinovich

AT&T Labs - Research, 180 Park Avenue, Florham Park, NJ 07932, USA

Abstract. Escalations refer to the actions taken when workflow activities miss their deadlines. Typically, escalations increase the cost of business processes due to the execution of additional activities, the compensation of finished activities, or the intervention of highly-paid workers. In this paper, we present two techniques for reducing costs related to escalations; namely, *dynamic deadline adjustment* and *preemptive escalation*. The former mechanism uses the slack accumulated during process execution to adjust the deadlines of the remaining activities, i.e., delay escalations. The latter mechanism predicts whether a process is going to escalate at some future point, and it decides whether and when to force escalation at an early stage during execution. Preliminary experimental results show the effectiveness of our techniques.

1. Introduction

Today, organizations use workflow management systems (WFMSs) to stream-line, automate, and manage business processes that depend on information systems and human resources (e.g., provisioning telephone services, processing insurance claims, and handling bank loan applications). WFMSs provide tools to support the modeling of business processes at a conceptual level, coordinate the execution of the component activities according to the model, monitor the execution progress, and report various statistics about the business processes and the resources involved in their enactment [GHS 95, KS 95].

A workflow is an abstraction of a business process. It consists of *activities*, which correspond to individual process steps, and *agents*, which execute these activities. An agent may be an information system (e.g., a database system), a human (e.g., a customer representative) or a combination of both (e.g., a human using a software program). The workflow specification may also specify execution durations, referred to as *deadlines*, for both the activities and the entire process. When an activity misses its deadline, special actions, referred to as *escalations*, may be triggered. Escalations increase the operational cost of a business process since, otherwise, they would have been specified as part of the normal execution path.

Escalations may have local scope or global scope. A local escalation affects the triggering activity (i.e., the one that triggered the escalation) and it may: (a) restart the triggering activity, (b) execute a new activity and then resume the execution of the triggering activity, or (c) replace the triggering activity with a new activity. A global escalation affects the whole business process and it may: (d) abort the process and compensate all finished activities, or (e) stop the normal flow of execution, compensate some of the finished activities, and execute an alternative sequence of activities to complete the process. In all cases, escalations increase operational costs due to the additional activities that may have to be executed, or because completed work is rolled back, or because intervention of highly-paid workers is required.

In this paper, we concentrate on ways to reduce escalation-related costs. The most obvious way to ensure that escalations are rare events is to assign very long deadlines or increase the available resources (e.g., the number of agents). However, this may not be always feasible from a business perspective (a customer would choose another telecommunications company if she were told that the service provisioning workflow may take a month to complete). Therefore, our goal is to try to reduce the escalation-related costs by better management of business process during their execution by a WFMS, assuming that business processes and the allocated resources are decisions outside our control. In particular, our approach combines two inter-related mechanisms: *dynamic deadline adjustment* and *preemptive escalation.*

Typically, deadlines are assigned to activities based on their *estimated* execution times, the need to meet the overall business process deadline, and to ensure that corrective measures, i.e., escalations, are invoked in a timely manner. On the other hand, the *actual* execution times of activities vary from one instance to the next due to variations in load, work conditions, etc. Therefore, if in a given workflow instance an activity finishes faster than its estimated execution time, the remaining activities can be given extra time before escalation is invoked. Based on the above observation, the dynamic deadline adjustment mechanism (initially outlined in [PR 96]), attempts to reduce the number of escalations during the execution of workflow processes by keeping track of the slack time accumulated during a partial process execution and using this slack to extend the deadlines (i.e., delay escalation) of the remaining activities.

In situations where escalations cannot be avoided (e.g., when the resources needed for the enactment of an activity are not available for an extended time period), it may be beneficial to escalate preemptively during the execution of an *earlier* activity, which has not missed its deadline yet. Often, escalations involve the compensation of finished activities and, hence, invoking them early entails less work and fewer wasted resources for executing and then compensating activities that are rolled back. Based on the above observation, the preemptive escalation mechanism attempts to predict whether a process is going to escalate at some future point and, then, decide whether and when to force escalations before they actually occur. Our approach exploits information about escalation costs as well as information provided by existing workflow systems such as statistical measurements based on past process executions and current status data (e.g., agent load and availability).

Our preliminary experimental results show that our approach reduces escalation costs. This is achieved without any modification to the process

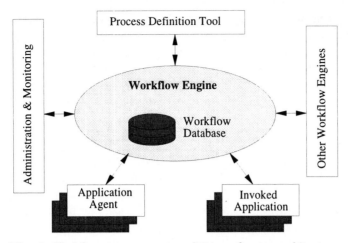

Fig. 1. Workflow management coalition: reference architecture

model or increase of allocated resources and, thus, it is completely transparent to the users of the workflow system. A limitation of our approach is that it assumes that the process model stays the same during the execution of a process instance. We thus exclude *ad hoc workflows* [GHS 95] where the schema of the process for a given process instance is altered during the instance execution. Instead, our approach targets *production workflows* systems, where escalation-related costs constitute a significant amount and an important concern. Our approach can also be applied to *administrative workflows* to the extend they do not dynamically change workflow specifications of workflow instances in progress.

The remainder of the paper is organized as follows. Section 2 offers an introduction to workflow concepts and describes the workflow process model we use in this paper. Section 3 presents our dynamic deadline adjustment algorithms. Section 4 describes our algorithm for invoking escalations early. Section 5 presents preliminary experimental results. Section 6 compares our work with related work and, finally, Section 7 concludes our presentation.

2. System Model

Figure 1 shows the WFMS reference model provided by the Workflow Management Coalition (WfMC) [WfMC 94a]. The WFMS consist of an engine, application agents, invoked applications, a process definition tool, and administration and monitoring tools. The process definition tool is a visual editor used to define the specification, i.e., the *schema*, of a workflow process. The same schema can be used for creating multiple *instances* of the same business process at a later time. The workflow engine and the tools communicate with a workflow database to store and update workflow-relevant data, such as workflow schemas, statistical information, and control information required to execute and monitor the active process instances.

Each application agent has a work queue associated with it. Activities submitted for execution are inserted into the work queue when the agent is busy. The agent may follow its own policy to select the next activity to execute (the most common policies are priority-based and FIFO). In addition, existing WFMSs maintain audit logs that keep track of information about the state of the various system components, changes to the state of workflow processes, and various statistics about past process executions. This information can be used to provide reports about the state of the system and the active workflow process instances, as well as various statistical measurements such as the average execution time of an activity belonging to the particular process schema. These statistical measurements can be used for predicting the timing characteristics of the active workflow instances.

2.1 Workflow Schema

A workflow is a collection of *activities, agents,* and *dependencies* between activities. Activities correspond to individual steps in a business process. Agents are responsible for the enactment of activities, and they may correspond to specific software systems (e.g., database application programs) or humans (e.g., customer representatives). Dependencies determine the execution sequence of activities and the data flow between these activities. The workflow model may also define *roles*, which serve as descriptions for human skills and software system services required for the enactment of activities. Formally, a role is a set of agents; each activity has an associated role, which determines the agents that can execute this activity. The notion of a role facilitates load balancing among agents and can flexibly accommodate changes in the workforce and the computing infrastructure of an organization, by changing the set of agents associated with roles.

Activities can be executed sequentially or in parallel. Parallel executions may be unconditional, i.e., all activities are executed, or conditional, i.e., only activities that satisfy a given condition are executed. In addition, activities may be executed repeatedly, and the number of iterations may be determined during the execution. The point where control splits into multiple parallel activities is referred to as *split point*. The point where control merges into one activity is referred to as *join point*. A join point is called AND-join when the activity immediately following this point starts execution only when all the activities preceding the join point finish execution. An unconditional split or a conditional split such that it can be statically, before execution, determined that all branches are taken is referred to as AND-split. A split for which is can be statically determined that exactly one branch will be taken is referred to as OR-split. Activities belonging to the path following an AND-split or an OR-split are referred to as AND-split and OR-split activities, respectively.

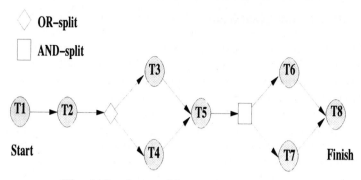

Fig. 2. Service provisioning workflow process

Many of the existing WFMS process definition tools allow the specification of arbitrary dependencies between activities. If these tools are used without a discipline, the resulting workflow schemas may be hard to debug, modify, and reason about [S$^+$ 96]. While we do not place any restrictions on workflow types that are allowed in the system, some of our algorithms for dynamic deadline adjustment are applicable only to well-structured workflows. A well-structured workflow consists of m sequential activities, $T_1 \ldots T_m$. Each activity T_i is either a primitive activity, which is not decomposed any further, or a composite activity, which consists of n_i parallel conditional or unconditional sub-activities $T_i^1, \ldots, T_i^{n_i}$. Each sub-activity may be, again, primitive or composite. The following example, illustrated in Figure 2, shows a well-structured telephone service provisioning workflow that we use in the remainder of the paper.

Example 2.1. An instance of the telephone service provisioning workflow is created when an operator collects from a customer the information needed to carry out the service, such as name, address, kind of service and requested options. $T1$ is executed to verify that the information is accurate, check if the requested service can be provided, and create a service order record. $T2$ uses the service order record created by $T1$ and consults the facilities database to determine whether existing facilities can be used for establishing the service. If existing facilities can be used, $T3$ is executed. Otherwise, a human field engineer is selected to execute $T4$, which may involve manual changes to some switch and the establishment of a new telephone line. Once $T3$ or $T4$ is completed, $T5$ is executed to verify that the installation was successful. Then $T6$ and $T7$ are executed in parallel to update the telephone directory database and generate billing information, respectively. Finally, $T8$ generates some summary data about the provisioning of the new telephone service.

2.2 Deadlines and Escalations

A workflow schema can be used to assign deadlines to activities and the entire process [LR 94, InConcert, TWF]. The schema may specify time-triggered activities, escalations, which are executed when the process or some of its activities miss their deadlines. For the entire process, the deadline is specified as the allowable execution time. When a process instance is initiated, this deadline is translated into an absolute time based on the starting time of the instance. For an individual activity, the deadline may be expressed as the allowable execution time, or the time by which the activity must complete relative to the starting time of the process instance containing the activity.

Existing WFMSs provide capabilities for specifying activity deadlines in either one or both of these ways. We will show that specifying the deadline as completion time relative to process start is equivalent to one method of deadline adjustment. Moreover, our performance study shows that this method does not always offer the best performance. Thus, we argue that even when activity deadlines are specified relative to the process starting time, it is beneficial to translate each activity deadline into its maximum allowable execution time, and then choose the right algorithm to adjust the latter. From now on, we assume that deadlines correspond to allowable execution times.

2.3 Assumptions

We now summarize our assumptions about the WFMS and the information that is available about the activities constituting a business processes.

- Scheduling of the activities that are ready for execution is not based on the deadlines assigned to them.[1] To the best of our knowledge, the above assumption is true for all commercial WFMSs and existing research prototypes.
- Each activity T has a deadline – $dline(T)$. The deadline specifies the allowable execution time for the activity, and is assumed to be assigned by the business analyst when defining the schema. When only the overall process deadline is specified, techniques similar to those proposed in [KGM 93a, KGM 93b] can be used to assign deadlines to individual activities at runtime, based on the overall process deadline and the agent loads. Finally, both the process and activity deadlines can be dynamically assigned based on the current system load [PR 97].
- For each activity T, an estimate of its average completion time is available – $avg\_completion(T)$. This estimate corresponds to the time it takes an agent, which can execute the activity, to complete the activity after

---

[1] Under the *earliest deadline first* scheduling policy, the scheduling priority of a task decreases as the task's deadline increases. Consequently, our dynamic deadline adjustment algorithms may increase the number of escalations because they extend deadlines.

the activity is submitted for execution, including any queuing time at the agent's work queue. Such estimates can be extracted from the audit logs maintained by existing WFMSs.

- Each activity T is assigned an escalation cost – $escal\_cost(T)$. Typically, WFMSs allow user-defined attributes to be associated with activities and, thus, one of these attributes could be used for specifying escalation costs. Escalation costs are assigned by business analysts based on the effects of escalation should an activity miss its deadline.
- At any point, the system can obtain, for each agent A, the current queue length – $cur\_queue(A)$ – and the average queue length – $avg\_queue(A)$ – based on past history. Most existing WFMSs provide this functionality.

3. Dynamic Deadline Adjustment (DDA)

In this section, we present several algorithms that adjust dynamically the deadlines assigned to workflow activities. For each activity T, the algorithms use T's effective deadline, $effective\_dline(T)$, which is set to $dline(T)$ when a new workflow instance is created. An activity T escalates when its actual execution time is greater than its effective deadline.

No Adjustment (NOA): This is the default algorithm followed by existing WFMSs. Under NOA, the deadline of an activity is not adjusted at all. NOA is used as the baseline for the experimental results we present in this paper.

Total Slack (TSL): This algorithm is implicitly followed by WFMSs that specify the deadlines of activities relative to the starting time of the workflow instances containing them [InConcert, TWF]. Under this algorithm, the deadline of an activity T_k that is going to be executed next is adjusted by adding the currently available slack to it.

$$effective\_dline(T_k) = dline(T_k) + slack$$

The value of $slack$ is computed as follows. The starting activity does not receive any slack since there is no slack available at that point. After an activity T finishes, $slack$ is computed as the difference between T's effective deadline and T's execution time. An important point to note is that if T is an AND-join, i.e., it has multiple predecessors, its effective deadline reflects the slack produced by the last completed predecessor. This is because T's effective deadline is calculated anew each time a predecessor activity finishes.

NOA and TSL algorithms can be applied to any workflow model because they do not use any information about the structure of the workflow. The algorithms we present next assume that workflows conform to the well-structured model we defined in the previous section. When considering a well-structured workflow schema, it is easy to see that for any given primitive activity T, all successors of T, including T, constitute a well-structured workflow schema, W_T. Therefore, if T_k is a primitive activity that immediately follows T, W_{T_k} consists of several sequential activities $T_k^1 \ldots T_k^{m_k}$, each of which is either primitive or composite.

Assuming that *slack* is known when T_k is ready to be submitted for execution, the following algorithms can be used for computing T_k's effective deadline.

Proportional Execution (PEX): The available slack is distributed among T_k and $T_k^1 \ldots T_k^{m_k}$ in proportion to their average completion times. The average completion time of a composite activity is the sum of the average completion times of the activities belonging to the critical path within the composite activity.

$$effective\_dline(T_k) = dline(T_k) + slack * \frac{avg\_completion(T_k)}{\sum_{j=1}^{m_k} avg\_completion(T_k^j)}$$

Proportional Escalation (PES): The available slack is distributed among T_k and $T_k^1 \ldots T_k^{m_k}$ in proportion to their escalation costs. For composite activities, the escalation cost is set to the maximum of the escalation costs among their sub-activities.

$$effective\_dline(T_k) = dline(T_k) + slack * \frac{escal\_cost(T_k)}{\sum_{j=1}^{m_k} escal\_cost(T_k^j)}$$

Proportional Load (PLO): If A_{T_k} is the agent that will execute T_k, PLO distributes the available slack in proportion to the loads (expressed as the average queue length) of the agents that will execute the remaining activities. For composite activities, these loads are set to be the maximum of the average queue lengths of the agents that will execute their sub-activities. In addition, when there are multiple agents that can execute the same activity, the average load among them is chosen.

$$effective\_dline(T_k) = dline(T_k) + slack * \frac{avg\_queue(A_{T_k})}{\sum_{j=1}^{m_k} avg\_queue(A_{T_k^j})}$$

The *slack* value used in the above algorithms is computed in the following way. When a workflow instance is submitted for execution, the value of *slack* is 0. When an activity T finishes execution, its slack, which is computed as the difference between T's effective deadline and T's execution time, is added to *slack*. The new value of *slack* is the available slack for every W_{T_k}, where T_k is an immediate successor of T. Then, some portion of *slack* is assigned to T_k, according to the above algorithms, and the new value of the available slack for W_{T_k} is decremented by this portion.

Finally, AND-joins are handled in the same way as in the TSL algorithm. Upon completion of each predecessor of T_k, the effective deadline of T_k is re-computed. Therefore, when T_k is ready for execution, its effective deadline has received the appropriate portion of the slack produced by the predecessor that finished last.

PreemptiveEscalation(W, T) : boolean
/* Executed when activity T of workflow W becomes ready */
    RETURN(NextStep(W, T, T);
END;

NextStep(W, T, T_c) : boolean
    $pred\_completion(T_c) = \frac{cur\_queue(T_c)}{avg\_queue(T_c)} * avg\_completion(T_c)$;
    IF $T_c == T$ AND $dline(T_c) < pred\_completion(T_c)$
        RETURN("YES");
    ENDIF
    IF $T_c \neq T$ AND $(1 - \frac{escal\_cost(T)}{escal\_cost(T_c)}) * pred\_completion(T_c) > dline(T_c)$
        RETURN("YES");
    ENDIF
    IF number of activities on the path from T to T_c is less than P AND
        T_c not followed by conditional activities AND
        $(T == T_c$ OR $escal\_cost(T) > escal\_cost(T_c))$
        FOR each successor T'_c of T_c in W
            IF NextStep(W, T, T'_c) = "YES"
                RETURN("YES");
            ENDIF
        ENDFOR
    ENDIF
    RETURN("NO");
END;

Fig. 3. The basic preemptive escalation algorithm

4. Preemptive Escalation

The algorithms presented in the previous section aim at reducing the number of escalations. However, escalations cannot be always avoided. In such cases, if we were able to *predict* that an escalation is likely to occur during the execution of a future activity, we could use this information to reduce the operational cost of the process containing this activity. Specifically, consider workflows with global escalations. If at some point during the workflow execution we determine that a future activity is going to escalate, it is often cost-effective to invoke escalation *immediately,* regardless of whether or not the currently executed activity misses its deadline, since this would allow more time for remedial actions and would reduce the cost associated with the compensation of finished activities.

Figure 3 shows the preemptive escalation algorithm. The algorithm uses parameter P to limit the prediction scope, and it is invoked every time an activity T becomes ready for execution. Consider a directed graph with nodes corresponding to activities in schema W, where an edge goes from node T_i to T_j if T_j can immediately follow T_i in some execution. The algorithm examines all activities reachable from T by a path of length not greater than P, and such that there are no conditional splits on the path. Conditional splits complicate prediction since the activities that will be executed in the future are not known in advance. The algorithm examines these activities in depth-first order and stops exploring each path when it finds an activity T_c that has lower escalation cost than T. In this case, even if T_c or any activity following T_c is likely to escalate, it is cost-effective to wait until T_c is ready for execution rather than escalating early.

For an activity T_c, the algorithm computes T_c's predicted completion time $(pred\_completion(T_c))$ as $avg\_completion(T_c)$ times the *load factor* of the system, which is the ratio $\frac{cur\_queue(T_c)}{avg\_queue(T_c)}$, where $cur\_queue(T_c)$ is the current queue length of the agents that can execute T_c averaged over all such agents, and $avg\_queue(T_c)$ is the average queue length of these agents that corresponds to the load conditions reflected in $avg\_completion(T_c)$. Intuitively, if the average completion time for T_c was observed when the average queue length was 3, and the current queue length averaged over the agents that can execute T_c is 6, we can expect that T_c will take twice as long, provided the current load conditions remain by the time T_c becomes ready for execution.

When examining the first activity, T, (i.e., $T_c = T$ in the algorithm), early escalation is beneficial if T is likely to escalate, i.e., $dline(T_c) < pred\_completion(T_c)$. Early escalation in this case means that we force escalation without starting T. For subsequent activities, the condition for early escalation reflects the idea that the less difference in escalation costs the more confident we want to be that T_c will miss its deadline before invoking an early escalation. One way to account for this could be to compute the confidence interval of our estimate for $pred\_completion(T_c)$ for the confidence level that would be set based on the difference in escalation costs. The unclear part here is how to set the confidence level. We plan to explore this method in the future.

Instead, we use a heuristic approach to measure indirectly the confidence in our prediction by how much the predicted completion time of T_c exceeds its deadline. For example, if $pred\_completion(T_c)$ exceeds slightly $dline(T_c)$, then even a small error in estimating $pred\_completion(T_c)$ will lead to the incorrect prediction that T_c will escalate. Then, if the escalation costs of T and T_c are close, we may not want to escalate early, to avoid an unnecessary escalation. However, if the escalation cost of T_c greatly exceeds that of T, we want to escalate immediately just because we have a reason to believe that T_c will escalate. We achieve this by introducing the factor $(1 - \frac{escal\_cost(T)}{escal\_cost(T_c)})$, which ranges from 1 when $escal\_cost(T_c) >> escal\_cost(T)$ to 0 when $escal\_cost(T_c) = escal\_cost(T)$, in which case early escalation is not beneficial.

The preemptive escalation mechanism can be used in conjunction with any of the DDA algorithms. For each activity T_c, the preemptive escalation algorithm predicts the value of $effective\_dline(T_c)$ that would be assigned to it by the DDA algorithm at hand, assuming that each activity

T_i on the path from T to T_c takes $pred\_completion(T_i)$ to complete. Then, $effective\_dline(T_c)$ replaces $dline(T_c)$ in Figure 3.

This calculation of $effective\_dline(T_c)$ is very optimistic because it does not take into account AND-joints. Consider, for example, the schema on Figure 2 and assume that we are about to execute $T6$. Assume for simplicity that there is no available slack when $T6$ become ready for execution. The algorithm will obtain $pred\_completion(T6)$, and then calculate $slack$ after $T6$ as $dline(T6) - pred\_completion(T6)$. It will then use this slack value for calculating the effective deadline of the next activity, $T8$. However, the actual available slack for $T8$ may be considerably smaller, because $T8$ will not be ready for execution until its other predecessor, $T7$, finishes. Thus, the effective deadline of $T8$ may be over-estimated. It is important to note, however, that over-estimating the effective deadline may only reduce the number of times early escalation is found beneficial. Thus, while it may reduce the benefits of predictive escalations, it will not cause erroneous escalations (i.e., the algorithm will not invoke an early escalation for a process that would have completed normally otherwise).

5. Experimental Evaluation

To study the performance of the deadline adjustment algorithms and the impact of the preemptive escalation technique, we developed a simulation model and carried out an initial experimental evaluation. In the following sections, we outline the simulation model, present the experimental setup as well as the assumptions made and, finally, analyze the collected results.

5.1 Simulation Model

An event-driven simulation toolkit was used in our study. Figure 4 shows the workflow management system model we used. The model consists of four basic modules: *process source, workflow engine, agent node,* and *local source.* A detailed description of each of these modules is given below.

Process Source: Generates instances of business processes and submits them to the workflow engine for execution using the arrival rate specified for each process schema.

Workflow Engine: Schedules the activities of every business process instance. When an activity is ready for execution, the engine selects the agent that can execute the activity and schedules its execution at that agent. When an activity finishes execution, the engine is notified and, then, it determines the activities, if any, to be scheduled for execution next.

Agent Node: Executes workflow activities. Agents may belong to different roles, including humans and computer applications.

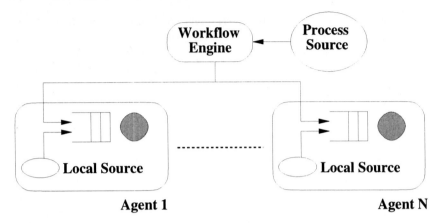

Fig. 4. Workflow simulation model

Local Source: Generates tasks to be executed at an agent. These tasks do not
belong to workflow instances, and they do not have deadlines associated
with them. Local tasks are introduced into the model for modeling real-
life scenarios where existing resources are shared by WFMSs and other
applications.

Each business process schema consists of several activities and has an
arrival rate, referred to as *instance generation rate.* For each activity, information about the statistical distribution of its execution time as well as
information regarding the agent(s) that can execute the activity is available.
The above-mentioned statistical distribution is used to compute the execution
time of a particular instance of the activity.

When an escalation occurs, the entire business process instance is aborted
and the escalation cost is equal to the cost of the activity that triggered the
escalation. We do not model the execution of escalations; the assumption is
that escalations are executed by agents that do not execute normal workflow
activities. In addition, we assume that each agent monitors its queue, which
contains workflow activities and local tasks, if any, and it maintains a running
estimate of the average size of the queue. The workflow engine, on the other
hand, is responsible for maintaining the average completion time for every
workflow activity.

Before an agent starts executing a workflow activity, it checks if the activity was queued longer than its allowable execution time. If it was, the
agent notifies the workflow engine about the missed deadline and escalation
is invoked. Otherwise, the activity is executed to completion. In this case,
the workflow engine checks upon the completion of the activity whether it
missed its deadline, in which case escalation is invoked. When the activity
completes without escalation, the activities that can be executed next are
computed, their deadlines are adjusted depending on the DDA algorithm

used, and they are submitted for execution at the appropriate agents. When an activity escalates, the entire process instance is aborted in a single step.

5.2 Experimental Setup

Table 1. Baseline simulation setting

Parameter	Setting
Number of agents	8
Workflow schemas	1
Number of activities per workflow schema	8
Instance inter-arrival rate	0.3
Local task inter-arrival rate	0.4

Typically, organizations have many business processes consisting of different number of activities. These activities can be considerably different in terms of their actual execution times and the resources they require, e.g., a telecommunications service provisioning process may involve human actions, real-time system actions, database application programs, and legacy applications. If we tried to capture all this diversity and complexity in our performance study, the results would have been obscured by too many parameters. Rather, we chose to model just one business process for studying our algorithms. In particular, we chose to model the telecommunications service provisioning workflow presented in Figure 2. The workflow system consists of single-threaded agents, which follow a non-preemptive FIFO scheduling policy.

The execution time of activities follows the *erlang* distribution. The execution time of local tasks follows the *exponential* distribution with mean equal to 1.0. The deadline of each activity is set to be twice its mean execution time. Table 1 summarizes the baseline parameter settings, and Table 2 shows the values for activity parameters used in the experiments. Each simulation experiment consists of three simulation runs, with each run initialized using a different seed. The statistics collected during each of the runs correspond to 100 000 process instances. In addition, during each run, we started collecting statistics after the simulator had reached a stable state.

5.3 Simulation Results

In this section, we present the results of our initial simulation study. The study investigates the cost benefits of the preemptive escalation mechanism when it is used together with one of the five DDA algorithms. When the prediction scope is 0, the preemptive escalation algorithm is not invoked at all and, hence, the results show the performance of the DDA algorithms alone. As performance measures, we use the percentage of executions that resulted in escalations and the escalation cost.

Table 2. Service provisioning activity attributes

Activity	Mean Execution	Deviation	Escalation Cost	Agent
T1	2.0	0.5	1	1
T2	2.0	0.5	2	2
T3	2.0	0.5	4	3
T4	10.0	5.0	4	4
T5	2.0	0.5	8	5
T6	2.0	0.5	16	6
T7	2.0	0.5	16	7
T8	2.0	0.5	32	8

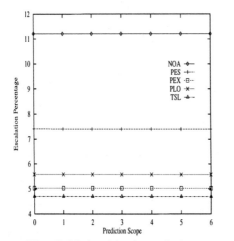

Fig. 5. No local load: escalations

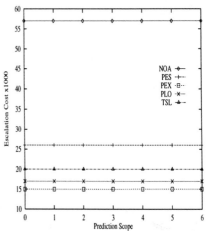

Fig. 6. No local load: cost

5.3.1 No Local Tasks. Here, we present the performance results when only workflow activities are executed by the agents. Figures 5 and 6 show the percentage of escalations and the escalation costs, respectively. While these graphs show that dynamic deadline adjustment reduces significantly the number of escalations and the escalation costs, these gains do not depend on the prediction scope of the preemptive escalation mechanism. In other words, preemptive escalation is not beneficial in this case.

The reason for this behavior is that, in the absence of local tasks, the system operates in a steady state, with agent queue lengths not varying dramatically. Moreover, the process arrival rate does not load the system enough to trigger early escalations (early escalations are triggered when the predicted completion time exceeds the deadline by a factor of $(1 - \frac{escal\_cost(T)}{escal\_cost(T_c)})$). Although some early escalations occur during the execution of $T4$ due to $T4$'s high mean execution and standard deviation values, they account for less than 1% of all escalations and, therefore, they do not affect the results.

Among the different DDA algorithms, Figure 5 shows that TSL outperforms all of them in terms of the number of escalations. However, as seen in Figure 6, TSL is not the most cost effective algorithm. In fact, it is 33% more expensive than PEX and 17% more expensive than PLO. By assigning the entire slack to the next activity, TSL reduces the escalations during the execution of initial activities. However, by letting early activities consume the whole slack, TSL increases the number of more costly escalations during the execution of the remaining activities. On the other hand, even though PEX and PLO cause more escalations than TSL, a greater percentage of their escalations occur during the execution of early activities, resulting in lower overall costs.

Finally, PES performs the worst among all DDA algorithms, both in terms of the number of escalations and escalation costs. It has 57% more escalations than TSL and 32% more escalations than PEX. The reason for this behavior is that, given the difference in escalation costs between earlier and later activities, PES assigns the least slack among all algorithms to activities and, consequently, it causes more escalations to occur. These escalations are too numerous to be compensated by a reduction of escalations at later stages, even though these escalations have higher costs.

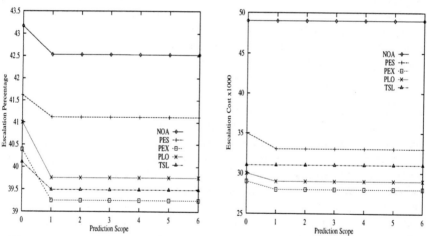

Fig. 7. Agent 1 loaded: escalations   **Fig. 8.** Agent 1 loaded: cost

5.3.2 Adding Local Tasks. We now turn our attention to the performance of the algorithms when agents execute local tasks as well. Figures 7 and 8 illustrate the percentage of escalations and the escalation costs for the early escalation algorithms when the agent executing $T1$ is loaded with local tasks. These figures show some small benefits due to early escalations, both in terms of the number of escalations and the escalation costs. In particular, early escalations account for about 1.5% of the total number of escalations for all algorithms.

One reason for the benefits in escalation costs being so small is the way we do accounting. Since the loaded agent in this experiment is the one executing the very first activity, early escalation here mostly means escalating *before* the first activity executes as opposed to *after* the first activity misses its deadline. In both cases, we, simplistically, assume the escalation cost to be the same and equal to the cost associated with the first activity. Thus, the cost benefits shown in Figure 8 are due to the reduction in the number of escalations only.

Interestingly enough, although the preemptive escalation mechanism is supposed to just replace a later escalation with an earlier one, Figure 7 shows a drop in the total number of escalations when the preemptive escalation mechanism is employed, i.e., the prediction scope becomes greater than 0. This is because a workflow instance that escalates early does not contribute to the load of the agents that would have to execute some of its remaining activities. Therefore, these agents can service more tasks from other instances. In other words, escalating early increases the total system capacity in terms of executing non-escalated process instances.

Furthermore, Figure 7 shows that one-step-ahead prediction in the preemptive escalation mechanism yields all the benefits (the graphs flatten beyond prediction scope 1). This is because only the agent that executes activity $T1$ is loaded and, hence, similar to the discussion we had in the previous section, extending the prediction scope increases early escalations marginally since the agents executing the remaining tasks are not loaded.

Comparing Figures 5 and 7, we notice that, while TSL outperforms the rest of the DDA algorithms when there are no local tasks, PEX results in the minimum number of escalations when the preemptive escalation mechanism is employed and the agent that executes $T1$ performs local tasks as well. In terms of the escalation costs, PEX is the best in both cases.

Figures 9 and 10 show the percentage of escalations and the escalation costs when the agent executing $T2$ is loaded with local tasks. The graphs exhibit the trends we noticed in the previous experiment, except for the fact that TSL outperforms all DDA algorithms in both the number and cost of escalations. This is because TSL assigns the whole slack produced after $T1$'s execution to $T2$ whereas the rest of the algorithms assign only a portion of it to $T2$ – Notice that in the previous experiment there was no slack to be assigned to the overloaded agent since this agent executed the very first activity. In addition, TSL benefits the most among all algorithms when early escalations take place.

As we would expect from the earlier discussion, the benefits from the preemptive escalation mechanism extend to prediction scope of 2, and are higher than in the previous experiments. In particular, the percentage of early escalations ranges from 6.3 for NOA to 12 for TSL. Finally, in contrast to the previous experiments, PLO outperforms PEX in both the number of

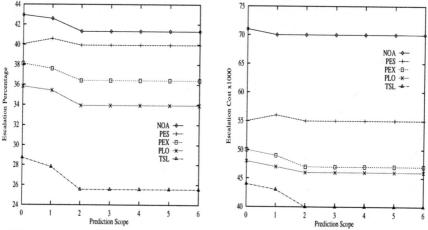

Fig. 9. Agent 2 loaded: escalations   **Fig. 10.** Agent 2 loaded: cost

escalations and the escalation cost. The reason for this behavior is that PLO assigns more slack to activities than PEX.

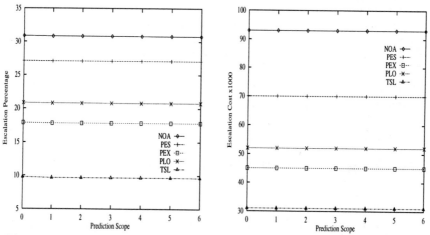

Fig. 11. Agent 3 loaded: escalations   **Fig. 12.** Agent 3 loaded: cost

When the agent that executes activity $T3$, which is enacted conditionally with frequency 80%, is loaded with local tasks, the performance of our algorithms is shown in Figures 11 and 12. These figures are very similar to the ones for the case where no load is placed on any of the agents. The difference is that, here, TSL has the best performance in both the number of escalations and the escalation cost. In particular, TSL results in 45% fewer escalations than PEX and 53% fewer escalations than PLO. In terms of costs, TSL is 31% less expensive than PEX and 40% less expensive than PLO.

Also, similar to the results shown in Figures 5 and 6, the prediction scope does not matter. The reason is as follows. When we apply the preemptive escalation algorithm on $T1$ and $T2$, the prediction scope does not matter because the agents that execute these activities are not loaded and the algorithm stops after examining $T2$ due to the OR-split. When we examine $T4$ and beyond, the prediction scope does not matter either because the agents are not loaded. When we are about to execute $T3$, the preemptive escalation algorithm is likely to announce that early escalation should be invoked at this point and will not examine any other activities. However, since the cost of the early escalation in this case is the same as $T3$'s escalation cost (because of our accounting strategy), early escalation does not affect the escalation cost.

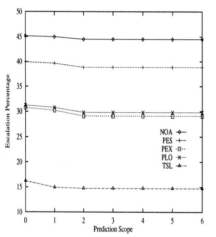

Fig. 13. Agent 5 loaded: escalations

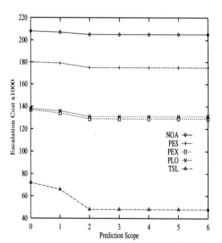

Fig. 14. Agent 5 loaded: cost

Turning to the case where the agent that executes $T5$ is loaded with local tasks, the percentage of escalations and the escalation costs are illustrated in Figures 13 and 14. The graphs demonstrate the same trends as the results presented in Figures 9 and 10, respectively. In particular, early escalation is beneficial for all algorithms, and increasing the prediction scope beyond 2 does not produce any additional benefits.

One might have expected that the performance of the DDA algorithms would continue to improve as the prediction scope becomes greater than 2. However, prediction scope greater than two does not have any effect when $T1$ or $T2$ are examined because they are followed by an OR-split and the prediction stops at the split. In addition, the preemptive escalation algorithm will rarely return "YES" when examining $T6$, $T7$, or $T8$ since the agents that execute these activities are not sufficiently loaded. The only situation where the preemptive escalation algorithm returns "YES" in the majority of executions is when examining $T5$ because the agent executing $T5$ is loaded. $T5$ is within prediction scope 2 from $T3$ and $T4$.

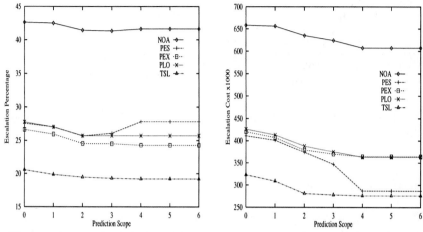

Fig. 15. Agent 8 loaded: escalations   **Fig. 16.** Agent 8 loaded: cost

We do not include the graphs produced for the cases where the agents that execute $T6$ and $T7$ are loaded with local tasks because they are very similar to the graphs when the agent that executes $T5$ is loaded (shown in Figures 13 and 14). However, we should note that in these cases preemptive escalation does not benefit the DDA algorithms any more when the prediction scope exceeds 3. The explanation is the same as the one given for the case where the agent executing $T5$ is loaded; namely, $T6$ and $T7$ are within prediction scope 3 from $T3$ and $T4$.

When the agent that executes the last activity, $T8$, is loaded, the performance of our algorithms differs significantly from the previous cases, as shown in Figures 15 and 16. In particular, PES is not as bad as in the previous experiments. Not only that, but PES outperforms PLO and PEX with respect to the escalation cost. This is because under PES, the percentage of early escalations is the greatest among all PEX and PLO, as shown in Table 3. TSL is still the best overall algorithm.

Table 3 shows the percentage of executions that result in escalations and the percentage of these escalations that are due to early escalations when the prediction scope is between 0 and 4. Beyond escalation scope 4, the percentage of early escalations does not change because the longest path used by the prediction mechanism in the provisioning workflow schema is 4 (remember that prediction always stops at OR-splits). As we see, as the prediction scope

Table 3. Local load on agent 8: percentage of escalations

Prediction Scope		NOA	PES	PEX	PLO	TSL
0	Total	42.62	27.57	26.63	27.76	20.57
	Early	0.00	0.00	0.00	0.00	0.00
1	Total	42.49	27.03	25.94	27.02	19.86
	Early	1.41	3.99	5.01	4.81	19.23
2	Total	41.43	25.68	24.53	25.70	19.47
	Early	7.82	12.38	14.88	13.85	31.99
3	Total	41.32	26.07	24.50	25.71	19.29
	Early	9.87	20.25	17.42	17.15	32.45
4	Total	41.61	27.81	24.28	25.70	19.20
	Early	14.05	38.40	18.28	20.43	32.81

increases, early escalations contribute more to the total number of escalations that take place.

6. Related Work

We are not aware of any work that directly addresses the issue of re-ducing costs due to process escalations in workflow systems. Nevertheless, dynamic deadline adjustment is somewhat similar to real-time scheduling [LL 73, AGM 88, HSTR 89]. Real-time systems use deadlines for scheduling system components such as CPU and I/O and, typically, they target ap-plications consisting of single tasks with known resource requirements and execution times. We view scheduling and dynamic deadline adjustment as complimentary mechanisms.

Our DDA mechanism is related to the work described in [MN 95]. In [MN 95], the authors present priority-driven CPU scheduling algorithms for transactional workflows. Each workflow process consists of several sequential tasks. Each task is an ACID transaction having an average response time goal. The assignment of priorities is based on the performance of the tasks relative to their original response time goals. In contrast to these algorithms, our DDA algorithms do not concentrate on CPU scheduling. In addition, our algorithms are not restricted to transactional workflows, and they allow both sequential, conditional, and parallel execution of tasks.

In [KGM 93a, KGM 93b], the authors study the problem of how the dead-line of a real-time activity is automatically translated to the deadlines of all sequential and parallel sub-tasks constituting the activity. Each sub-task deadline is assigned just before the sub-task is submitted for execution, and the algorithms for deadline assignment assume that the *earliest deadline first* scheduling policy is used. Similar to our work, the goal of the proposed al-gorithms is that of minimizing the number of missed deadlines. In contrast to these algorithms, our work assumes that all sub-tasks have been assigned deadlines before the activity is submitted for execution and, thus, we focus on adjusting sub-task deadlines on-line rather than assigning deadlines. In addition, [KGM 93a, KGM 93b] assume a soft real-time environment where sub-tasks may miss their deadlines without triggering other sub-tasks. In our environment, however, escalations caused by missed deadlines may result in the execution of new activities, and our algorithms take into account the cost associated with these escalations.

In active real-time databases transactions may trigger new transactions during their execution. The triggered transactions are executed immediately or after the original transaction finishes execution. In [Si+ 96], the authors present algorithms that try to minimize the number of triggering transactions that miss their deadlines when a priority-driven scheduling policy is employed. The proposed algorithms assign priorities to the triggered transactions, and they dynamically reassign the priorities of the triggering transactions. In contrast, our DDA algorithms modify the deadlines assigned to activities without altering their priorities, if any. Consequently, our DDA algorithms could be complemented with the scheduling algorithms proposed in [Si+ 96].

7. Conclusions

In this paper, we concentrated on ways to reduce operational costs due to escalations by combining *dynamic deadline adjustment* and *preemptive escalation*. Dynamic deadline adjustment reduces the number of escalations that occur during workflow executions by using any available slack time to extend the deadlines of the workflow activities that are going to be executed in the future. The distribution of the slack time is based on the estimated execution time of the activities, their escalation cost, and the loads of the agents responsible for their enactment.

Our preemptive escalation mechanism tries to reduce the escalation-related costs by invoking escalations early. Our technique uses statistics from past executions as well as current state information, such as current agent loads, to predict if a future activity is going to miss its deadline. It then exploits the knowledge about the costs of escalation provided by the business analyst to decide if it is beneficial to force escalation early, without waiting for the execution to reach the trouble point.

We have also presented preliminary performance results which evaluate the performance of our algorithms under different workload conditions. The results show that preemptive escalation combined with DDA is an effective approach for reducing escalation-related costs. All DDA algorithms resulted in substantial savings compared to the system with no adjustment, both in the number of escalations and the escalation costs. Among the DDA algorithms, TSL and PEX appear to perform well overall. Nevertheless, more work is needed to investigate the trade-offs between the DDA algorithms presented in this paper.

In addition, the results showed that using the preemptive escalation mechanism in conjunction with DDA offer additional cost reduction of up to 33% (see Figure 14), compared to DDA alone. It even reduced the number of escalations by up to 10% (see Figure 9), due to decrease in the system load. We expect to be able to improve these numbers further by being more aggressive in invoking early escalations. Indeed, our preemptive escalation algorithm, in its present form, invokes early escalation only when the predicted completion time of a future activity exceeds its deadline by a significant factor, especially if the escalation costs of the current and future activities are close. We deliberately chose this conservative heuristic so that, in our first approach to the problem, we do not cause unnecessary escalations. We plan to explore other heuristics in the future.

The Workflow Management System Panta Rhei *

Johann Eder, Herbert Groiss, Walter Liebhart

Department of Informatics, University of Klagenfurt, Austria
email: {hans, herb, walter}@ifi.uni-klu.ac.at

Abstract. We present the prototypical workflow management system Panta Rhei which was designed to support various types of workflows in an uniform and elegant way. The main characteristics of this system are its flexibility, the lean architecture, the integration in the Web, the transactional features and its support of process management. We discuss the basic concepts of the system, its architecture and its implementation.

1. Introduction

With hundred workflow management systems on the market [Law 97] and even more workflow prototypes in research labs the question arises: Why design and implement another one? If we have a closer look on workflow systems, we discover that this term is used for quite different concepts ranging from documented email to scripting languages and workflow management systems offer very different functionalities.

A popular classification ([GHS 95]) distinguishes three types of workflows:

- *ad-hoc workflows*
  Workflows are controlled by users at runtime. Users can react to situations not considered at build-time.
- *administrative workflows*
  Predictable and repeatable workflows described in simple description languages. Activities are mainly performed by humans.
- *production workflow*
  Predictable and repeatable complex workflows which are predefined completely and in great detail using complex information structures and involve application programs and automatic activities.

Although this classification seems to be very helpful at first glance and suggest a need of different workflow management systems we have some objections against this conclusion. The first observation is that in most organizations we found different types of workflows. Some are ad-hoc, some administrative, some of production type. And we observe that persons usually are involved in different types of workflows. We regard it as disadvantage, if they had to use different systems. The other observation is that the classification does not hold in practice. Take for example an highly structured

---

* Heraclitus: "Everything flows"

and often-repeated production workflow. It is simply impossible to preplan all exceptions that could arise since workflows are models of real world processes. Folklore in workflow systems says that exceptions are not exceptional. Therefore, ad-hoc intervention in production workflows has to be possible too to avoid workflow system to become bureaucratic nuisances.

These observations and considerations as well as our experiences with an earlier prototype which was based on form flow metaphor and active databases [EGN 94] led us to design a new system. We claim that it is possible to support all these different types of workflows with diverse and seemingly contradicting requirements with a single workflow management system. And with our workflow system Panta Rhei we show that this can be achieved without an inflation of features. Our main contributions are:

- The design of a set of concepts which fit well together and allow the support of different types of workflows.
- A set of features for improving the management of workflows that work well together with the basic concepts, in particular workflow transaction, time management and process management.
- An open architecture supporting user interaction as well as collaboration of workflow systems of different organizations.
- A lean architecture and a comparably simple implementation.

The remainder of this paper is organized as follows: in the next section we present and discuss the basic concepts of Panta Rhei and highlight some of the additional features. In section 3 we present our workflow definition language WDL. Section 4 contains the architecture and implementation aspects of Panta Rhei. Section 5 concludes this paper by giving a summary and presenting some ideas of further research.

2. The Concepts of Panta Rhei

2.1 Classification of Workflows

We consider workflow systems as man-machine systems with the following ingredients: Agents perform activities which means among other possibilities the manipulation of data. Processes are partial orderings of activities. The workflow systems organizes who performs which activity with which data at which time.

We can classify workflow management systems along several dimensions:

- *initiative*
  In user centered systems the initiative is with the user. He decides on the continuation of the process, who is next, etc. In the extreme the workflow management system is a rather passive delivery and bookkeeping device. The initiative could also be with the system. In the extreme the users

cannot influence the process and merely fulfill tasks they receive from the system.

- *structure of data*

  Data can be structured or unstructured. Structured data can be accessed and interpreted by the system, while unstructured data (like text documents) cannot.

- *data classes*

  We distinguish between case data (e.g. client name in an insurance claim process) and process data (e.g. termination state of an activity).

- *activity types*

  Manual activities are performed by users without further support from the system. Automatic activities are carried out by IT-systems without human intervention. For semiautomatic activities humans use specific interactive programs for performing an activity.

- *process specification*

  Here we distinguish how processes are specified and when. They could be completely ad-hoc which means the process is defined at run time step by step by the agents. The other extreme is a fully specified process where agents cannot make decisions about the continuation of the process at all. We distinguish also according to the expressiveness of the process specification language, in particular, whether the process can be defined dependent on case or process data.

- *agents*

  Agents are the ones performing activities. Agents can be humans or IT-systems, or abstractions thereof, like roles or organizational units.

It is easy to see that these dimensions are all but orthogonal. For an example, if the system should make decisions based on case data it is mandatory that case data are available to the system in form of structured data. Another example shows the dependencies between the dimensions initiative and process specification: if workflows are defined undeterministically then the user has to take the initiative.

2.2 Basic Concepts

Our aim was to develop a small set of basic concepts which allow to express all workflows which are possible according to the classification above in an uniform way. The basic decisions for achieving this goal were the following:

- All process information is mapped to the data space. Process schema as well as process instance data are stored in the database. Thus processes can be manipulated as data which offers enormous flexibility.
- Case data and process data are represented in a uniform way. We use the form metaphor for representing data. From a programming point of view a form is a data type. From an implementation perspective, a form is a view on the database.

- Processes are defined in a highly generic workflow definition language with the usual control structures. The only variables in this language are of type form, such that all data used in processes is stored in the database.
- We rigorously tried to abstract and parameterize concepts. All concepts are first class citizens in our workflow language. Agents, forms, activities and even process definitions and control structures can be taken from form items.

These decisions brought several advantages. Above all we achieved great flexibility and expressiveness with a comparably small set of concepts. We do not have to distinguish between ad-hoc processes and predefined processes at this level. For an example, the name of an agent and the name of the next activity and the forms it should manipulate can all be taken from a form manipulated by an agent in a previous activity. With this concept we tightly integrate ad-hoc and production processes. The workflow engine is kept small and generic. It can be seen as an automaton operating on workflow specification data, process data and case data representing the state space of the workflow system.

2.3 Additional Features

Panta Rhei offers several possibilities in order to guarantee a consistent and reliable execution of business processes, i.e. the handling of failures and exceptions (see [EL 95, EL 96, EL 97]). Therefore it is necessary to distinguish between possible failure and exception classes, like system failures (e.g. a client breakdown), semantic failures (if an activity terminates unsuccessfully) or unexpected exceptions at runtime, like changing the order of activities within a workflow. The *advanced transaction* system of Panta Rhei tries to automate the recovery from failures and exceptions as much as possible. The transaction system is both, a runtime feature and a build time feature. As build-time feature it offers additional possibilities for a workflow designer to specify valid processes. The workflow schema can be enriched by additional information which is used in case of an exceptional situation. As runtime feature it (automatically) recovers from (semantical) failures, compensates activities and triggers alternative executions. Many of the underlying concepts are borrowed and adapted from advanced transaction models [Elm 92, Alo 96].

Although most workflow management systems offer sophisticated modeling tools to specify and analyze workflows, they suffer from an important shortcoming: they are not capable to handle the concept of time adequately [PEL 97, JZ 96, ELP 97]. *Time* appears in Panta Rhei in two notions. Structural time aspects express the (estimated) duration of activities and structural time dependencies between activities. Explicit time aspects are used to formulate time constraints of the real world (e.g. an activity d has to be finished 5 days after activity a has finished). For the integration of these time aspects a new method called ePERT, based on the optimization method

PERT (Program Evaluation and Review Technique) was developed [PEL 97]. The time information which becomes available by this approach can be used to find the critical path within a workflow, to determine which alternative executions are still valid and what are the latest start time for activities in order to meet some deadline. The system is capable of monitoring deadlines and generates time errors in the case that deadlines are missed. Another aspect is the possibility to delay tasks for a certain amount of time or to a specified data.

Modern businesses build the whole organization around their key business processes. Important for the success of process centered organizations is that each process has a responsible manager. Similar we see the management of workflows. A *workflow manager* is assigned to each workflow. He is in charge of monitoring workflows, handle exceptions and failures which cannot be resolved automatically and has several possibilities to manipulate the execution of workflows. In particular he should be able to quickly analyze the current status of a workflow, stop and resume a workflow, abort a workflow, change a workflow specification, map a workflow to a different one, start an ad-hoc process, make decisions about priorities, etc. Of course, all these manual interventions should not violate the consistency of the overall workflow and therefore they are based on the systems internal advanced transaction mechanism. To enable workflow managers to achieve all this, a special workflow client application is needed which offers all this functionality. Furthermore, the time information computed with the ePERT method can be used to calculate priorities within worklists of users and thus it contributes to avoid time errors beforehand. It allows to discover potential timing problems early such that a process manager can take steps to avoid them.

2.4 Open Architecture

One design decision of Panta Rhei was to make the participation in a workflow as easy as possible. First, the interaction between the workflow system and the outside world (users, applications, other workflow systems at the same site or at remote sites) is solely realized by exchange of forms. This has two important advantages: The interface of a user to Panta Rhei is completely integrated in a web browser. This makes the system open such that anybody with access to the WWW can participate in a workflow. This feature is important, if one realizes that workflows are frequently started as a reaction to some request from outside of an organization (e.g. an order is received). Second, the communication between the workflow system and other systems is realized through the exchange of forms. Panta Rhei does not make any assumptions on client applications and remote systems but that they are able to receive forms and return or send forms. All process specific information is represented in forms. So there is no need for complex suite of APIs to make workflow systems collaborate.

3. Workflow Description Language

The formal representation of processes within Panta Rhei is based on the Workflow Definition Language WDL. This language was explicitly designed for the system Panta Rhei and its "look and feel" is similar to that of traditional programming languages. Since workflow designers are not necessarily programmers, Panta Rhei also offers an easy to use graphical interface to specify workflows. Such a specification can be mapped to WDL and vice versa. WDL itself consists of 5 basic units: the workflow specification part, the definition of activities, roles, organization structures and inter-process communication.

3.1 Workflow Specification

The workflow specification part of WDL enables the formal description of a workflow (process). Primarily this means to specify the control and data flow of a workflow. Additionally, transactional and time relevant aspects are specified within this part.

3.1.1 Structure of a workflow specification. The structure of a typical workflow specification is similar to the structure of ordinary procedural programs:

- *Header:* Every workflow has a name and any number of optional arguments. Arguments are forms which are passed into the workflow and/or produced by the workflow.
- *Declaration part:* The declaration part consists of two units: workflow declaration and data declaration. The *workflow declaration part* serves for the specification of general process information. This type of information is equal for all processes and comprises information of the process owner, a subject text, a short description of the current process, the specification of the maximal execution time and the specification of some action (e.g. the execution of a special time activity) in case of a time failure.
  Forms which are produced within a workflow have to be declared in the *data declaration* part. This is simply be done by assigning form-types to form variables. Fields within the form can be accessed via the dot notation. The scope of a data declaration is the whole workflow.
- *Body:* This is the main part of a workflow specification. Included between the keywords begin and end the description of the control and data flow of the process is expressed. Within the workflow context this means to answer the following W-questions: *who has to do what and when and with which data.* Based on this paradigm, typical statement sequences in WDL are of the following simple structure (see also Fig. 1):
  agent_name activity_name (form_names);
  The semantics of this is: The workflow agent user_name performs the activity activity_name with the forms defined by the arguments form_names.

3.1.2 Assignment of agents to activities. The assignment of agents (human or machines) to activities is a fundamental concept within workflow management systems. At run time, flexible and dynamic assignment resolution techniques are necessary to react adequately on organizational needs and changes. WDL fulfills this requirement by the following assignment techniques:

- The agent is defined directly by the user name of the responsible person.
- The agent is defined indirectly via a role concept. Any user who belongs to such a role is allowed to execute the activity. Of course, roles within different organization structures (e.g. departments) may have the same name. Therefore, in WDL the workflow designer can extend the role name by a department name in order to avoid such conflicts.
- Often there are different activities within a process which should be executed by one and the same agent. In most cases, it is not known at process definition time, which agent this will be. WDL offers a simple concept to handle this requirement.
- The highest degree of flexibility is achieved by assigning agents dynamically during run time (especially for weak structured workflows). Since forms are first class citizens within WDL, it is easy to support this by introducing an extra field within the form into which the name of the next agent can be written or executed out of some other information at run time. Consider the following example: If a request for a credit is accepted then the applicant should be informed by the person who always takes care of this applicant. At run time the actual name of this person is stored in the field `responsible_agent` within the form `credit_form`. The WDL command is:

```
credit_form.responsible_agent accept(credit_form);
```

3.1.3 Control flow specification. As explained earlier, the basic statement sequence in WDL is the assignment of agents to activities and the data specification in the form of `agent activity(form1, form2)`. Let's call such an assignment a "workflow step". WDL now offers a variety of control structures to specify the execution order of workflow steps. The most relevant control structures are:

- *sequence:* A sequential execution order of workflow steps is specified by listing the corresponding workflow steps one after another, each separated by a semicolon.
- *alternative:* For the definition of alternatives the well known `if` - `then` - `else` construct is available. For the specification of expressions, WDL offers almost all the concepts which are known from procedural languages. Above all, the usage of form fields within expressions is a very convenient feature to construct expressions. An example of an expressions within a control structure is:

```
IF credit_form.sum > 1000 and credit_form.judge = ''True''
THEN boss approve(credit_form);
ELSE ... ENDIF
```
– *loop:* Two types of loops are realized in WDL: while-loops and repeat-until-loops. Within a loop, workflow steps are repeated as long as a certain condition holds.
– *parallelism:* Parallelism helps to reduce workflow execution time and is therefore an important control flow construct. In WDL two types of parallelism are available: and-parallelism (`andpar`) and or-parallelism (`orpar`). The difference between these two types is the synchronization of parallel paths. In the first case, synchronization means that all parallel executing paths have to be finished in order to continue with workflow execution after the synchronization point. In the second case, workflow execution can continue as soon as one parallel execution path finishes.
– *nesting:* In order to reduce complexity and to reuse already defined workflows, Panta Rhei supports the nesting of activities. Activities within a workflow can themselves again be a complex workflow.

3.1.4 Transaction support. WDL allows the specification of workflow transactions [EL 95, EL 96, EL 97] which are very helpful to support reliable and consistent workflow executions. The main idea is to compute workflows within relaxed ACID transactions in order to guarantee the consistency of the business process. The following concepts are necessary to express workflow transactions and are hence fully integrated within WDL:

– *transaction specific control structures:* Besides the already mentioned control structures there are two transaction specific control structures: `free choice` and `ranked choice`. These constructs enable the modeling of contingency paths which are executed in case the previous execution path cannot be executed successfully. A contingency path is intended to accomplish a similar goal as the original path. The difference between the two choice constructs is the selection - fixed or dynamically - of the different paths at run time.
– *vitality:* Typically, workflows have a hierarchical structure. Within such a structure, one (parent) process may exist of several other (child) processes or elementary activities. Whether a parent process achieves its goal or not, mainly depends on its child components. The relation between parent and child components can be specified as vital or non-vital, meaning, that vital connected childs have to terminate successfully in order to enable a successful termination of the parent. Non-vital connected components do not directly influence the result of the parent component.
– *compensation:* Since workflows are long-running applications it is necessary to split the execution into multiple transactions. Doing this, the benefits of single ACID-transactions, isolation (i.e., serializability) and atomicity (i.e., all-or-nothing behavior) is lost. Therefore the concept of compensa-

tion must be introduced in order to cope with the problem of partially executed workflows. WDL supports the specification of workflows with compensation activities. During activity definition, the workflow designer can assign a corresponding compensation activity which semantically undoes the effects of the original activity. Unfortunately, there are different levels of compensation. Therefore in WDL the compensation type must be specified with the special keyword `stornotype`. Four different stornotypes are possibilities: Type `none` (1) means, that the committed activity does not need to be compensated because it is not necessary from an application point of view. Type `undoable` (2) means that a committed activity can be undone by a corresponding compensation activity without any side-effects, in the sense of an inverse operation. Type `compensatable` (3) means that the compensation of an activity leads to some side-effects (e.g. money transfer and back transfer with transfer fees). Type `critical` (4) means that an activity which has already terminated cannot be undone or compensated afterwards because its effects are irreversible within the current context (e.g., drilling a hole, mailing a sensitive information). The following example shows a cutout of an activity definition with compensation in WDL:

activity *money_transfer* (f1) stornotype compensatable
money_back_transfer(f1);

In Panta Rhei *concurrency control* is supported on the level of forms. For every form and all fields within a form various access rights can be specified. At runtime the system monitors the compliance of these rights.

As an example we briefly describe a simple process for a credit application (see Fig. 1). After the header some properties of the process are defined (owner, description, maxtime, subject). The data container for this process is a form of type `c_appl` (credit application form), declared as `appl`. The process is initiated by a `salesperson` performing the task `insert` with the form `appl`. If the field `judge` of this form is set to `'refuse'`, a secretary will perform the step `make_refusal`. Otherwise the else-block is executed in the same fashion.

3.1.5 Definition of Activities, Roles and Organization Structures.
The definition of activities consists of a header part and a declaration part. In the header the name of the activity and the forms which are passed to or from the activity are specified. The declaration part contains the following information:

- *procedure*: If the activity uses external applications then this must be specified at this position.
- *postcondition*: This area allows the definition of a postcondition (i.e., any complex expression) which is evaluated when the activity is finished. The activity will terminate successfully if this condition is satisfied.
- *description*: Short description of the activity.
- *maxtime*: Allows the definition of the maximum execution time of the activity.

```
process credit
owner herb;
description 'simple treatment of credit application';
maxtime 10 days;
forms appl c_appl;
subject f.applicant;

begin
 salesperson insert(appl);
 if appl.judge = 'refuse' then
        secr make_refusal(appl);
    else
        clerk check(f);
        if appl.c_sum > 1000000 then
                boss check(appl);
        end;
        if appl.judge = 'refuse' then
                secr make_refusal(appl);
          else
                secr accept(appl);
        end;
 end;
```

Fig. 1. Credit application workflow

- *formprops*: This attribute allows the specification of access rights on the forms which are manipulated within the activity. The granularity of access rights are form fields.
- *costfunction*: For run-time optimization purpose, cost-information (e.g., how expensive is an activity, what is the success probability of an activity) is necessary. This information is either specified by a numeric constant or by a program which computes the cost of the activity at run time.

Example: Definition of the activity order_entry:

```
ACTIVITY order_entry(f order-form)
DESCRIPTION 'Fill in the order form';
PROCEDURE start_order_application;
POSTCONDITION f.judge = 'OK';
MAXTIME 1 DAY;
FORMPROPS f.customer_data write, f.order_number read,
f.security invisible;
```

The assignment of users to roles is in WDL realized by the construct:

```
agent <user> has <role> in <dept>
```

Additionally, there are two special roles: all and system. Every user automatically belongs to the role all. The role system means that the role is not occupied by a human being but by a system. The *definition of organization structures* is possible via the construct:

department <dept> contains <dept>

3.1.6 Inter-process communication. Panta Rhei allows two types of distribution of process execution. First, a process can be triggered by sending a form to the workflow server. This can be done from another workflow system or an arbitrary application. The WDL-construct for defining the behavior when receiving a form is:

on receive <form-type> start <process> in <dept>

The second kind of inter-process communication is the remote execution of an activity or a subprocess. It is performed when the agent of the activity is an URL, i.e. a pointer to another workflow system. In this case, all process relevant data are sent to the other workflow system, the results are sent back after execution.

3.2 Execution of WDL

A process description defined in WDL is transformed to an execution graph, Fig. 2 shows the graph of the credit process. Every activity or call of a subprocess is translated to a node. Additional special nodes are defined for handling of control structures, if-nodes for conditional statements and loops, andjoin and orjoin for the *anpar* and *orpar* constructs. For the workflow engine these control structures are another type of activities, the only difference to other activities is that they are directly executed in the engine. Three types of edges connect the graph: unconditional edges, true-edges followed if the expression of the preceeding node evaluates to true, and false-edges followed in the other case.

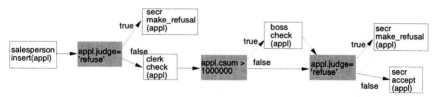

Fig. 2. Execution graph of process credit

Fig. 3 shows the two procedures, which make up the interpreter of this graph. When a workflow is initiated, the procedure start_activity is called. It selects the initial activity of the process and calls the procedure recursively. If the activity is not a special one (like if), the following steps are performed: the (optional) procedure defined for this activity is executed, the user is assigned. If the agent is *system*, we are finished and call the procedure finish_activity. Otherwise the activity is now visible in the worklist(s) of the assigned agent(s) and the (manual) execution of the activity can begin.

If a user finishes an activity, the procedure finish_activity is called, it checks the post-condition and starts the successor activities, if such exists. When the execution of the postcondition fails, the exception handling procedure is called.

This architecture allows the modification of processes at run-time. If a user wants to change the execution of the current process, he is able to change the execution graph of the process instance. This possibility allows the definition of ad-hoc processes and process versions and is an advantage over our first approach, where process descriptions have been compiled into active database rules [EGN 94].

```
procedure start_activity(act)
    case type_of(act)
        process:
            start_activity(init_activity(act));
        activity:
            execute_procedure(act);
            assign_agent(act);
            if agent = system then
                finish_activity(act,0);
            end if;
        if:
            branch := execute_expression(act);
            finish_activity(act, branch);
            ...

    end case;
end;

procedure finish_activity(act, b)
    if act = null then
        return;
    end if;
    status := execute_postcondition(act)
    if status ='success' then
        if no successors of act then
            finish_activity(parent(act));
        else
            for all successors succ of act in branch b do
                start_activity(act);
            end do;
        end if;
    else if status = 'fail' then
        handle_exception(act, status);
    end if;
end;
```

Fig. 3. Execution of workflows

4. Architecture and Implementation

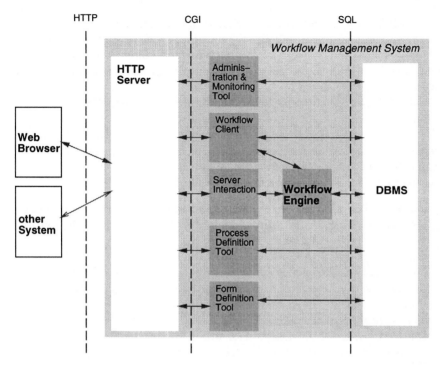

Fig. 4. Architecture of Panta Rhei

The architecture of Panta Rhei is based on the Web technologies. Three concepts make up the World-Wide Web (WWW): uniform addressing of information in the Internet via the Uniform Resource Locator (URL), presentation of information in the Hypertext Markup Language (HTML), and transmission of data using the Hypertext Transfer Protocol HTTP.

The HTML format [BLC 95] allows the integration of different media type into a document. So-called hyper-links enable the integration and connection to other documents or media types. Important for using the WWW for workflow systems is the feature of fill-in forms in HTML, which allows a form based interaction between the user and a program.

HTTP [BLFF 95] is a simple protocol for transmitting information over the net. The client (browser) requests a document from a server, by opening a socket connection and sending the URL of the document to the server. The server sends back the content of this document together with some status information. If the URL points to an executable program the server executes this programs and sends the output back to the client. The HTTP-Server calls this programs using the Common Gateway Interface (CGI). Moreover, the HTTP protocol provides a mechanism for user authorization allowing to restrict access to a group of users or hosts.

Recently, the mechanism of mobile code got significance. Small programs, so-called Applets are integrated in HTML pages and executed at the client machine. These programs enhance the functionality of the browsers and allow the implementation of arbitrary complex user interfaces. The programming language Java [Sun 95] is used for this purposes, most browsers allow the execution of Java Code.

Fig. 4 shows the components of the Panta Rhei system. The architecture differs from the well-known reference model of the Workflow Management Coalition [Hol 95]. Here, the workflow engine is a relatively small component containing the process interpreter. All other components are directly connected to the database and make modifications in it. The workflow management system comprises the following components:

- *database:* The database contains all data relevant for process execution, process definition, organizational hierarchy, roles, as well as the dynamic data of the process instances.
- *workflow engine:* This component contains the interpreter for the defined processes, it is called whenever a process is started or an activity is finished through the user interface. Additionally, the engine comprises the advanced transaction facility and a special time component for monitoring structural and explicit time information.

  Due to the usage of the database for storing the process descriptions as well as the status information of process instances we gain several advantages: every process state is persistent, process and case data are under control of the transaction system of the DBMS, and dynamic changes of workflow specifications are possible during execution.
- *administration and monitoring tool:* It contains functions for creating, modifying and deleting users, roles, and departments. It also allows the inspection and modification of running processes, like terminating instances, reassigning steps, etc. Like the other components communicating with the HTTP Server, the interactions with the user are done by creating and receiving HTML pages and forms.
- *workflow client:* It generates the HTML pages and forms used for interaction with the user. The main page is the user worklist (see Fig. 5), which contains links to the other relevant information, i.e. the forms, process descriptions, history, etc.

  This component calls the workflow engine if the user wants to start a process or finishes an activity. Other interactions, for example viewing the worklist, access the database directly.
- *server interaction:* Activities or subprocesses can be executed on another workflow server. The system sends the required forms to the other server

and the results are sent back. Both interactions are performed using the HTTP protocol.

- *process definition:* Two interfaces are available for process definition: Workflows defined as WDL scripts can be compiled and loaded into the system. Additionally, a graphical process designer has been implemented. Both components are accessible using a Web browser. The WDL description can be uploaded using an input field of type file in the HTML form. The process designer is written as a Java Applet, and therefore accessible from the browser (see left window of Fig. 5).
- *form definition:* Forms are created using a standard HTML editor. A parser extracts all input fields from the form and presents the user with a suggestion for the definition of the corresponding database table. The user can alter the data-types and creates the form table. The HTML form is stored in the database.
- *HTTP Server:* The HTTP server is the interface between the Web and the workflow system. It translates the requests from the users to calls of the corresponding procedures of the workflow system using the CGI Interface.
- *Browser:* Every interaction with the system is done by a Web browser. This allows wide availability and platform independence and made system implementation easier.

The current version is implemented in Java connecting the database using JDBC (Java Database Connection). We also use the NCSA HTTP-Server and an ORACLE 7 database. However, by using standard interfaces between the components (HTTP, CGI, JDBC) the implementation is fairly independent of a specific HTTP server or database management system.

5. Conclusions

We achieved our goal to find a small set of basic concepts to support a wide range of different workflow types. We validated our ideas by actually building a workflow management system. We also found it quite easy to extend the core system with some additional features like time management, transactions, and support for workflow administration and management.

Ongoing research, therefore, concentrates on providing additional features to facilitate the application of the workflow management system in organizations. We plan to complement workflow management with resource management. By resources in this project we mean business resources like budgets, machines, work-time, etc. The goal is to manage, monitor and control the assignment of resources to processes to better support business transactions and the management of workflows. Furthermore, we intend to design a more sophisticated workflow client. It should support the user in planning his/her work and making decisions about priorities. Such a system serves as a personal productivity tool which assists the empowerment of employees and con-

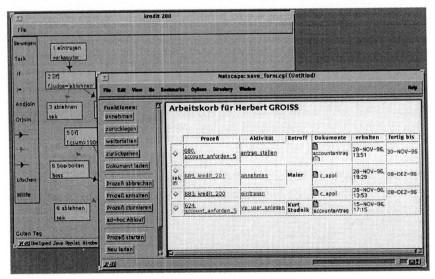

Fig. 5. Worklist and process designer of Panta Rhei

trasts the fear that workflow systems install virtual conveyor belts through offices.

To summarize, the basic concepts for a workflow management system developed in our Panta Rhei project proved to be very useful. They led to the design of a rather clear and lean architecture and implementation. The Panta Rhei prototype system was implemented with the effort of about two person-years. It is operational and runs fairly stable. Currently it is evaluated by third parties for potential use in industrial applications.

The WASA Approach to Workflow Management for Scientific Applications

Gottfried Vossen, Mathias Weske

Lehrstuhl für Informatik, University of Münster
Grevener Strasse 91, D-48159 Münster, Germany
{vossen,weske}@helios.uni-muenster.de

Abstract. Workflow management has gained increasing attention recently, since it allows one to combine a data-oriented view on applications, which is the traditional one for an information system, with a process-oriented one in which activities and their occurrences over time are modeled and supported properly. While workflow management has mostly been considered in business applications so far, the focus of the WASA project is on *scientific* applications such as geoprocessing, molecular biology, or laboratory environments. In particular, WASA aims at flexible and platform-independent workflow support, with respect to both specification and execution of workflows. It turns out that the modeling and execution of workflows in traditional and in scientific applications exhibit significant differences. In particular, the need for dynamic modifications of workflow models while workflows are running is an important feature in scientific applications. Observations like these have resulted in a generic WASA architecture, which can be tailored towards various specific application domains. The conceptual design and functionality of a WASA prototype is outlined, in particular that of its core workflow engine, and it is shown how the requirements of flexibility in modeling and executing workflows, imposed by scientific applications, are met by this prototype.

1. Introduction

Workflow management aims at modeling and controlling the execution of processes in both business applications [GHS 95, LA 94] and scientific applications [I 93, RD 94, WVM 96, RVW 97]. It has gained increasing attention recently, since it allows to combine a data-oriented view on applications, which is the traditional one for an information system, with a process-oriented one in which (human or machine) activities and their occurrences over time are modeled and supported properly [VB 96]. While a number of workflow management systems for business applications are commercially available already, systems for scientific applications are still in their infancy. A major goal of the WASA[1] project is to remedy this situation. Specifically, WASA tries to take the particular requirements of these applications, such as high modeling and specification flexibility as well as platform independence [MV+ 96, MVW 96], into account. In this paper we survey the WASA project. In particular, we characterize the specific properties of scientific workflows as opposed to business workflows. We develop a generic WASA architecture and describe the conceptual design and functionality of a prototypical implementation.

---

[1] Workflow-based Architecture to support Scientific Applications

In business applications, workflow management is of increasing strategic importance. Indeed, the identification of *business objects* and the process of *re-engineering* business procedures is considered highly relevant to the future development of commercial enterprises. On the other hand, the transition from data modeling to process modeling appears relevant in a variety of non-business applications as well. Indeed, there is an increasing number of experimental sciences that rely on computers and software, and that needs guidance through the appropriate exploitation of this technology; as it turns out, workflow management can provide such guidance. The applications we refer to include experimental physics, molecular biology, and geoprocessing; more generally, we are interested in applications in which experiments are done in a laboratory environment and hence the experiments themselves as well as the information they consume or produce need to be managed properly. Surprisingly, there are not yet too many system developments which try to take care of these domains. The systems we have identified generally fall into the following categories:

1. Environments that are tailored towards a specific application domain: OASIS [M+ 96], ZOO [ILGP 96, AIL 96]. Application specific environments built on top of database systems are Moby Dick [RD 94] or XBio [KSK 93].
2. Workflow management systems primarily for traditional (business-type) applications which could be used in scientific environments, although the latter were not foreseen as targets initially: Mentor [Wod 96a], Meteor$_2$ [SK+ 96], Mobile [J 94, BJS 96], and Panta Rhei [EGN 94]; clearly, commercial systems such as IBM's FlowMark [LA 94, IBM 96] also fall into this category.
3. "Workflow-aware" systems for scientific applications: LabBase [SRG 94], CRISTAL [Clat], MapBase [G 94].

OASIS is an environment for data analysis, knowledge discovery, visualization, and collaboration, and is directed towards geo-applications. Its implementation is based on a CORBA-compliant distributed object management system. The geo-sciences are also a target of the WASA project; however, the WASA project focuses on support for pre-defined processes (which may change over time), while the OASIS project lays an emphasis on a loose cooperation of agents to achieve a common goal. ZOO is essentially a software package that allows scientists to manage experiments and data related to an experiment from a desktop machine through a uniform interface. However, ZOO emphasizes data modeling and experiment modeling at a high language level and at an individual basis, and ignores workflow aspects; we try to prove that a process orientation right from the beginning is a more appropriate way to go.

Besides OASIS, several other system developments also exploit CORBA technology and hence distributed object management facilities. This particularly applies to experimental workflow management systems such as Meteor$_2$

and Mentor appearing in the second category. In Meteor$_2$, workflow programs are generated from workflow specifications, and CORBA is used for executing workflows in distributed environments. Mentor incorporates a CORBA-compliant broker to integrate external applications into a workflow execution environment. Here the major development goals include good scalability, high availability, heterogeneity, and distributed workflow executions which even allow for formal verification [Wod 96a]. In our project these aspects, although important, are currently not an issue, since our emphasis is different. The idea of using a Web browser as end-user interface pops up in the next two systems mentioned in Category 2, Mobile and Panta Rhei. Mobile takes the Web as a service for building user interfaces and for integrating or implementing external applications, while Panta Rhei primarily uses the Web for exchanging forms between an end-user, i.e., a person involved in a workflow execution, and the workflow engine. The difference to WASA is that our system is implemented entirely in Java and hence not only usable through any ordinary Web browser, but also vastly machine-independent and open to all kinds of enhancements brought along by the Java world. Finally, commercial workflow tools such as FlowMark are, as has been argued in [BW 96], an obstacle to dynamic workflow modifications, as they are typically based on a built-time/run-time-approach; as a consequence, specifications must be complete before they can be executed, and changes always require a halt followed by a system restart.

The developments that we consider closest to our project are those in the third category. Indeed, LabBase and CRISTAL also try to bring workflow concepts into scientific applications. LabBase is a system for managing workflows in large semi-automated laboratory projects which sits on top of the MapBase database system. Its workflow manager essentially controls the execution of laboratory protocols in which experiments to be conducted are described. Protocols may change frequently, since the sequencing or composition of their experiments are altered. The workflow manager is able to take care of this by taking appropriate input from the respective application at its interface; basically, it is programmed from outside for each experiment that is executed. As will be demonstrated, WASA takes a significantly different route; it does not have an API for workflow control, but a dedicated workflow engine that responds to database updates representing dynamic changes in workflow models. Finally, the CRISTAL system (Concurrent Repository and Information System for the Tracking of Assembly Lifecycles) emerged from the Compact Muon Solenoid (CMS) experiment in particle physics [Clat]. The preparation and instrumentation of that experiment evolves dynamically, mostly as the result of preliminary tests that are made, and needs to integrate resources from remotely located research centers. Here the approach is to employ product data management tools, which are able to organize and control product data as well as product life-cycles, and to extend these by workflow management capabilities for being able to keep track of production system activities. Again, this is different from the WASA approach, since workflow management comes in as an aid to product data management, while we consider databases or files subordinate to workflow engines and emphasize activity descriptions and control.

The paper is organized as follows: In Section 2. we discuss the commonalities and differences of workflow modeling in traditional applications and in scientific applications, and we present a case study of a scientific workflow from the area of molecular biology. Section 3. describes a key property of scientific workflows, namely dynamic change of workflow models while workflows run. The WASA architecture is presented in Section 4.; in Section 5. we discuss the conceptual design and the functionality of a prototypical implementation of the WASA workflow engine. Concluding remarks in Section 6. complete the paper.

2. Workflow Modeling

In this section we discuss specific properties of the workflow modeling process and of the resulting workflow models in business applications and scientific applications. In particular, we discuss properties of scientific workflows, and provide a set of features which are present in scientific workflows but which are not present in business workflows. To support our statements, examples from the areas of molecular biology and laboratory information systems are provided. These observations will serve as a motivation for two basic dynamic change operations that are useful for the application areas in question. These operations are discussed in Section 3.

2.1 Workflow Modeling in Business Applications

So far, the major application area of workflow management has been the business field [GHS 95, LA 94, VB 96]. In particular, modeling and re-engineering of business processes has become a strategic goal in many enterprises, with the final goal of enhancing flexibility and efficiency of business processes and thereby improving customer satisfaction as well as enterprise performance.

Workflow applications are developed in complex processes, roughly characterized as follows. After initial information gathering on the relevant business procedures, the modeling and specification of business processes is performed. When this phase is completed, the resulting process model is transferred into a workflow model, which is a computerized representation of activities and their execution relationships used by a workflow management system for the controlled execution of workflows [GHS 95, SI 95]. Various tools are now commercially available which support the development of workflow applications. Business process modeling and re-engineering tools focus on the early phases, while workflow management systems support the later phases of the workflow development process.

Specific properties of application processes have implications for the required functionality of a workflow management system. In general, business processes to be modeled and analyzed are usually well understood. The major aim of modeling is to find bottlenecks with the goal of increasing efficiency and reducing cost of doing business. This means once the business modeling phase is completed, a workflow model is created to implement the process. It is important to notice that the structure of the workflow model is fixed and does not change over time. Workflow models with this property are called *static*. Static workflow models might be changed during future re-engineering processes, which then also involve earlier phases, namely business process modeling. In this context, changes to the structure of workflows are not permitted during workflow executions; they usually require a re-compilation with subsequent re-execution.

Since static workflow models are well-suited to describe most business processes, current workflow management systems provide appropriate support for controlling workflows described by static workflow models. These are brought onto the workflow management system, which is used to control the executions of many (often hundreds of) workflow instances of a given static workflow model.

We next focus on scientific applications and show that their requirements render workflow management systems unable to realize dynamic changes inappropriate for the controlled execution of scientific workflows.

2.2 Workflow Modeling in Scientific Applications

As mentioned before, new applications for workflow management are emerging, among which scientific ones seem to play a major role [WVM 96, BW 96, Clat]. Workflows in these domains differ significantly from business workflows. This is mainly due to the fact that concepts in scientific applications are not as stable, and processes often are not completely known in advance. The lack of complete knowledge about the processes in scientific applications has implications for the modeling of scientific workflows. The main issue is that workflow models are inherently incomplete, or they may even change over time, either in predictable or unpredictable ways. We discuss several examples where these properties show up before presenting a case study of a scientific workflow from the domain of molecular biology.

– *Order Processing in Laboratory Environments:* Consider a chemical analysis enterprise, which processes orders for sample analysis. Assume an order represents the chemical analyses of a number of samples, ranging from soil to crops and animal feed. The high volume (10^6 samples per year) makes workflow management useful to enhance throughput. The samples are processed independently within an order workflow. For each sample there is a default structure of the steps to be carried out, i.e., of the workflow to be executed for processing the sample. This default structure can change. A common form of change occurs when the customer wants additional analyses performed on a given sample, or wants some analyses redone to validate the results.

These changes cannot be foreseen completely, they are vastly *ad-hoc*. Hence, changing the workflow dynamically is needed to (i) be able to use the controlled execution of workflows to enhance efficiency of throughput while (ii) supporting dynamically changing procedures. The situation characterized can be coped with by a feature called *dynamic modification*, which means the ability of a workflow management system to change workflow models while workflows of this model are running.

– *Experiment Design:* A common property of scientific experiments is incomplete specification. In particular, the activities of some initial part of an experiment are typically known before the experiment starts. However, the researcher decides on the continuation of the scientific experiment only after execution (or even a preliminary evaluation of the results) of the first part of the experiment, i.e., after the completion of the partial workflow. In this case, the point in time when the decision is taken may be available before the workflow starts. Thus, a dynamic change of the workflow model is now known *a priori*.

2.3 Case Study: Scientific Workflows in Molecular Biology

We now provide a specific example of an application in which WASA is relevant and its use appropriate – the area of *DNA Sequencing*. We give a brief introduction to the field and describe how to perceive DNA sequencing as a workflow problem. For further details on the material presented in this section, the reader is referred to [MVW 96]; a complete report on our findings regarding the use of a commercial product is [BW 96].

The issues dealt with in DNA Sequencing can roughly be summarized as follows. Recall that all genetic information of organisms is stored in nucleotide sequences. One form is desoxyribonucleid acid (DNA), which consists of two parallel strands, each of which is a sequence of bases, identified by A, C, T, and G. Finding and interpreting the base sequence of an organism is an important and fundamental task in molecular biology [F 91]. Today, short sequences of DNA (≤ 500 base pairs) can be generated semi-automatically, using specific devices; these sequences are known as *fragments*. Among the complicating factors of DNA Sequencing are *errors* (device inaccuracies and spontaneous mutations), *contamination*, *lack of coverage*, or *repeats* (long, repeated strings in the target DNA sequence). Because of these inaccuracies, the base sequence returned by a sequencing device may not be entirely correct; it is therefore considered as *raw data*. One task of scientists is to correct the errors in such a sequence, and to produce data sets of higher quality.

This is done using predefined validation procedures as well as the scientist's expert knowledge.

Since direct sequencing is possible only for relatively small DNA fragments, a divide-and-conquer strategy has to be used in order to determine the base sequences of larger stretches of DNA (e.g., 10Kbase pairs). It is such strategies that are known as *fragment assembly*; they basically consist of the following steps:

1. Generate multiple copies of DNA (cloning),
2. cut clones into pieces (fragments),
3. sequence fragments directly,
4. assemble fragments.

After sequencing and validating a number of fragments, the assembly process starts (note that, due to resource limitations, typically not all fragments can be sequenced). Sequences that consist of a number of assembled fragments are known as *contigs*. Having produced a number of contigs, and trying to find a place for the next fragment, there may be zero, one, or more places to put it; the latter may happen due to repeated sequences in the genome. To solve ambiguities of this kind, or to fill remaining gaps, new fragments have to be sequenced. The information on the next steps to take becomes available only while the experiment is being conducted.

We now look at the DNA sequencing process and its subprocess "fragment assembly" and specify them using workflow terminology. The underlying idea of our approach is the following. Fragment assembly tools are typically programs composed of many modules that have to perform the various steps mentioned in the previous subsection. However, since there is not a unique accepted strategy for doing fragment assembly, people perform several experiments, and do so, among other things, by configuring distinct program modules into new assembly programs. It is here that workflows come into play: we consider that each such configuration activity corresponds to specifying a workflow. In other words, composing a fragment assembly tool from given modules is treated as a workflow specification. Consequently, the workflow management system used executes the resulting program system, hence driving the various modules it comprises. Moreover, it can feed input and receive output data to and from the various assembly steps, and may even be capable of triggering external devices.

To specify workflow models, we use a simple graphical notation based on directed graphs, whose nodes represent tasks, and whose edges represent relationships between tasks, e.g., control flow. Tasks can be nested in an arbitrary fashion, by unfolding nodes into subgraphs. The overall structure of the DNA Sequencing workflow, i.e., the top-level workflow, is shown in Figure 1; each task shown will undergo one level of refinement.

The *initial generation* task specifies the scientific experiments that aim at extracting sequence information from a given chemical molecule. This usually

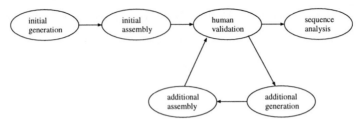

Fig. 1. DNA Sequencing seen as a Workflow.

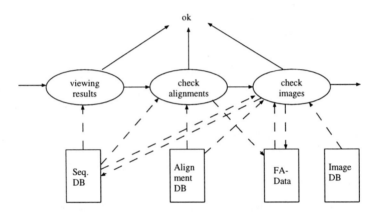

Fig. 2. The Step of Human Validation.

consists of a number of steps that result in the production of a film from which the base sequence of the molecules under consideration are read and entered into a sequence database. *Initial assembly* uses the set of fragments generated by the first step and tries to assemble them to generate the desired sequence. The result of this activity is validated by a human. If satisfied, *sequence analysis* can be launched, which runs the sequence found against one or more community databases, and performs various analysis tasks, like examining the sequence for the presence of genes.

Each of these global activities is refined in [MVW 96]. We here restrict our discussion to the *human validation* activity, as shown in Figure 2. This activity is especially important whenever two or more consensus sequences are generated during initial assembly, since the goal of the assembly is to return a single sequence, not a number of partial sequences of the sequence under consideration. Human validation starts with viewing the results of the assembly process.

If the assembly produced a single consensus sequence that has a high percentage of correct overlaps, then the human can decide whether the assembly process was successful and thus that the next task of the top-level workflow can start. In Figure 2 this is indicated by an edge to "OK". If, however, the human is not satisfied, certain alignments (matching of fragment patterns) have to be checked. In order to do so, the human accesses sequences stored in the sequence database as well as the set of alignments that were used to perform the alignment. Looking at the alignments may render the objections obsolete, again leading to "OK". However, the scientist may suspect an error in the task that led to the incorrect alignment. In this case, the *check images* task is performed. In this task, the human accesses the film images stored in the image database and fragment assembly data (FA-Data) to validate the reading process or to detect reading errors. To decide for the latter, accessing the sequence database and the alignment database is necessary, in which case the loop of the top-level workflow is iterated and additional fragments are generated and added to the consensus sequences found so far. The loop is exited when a human validates the results, in which case the consensus sequence found is analyzed. As already mentioned, further refinements of the workflow model shown in Figure 1 can be found in [MVW 96].

3. Dynamic Change Operations

We next identify two forms of dynamic change operations to cope with the issues stated above. In Section 5. we will explain how our prototype is designed to support the dynamic change operations required, and how these can be executed by the user. (A more detailed discussion of flexibility issues in workflow systems appears in [W 97].)

3.1 Anticipated Dynamic Change

The first form of dynamic change deals with *anticipated, predicted* dynamic changes. Operations of this form appear whenever the modeler of a workflow knows the exact position at which a modification of the workflow model might appear (and will be appropriate). In this case the workflow model explicitly includes modeling activities which are executed within the workflow. Anticipated dynamic changes are necessary when there is no complete knowledge of the workflow before the workflow starts, i.e., if the workflow model is incomplete. To cope with this situation, the modeler explicitly specifies a modeling activity as one activity of the (incomplete) workflow model (typically the one that completes the specified part of the workflow). During the execution of the workflow, the modeling activity is started. When the modeling activity starts, the system offers a number of sub-workflows to implement the activity, which were defined beforehand. The modeler may choose one of the pre-defined sub-workflows to implement the activity by accessing the workflow library. However, if none of the pre-defined workflow models seems suitable to continue the workflow properly, he or she may decide to specify a new workflow to implement the activity. In this case, workflow modeling

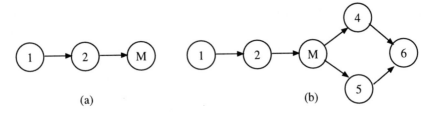

Fig. 3. Anticipated Dynamic Change, Implemented by Modeling Activity M.

is done *while the workflow executes*. Finally, the chosen workflow is started, and the workflow execution resumes.

Anticipated change of workflow models is a common property of scientific workflows [WVM 96], where scientists decide on future experiments only after initial experiments have been performed and – at least partially – evaluated. The modeling activity of the scientific workflow corresponds to choosing an experiment to execute next, or to designing a new experiment. A simple and abstract workflow model including a modeling activity is depicted in Figure 3(a). The incomplete workflow consists of activities 1, 2 and a modeling activity M. During the modeling activity the agent performing it decides to continue the incomplete workflow with the concurrent execution of activities 4 and 5, followed by an activity 6; the workflow model that results from the dynamic modification is given in Figure 3(b). The final activity of an incomplete scientific experiment is a modeling activity which involves choosing activities to continue the scientific workflow.

Note that in a situation like the one just described, workflow parts will typically be known in advance, as will be rules that guide the process of combining them into larger workflows.

3.2 Ad-hoc Dynamic Change

The second form of dynamic change deals with *ad-hoc*, i.e., not anticipated dynamic changes. It is characterized by the need to change the future behavior of a running workflow at an unpredicted point in time during the execution of the respective workflow.

This situation has commonalities with exception handling in traditional programming. However, in programming the programmer defines a set of situations for which an exception is raised, and a set of procedures to be executed when the exception is raised. In contrast, ad-hoc changes of workflow models do not need to be specified *a priori*. In many applications, specifying all possible reasons for an ad-hoc change is a cumbersome if not impossible task. Moreover, modelers do not want to model situations that may or may not happen in the future. Hence, support for these kind of exceptions by ad-hoc changes is important for a flexible workflow system.

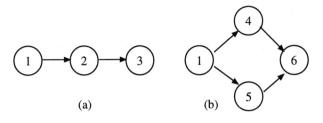

Fig. 4. Ad-hoc Modification.

In ad-hoc change, a modeling activity can be started at any time during the execution of a workflow. An example from the area of scientific workflows is a complex experiment that involves numerous persons and resources, for instance specialized devices. When, during the execution of a scientific experiment, some devices or chemical agents are not available and the experiment cannot be delayed until the devices are operational again, there has to be an ad-hoc change of the model of the scientific workflow. For instance, additional clean-up activities have to be started to shut down the experiment properly. We mention that ad-hoc changes are not limited to scientific experiments. In certain business applications, ad-hoc changes are also required [ER 95], with the aim of saving modeling effort and providing high flexibility for the application by allowing for unpredicted, ad-hoc changes.

A sample workflow model with an ad-hoc change is given in Figure 4. Assume a workflow has been started based on the workflow model given in Figure 4(a). After executing activity 1 an ad-hoc change occurs. The person responsible for the workflow decides not to continue the workflow as specified (continue the workflow with activities 2 and 3) but to execute activities 4 and 5 concurrently before completing the workflow with activity 6. The resulting workflow model is given in Figure 4(b). Notice that the workflow model does not contain any explicit modeling activities as in the previous example.

The situation just described occurs, for example, in order processing applications in laboratory environments, as discussed above. The ad-hoc change is usually initiated by a customer who decides to add some analysis procedures to an order. This change may occur at any point in time while the workflow runs, i.e., while the samples of the order are analyzed. Returning to the example of Figure 4, instead of performing, analysis 2 and 3 on a given sample, the customer decides that he wants analyses 4 and 5 performed concurrently before analysis 6 is done. (Performing analyses concurrently is attractive since analyses may take days or even weeks.) In this scenario, the dynamic change should only apply to the workflow instance under consideration; other workflows should not be affected by that dynamic change.

3.3 Related Work on Dynamic Change

In terms of flexibility in modeling and executing workflows, our approach relates to several approaches that have been reported in the literature. This does not come unexpected, as workflow management combines influences from a variety of disciplines, including cooperative information systems, computer-supported cooperative work, groupware systems, and active databases [VB 96]. Ellis et al. [ER 95] show that the need for dynamic change is present in office workflows, in order to circumvent or augment standard procedures. As stressed by Craven and Mahling [CM 95], work environments nowadays are becoming increasingly dynamic, which requires new types of support for cooperative work. This motivates that, while these properties are important for workflow management in scientific applications [I 93, WVM 96], modern requirements in business computing also benefit from them. In particular, specifying error conditions may not be feasible in business applications, and dynamic change of workflow models is an important functionality of a workflow management system to cope with exceptions [ER 95]. Reichert and Dadam present ADEPT$_{flex}$, an approach for controlled dynamic modifications of workflow specifications based on non-nested, symmetric workflow specifications [R 97].

We conclude this section by mentioning that dynamic modifications raise a number of questions, ranging from modeling issues to system requirements for an implementation of this concept. One question addresses the workflow instances which should be effected by a dynamic change. Changes of workflow models may apply to a single workflow instance, to multiple workflow instances, or to all workflow instances of a given workflow model. An example of the latter is the adjustment of a workflow model to the change in the environment of the process, e.g., the installation of a new laboratory procedure which is obligatory for all scientists of a given laboratory. In this case it is very important that all future workflow instances reflect the changes. Furthermore, the active workflow instance of this model which are not yet executing the changed part of the workflow should also be affected.

4. The WASA Architecture

In this section we describe the WASA architecture, whose overall goal is to provide an integrated, workflow-based environment for scientific work.

4.1 The WASA Layers

In the WASA architecture, the following four layers can be distinguished (see Figure 5):

1. User Interface Layer
2. Internal Tools Layer
3. Enhanced Database Functionality Layer
4. Database Layer

The users for which this environment has been designed are expected to be scientists which are experts on some domain, and to have experience in designing new experiments and controlling the execution of existing ones. Also, users will be supposed to have a basic familiarity with the workflow paradigm, so that they are able to express their needs and plans in a corresponding formalism. A general assumption underlying the WASA architecture is that all data manipulations are done via the WASA interface.

The *User Interface Layer* is responsible for communication between users and the rest of the system. It consists of four main functional blocks which communicate with each other (and with the internal tools, see below). The *Specification and Design* facility provides users with tools to specify and design experiments by means of workflows; in addition, it is intended to provide access to previously designed workflows for re-use, to support shared workflow design, and to allow the configuration of partially specified workflows into a new one. The *Data Manipulation* facility provides users with means for accessing and updating data concerning applications and experiments. This includes navigation through reported experiments and their results as well as the invocation of analysis procedures (e.g., through method execution calls). This module would typically encapsulate facilities such as those provided by a database query language processor.

The *Browsing and Visualization* module allows users to browse and visualize different kinds of application data as well as management data. It allows access to application specific data as well as to general data. Clearly, visualization is highly domain-specific. For example, in molecular biology, visualization of DNA sequences and of protein structures may be relevant; in medical experiments, physicians may need to visualize 3D renderings of objects; in geography, maps of different resolution and levels may need to be displayed. Finally, the *Runtime Monitor* allows users to execute previously defined workflows, and to monitor and control their executions.

The *Internal Tools Layer* consists of the workflow management system and of a set of auxiliary managers to support experiment specification, documentation, and execution. The *Workflow Engine* is the core component of the WASA system. It provides the core functionality for scientific workflow management. The *Documentation* manager provides the means to document the conduction of an experiment as well as its specification. It also allows recording of relevant events that occurred during the specification or execution of the experiment. The *Analysis* manager is responsible for managing the interface to application-specific analysis procedures, and for controlling their execution as requested by users. We imagine this to be a loose coupling only, in the sense that this manager will generally know where to find

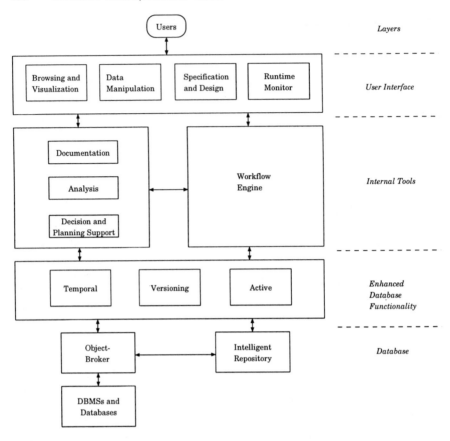

Fig. 5. The Architecture of WASA.

relevant procedures and analysis tools, to export input data to such tools, and to import their results and findings into the WASA system. The *Decision and Planning Support* manager helps to guide users in designing and conducting experiments. Decision support on how to continue a given experiment would also be a task of this component, i.e., which step to take next in a given experiment. Thus, it contains knowledge that is domain specific, as well as knowledge about workflow construction. This is extremely relevant to situations in which an experiment starts by executing a partially specified workflow, but where its continuation and successful completion will depend on intermediate results and decisions based on these results.

Scientific experiments generally need the capability to manage a variety of data using different types of facilities. Although the WASA architecture is based on multiple database systems which can be incorporated as data sources, we cannot assume that all these database systems will provide advanced functionality; indeed, it is common nowadays to build scientific applications on legacy systems such as relational databases, or data files. As a consequence, the enhanced database management layer of WASA consists of a set of mechanisms that provide the relevant advanced functionality in a system-independent way. We consider three types of functionality of particular importance here: (i) Being able to handle *temporal* aspects, (ii) being capable of distinguishing versions (of both data and workflow models), and (iii) being able to support *active* features for controlling the execution of a given task or workflow. In order to make this layer portable and independent of pre-existing databases in particular application domains, WASA is intended to provide access to individual databases through a standardized interface. To this end, it is reasonable to assume that underneath WASA there is typically a federation of multiple databases with a common interface such as an object request broker [OMG 91, OHE 96] on top. This broker is responsible for retrieving the appropriate data and control descriptions from stored data sets, and is expected to support a variety of data models and query languages.

As described above, the underlying databases which store and provide relevant data are not part of the WASA architecture; instead, they will be handled through the object broker interface. However, the system creates numerous internal data and information, which is relevant, for example, to the various workflows it handles. So it is clear that the database layer of WASA has to contain two categories of data and, hence, two types of databases: (i) data used by applications, which is supposed to be stored in a number of databases whose details are hidden from the system through the broker, and (ii) an intelligent data repository, i.e., a WASA-specific database, which is used to store data needed to run the upper levels of the architecture (e.g., constraints on workflow construction, documentation) as well as special structures which are used by the database layer to perform its functions.

5. The WASA Prototype

In this section we discuss the conceptual design of a WASA prototype, its system architecture and functionality. We first focus on modeling capabilities and on dynamic modification operations, as discussed earlier. The system functionality also includes support for further aspects, such as the organizational aspect used for role resolution. The prototype allows to execute workflows based on workflow models, including management of work-item lists of workflow clients and automatic start of applications to perform activities within workflows. We discuss the architecture of the system and the functionality of its components below.

5.1 General Considerations

The traditional approach to workflow management is based on the "built-time/run-time"-paradigm: During the built-time workflow models are specified completely. Complete workflow models are used at run-time to control the execution of workflows. Since dynamic modification requires more flexibility than this approach has to offer, we believe that an interpretational approach is more feasible. In this approach, the system interprets workflow models successively, whereas in the compilation approach the whole specification of the workflow is transferred into an executable format, and only then workflow executions are started. The step-by-step interpretation allows more conveniently to react to unpredicted changes in the application. The prototype is based on the interpretation approach and hence satisfies this criterion.

Modeling as well as dynamic modification are supported by representing workflow models in a relational database. In particular, the constituents are described in corresponding relations and tuples. Thus, *creating* a workflow model amounts to an *insertion* of tuples, while *modifying* is done by appropriate database *updates*. Moreover, combining pieces of workflow models into larger workflow models boils down to performing *retrievals*, subject to selections which test relevant assembly conditions.

Anticipated dynamic changes (cf. Section 3.) are done within a single workflow instance and, hence, should have effects only on this workflow. Consider again the workflow model shown in Figure 3; the modeling activity M is performed as follows: First, a number of pre-defined workflow models are displayed (subject to data flow requirements), from which the modeler can choose one to continue the incomplete workflow. The activity then sends SQL statements to the specification database to attach the chosen sub-workflow to the incomplete workflow. If an adequate workflow model is not available in the workflow library, the modeler can define a new workflow model by using the workflow specification tool. After defining the new sub-workflow, the system registers it as the continuation of the incomplete workflow, whose execution is resumed with the newly specified workflow model.

We now sketch the functionality a workflow system has to provide to support ad-hoc changes. Traditionally, for each workflow execution, there is one workflow model that is used by the system for controlling it. However, when changes to the workflow model are applied, the workflow model changes. Since there may be other workflow executions based on this workflow model, simply changing it is not feasible. In this case, all workflow executions based on the workflow model given would be changed, something that we assume is not intended by the ad-hoc change. Therefore, a new workflow model (or a new version of the workflow model) has to be created, and the changed workflow execution is now controlled by the new workflow model. This implies that the system has to be able to use different workflow models at different times during the execution of a workflow.

The prototype allows a restricted form of dynamic change. In particular, the refinement of the sub-workflows of a given workflow may be changed. However, the change has to occur before the the start of the sub-workflow. Once the sub-workflow is started, the system does not allow changes. Future versions of the prototype will provide more flexibility for ad-hoc workflows.

5.2 System Architecture

The following design decisions have been taken, in order to achieve our main goals of flexibility and platform independence:

- *Relational representation of workflow models:* In the application domains we consider, workflows are composed of steps or collections of steps whose exact sequencing is not necessarily known in advance. We store descriptions of such steps or sub-workflows in a relational database that has relation schemas for workflow types, their constituents, I/O, data and control connectors, variables, roles, agents, etc. (see [W 96] for details).
- *Interpretation approach to workflow execution:* Workflow specifications are interpreted for the purpose of execution, simply by retrieving the relevant information from the workflow database. Thus, no compilation of a complete specification is done. The implication is that models can easily be changed, even while a workflow is being executed.
- *Exploitation of Java:* The workflow system has a client/server architecture, where both the workflow server and the clients are written in Java. Java byte code can be interpreted on a large variety of platforms (including the Sun Solaris and Windows95 platforms used by us).
- *Database access via JDBC:* Workflow models are currently stored in an Oracle database, and the workflow server accesses these models using a JDBC interface (Java DataBase Connectivity). Using this middleware component, different underlying relational database products can be used without changing the code.
- *Web browser as Workflow Client:* HTTP (Hyper Text Transfer Protocol) is today an industry standard for communication between Internet-connected computers. Web browsers (like Netscape Navigator or HotJava) can be used as front-ends to the HTTP protocol; these are available for a large number of platforms. We use standard Web browsers interpreting Java applets or stand-alone Java applications as workflow clients.

The design decisions and features discussed above have led to the system architecture shown in Figure 6. Essentially, this is a client/server architecture, where the server reads workflow models from the database, controls the execution of workflows, and performs other important services like role resolution. Internally, it is composed of the core component, the workflow engine, and the database server which accesses application data stored in the underlying database. Both components are connected to the database by a JDBC interface, and the database contains workflow-related data (like workflow models and role descriptions) as well as application specific data.

The workflow engine is the core part of the prototype (called "Kernel" in Figure 6). When the system is started, the workflow engine reads workflow models from the workflow library. Since workflow models without any incoming control connectors can be started in an ad-hoc fashion, workflow models with this property are displayed. At any point in time, the system may control multiple instances of a given workflow model. Hence, the system supports concurrent executions of multiple workflows. The key functionality of the workflow engine is to control the execution of executing workflows using information on the structure of the workflow and on the agents ready to perform activities. In general, for each activity a role is defined, and when the activity is about to be started, the workflow engine determines the agents ready to perform it. This functionality is called role resolution.

We have also developed a specification tool which allows the graphical specification of workflow models. Workflow models may be built from scratch, or existing workflow models may be re-used, e.g., as sub-workflows in complex workflows. On start-up, the specification tool connects to the database via JDBC and retrieves workflow models from the database if requested by the user. The specification tool can be invoked as a stand-alone application or it can be invoked by a workflow application. The latter corresponds to an implementation of an anticipated dynamic change activity using the WASA prototype. When the modeling activity is completed and the modified workflow model is saved, the workflow model is effectively entered into the database. Since workflow models are successively retrieved from the database while workflows execute, the current workflow instance and all future instances of that model will be effected by the dynamic modification.

Users access the workflow system using workflow clients. The basic functionality of a workflow client is to inform users (agents in general) of activities to perform. We have implemented two types of workflow clients:

- *Java Applications:* For this type, a Java interpreter has to be present on the client side. Since there are no restrictions on the accesses of Java applications, implementations of workflow clients may access local data and may start external applications.
- *Java Applets, interpreted by standard Web browsers:* For this type, the presence of a standard Web browser suffices on the client side. The Java applet is down-loaded to the client Web browser and interpreted by it. Like the other type of client, it communicates with the workflow server using the TCP/IP protocol. However, security restrictions apply to Java applets, e.g., access to local data and starting external applications may not be performed by workflow clients implemented by Java applets.

Further details on the server, the two types of clients, and also on workflow applications can be found in [VWW 97].

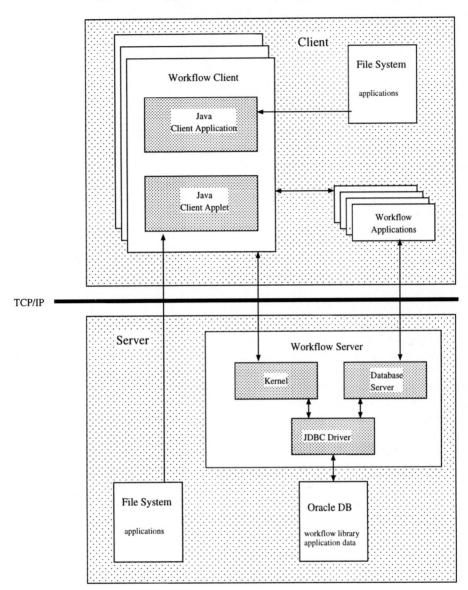

Fig. 6. System Architecture.

6. Conclusions and Future Work

In this paper we have surveyed the WASA project at the University of Muenster, its goals, design decisions, and current status. The key feature is that the WASA workflow manager is capable of supporting different dynamic change operations which are useful for a wide range of non-traditional applications of workflow management systems. Indeed, WASA has been designed with scientific applications in mind, and is supposed to take care of their specific workflow requirements. Our current prototype is a first step in realizing our goals, and it obviously gives rise to a number of future enhancements.

Since workflow specifications, even after dynamic changes, can often be considered as being different versions of the same underlying model, we plan to investigate the applicability of the database version approach of [CJ 90] and its extension into a tool for configuration management described in [CVJ 94]. In the database version approach, versioning in a (relational) database is achieved by distinguishing versions of *entire* database instances, not just individual relations or tuples in it. Thus, whenever a new version of some object in a given database is created, a new version of that database as a whole comes into being. However, the management of these versions is based on a simple and clever naming scheme so that the overhead can be neglected, and that issues like database consistency are easy to enforce. We expect that, since we use a relational database for storing workflow models, a combination of the database versioning scheme with the configuration management approach of [CVJ 94] will be fruitful.

For bringing the prototype to real-world applications, we are implementing a variety of workflows from the geoprocessing domain as well as from the area of laboratory information and management systems. We also plan to extend our case studies to particle physics and medical applications. These will provide a field study of the applicability of the prototype. Underneath the workflow engine, we are exploring CORBA functionality for both support of the workflow engine and uniform access to external storage systems, including database managers and file systems.

Acknowledgements

We are grateful to our students G. Wittkowski and B. Focke for having carried out the implementation work that was described above, and to our Brazilian partners C.B. Medeiros and J. Meidanis for helping us in designing WASA and introducing us to specific application domains.

Security Enforcement in Activity Management Systems*

Kamalakar Karlapalem, Patrick C. K. Hung

Department of Computer Science, Hong Kong University of Science and Technology, Clear Water Bay, Kowloon, Hong Kong, China

Abstract. Security enforcement is an issue of paramount importance for any system that facilitates computer supported cooperative work. An activity management system is a software that facilitates specification and decomposition, and execution of activities. An activity is a set of coordinated tasks (atomic activities). The focus of this paper is on supporting security in activity management systems. In particular, we present an architecture, and describe the mechanisms that need to be incorporated for enforcing security for activity specification and decomposition, and during activity execution. This paper provides a task-centered approach towards security enforcement, wherein, the security constraints are checked and the task is allowed to be executed only if none of the security constraints are violated. This is handled by the event-condition-action rule paradigm from active database systems.

1. Introduction

An activity consists of multiple inter-dependent tasks that need to be coordinated, scheduled and executed by a set of problem solving agents (PSAs). A problem solving agent (PSA) is either a computer system (hardware or software) or a human capable of performing some tasks. A task is an atomic activity performed by exactly one PSA. Activity management consists of decomposition of activities into tasks, coordination and data sharing among multiple PSAs executing the activity, and monitoring, scheduling and controlling the execution of multiple tasks of an activity. A software system that facilitates the specification, maintenance, and execution of activities is known as an Activity Management System (AMS).

Example of an Activity: *The graduate admission office processes the applications of the potential graduate students twice a year by using a set of university and departmental guidelines. The graduate admissions committee headed by the Graduate Coordinator, supported by the Graduate Secretary and consisting of a few faculty members, review the applications. The graduate admission activity proceeds as follows. Each time a batch of new student application forms come, the clerk will check the completeness of the student's applications. If a student's application is incomplete, a message requesting additional documents by a due date is sent to the candidate. If there is no receipt of additional documents from the student by the due date, the student*

---

* This work is partly supported Hong Kong Special Admistrative Region Research Grants Council's Earmarked Research Grant HKUST 747/96E

application record is deleted. If the application is complete, the graduate co-ordinator initiates a task to review the application by a decision due date, during which time the status of student's application is "pending". The result of the review process can be i) accept the student, and a letter of acceptance is sent to the student, ii) reject the student, and a reject letter is sent to the student, and iii) interview the student, and an interview call letter is sent to the student. The result of the interview process is either to accept or reject the student. If the review of the student's application is not completed by decision due date, a reminder is sent to the Graduate Coordinator and a new decision due date is set.

The above example shows the distributed and heterogeneous computing and human interaction that is required for executing an activity. The particular nature of an activity makes the security and integrity enforcement a challenging and important problem. For example, information pilferage or illegal violation of privacy through accessing of specification time, compile time, or run time data about activities from activity management system and/or distributed PSAs must be prohibited. The distributed execution of multiple inter-dependent tasks by different PSAs using different software and hardware resources requires enforcement of additional global security requirements. These requirements encompass matching the PSAs to tasks and to specification and decomposition of activities. In many sensitive applications like the tendering process, an organization would not want knowledge about an activity and its component tasks to be divulged. A PSA is required to fulfill additional security requirements, such as maintaining integrity and data security during and after executing a task. If a PSA can not satisfy the security requirements, it can use an external mechanism to enhance its security abilities to become a secure PSA. For example, an "E-mail System" may need to be enhanced by an external "Encryption Mechanism" to protect out-going mail. Therefore, the "E-mail System" combined with the "Encryption Mechanism" will form a secure PSA. Also a task can potentially involve some processing of documents, especially when executing a document intensive task. Since many of the documents have sensitive information, document security needs to be modeled, specified, and managed by the activity management system.

There are three major aspects to security and integrity in activity management systems:

Security: Security deals with protecting the hardware systems, software systems, and data from illegal use and break-ins. Many of the standard techniques like login identifiers, passwords, and encryption do provide some basic security for individual systems. But for an activity management system, wherein different PSAs are executing different tasks at different times, on different hardware and software systems, it is pertinent that some form of global control is required to allow a PSA to access only those systems required for task execution for an interval of time during the task execution. This gives rise to a difficult problem of controlling the access privileges of the PSAs. This is required when there is a need for confidentiality and separation of duties.

Integrity: Integrity deals with the integrity of the PSAs in performing the task according to the specification, which depends on the integrity of the data processed and handled by PSAs. For example, each request for data and each modification of data needs to be an authentic legal request. That is, no user/PSA should be able to generate fake requests or initiate fake activity executions. Masquerading as a PSA or counterfeiting of data should not be allowed. Some of the integrity checking can be supported by existing technology, such as digital watermarks.

Authorization: Authorization deals with the certification of the authenticity of an activity being executed. For example, ACID properties guarantee the authentic completion of a transaction in a DBMS. That is, there are no side effects after the transaction execution, and it was executed according to the sequence of read/write operations specified by the transaction. Similarly, when an activity is executed, it should be possible to guarantee, or show that it was executed completely and in a manner as envisaged by the user, without which it is not possible to trust the completion of activity. This gives rise to the problem of task authorization and rigid control, sequencing, and maintenance of atomicity in authorization procedures of the activity. For example, a PG student is admitted only after a thorough review, possible interview, and a legal authentic offer letter. Unless all the above tasks are completed, one cannot say that the postgraduate admission activity is completed in a trustworthy manner. For example, it should not be possible to admit a postgraduate student with-out thorough review. Authorization can be supported by audit trails and digital signatures and validation protocols.

In this paper we show how we handle security and integrity issues in activity management systems. In particular, we shall present our approach in the context of CapBasED-AMS (Capability Based and Even Driven Activity Management System) .

1.1 Related Work

There are two approaches developed by researchers [H 93, P 92a, P 92b, TS 93, ThS 94, TF 95] to managing access control of resources and adapted in CapBasED-AMS. Discretionary Access Control (DAC) is used to model the security of objects on the basis of a subject's access privileges defining what kind of access a subject has to an object, and a set of predicates to represent content-based access rules such as read, write, delete, create and copy. In Mandatory Access Control (MAC) the security objects and subjects are assigned to a security level. The access rule is based on a pre-defined predicate which compares the security levels between objects and subjects.

In the context of agent based technology, security models such as IBM Aglets [Kar 97] were proposed which only concentrate on the resource access control and secure communication during execution, but do not present any centralized model to manage and enforce the security requirements during agent driven task execution. Furthermore, the details about the specification of security requirements are lacking. In computer supported collaborative work [F 97] the security aspects are concentrated on the language-oriented conceptual model, and do not address security enforcement mechanisms during activity execution.

In [HK 96] we addressed the security model in the context of tasks which need to access documents during activity execution. In particular we presented a task-oriented document security model which pertains to modeling the security related dependencies before a task (which needs to access a set of documents) can be executed. In [KGH 98], we presented issues in document security enforcement during activity execution by enumerating problems of least privileges, dynamic authorization of document access and deduction of document privilege information from event observation. The above work facilitated further work on secure CapBasED-AMS system presented in [HK 97a, HK 97b] whose major contribution is to integrate the security requirements and security handling mechanisms by taking into consideration above aspects to develop a logical framework which can be used to model, manage, and impose security-driven activity execution. Here we present a secure CapBasED-AMS by taking into consideration the system infrastructure, match-making under security requirements, security policies and secure PSA. Further, we introduce the basic concepts of CapBasED-AMS and present a task centered approach towards security enforcement, wherein, the security constraints are checked and the task is allowed to be executed only if none of the security constraints are violated.

The rest of the paper is organized as follows: Section 2 covers the architecture of a secure CapBasED-AMS, Section 3 covers the security issues in activity specification and decomposition, Section 4 presents an execution model for activity execution, Section 5 covers the security enforcement during task execution, and finally Section 6 presents a brief summary and discusses open problems.

2. Secure CapBasED-AMS

Activity management consists of decomposition of activities into tasks, coordination and data sharing among multiple PSAs executing the activity, and monitoring, scheduling and controlling the execution of multiple tasks of an activity. A software system that facilitates the specification, maintenance, and execution of activities is known as an Activity Management System (AMS). A secure activity management system must satisfy at least the following fundamental security requirements:

- *Confidentiality:* All aspects of activity specification, decomposition and execution must be restricted to the PSAs involved.
- *Authorization:* Data or document should not be modified or written by unauthorized PSAs at anytime.
- *Availability:* Data and document must be at PSAs disposal when needed for legitimate use.
- *PSA Anonymity:* No PSA will know other PSAs work and status, or communicate with other PSA directly during task execution.
- *Data Anonymity:* No PSA knows (except security administrator) who has produced the data or transmitted them, unless required.
- *Authenticated PSA:* The PSA executing task must be the original PSA which is known by system. No impersonating allowed.
- *Authenticated Activity:* It should be able to certify that the activity is executed according to the specification by an authenticated set of PSAs.

In order to support above set of fundamental security requirements we aim towards building a secure CapBasED-AMS based on following two functionalities that form core of an activity management system.

Capability-based activity specification and decomposition [Hu 95]: Each PSA has its competence defined by set of *capabilities* it has to execute tasks. Each activity requires a certain competence from the PSAs specified as a set of *needs* for executing each of its tasks. Each activity is decomposed into a set of tasks by using the property that each task must be executed by exactly one PSA. Further each task is matched to a PSA by selecting a PSA that has the capabilities to meet the needs of the task. In CapBasED-AMS, we use tokens to model the capability/need of a PSA/task respectively. This is the new idea which has not been applied in related work [F 97], because most of the related works model this concept by applying role based or hard-coded solutions. We present a new philosophy of applying capability-based approach as the bridge mechanism for matching a PSA to a task. The match making of each task to an appropriate PSA can be done automatically by simple SQL queries on the Capability Database. The specification of activities, sub-activities, tasks and PSAs are all user-driven. We define this aspect of activity management as capability-based activity specification and decomposition. In this paper, we extend the concept of abilities and needs to model the security privileges granted to the PSAs and needed by the tasks.

Event-driven activity execution [Y 95]: An activity consists of multiple interdependent tasks that need to be coordinated, scheduled and executed. The dependencies between tasks can be one or more of the following: i) data/control dependency - the execution of the task depends on some data or outcome of another task, ii) temporal dependency - the execution of the task depends on some temporal occurrences, and iii) external dependency - the execution of the task depends on the input from outside the AMS domain. All these dependencies can be expressed by means of a uniform framework of events. For each task, there are two types of events associated with it, namely *In-events* and *Out-events*. In-events are the situations in which the task is initiated to execute whereas Out-events are the effects after the execution of the task. Both In-events and Out-events can be one or more of the event categories described above. Note that both In-events and Out-events can correspond to receipt and delivery of documents processed by a task. Based on the events raised, an Event-Condition-Action Rule [CM 94] (ECA Rule) is triggered that leads to initiating the execution of the relevant tasks. When events are raised, conditions in the corresponding ECA rules are evaluated, and corresponding actions are triggered if the conditions are satisfied. Note that the ECA rules are also used to specify the security authorization requirements imposed on a task, and are used to authenticate the execution of a task by a PSA. Therefore, the execution and coordination of tasks of an activity is orchestrated by the occurrence of the events. We define this approach to execute activities as *event-driven activity execution*. In this paper, use the ECA rules to provide for the run-time security enforcement during activity execution.

2.1 Architecture of Secure CapBasED-AMS

Figure 1 shows the secure CapBasED-AMS architecture which consists of two parts: (1) capability-based activity specification and decomposition, and (2) event-driven activity execution.

The capability-based activity specification and decomposition component consists of an Activity Specification Language (ASL) processor, a Security Constraint Specification (SCS), an Activity Decomposer (AD), a Match Maker (MM) and Security Policy Decider (SPD) . ASL facilitates the description and specification of the activities. The Document Management System facilitates the specification and management of documents involved in ASL. SCS facilitates the description and specification of the Security Constraints (SC) imposed in the activities, and SPD assembles all the security constraints and generates a Security Policy (SP) to satisfy the security requirements from the information stored in Security Knowledge Base. AD decomposes an activity into tasks. MM interacts with SPD to identify secure PSAs (that execute the tasks) which will be stored in Secure PSA Base (SPB). AD and MM generate a specification of coordination plan using a Task Specification Language (TSL) as addressed in [Hu 95, KYH 95]. The event-driven activity execution component deals with propagating information, coordinating PSAs, scheduling and monitoring execution of tasks of an activity. In AMS, the activity execution is supported by four modules, namely the Document Manager (DM), Event Manager (EM), Activity Generator (AG) and the Activity Coordinator (AC). The DM manages the document flows and enforces the security specification of document in activity execution. The EM manages the event transmission to the PSAs. The AG acts as a pre-compiler. It takes a specification in TSL (the ActivityID.tsl in Figure 1) to generate the activity graph, ECA rules and define runtime database schema. The AC

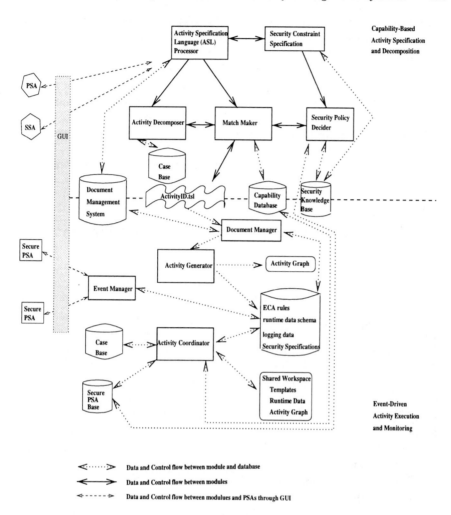

Fig. 1. Architecture of Secure CapBasED-Activity Management System

acts as an execution manager for activity execution and monitors security
enforcement by ECA rules when executing tasks. As the focus of this paper
is on security issues, we refer to [Hu 95, Y 95] for further details on activity
specification, decomposition and execution.

The salient features of the secure CapBasED-AMS are:

- the module for specification of security constraints on activities and documents is independent of the module for selection and enforcement of security policy during task execution.

- we provide a dynamic and automatic mechanism to match the task with the secure PSA based on tokens by taking into consideration security constraints.
- while most of the related work concentrates on the role based modeling document security, we use the task oriented modeling of document security which takes into account the task semantics, and the security requirements imposed by the activity/task.
- flexible PSA role based document security modeling using logical and physical documents for facilitating PSAs access to documents.
- present task oriented, document-based security enforcement framework for executing activities in secure CapBasED-AMS.

3. Security Requirements for Activity Specification and Decomposition

Each token is an unique fixed-length character string that symbolizes a capability possessed/needed by a PSA/task respectively. The token hides how a PSA achieves the capability and just specifies what this capability is. Note that how a PSA achieves that capability is internal to the PSA and may not always be revealed to the outside environment. During match making additional constraints can be specified to identify the PSA that achieves a capability according to some user specified constraints. In secure CapBasED-AMS, a PSA's security capability is also represented by token.

Example (cont.) *The following table describes some of the tokens for the Graduate admission activity.*

Token Id.	Token Description	Token Type
KPR	knowledge about university and departmental guides for Graduate Admissions.	Human
KFA	knowledge about faculty's research areas and current projects.	Both
CTA	ability to approve students admission.	Human
COC	ability to use computer system for word processing, spreadsheet, and database access.	Human
SBD	Database management system.	System
DAC	Able to perform Discretionary Access Control.	Security
MAC	Able to perform Mandatory Access Control.	Security
TDE	Able to transmit data with encryption.	Security
AB1	Able to apply B1 security standard.	Security
AB2	Able to apply B2 security standard.	Security

Each task of an activity is executed by exactly one PSA. PSA role abstraction is used to specify the basic set of capabilities for a set of similarly capable PSAs. A PSA can be an active PSA (like a human) or passive PSA (like a word processing system) specified by (role-) type. Each PSA role has a set of tokens denoting the set of capabilities PSAs taking this role have. Each PSA must have at least one role; each role may have several PSAs. On the other hand, two PSA roles can be specified as mutually exclusive. That is, the same PSA instance is not permitted to be assigned both PSA roles. For example, an employee in the department of computer science cannot be assigned to both "Research Assistant" and "Demonstrator" roles. For each of the PSA roles, the user can also assign cardinality constraints on it. That is, for some specific PSA roles, there may be maximum number of instances in a role. For example, there will be only one "Dean" in school of engineering who authorizes the initiation or completion of activities.

Example (cont.) *The list of PSA Roles for the Graduate admissions activity.*

PSA_Role Name	Graduate Coordinator.
Description	Coordinator of PG admission committee.
Type	Active.
Capabilities	{KPR, KFA, CTA}
Security Profile	{AB1, AB2}
PSA_Role Name	Graduate Secretary.
Description	Departmental administrative staff.
Type	Active.
Capabilities	{COC}
Security Profile	{}
PSA_Role Name	DBMS.
Description	Database management system.
Type	Active.
Capabilities	{SBD}
Constraints	Relational Database.
Security Profile	{DAC, MAC}

Example (Cont.) *The list of PSA Instances for the Graduate Admissions activity.*

PSA_Id.	Roles	Location	Constraints
Prof. Smith	Graduate coordinator	Room 233	Null
Miss Chow	Graduate Secretary	Department Office	Null
Sybase Server	DBMS	Room 4231	10G Byte Storage

In a secure CapBasED-AMS, different types of events occur and are used to coordinate, schedule and execute the tasks of an activity. Furthermore, threats, such as unauthorized access or modification of data, document, resource and system are identified as events. An event can be composed of multiple events by using operators, namely disjunction (∇), conjunction (Any, All), aperiodic Event Operators (A, A*), and periodic Event Operator (P, P*) of the SNOOP language [CM 94]. The event specification consists of an unique *Event Id*, the *Event Expression* and the *Type* of the event.

Example (Cont.) *Here is a list of Events for the Graduate Admissions Activity.*

Event Id	Event Expression	Type
E100	Insert("Application_Complete")	Normal
E200	Insert("Application_Incomplete")	Normal
E300	Review_Due_Date	Normal
D100	process(operation, document)	Document
T100	Access("Unauthorized Data")	Threat

In the activity specification and decomposition module, the high level activity specification language (ASL) defined in [Hu 95, KYH 95] is used to describe the activities by using a set of declarative constructs. The sub-activities, as activities themselves, are specified using ASL just like activities. During the activity decomposition phase, the sub-activities are decomposed recursively until the specification of tasks. The coordination among the sub-activities of an activity is derived and verified by using the input and output of external events of the sub-activities. In a secure CapBasED-AMS, we do not distinguish the data and control flow in the event as the receipt or delivery of a document is embedded in the input or output event.

Example (cont.) *The specification of graduate admission activity in ASL is given below. The top level activity is "Graduate_Admission", which consists of two sub-activities "Application_ Completeness_Check" and "Application_Review". The descriptions of the sub-activities are derived during the activity decomposition phase. The decomposition of sub-activities "Application_Completeness_Check", into "Application_Review" gives rise to following activity specification for "Graduate_Admission" activity. Note that by matching the output external events and input external events of the (sub-)activities, we can derive the coordination plan at this level of specification.*

Activity Id.	Graduate_Admission;
Description	Processing of applications to Graduate Studies, executed during Oct-Nov and Feb-Mar each year;
IE Events	Receipt_of("Application_Forms");
Sub-Activities	Application_Completeness_Check, Application_Review;
OE Events	Send("Acceptance Letter") ∇ Send("Reject Letter") ∇ Delete("Application");
Date Created	7/12/94.
Activity Id.	Application_Completeness_Check
Description	Check the completeness of the application
IE Events	Receipt_of("Application_Forms") ∇ Insert("Application_Incomplete");
OE Events	Insert("Application_Complete") ∇ Insert("Application_Incomplete") ∇ Delete("Application")
Activity Id.	Application_Review;
Description	Review the applications;
IE Events	Insert("Application_Complete");
OE Events	Send("Acceptance Letter") ∇ Send("Reject Letter").

The activity that has been specified at the high level as shown in Figure 2 must be recursively decomposed to generate a coordination plan at the task level by the algorithm given in [KYH 95]. This coordination plan is specified by using Task Specification Language developed in [Hu 95, KYH 95] where a task is an atomic activity executed by exactly one PSA. The graphical representation of task level specification of graduate admission activity is shown in Figure 3.

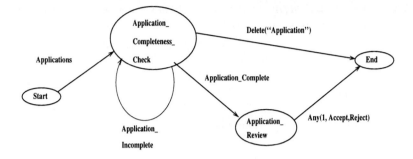

Fig. 2. The Coordination Plan of Graduate Admission Activity

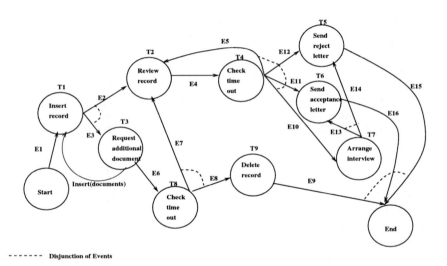

Fig. 3. Graphical Representation of Task Level Specification of Graduate Admission Activity

Example (cont.) *Here is the specification of some of the tasks for graduate admissions activity.*

Task Id.	Insert record (T1);
Description	To insert the records of the application forms;
Needs	{SBD};
Task Type	User-defined;
Input Events	Receipt_of("Application_Forms") ∇ Insert("Application_Incomplete");
Output Events	Insert("Application_Complete") ∇ Insert("Application_Incomplete");
PSA	SELECT PSA.Identifier FROM PSA, PSA_Role WHERE PSA.Role = PSA_Role.Name AND PSA_Role.Capabilities = SBD;
Task Id.	Review record (T2);
Description	To review the status of each application;
Needs	{KPR, KFA, CTA};
Task Type	User-defined;
Input Events	Insert("Application_Complete") ∇ Review_not_complete;
Output Events	Review_Due_Date;
PSA	SELECT PSA.Identifier FROM PSA, PSA_Role WHERE PSA.Role = PSA_Role.Name AND PSA_Role.Capabilities = {KPR, KFA, CTA};

In Figure 4, a hierarchy of activity specification and decomposition is shown. Each node in the hierarchy is either ASL or TSL specification of activity, and each level in the hierarchy is one level of decomposition.

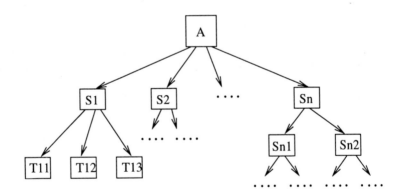

A - Activity Specification
S - Subactivity Specification
T - Task Specification

Fig. 4. Logical Hierarchy of Activity Specification and Decomposition

3.1 Security Control in Activity Specification

A set of users can be involved in activity, subactivity and task specification for different levels of activity decomposition. In the secure CapBasED-AMS, we assume an activity/subactivity/task can only be specified by exactly one user, e.g., *User_1* may define the activity *A*, another user *User_2* may define the subactivity *S1* and task *T11*, and so on. In our example, the user defines the Graduate_Admission activity may not be the same person who defines the Application_Completeness_Check or Application_Review subactivities. Therefore, there is a need to control the access for viewing and modifying the activity specification in order to disallow unauthorized user's access to the activity specification. Activity description can contain sensitive data pertaining to competitiveness of the organization, and hence should have restricted access. The complete activity specification can be illustrated by a hierarchy as shown in Figure 4. The root node stands for the highest level of ASL specification of activity, the intermediate nodes stand for ASL specification of subactivities, and the leaf nodes stand for the TSL specification of the tasks of the activity. The user who defines the node (i.e., activity, subactivity, or task) is the owner, and he/she has the right to view or modify it. By default, the owner also has the authorization to view all the descendent subactivity/task specification under its node since the owner needs to validate the decomposition of its node in order to maintain the original specification. For example, the user who defines the node *subactivity S1* has the right to view the *tasks T11, T12 and T13*. On the other hand, the owner or security administrator has the right to grant other users to view or modify the activity/subactivity/task by using the declarative constructs as shown below. The granter can also specify additional constraints if required. But the user who is granted access to the node does not inherit the authorization to view the child nodes (if any) by default, except when it is granted explicitly by the owner or security administrator. Also, the PSA who is matched to the task has the inherent authorization to view the constructs of the task.

Identifier	/* Activity, Subactivity or Tasks Name*/
Type	/* Activity, Subactivity or Task */
Privilege	/* View or Modify */
View Descendant	/* Grant,NotGrant or None(for Task) to view the decomposed entity*/
User's ID	/* User'ID(s) in CapBasED-AMS */
Constraints	/* Specified Constraints */

Example (cont.) *Here is the example of granting authorization for the Review record task.*

Identifier	Review record
Type	Task
Privilege	Modify
View Descendant	None
User's ID	CSHCK
Constraints	Only permit to modify the needs of the task.

3.2 Security Constraints Specification

Security constraints are rules that state the security requirements to be enforced during the execution of activity. We have defined six types of security constraints incorporated in secure CapBasED-AMS. The Security Specification Administrator (SSA) is responsible for specifying the security constraints during the specification of activity, subactivity and task at different levels of activity specification and decomposition. The security constraints are stored into a Security Knowledge Base and include the following:

- *Simple Constraints:* are ethics rules that are imposed on a PSA that need to be enforced and followed during task execution. For example:

Identifier	C100
Type	Simple
Statement	Prohibit the release of student's particulars to third party

- *Execution Constraints:* are the requirements on the PSA with specific security abilities/tokens to satisfy a security level restriction when executing task. For example:

Identifier	C200
Type	Execution
Security Tokens	TDE (i.e., Able to transmit data with encryption)

- *DAC Based Access Constraints:* are the constraints to model the security of objects on the basis of a subject's access privileges defining what kind of access a subject has to an object, and a set of predicates to represent content-based access rules. For example:

Identifier	C300
Type	DAC
Subjects	System Administrator
Objects	DBMS
Access Privileges	Read, Write, Update

- *MAC Based Access Constraints:* are the constraints to model when the security objects and subjects are assigned to a security level. The access rule is based on pre-defined predicate that compares the security levels between objects and subjects.

Identifier	C400
Type	MAC
Entities	Research Assistant, Clerk
Level	18

Identifier	O600
Type	MAC - Object
Entities	Application Form, SOP Letter
Level	17

- *Event Based Constraints:* are the ECA rules to define what action will be triggered based on the occurrence of events.

Identifier	C500
Type	Event
Event	Raised(T100)
Action	Append to Audit Log

— *Composite Constraints:* are the combination of constraints stated above by using operators, namely, disjunction (∇) and conjunction (Any, All).

Identifier	C700
Type	Composite
Composition	C500 ∇ C400

In Figure 4, the SSA may define different security constraints at different levels of the activity decomposition hierarchy. The lower level node will inherit all the security constraints imposed at the higher level nodes with the additional locally imposed security constraints. Therefore, the security constraint inheritance makes the security requirements for an activity from being vague at a higher level to being precise at a lower level in the hierarchy. One needs to handle security constraint conflicts among different levels. In the secure CapBasED-AMS, if there is any conflict between two levels of security constraints, the lower level security constraints will supersede the higher level security constraint. For example, in the higher level of "Graduate Admission" activity specification, it may have a simple constraint stating that "The applicant's information can only be released to the staff in departmental office". However, in the lowest level of "Review Record" task specification, the simple constraint states that "The applicant's information can be viewed only by the Executive Officer and PG committee in the departmental office", which further restricts the inherited constraint from activity specification level. Therefore, the constraint specified at the lower level will be the constraint imposed on the task. The specification of security constraints for activity specification can be the combination of the different types of security constraints stated above.

4. Framework for Activity Execution

4.1 Activity Graph

For each activity in the AMS, there exists an activity graph which shows the partial execution order of the activity (i.e., the dependencies among tasks within an activity). For example, a given task cannot be initiated until all its dependencies (i.e., the events) are met (occur) or no conflicts among tasks are detected. Each type of activity is defined as an *activity class*. The graph is represented as a directed graph in which each node represents a task and the directed edge represents the execution order. The activity graph also depicts alternative ways (alternative execution paths) to execute an activity, i.e., all possible ways that an activity could be executed are specified by including tasks for both normal activity execution and activity execution in case of exceptional conditions and failures. An alternative execution path is defined as an *activity instance*. Each activity execution corresponds to an activity instance being executed.

The activity graph is generated before the actual task execution and is stored in the system catalog in the database. The activity graph is represented at the granularity of the task level. At runtime, a copy of the activity graph is retrieved and gets updated during runtime to give the overall activity execution status. The activity graph provides the following information:

1. the schedule of *tasks* of an activity that need to be executed;
2. all the relevant In-events (the events that trigger the execution of the task) and Out-events (the events raised by the task after its execution) for a task; and
3. exceptional handling tasks when exceptional conditions or failure occur.

There are basically two types of tasks involved:

– human/active task (represented by a rectangle), which is performed by a human PSA,
– system/passive task (represented by a circle) which is performed by a system PSA.

The synchronization and control structures used in representing the activity are as follows:

Given a set of activities $A_1, A_2, \ldots, A_n$, each of which is an activity or a task:

1. $A = \text{AND}(A_1, A_2[, A_3..., A_n]; A_{n+1})$ is an activity: all the activities A_i, $i = 1, 2, \ldots, n$ have to be executed and then A_{n+1} must be executed for activity A to be executed.
2. $A = \text{ANY}(A_1, A_2[, A_3..., A_n])$ is an activity: any one of the activities A_i, $i = i, \ldots, n$ must be executed for activity A to be executed.
3. $A = \text{SEQ}(A_1, A_2[, A_3..., A_n])$ is an activity: activity A_{i+1} must be executed after A_i, for $i = 1, 2, \ldots, n$ for activity A to be executed.
4. $A = \text{REP}(A_1[, A_2, ..., A_n]; Event^*)$ is an activity: A_i, $i = 1, \ldots, n$ must be repeatedly executed until the $Event^*$ occurs for activity A to be executed.
5. $A = \text{PAR}(A_1[, A_2, ..., A_n])$ is an activity: all activities A_i, $i = 1, \ldots, n$ must be executed simultaneously for A to be executed.
6. Any number of invocations of the above five rules.

4.2 ECA Rules

ECA rules are defined in our AMS as follows:

1. event belongs to either In-event or Out-event of a task. The event can be a system event (event raised within the AMS), external event (event raised externally outside the AMS), or temporal event (event raised due to time constraint).

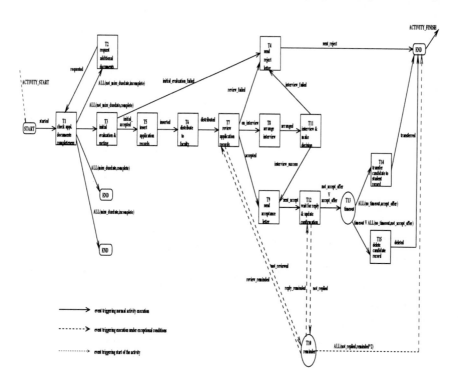

Fig. 5. Activity graph for Postgraduate Admission Activity

2. condition refers to the status of resource or external data sources, or PSA relevant to the task during runtime.
3. action refers to the subsequent task to be executed.

Activity execution is guided by the chain of ECA rules triggered by the events raised by the tasks. The set of ECA rules generated for the activity gives the execution plan. This approach is called event-driven activity execution. To illustrate this concept, we can use an event graph to represent the relationship between a task and its relevant events and rules. Figure 6 gives a mapping of the activity graph to its corresponding event graph representation.

Example (cont.) *Figure 7 shows how an ECA rule is triggered when some events are raised by T1 of the PA activity. For example, after the execution of T1, E3 and E5 are raised such that R3 is triggered and the action part in R3 specifies that T2 is the task to be initiated.*

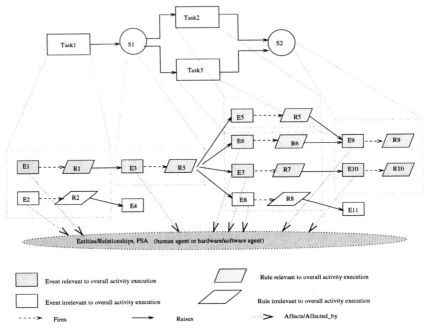

Fig. 6. Event Graph

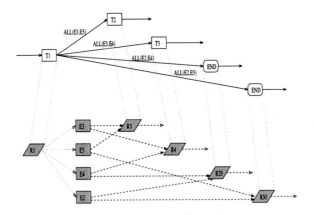

Fig. 7. Event Graph for Postgraduate Admission Activity

4.3 Activity Coordinator

The activity coordinator acts as both a facilitator and a mediator during activity execution in the *AMS*. It acts as a facilitator to coordinate PSAs to finish the activity. Based on a PSA's capabilities and requirements of a task, it acts as a mediator to select and initiate the PSA to do the task and gets the response from the PSA after finishing the task.

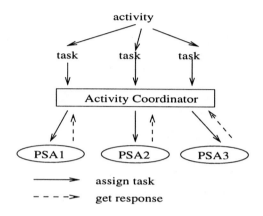

Fig. 8. Role of Activity Coordinator as a mediator

The activity coordinator is responsible for:

- Creating runtime templates which are used for keeping track of runtime execution and coordination information for an activity;
- Selecting PSAs, initiating, sequencing and controlling execution of tasks as detected by the occurrence of events and trigger corresponding ECA rules;
- Monitoring task execution status;
- Updating and populating relevant runtime databases;
- Supporting activity progress enquiry;
- Serving as a communication agent among PSAs;
- Logging task execution for recovery purposes; and
- Handling exceptional conditions.

Figure 9 gives the algorithm for the activity coordination in order to execute activities. In the following subsections, each of the functions listed previously is detailed along with the running example.

Algorithm to execute activity by the activity coordinator:

```
on start(activity) {
    activity.execution_status = EXECUTING;
    create and initialize activity template;
    for each task in the activity {
        create and initialize task template;
        for each event raised by the task {
            create and initialize event template;
        }
    }
    while activity.execution_status ≠ FINISH
        for each task in the task list {
            if the PSA is the activity coordinator then
                activity coordinator executes the task;
            else
                sends message to the PSA to execute the task;
            update activity graph;
            update templates;
            update runtime databases;
            do logging;
            on receiving message from the PSA {
                if task.execution_status = FAIL
                    initiate exception handling procedure;
            }
            update activity graph;
            update templates;
            updates runtime databases;
            do logging;
            on receiving enquiries from users
                retrieve relevant information from templates;
            if task.ID = "END" then
                activity.execution_status = FINISH
            else
                continue;
        }
}
```

Fig. 9. Activity Coordination Algorithm

4.4 Communication Between the Activity Coordinator and PSAs

There are basically two types of PSAs, known as human PSA and system PSA (the system could be hardware, software or the AC itself). For each type of PSA, the communication protocol is described as follows:

4.4.1 Communication between Activity Coordinator and Human PSA. Each human PSA capable of doing a task of an activity will communicate with the activity coordinator as follows:

1. The activity coordinator notifies the human PSA to perform the task by (1) **email** if the PSA is not currently logged on. (2) **popping up a window** on the workstation on which the PSA is logged on.
2. The PSA can either perform the task after getting the notification or at a later time select the task from the worklist and thus perform the task at his/her convenience.
3. The PSA processes the task.
4. After finishing the task, the PSA reports the final execution status, which is modeled in terms of events.

Figure 10 shows the protocol between the activity coordinator and PSAs. Note that all the above communication between the PSAs and the activity coordinator is orchestrated by the occurrence of events, satisfaction of corresponding conditions, and triggering of corresponding actions.

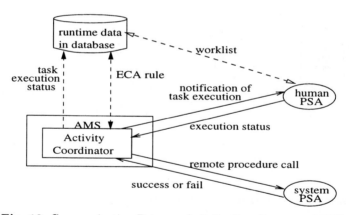

Fig. 10. Communication Between Activity Coordinator and PSA

Example (cont.) *When task T1 is finished by Mary, she will trigger the* TASKORGANIZER *program (a subsystem of the AMS installed at each human PSA site), which gives the worklist for Mary. Mary then sends the event ALL(E3,E4) (events E3 and E4 are specified in terms of the event descriptions such that Mary knows the semantics of the events) to the activity coordinator. Upon receiving the event from the PSA, the activity coordinator* *will update all the templates and the EXECUTION_STATUS table where the execution status of T1 is updated to FINISHED.*

4.4.2 Communication between the Activity Coordinator and a System PSA. If the PSA is a system (software, hardware, or the AMS itself), the activity will issue a *remote command execution* that triggers the corresponding PSA to execute the task as depicted in Figure 10. The activity coordinator will receive either success or failure upon completion of the task.

4.5 Task and Event Logging

There are two types of logging in the AMS, namely, *task logging* and *event logging*. The logging is used mainly for recovery purposes in case of failures.

Each task is logged whenever it is started and finished. After sending the message to a PSA for initiating the task execution, a log record for that task is populated in the database by the activity coordinator. Similarly, upon receiving a message from the PSA signaling the execution status of the assigned task, a log record is written. Similarly, an event is logged when it is raised.

Example (cont.) *Table 1 gives log records for T1 and E1 which are populated into the TASK_LOG and EVENT_LOG respectively.*

Table 1. Task and Event Log for Postgraduate Admission Activity

$Task_{time}$	$Activity_{id}$	$Task_{id}$	PSA_{role}	$PSA_{instance}$	ExeStatus
Fri May 26 13:48:53 1995	pal	T1	secretary	Mary	EXECUTING
Fri May 26 16:12:13 1995	pal	T1	secretary	Mary	FINISHED

$Event_{time}$	$Event_{id}$	$Activity_{id}$	RaisedByTask
Fri May 26 13:48:53 1995	E1	pal	START

4.6 Exception Condition Handling and Error Recovery

The AMS initiates different handling procedures when exception conditions or execution errors arise. However, any error internal to the PSA is detected and recovered only by the corresponding PSA itself instead of by the AMS system. The activity coordinator carries out the sequences of actions to execute the activity. If a task is completed successfully, the activity coordinator launches the next task; otherwise, an exception handling action for this particular failure of the task is initiated. One of the exception handling actions could be that the activity coordinator passes control back to the match maker to select another PSA who has the same capabilities to complete the task execution. Different types of failures that might occur in the AMS and how they are handled by the AMS are listed in Table 2.

Table 2. Exceptional Handling Techniques in CapBasED-AMS

Types of Failures	Handling Techniques
critical task execution failure	- redo the task by another PSA or the original PSA - signal failure of the whole activity, and consult users whether to restart the activity execution
non-critical task execution failure	- redo the task by another PSA or the original PSA - task substitution technique based on the token equivalence theory addressed in [Hu 95]
semantic task execution failure, i.e., the task finished in an unplanned manner, irrecoverable or exceptional case	- predefined contingency plans specified prior to execution are used - instead of aborting the whole activity, consult the user for partial rectification of the activity execution
PSA instance selection failure during task execution	- PSA substitution based on the token equivalence theory
PSA instance internal failure	- not handled by the AMS, but by the PSA itself - the PSA signals the activity coordinator to select another PSA to carry out the task - the AMS implements a timeout mechanism to prevent unresponsive PSA
AMS failure including its hardware, OS and other software	- recovery from the task log file and event log file after system repair (not implemented)
Any database failure, e.g., media failure in active database which might affect all tasks/activities that using that portion of the active database for execution	- database manager for the corresponding database is responsible for its recovery

Example (cont.) *Refer to Figure 5, when E14 or E22 is raised, task T10 defined as an exception handling task is activated. Note that the dotted directed line represents the execution path for exceptional condition.*

5. Security Enforcement During Task Execution

During the execution of activities, all the security requirements on the activities must be enforced. The CapBasED-AMS must be able to enforce the security constraints when executing the task.

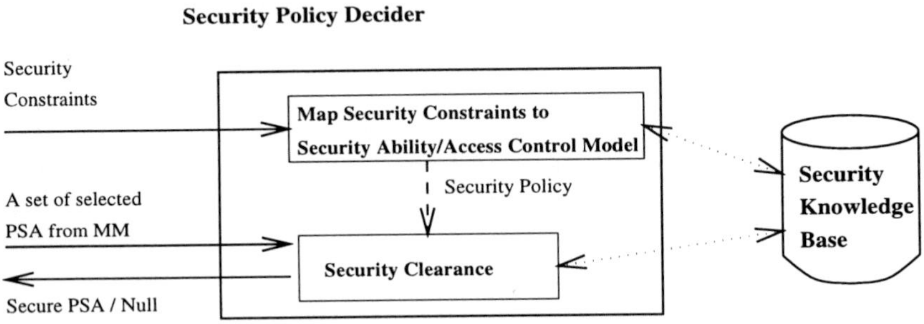

Security Policy Decider

Fig. 11. Security Policy Decider

5.1 Security Policy Decider and Secure PSA

A Security Policy is a set of security constraints to be enforced during the execution of task. It identifies the set of rules that regulate how a PSA manages, protects and distributes confidential and sensitive information and accesses the resources during the execution of tasks. A Security Policy is valid or applicable only during a predefined temporal interval. Furthermore, additional temporal dependencies among security policies can be specified stating that a PSA has to enforce a security policy as long as another PSA has a certain security policy. In Figure 11, the Security Policy Decider takes the security constraints of a task and then maps them into a security policy by the algorithm shown in Figure 12.

In the Map_Security_Constraints_to_Security_Policy algorithm, the Security Policy Decider (SPD) will retrieve the constraint from a set of specified constraints and check its type. If its type is "Simple", "Execution", "DAC" or "MAC", then SPD will insert the constraint into the group based on its type, e.g., Simple_Group, Execution_Group, DAC_Group or MAC_Group. Within each of the groups, if there are any conflicts detected between the newly inserted constraint and existing constraints, then SPD will resolve the conflict by applying a dominance rule, e.g., if there is a DAC constraint in the activity level stating that "Dr. Smith" has access privileges to a resource but at the task level it is stated that PSA role "Lecturer" cannot access such

```
Algorithm
Map_Security_Constraints_to_Security_Policy(Constraint_Set)
FOR ∀ Identifier ∈ Constraint_Set DO
BEGIN
    IF Type = (Simple OR Execution OR DAC OR MAC) THEN
    BEGIN
        Constraint_Group(Identifier, Type)
        IF Conflict_Detected(Type_Group) THEN
            Resolve_By_Dominance OR Resolve_By_Human_Intervention
    END
    ELSE IF Type = Event THEN
    BEGIN
        Establish_ECA_Rules(Identifier)
        Constraint_Group(Identifier, Type)
        IF Conflict_Detected(Type_Group) THEN
            Resolve_By_Dominance OR Resolve_By_Human_Intervention
        Check_ECA_Rules
    END
    ELSE IF Type = Composite THEN
    BEGIN
        Decompose_Composite_Constraint(Identifier)
    END
END
```

Fig. 12. Algorithm Map_Security_Constraints_to_Security_Policy

resource. Since "Dr. Smith" is the instance of PSA role "Lecturer", the constraint stated at the task level will dominate the constraint of the activity level (i.e., Dr. Smith will be denied access to the resource). If there is no clear dominance, human intervention is sought. If the type is "Event", then the Security Ability/Access Control Model (SAACM) will create the ECA rule and store it into "ECA_Group". The SAACM will also detect conflicts and resolve them if they occur by applying the dominance rule as stated above. These ECA rules will be used during the execution of the task. On the other hand, if the type is "Composite" then the constraint will be decomposed into a set of validated constraints and inserted into various groups as stated above based on the type. And then the Security Clearance model in Security Policy Decider takes the security policy and a set of selected PSAs from Match Maker to determine and return a PSA, which can also satisfy the security policy for the task by the algorithms shown in Figures 13 and 14.

In the algorithm of security clearance, a set of selected PSAs from Match Maker are checked in each constraint group (Simple, Execution, DAC, MAC and Event) for adherence to the security policy. If the Execution constraint group is not empty, then it will check if the security profile of the PSA has the security tokens as specified in the group. If the DAC/MAC constraint

```
Algorithm Security_Clearance(Selected_PSA_Set)
FOR ∀ PSA_ID ∈ Selected_PSA_Set DO
BEGIN
     IF Execution_Group in Security_Policy ≠ ∅ THEN
     BEGIN
          IF Execution_Group(Security_Tokens) ⊄
              Check_Profile(PSA_ID) THEN
                   Check_Next_PSA OR
                   Enhance_Security_Policy_Enforcer(PSA_ID,
                                   Execution_Group(Security_Tokens))
     END
     IF DAC_Group in Security_Policy ≠ ∅ THEN
     BEGIN
          IF DAC ⊄ Check_Profile(PSA_ID) THEN
               Check_Next_PSA OR
               Enhance_Security_Policy_Enforcer(PSA_ID, DAC)
          ELSE
               Grant the access control to PSA using DAC
     END
     IF MAC_Group in Security_Policy ≠ ∅ THEN
     BEGIN
          IF MAC ⊄ Check_Profile(PSA_ID) THEN
               Check_Next_PSA OR
               Enhance_Security_Policy_Enforcer(PSA_ID, MAC)
          ELSE
               Set the security level to PSA using MAC
     END
     IF Event_Group in Security_Policy ≠ ∅ THEN
          Store_into_Security_ECA_Files into Security_Knowledge_Base
     IF Simple_Group in Security_Policy ≠ ∅ THEN
          Store_into_Security_Rules_Files into Security_Knowledge_Base
     Secure_PSA = PSA_ID
END
```

Fig. 13. Algorithm Security_Clearance

```
Algorithm Enhance_Security_Policy_Enforcer(PSA_ID, Token_Set)
Security_Catalyst = Security_Knowledge_Base(PSA_ID, Token_Set)
IF Security_Catalyst ≠ ∅ THEN
BEGIN
     Enforce_PSA_ID := Select_One(Security_Catalyst)
     PSA_ID := Secure_PSA(Enforce_PSA_ID, PSA_ID)
END
```

Fig. 14. Algorithm Enhance_Security_Policy_Enforcer

group is not empty, then it will check if the security profile of the PSA has "DAC"/"MAC" security tokens as specified in the group. If the PSA does not satisfy the security constraint, the Enhance_Security_Policy_Enforcer will attempt to augment the PSA so as to facilitate satisfaction of the security constraints. If security of the PSA can be augmented, then Security_Clearance algorithm will create the access control/security level scheme for the PSA to enforce. If the Event/Simple constraints group is not empty, then it will store all the information into security knowledge base to be applied during the task execution. If a PSA satisfies all the conditions stated above, then the PSA is selected as the Secure PSA to execute the task.

A Security Policy Enforcer (SPE) enforces the security policy, and it can be treated as a PSA which has security abilities. This security enforcement is done by augmenting a security catalyst to a passive PSA. A Secure PSA allows information to flow as needed during task execution by disallowing unauthorized release of information.

5.2 Enforcement of Task Oriented Modeling of Security

All the security information will be stored using ECA rules in the security knowledge base, and will be used by the execution module of secure CapBasED-AMS. The security process subactivity is responsible for enforcing and monitoring the security policy during the execution of tasks of an activity. Security control is enforced by using Event-Condition-Action (ECA) rules. During the execution of tasks, ECA rules will be triggered when the resource is accessed for performing some operations by the PSA. The event "process(operation, resource)" is generated by the PSA, which involves an instance of the "Security Process Subactivity" to be created by the system. Three tasks "Resource Process", which is executed by the PSA, "Security Policy Enforcement" and "Exceptional Handling", which are executed by the activity coordinator, will be decomposed from the security process subactivity as shown in Figure 15. And then in the task "Security Policy Enforcement", the conditions such as whether the PSA can perform the operation on the resource or not will be checked. Based on the satisfaction of these conditions, an action will be taken to allow the operation on the resource. If the PSA has certain privileges on the resource, the action will be to allow the PSA to perform the operations on the resource in "Resource Process". SNOOP language [CM 94] is used to specify events for accessing the resource by the PSA. By using the event detector in the system, once the event is detected, the condition evaluator will evaluate and verify whether certain operations can be performed on the resource by the PSA. In our example, the "Graduate Coordinator" needs to read the applicant's form during the execution of the task "Review Record", then the *Event: process(read, applicant's form)* will trigger the execution of *Condition: Security Policy Enforcement* to validate if the "Graduate Coordinator" has the authorization to read this resource or not. If the "Graduate Coordinator" has the authorization to read it, then the

Action: read(applicant's form) is performed. Note that there can be separate events for satisfying the security constraints from the point of view of the activity, task, PSA, and the resource, before the resource is processed by the PSA. Thus ECA rules enable independent and integrated treatment towards security enforcement from different view points. On the other hand, if the PSA is denied to access the resource, then the "Exceptional Handling" task will be triggered. If the "Exceptional Handling" can resolve the conflicts, then it will trigger the event "retry" to "Security Policy Enforcement" again. Otherwise, it will trigger the event "failed" and return back to the original task. In order to prevent a cyclic process between the two tasks "Security Policy Enforcement" and "Exceptional Handling", the user can specify meta constraints on it, e.g., the maximum number of repeated executions of task Security Policy Enforcement, time out, etc.

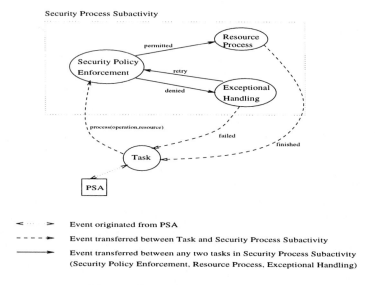

Fig. 15. Security Process Subactivity

Event logging for resource operation is done during the execution of tasks by the security administrator as elaborated in Section 4. This event logging is used for recovery if there is any failure during task execution and also for checking the authenticity of activity execution and certifying it. This allows for active security enforcement, monitoring, and control, which is very essential for activity management systems.

6. Open Problems and Summary

The focus of this paper has been on elaborating on a framework for supporting security in activity management systems. In particular, we presented an architecture and described the mechanisms incorporated for enforcing security for activity specification and decomposition, and during activity execution. Further, we elaborated on the importance of security enforcement for maintaining the integrity of activities being executed. This paper provided a task-centered approach towards security enforcement, wherein the security constraints are checked and the task is allowed to be executed only if none of the security constraints are violated. This is handled by the event-condition-action rule paradigm from active database systems. We are currently implementing the secure CapBasED-AMS system.

There are many issues related to management of security for activity execution that still need to be addressed, such as,

Agent-based Access Control: Traditionally, there have been three mechanisms for handling access control to resources, namely, discretionary access control, mandatory access control, and multi level access control. Recently, there has been a move towards role-based access control. In the case of a role based approach, each role has a fixed set of accesses to various resources, and there is a pre-defined and static assignment of access privileges to the roles. But for activity management systems, each PSA can take up many roles, and depending on the task being executed, would need specific access privileges. This would give rise to large number of roles, or would employ exceptional handling mechanisms if a role based access control mechanism were used. Therefore, there is a need for developing a formal model for agent-based access control for task specific access security enforcement. Further, since an activity consists of a set of coordinated tasks, each of which is executed by different agents, there needs to be a propagation mechanism for access privileges among the agents for the continuation of activity execution.

Assignment of Access Privileges: The PSAs in the activity management systems are also the potential users of the information and also are potential security leakage sources. Due to the confidentiality and sensitive nature of activities, it is of paramount importance that PSAs are kept at "need to know" basis while providing enough privileges so that they can execute the tasks. This issue of assigning minimal access privileges (i.e., concept of least privileges [KGH 98]) to PSAs so that they can execute the tasks while disallowing extra privileges is a very difficult problem. Further, additional constraints such as "separation of duties" and sequencing of authorization by different PSAs makes this problem even more difficult.

Privacy and Confidentiality: One of the major issues with computerized support for activity execution is the assurance provided to users about the privacy of the information. This problem is also related to assignment of access privileges to PSAs. But is much more general, because of indirect inferencing of information from partial knowledge, which could divulge private information. Hence, handling privacy of information requires appropriate modeling of information and appropriate mechanisms for specifying the information that is deemed to be private. it also requires devising appropriate mechanisms to maintain the privacy of information. Lastly, it should be possible to verify and validate that the mechanisms in place actually work.

All of the above problems concentrate on the logical level of security enforcement without getting to specific physical system level details. Therefore mechanisms at the logical level would have to be translated to physical system level constraints and an efficient implementation. Further, any proposed agent-based access control mechanism must have a physical implementation plan.

Towards a Platform for Distributed Application Development

Gustavo Alonso, Claus Hagen, Hans-Jörg Schek, Markus Tresch

Database Research Group
Institute of Information Systems
ETH Zentrum, Zürich CH-8092, Switzerland
E-mail: {alonso,hagen,schek,tresch}@inf.ethz.ch

Abstract. This paper describes the architecture of a generic platform for building distributed systems over stand alone applications. The proposed platform integrates ideas and technology from areas such as distributed and parallel databases, transaction processing systems, and workflow management. The main contribution of this research effort is to propose a "kernel" system providing the "essentials" for distributed processing and to show the important role database technology may play in supporting such functionality. These include a powerful process management environment, created as a generalization of workflow ideas and incorporating transactional notions such as spheres of isolation, atomicity, and persistence and a transactional engine enforcing these "quality guarantees" based on the nested and multi-level models. It also includes a tool-kit providing externalized database functionality enabling physical database design over heterogeneous data repositories. The potential of the proposed platform is demonstrated by several concrete applications currently being developed.

1. Introduction

Hardware architectures for information systems seem to be evolving towards infrastructures based on multiple stand alone computers linked by a network. From a research point of view, such clusters are interesting as platforms for implementing truly distributed systems. From a practical standpoint, the problem is how to build something coherent out of systems that were not necessarily designed to work together [COR 95a, Hol 96, BN 97]: existing products tend to be unsatisfactory because they are, in most cases, only partial solutions to a fairly general problem. For instance, CORBA [COR 95a] needs the transactional services a TP-monitor provides [BN 97, Obe 94]; a TP-monitor could greatly benefit from the standard interface defined by CORBA; both TP-monitors and CORBA implementations need a workflow tool to help specifying complex sequences of interactions between the different system components [Hsu 95]; distributed execution over the internet needs transactional guarantees [Le 97]; and so forth. The problem is not the lack of solutions but the lack of integrated solutions. To address this issue, this paper describes a basic kernel integrating ideas and technology from distributed and parallel databases, transaction processing systems, and workflow management. While the paper describes ongoing work, a prototype being developed, and some preliminary results, its main contribution is to propose a set of "essential features" in a distributed system and show the important role database technology may play in supporting such functionality.

The kernel features considered in here are *process management, execution guarantees*, and *exported database functionality*. Process management refers to the need to have an adequate environment in which to express and execute coarse distributed computations. To this end, OPERA, a kernel process management system, is being developed. OPERA generalizes many ideas from workflow management related to both transaction processing [BN 97, GR 93] and business re-engineering [AAEM 97, AAEM 97, AS 96]. It provides a sophisticated exception handling mechanism, incorporating transactional notions such as spheres of isolation, atomicity, and persistence. Regarding execution guarantees, we believe with [GR 93] and [BN 97] that transactions should be one of the basic building blocks for distributed applications. Hence, as a first step, we have developed a reformulation of nested and multi-level transactions geared towards exploiting the inherent parallelism of distributed applications. These ideas are currently being incorporated into OPERA to form the core of the execution guarantees it provides. Additional database functionality is incorporated into OPERA in the form of query management and physical database design. In this point, OPERA has taken advantage of the work done within the CONCERT project. Both CONCERT [BRS 96] and composite transactions [ABFS 97, AVA+ 94] have been described elsewhere, thus, in this paper we concentrate on OPERA and show how it integrates all these ideas into a coherent system by providing three application examples, one of them used as the running example to motivate the discussion.

The paper is organized as follows. Section 2 motivates the paper with an example. Section 3 presents OPERA, its general goals, architecture, and most relevant aspects. Section 4 discusses a number of application areas in which OPERA is being used by extending and tailoring the basic system with additional functionality. These application areas include higher level object management, and a distributed object manager for heterogeneous data repositories. Section 5 provides additional information regarding the status of the project and concludes the paper.

2. Motivation

One of the basic platforms in which to implement generic multiprocessor systems is commodity hardware and software, usually in the form of clusters of workstations connected via a network. In such environments, scalability and reliability are ideally only limited by the number of elements in the system. They also have the advantage that most of the necessary infrastructure is already in place.

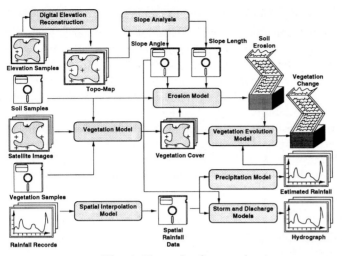

Fig. 1. Example of an earth sciences process

2.1 Application Example

As a running example of such environments, and to use one not directly related to traditional databases, consider earth sciences processes [SSE+ 95, SW 93, HGM 93], a concrete instance of which is shown in Figure 1 [AH 97, AE 94]. The interesting aspect of this example is that it shows how scientific data is handled, i.e., it is often subject to multiple transformations involving different applications and platforms. For instance, in the example shown, the purpose is to study the changes in the erosion patterns, vegetation and hydrographic characteristics of a given area. It is basically a series of transformations over base and derived data that, taken together, represent an interpretation of several interrelated geographic phenomena (erosion, rain storms, flooding). These processes are executed step-wise using a variety of GIS applications over a cluster of computers. Execution is controlled, at best, through scripting languages or, more often, manually. Any logging, accounting, indexing, classification, record keeping, or failure recovery is done, if at all, manually. These are, however, areas in which databases excel and that open up interesting opportunities for using databases in distributed environments. For instance, they could be used to support distributed computations in the same way that today's databases are used to support traditional data management. In other words, database technology could form the core of a "distributed operating system" facilitating the integration of independent systems into a single coherent whole. Some of this functionality (Figure 2) includes persistent execution with the database acting as a sophisticated data repository. This will certainly increase performance in environments in which many processes are run concurrently and in which it is necessary to provide sophisticated querying facilities to keep track of events in the system and to analyze the characteristics of already executed processes. Basic functionality also includes transactional guarantees, not only regarding atomic commitment, but also issues like forward and backward navigation using the database as a sophisticated log, high level compensation, and process synchronization. This immediately raises the question of which language to use to express the desired behavior and execution semantics. Databases can also provide much needed availability and resilience to failures, as well as helping in providing reasonable performance in complex distributed environments by separating the execution data from automatic record keeping, logging and auditing data. All these ideas indicate the important role databases could play in executing distributed processes like the one in Figure 1.

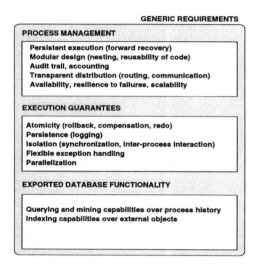

Fig. 2. Functionality necessary to support distributed process execution

2.2 Software Solutions

Existing solutions to distributed execution are commonly grouped under the name of *middleware*. Middleware products related to databases are, for instance, federated and multi-databases systems [SSW 95, DSW 94], TP-monitors [Obe 94], persistent queuing systems [MH 94], CORBA implementations [COR 95a], workflow management systems [Hsu 95, Hsu 93], and process centered environments for software engineering [TKP 94, BK 94]. They can support the process in the example in a variety of ways. For instance, a CORBA implementation would impose an object oriented interface over each application, and the process would then be coded in C++. A TP-monitor would treat each separate step as a service provided by one or more servers and the process would be coded as a series of service invocations with some transactional semantics. Each of these approaches has advantages and

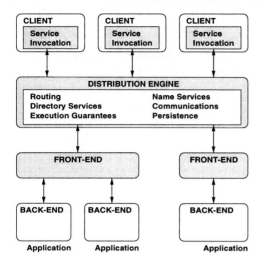

Fig. 3. Generic architecture of a middleware tool as a 3 -tier architecture

disadvantages, but none of them provides an integrated solution and there is always functionality missing. The main hypothesis behind this paper is that middleware systems have a lot in common. This shared functionality is mainly database related and, therefore, it should be possible to design a kernel system to provide it. As a first approach, the kernel can be based on the common aspects of existing middleware systems. An analysis of their functionality clearly shows a common generic architecture: the traditional 3-tier organization (Figure 3) and the typical configuration within a cluster of workstations (Figure 4) [Cor 95c, COR 95a, Cor 95b, IBM 95]. In both cases, there are four main components to consider: *Clients*, the *Distribution Engine*, *Front-Ends*, and *Back-Ends*.

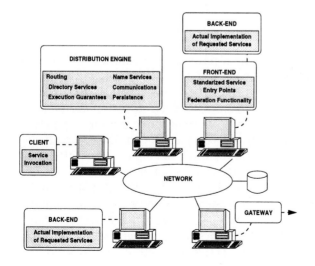

Fig. 4. Generic architecture of a middleware tool distributed in a cluster of workstations

Instance	Client	Distribution Engine	Front-End	Back-End
CORBA	Client	Object Request Broker	Object Adaptor	Server
Workflow Systems	Worklist Manager	Workflow Engine	Application Interface	Activity / Task
TP-Monitors	Client	TP-monitor	Server	Resource Manager
Queuing Systems	Client Application	Queue Server	Client Application	Client Application
Federated Databases	Client	Global Transaction Manager	Agent or Wrapper	Local Database

Fig. 5. Mapping between the generic components and the notations of several instances of middleware

The functionality of these components is as follows. The *client* interacts with the system through *service invocations*. The service invocations are handled by the *distribution engine*, which forms the core of the system. The distribution engine determines the nature of the system since it provides the main functionality: load balancing, routing, communication handling, protocol translation, name and directory services, system administration, client interaction, and so forth. The distribution engine passes the service requests to the *front-ends*, which provide a standarized entry point and generic interface to the *back-ends*, i.e., to the applications underlying the middleware system. It is a simple exercise to map these generic architecture to concrete products (Figure 5). With this generic architecture in place, the next step is to determine the functionality the kernel should provide.

2.3 Kernel Functionality for Distributed Systems

We are particularly interested in the aspects in a distributed system that can be supported by database technology. In particular, and as pointed out above, there are three aspects we consider "essential functionality": *process management, execution guarantees* and and *exported database functionality*. The reason to focus on these three aspects comes from our observations of current trends in existing products, which reveal a high degree of affinity among middleware systems. For instance, workflow systems and CORBA environments are slowly being merged under the notion of business objects (for process management), TP-monitors are being used to provide the execution guarantees in CORBA, and queuing systems are being added to workflow management systems to increase reliability (exported database functionality). By exploiting this affinity, we aim at designing a generic kernel providing the following "essentials":

Process management. Distributed computation is to be based on the concept of process. Processes are arbitrary sequences of application invocations over different locations and platforms. Hence, the main hardware infrastructure behind the system is a cluster of workstations used as a shared nothing multi-processor environment in which the kernel plays the roles of scheduler and resource allocator. The kernel should provide sufficient reliability, availability and scalability and, for this purpose, should take advantage of the underlying hardware platform to distribute its functionality. Ideally, all the components could be moved from node to node to enhance the overall robustness, availability, and scalability. For instance, in the example of Figure 1, if a node in which a step is usually executed is not available, it may be possible to run the same step at a different location. This should happen transparently so as to allow the system to dynamically adjust itself to configuration changes due to failures or scheduled shut-downs. Similarly, if a failure occurs midway during the execution of the process, it should not be necessary to restart executing from the beginning when the failure is repaired. Intermediate results should have been stored and execution resumed at the point where it was left off when the failure occurred. Moreover, in some cases it should even be possible to resume execution before the failure is repaired by using a reliable backup strategy. All this, of course, must be provided with reasonable performance and without introducing significant overheads.

Execution Guarantees. The kernel should guarantee correct results in spite of the fact that the execution is concurrent and involves autonomous and often uncooperative systems. Correctness includes concepts such as atomicity, "exactly once" semantics, concurrency control, recoverability, etc. Thus, the kernel should place a significant emphasis on the transactional aspects of distributed computations. It should provide not only language constructs to incorporate transactional notions into processes (spheres of isolation, atomicity, and persistence), but also support for composite transactional interactions [ABFS 97] among the different components of the distributed system as a way of guaranteeing overall correctness. In addition, mechanisms are needed to exploit as much as possible the inherent parallelism of processes like the one in Figure 1.

Externalized Database Functionality. One of the main problems of today's databases is that they behave like black boxes. Their services are available only to the data that resides within the database. In practice, however, most data does not reside within databases and applications using this data must implement their own database services. This is certainly the case in many applications running over clusters of workstations. Part of the basic support the kernel should provide is database functionality such as indexing and query processing [BRS 96]. The advantage of exporting database functionality is that it provides a very powerful mechanism to interact with data and applications residing outside of the system. It not only alleviates the task of writing new applications (since there is no need to incorporate this database functionality in them) but it also establishes the basis for keeping track of the many elements involved in distributed environments (both data and applications).

3. The OPERA Kernel

OPERA is being designed as a kernel providing the core functionality described above. This kernel will be extended to build distributed solutions such as shared nothing parallel database systems, experiment management environments, or distributed object management engines (see below).

3.1 Architecture

The architecture of OPERA is organized around three service layers (Figure 6): *database services, process services* and *interface services.* The database service layer acts as the storage manager. It encompasses the storage layer (the actual databases used as repositories) and the database abstraction layer (which makes the rest of the system database independent). The storage layer is divided into five *spaces*: template, instance, object, history, and configuration, each of them dedicated to a different type of system data. Templates contain the structure of the processes. When a process is to be executed, a copy of the corresponding template is made and placed in the instance space. This copy is used to record the process' state as execution proceeds. For each running instance of a process the instance space contains a copy of the corresponding template. Storing instances persistently guarantees forward recoverability, i.e., execution can be resumed as soon as the failure is repaired, which solves the problem of dealing with failures of long lived processes [ST 96, DHL 91]. Instances also constitute the basic unit for operations related to process migration and backup facilities [KAGM 96]. Objects are used to store information about externally defined data. They allow OPERA to interact with external applications by acting as a proxy containing the information indicating how to access external data [BRS 96, AH 97]. The history space is used to store information about already executed instances. It contains a detailed record of all the events that have taken place during the execution of processes, including already terminated processes. Finally, the configuration space is used to record system related information such as configuration, access permissions, registered users, internet addresses, program locations, and so forth.

   The database abstraction layer implements the mechanisms necessary to make the system database independent. The experience with workflow systems shows that this is a crucial issue affecting scalability and the overall openness of the system [AAEM 97]. Hence, OPERA uses internally a canonical representation [KAGM 96] optimized for performance and expressibility.

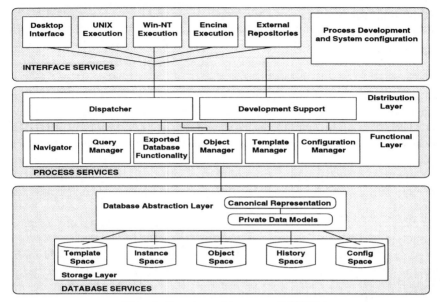

Fig. 6. System architecture of OPERA

This canonical representation is not suitable, however, for either commercial databases or user interaction. The database abstraction layer translates the canonical representation to the private representations of the underlying repositories (SQL, C++, system calls) as required by the physical implementation of the underlying database (Figure 7).

The process service layer contains all the components required for coordinating and monitoring the execution of processes. The most relevant components for the purposes of this paper are the *dispatcher*, the *navigator*, the *object manager*, the *query manager*, and the *exported database functionality* module. The dispatcher and the development support constitute the distribution layer, which deals with physical distribution. The dispatcher acts as resource allocator for process execution. It determines in which system the next step will execute, locates suitable nodes, checks the site's availability, performs load balancing, and manages the communication with remote system components. The development support performs similar tasks for process definition, forming the basis of OPERA's development environment. These two components are an example of the advantage of separating the database spaces. The development support module works mainly over the template space, the dispatcher mainly over the instance and configuration spaces. Separate spaces implies that these two components do not compete for the same resources.

The rest of the components form the functional layer, which implements most system's capabilities. The navigator acts as the overall scheduler: it "navigates" through the process description stored in the instance space, establishing what to execute next, what needs to be delayed, and so forth. It enforces the transactional aspects of the execution. During navigation, the variables in the process instance are updated to keep track of every step taken in the execution of the process. When the process terminates, this information is moved to the history space to avoid interferences between process execution and history analysis. The system interacts with the data spaces through the query manager. The query manager provides a suitable interface for complex queries, which in many cases are standard. Instead of including them as part of all the modules where they are used, they are centralized in the query manager, which offers them as services to other components. We expect that most of these queries will be executed over the history space. In some applications this aspect of process support is heavily used, hence the advantage of separating the instance space, used to drive the execution of processes, and the history space, used for record keeping purposes.

Interaction with external objects takes place through the object manager and the exported database functionality module. The latter is is based on CONCERT [BRS 96], a system designed to provide database functionality to data external to the database. The former is much more application dependent, acting as the repository for metadata information. Examples of this metadata include any dependency between external objects, lineages, versioning, etc.

Finally, the interface service layer encompasses all the mechanisms that allow OPERA to interact with applications in different hardware and software platforms. Users interact with the system via *desktop interfaces*, which are also used to inform the user of any activity that they need to execute as part of a process (like worklists in workflow engines). The interaction with external applications takes place through *execution interfaces* supporting several operating systems and specific tools. These execution interfaces communicate with the dispatcher, translating the commands sent by the dispatcher into the corresponding commands required to start an application, and notifying the dispatcher of the termination of the application.

3.2 Process Management: Model

The notion of process is central to OPERA. A process is a sequence of computer programs and data exchanges controlled by a meta-program (the process itself). Typical examples of processes are business processes, software processes, manufacturing processes, scientific experiments, and geographic modeling. The problem with existing process management systems is that they tend to focus on a particular type of process. The situation resembles in many ways that of databases before the adoption of the relational model. It is difficult to generalize individual solutions as proven by recent attempts to use commercial workflow products to support scientific applications [MVW 96, BSR 96]. Indeed, a generic notion of process can be compared with

SQL. SQL alleviates the task of data management by providing a universal interface to data management tools (the database). A generic notion of process would alleviate the task of defining the control flow between different applications by providing a common interface to process management tools. This is the idea, for instance, behind the joint efforts of the OMG (Object Management Group) and the Workflow Management Coalition to define a standard for process management in CORBA. Similarly, OPERA provides a generic way of representing arbitrary processes, as a first step towards becoming the engine behind many distributed applications. The crucial role process management could play in the design of server and client code is an example of the advantages of this approach. For the servers, it provides a mechanism to federate applications, as it happens today in workflow systems. This can greatly simplify the task of writing servers in the TP-monitor sense, which tends to be the most complex task from a designer's point of view. For the clients, process management opens up interesting new ways of interacting with the system. Processes can be seen as a sophisticated form of scripting, allowing the users to quickly build applications over distributed systems. Using the same concept for coding at both the client and the server blurs the distinction between them, allowing arbitrary nesting of systems, which we expect to become a very useful feature in practical applications.

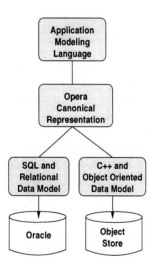

Fig. 7. The different language representations in OPERA

In order to provide a generic notion of process, OPERA contains a hierarchy of process representations rather than a single model (Figure 7). At the top of the hierarchy, and used at the interface service layer, is the application specific language. This is the language that can be customized to processes such as those shown in Figures 15 and 1. In most process support systems, this language has a strong graphic component. User representations, however, are not suitable for handling processes efficiently. Therefore, OPERA works internally using OCR (*Opera Canonical Representation*), which constitutes the second level of process representation. The third level appears when OCR is translated into the private representations of the underlying databases (currently ObjectStore and Oracle). The following are the most relevant components of OCR.

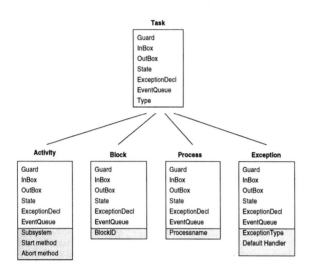

Fig. 8. Class hierarchy of tasks in OPERA

A *process* consists of a set of tasks and a set of data objects. Tasks can be activities, blocks, or processes. The task class hierarchy (Figure 8) also includes exceptions as a special type of internal tasks. The data objects store the input and output data of tasks and are used to pass information around. The connectors indicate the order in which the tasks are to be executed. To better understand how some of these notions fit together, Figure 9 shows how the example of Figure 1 as an OCR process (with some unavoidable simplifications for reasons of space, for instance, OCR does not implement connectors explicitly but implicitly).

Activities are the basic execution steps. In the example of Figure 1, each shaded box corresponds to an activity. An activity provides a *navigation interface* (Figure 8) to access information about its state, parameters, return values, raised events, possible exceptions, etc. This information is stored as part of the process template and is used during navigation. In addition, each activity has an *external binding*, which specifies the program(s) to be executed, users responsible for the execution, and/or resources to be allocated for its execution. This information is used by the dispatcher to execute external applications. The external binding is stored in the configuration space as several activities may use the same external program. The procedure to

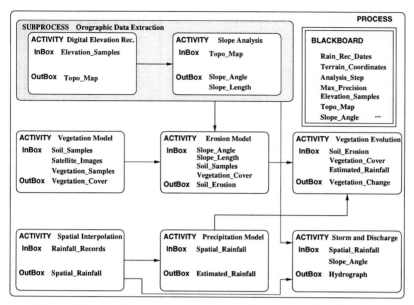

Fig. 9. The earth science process example in terms of OCR components

create the external binding is similar to that of registering programs in an operating system so they can be properly invoked.

Blocks are sub-processes defined only in the context of a process. They are used for two purposes, for modular design and as specialized language constructs such as loop blocks (for, do-until, while, fork), spheres of atomicity, spheres of isolation, or spheres of persistence.

Subprocesses are processes used as components of other processes. As an example, in Figure 9 two activities have been grouped into a subprocess called "Orographic Data Extraction". Subprocesses allow, like blocks, the hierarchical structuring of complex process structures. Late binding (the referenced process is read only when the sub-process is started) allows dynamic modifications of a running process by changing its sub-processes [IBM 95].

Control flow inside a process is based on *guards* attached to each task. The guard concept borrows heavily from the ECA rule mechanism of active databases. A guard consists of an *event description* describing the process state(s) that activate the execution of a task. The task's execution can be restricted by an *activation condition* expressed as a predicate on output data of other tasks. Event descriptions can only refer to execution states and events raised by tasks within the same process. This helps to avoid many of the complexity problems associated to ECA rules. The reason to use guards comes from our experience in workflow systems. For instance, in the case of Object-Store, it was determined that the cost of pointer chasing caused significant overheads and, therefore, an active mechanism was used (guards) instead of the traditional control connector approach (in which a control connector implies several steps in a chain of pointers). In Figure 9 guards have been omitted for simplicity. Control flow is instead represented through connectors similar to those used in workflow engines.

Data flow is possible between tasks and between processes. Each task has an *input data structure* describing its input parameters and an *output data structure* to store any return values. The input parameters of a task can be linked to data items in the process' global data area (the blackboard) or in other task's output structures. When a task starts, these bindings are analyzed and the necessary values passed to the task. After the successful execution of a task, a *mapping phase* transfers data from its output structure to the global data area. The input and output data structures of a process are part of the *blackboard* which acts as the global data area for the process (Figure 9).

Events: OCR incorporates an event mechanism that allows the communication between processes as well as the externalization of intermediate results of activities. Processes and activities must declare the *events* they may signal during their execution. Processes subscribe to these events, with the process engine behaving as a broker that notifies subscribers of relevant. The guard of a task can also contain references to events, allowing to make the flow of control dependent on intermediate states of other processes or activities. Events are parameterized, which facilitates exchanging data between processes. For automatic activities, the OPERA API provides a call to signal events. Users may also raise events through the desktop interface.

Exceptions: Exceptions are raised by tasks when unexpected situations occur, or when external intervention is needed to either decide on the further flow of control or to change data values passed to a task [HA 97]. Exceptions serve as a unique mechanism to parameterize the behavior of processes. The declaration of possibly exceptions is part of the navigation interface. A task defines default handlers for each exception it throws. A calling process can modify the behavior of a task by specifying *override handlers* that replace the predefined handlers. This mechanisms provides a very powerful way of coping with exceptions, one of the most pervasive problems of process management. Details of the exception handling mechanisms in OPERA have been published elsewhere [HA 97] and they will not be discussed further in here.

3.3 Transactional Execution Guarantees

The transactional aspects of OPERA are embedded in the notion of *spheres* and in the scheduling performed by the navigator. The former addresses the problem of providing a way of bracketing operations as units with transactional properties. The latter forms the basis for actual transactional scheduling.

The concept of ACID transactions [GR 93] has been very successful in databases. But once transactions are used outside the database, there is a strong need for *light-weight* transactions in which some of the ACID properties are not enforced [BRS 96]. In particular, in the case of OPERA processes, OCR tries to avoid a unique construct encompassing all properties, e.g., *BOT/EOT*. Instead, blocks are used to group tasks according to the desired semantics. From a transactional point of view, there are currently three possibilities (and combinations thereof): blocks as atomic units with the standard all or nothing semantics (sphere of atomicity), blocks as isolation units (sphere of isolation), or blocks as persistence units (spheres of persistence). In this regard, OPERA borrows heavily from existing work on advanced transaction models [Elm 92, Kle 91, CR 91, BDG+ 94].

Regarding atomicity, the information about the properties of the corresponding application must be provided by the user when the activity is registered. There are several options when selecting a task interface: *Basic* (non-atomic), *Semi-atomic, Atomic, Restartable*, and *Compensatable*. Basic tasks are the default and correspond to non-atomic applications, i.e., those for which OPERA cannot guarantee atomicity. Semi-atomic tasks are those providing enough information to implement a rollback method to be executed if the task fails before completing its execution. Atomic tasks are those that preserve atomicity by themselves, for instance, a transaction executed over an X/Open XA interface. Restartable tasks [ELLR 90] are those that can be invoked repeatedly until they eventually succeed. Compensatable tasks are those that can be undone after they have finished using an user provided method attached to the task interface[ELLR 90]. Note that these categories apply to activities, blocks, and sub-processes. Thus, it is possible to group a set of tasks into a semi-atomic block, for instance, or provide high level compensation for an entire sub-process by declaring it to be compensatable.

Spheres of persistence are used to avoid the overhead incurred by storing all process information in the instance space. The size of a process and the significance of the delay due to I/O while accessing the instance space is largely application dependent. When a task or a group of tasks is embedded within a sphere of persistence, every step of the execution is recorded in the instance space. This guarantees forward recovery in the event of failures. By default, all tasks are embedded within a sphere of persistence. It is possible, however, to switch this option off, in which case the information about the execution is maintained only in main memory. Upon completion, this information is stored in the instance or the history space for record keeping purposes but this is done off-line, thereby avoiding the I/O overhead.

The semantics behind the notion of spheres of isolation follow the ideas suggested in [AAE 96], which point out that processes may require more a notion of synchronization in the traditional operating systems sense than the traditional database concept of serializability. But there are also applications that clearly demand a database like approach (see below the description of HLOM). For these cases, spheres of isolation and spheres of atomicity are used in the scheduling performed by the navigator. Note that processes are essentially nested structures. This is best captured by using a nested transaction or multilevel model [Wei 91, M 81], which provides a powerful mechanism to reason about recovery in applications with a complex structure [GR 93]. A similar conclusion has been reached in several instances of middleware [BN 97, Cor 95c, CD 96, SSW 95]. Thus, the navigator in OPERA is based on recent work that extends the existing notions of nested and multilevel transactions and applies them to *composite systems* [ABFS 97]. The goal is to exploit the parallelism inherent in processes, guaranteeing at the same time that the order of execution specified by the process designer is respected. For this purpose, OPERA allows to label the control flow between two tasks as a *strong ordering* or a *weak ordering*. The strong ordering forces OPERA to match the externally derived ordering when scheduling tasks. This order reflects external dependencies that OPERA cannot ignore. The weak order, however, is used to indicate a particular order that becomes meaningful when tasks actually conflict. When conflicts do not exists, the weak order can be ignored. The advantage of differentiating between the strong and weak orderings is that OPERA has yet another degree of freedom to parallelize the execution of processes.

From a practical point of view, the theory of composite systems has the following implications: conventional parallel programming gives the choice of executing operations sequentially or in parallel ("do in parallel"). The mechanisms described allow to add a third possibility, "do in parallel in a given order", which executes operations in parallel but preserves the order in terms of externally observable effects. The OPERA navigator then becomes yet another layer on a hierarchy of schedules enforcing *stack conflict consistency* as explained in [ABFS 97].

3.4 Availability and Scalability

Unlike existing workflow management systems, OPERA provides support for generic processes. Business processes are a very special case in which issues like isolation or performance do not have significant role. In the same way that OPERA provides isolation capabilities for those processes that may need them, a significant effort has been made in OPERA to make it a robust and scalable system although this may not be a big issue in some cases [AAEM 97, AS 96]. Note that OPERA is to be interpreted more as a distributed operating system than as a workflow engine.

In terms of both scalability and availability, process support systems relying on a single database have a clear scalability limit and a single point of failure [KAGM 96]. To avoid these problems, OPERA relies on OCR to make its operations database independent. This has the advantage that several databases can be used at the same time and there is no need for them to be the same. For instance, the current prototype can use Oracle and Object Store simultaneously. OCR also allows the separation of spaces, which is probable one of the most significant factors when performance and scalability is considered. In a large system, it is not feasible to install the five spaces in a single machine. This would result in clear competition for resources. Since the five spaces are in practice orthogonal to each other, they can be located in different nodes. In this way, operations related to data mining and audit trail analysis (very significant in business and scientific processes) and operations related to execution use different databases. This reduces the system overhead but, as a result, certain non-key operations become more expensive. For instance, when a process is started, a copy has to be made from the template space into the instance space. If they are in different locations, this takes some time. For the cases in which this may become a problem, it is possible to prefetch process templates in advance.

As a further step towards enhancing scalability, OPERA allows to have several navigators working on different instance spaces. Such sub-systems share all the static information (template, history, object, and configuration) and may even share the same dispatcher (if the dispatcher becomes a bottleneck, several of them may also be run in parallel at the locations where the navigators are running). This opens up the possibility for OPERA to perform automatic load balancing by spawning new navigators and new instance spaces at other sites as the load increases. Several OPERA systems can also be interconnected to form a larger system.

In terms of availability, OPERA follows the suggestions of [KAGM 96]. The user can chose among three levels of availability for each process. The highest level of availability (*critical*), guarantees a hot-standby, 2-safe backup. If the primary system fails, the backup can take over immediately. The intermediate level of availability (*important*) guarantees a cold-standby, 2-safe backup. After a failure at the primary, execution can be resumed at the backup once the state of the process is brought up to date. It is also possible to run processes as *normal* processes, in which case no backup mechanism is used (but the process is still persistent, thereby allowing to resume execution as soon as the failure is repaired). These same mechanisms can be used to implement dynamic process migration.

The mechanisms used for backup and process migration have already been implemented and are on the testing phase. These tests will serve as a sort of validation of the OPERA concept as its generality and validity depend heavily on its ability to provide reasonable performance, scalability and availability. They will also help to optimize the design and detect potential bottlenecks. In particular, we are specially interested on possibility of using the backup mechanism to dynamically migrate processes from node to node, a feature that will considerably enhance the load balancing capabilities of OPERA as well as its overall scalability. Preliminary results look promising. Figures 10, 11, 12, and 13 show the cost associated with starting an activity, terminate an activity, starting a process, and the relative cost of these three operations for processes executed with availability level of normal, respectively. As far as current experiments show, the cost is quite reasonable. The most expen-

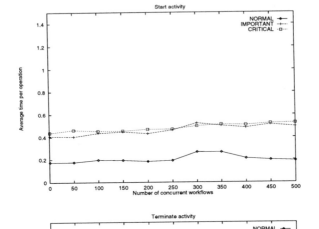

Fig. 10. Delay (in seconds) incurred when starting an activity.

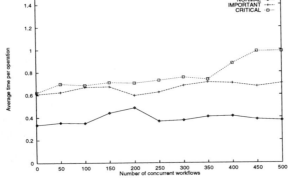

Fig. 11. Delay (in seconds) incurred when terminating an activity.

sive operation is starting a process, since this implies making a copy of the template and installing it in the instance space, in addition to performing the initial navigation steps. For applications in which the process duration is comparable to the figures shown, several optimizations are possible. For instance, the idea of providing spheres of persistence arises from the difficulty of providing reasonable response times if the process is kept in the instance space and each navigation step involves several access to the disk. The overhead incurred in these cases is not significant in business processes, but it will certainly have a considerable impact on applications like the ones described below. This will also reduce the time it takes to start a process. Another possible optimization is to keep the template in main memory to avoid having to copy it from the template space when the process is started. Similarly, the cost of terminating an activity can be reduced by performing navigation in main memory, without having to access the instance space. Note that terminating an activity involves determining what is to be executed next, a fairly complex operation requiring to evaluate several guards. A number of other

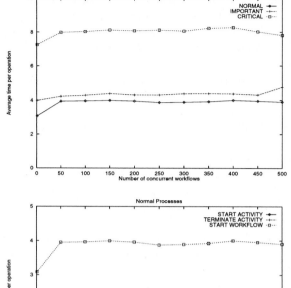

Fig. 12. Delay (in seconds) incurred when starting a process.

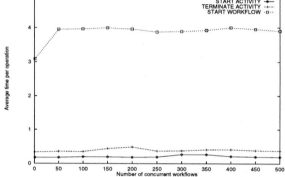

Fig. 13. Delay (in seconds) incurred when (a) starting an activity; (b) terminating an activity; (c) starting a process, shown for a process executed at availability level normal.

similar optimizations are possible, which gives us enough confidence in being able to improve those figures significantly.

3.5 Externalized Database Functionality

The advantages of the externalized database functionality provided by OPERA are best shown with a concrete application. Geo-Opera [AH 97] is an extension of OPERA for earth sciences processes. The most relevant aspect of Geo-Opera is the use it makes of OPERA functionality to track data dependencies. A process like the one in the example produces derived data that cannot be interpreted without knowledge about the process itself [Arm 88, Lan 88, LV 90]. This is related to the problems of lineage-tracking, change propagation and versioning [GG 89, Rad 91, SSAE 93]. Queries such as "which models use algorithm X", "which results may change if dataset Y is updated", and "which data sets are used to derive result Z" are typical of such environments. The mechanisms provided to deal with such queries are implemented as extensions to the exported database functionality module and the object manager.

In the object space, each external dataset is represented as an object. As shown in Figure 14, a number of attributes in each object allow maintaining detailed information about existing versions, lineage, and usage [AH 97, AE 94]. This information is updated by the navigator every time one of the objects is used, thereby creating a record of all possible dependencies between objects. As we foresee systems handling a large number of objects and processes, the effective management of the object space requires to be able to build indexes over this information. This, as well as building indexes over information externally stored, can be done using the exported database functionality module as explained in [BRS 96]. As an example of the functionality that can be provided, consider the active mechanisms implemented in Geo-Opera: *active objects* and *active tasks*. Active objects are automatically recomputed if some object they depend on has been modified. For instance, in the process of Figure 1, if the object "Hydrograph" is declared as active, it will be recomputed whenever a new version of the object "Rainfall Records" is available. To avoid expensive checks, the update takes place in a lazy manner. Instead of doing a search of all related objects every time an object is modified, the update takes place when an object is accessed. Detecting that an object needs to be recomputed is done by first calculating its lineage, which can be done by following the appropriate chain of pointers (Figure 14), and then looking for new versions of the objects found in the lineage, which is done by checking the corresponding attribute of each object in the lineage.

Similarly, active tasks are recomputed when some of their inputs are modified. This allows to get derived data automatically every time new input is available. As with active objects, the mechanism is recursive but, unlike active

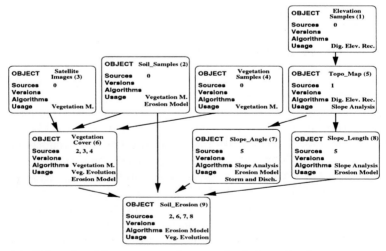

Fig. 14. Using the object space to keep track of dependencies among external datasets.

objects, is based on eager propagation, i.e., the task is recomputed every time one of the inputs changes. Thus, if the example of Figure 1 is defined as an active process, the entire process is recomputed whenever a new version of the object "Rainfall Records" is available, for instance. Note that the mechanism applies to tasks. This makes possible to apply the same idea to subprocesses and activities. Spheres of atomicity are used to avoid re-execution before the entire set of new input data is ready.

4. Application Examples

There are many examples in which functionality like the one provided by OPERA is needed. These include job scheduling in distributed systems, workflow applications, CORBA environments, OLAP and OLTP. The examples described below correspond to two research projects being carried out at ETH as extensions to the OPERA kernel.

4.1 High-Level Object Management (HLOM)

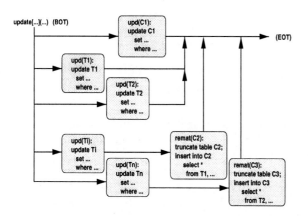

Fig. 15. Mapping of an object model operation to an OPERA process: execution dependencies on an update statement.

A first application of OPERA is within the HLOM project. OPERA treats clusters of workstations as heterogeneous shared-nothing multiprocessor platforms. HLOM is a research project in which higher-level parallelism is implemented over such clusters. Unlike other parallel database projects, the HLOM prototype is being built over stand-alone, off-the-shelf, commercial database systems which are treated as black boxes providing database services. Contrary to federated databases, HLOM is designed in a top-down manner, i.e., the designer has control over the data placement strategies, data partition, schema organization, etc. Some of the advantages of this approach have been demonstrated recently by implementing an object oriented database on top of a relational system [RNS 96]. In this preliminary work, the underlying database (Oracle) runs over a multiprocessor machine (Sun-Sparc Center 2000 with 10 processors). The operations specified in an object algebra (COOL) [TS 94], are translated into SQL statements executable in the relational database. The available parallelism is exploited by, first, using a physical design in which tables are replicated, and, second, by transforming intra-transaction parallelism (within the object algebra operations) into inter-transaction parallelism (among the resulting SQL statements). Compensation and a multilevel scheduling is used to enhance parallelism and avoid retaining locks for the duration of a top level transaction.

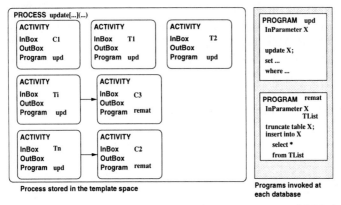

Fig. 16. Mapping of an object model operation to an OPERA process: the corresponding OPERA process.

HLOM is a generalization of this idea. It has been pointed out [Gra 95], that one of the main performance limitations of parallel databases is the fact that the client interacting with the database is not a parallel application. Asynchronous SQL, for instance, is a step towards addressing such problem. An alternative approach is to consider the sequences of operation invocations as processes and let OPERA manage their execution. In other words, OPERA acts as the database scheduler and distribution engine for HLOM, which is built from a collection of stand-alone databases. Figures 15 and 16 show an example of how a generic update statement (borrowed from [RNS 96]) can be expressed as an OPERA process (for simplicity the compensation mechanisms, also expressed in OCR have been omitted, for a more detailed explanation of how they can be used see [HA 97]). Since the designer has control over the data placement and schema distribution, the execution plan for each COOL statement can be predetermined. Thus, in the same way that in [RNS 96] COOL statements are translated into several Oracle transactions, in HLOM each COOL statement is mapped to a process. When a COOL statement is issued, it is parsed to determine the objects being accessed. This information is used as input parameters to the process, which will forward it to each individual task. Each task learns about which tables are to be accessed by consulting its InBox. The actual execution of each step takes place by invocating generic programs that can be parameterized. These can be implemented in a variety of ways, for instance, as stored procedures defined over each of the participating databases. A rough outline of how these programs look like is shown in Figure 16.

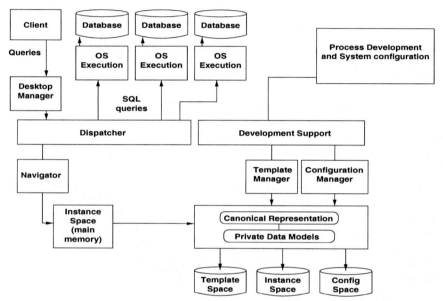

Fig. 17. Extensions and modifications to OPERA for HLOM

For the purposes of HLOM, OPERA is extended as indicated in Figure 17 (the OPERA components not represented are optional in HLOM). The desktop manager is converted into an interface for external clients (either as a console, or as an API). Clients submit queries through the desktop manager, who parses them and transforms them into process invocations, which are forwarded to the navigator. The query language (COOL in the case of [RNS 96], asynchronous SQL in future versions of HLOM) becomes the Application Modeling Language. The translation of the Application Modeling Language into OCR is performed using the same compiler and scheduler as in the centralized case [RNS 96]. Each resulting SQL statement is considered as a task, and each object statement is mapped to a process encapsulated within a single sphere of atomicity. Since SQL statements are treated as tasks (not activities) it is possible to further refine them into a subprocess to exploit the intra-query parallelism. HLOM uses as its concurrency control engine a multilevel scheduler [Wei 91] augmented with the ideas described in

[ABFS 97]. This engine is implemented as part of the navigator, using the transactional functionality of OPERA. In this model of correctness, locks are released before the parent transaction commits and compensation is used to undo any changes if needed. The functionality of OPERA is also useful in this regard. Every step of the execution plan (the process corresponding to the transaction) has a compensation action associated with it which is executed in the case of rollback. For the purposes of HLOM, the dispatcher needs additional information to be able to determine to which node a given SQL statement needs to be sent. This information is registered within OPERA using the standard interface provided. To help increase performance, a number of options provided by OPERA are turned off. The execution plans for object queries are not large processes. They can be easily kept in main memory to avoid the overhead of having to interact with the underlying repository after every activity terminates. One of the advantages of doing this is that the processes can be directly manipulated in OCR representation and there is no need to translate the operations into database operations. This, however, implies that the process execution is no longer persistent. Depending on the load at the navigator, it may be possible to checkpoint the state of the process by updating its image in the instance space. The decision about when to incur in this overhead is left to the user who can set the persistence level on a process (query) basis. It is here that the notion of spheres of persistence will play a major role. In addition, several navigators can be installed at different locations to help distribute the load. Although in principle OPERA supports databases of different type and residing in different networks (which can be exploited to build multimedia databases), the idea in HLOM is that the databases will be homogeneous and residing within the same LAN. This minimizes the cost of having to translate communication protocols and connecting different operating systems.

4.2 Distributed Object Management (DOM)

A similar idea to that of HLOM can be applied to heterogeneous data repositories. While HLOM is based on homogeneous components, the DOM project aims at integrating heterogeneous repositories by representing the information contained in them as virtual global objects. The idea is to provide database services to data residing outside the database. Such services include uniform object data modeling, view definition over multiple repositories, physical database design, query processing and optimization, and integrity constraint management. Some of these aspects have already been implemented as part of the Concert prototype, specially those related to physical database design [BRS 96], in which the database is seen as a dataless repository exporting its services to data residing in external repositories. Of particular interest in DOM is the fact that external repositories do not need to be databases. Basic building block within DOM can be file-, email-, project management, or library information systems. Since the advantage of using an object-oriented common data model is widely accepted [PBE 95], DOM is based on the ODMG data model [Cat 94], extended for a distributed environment [Rad 86].

Integration of such repositories into a global system requires a translation mechanism between their internal representation and the DOM model and vice versa. As an example consider a Unix file system and a library information system over which we would like to perform cross queries. The *Unix File System* holds files organized in a hierarchical directory structure. Files may have many internal structures, often known to a particular application only. Consider, for example, the BibTEX format used by the TEX system for storing literature references. A BibTEX file can be seen as lists of entries with a well-defined structure for each entry. Thus, such files can be accessed through an iterator interface providing operations like getting the first/next object, deleting/updating the current object, or inserting a new object (object meaning files, directories, BibTEX entries, etc.). Typical queries over such an interface are "retrieve the n_{th} object" or "how many objects are available". On the other hand, the *Library Information System* consists of a database with record-oriented data about publications (books, papers, and journals) and an information retrieval system for querying purposes. Both act as a black box system, in the sense that no interface for direct access to data records is provided. Access is only gained through a WWW search interface with very limited capabilities: search is based on particular attributes and similarity, always producing a list of publications. Such an interface does not provide concepts like *current object*, or navigation following a prescribed order, and does not allow to count the number of objects stored in the library, or ask for the next object. It is even not possible to ask for all attributes of the objects.

To solve this and similar problems, (semi-) automatic integration methods have in most cases shown to be impractical. DOM, instead, pursues a different approach in which repositories can be integrated gradually. In contrast to related work, we do not focus on schema integration. Instead, only selected required parts of the repository need to be wrapped and integrated. This is done on demand, such that a more and more refined object-oriented view of external repository data is achieved over time in a stepwise manner. In the example above, for instance, the goal is to be able to query BibTEX files for specific entries and join these information with the book entries in the library system. Consider the following query, asking for the names of authors (stored in BibTEX-files), the ISBN number of books (stored in the library system), and the name of the corresponding BibTEX-file, for all publications of 1997. The resulting publications are ordered by their relevance to the keywords "objects" and "distributed".

```
select b.author, o.isbn, f.fname
from BibEntries b, Books o, Files f
where b.key = o.ident
and b.year = 1997
sort by o.abstract.about("objects","distributed")
```

In DOM, the objective is to optimize the execution of such query minimizing communication cost, I/O cost, global and local processing cost. For this purpose, first the object SQL query is parsed and translated into an object algebra expression [TS 94]. These object algebra expressions (an example is shown in Figure 18a) serve as the starting point for query optimization. The result of this first step, an operator tree, is further optimized by a non-algebraic optimizer, that assigns concrete algorithms to the nodes of the operator tree and decides where to execute each of these nodes. The result is an execution plan such as that shown in Figure 18b. This execution plan is translated into an OPERA process and, henceforth, its completion is carried out as any other process within OPERA. The procedure is very similar to that described for HLOM.

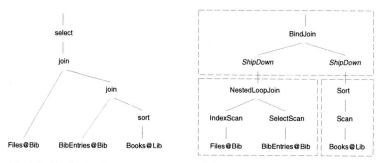

Fig. 18. (a) Algebraic Operator Tree and (b) Distributed Query Execution Plan

The extensions to OPERA necessary to implement DOM involve mainly those necessary to interact with heterogeneous data repositories. First, the desktop manager must incorporate the tools to translate queries into OPERA processes. This involves a language parser, algebraic optimizer, and non-algebraic optimizer. Unlike in HLOM, in DOM the mapping cannot be easily predetermined, hence the need to include an optimizer so as to avoid mapping a query into a process with too much overhead. In addition, since the external repositories may not provide any support for optimizing the execution plans, the object and query managers within OPERA are used to build indexes over external stored data. The mechanisms are similar to those described in the case of Geo-Opera. Similarly, the history space can be used to collect statistics and selectivity estimations to be used by the query optimizer. The interaction with external repositories takes place through the standard interface layer. In the case of DOM, these interfaces must be explicitly written to state the capabilities supported by the underlying system. This is a standard procedure when dealing with legacy applications since these interface can be seen as a wrapper. An example of such interface would be the iterator built over BibTEX files. If updates are considered, these interfaces need to be augmented to allow update operations. In this case, the same transactional functionality discussed for HLOM can be used in DOM to guarantee correct execution of update operations.

5. Conclusions

Surprisingly, and to our knowledge, there is no real attempt at tackling the general problem of designing and building a general platform for distributed processing using stand alone systems and applications. Many partial solutions exist, but there is an urgent need to integrate these solutions. In this regard, the paper has tried to specifically motivate OPERA taking as starting point the current situation of middleware products. Any serious analysis of this situation points out the need to integrate all this functionality. This is not just a hypothesis, many commercial and research efforts are moving towards such a goal. But, to our knowledge, there is no in depth study of how such systems should be built and what functionality they should incorporate. The proposed system is a first step towards evaluating such questions.

The Integration of Workflow Systems and Collaboration Tools

Nuno Guimarães, Pedro Antunes, Ana Paula Pereira

Instituto Superior Técnico (IST)
Instituto de Engenharia de Sistemas e Computadores (INESC)
R. Alves Redol 9, 1000 Lisbon, Portugal
email: {nmg,paa,app}@inesc.pt,guimaraesn@acm.org

Abstract. The design and development of computer support for work environments must consider both the coordination of individual activities and the collaboration that occurs among individuals in organizations. This paper presents our research efforts towards the understanding, design and implementation of a technological framework designated by "augmented work environments". These efforts build bridges between computational support for formal processes in organizational work (workflow) and computational support for interactive and informal processes (collaborative tools for group facilitation, decision or negotiation).

1. Introduction

This paper presents a particular dimension of our research efforts towards the understanding, design and implementation of a technological framework that we classify as "augmented work environments". These efforts aim at building bridges between computational support for formal processes in organizational work, which we see materialized in current

workflow technology, and computational support for interactive and informal processes, which we identify with collaborative tools for group facilitation, decision or negotiation. This is the fundamental motivation for the work presented here.

The concepts, designs, prototypes, and experiments that are reported in the paper were mostly produced in the scope of the Orchestra project [G 97]. The concerns expressed and addressed in this paper were already approached in two other publications related with the project's activities [AG 95a] and [GP 96].

The next section makes the concerns more explicit and lays a set of theoretical and conceptual arguments that justify our approach. The core arguments are a specialization of fundamental notions related with the design of interactive systems and human machine interaction. The two following sections describe the technological environment were we stand. The first of these two sections addresses workflow systems and technology, while the second overviews collaboration techniques and tools. The fifth section presents approaches to integration of those two independent but unseparable technologies. The core of this section is the report of our previous experience and the presentation of our current thinking on the subject. The final section summarizes the paper and highlights the main conclusions.

2. Concerns and Theoretical Foundations

The work described in this paper was influenced by a number of theoretical principles. Amongst those notions are the duality between coordinated and collaborative activity, the situated nature of work, and the perspectives of organizational structures and dynamics.

2.1 Coordination Versus Collaboration

A frequently used quote in the field of CSCW (Computer Supported Cooperative Work) is a statement of C. Ellis [EW 94], according to which *Workflow Systems automate a fiction*. The statement highlights the notion that organizational work is seldom a fixed flow of individual actions, but rather includes informal activities and spontaneous interaction between persons as members of a group.

Underlying the above quote is also a dichotomy between two related concepts: *coordination* and *collaboration* (as subclasses of Cooperation). Coordination is understood as a process by which the individual activities of the members of a group become organized (in terms of inputs, outputs and scheduling) by an external entity, in such a way that this organization leads to the predefined goal. Collaboration emphasizes the capability of self organization of those group members, which progress to the final goal through informal and mutual adjustment. Defined as such, workflow systems can be labeled coordination technologies, while tools for informal interaction like group decision and negotiation support systems are better defined as collaborative. A basic assumption in this separation, and in the remainder of this paper, is a rejection of any bias towards one or the other type of systems. Both are adequate in particular circumstances and address complementary issues in the computer support for organizational work.

2.2 The Situated Nature of Work

The title of this subsection points to the foundational notions presented by [S 87]. Those notions, presented in the scope of human machine communication, matches particularly well with the dichotomy mentioned above. In the context of group work, the automation provided by traditional workflow systems can be associated to *plans*. Just as for face-to-face or human-machine communication, *plans are inherently vague*. Workflow systems provide plans, as *resources*, for group interaction and work. However, these plans never define the complete details of the interaction, which are ultimately defined by the actual circumstances or situation.

Another important concept in this framework is the concept of *breakdown*. This concept is also central in [WF 86], and has its roots in reflections on cognition and language. According to these authors, *a design constitutes an interpretation of a breakdown and a committed attempt to anticipate future breakdowns*.

The contextualization of the above reasoning to the design and use of workflow systems in organizational settings leads us to the following questions: which resources are made available to groups and group members when prescribed plans breakdown in a workflow environment? Which alternate courses of action are provided to the group? Our suggestion is to provide support for informal group interaction, communication and decision.

2.3 Organizational Structures and Flows

A relevant body of theory is presented in [M 79, M 93] on organizational structure and dynamics. The general model for the structure of organizations includes five basic parts: (1) the operating core, (2) technostructure, (3) support staff, (4) strategic apex and (5) middle line. Based on the five part structure, linkages between the parts are defined, which characterize the organization as a system of flows: a flow of formal authority; a set of regulated flows; a system of informal communication; a system of work constellations; and a system of *ad hoc* decision processes.

This classification scheme for organizational structures and dynamics, suggests that regulated or formal flows are associated with coordinated actions, and therefore prone to be supported by workflow systems, while informal flows, work constellations and *ad hoc* decision processes, as essentially unplanned or situated, seem to be better suited to profit from collaborative technologies. Once again, and drawing on Mintzberg holistic view of the organizational life, the former cannot exist without the later, a conclusion that reinforces our integrative efforts.

2.4 Empirical Evidence

Another ground for our approach is the evidence drawn from observing workflow systems in use. The observations can be summarized as:

- Workflow systems eliminate paper based forms in standard processes.
- Control becomes easier and awareness of the processes status is increased. However, speed is not a major gain.
- The number of automated processes has a steep growth when a workflow system is put at work. However, the coverage of the workflow automation saturates: obviously automatable processes are no longer available, and the remaining ones are not obviously supported.

This observation leads to the conclusion that coordination-only systems have, in spite of its relevance and usefulness, a constrained space of intervention and therefore a limit to their impact in the organizational activities. A significant amount of group activities is related with the informal collaborative processes.

3. Orchestra: a Testbed Environment

The concepts presented in this paper have been consolidated in the Orchestra ·project. This project, its rationale, activities, partners, a nd results are described in [G 97]. Orchestra stands for ORganisational CHange Evolution, STRucturing and Awareness, and was an
EC funded project (ESPRIT 8764), involving a large number of partners (12), lead by INESC (94-96).

3.1 Objectives

The objectives of Orchestra can be interpreted in multiple ways. The conceptual framework of Orchestra was designed with the organizational theories in background and with the concern for organization-centered application of information technologies. Other more pragmatic reasons underlie the definition of the Orchestra project. Previous experience in the development and deployment of office systems, understood as primitive forms of organizational systems, allowed us to identify a set of needs that shaped the project:

- The lack of awareness about the organizational structure and dynamics has to be overcome with the inclusion of knowledge coming from social sciences and management experts.
- This knowledge must be incorporated in the tools provided to the organization, improving flexibility and support for re-organizati on decisions,
- Office, workflow and corporate information systems must be integrated to provide a seamless interface to the organizational worker.
- Communication must be flexible, both at the infrastructure level and at the user level, integrating the organizational knowledge mentioned above.
- Decision and negotiation tools can not be stand alone tools, but rather integrated in the context of organizational daily work.

The objective of the project was then summarized as: *to design and develop a group work environment that increases organizational effectiveness through better management of organizational information, improvement of the communication among individuals and groups, and support to the group decision and negotiation processes.*

3.2 Participants and Activities

The participants in the Orchestra project were software producers, social sciences experts, research and development institutions and user organizations. The user organizations were departments of large organizations: the administrative department of a Thermal Powerplant in Sines, Portugal, a holding organization for the Telecommunications sector in Lisbon, Portugal, and a department concerned with the planning of the Nuclear Fuel Purchases in Madrid, Spain.

The project as a whole addressed the following areas: organizational analysis, automation of organizational procedures, security, workflow management and information systems integration, interpersonal and organizational communication, negotiation and decision processes. The activities directly related with the purpose of this paper are described below.

3.2.1 Organizational Analysis and Modeling. The task of organizational analysis was undertaken by a social sciences team. This analysis was performed in the three pilot organizations. To guide the analysis, the Stream Analysis Model citePorras87 was adopted. The data collection process, based on semi-directive interviews to the key elements of the organizational units, allowed to capture the work and communication flows.

Given the organizational information, the project approached the problem of modeling workflow in the larger scope of organizational description and modeling. To support organizational and workflow modeling, the Taskon OORAM (Object Oriented Role Analysis and Modeling) [RWL 96] tool was used. The result was the production of a significant sample of workflow models (60-80) in computational form.

3.2.2 Workflow System Design and Development. The definition of the workflow functionality based on the initial prototypes, the evaluation of competing products, and the result of the project reviews, led to the design of a workflow system as an open and integratable component. The effort was put in the design and construction of a Workflow Engine, upon which specific applications could be designed and implemented. This design was a precursor of the approach currently promoted by the WfMC (Workflow Management Coalition).

3.2.3 Interactive Negotiation Tools. The construction of interactive negotiation tools or facilitation tools, had two dimensions in Orchestra: the first includes the design of a suite of tools for the specific computing environment of Orchestra. While related tools exist, the requirements for integration with other components, as well as the wish to elaborate on the interaction approaches, led us to these developments. Computer-based tools for three types of group interaction techniques were designed and implemented (Voting, Brainstorming and Nominal Group Technique). The second dimension relates with the problem, which relevance became clearer and clearer along the project, of linking together support for regulated of formal processes (traditional workflow) and support for informal and *ad hoc* decision processes.

4. Workflow Systems and Technology

This section reviews several classes of workflow technology. We first highlight aspects of some existing workflow systems (Flowmark, Staffware, Action and Action Metro) and groupware platforms. The modeling approaches are of particular relevance to us since they provide a departure point for our integration efforts. The proposals of the Workflow Management Coalition are another contribution to consider.

4.1 A Sample of Workflow Systems

4.1.1 IBM Flowmark. Flowmark [IBM 96, SHLL 95] is a client-server workflow management system based on workflow process models. An enactment service controls the execution of these models, which are linked to application programs using FlowMark's APIs. Application programs support the work to be done in a process activity and are defined by the developer.

Design Concepts The top level element of a FlowMark workflow model is the Process. A process is a sequence of activities that must be completed to accomplish a task. It defines how work is to progress from one activity to the next, who or what performs the activities, nested processes and how these subprocesses are distributed among servers, clients and databases. Activities are steps within a process. A Block is a modeling construct used for reducing the complexity of a process diagram, loop through a series of activities or implementing bundles. Connectors link activities in a workflow model. Control Connectors have transition conditions associated with it that direct the flow. Data Connectors specify the flow of data in a workflow model and Default Connectors specify where control should flow in the case of exceptional events.

4.1.2 Staffware. Staffware is a client-server workflow tool and one of the earliest workflow products. The most significant aspects of Staffware [SHLL 95] are its ability to support a distributed workflow environment containing a mixture of platforms and the possibility of installing the server in any number of nodes. A workflow process can span several servers and Staffware ensures the integrity of communications between the servers involved.

Design Concepts Staffware procedures are process definitions of workflow applications and are composed of steps. All data required for a procedure is defined into a case. Each time a Staffware workflow is initiated an individual case is created. Steps are used to model routing conditions and are a placeholder for scripts. Three types of steps are defined: normal steps, require user interaction and appear in the work queue for the user or group; automatic steps are designed into the procedure and invoke external applications that do not need user intervention; event steps are triggered by specific events and can be used to pause or suspend a case , deal with exceptions or change task data.

4.1.3 ActionWorkflow. ActionWorkflow [Act 96] is a client-server application that routes forms. Forms are the front end to a Lotus Notes or Microsoft SQL Server database. The Action workflow system is strongly based on a specific methodology. It enacts processes based on *conversation cycles* between entities generically designated as *customers* and *performers*.

Design Concepts ActionWorkflow modeling is rooted on the *speech acts* theory. This theory reduces interactions between people to conversations that are represented graphically as workflow loops. A conversation has four phases (preparation, negotiation, performance and satisfaction), two participants (a customer and a performer) and one objective (the performer must satisfy the customer within a defined period of time). The preparation is the initiation of the dialog. In the negotiation phase, the customer and the performer agree upon unique conditions of satisfaction for the particular instance of work. The performance phase is where the actual work is carried out, and it ends with the report that the work is complete. Finally, the acceptance phase closes the dialog loop, the customer accesses the deliverable and declares satisfaction or refuses to accept. Workflow loops can also include observers, which are not directly involved in the workflow but have access to information and data associated with it.

Processes are called business process maps and consist of a hierarchy of linked workflow loops. The first workflow loop to be initiated in a process defines its main objective and it is called the primary workflow. Secondary workflow loops are created when it is necessary to do something that cannot be adequately expressed in the primary workflow, thus replacing a phase of the primary workflow. Secondary workflows can also have secondary workflows and so on.

4.1.4 Action Technologies Metro. Action Metro is a process management solution available for the Internet environment, addressing the needs of organizations that wish to automate their business processes across a virtual enterprise. Action Metro is based on the Action Workflow coordination engine. Action Metro has several components that enable a standard Web browser to participate in an application. The core services of workflow are provided by two components: a personality module that translates data and commands from a Web browser to the Action workflow system and vice versa; and a set of HTML form templates, form responses and WorkBox form lists by which Metro receives information from, displays information to, and solicits responses from users.

4.2 Groupware Environments and Workflow Support Mechanisms

Recent years have witnessed the widespread use of what has become to be known as Groupware platforms. Two representative examples of this type of systems are Lotus Notes and recent evolutions of Microsoft Exchange. These platforms provide high level communication support, both inter-personal and inter-application, some degree of document management, and tools to build special purpose applications that use the base functionality. As such, workflow becomes one of the obvious directions of evolution.

4.2.1 Lotus Notes. Lotus Notes R4 [Lotus 96a, Lotus 96b] is a client-server application development, integrating a database and a messaging infrastructure. The Notes Application Development Environment (ADE) enables development of applications that store and route information objects using these database and messaging services.

The document database Notes is comprised of databases of *documents*. A Notes document is defined as an object containing text, graphics, video, and/or audio objects or any other kind of *rich text* data. Notes databases are semi-structured records consisting of basic design elements like Forms (for information entry and storage in the document), Subforms (objects in a Form that can be reused across applications), Collapsible sections (sections within a Form that can be expanded or collapsed depending on the need to view that particular piece of information), Fields (parts of a Form that contain a single type of information), Views (user-defined ways of looking at information), and Navigators (graphical tables of contents for a database).

The messaging infrastructure Notes databases are animated by the messaging infrastructure. Information is not just stored in or retrieved from databases but can be routed between users or even other databases. The Notes messaging infrastructure consists of a transport back-end that runs on almost any wiring topology and/or network operating system.

4.2.2 Microsoft Exchange Server/ Microsoft Outlook Client. Microsoft Outlook'97 [C 97] is a workgroup client combined with Microsoft Exchange, that combines messaging, group scheduling, personal information management and a form-design environment.

Outlook enables creation of custom groupware and workflow applications based on customized forms. Typically, custom forms will be stored in a Microsoft Exchange Server forms registry along with forms created using Microsoft Exchange Forms Designer. Outlook Forms can also be included as part of an e-mail message that can be sent across the Internet. The groupware applications can be made richer through the use of the Microsoft Visual Basic programming system, Scripting Edition (VB Script) and ActiveX Controls.

4.3 Workflow Modeling Approaches

The modeling facilities of workflow systems have a fundamental impact on the power and usability of such systems. Just as software programs and systems, workflow as an inherent complexity that grows together with the organizational complexity. Workflow modeling is the process of capturing the work processes and describing them in a machine understable form. Every workflow system tends to have its own modeling component. On the other hand general tools for systems analysis and modeling can be considered as providers of modeling support. Three basic categories of process modeling methodologies are considered:

- Activity based methodologies focus on modeling activities and tasks. Workflows consist of tasks and each one may be comprised from subtasks. This is the model used by most of the commercial workflow management systems but it does not capture process objectives such as customer satisfaction.
- Commitment based methodologies are based in an interpretation of work as the coordination of actions where the flow of work can be specified through speech acts. A process in a workflow is an interaction between a customer and a performer. This is the approach of the Action family of products and systems.
- Object-oriented methodologies model workflow as communicating objects. Jacobson=B4s model is made of actors and use cases [JEJ 95]. The *role model* is the basic abstraction used in OORAM [RWL 96]. A role model describes the subject of object interaction, the relationships between objects, the messages that each object may send to its collaborators, and the model information processes.
  Each object can play several roles in different role models.
  Object orientation provides no explicit support for workflow process modeling. The object designer typically must define workflow model specific objects from scratch (eg, customer, employee, document, step, etc) as it was done in the models described in [GP 96] and [FC 96].

The first two types of modeling approaches were illustrated in the previous section. Workflow systems like Flowmark or Staffware reinforce Activity-based modeling methodologies. Action and Metro are the most striking examples of a Commitment based methodologies. The use of object oriented methodologies in modeling workflow systems is an approach that is being pursued in multiple contexts. In Orchestra, we adopted the Taskon OORAM methodology and tool as an open approach to workflow modeling. For further details on the use of this methodology, see [G 97] and [RWL 96].

4.4 The Workflow Management Coalition

The Workflow Management Coalition[1] was established in August 1993 as a non-profit international body for the development and promotion of standards for software terminology, interoperability and connectivity between workflow products. A glossary and a framework for workflow systems have been proposed.

4.4.1 Models and Architectures. All workflow systems contain a number of generic components which interact in a variety of ways. The model (fig. 1), identifies the major components and interfaces:

---

[1] http://www.aiai.ac.uk/WfMC

- Process Definition Tools are used to analyze, model and describe business processes, as mentioned in the previous sections.
- Workflow Enactment Service is the run-time environment where workflow processes are executed (or enacted). This may involve more than one work-flow engine. This service is responsible for reading process definitions, and creating and managing process instances.
- Workflow Client Applications are the software entities which present work items to the end user, invoke application tools which support the task and the data related to it, and allow the user to take actions before passing the case back to the workflow enactment service.
- Administration and Monitoring Tools can be used to track process status, for control, management and analysis purposes.

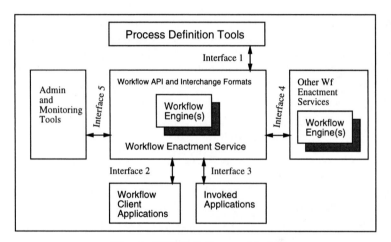

Fig. 1. WfMC Reference Model

The standardization efforts of the WfMC is focused on the five interfaces to the workflow enactment service:

- Interface 1: process definition import/ export interface
- Interface 2: interaction with workflow client applications and software for presentation of worklists
- Interface 3: tools and external application invocation
- Interface 4: interoperability between several workflow management systems
- Interface 5: interaction with Administration and Monitoring Tools

4.4.2 Openness and Reusability Directions - WPDL. One of the in-terfaces being standardized that has, in our perspective a direct impact on the proposals that we make in this paper, is the Process definition import/export interface. This interface normalizes the final format of a work process descrip-tion. This definition led to a common interchange format, the Workflow Process Definition Language (WPDL), which supports the transfer of workflow process definitions between separate products.

The WPDL definition proposes a set of extensibility mechanisms to support vendor specific requirements. This is based on the definition of a Workflow Meta-Model, a limited number of entities that describe a workflow process definition (the "Minimum Meta Model"). The meta-model identifies a basic set of entities and attributes for the exchange of process definitions: Process Definition, Process Activity, Participant Definition, Transition Information, Application Definition, and Process Relevant Data. These entities contain attributes which support a common description mechanism for processes. Further entities and attributes may be added to the model to create future conformance levels.

The WfMC proposal document includes one representative business case that can be used to verify the feasibility of the implementation of the standard, as well as to constitute a preliminary test of a conformance assessment procedure. The business example describes a fictitious company, FBN Sports Equipment Company, its departments, and business or work processes. The example details the analysis and definition of the work processes, and its further specification in the WPDL format. Just for the sake of providing the reader with a flavor of the language, see extract below.

```
WORKFLOW At the Sales Department
        WPDL_VERSION    1.0
        VENDOR  Vendor:Product:Release
        CREATED 1995-12-06
// <Activity List>
// <Transition Information List>
END_WORKFLOW
PARTICIPANT Tim White
        TYPE            HUMAN
        USERID          tw456
        SURNAME         White
        FORENAME        Tim
        DESCRIPTION     Mail Room Clerk
END_PARTICIPANT
PARTICIPANT Presidents_Secretary
        TYPE            ROLE
        PERSONDESCR     France Baroque
        DESCRIPTION     handles presidents mail
END_PARTICIPANT
APPLICATION scan_document
        TOOLNAME        winscan.exe
        OUT_PARAMETERS  scanned_document
END_APPLICATION
DATA document_type
        TYPE            string
        DEFAULT_VALUE   Sales Order
END_DATA
DATA scanned_document
        TYPE            reference
END_DATA
```

5. Collaboration Approaches and Technologies

This section addresses the support for collaboration in three dimensions: existing collaboration technology, techniques for group decision and interaction, and high level decision models that regulate group interaction. These are the elements of a framework required for effective support to group collaboration, as well as for adequate integration with coordination technology.

5.1 Collaboration Technology

Technology support for informal processes can be associated with a broad range of computer based technologies. Electronic mail has been the technology with broadest dissemination and a large number of studies have been published on the specific issues related with the impact of electronic mail in organizational life. Similarly, teleconferencing and videoconferencing has progressively been introduced to overcome the physical limitations of interpersonal and intergroup communication. These technologies are however limited to the physical dimensions of the communication, either time, such as electronic mail, or space, such as the telephone or conferencing facilities. In particular, no attention is given to the interactive process that may be carried out over those physical supports.

Beyond the above mentioned technology, the most relevant nature of current and emerging collaboration technology is the support for particular styles of group interaction processes. Examples of this styles are argumentative processes that occur for example in collaborative authoring environments [SGHH 94], or decision or negotiation processes that can be found as the object of support in multiple GDSS's (Group Decision Support Systems)[N+ 91].

Several classification tags exist for collaborative technology. The basic classification divides the possible systems into four (4) classes according to the time-space x same-different combinations. Other aspects that have impact on the classification of collaborative systems include size of the group, types and structure of the groups, process support, etc.

5.1.1 GroupSystems. GroupSystems, from Ventana Corporation[2] , is one of the most successful electronic meeting support software systems. The system runs on a generic infrastructure of networked personal computers. The functionality is provided by a set of complementary components that includes: Agenda (supporting electronic brainstorming, idea categorizer, voting tools, topic commenter, and group outliner), People (supporting the management

---

[2] http://www.ventana.com

of group's information), Whiteboard (for group interaction through a shared drawing space), Handouts (for structured information sharing), Opinion meter (quick polling), Briefcase (for auxiliary tools), Personal Log and Event Monitor.

5.1.2 MeetingWorks. MeetingWorks, from Enterprise Solutions[3], is another electronic meeting system that provides tools for managing the several steps of a meeting, with specific support for brainstorming sessions. This support includes idea organization, ranking, voting, impact analysis and other tools. A distinction is made between facilitator (*chauffeur*) and participants.

Fig. 2. The Ocean Lab at GMD-IPSI - printed with permission.

5.1.3 Dolphin and the Ocean Lab. Dolphin [SGHH 94, MHS 95] is the system used in the Ocean Lab[4], at GMD, Darmstadt, Germany. The Ocean Lab is an electronic meeting room designed to study multiple types of computer based support for cooperative work. From the infrastructure point of view, the lab is characterized by the coupling of personal workstations with electronic boards (LiveBoard or Smart Board). Dolphin is the interactive hypermedia system that provides support for private and public interaction, idea and work organization, and multiple levels of sharing . The environment has been used intensively and continuously in the research of the new cooperation modalities [SRH 97].

---

[3] http://www.accessone.com/entsol
[4] http://www.darmstadt.gmd.de/publish/ocean

5.2 Techniques for Group Decision and Collaboration

Techniques for group decision and negotiation are based on the social behavior of people in small groups. This subsection presents a sample of those techniques. The objective is to point out multiple choices for a given group decision situation.

5.2.1 Brainstorming. Brainstorming is the most known method of idea generation and is in worldwide use [HL 87]. Webster defines it as: to practice a conference technique by which a group attempts to find a solution for a specific problem by assuming all the ideas spontaneously contributed by its members . The technique employs four basic rules [PGP 89]: criticism is ruled out; Free-wheeling is welcomed (the wilder the idea, the better); Quantity is wanted (the greater the number of ideas, the more like-hood of winners); Combination and improvement are sought.

A number of variations of the technique have been devised [HL 87, N+ 91]: anonymous brainstorming, electronic brainstorming, brainwriting, the Trigger Method, the Sil Method. Studies of brainstorming suggest that it produces a wide range of ideas while promoting group enthusiasm.

5.2.2 Delphi. The Delphi process is applied to complex and unstructured problems, in order to develop the strongest pro and con arguments for a set of alternative solutions [T 91]. The Delphi process is based on individual and silent indexDelphi generation of suggestions and arguments which are solicited by a facilitator to the group members. The phases followed by the facilitator are [HL 87]: (1) Initial questionnaire. This questionnaire is intended to collect a broad spectrum of answers to a particular problem; (2) Analyis of the questionnaire. From this analysis, executed by the facilitator, results a list that summarizes the objects identified by answers to the questionnaire. The list is presented to participants, preserving anonymity. (3) Second questionnaire. The facilitator develops a new questionnaire, which allows to identify areas of agreement and disagreement. The participants are requested to present opinions and vote the list of objects; (4) Analysis of the second questionnaire. Votes are counted and a summary of comments is associated to each object; (5) Third questionnaire. A new questionnaire is developed, allowing to identify agreements and disagreements among participants; (6) Final report. The final report allows to summarize the process results and legitimate future actions.

Delphi is based on the anonymity of the group members and is particularly oriented towards avoiding direct confrontation. Decisions with Delphi express opinions rather than facts which requires group members to be experts. One other important characteristic is that Delphi does not require physical presence [R 92].

5.2.3 Nominal Group Technique. The NGT is a participative data collection and consensus-forming device [S 83]. The basic format of a NGT meeting is based on a facilitator which ensures that the group development runs through the following phases: (1) Individual silent generation of a list of ideas; (2) Individual round-robin feedback, where each group member describes one idea from the individual list. A global list is then generated; (3) Group clarification of the ideas in the list, removing overlapped ones and clarifying any inconsistencies; (4) Individual voting and prioritizing of ideas; (5) Discussion of results, perception of consensus and focus on potential next steps; (6) The NGT meetings are designed to generate a high quality list of prioritized ideas but has been found to be very sensitive to the performance of the group facilitator [HL 87].

5.2.4 Survey. This technique allows managers to ask for information while taking decisions alone. Subordinates may or may not be told about what the problem is [ML 87]. The Vroom & Yetton's model describes the situations where this level of participation is appropriate [VJ 88]. One major requirement is that the problem should be structured.

5.2.5 Voting. Voting is a group decision-making method in a democratic society, an expression of the will of the majority. It is a multiple criteria decision making process whenever a voter casts a vote to select a candidate or alternative policy. There are two basic voting systems: the non-ranked voting in which each voter has one and only one vote, and the preferential voting in which the voter indicates in what order of preference he/she would place the candidates. The first system is indicated when the number of candidates are two, and the second system when the number of candidates are more than two and it is necessary to protect the minorities and the spreading of representation over a reasonably wide range of interests [R 55].

A large number of other techniques are available for consideration in every group decision making situation, but the above are already an illustration of alternate forms of social techniques that we should consider in designing and developing computer based tools for group work.

5.3 Decision Models

Decision models provide systematic views on how people and groups handle several variables in the course of a decision processes. This subsection outlines specific perspectives of the decision processes that are relevant for the integrative approaches we are presenting.

5.3.1 Contingency view of decision processes. One important model that characterizes decision making processes in organizations and groups is the Thompson & Tuden's contingency model for group decision making [B 91]. This model is concerned with the understanding of decision making from the intended solution point of view. It considers two criteria related with the problem that asks for a solution, or decision: (1) Uncertainty about ends (the intended outcomes); and (2) Uncertainty about means (the solutions used to achieve the desired ends). Based on this distinction, it maps the combination of high and low scores on these criterias in four types of decision making processes:

- Computation. Well known ends and solutions.
- Judgment. Selection of solutions for well known ends.
- Bargaining. Resolving of disagreement over ends.
- Inspiration. Unknown ends and solutions.

5.3.2 Task view of decision processes. The McGrath's typology of group tasks [ML 87] classifies what a group is expected to do: (1) Generate plans or ideas; (2) Execute some task; (3) Negotiate disagreements; and (4) Choose any issues or answers. These four classes are further refined according to the level of required cooperation (cooperation versus conflict) and skills (behavioral versus conceptual).

5.3.3 System's view of decision processes. The Hwang & Lin's approach to expert judgments/group participation [HL 87] focuses on decision making from a system viewpoint, regardless of organizational, political and social factors. The model considers four types of problems: (1) Idea stimulation; (2) Issue clarification; (3) Problem structuring; and (4) Problem solving. The model then maps these problems onto four types of facilitation: (1) Creative confrontation; (2) Polling of experts/participant ideas; (3) Systematic structuring; and (4) Simulation. The mapping is based on the following criteria:

- Definition of the problem: well defined, semi-defined or ill-defined.
- Scope of the problem: narrow, medium or broad.
- Time required to accomplish the task: hours, days, weeks.
- Training of participants: needed, not needed.
- Tools required to accomplish the task.

5.3.4 The Participation view of decision processes. The Vroom & Yetton's model[5] addresses the different degrees of group participation in decision making from the manager's viewpoint [VJ 88]: (1) Manager decides alone; (2) Manager asks individually for information but decides alone; (3) Manager asks individually for information and evaluation but decides alone; (4) Manager meets with group to discuss a problem but decides alone; and (5) Manager meets with group to discuss a problem and the group makes the decision.

The decisions suggested by this model are based on the following criteria: (1) Quality requirements; (2) Information available; (3) Problem structure; (4) Acceptance by those affected by; (5) Subordinate implication; and (6) Probability of conflict among members.

---

[5] A software tool exists that implements this model and provides aids to a manager.

5.3.5 The Group Membership and Interaction. The Stumpf et al. [ML 87] model focuses on the typology of group processes in two aspects that complement the participants' view: membership and interaction. The model uses the following criteria: (1) Quality of the decision; (2) Acceptance by those affected by; (3) Requirement of a creative or original decision; (4) Span of the decision; (5) Knowledge and information needs; and (6) Probability of conflict among members. Based on the above criteria, it decides on group membership: experts, coworkers, and/or representatives of all relevant constituencies. The model also suggests the type of group interaction: face-to-face interchange during the whole process, face-to-face interchange only in evaluation phase, or no face-to-face interchange at all.

The fundamental conclusion from this section is that we have available a large spectrum of knowledge and approaches that provide systematic views on the decision processes. The se allow us to conceptualize the computational support to group interaction, and, in turn, relate it with the coordination approaches and technologies presented in the previous sections.

6. The Integrative Approaches

The previous sections presented the scenario for the integrative approaches On the first hand, we have available a significant set of methodologies and technologies for supporting essentially formal and coordinated processes or workflow. On the other hand, we are aware of the existence of models and techniques that characterize group decision as an essentially informal or collaborative process. The issue to be addressed in the design of an integrative approach is the bridge between the multiple models and techniques.

This section identifies the dimensions of this specific problem. First, it summarizes a perspective that considers collaboration tools as a mechanism to handle coordination exceptions. Then, it generalizes the notion of alternate coordination and collaboration. Finally, it explores the idea that some sort of equivalence, or mapping, must be found between coordinated and collaborative work.

6.1 Identifying Exceptions

Exceptions in organizational work are explicitly addressed, for example, in [SW 95]. It this work, exceptions are classified as follows:

- *Established exceptions* are events where appropriate handling rules exist but they are either incomplete or the exact set of rules to be applied cannot be identified.
- *Otherwise exceptions* are events that lack handling rules but, given the rules for the normal cases, the goal of handling the exception is clearly defined

– *True exceptions* are completely unanticipated events where no preparation exists, and neither the normal situation, nor the specific goal or state that results from handling the exception is defined.

Another dimension of exceptions is the effect that their handling has on the rule base of an organization. In this context, exceptions can have the following types:

– They *do not affect* the rule base.
– Exceptions *cause instance level updates* (e.g. odd invoices are handled specifically, but do not change the way invoices are handled in general)
– Exceptions *cause type level updates* (e.g. general rules for handling invoices are changes due to the occurrence of some kind of relevant exception).

This short classification of exceptions allows us to define the problem space of our initial integrative approach. Some coordination-support systems will be more flexible in handling less dramatic exceptions (the first ones in the above lists), in which case the switch to a collaborative scenario can be minimized. For higher complexity exceptions (the later types in the above lists), collaborative action is the adequate exception handling approach.

6.2 Collaboration as a Handler for Coordination Problems

In Orchestra, the project mentioned in the beginning of the paper, the integrative approach was taken in the design of integration mechanisms between the workflow systems and a set of interactive negotiation and decision tools [AG 95a].

The Orchestra approach can be summarized as follows: the workflow system must be able to identify situations where formalized solutions do not exist.

Once identified, and categorized as a problem to be solved through an informal interaction, several group interaction techniques are available for supporting that interaction. A match between problem characteristics and available group interaction techniques has to be found. As a consequence, an informal process is activated through the execution of the computer-based tool that supports the selected technique [AG 95b]. The outcome of the informal process is then fed back into the workflow system which progresses with the execution of the formal flow. The concept is illustrated below in fig. 3.

6.2.1 The Integration Architecture. The architecture that supports this approach is depicted in fig. 4 and performs as follows: first, the Workflow engine detects an exception during the execution of an organizational procedure. Assuming that it is not able to handle the situation, it gathers all the available information concerning the exception and generates a flow interrupt. The interrupt is delivered to the Negotiation system which handles the situation through cooperative techniques and tools. When the problem

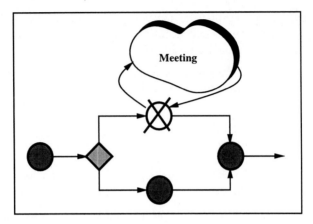

Fig. 3. Meetings or informal processes as solutions to breakdowns

that raised the interrupt is solved the workflow engine may continue with the execution of the procedure.

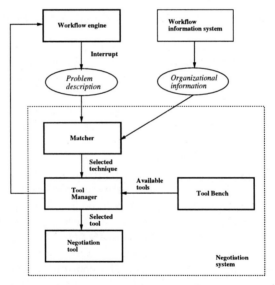

Fig. 4. An architecture for the Integration of workflow systems and GDSS tools

The Negotiation system is composed by the Matcher, the Tool Bench and the Tool Manager. The Matcher receives interrupts from the workflow engine and gathers relevant information. Based on this information, it classifies the problem, identifies the agents to be involved in a group decision process, and the most adequate technique solve the problem. This results in the selection of one group interaction technique and the delivery of that information to the Tool Manager. The Tool Manager instantiates a tool from the Tool Bench and connects the agents with the tool.

6.2.2 Criteria for Problem-Matching Techniques. The decision models described above were considered in the design of the Matcher functionality : Thompson and Tuden's contingency model for group decision making; Hwang and Lin's systems approach to expert judgments and group participation; McGrath's typology of group tasks; Vroom and Yetton's contingency model of participation; and the Stumpf, Zund and Freeman's contingency model for group decision making.

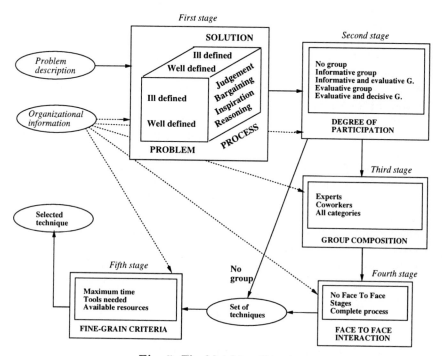

Fig. 5. The Matching Criteria

The Mapping from Problem to Technique The mapping from problem to technique is made by the Matcher in the following five stages (see fig. 5):

– First Stage: the first stage deals with fundamental and general criteria. This stage considers different values for three basic aspects of:
  1. Problem - Ill defined or well defined;
  2. Solution - Ill defined or well defined;
  3. Process - judgment (selection of solutions), bargaining (resolving of disagreement over solutions), inspiration (search for inspired solutions) or reasoning (rational approach).

The output of this stage corresponds to the selected subset of techniques that results from crossing the values for Problem, Solution and Process. One can argue about how appropriate values for Problem, Solution and Process are assigned. This assignment can be based on several attributes which should be extracted from the Workflow system or otherwise requested to a human agent.

– Second Stage - Degree of Participation: the degree of participation needed to solve the problem is identified. The major concern is the formation or not of a group or committee to make the decision. The degree of participation of the members of this group in the final decision is also defined, since its members may act as simple consultants or as more active participants. The possible degrees of participation follow the guidelines of the Vroom and Yetton model. When there is no need for a group, the Matcher will jump over the third and fourth stages, which are dedicated to group oriented techniques. Some of the techniques identified in this stage require a facilitator. The output of this stage will specify the need and qualification of this manager. The Matcher will also suggest a name of a person who could act as the manager.

– Third Stage - Group Composition : at this stage, the Matcher has already identified the need for a group or committee. It then decides on the qualification of the group. This decision is based on the Stumpf et al. model. The names of people who could be part of the group are also provided.

– Fourth Stage - Face to Face Interaction : at the fourth stage, the need for face to face interaction is considered. The output will be a subset of the group of techniques which fulfill the requirement established in the stage about the face to face interaction. The possible requirements were extracted from the Stumpf et al. model.

– Fifth Stage - Fine-Grain Criteria : in this last stage the Matcher assigns values to fine-grain criteria, in opposition to the other more formal criteria considered in the previous stages. The output of this stage will designate a single selected technique, without discarding the previous selections notwithstanding.

The complete output of the Matcher is the following:

1. A subset of techniques selected by the first stage.
2. The need or not for a group to solve the problem.
3. If needed, the qualification of a human facilitator and, optionally, the name for this facilitator.
4. If needed, the qualifications of the group members and, optionally, their names.
5. A subset of techniques complying to the required face to face interaction.
6. A single technique complying with the above and the fine-grain criteria.

6.2.3 The Tool Manager and the Tool Bench. The description of the functionality of the Tool Manager is of particular interest here, since it directly mediates the operations of the Workflow with the group negotiation processes.

The Matcher does not select a tool for executing a particular negotiation process but rather identifies a set of techniques and a set of actors. The Tool Manager is responsible for selecting and launching a tool that will execute the selected technique. It is also responsible for returning control to the workflow system when the group interaction is finished.

The Tool Manager selects tools according to a catalog provided by the Tool Bench. First, the Tool Manager inquires the Tool Bench on the availability of tool support for the single selected technique. If the technique is not implemented, the alternative techniques indicated by the Matcher are inquired in order: face to face interaction, group composition, degree of participatio and, finally, the first stage of the Matcher. As new tools are implemented and incorporated to the Tool Bench, the Tool Manager should be able to select them and the Matcher should be able to discriminate them. If not, the Matcher has to be upgraded with new criteria in the second level.

The Tool Bench is the repository of tools implementing group interaction techniques. Only a small number of the identified techniques has presently been selected for implementation and inclusion in the Tool Bench. At this moment, the intention is to achieve a minimum coverage of the possible selections of the first stage of the Matcher. Five techniques have been selected: Delphi, Nominal Group Technique (NGT), Brainstorming, Voting, and Survey.

6.3 Beyond Exceptions

The view of work as a cooperative and group interaction process suggests a generalization of the computational support that encompasses formal-coordinated actions and informal-collaborative meetings as equal contributors for the efficacity of organizational work. This perspective is depicted in the figure 6(a) below. Coordinated steps are defined as complementary to informal meetings.

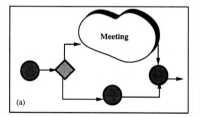 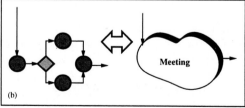

Fig. 6. (a) Meetings (informal processes) as steps is real life work; (b) Meetings and Flows as equivalent forms of work.

This view is not currently supported by most of the available workflow technology. Some systems, specially the ones we classified as Commitment-based methodologies, may have an advantage in this context.

In fact, the foundation provided by a conversational model allows a level of abstraction that encompasses both formal and informal interaction. The problem, however, is that the commitment based approach (in particular, the Conversations-for-Action models) is hard to extend to groups of participants, and we would still be left with a wide range of undefined parameters, namely the ones addressed by the Orchestra integration approach (Matcher) and described above.

If we consider coordination and collaboration as particular sub-classes of cooperation, then we should search for higher level models that allow the mapping of a given cooperative process onto a given coordination or collaborative system. This further level of abstraction is even more relevant, insofar it opens the possibility of transformations between coordinated processes and collaborative processes, which in fact translates to transformation, at the level of the computational support, between formal and informal processes (see fig. 6(b)).

We believe that this is the fundamental progress to be sought, given its relevance to the integration of cooperative technology with the organizational change and transformation processes (the so called reengineering). Much of the reenginering processes affect the formality degrees in several places in the organizational structure. This bridge enables what we designate as *reengineering for participation.*

The design of the transformation mechanisms is currently under research. The initial approaches consider the following baseline:

- The recent progresses in the structuring of the workflow systems and technologies, namely the Worflow Management Coalition models and interfaces, provide an important framework for the identification of the different components and types of information that have a role in coordination systems. In particular, the Workflow Process Definition Language (WPDL) is an example of a structuring tool that can be used to other ends than just the enactment of a process through a workflow engine. WPDL descriptions are descriptions of coordinated work processes and include much of the information (recall the WPDL example) required to refine an integrative approach such as the Orchestra one.
- The framework developed in Orchestra, that associates group interaction tools with the requirements of group decision techniques, is another departure point for the analysis of the relation between those tools and the descriptions of work mentioned above.

The missing links in the integration, which we are currently seeking, are:

– A fine-grained set of criteria that allows to encapsulate a work process is such a way that it can be generalized as a group process, independent of its coordinated or collaborative nature.
– A significant amount of empirical studies, made on information concerning real work processes of a wide range of organizations. This effort is capitalizing on the Orchestra data, but requires further contributions.

7. Conclusions

The concepts and approaches presented in this paper address the problem of improving work environments. Work environments are understood as scenarios for cooperation among people that participate in group and organizational activities. The cooperation has two fundamental facets: a coordinated and a collaborative one. After defining this dual nature, the paper demonstrated that there are both theoretical and empirical grounds to define this separation. Moreover, we stated that, in what concerns computer-support, workflow systems are coordination support systems and tools like electronic meeting rooms or conferencing tools are designed to support collaboration.

In both areas, workflow and collaboration tools, we are faced with a growing dissemination of technologies, standards, methodologies and models. The paper has presented some examples of those, and pinpointed the relevant areas where integration between these two types of systems can be sought.

One of the main conclusions of the paper is the design of viable approaches to the integration of workflow systems and collaborative tools. The first approach was designed and prototyped in the Orchestra project. It essentially links the functionality of a workflow engine with a set of interactive discussion and negotiation tools. The collaboration tools take the role of an exception handler for the workflow system. The innovation lies in the concepts upon which the "linking" mechanism is

built namely, a clear knowledge of the purpose of the several collaboration techniques, and a computational integration of hints provided by organizational decision models.

The experience with the design of this first approach led us to the proposal of a more generalized and challenging approach which tries to integrate coordination and collaboration as alternative forms of cooperation. The design and implementation of the mechanisms for this type of integration is an open question. However, based on the theoretical foundations, on the empirical data, and on the experience with our own projects and prototypes, we believe that this type of integration carries a significant added value and will become an enabling factor for what we have coined as "reengineering for participation".

Interoperability in Large-Scale Distributed Information Delivery Systems

Ling Liu, Ling Ling Yan, M. Tamer Özsu

University of Alberta, Department of Computing Science
Edmonton, Alberta, Canada T6G 2H1

Abstract. In this paper we address interoperability issues in large-scale distributed information delivery systems. Architecturally, we classify existing approaches and systems into two paradigms: *Multidatabase management-based* paradigm and *Mediator-based* information delivery paradigm, and analyze the techniques used in each. Technically, we describe a number of data delivery characteristics in terms of delivery protocols, delivery modes, and delivery frequencies. We further use these characteristics to discuss and compare several data delivery schemes. We argue that an advanced distributed information system must incorporate different types of information delivery so that the system can be optimized according to various criteria, such as network traffic and heterogeneity and constant evolution of online information sources. To illustrate the architectural and technical aspects of distributed information delivery systems, we review a number of research prototypes to demonstrate the various implementation approaches used in practice, and the different solutions to the interoperability issues addressed in the paper.

1. Introduction

In the past few years there has been an explosion in the amount and diversity of information available across networks. The proliferation of Internet and intranets and the ongoing advances in the World Wide Web (WWW or Web) have fueled the development of a wide range of data-intensive applications and information dissemination systems. Many new ways are being explored to deliver information contents to users in office, at home, and on the road.

A common problem facing many organizations and enterprise computing systems today is the uniform and scalable access of multiple, disparate information sources and repositories, including databases, object stores, knowledge bases, file systems, digital libraries, and information retrieval systems. It is widely recognized that information sources change constantly, and users are faced with the daunting challenges of navigating, collecting, evaluating, and processing data in this dynamic and open information universe. Decision makers often need information from multiple information sources but are unable to get and fuse information from multiple information sources in a timely fashion, not only due to the unpredictable state of networks and the contention at information sources, but also due to the heterogeneous and evolving nature of information sources.

An "advanced" distributed information system is an open and interoperable system, rather than a static data delivery system. Two immediate functional requirements of such a system is the support of extensible distributed object management and dynamic interoperability among diverse information sources and between information consumers and information producers.

In terms of object-oriented terminology, *interoperability* refers to the ability to exchange requests between objects and the ability to enable objects to request services of other objects, regardless of the language in which the objects are defined and their physical location (e.g., hardware platforms, operating systems, DBMS's). *Distributed interoperable objects* are objects that support a level of interoperability beyond the traditional object computing boundaries imposed by programming languages, data models, process address space, and network interface [Bet 94]. The abstractions of distributed interoperable objects are captured and utilized by the distributed object management services to schedule and control the remote data access and delivery.

A key objective in providing interoperability and distributed object management in a dynamic and open information universe is the *scalability* and *effectiveness* of remote data access and delivery.

- Scalability refers to the ability of distributed object management services to scale the process of delivering information (in the form of objects) from a set of data sources to a typically larger set of consumers, with respect to both the heterogeneity in hardware platforms, process address spaces, operating systems, data models and programming languages, and the evolving nature of information sources.
- Effectiveness of remote data access and delivery refers to the ability of distributed object management services to incorporate the constant information evolution and explosion, the network traffic, and the availability of information sources or communication links, into the distributed query optimization and execution strategies.

Query optimization and evaluation strategies have long been studied in centralized, parallel, and tightly-coupled distributed environments. However, data access across widely-distributed and highly autonomous information sources imposes significant new challenges for distributed object management for a number of reasons. First, there are semantic and performance issues that arise due to the heterogeneous nature of the data sources. Second, the amount and diversity of online information available across networks is exploding. Users today are faced with increasing difficulty in collecting, processing, and integrating information effectively and in a timely fashion. As the scale and rate of change for online information continues to grow, the user-initiated, comprehensive searching is no longer sufficient as a dominant mode of information access and delivery. To improve the query responsiveness, remote data access and delivery must combine user-initiated, comprehensive searching with source-initiated dissemination of relevant information, and migrate from pre-established communication endpoints to anytime-access-anywhere on the globe. Finally, data access over wide-area networks today depends heavily on the specific data sources accessed and the current state of the network at the time that such access is attempted, including the availability of information sources, intermediate sites, and communication links.

In this paper we describe a number of techniques and strategies that are used or can be used to address these technical challenges. We also present a brief review of the state-of-the-art in research and development for accessing multiple and heterogeneous information sources. The reminder of the paper is organized as follows. We outline the architectural issues in supporting inter-operability of multiple and heterogeneous information sources in Section 2, and outline a number of mechanisms for effective information delivery in distributed and interoperable information systems in Section 3. In Section 4 we overview several representative systems or ongoing research projects that contribute to the issues of dynamic interoperability and scalable distributed object management . A few popular enabling technologies for deployment and implementation of interoperable distributed object management services is summarized in Section 5. In Section 6 a brief overview of the AURORA project that we are currently developing for the electronic commerce domain is presented. We end the paper with a summary and some remarks on the role of database technology within the global information infrastructure, in particular the wide-range of data-intensive applications being deployed on the Internet and intranets.

2. Architectural Issues

Over the last decade, several approaches and paradigms have been proposed for information access and delivery from multiple heterogeneous information sources. To simplify the review, we classify the state-of-the-art of research and development into two paradigms: *Multidatabase management-based* paradigm and *Mediator-based* information delivery paradigm. In this section we concentrate on the architectural issues of data access and delivery with respect to these two paradigms. We discuss the techniques and challenges for delivering information effectively and responsively, in Section 3.

2.1 Multidatabase-Based Paradigm

Multidatabase management has evolved over years and through several stages. A classic approach [R 91, S 91] for multidatabase management relies on building a single global schema to encompass the differences among the multiple local database schemas. The mapping from each local schema to the global schema is often expressed in a common SQL-like language, such as HOSQL in the Pegasus system [Aea91] or SQL/M in the UniSQL/M system [Kea93]. Although the enforcement of a single global schema through data integration yields full transparency for uniform access, component databases have much restricted autonomy, scalability and their evolution becomes difficult.

The federated approach [SL 90] improves the autonomy and the flexibility (composability) of multidatabase management by relying on multiple import schemas and the customized integration at various multidatabase levels. However, the integration of component schemas at each multidatabase level is enforced by the system. The integrated schema is static. The heterogeneity problems are resolved at the schema integration stage. This approach cannot scale well when new sources need to be added into an existing multidatabase system. Also the component schemas cannot evolve without the consent of the integrated schema.

The distributed object management approach [Man92, ODV 93] generalizes the federated approach by modeling heterogeneous databases of different levels of granularity as objects in a distributed object space. It requires the definition of a common object model and a common object query language. Recent activities in the OMG and the ODMG standard [Cat 94], which extends the OMG object model to the database interoperability, are important milestones for distributed object management .

2.2 Mediator-Based Paradigm

Mediator-based information integration architecture has evolved from an initial proposal by Gio Wiederhold in [Wie 92] and elaborated through the intelligent information integration (I^3) program [Wie 95]. A mediator-based system consists of a network of mediators. *A mediator is a software module that exploits encoded knowledge about some sets or subsets of data to create information for a higher layer of applications* [Wie 92]. Intuitively, each mediator offers a specific data service and acts as an information "broker" in a particular application domain. Mediators often have knowledge-based capabilities.

The most interesting features that distinguish the mediator-based paradigm from conventional multidatabase management approach are the following:

– On the information source side
  1. The information universe it addresses is large-scale, dynamic, and open in nature, rather than small-scale, static, and closed.
  2. Information sources considered in mediator-based systems include not only *structured* sources such as relational databases, object stores, and knowledge-bases, but also *semi-structured* information sources such as HTML files, WWW pages, or *unstructured* data sources such as plain text documents, images, video clips.
  3. Information sources are highly autonomous. The amount of information sources and applications available online is very large and grows rapidly.

The content, the number, and the connectivity of information sources change constantly. Heterogeneity problems become a natural and unavoidable consequence.

– On the interoperability management side

1. The set of functions for interoperability management are divided and packaged into two architectural tiers: mediator-tier and wrapper-tier . The mediator-tier is responsible for interfacing with applications and end-users. The wrapper-tier is responsible for interfacing with underlying information sources. A wrapper can be seen as a special type of mediator that deals with idiosyncrasies of the individual data sources such as translating a mediator tier request to executable instructions at the source.

2. There is no single global view or system that can serve for all applications. Different mediator-based systems may access shared information sources. All information sources accessed within a mediator system are wrapped using the mediator system-specific interface language. The same information source may be wrapped differently for different mediator systems. A wrapper serves as an agent or a delegate of a particular mediator system to communicate with the underlying (wrapped) information sources.

3. The scalability and extensibility issues become a major concern and an important evaluation criteria for interoperability management. Object-oriented design, programming, and development technology is a powerful and yet practical paradigm for building distributed information systems.

4. The role of ontology and classification hierarchies becomes increasingly important for dynamic interoperation and heterogeneity resolution between information consumers and information producers.

Architecturally, mediator-based systems are more flexible since wrappers are built independent of one another and are used to serve for all accesses to the corresponding data sources in the system.

There are many prototype systems and ongoing projects for developing mediator-based interoperability management systems. They vary in the way mediators and wrappers are built, functionality and capability that different mediators may provide, and ways of dividing functional components between mediator-tier and wrapper-tier. We will discuss some of the representative systems in Section 4.

3. Technical Issues

With the ongoing advance in WWW technology, everyone today can publish information on the Web at any time. The flexibility and autonomy of producing and sharing information on WWW is phenomenal. On the other hand, one has to learn to deal with the rapid increase of volume and diversity of online information and the constant changes of information sources in number, content, and location. Thus, queries to the current WWW search tools are mostly specified independent of the structure, location, or existence of requested information. One simply types in the keywords, the search tools will handle the request and find the sources that match the given keywords. However, the scalability is achieved at the price of effectiveness of queries, namely the quality and the responsiveness of the answers, for several reasons. First, responses returned by WWW search tools often contain too much irrelevant information (noise). Second, queries in network-centric information systems are more vulnerable to failure due to the congestion of networks, traffic at the intermediate sites and the contention at the sources. Thus frequently one needs information from multiple information sources but is unable to get and fuse the information from information sources in a timely fashion.

A practical optimization solution to these problems is to provide technologies that support a variety of data delivery schemes and allow the scheduling process of queries to be tuned at run-time according to the state of networks and the availability of intermediate sites and source sites. One example of such technology is to combine and interleave the user-initiated, comprehensive search-based data delivery with the server-initiated dissemination of relevant information.

In this section we describe a number of data delivery characteristics [FZ 96] in terms of protocols, delivery modes, and delivery frequencies, and use these characteristics to discuss and compare several data delivery schemes.

3.1 Data Delivery Protocols

Data delivery is defined as the process of delivering information from a set of information sources (servers) to a set of information consumers (clients). There are several possible ways that servers and clients communicate for delivering information to clients, such as clients request and servers respond, servers publish what are available and clients subscribe to only the information of interest, or servers disseminate information by broadcast. Each way can be considered as a protocol between servers and clients, and has pros and cons for delivering data in an open and dynamic information universe.

3.1.1 Clients Request and Servers Response. The *request/response* protocol follows the data delivery mechanism that clients send their request to servers to ask the information of their interest, servers respond to the requests of clients by delivering the information requested.

Current database servers and object repositories deliver data only to clients who explicitly request information from them. When a request is received at a server, the server locates or computes the information of interest and returns it to the client. The advantage of the *request/response* protocol is the high quality of data delivery since only the information that is explicitly requested by clients is delivered. In a system with a small number of servers and a very large number of clients, the *request/response* mechanism may be inadequate, because the server communication and data processing capacity must be divided among all of the clients. As the number of clients continuous to grow, servers may become overwhelmed and may respond with slow delivery or unexpected delay, or even refuse to accept additional connections.

3.1.2 Servers Publish and Clients Subscribe. The *publish/subscribe* protocol delivers information based on the principle that servers publish information online, and clients subscribe to the information of interest. Information delivery is primarily based on the selective subscription of clients to what is available at servers and the subsequent publishing from servers according to what is subscribed.

As the scale and rate of changes for online information continues to grow, the *publish/subscribe* mechanism attracts increasing popularity as a promising way of disseminating information over networks. Triggers and change notifications in active database systems bear some resemblance to the *publish/subscribe* protocol based on point-to-point communication [AFZ 97]. The *publish/subscribe* mechanisms may not be beneficial when the interest of clients change irregularly because in such situations clients may be continually interrupted to filter data that is not of interest to them. A typical example is the various online news groups. Another drawback is that publish/subscribe is mostly useful for delivering new or modified data to clients, but it cannot be used to efficiently deliver previously existing data to clients, which the clients later realize they need. Such data are most easily obtained through the request/respond protocol.

3.1.3 Servers Broadcast. The *broadcast* mechanism delivers information to clients periodically. Clients who require access to a data item need to wait until the item appears. There are two typical types of broadcasting: *selective broadcast* (also called *multicast*) and *random broadcast* [FZ 96]. Selective broadcast delivers data to a list of known clients and is typically implemented through a router that maintains the list of recipients. Random broadcast, on the other hand, sends information over a medium on which the set of clients who can listen is not known *a priori*. Note that the difference between selective broadcast and *publish/subscribe* is that the list of recipients in selective broadcast may change dynamically without explicit subscription from clients.

The *broadcast* protocol allows multiple clients to receive the data sent by a data source. It is obvious that using broadcast is beneficial when multiple clients are interested in the same items. The tradeoffs of broadcast mechanisms depend upon the number of clients who have common interests and the volume of information that is of interest to a large number of clients [FZ 96, AFZ 97].

3.2 Data Delivery Modes

With the rapid growth of the volume and variety of information available online, combined with the constant increase of information consumers, it is no longer efficient to use a single mode of data delivery. A large-scale modern information system must provide adequate support for different modes of data delivery in order to effectively cope with the various types of communications between clients and servers to improve query responsiveness. Another benefit of providing different modes of data delivery is to allow the system to be optimized for various criteria according to different requirements of data delivery. In this section we identify three potentially popular modes of data delivery and compare them with the types of delivery protocols that can be used. They are client pull-only option, server push-only option, and client pull with server push combined option.

3.2.1 Pull-only Mode. In the *pull-only* mode of data delivery, the transfer of data from servers to clients is initiated by a client pull. When a client request is received, the server responds to it by locating the requested information. The *request/respond* style of client and server communication is *pull-only*.

The main characteristic of pull-based delivery is that the arrival of new data items or updates to existing data items are carried out at a server without notification to clients unless clients explicitly poll the server. Also, in pull-based mode, servers must be interrupted continuously to deal with requests from clients. Furthermore, the information that clients can obtain from a server is limited to when and what clients know to ask for. Conventional database systems (including. relational and object-oriented database servers) offer primarily pull-based data delivery.

3.2.2 Push-only Mode. In *Push-only* mode of data delivery, the transfer of data from servers to clients is initiated by a server push in the absence of specific request from clients. The main difficulty of push-only approach is to decide which data would be of common interest, and when to send them to clients (periodically, irregularly, or conditionally). Thus, the usefulness of server push depends heavily on the accuracy of a server to predict the needs of clients. *Broadcast* style of client and server communication is a typical *push-only* type.

In push-only mode, servers disseminate information to either an unbounded set of clients (random broadcast) who can listen to a medium or a selective set of clients (multicast) who belong to some categories of recipients that may receive the data. It is obvious that the push-only data delivery avoids the disadvantages identified for client-pull approaches such as unnoticed changes. A serious problem with push-only style, however, is the fact that in the absence of a client request the servers may not deliver the data of interest in a timely fashion. A practical solution to this problem is to allow the clients to provide a profile of their interests to the servers. The *publish/subscribe* protocol is one of the popular mechanisms for providing such profiles. Using publish/subscribe, clients (information consumers) subscribe to a subset of a given class of information by providing a set of expressions that describe the data of interest. These subscriptions form a profile. When new data items are created or existing ones are updated, the servers (information providers) publish the updated information to the subscribers whose profiles match the items.

3.2.3 Hybrid Mode. The hybrid mode of data delivery combines the client-pull and server-push mechanisms. The continual query approach described in [LPBZ 96] presents one possible way of combining the pull and push modes, where the transfer of information from servers to clients is first initiated by a client pull and the subsequent transfer of updated information to clients is initiated by a server push.

The hybrid mode represented by continual queries approach can be seen as a specialization of push-only mode. The main difference between hybrid mode and push-only mode is the initiation of the first data delivery. More concretely, in a hybrid mode, clients continuously receive the information that matches their profiles from servers. In addition to new data items and updates, previously existing data that match the profile of a client who initially pull the server are delivered to the client immediately after the initial pull. However, in push-only mode, although new data and updates are delivered to clients with matching profiles, the delivery of previously existing data to clients that subsequently realize that they need it is much more difficult than through a client pull.

3.3 Data Delivery Frequency

There are three typical frequency measurements that can be used to classify the regularity of data delivery. They are

- *periodic*: Data is delivered from server to clients periodically. The period can be defined by system default or by clients using their profiles.
- *conditional*: Data is delivered from servers whenever certain conditions installed by clients in their profiles are satisfied. Such conditions can be as simple as a given time span and as complicated as sophisticated ECA rules.
- *ad-hoc* or *irregular*: A data delivery is requested at any time from clients to servers and the matched data items are sent to clients from servers within a reasonable response time.

3.3.1 Periodic Data Delivery. Both pull and push can be performed in periodic fashion. Periodic delivery is carried out on a regular and pre-specified repeating schedule. A client's weekly requests for the stock price of IBM is an example of periodic pull. Periodic pull is a simpler case of the request/respond protocols. An example of periodic push is when an application can send out stock price listing on a regular basis, say every morning. Using period push, a set of data items is sent out periodically according to a pre-defined schedule.

Since the pattern repeats, a client who misses a data item in one period of the pattern can get it in the next one.

Periodic push is particularly useful for situations when clients might not be available at all times or might be unable to react to what has been sent, such as in the mobile setting where clients can become disconnected.

3.3.2 Conditional Data Delivery. Conditional delivery is mostly used in the hybrid or push-only based delivery systems. Using conditional push, data are sent out according to a pre-specified condition rather than any particular repeating schedule. An application that sends out stock prices only when they change is an example of conditional-push. An application that sends out the balance statement only when the total balance is %5 below a pre-defined balance threshold is an example of hybrid conditional push. Conditional push assumes that changes are critical to the clients and that clients are always listening and need to respond to what is being sent. Hybrid conditional push further assumes that missing some update information is not crucial to the clients.

3.3.3 Ad-Hoc Data Delivery. Ad-hoc delivery is irregular and is performed mostly in a pure pull-based system that uses traditional request/ respond protocol of data delivery. Data is pulled from servers to clients in an ad-hoc fashion whenever clients request it. In contrast, periodic pull arises when a client uses polling to obtain data from servers based on a regular period (schedule).

3.4 General Remarks

An advanced distributed information system must incorporate different types of information delivery so that the system can be optimized according to various criteria, such as network traffic and heterogeneity and constant evolution of online information sources. Based on a number of important characteristics of distributed information delivery discussed in the previous sections, we provide below a brief comparison of data delivery mechanisms.

The three protocols that are considered here are *request/respond*, *publish/subscribe* and *broadcast*. Table 1 shows a comparison of the use of different protocols or frequencies of data delivery with respect to the modes of data delivery.

As we mentioned in Section 3.1, most of the conventional database systems are pull-based data delivery systems and use the request/respond protocol for data delivery, where clients pull servers by sending requests to the servers and servers respond by locating and computing the data items that match the requests and delivering the results to the corresponding clients. Clients can pull the servers anytime (including a periodic time span controlled by clients) whenever there is a need for information from servers. Since the pulling of servers is always initiated by users in an ad-hoc fashion, rather

Table 1. A combination of techniques applicable to different modes of data delivery

	request/ respond	publish/ subscribe	broadcast	periodic	conditional	ad-hoc
pull only	Y			Y		Y
push only		Y	Y	Y	Y limited	
hybrid	Y	Y	Y	Y	Y limited	Y

than monitored by a computer program automatically, neither broadcast, publish/subscribe nor conditional delivery is relevant.

The pure push style of data delivery is very useful when the volume of information of common interest is huge and/or the number of clients who are interested in the same amount of information is large. The push-only delivery can also be seen as an optimization strategy that reduces the traffic and server load when the volume of information of common interest at a particular server continues to grow. The publish/subscribe protocol is typically used for server-initiated information dissemination, where data is delivered automatically (push-only) or semi-automatically (hybrid mode). The frequency of such server push is either according to a periodic (regularly repeated) schedule or based on a conditional schedule. Ad-hoc delivery frequency does not make much sense in practice for push-only mode. The broadcast protocol is also a push-only delivery protocol. But it is mostly used for server-initiated periodic delivery. The publish/subscribe protocol can be seen as a specialization of the broadcast protocol by incorporating profiles of clients that specify what groups of information to subscribe, such that the servers only publish the information to the clients, which match their profiles.

4. Overview of Some Existing Projects

We discuss in this section a few projects that are either the well-known systems (such as Carnot), or mostly related to the mediator-based architecture discussed in Section 2. (such as TSIMMIS, DIOM, DISCO, InfoSleuth), or to the data delivery mechanisms outlined in Section 3. (such as Broadcast Disks project). Space limitation prevents us from being exhaustive.

4.1 Broadcast Disks Approach to Information Dissemination

The broadcast disks approach [AAFZ 95, AFZ 97, FZ 96] to information dissemination uses a periodic push-only data delivery with broadcast protocol. The broadcast disks paradigm is based on a cyclic broadcast of objects (e.g., pages) and a corresponding collection of client cache management techniques.

The main idea is to explore multi-level frequencies of disks and their relationship to cache management. For example, using broadcast disks, groups of objects (e.g., pages, disks) are assigned different frequencies depending on their probability of access. By broadcasting higher priority items more frequently, their access times can be reduced at the expense of increasing the latency for lower priority items. A key issue here is the generation of a broadcast schedule that can deliver the data items of different priority requirements most efficiently.

A broadcast schedule is generated based on the number of disks, the relative frequencies of each disk and the assignments of data items to the disks on which these items are to be broadcast [AFZ 97]. Interesting to note is that the multi-levels are in fact superimposed on a single broadcast channel by interleaving the data items of the various levels in a manner that results in the desired relative frequencies. For instance, consider a simple broadcast of three objects (pages), say A, B, C, arranged on two disks, where A is on a disk that is spinning twice as fast as the disk where B, C are located. If we have two levels of disk frequency, say 2:1, data item A has a higher priority than data items B and C. Thus, a broadcast schedule would generate the following broadcasting pattern: "A, B, A, C, ..." [FZ 96]. One of the difficulties in deciding how to structure a broadcast schedule is that the server must use its knowledge to reason about the needs of the clients who require disseminated data. Intelligent management of client caches is a key to solving this problem.

As we mentioned earlier, most of database systems and current Internet browsers are pull-only style of data delivery systems. The Broadcast Disks project developed a set of strategies and algorithms for a periodic push style of data delivery. Currently, an integrated dissemination-based information system is under development as a continuation to the Broadcast Disks project at Brown University and University of Maryland, aiming at supporting a wider range of ways to deliver data to clients [AFZ 97].

4.2 Carnot

The Carnot Project [CHS91, WCH+93] at MCC has developed and assembled a large set of generic facilities for managing integrated enterprise information. These facilities are organized into five sets of services: communication services, support services, distribution services, semantic services, and access services. The Carnot architecture is shown in Figure 1.

The communication services provide the user with a uniform method of interconnecting heterogeneous equipment and resources. These services implement and integrate various communication platforms that may occur within an enterprise. Examples of such platforms include ISO OSI session and presentation layer protocols running on top of ISO TP4 with CLNP, TCP/IP via a convergence protocol, or X.25. Additional platforms being considered are OSF's DCE and UI's Atlas.

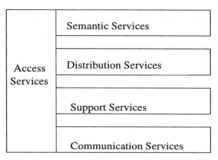

Fig. 1. Architecture of Carnot

The support services implement basic network-wide utilities that are available to applications and other higher level services. These services currently include the ISO OSI Association Control (ACSE), ISO OSI Remote Operations (ROSE , CCITT Directory Service (X.500), CCITT Message Handling System (X.400), ISO Remote Data Access (RDA), and MIT Project Athena Authentication Service Kerberos). Work is progressing on support for additional services, such as ISO Transaction Processing, OMG's Object Request Broker (ORB) and Basic Object Adapter (BOA), interfaces to Information Resource Dictionary Systems (IRDS), and Electronic Data Interchange (EDI).

The distribution services layer supports relaxed transaction processors and a distributed agent facility that interacts with client applications, directory services, repository managers, and Carnot's declarative resource constraint base to build workflow scripts. The workflow scripts execute tasks that properly reflect current business realities and accumulated corporate folklore. The declarative resource constraint base is a collection of predicates that expresses business rules, inter-resource dependencies, consistency requirements, and contingency strategies throughout the enterprise. Carnot's Distributed Semantic Query/Transaction Manager (DSQTM), based on the work of OMNIBASE [R 89], provides relaxed transaction processing services. It dynamically expands a query to include access to all semantically equivalent and relevant information resources, and also groups any updates to these resources as a set of independent transactions that interact according to a dynamically defined relaxed transaction semantics.

The semantic services provide a global or enterprise-wide view of all the resources integrated within a Carnot-supported system. This view, or portions of the view, can be compiled for use within the distribution services layer. The Enterprise Modeling and Model Integration facility uses a large common-sense knowledge base as a global context and federation mechanism for coherent integration of concepts expressed within a set of enterprise models. A suite of tools uses an extensive set of semantic properties to represent an enterprise information model declaratively within the global context and to construct bidirectional mappings between the model and the global context. There are two interesting features of semantic services: First, a key to coherent integration is Carnot's use of the Cyc common-sense knowledge base as a global context. Further, Carnot uses the knowledge representation language of Cyc to express both the information structures and the processes of an enterprise. The broad coverage of Cyc's knowledge enables it to serve as a fixed-point for representing not only the semantics of the formalisms, but also the semantics of the modeled domains. Second, the relationship between a domain concept from a local model and one or more concepts in the global context is expressed as an articulation axiom equivalence mapping. Enterprise models are then related to each other – or translated between formalisms – via this global context by means of the articulation axioms. As a result, each enterprise model can be integrated independently, and the articulation axioms that result do not have to change when additional models are integrated. This same technology can also be used to integrate database schemas and database views. Besides its common-sense knowledge of the world, Cyc knows about most data models and the relationships among them. This enables database transactions to interoperate semantically between, for example, relational and object oriented databases.

The access services provide mechanisms for manipulating the other four Carnot services. The access services allow developers to use a mix of user interface software and application software to build enterprise-wide systems. Some situations (such as background processing) utilize only application code and have no user interface component. In other situations, there is a mix of user interface and application code. Finally, there are situations in which user interface code provides direct access to functionalities of one or more of the four services.

4.3 DIOM

The DIOM project [LPL 96, LP 97] presents a concrete implementation of the mediator-based interoperability management infrastructure described in Section 2.2. Users may pose queries to DIOM on the fly, namely queries can be specified independently of the structure, the content, or the existence of information sources. The DIOM query mediation manager first filters the queries by creating user query profiles and then dynamically matches the queries to the information sources that are relevant at the time the query is processed. Additional features that distinguish DIOM from other systems include the dynamic query scheduling strategies, such as the dynamic query routing algorithms, the dynamic query execution planning strategies, and the set of result assembly operations. In DIOM application-specific mediators are created through specialization of meta mediator query processing framework, which includes DIOM metadata manager for managing user query profiles and source capability profiles, the distributed query scheduler, and the generic wrapper manager functions. Figure 2 presents a sketch of the DIOM system architecture currently developed using SunJDK version 1.1 and accessible from `http://ugweb.cs.ualberta.ca/diom/`.

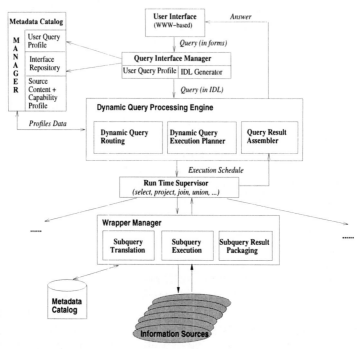

Fig. 2. The distributed query scheduling framework in DIOM

The main task of DIOM distributed query mediation manager is to coordinate the communication and distribution of the processing of consumer's queries between a mediator and wrappers to the relevant data sources. The processing at mediator layer includes query routing, query execution planning, and result assembly. The processing at wrapper layer involves the subquery translation and execution and the subquery result packaging.

Query routing is responsible for locating and selecting relevant information sources that can actually contribute to answering a query. *Query execution planner* is responsible for the decomposition of a user query into a set of subqueries, each targeting at a single source, and then generating a query execution schedule that is optimal in the sense that it utilizes the potential parallelism and the useful execution dependencies between subqueries to restrain the search space, minimize the overall response time, and reduce the total query processing cost. *Subquery translation and execution* process basically transforms each subquery into an executable program that can be executed at the source. The DIOM *query result packaging and assembly* process involves two semantic resolution phases for resolving the semantic variations among the subquery results: (1) packaging each individual subquery result into a DIOM object (done at wrapper level) and (2) assembling results of the subqueries in terms of the consumers' original query statement (done at mediator level). The semantic attachment operations and the consumers' query profiles are the main techniques that are used for resolving semantic heterogeneity implied in the query results [LP 97].

4.4 DISCO

DISCO, the Distributed Information Search COmponent [TRV 96, TRV 97], adopts the general mediator-based paradigm, and can be seen as another concrete instance of the mediator-based approach. The DISCO mediator data model is based on ODMG-93 data model specification. It extends the ODMG-93 Object Definition Language (ODL) with two constructs:

1. *Extents.* An interface in DISCO may have a bag of extents. Each extent in this bag mirrors the extent of objects of a particular data source, associated with the interface. This extension is fully integrated into the ODMG model, the full modeling capabilities of the ODMG model are available for organizing data sources. DISCO evaluate queries on extents and thereby on data sources.
2. *Type mapping.* This extension associates type mapping information between a mediator type and the type associated with a data source.

In addition, DISCO defines two standard ODMG interfaces: `Wrapper` and and `Repository`. A DBA can add a new data source into DISCO in a few steps. First, the DBA creates an instance of the `Repository`:

```
r0 := Repository (host="rodin.inria.fr", name="db",
       address="123.45.6.7")
```

Second, the DBA locates a wrapper , implemented separately, for the data source. A wrapper is an object with a standard interface that identifies the schema and functionality of a source. It is also able to answer queries, such as `w0 := WrapperPostgress()`. In the third step, the DBA defines the type in the mediator which corresponds to the type of the objects in the data source.

```
interface Person {
      attribute String name;
      attribute Short salary;}
}
```

Finally, the DBA specifies the extent of this mediator type: `extent person0 of Person wrapper w0 repository r0;` This adds extent `person0` to the `Person` interface. The name `person0` is determined by the name of the data source in the repository, it could be a relation name or an object type name. To add a new data source containing `Person` objects, say `person1`, one needs to add an extent called `person1` to the mediator type `Person` explicitly, i.e., `extent person1 of Person wrapper w0 repository r1;` DISCO provides constructs to specify a name for the `Person` extent that includes all the sub-extents specified as above. Assume this extent is defined to be `person`. Then DISCO is able to process queries such as `select x.name from x in person where x.salary > 10`.

Whenever a new source becomes available or a new relation or class type is added to an existing source, it is DBA's task to include the new object (class or relation or data source) into the existing mediator types by following the above procedure. This process can become expensive when a large number of mediators need to include this new class or this new source.

Query processing in DISCO is performed by cooperation between the mediator and the wrappers in two ways: (1) Determine whether a subquery can be evaluated by the wrapper; (2) Determine the cost of a query execution plan where the wrapper evaluates some subqueries. A partial query evaluation model where *the answer to a query is another query* is also studied, which defines semantics of accessing unavailable data sources [TRV 96].

4.5 InfoSleuth

InfoSleuth [BBa 97] is a mediator-based project at MCC that extends Carnot technology to meet the challenges presented by the World Wide Web. Although Carnot has developed semantic modeling techniques that enable the integration of static information resources and pioneered the use of agents to provide interoperation among autonomous systems, it was not designed to operate in a dynamic environment where information sources change over time and new information sources can be added autonomously and without central control.

InfoSleuth integrates the following new technological development in supporting mediated interoperation of data and services over information network:

- Agent Technology. Specialized agents that represent the users, the information resources, and the system itself cooperate to address the user' information requirements. Adding a new source implies adding a new agent and advertising its capabilities. This provides a high degree of decentralization of capabilities, which is the key to system scalability and extensibility .
- Domain models (ontologies). Ontologies give a concise uniform and declarative description of semantic information, independent of the underlying syntactic representation or the conceptual models of information bases.
- Information brokage. Broker agents match information needs with currently available resources, so retrieval and update requests can be properly routed to the relevant sources.
- Internet Computing. Java and Java Applets are used to provide users and administrators with system-independent user interfaces, and to enable ubiquitous agents that can be deployed at any source of information regardless of its location or platform.

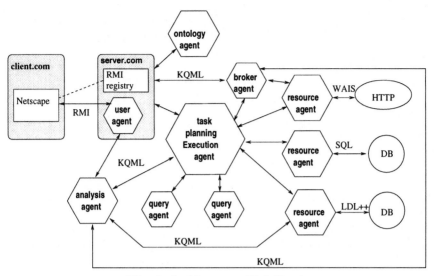

Fig. 3. Architecture of InfoSleuth

As shown in Figure 3, InfoSleuth is comprised of a network of cooperative agents communicating by means of the high level query language KQML. Users specify requests and queries over specified ontologies via applet-based user interfaces. The dialects of the knowledge representation language KIF and SQL are used internally to represent queries over specified ontologies. Queries are routed by mediation and brokage agents to specialized agents for data retrieval from distributed resources, and for integration and analysis of results.

Agents process requests either by making inferences based on local knowledge, by forwarding the request to a more appropriate agent, or by decomposing it into a collection of subrequests and then routing these to other agents and integrating the results. Decision on relevant source selection is based on the InfoSleuth ontology, a body of metadata that describes agents' knowledge and their relationships with one another.

4.6 MIND

The METU INteroperable DBMS (MIND) [DDO96] is a multidatabase system that supports integrated access to multiple heterogeneous and autonomous databases. MIND can access Oracle 7, Sybase, Adabas and MOOD, a home grown OODB developed at METU, Turkey. The canonical data model and query language of MIND are object-oriented. MIND differs from other multidatabase systems in that it uses CORBA as the model for managing the distribution and system level heterogeneities. MIND has a distributed and object-oriented architecture as shown in Figure 4.

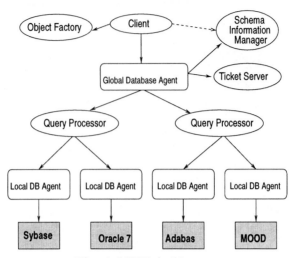

Fig. 4. MIND Architecture

The central components of MIND are two object classes: the Global Database Agent (GDA) class and the Local Database Agent (LDA) class. Objects of these classes can be created by an object factory. A LDA object acts as a local DBMS driver, and is responsible for maintaining export schemas provided by the local DBMSs, and translating queries received in the canonical query language to the query language of the local DBMSs. A GDA object is responsible for parsing, decomposing and optimizing the queries according to the information obtained from the Schema Information Manager object. It also provides global transaction management that ensures serializability of multidatabase transactions without violating the autonomy of local databases. When a user wants to query MIND, a GDA object is created by the object factory. The location and implementation transparency for this object is provided by ORB. A GDA object contains an object of the Global Query Manager (GQM) class, which processes queries, and an object of the Global Transaction Manager (GTM) class which performs global transaction.

MIND views each participating database as an DBMS object registered with an ORB with a standard interface (but different implementation). Objects in individual databases are not registered with the ORB, that is, they are not accessible via the ORB; they are only accessible by the local DBMS where they reside. For example, consider a data source storing `Person` information. With the MIND approach, the interface of `Person` objects is not known to the ORB. The fact that MIND does not allow registration of fine-granularity objects makes MIND different from the distributed object management approach towards database interoperability as described in [Man92], where all objects in all databases form an object space that is accessible via the ORB. The way MIND uses CORBA is largely as a sophisticated communication backplane, and it has little impact on the major technical aspects of MIND, such as schema integration and query processing.

Schema integration in MIND is performed by DBAs using an object definition language that allows specification of interfaces of objects in the global schema and how they relate to objects exported by various data sources. MIND also develops some query processing techniques, especially in global query optimization [EDNO 96, ONK$^+$ 96], including (1) cost-based global query optimization in case of data replication. This technique deals with site selection issues in cases when a subquery can be executed at more than one site. (2) cost-based inter-site join optimization. This technique starts from a left-deep join tree and tries to transform this tree into a more bushy tree so that response time can be reduced by exploiting parallelism. (3) dynamic optimization of inter-site joins. This technique is still cost-based but is dynamic in that it uses partial results at run time, do some cost estimation and determine the next step. This approach reduces uncertainties in cost estimation.

4.7 TSIMMIS

The TSIMMIS project at Stanford [PGMW 95] [PGGU 95] [PGMU 96] [PAGM 96] represents a big step away from most previous work. Rather than a semantically rich, structured data model, TSIMMIS uses a self-describing model, the *Object Exchange Model* (OEM) for expressing integration and for querying. OEM is an information exchange model; it does not specify how objects are stored, it only specifies how objects are to be sent and received.

In TSIMMIS, one does not need to define in advance the structure of an object and there is no notion of schema or object class. Each object instance contains its own schema. An OEM object consists of four fields: an *object id*, a *label* which explains its meaning, a *type* and a *value*. Mostly, the object ids are internal strings that are used for linking objects. The following OEM object describes a person Fred:

$< p1,$ *person-record, set,* $\{component_1, component_2, component_3, \} >$
$< component_1,$ *name, string, "Fred">*
$< component_2,$ *office-number-in-building-5, integer, 333>*
$< component_3,$ *department, string, "Toy">*

Each data source to be accessed are viewed as a collection of OEM objects in the above form, with no predefined structure. Querying in OEM is via *patters* of the form $<$*object-id, label, type, value>*, where constants or variables can be put in each position. When a pattern contains constants in the label (value) field, it matches successfully only with OEM objects that have the same constant in their label (value). For instance, the following pattern would match successfully with person Fred given earlier:

$$<person\text{-}record,\ \{<name\ ``Fred">,\ <department\ ``Toy">\}>$$

Essentially, this pattern matches with all *person-record* that has a component *name* with value "Fred" and a component *department* with value "Toy". Notice that this pattern matching assumes no structure on the objects, as long as the object has the right label with the right value, it matches successfully. This effectively makes the labels (*person-record, name, office-number-in-building-5, department*) first-class citizens. Labels do not put any constraints on what type of queries are acceptable, rather, they can be queried themselves.

Queries and view specifications in TSIMMIS are also formed using patterns. The TSIMMIS Mediator Specification Language (MSL) is a rule-based language. For instance, the following rule defines a view *ToyPeople* that contains names of all people who work in the Toy department:

$$<ToyPeople,\ \{<Name\ N>\}>:\text{-}\ <person\text{-}record,\ \{<name\ N>,\ <department \\ ``Toy">\}>.$$

The following query finds all persons who have name "Fred":

$$FredPerson\ :\text{-}\ FredPerson\text{:}<person\text{-}record,\ \{<name\ ``Fred">\}>$$

In this query, *FredPerson* is an *object variable*. The formula to the right of :- says that *FredPerson* must bind to all *person-record* with a sub-object by the label of *name* and value of "Fred". The symbol :- says that all such objects are included in the query result. Notice that the query result is potentially heterogeneous with objects with all sorts of structures, except that each object must have a label *person-record* and a *name* sub-object with value "Fred".

TSIMMIS wrappers must be built for every data source in the access scope. TSIMMIS provides a *wrapper implementation toolkit* to support fast generation of wrappers. These wrappers are indeed an OEM query processor. The wrapper implementer is required to (1) describe the types of OEM queries that the source can handle using query templates; and (2) map these query templates to local queries/actions at the data source.

Intuitively, OEM is so simple and flexible that it can represent data of any type, from unstructured random records, to relational data, to complex objects. After all types of data is represented in OEM, they can then be integrated using the set of techniques developed in TSIMMIS. The TSIMMIS approach uses logic rules that transform and merge OEM objects from various data sources to form a mediator view. This view can then be queried. Query processing in TSIMMIS leverages deductive database techniques; it includes view expansion and execution plan generation. In [PGMW 95], various aspects of the OEM model are defined and discussed. In [PGGU 95], an approach for developing OEM wrappers for semi- or unstructured data sources is described. In [PGMU 96], an OEM-based mediation language and its implementation is described. This language allows creation of integrated views in the mediator that removes various types of semantic conflicts. In [PAGM 96], an approach for object matching (referred to as object fusion in this paper) using OEM is described. This approach allows resolution of instance level conflicts. An approach for global optimization of queries posed against these "fused" object is also described.

In the database community, OEM is also the representative of an emerging data model that is not constrained by database schemas. This feature alone removes a major representational heterogeneity among data sources. The labelled-tree structures like those in OEM can represent all sorts of data structures equally well and have a great potential in supporting integration of heterogeneous data. Query and manipulation language and optimization techniques are being developed for this new data model [BDHS 96].

4.8 Comparison with Respect to Data Delivery Capabilities

In previous sections we have described several projects or prototype systems in terms of the capabilities and mechanisms they use to process queries through mediators and wrappers and the support they provides for interoperability and scalable distributed object management .

In addition to Broadcast Disks project which implements a push-only data delivery system with broadcast protocol, all the others are pull-only data delivery systems, although the DIOM project has developed techniques for supporting continual queries [LPBZ 96], which use hybrid mode of data delivery with publish/subscribe protocol. Table 2 shows a brief comparison of these systems with respect to the variety of data delivery capabilities.

Table 2. A comparison with respect to delivery capabilities

	request/ respond	publish/ subscribe	broadcast	pull	Push	hybrid
Broadcast Disk		Y	Y		Y	Y
Carnot	Y			Y		
DIOM	Y	Y		Y		Y limited
DISCO	Y			Y		
InfoSleuth	Y			Y		
MIND	Y			Y		
TSIMISS	Y			Y		

5. Enabling Technology for Interoperability

5.1 CORBA

The CORBA (Common Object Request Broker Architecture) technology enables object-oriented computing in distributed heterogeneous environments.

The main features of CORBA include the ORB Core, the Interface Definition Language (IDL), the Interface Repository (IR), the language mappings, the stubs and skeletons, dynamic invocation and dispatch (DII and DSI), the object adaptors and the inter-ORB protocols. The general structure of an ORB is illustrated in Figure 5.

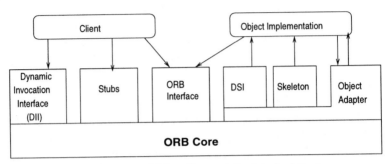

Fig. 5. Common Object Request Broker Architecture

The ORB core delivers requests to objects and returns any responses to the callers. The key feature is to facilitate transparent client/object communication by hiding object location, implementation, execution states, and communication mechanisms. To make a request, the client specifies the target object by using an *object reference*. These are created upon CORBA object creation; they are immutable and opaque references that only ORB cores know how to manipulate.

Before a client can make requests on an object, it must know the types of operations supported by the object. The Interface Definition Language (IDL) is used to define an object's *interface*. IDL is a *language independent*, declarative language, not a programming language. It forces interfaces to be defined separately from object implementations. Objects can be constructed using different programming languages and yet communicate with one another. *Language Mappings* determine how IDL features are mapped to facilities of a given programming language. OMG has standardized language mappings for C, C++ and Smalltalk. IDL language mappings are where the abstractions and concepts specified in CORBA meet the "real world" of implementation.

A CORBA-based application must have a way to know the types of interfaces supported by the objects being used. The CORBA Interface Repository (IR) allows the OMG IDL type system to be accessed and written programmatically at runtime. IR is itself a CORBA object that has a standard interface. Using this interface, an application can traverse an entire hierarchy of IDL information. IR is usually used together with the CORBA dynamic invocation interface and as a source for generating static support code for applications.

OMG IDL language compilers and translators generate client-side *stubs* and server-side *skeletons*. These are interface specific code segments that co-operate to effectively exchange requests and results. A stub is a mechanism that effectively creates and issues requests on the client's behalf. A skeleton is a mechanism that delivers requests to the CORBA object implementation. Communicating through stubs and skeletons is often called *static invocation* because the stubs and skeletons are built directly into the client application and object implementation. For clients, a stub is an *adapter* that adapts the function call style of its language mapping to the request invocation mechanism of the ORB. To object implementation, the skeleton is a *proxy* that handles translation issues in passing request in the right format to an object implementation and also passing result back to the ORB. In addition to the static invocation via stubs and skeletons, CORBA supports two interfaces for dynamic invocation: *Dynamic Invocation Interface* (DII) and *Dynamic Skeleton Interface* (DSI). DII allows clients to invoke requests on object without stubs. DSI allows servers to be written without skeletons.

The Object Adaptor (OA) is the "glue" between CORBA object implementation and the ORB itself. OA is an object that adapts the interface of another object to the interface expected by a caller. It is an object that uses delegation to allow a caller to invoke requests on an object even though the caller does not know the object's true interface.

Prior to CORBA 2.0, one of the biggest complaints about commercial ORB products was that they did not interoperate. Lack of interoperability was caused by the fact that earlier CORBA specification did not mandate any particular data formats or protocols for ORB communications. CORBA 2.0 specifies an interoperability architecture based on the *General Inter-ORB Protocol* (GIOP), which specifies transfer syntax and a standard set of message formats for ORB interoperation over any connection-oriented transport. CORBA 2.0 also mandates the *Internet Inter-ORB Protocol* (IIOP), which is an implementation of GIOP over TCP/IP transport. With IIOP, ORBs can interoperate with one another over the Internet.

5.2 COM/OLE

This is the alternative standard to CORBA that is developed by Microsoft. COM (Common Object Model) is similar in functionality to CORBA ORB, while OLE (Object Linking and Embedding) is the complete environment for componentization for handling compound documents. COM/OLE is less well-defined than CORBA and since it is a single vendor proposal, its contents are fluid and changing. Currently, it is a single machine environment with distribution to come with the release of *Cairo*.

COM object model is quite different than CORBA's; COM objects are really not "objects" in the commonly accepted sense of the term. The main differences with CORBA object model are the following:

- A COM (or OLE) object is one which supports one or more interfaces as defined by its class. Thus, there could be multiple interfaces to an object.
- All objects support one interface called **IUnknown**.
- COM objects have no identifiers (OIDs).
- There is no inheritance defined among object classes. The relationship among them is defined by means of containment/delegation and aggregation.
- COM objects do not have state; applications obtain a pointer to interfaces that point to the methods that implement them.
- There are two definition languages: IDL for defining interfaces and ODL for describing object types.

Clients access COM objects by means of the interfaces defined for each object. This is accomplished by indirection through an *Interface Function Table* each of whose entries points to an interface implementation inside the COM object. There is one Interface Function Table per each interface that the object supports. The client obtains a pointer to the Interface Function Table that corresponds to the particular interface that it wishes to access and invokes the interface functions contained therein. This method isolates clients from interface implementations.

A *COM server* performs a number of functions. It encapsulates a COM object and a class factory. In addition to the COM object interfaces that it supports, it provides an **IClassFactory** interface to interact with the class factory. The functions that the server performs are the following: (a) it implements a class factory interface, (b) it registers the classes that it supports, (c) it initializes the COM library, (d) it verifies that the library version is compatible with the object version, (e) it implements a method for terminating itself when no clients are active, and (f) it terminates the use of the library when it is no longer needed.

There are three types of COM servers. An *in-process server* is one that shares the same process space as the clients that connect to it. A *local server* runs on the same machine as the clients, but in a different process space. The interconnection between the clients and the COM server in this case is by means of lightweight RPC. Finally, a *remote server* is one that runs as a separate process on a separate machine. In this case, the connection between the clients and the server is by means of DCE RPC.

6. AURORA and its Application to Electronic Commerce

The AURORA project at the University of Alberta, in collaboration with IBM Canada, is developing a collection of mediators that can be used for constructing integrated (read only) access to heterogeneous and autonomous data sources. The goal of the project is to make such access scalable and efficient. The target application driving the research in AURORA is electronic commerce.

6.1 A Motivating Example: Virtual Catalogs in Electronic Commerce

A virtual shopping mall is a typical electronic commerce (EC) application. A key component in a virtual mall is a catalog system. Companies organize their catalogs differently. This gives rise to a set of heterogeneous and autonomous catalogs. When the number of participating catalogs is large, it is difficult for a shopper to perform cross-catalog searching or comparative shopping in order to locate items of interest. One possible solution to this problem is to require all vendors to re-organize their catalogs in a common format and merge all the catalogs into a central catalog database which allows customers to perform sophisticated searching without dealing with individual catalogs. This requires re-engineering of existing catalogs. In general, vendors want to participate in the central catalog without making changes to their existing catalogs. One solution is to create a *virtual catalog* that has the look and feel of a central catalog but holds no physical catalog information. Upon a customer request, this catalog retrieves relevant information from (multiple) individual catalogs and assemble an answer. Such a virtual catalog should satisfy the following requirements:

- It is up-to-date but does not violate the autonomy of the participating catalogs.
- Its search performance does not degrade as the number of participating catalogs increases.
- It allows easy inclusion of new catalogs and integrates with other EC applications.
- It is easy to construct. Tools should be provided to assist in construction.

The AURORA project potentially allows construction of such virtual catalog. AURORA adopts the mediator paradigm as described in [Wie 92]. It has two main themes: (1) a scalable mediation model ; and (2) the enabling techniques.

6.2 Homogenization and Integration Mediators: A 2-tier Mediation Model

A *mediation model* describes how heterogeneities among data sources are perceived and handled. The AURORA mediation model, shown in Figure 6, is a 2-tier model . It is 2-tier because it models mediation as a 2-step process: homogenization followed by integration, performed by respective mediators. The original mediator framework proposed by [Wie 92] encourages specialization of mediators but using specialized mediators for accessing heterogeneous data sources has not been explored before. Most previous mediator systems are 1-tier, providing a single type of mediator. AURORA's 2-tier mediation model is designed to allow scalable mediation.

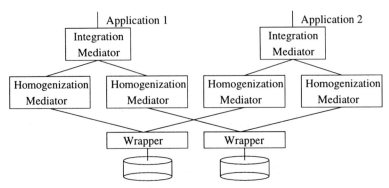

Fig. 6. The AURORA Mediation Model

6.2.1 AURORA's 2-tier Mediation Model. We distinguish between two categories of heterogeneities among data sources: *schematic mismatches* that arise when the same application domain is modeled differently; and *instance level conflicts* that arise when inconsistent values on the same real world object are recorded. Schematic mismatches must be resolved first, otherwise there is no basis for further integration. The process of resolving schematic mismatches is referred to as *homogenization*. In AURORA, specialized mediators, the *homogenization mediators* , support this process. The task of homogenization is to map a common application model onto a participating data source that models the same application (differently and partially) by constructing a *homogenizing view* on top of it. The *integration mediator* "glues" a large number of data sources together by combining all the homogenizing views into an integrated view. In this process, instance level conflicts must be resolved.

6.2.2 The 2-tier Mediation Model and Scalability. To include a new data source into the access scope, one must resolve two issues:

1. *Communication.* It must be possible to "talk" to the data source. A wrapper is used to remove idiosyncrasies of the data source.
2. *Semantic integration.*

Scalability requires that both steps be performed rapidly. For 1, this requires rapid, if not automatic, wrapper generation . Various enabling techniques have already been developed [PGGU 95]. Much is known about *how* 2 can be done; the scalability aspect of it has not been well addressed. The traditional approach is to *derive* an integrated view from all the data sources in a monolithic integration specification. This approach does not favor scalability because adding or removing a data source potentially requires the integration specification to be modified. There has been no methodology that prescribes incremental modifications. When the number of data sources involved is large, the specification is difficult to modify or reconstruct.

AURORA's 2-tier mediation model requires that data sources be *homogenized* before being integrated. The scalability issue in AURORA is reduced to the issues of rapid homogenization of individual data sources and the rapid integration of multiple data sources. Homogenization can be performed in parallel among sources. It is a process that concerns single data sources; it has good potential to be fast. AURORA provides tools to assist in this process. Integration handles multiple but homogeneous (although still autonomous) sources. To achieve scalability of this step, AURORA integration mediator assumes that the integrated view is pre-defined by the application requirement. Let this view be pre-defined as V_W. To integrate objects in each data sources (these data sources now appear as homogenization mediators) into V_W, AURORA requires these objects to be *registered* as *fragments* of objects defined in V_W. Removing a source from the access scope only requires the relevant registrations to be cancelled. This way the integration can be performed in a plug-and-play fashion.

6.3 AURORA Mediators as Distributed Components

AURORA does not restrict the canonical data model to a specific one that is deemed to be most "suitable". Rather, AURORA provides mediators and wrappers in two popular data models, the relational data model and the ODMG object data model. Necessary facilities are provided to allow the two data models to coexist seamlessly. AURORA mediators are classified along two dimensions: the canonical data model and the specialty, homogenization or integration. Figure 7 shows this classification.

Mediator Type \ Canonical Data Model	Relational	Object-Oriented
Homogenization	AURORA-RH	AURORA-OH
Integration	AURORA-RI	AURORA-OI

Fig. 7. AURORA Mediator Classification

AURORA designs and develops three types of software components: the wrappers , the homogenization mediators and the integration mediators. These are provided as distributed components that communicate and cooperate via an Object Request Broker (ORB), as shown in Figure 8. AURORA wrappers and mediators support pre-defined interfaces, as shown in Figure 9.

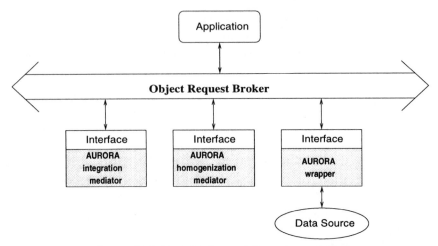

Fig. 8. AURORA Mediators/Wrappers and ORB

These are the only interfaces via which a wrapper/mediator can be accessed by the application or by other AURORA mediators.

Schema Export Service	Query Service	Event Notification Service
AURORA Wrapper		

Schema Export Service	Query Service	Materialization Service	Event Notification Service
AURORA Homogenization/Integration Mediator			

Fig. 9. The AURORA Mediator Interfaces

A middleware that facilitates integrated access to multiple heterogeneous data sources can be constructed by using a network of mediators that cooperate with one another to provide an integrated data service. With AURORA, one can choose between relational and object-oriented components. The use of AURORA mediators in building middleware is best illustrated by Figures 10 and 11. AURORA-O mediators have the built-in capability of accessing AURORA-R components.

6.4 AURORA Mediator Development Workbench

Each AURORA mediator is a *mediator development workbench* consisting of a mediator skeleton and a toolkit named MAT.

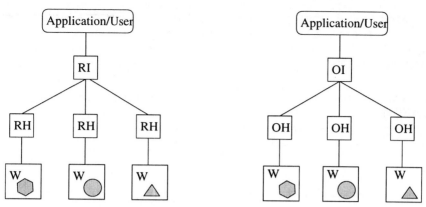

Fig. 10. Application Using AURORA Mediators (Uniform)

Mediator Skeletons. The most important components in a mediator are an integrated view over (multiple) data sources and a query processor that answers queries posed against this view. Building a mediator means building the view, the query processor, and software modules that support other standard services. In AURORA, mediators are constructed from *mediator skeletons* that have all the necessary components of a mediator except for the view.

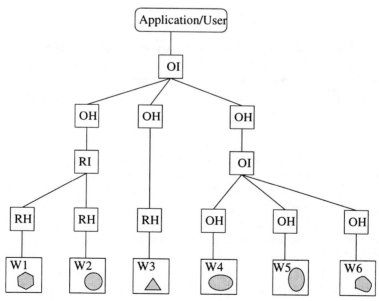

Fig. 11. Application Using AURORA Mediators (Mixed)

Mediator Author's Toolkits (MATs). In AURORA, a *mediator author* chooses a mediator skeleton, identifies heterogeneities among the sources, and defines views into the mediator skeleton to resolve the heterogeneities . AURORA MATs assist the mediator authors in performing such tasks. This scenario is shown in Figure 12. A MAT has two main functionalities: it mandates a *mediation methodology* and it provides *Mediation Enabling Operators* (MEOs).

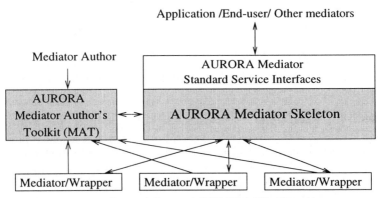

Fig. 12. General Form of AURORA Workbenches

6.5 Homogenization Mediators

The architecture of AURORA-RH is shown in Figure 13. **MAT-RH** is a toolkit that assists a mediator author in constructing a homogenizing view. It provides a set of MEOs and mandates a homogenization methodology. Each tool in the toolkit allows specification of *transformations* and *domain mappings*. Transformations are expressions consisting of the AURORA-RH MEOs and the usual relational operators. Domain mappings are arbitrary mappings. This information is captured in the **View Definition Repository** and are used for query processing. **AURORA-RH Primitives** are MEOs; they extend the relational algebra to form a *Mediation Enabling Algebra* (MEA), MEA-RH. **AURORA-RH Query Processor (AQP)** processes mediator queries posed against the target database. It rewrites such a query into a (optimal) set of queries over the source database, sends these queries for execution and assembles the answer to the mediator query from the returned data.

6.5.1 MAT-RH and AURORA-RH Query Processing. MAT-RH

identifies a wide range of domain and schema mismatches and mandates a methodology to resolve them systematically. It also provides constructs for expressing such resolutions. The types of mismatches considered by MAT-RH are the following:

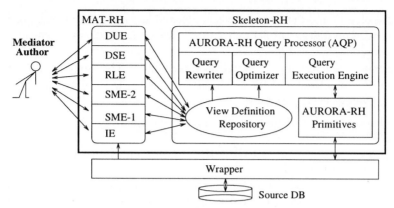

Fig. 13. AURORA-RH Workbench

Cross-over schema mismatches. A **type 1** cross-over mismatch happens when a concept is represented as data in M but as relations in B. A **type 2** cross-over mismatch happens when a concept is represented as data in M but as attributes in B.

Domain structural mismatches. This mismatch happens when a domain in M corresponds to a domain with a different data type or several data domains in B.

Domain unit mismatches. This mismatch happens when a domain in M assumes different unit of measurement from the corresponding domain(s) in B.

Domain population mismatches. This mismatch happens when a domain in M assumes different population from the corresponding domain(s) in B.

MAT-RH mandates a 6-step methodology for homogenization. It supports each step by a specialized tool (environment) that accepts certain types of transformations and domain mappings. This is shown in Figure 13 and is further described below:

1. Construct an import schema. The supporting environment is the Import Environment (IE).
2. Resolve type 1 schema mismatches. The supporting environment is the Schema Mismatch Environment 1 (SME-1).
3. Resolve type 2 schema mismatches. The supporting environment is the Schema Mismatch Environment 2 (SME-2).
4. Link relations. The supporting environment is the Relation Linking Environment (RLE). RLE mandates that for each relation in the homogenizing view, a prototype relation must be specified. This relation is close to the target relation modulo domain mismatches.

5. Resolve domain structural mismatches. The supporting environment is the Domain Structural Environment (DSE). DSE allows specification of *domain structural functions*.
6. Resolve domain unit/population mismatches. The supporting environment is the Domain Unit Environment (DUE). DUE allows specification of *domain value functions*.

Detailed description of these environments and their application are given in [YOL97].

Query processing in AURORA-RH is based on MEA-RH. MEA-RH extends the relational algebra with operators specially designed for homogenization. These new operators are *retrieve*, *pad*, *rename*, and *deriveAttr*. Homogenizing views are defined using these operators. When processing a mediator query, AQP uses these view definitions to rewrite the query into an algebraic formula in MEA-RH, transforms this formula into an "optimal" form, and evaluates it with the participation of a relational wrapper . Details of AQP are described in [YOL97].

6.6 AURORA Integration Mediators

AURORA integration mediators, AURORA-RI and AURORA-OI (Figure 7), are responsible for integrating a large number of *homogenized* sources. Since the sources are homogenized, the types of heterogeneities that the integration mediator must handle is limited. First, lets give a closer look at the 2-tier mediation model and the meaning of homogenization.

6.6.1 A Plug-and-Play Integration Mechanism. Lets assume that the application view consists of a single relation R_g. A data source is said to be *homogenized in regard to R_g* if:

1. It is structurally homogenized. It contains a single relation R_s that is a *fragment* of R_g, that is, $ATTR(R_s) \subseteq ATTR(R_g)$.
2. It is semantically homogenized. Each attribute in R_s is the *same* as that in R_g with the same attribute name.

Now the following plug-and-play integration mechanism can be imagined: To "plug" a data source into the the integration mediator, we first homogenize this data source in regard to the application view, that is, construct a *homogenizing view* on top of the data source. We then *register* each relation in this view with the integration mediator as a fragment of a global relation. To "unplug" a data source from the integration mediator, we remove all fragments from this source. When a particular source is down, all fragments from this source are considered to be empty.

6.7 Constructing Virtual Catalogs with AURORA

Consider a number of vendors each having an autonomous catalog database. A virtual catalog effort can be initiated by a third-party broker who seeks to offer value-added services. The broker first design a common catalog structure, its data model and query language. To include a vendor into the virtual catalog, the broker first homogenizes the vendor's catalog using an AURORA homogenization mediator. This process maps the vendor catalog structure and semantics into that in the common catalog. After homogenization, it should be straightforward to "plug" a catalog into an AURORA integration mediator that supports the common catalog. While homogenization is a more complex process, the broker can hire a few people to homogenize individual vendor catalogs in parallel. Integration mediator is where large number of virtual catalogs merge but the integration is a simple mechanism. Overall, construction of the virtual catalog is scalable.

7. Conclusion

We have discussed several interoperability issues in large-scale distributed information delivery systems from both architectural and technical perspective. We present two representative architectural paradigms: *Multi-database management-based* paradigm and *Mediator-based* information delivery paradigm. The former contributes to the interoperability research in terms of techniques for resolution of semantic heterogeneity and techniques for distributed query optimization in tightly-coupled and somewhat closed distributed environments [S 91, SL 90]. The later contributes to the interoperability research in terms of techniques for handling both structured data sources and semi-structured or unstructured data sources, and techniques for providing scalable and adaptable data delivery services in loosely-coupled and open distributed environments.

Technically, we identify a number of data delivery characteristics in terms of (1) *delivery protocols*, such as Client Request/Server Response, Server Publish/Client Subscribe, and Server Broadcast, (2) *delivery modes*, such as Pull-only, Push-only, and Hybrid, and (3) *delivery frequencies*, such as periodic, conditional, and ad-hoc. We analyse several data delivery schemes using different combinations of these characteristics (Section 3.4). For example, the publish/subscribe protocol is typically used for server-initiated information dissemination, where data is delivered automatically (push-only) or semi-automatically (hybrid mode). The frequency of server push can be either periodic or conditional. Ad-hoc delivery frequency does not make much sense in practice for push-only mode. We argue that an advanced distributed information system must incorporate different types of information delivery so that the system can be optimized according to various criteria, such as network traffic and heterogeneity and constant evolution of online information sources.

We illustrate the architectural and technical aspects of distributed information delivery systems through a review of several existing research prototypes and demonstrate the different implementation approaches used in practice, and the various solutions to the interoperability issues. We also report our research and experience with AURORA, a mediator-based information integration project, in collaboration with IBM Canada, and its application to electronic commerce domain.

We believe that interoperability in large-scale distributed information delivery systems is one of the most critical functional requirements for many enterprise-wide cooperative applications, such as business workflow automation, computer-aided software engineering (CASE), computer-aided design (CAD) and manufacturing (CAM), and interactive programming environments.

Enterprise-Wide Workflow Management Based on State and Activity Charts

Peter Muth[1], Dirk Wodtke[1], Jeanine Weissenfels[1], Gerhard Weikum[1],
Angelika Kotz Dittrich[2]

[1] University of the Saarland
Department of Computer Science
P. O. Box 151150, D-66041 Saarbrücken
E-Mail: muth, wodtke, weissenfels, weikum@cs.uni-sb.de
[2] Union Bank of Switzerland
P. O. Box 2336, CH-8033 Zürich
E-Mail: kotz-dittrich@ubs.ch

Abstract. This paper presents an approach towards the specification, verification, and distributed execution of workflows based on state and activity charts. The formal foundation of state and activity charts is exploited at three levels. At the specification level, the formalism enforces precise descriptions of business processes while also allowing subsequent refinements. In addition, precise specifications based on other methods can be automatically converted into state and activity charts. At the level of verification, state charts are amenable to the efficient method of model checking, in order to verify particularly critical workflow properties. Finally, at the execution level, a state chart specification forms the basis for the automatic generation of modules that can be directly executed in a distributed manner. Within the MENTOR project, a coherent prototype system has been built that comprises all three levels: specification, verification, and distributed execution.

1. Introduction

Business Process (Re)Engineering (BPR) [HC 93] is an important driving force for *workflow management.* It aims at increasing the efficiency of business processes and making them easily and quickly adjustable to the ever changing needs of customers. Today, business processes are mostly modeled in a high-level and informal way. BPR tools such as the ARIS-Toolset [SJ 96] serve to construct graphical representations of business processes, including organizational properties of an enterprise. Some BPR tools also support the analysis of quantative metrics of business processes, such as turnaround time, if the required statistical data is provided.

In contrast to specifications of business processes, *workflow specifications* serve as a basis for the largely automated execution of processes. Workflow specifications are often derived from business process specifications by refining the business process specification into a more detailed and more concrete form. Automated and computer-assisted execution means that a *workflow management system* (WfMS) [GHS 95, Hsu 95, JB 96, Moh 96, VB 96] controls the processing of work steps -denoted *activities*- which have to be performed in the workflow. Some activities may have a manual or intellectual part, to be performed by a human. But the workflow management system is in charge of determining the (partial) invocation order of these activities. In contrast to business process specifications, this requires a formal specification of control flow and data flow. Based on organizational properties of an enterprise, *roles* are assigned to those activities that require human interaction. At runtime, a human *actor* who can fill the given role is chosen to execute an activity.

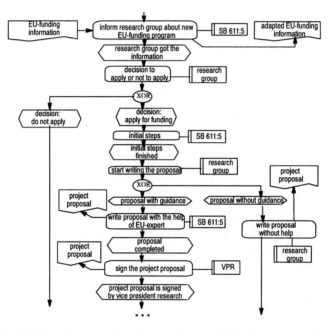

Fig. 1: ARIS Specification of the Business Process 'EU project proposal'

Figures 1 and 2 show a part of a business process specification for a university research group submitting R&D project proposals to the European Union (EU). The specification of Fig. 1 has been created with the BPR tool ARIS-Toolset, whereas Fig. 2 shows the same part of the specification given as a state chart, i.e., by using a formal specification method. Both specifications show activities such as signing the proposal by the university's vice president of research, and both show the control flow in a graphical way. In Fig. 1, conditions for choosing different paths in the execution are given as plain text. Therefore, the specification might be incomplete and ambiguous. In Fig. 2, the formal specification method of state charts requires all conditions to be explicitly given in expressions based on predicate logic. This makes the workflow executable by a workflow management system.

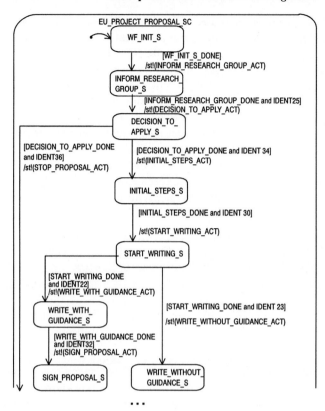

Fig. 2: State Chart Specification of the Workflow 'EU project proposal'

A coexistence of different specification methods on different levels of abstraction is common in computer science. In early stages of the design process, analyzing and designing complex applications is often based on informal methods. However, in the case of workflow management, there exist two important arguments for using formally founded specification methods:

- A seamless integration of business process reengineering and workflow management is desirable to enable an automatic transformation of business processes specified by BPR tools into executable workflows. This should be possible without additional specification effort. Some BPR tools already support such an automatic transformation of business process specifications written in their specification language into workflow specifications suitable for commercial workflow management systems. However, such a conversion is successful only if the original specification has been developed in a disciplined manner, having the desired conversion already in mind. For example, the specification of Fig. 1 can be treated as a formal specification by considering the control flow conditions, which are given in a textual form, as predicate symbols to be evaluated at runtime by human interaction. However, this requires that all conditions are complete and consistent, i.e., there are no contradictions. Today's BPR tools do neither guide the designer towards this goal, nor do they enforce such specifications.

– Business processes often represent high values for an enterprise, as they have a strong impact on internal costs and on customer satisfaction. For example, consider the processing of credit requests in a bank. Especially in the case of companies as customers, an erroneous processing of a credit request or an unreasonable delay might cause huge losses, now and in the future. Hence, it is mandatory that mission critical properties of workflows can be verified in a rigorous, formal manner. In addition, it should be possible to carry out the verification automatically. Of course, this dictates a formal specification method.

In this paper, we show how to employ the formal method of state and activity charts [Har 87, Har 88, Har 90] for the specification of workflows, for the formal verification of workflow properties, and for the distributed execution of workflows. We discuss experiences and results of the research project MENTOR (Middleware for Enterprise-wide Workflow Management) [Wod 96, Wod 96a, Wod 97, Wei 96]. MENTOR is a joint project with the Union Bank of Switzerland. The main contributions of this paper are as follows:

– By using state and activity charts as our specification method, we are able to automatically verify mission critical workflow properties with the method of model checking. Model checking is a well known approach in the field of reactive systems. Our contribution is to exploit model checking in the area of workflow management.

– Tools for formal specifications, including tools for model checking, typically have a centralized view on the specification. However, in practice huge and complex workflows have to be executed in a distributed environment. This is due to the decentralized structure of an enterprise or due to the different organizations that participate in a workflow spanning several enterprises. In order to integrate these different views and requirements, we have developed a method for partitioning a centralized workflow specification in an automated manner. Again, the formal nature of state and activity charts can be exploited for proving that the partitioned specification is equivalent to the original, centralized one. Therefore, properties proven for the centralized specification provably carry over to the partitioned one.

The paper is organized as follows. Section 2 summarizes basic requirements on workflow specification methods, and Section 3 gives a brief overview of specification methods used in research and industry. Section 4 introduces state and activity charts and shows how to model workflows in this formalism. Section 5 presents our approach of utilizing model checking for the formal verification of workflow properties, and experiences with this approach are discussed. Section 6 presents our method for partitioning workflow specifications and discusses the corresponding distributed execution. In general, we focus on aspects of control flow and data flow which are specific to workflow management. We do not discuss the organizational aspects of an enterprise and do not consider issues of the underlying information systems infrastructure, e.g., an enterprise-wide data model.

2. Requirements on Workflow Specification Methods

In general, a 'good' workflow specification method should have the following properties:

1. The method must be able to specify the control flow and data flow of a workflow in an unambiguous and complete manner. This enables the execution of the specification by the workflow management system.
2. The method must have a well founded formal basis. In particular, a mathematically defined semantics is required. This is in contrast to methods having their semantics defined by the code of the corresponding workflow management system. The better the formal basis, the more formal results and tools typically exist (e.g., for an automatic verification of properties of a workflow).
3. In order to support an incremental specification process, the specification method must support the stepwise refinement of specifications. Likewise, the composition of existing specifications into larger, more complex ones must be possible within the formal framework.
4. It should be possible to visualize workflow specifications in a graphical manner, and to animate a workflow execution accordingly.
5. It should be possible to modify specifications at runtime. This is important for ad-hoc workflows, where the set of activities to be executed along with the data and control flow between them can be modified dynamically during execution.
6. The quality of a specification method typically depends on the application scenario as well as on personal preferences of the workflow designer. Hence, it should be possible to automatically convert specifications given in one method into other methods. This is also important in heterogeneous workflow environments [WfM 96], for the interoperability of different workflow management systems [Cas 96], and for building comprehensive process handbooks [Bern 95].

3. Formal Methods for Workflow Specification

This section gives a brief overview of specification methods used in products and research prototypes of workflow management systems. We distinguish the following types of methods: script languages, net-based methods, logic-based methods, algebraic methods, and ECA rules.

Script Languages: Workflow specifications based on *script languages* contain control flow and data flow constructs which are specifically tailored to workflow applications. Such script languages are popular in current WfMS products. They provide a compact representation and are therefore easy to use. Experienced workflow designers even seem to prefer script languages over graphical interfaces, which are also offered by almost all WfMS products. A drawback of most script languages is their lack of a formal foundation. Their semantics is mostly 'defined' by the code of the script interpreter used.

Net-based Methods: When a graphical visualization of workflow specifications has top priority, *state transition nets* are a good choice. In state transition nets, activities are represented by nodes, and control flow is represented by edges. In fact, almost all WfMS products provide means for graphical specifications similar to state transition nets. However, an important question is whether these net-based methods have a formally founded semantics. Unfortunately, this is not the case for most WfMS products ([LA 94] being an exception).

Considering only net-based methods with a formal foundation, we have to restrict ourselves more or less to *state charts* [Har 87, Har 88] and *Petri nets* [Gen 86, Rei 85]. Variants of Petri nets, especially *predicate transition nets* , are used in a number of research prototypes as well as in several WfMS products [DG 94, EN 93, Obe 96, OSS 94]. Some workflow management systems use variants of Petri nets for the internal representation of the workflow engine, e.g. [RS 95]. State charts [Har 87, Har 88, Har 90] have received little attention in workflow management, but they are well established in software engineering (e.g., [CKO 92]), especially for specifying reactive systems. In the MENTOR project [Wod 96, WW 97, Wod 96a, Wei 96], we have chosen state charts as a formal foundation for workflow specification. In Section 4, we will discuss state charts in detail.

Logic-based Methods: For a *logic-based* specification of workflows or for specifying dynamic aspects of information systems in general [LM 96], *temporal logic* is a commonly used method [Eme 90, MP 92]. Temporal logic has an excellent formal basis. A potential problem is the execution of specifications in temporal logic if the expressive power is too high. In addition, it is hard to visualize specifications in temporal logic, and it is often impossible to transform them into other specification methods. Simple forms of temporal logic, especially *computation tree logic* (CTL) [ES 88], have been used as a formal model for specifying execution dependencies in extended transaction models [Att 93, Kle 91, Gue 93], and are also important for the verification of properties of workflow specifications (see Section 5).

Algebraic Methods: Process algebras [Mil 89] have been considered only in the theory community and are not widely known in the field of workflow management. As an exception, in [FEB 96] the specification language LO-TOS, which is based on a process algebra, is extended towards workflow management. The drawbacks of algebraic methods are similar to logic-based methods, but logic-based methods are superior to process algebras in terms of automatic execution and the potential for formal verification. In addition, specifications given in a process algebra are often not intuitive and hard to understand for practitioners.

ECA Rules: Event-Condition-Action-Rules , shortly termed *ECA rules* , are used in active database systems [WCD 95] and have been adopted by a number of projects in the workflow area (e.g., [BJ 94, GKT 95, Kap 95]). ECA rules are used to specify the control flow between activities. Like for other methods that are not based on nets, the graphical visualization of sets of ECA rules is a non-trivial task. Large sets of ECA rules are hard to handle, and a step-wise refinement is not supported (see [App 96, SK 95]). In terms of their formal foundation, ECA rules are typically mapped to other specification methods, especially variants of Petri nets or temporal logic.

Many relationships exist between the above categories (see, e.g., [Old 91] for a formal analysis of such relationships). Hence, beyond the "pure" approaches that fit into the given categories, hybrid methods have also been proposed. Such hybrid methods are especially attractive when a graphic representation of a non-net-based method is desired. Because of its designated role as an industry standard, the Workflow Process Definition Language (WPDL) of the Workflow Management Coalition is an especially notable hybrid method [WfM 96]. The Workflow Management Coalition, an industry consortium, aims at a unified terminology and a standardization of interfaces between key components of workflow management systems. WDPL, currently available as a draft only, can on one hand be viewed as a textual representation of (highly simplified) state charts or state-transition nets. On the other hand one can view single statements as (again highly simplified) ECA rules. Finally, a complete WDPL specification could also be interpreted as a script.

4. Workflow Specification with State and Activity Charts

4.1 Introduction to State and Activity Charts

In this section, we will describe the specification of distributed workflows based on the formalism of state and activity charts [Har 87, Har 87a, Har 88, Har 90, HN 95]. State and activity charts have originally been developed for reactive systems (e.g., embedded control systems in automobiles) and have been quite successful in this area. They comprise two dual views of a specification.

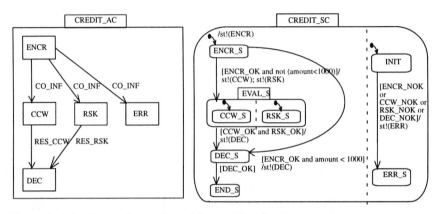

Fig. 3: Activity chart and state chart of the workflow 'credit processing'

Activities reflect the functional decomposition of a system and denote the "active" components of a specification; they correspond directly to the activities of a workflow. An *activity chart* specifies the data flow between activities, in the form of a directed graph with data items as arc annotations. An example for an activity chart is given in the left part of Fig. 3. It represents a simplified workflow for the processing of credit requests of companies in a bank. A request for a credit involves, among other things, the checking of the company's current credit balance, the company's credit rating, and a risk evaluation. The activity chart of Fig. 3 defines the activities $ENCR, CCW, RSK, DEC$, and ERR, and the data flow between these activities. In activity $ENCR$ (enter credit request) the company's credit request is entered into a credit database. The company information CO_INF constitutes the data flow from $ENCR$ to activities CCW, RSK and ERR. Activity CCW checks the company's credit worthiness by looking up the appropriate account and balance sheet data of the company. Activity RSK evaluates the potential risk that is associated with the requested credit. RSK takes into account the bank's overall involvement in the affected branch of industry (e.g., the total of all credits already granted to computer companies) and the requested currency. Finally, the decision activity DEC records the decision that is eventually made on the credit request (i.e., approval or rejection); this would typically be an intellectual decision step based on the results RES_CCW and RES_RSK of the activities CCW and RSK. These four activities are complemented by a fifth activity ERR, which may be invoked as a generic error handler, for example, to stop the processing of the workflow when the credit applicant goes out of business.

State charts capture the behavior of a system by specifying the control flow between activities. A state chart is essentially a finite state machine with a distinguished initial state and transitions driven by Event-Condition-Action rules (ECA rules). Each transition arc between states is annotated with an ECA rule. A transition from state X to state Y, annotated with an ECA rule of the form $E[C]/A$, fires if event E occurs and condition C holds. The effect is that state X is left, state Y is entered, and action A is executed. Conditions and actions are expressed in terms of variables, for example, those that are specified for the data flow in the corresponding activity chart. Conditions and events may also refer to states by means of special predicates such as $IN(s)$ which holds if and only if state s is currently entered. In addition, an action A can explicitly start an activity, expressed by *st!(activity)*, and can generate an event E or set a condition C. Each of the three components of an $E[C]/A$ triple may be empty. Every state change in a state chart execution is viewed as a single step; thus, state changes induce a discrete time dimension.

Two important additional features of state charts are *nested states* and *orthogonal components*. Nesting of states means that a state can itself contain an entire state chart. The semantics is that upon entering the higher-level state, the initial state of the embedded lower-level state chart is automatically entered, and upon leaving the higher-level state all embedded lower-level states are left. The capability for nesting states is especially useful for the refinement of specifications during the design process. Orthogonal components denote the parallel execution of two state charts that are embedded in the same higher-level state (where the entire state chart can be viewed as a single top-level state). Both components enter their initial states simultaneously, and the transitions in the two components proceed in parallel, subject to the preconditions for a transition to fire.

An example of a state chart is given in the right part of Fig. 3 for the credit processing workflow. For each activity of the activity chart there exists a state with the same name, extended by the suffix _S_. Furthermore, the workflow consists of three major sequential building blocks, *ENCR_S*, *EVAL_S,* and *DEC_S*, where *EVAL_S* consists of two orthogonal components, *CCW_S* and *RSK_S*. Hence, the activities *CCW* and *RSK* are executed in parallel. For each activity, its outcome in terms of an error variable is available. For example, variable *ENCR_OK* is set to true after termination of activity *ENCR* if no error occurred. Otherwise, the variable *ENCR_NOK* is set to *true* and an error handling activity is started. Initialization and error handling of the workflow are specified in an orthogonal component.

A detailed presentation of state and activity charts including a formal semantics can be found in [Har 87a, HN 95]. [WW 97] presents a formal semantics for a variant that is tailored to the specific needs of workflow management.

4.2 Design Methodology for Workflow Specifications

In the MENTOR project, we have gained experiences in using state and activity charts for specifying complex workflows in banking applications. From these studies, we have derived the following simple methodology for specifying workflows with state and activity charts. We consider two cases. In the first case, the initial workflow specification is developed as a state and activity chart. In the second case, a state and activity chart is derived from a specification of a business process, given in the specification language of a BPR tool.

4.2.1 Design with State and Activity Charts. When state and activity charts are chosen as the initial specification method, we proceed in the following steps:

1. *Definition of Activities:* First, the activities are defined. An activity might be a fully automated system call such as creating a new customer id, or a manual, interactive work step such as writing a memo by using an editor, or an intellectual work step such as deciding on a customer's discount.
2. *Assigning Activities to Roles:* For each activity, a corresponding role is assigned to it. This guarantees that at the time the workflow is executed, an adequate actor is selected for performing the activity.
3. *Definition of the Data Flow between Activities:* Here, we consider all data and all object identifiers which are relevant for the control flow. For example, in credit processing applications the amount of a credit request can determine subsequent processing steps.
4. *Coarse Definition of Control Flow:* In this step, the (partial) execution order of activities is determined. Activities with no precedence between them can be executed in parallel.
5. *Precise Definition of Control Flow:* For each activity, the preconditions for its execution have to be determined. Such conditions can refer to elements of the data flow (e.g. the credit amount), to the termination of other activities, or to temporal data such as deadlines.

The above steps can be iterated until a complete specification is determined. In our case studies, state and activity charts have proven their suitability, as they enforce precise specifications on one hand, but allow a later refinement of the specification on the other hand.

4.2.2 Transformation of BPR Specifications into State and Activity Charts. When discussing the above methodology with business practitioners such as bank staff, we have encountered problems in accepting the formal nature of state and activity charts for specifying business processes. Some practitioners prefer (informal) BPR tools because they are more intuitive to understand and easier to handle. Therefore, we have also investigated transformations from workflow specifications developed with BPR tools into state and activity charts. In this case, state and activity charts become a 'canonical', internal representation for workflows specified with various BPR tools.

In addition, in such an environment state and activity charts can also serve as an interchange format for workflow specifications between workflow management systems that use different specification languages. This transformation approach is feasible only if the control flow conditions in the BPR specification (given as text) can be interpreted as predicate symbols of a formal model of conditions which are evaluated at runtime. Since typical BPR tools would also accept contradicting or incomplete conditions, manual interaction may be required for transforming the BPR specification into state and activity charts.

As an example, we have investigated the following three tier transformation. Initially, business processes have been specified as event-process chains with the BPR tool ARIS-Toolset [SJ 96]. In a second step, these specifications have been transformed into FDL, the specification language of IBM's workflow management system FlowMark. This step was performed by a tool contained in the ARIS-Toolset. In the third step, the FDL specification served as input for an automatic conversion into state and activity charts, using a tool that we developed ourselves. Figures 1 and 2 show a specification developed with the ARIS-Toolset and the corresponding state and activity chart that was automatically generated. The underlying business process was taken from a set of business processes which model the administrative processes of the University of the Saarland. The example of Fig. 1 is (to a large extend) authentic. It describes the process of writing a project proposal addressed to the European Community (EU). The business process starts by gathering information about proposals for a new EU-funding program, performed by the administration of the university (role *SB 611:5*). The gathered information is posted to the research groups. Based on this information, research groups decide whether a project proposal should be submitted or not. If the decision is positive, initial steps are taken, involving the administration of the university. At the end of these initial steps, it is decided whether the project proposal should be written with help from EU-experts of the university or by the research group alone. Subsequent steps are not shown.

According to the ARIS terminology, in Fig. 1 rectangles with rounded edges represent functions, the hexagons represent events. Parallelism in the control flow is expressed by AND connectors, XOR connectors specify alternative executions. Assignments of roles to functions are expressed by edges between the rectangles representing functions and rectangles representing roles, the latter having an additional vertical line. Input and output in terms of documents is visualized by the usual document symbol. Figure 2 shows the part of the generated state chart that corresponds to the ARIS specification of Fig. 1. Some information contained in the ARIS specification is mapped to an activity chart, which is not shown. In order to save space, the transitions given in the state chart have been partly simplified, e.g., *IDENT34* is actually defined as: $DECISION\_APPLY\_FOR\_FUNDING$.

The completeness of the resulting state and activity chart, i.e., its direct executability, depends on the quality of the original specification of the business process. Hence, it is crucial that the specification developed with a BPR tool is as complete and precise as possible.

5. Utilizing Tools for Formal Verification

BPR tools often support the analysis of business processes from a business management point of view. In particular, they evaluate statistical data, e.g., about the execution times and the execution frequencies of activities. Verifying the correctness of workflow specifications, on the other hand, is still a rather unexplored issue of workflow management. The state of the art merely boils down to simulating workflow executions, based on a given set of input parameter patterns. The problem here is to find a set of input parameter patterns that is small enough to guarantee short simulation times but contains all necessary test patterns. To determine a good set of input parameters is up to the designer. A systematic approach to the verification of critical workflow properties must be based on formal verification methods. Such methods necessarily require a formal workflow specification.

5.1 Workflow Properties

Even with a formal approach, reasoning about a perfect match of workflow specifications and reality is impossible. Instead, we are aiming at the verification of selected, particularly critical properties of workflows which have to be represented formally as well. A number of proposals for the classification of properties of dynamic systems can be found in the literature. The probably most prominent one is Lamport's dichotomy of *safety* properties ("some bad thing never happens") and *liveness* properties ("some good thing eventually happens") [Lam 77]. In our example of the project proposal workflow, two safety properties would be:

- 'A project proposal cannot be accepted and rejected at the same time.'
- 'Funds cannot be transferred to the research group before a written cost statement is presented'

An example of a liveness property that considers possible terminations of the workflow would be:

- 'For each proposed project, either a contract is signed or the proposal is rejected.'

Note that these properties refer to process executions and cannot be expressed as dynamic integrity constraints on the data of the underlying information systems. Hence, the required properties cannot be enforced by standard database mechanisms. In principle, active database systems may be able to address this problem, but they suffer from other drawbacks (see Section 3).

5.2 Specification of Workflow Properties

A prerequisite for the verification of workflow properties is the modeling of these properties in a formal language. For this purpose, variants of temporal logic are well established [Eme 90, MP 92]. Temporal logic extends predicate logic by temporal operators. With these operators, conditions about the past or future can be modelled, for example: 'If p was true in the past, q will be true at some point in the future'. A temporal logic with an expressive power suitable for properties of workflows (according to our experience) is CTL (*Computation Tree Logic*) [ES 88]. In CTL, each temporal operator (X, F, G, U) is directly preceded by an existential quantifier E or an universal quantifier A. These quantifiers refer to the set of possible execution paths that branch out from the current state. The temporal operators have the following semantics: Xp ('neXt p') means that in the next step p holds; Fp ('Finally p') means that p will hold eventually; Gp ('Globally p') means that p will always hold; pUq ('p Until q') means that q will hold eventually, and until then p holds.

The informally stated properties of Section 5.1 for the EU project proposal workflow can be expressed in CTL as follows:

$$AG \neg EF(REJECT\_PROPOSAL\_S \; \& \; ACCEPT\_PROPOSAL\_S)$$

and

$$AG(FUNDS\_TRANSFER\_S \Rightarrow COST\_STATEMENT\_S)$$

and

$$AG(((EF \; DECISION\_TO\_APPLY\_DONE\_S)\&$$
$$(EX \; DECISION\_APPLY\_FOR\_FUNDING))$$
$$\Rightarrow EF(SIGN\_CONTRACT\_S \mid REJECT\_PROPOSAL\_S)).$$

The term AGp means that at all future time points of all possible executions p holds. EXp means that there exists at least one execution path where p holds in the next execution step on this path. EFp means that on at least one execution path p will eventually hold.

5.3 Model Checking

Once the critical workflow properties are formally stated, they can be verified against the formal specification of the workflow. Two different approaches are possible here. The first approach is using theorem provers, which automatically verify that a given specification has the desired properties. However, in many cases this approach is computationally infeasible. As a less powerful, but much more efficient approach, *model checking* can be used. In essence, model checking verifies whether a given finite state automaton (the workflow specification) is a model of a given temporal logic formula [Cla 86]. The most efficient variant of model checking is known as symbolic model checking [McM 93]. Symbolic model checking is based on a compact, symbolic representation of a finite state automaton in terms of an *ordered binary decision diagram (OBDD)* .

Because state charts are closely related to finite state automatons, model checking can be applied to state charts. Tools for symbolic model checking already exist (at least as research prototypes) and are used mainly in hardware design and for reactive embedded systems. In the MENTOR project we have used a tool for symbolic model checking described in [HK 94]. When using this tool, main memory turned out to be the decisive bottleneck. Verifying the formulas given in Section 5.2 required approximately 60MByte of main memory (the OBDD consisted of 39.467 nodes), and determining the result (tautology in all cases) took between 1 and 11 seconds. Although the resource requirements were high, the example shows that symbolic model checking is suitable even for the interactive verification of workflow specifications of non-trivial size. However, verifying critical workflow properties by means of model checking requires the workflow designer to be familiar with CTL. As a consequence, we anticipate that at least for the near future, model checking will remain a tool for experts among the designers of workflows. But it is also reasonable to assume that especially for the design of complex, mission critical workflows such experts will in fact be consulted.

6. Distributed Workflow Execution

Formal verification methods have an inherently centralized view of a specification: independently of the formal specification method used, they are based on a specification which comprises the whole system and does not reflect aspects of distribution. Complex workflows will, however, often be executed in a distributed fashion for the following reasons:

- Applications with a high number of concurrently active workflows, e.g., in insurance companies or medical applications, will impose a high workload on the underlying workflow management system which is responsible for maintaining the state and context information of all active workflows. Scalability and availability demands thus that the workflow management system be distributed across several servers.
- In complex workflows, activities of different departments or even autonomous branches of an enterprise cannot be freely assigned to workflow servers. Instead, the execution of an activity is often restricted to the workflow server 'owned' by the department where the activity belongs to. Hence, the organizational decentralization of an enterprise may explicitly demand a partitioning and distributed execution of a workflow.

We now present our method for the partitioning of workflow specifications. As we will see, partitioning the state chart is the most challenging part. The partitioning transforms a state chart into a behaviorally equivalent state chart that is directly amenable to distributed execution in that each distributable portion of the state chart forms an orthogonal component. The first step towards a partitioned specification is thus called *orthogonalization*. The outcome of this step is another state chart that can easily be partitioned. The proof that this transformation is indeed feasible in that it preserves the original state chart's semantics is cast into showing that the resulting orthogonalized state chart is a homomorphic image of the original specification. Note that we do not address the issue of 'streamlining' or optimizing business processes by altering the invocation order of activities. We are solely concerned with preparing workflow specifications for distributed execution.

6.1 Partitioning of State and Activity Charts

The partitioning of a workflow specification consists of two elementary transformations: the partitioning of the activity chart and of the state chart. We assume that for each activity of the activity chart there exists an assignment to the corresponding execution role and thus an assignment to a department or business unit of the enterprise. Therefore, each activity can be assigned to a workflow server of the corresponding department or business unit. Consequently, the partitioning of the activity chart falls out in a natural way in that all activities with an identical assignment form a partition of the activity chart.

While this is straightforward, the partitioning of the state chart requires more than simply assigning states to partitions. State charts can be state trees of arbitrary depth where parent states may have assignments that differ from the assignments of their children states. Furthermore, transitions may interconnect states at different levels of the state tree and/or with different assignments. In order to partition a state chart without changing its behavior, we pursue an approach which is different from the partitioning of the activity chart and is organized in three major steps:

(1) Assignment of states to activities
    In this step, each state is assigned to an activity of the activity chart. For each state, this assignment allows to derive to which execution role and department or business unit it belongs. In the case of nested state charts where a state can contain an entire state chart the higher level state will correspond to a higher-level activity chart with embedded subactivities.
(2) Orthogonalization of the state chart
    For each state of the state chart an orthogonal component is generated. Each generated orthogonal component emulates the corresponding original state S by means of two states, in_S and out_S, which are interconnected by transitions in both directions. These transitions correspond

to the transitions that lead to or originate from state S. The transition labels of these transitions are extended by conjunctive terms that refer to the source states of the original transitions. Figure 4 illustrates the orthogonalization for the state and activity chart of Fig. 3. For example, for the transition that interconnects states $ENCR\_S$ and $EVAL\_S$ the following transitions are generated: a transition from in_ENCR_S to out_ENCR_S, a transition from out_CCW_S to in_CCW_S, and a transition from out_RSK_S to in_RSK_S. The first transition has the same condition component in its transition label as the original transition, $ENCR\_OK$ and $not(amount < 1000)$. The other two transitions have the condition $ENCR\_OK$ and $not(amount < 1000)$ extended by a conjunctive term $IN(in\_ENCR\_S)$ as condition components and the start instructions for the corresponding activities as action components of their transition labels. This extension of condition components guarantees that in the orthogonalized state chart, all transitions which are generated from the same original transition fire at the same time. Consequently, in the example the activities CCW and RSK are started if and only if state $ENCR\_S$ is left, and $amount$ is not less than 1000. If $amount$ is less than 1000, the decision will be made without requiring an analysis of the company's credit worthiness and the risk, and state DEC_S is entered when $ENCR\_S$ is left. In this case, activities CCW and RSK are not invoked. Note that the orthogonal components in Fig. 4 have been automatically generated by our partitioning algorithm. This is the reason for the two transitions from state in_ENCR_S to state out_ENCR_S which could be merged into a single one with just $ENCR\_OK$ as condition component.

(3) Assignment of partitions to workflow servers

In this step, the orthogonal components that have been generated in step (2) are grouped into state chart partitions. The criterion for grouping a set of orthogonal components to form a state chart partition is the assignment of their underlying original states to the same department or business unit of the enterprise.

Note that for the example of Fig. 4, we assume that the activities CCW and RSK belong to the same partition, whereas the remaining activities belong to different partitions. The data flow between activities belonging to different partitions is indicated by data flow connectors that start or end at the borders of the boxes that represent partitions. If a partition contains several orthogonal components which have formed a coherent part in the original state chart, it is possible to merge these components. Consider, for example, partition $P4$ in Fig. 4. State in_INIT and out_ERR_S are left if one of the activities $ENCR$, CCW, RSK and DEC fails, i.e., the corresponding '$\_NOK'$ variable becomes $true$. The transition from out_ERR_S to in_ERR_S contains the term $IN(in\_INIT)$. If we change the source of this transition to the state in_INIT, and remove the now unnecessary states

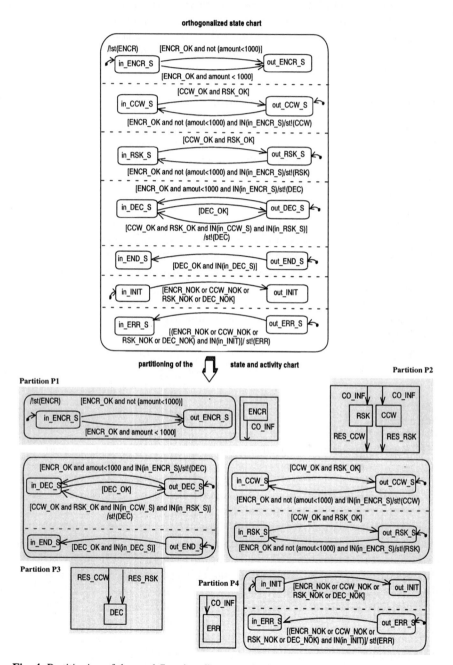

Fig. 4: Partitioning of the workflow 'credit processing'

out_INIT and *out_ERR_S*, we have reconstructed the corresponding part of the original state chart, namely the orthogonal component on the right side of the state chart in Fig. 3. An algorithm for this optional merging step is given in [Wod 96]. For the sake of simplicity, we do not consider such merges in the rest of the paper.

6.2 Correctness of the Partitioning

The feasibility of the described transformation depends on the assumption that the semantics of the original state chart is preserved. What is needed is a formal correctness proof that this is indeed the case. We will concentrate on the correctness proof of the orthogonalization (step (2)), which is the most critical step with regard to possible changes of the behavior of the state chart.

First, we will refer to a formally defined operational semantics of state charts, which is a simplified version of the semantics given in [HN 95]. It is tailored to our context of workflow specification (see [Wod 96] for full details). To this end, we define the set SC of *system configurations*. At each point, the system configuration describes the set of currently entered states and the context, i.e., the current values of conditions, events, and variables that are part of the state chart. For the execution of a state chart, we define a step operator, *step*, which maps a system configuration to its successor system configuration.

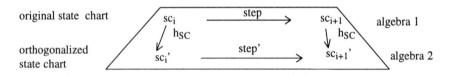

Fig. 5: Interrelationship between original state chart and orthogonalized state chart

Figure 5 illustrates the interdependence between the operational semantics of the original state chart and the operational semantics of its orthogonalized representation. We view both state charts as algebras with identical signatures. The carrier sets are the sets of system configurations, and the only operator is the step function. In order to distinguish between both carrier sets and operators, the carrier set and the operator of the algebra of the orthogonalized state chart (i.e., algebra 2) are denoted by SC' and *step'*, respectively. The interdependence between the two algebras is described by the mapping h_{SC}, which maps each system configuration of algebra 1 onto a system configuration of algebra 2. For the contexts this mapping is the identity mapping. With regard to the state configuration, h_{SC} maps each state Z that is currently entered onto the corresponding state *in_Z* of the orthogonalized state chart and each state Z that is currently not entered onto the corresponding state *out_Z* of the orthogonalized state chart.

If the diagram given in Fig. 5 commutes then algebra 2 of the orthogonalized state chart is a homomorphic image of algebra 1 of the original state chart. In this case, we say that the orthogonalized state chart is *behaviorally equivalent* to the original state chart, i.e., has the same properties as the original state chart. For example, the activities are started at the same time whenever both state charts are executed under identical external input. The following theorem states the above formally:

Theorem 1

The mapping h_{SC}, which maps each system configuration of an arbitrary state chart S onto system configurations of the orthogonalized state chart S' is a homomorphism. That is, for each timestep $i, i \geq 0$ and for each system configuration sc_i of S the following holds:

$$h_{SC}(step(sc_i)) = step'(h_{SC}(sc_i)),$$

with step being the step operator of S, $step'$ being the step operator of S', and both step operators being defined by the operational semantics of state charts.

A detailed presentation of the formal model and the proof can be found in [Wod 96] and [WW 97].

6.3 Synchronization

In distributed workflows, the execution of workflow partitions has to be synchronized. For a partition to execute the next step, the system configuration of other partitions, i.e., their state and context information, may be necessary. This is the case if information written in other partitions is used in a local condition or read by a local action. In the original state chart semantics, all updates to the system configuration are immediately and ubiquitously available for the evaluation of conditions and the execution of actions. This scheme can be implemented in a distributed environment by broadcasting all changes of local system configurations to all other partitions after a step is performed. The next step must not be performed before the corresponding information, the *synchronization data* from all other partitions, has been received.

In the following, we will discuss a simple communication scheme implementing the exchange of system configurations by sending synchronization messages between partitions according to the above rules. Issues of fault tolerance are considered in the next subsection. A more advanced scheme aiming to reduce the number and size of the required synchronization messages is presented in [Mut 97].

The computation and exchange of synchronization data between partitions is performed by the following three steps. The first two steps take place in the workflow engine executing the sending partition, the third takes place in the workflow engine executing the receiving partition.

(1) **Collecting updates:** All updates to state and context information are collected. This involves the detection of local updates in the executing state charts and activities, and the temporary storage of update information.

(2) **Communicating update information:** The synchronization data is send to the receiving partitions. If no synchronization data exists, an empty message is sent.

(3) **Propagating the updates in the receiving partition:** The received synchronization data is is used to update the system configuration of the receiving partitions. After synchronization messages from all remote partitions involved in the workflow have been received, a receiving partition is ready to perform the next step.

6.4 Fault Tolerance

We consider two kinds of failures, namely loss of messages and site failures. Consider the credit processing workflow and assume that the synchronization message that propagates the successful completion of the activity $ENCR$ (i.e., the update that sets condition $ENCR\_OK$ to *true*) is lost. In this case, the activities CCW and RSK will never be started. A similar problem arises if only a subset of these activities receives the synchronization message and thus starts executing. Both situations imply that the activity DEC will never be executed and the company will never be notified about whether the credit request is granted or rejected.

Now consider a different failure scenario in which the synchronization messages are successfully delivered but the site where the activity $ENCR$ is executed fails immediately after sending the messages. As an effect of this site failure, the data that was inserted by the $ENCR$ activity into a credit database may become corrupted (unless sufficient steps are already taken to make the data recoverable). Then, the activities CCW and RSK would start executing, but would possibly not be able to access their input data in the credit database. All these unacceptable situations can be avoided if there exists a mechanism that detects that a message is lost or data is corrupted and retransfers the message or reconstructs the data, respectively.

One prerequisite for reliable communication is that all messages are saved onto durable storage, i.e., a reliable message queue , so that they can be resent if necessary, even in the presence of site failures. However, this alone does not prevent the second one of the above two failure scenarios. To overcome this problem, it is necessary to combine the database update of the $ENCR$ activity and the two synchronization messages into a single atomic unit. This property is exactly what distributed transactions can provide [GR 93, BN 97]. Hence, in a workflow environment, transactions do not only refer to database updates but should also control message deliveries. A message should actually be delivered only upon the commit of the transaction. Thus, if the $ENCR$ site fails before the commit of the transaction, the database update will be undone if necessary and the "pending" messages will be discarded. If the $ENCR$ site fails after commit, the database updates will be redone if necessary and the messages that are marked as pending will be actually delivered to their recipients.

In case of a failure after commit, it is unfortunately impossible to identify, in retrospect, the exact point of failure. Therefore, it may happen that a message is both sent upon the original commit and resent again as part of the recovery . Such a generation of duplicate messages may be a problem as well, since each of the two message arrivals may trigger non-idempotent effects in the receiving activity. Unless the activity is explicitly implemented to cope with duplicate messages, a system mechanism is needed to detect and eliminate duplicates, for example, based on message sequence numbers.

In MENTOR , we address the above problems by employing a TP monitor [Wei 96], namely, Tuxedo [Pri 94, Tux 94]. A TP monitor essentially provides the following functionality:

(1) It offers facilities for saving messages onto durable storage. The *System/Q* component of Tuxedo provides *enqueue/dequeue* operations on *reliable message queues* . Messages that have been saved onto such a queue are resilient to site failures.
(2) It guarantees the atomicity of all operations within a transaction. To be precise, the atomicity guarantee refers to all operations that are invoked on transactional resource managers that can participate in a distributed transaction and comply with a standardized commit protocol like *X/Open XA*. This requirement is satisfied by most commercially relevant database systems and also by the System/Q component of Tuxedo, which thus serves as a special resource manager under the coordination of Tuxedo.
(3) By embedding the sender's enqueue and the recipients' dequeue operations in transactions , it can be ensured that a message is delivered exactly once.

There is one more problem incurred by site failures that requires further recovery procedures beyond those provided by the TP monitor and the underlying resource managers. A site failure causes the loss of all information on the state chart execution of a failed workflow engine (i.e., the current state and the current context). This information is needed for continuing the workflow when the failed site is brought up again. To overcome this problem, all state transitions and updates to variables are recorded in a special *workflow log* . During the restart of a workflow engine, this log provides the necessary redo information for re-establishing the most recent state before the failure. Insertions into the workflow log are part of the Tuxedo-coordinated transactions which serve to propagate update information between the workflow engines. So, during recovery a failed workflow engine will be rolled forward exactly to its most recent synchronization point.

7. Conclusions

In this paper, we have advocated formal methods for the specification of workflows. We have demonstrated the usefulness of this approach by investigating the method of state and activity charts. For workflow specifications, the advantages are twofold: First, formal methods enable the automatic verification of critical workflow properties. Secondly, a formally founded workflow specification is an important asset for the distributed execution of workflows: we have presented a transformation scheme for partitioning a centralized workflow specification such that the resulting partitions are again state and activity charts that are provably equivalent to the original execution. In summary, we have achieved a seamless integration of the workflow specification, the use of tools for verifying workflow properties, and the distributed workflow execution.

In addition to the specification issues, we have investigated aspects of scalability, fault tolerance and availability. With the exception of a brief discussion of fault tolerance, these issues could not be discussed in this paper.

Further problems we want to consider in the future include the specification of transactional properties in workflows as well as dynamic modifications of workflows during execution:

- Many applications demand a facility for grouping a number of workflow activities into an atomic unit. Besides the required runtime mechanisms such as distributed transactions, compensation etc., the problem is to integrate the specification of transactions into the workflow specification and to analyze the impact of the specification of transactions on properties of the original specification [Alo 96, Ley 95, Ley 96, RS 95, Wei 93, WR 92].
- In applications such as concurrent engineering [MHR 96, OD 95] or medical information systems, there is a strong need for dynamic modifications of processes and interoperability with CSCW (computer-supported cooperative work) tools whenever unforeseen situations arise and intellectual interception is required. Applications should allow to add or remove activities or even change the control flow between activities while a workflow is already in progress. In principle, the method of state and activity charts as used in the MENTOR project supports such dynamic modifications. However, the seamless transition from rigid workflow specifications to CSCW raises more demanding issues beyond the scope of this paper.

Acknowledgements

We wish to thank the UBILAB of the Union Bank of Switzerland for the scientific and financial support of the MENTOR project as well as the Institut für Wirtschaftsinformatik at the University of the Saarland for contributing the business process specification of the EU project proposal example.

Transactional Support for Cooperative Applications

Jürgen Wäsch, Karl Aberer, Erich J. Neuhold

German National Research Center for Information Technology
Integrated Publication and Information Systems Institute (GMD-IPSI)
Dolivostraße 15, D-64293 Darmstadt, Germany
Email: {waesch,aberer,neuhold}@darmstadt.gmd.de

Abstract. Cooperative work on shared, persistent data requires computing system support to coordinate the work of multiple users and to ensure data consistency. Conventional database transaction models do not meet the requirements of cooperative applications. Isolation of transactions, as guaranteed by the ACID properties, contradicts the need of cooperation between users. In this paper, we investigate different advanced transaction models that target at improved support for cooperative applications. To that extent we analyze typical cooperative application scenarios and derive from that basic requirements for consistent access to shared databases. In particular we discuss in detail the cooperative transaction model that has been developed within the TRANSCOOP project. This model supports alternating periods of individual and joint work, and allows to exchange and share information consistently. It provides transactional execution guarantees both for the work of single users and for the overall cooperative effort. The model is applicable to a wide spectrum of cooperative applications ranging from creative design applications to structured workflow-like applications.

1. Introduction

The global information infrastructure – open networks, intranets as well as mobile networks – opens a growing number of opportunities to perform joint work efforts in locally distributed environments and within virtual organizations. This requires to support human interaction in cooperative working environments increasingly at a computing system level, in addition to conventional means, like phone or electronic mail. Examples of applications, where globalization of cooperative work is taking place, are design applications (like cooperative document authoring, CAD, CASE, or design for manufacturing), groupware systems (like shared whiteboards, corporate calendar managers, or meeting schedulers), business workflow management, and mobile information systems.

Most of these cooperative applications are based on shared databases, providing documents, design data, or business data. Usually, database management systems (DBMS) are used to model and store this information. Thus, DBMSs have to support the typical modes of interaction of cooperating users with each other and with the computing system. These interactions require support for multi-user cooperation on persistent, shared documents, long duration activities, and interactive user control. In mobile environments, work has to be possible when mobile co-workers are disconnected from the network. At the same time data and application constraints need to be enforced.

Ensuring consistency of persistent data in multi-user environments is the classical problem of concurrency control and transaction management in database research. The concept of transactions has been investigated in computer science from the early 1970s [Bjo 73, Dav 73]. Conventional transaction models are based on the assumption that a large number of relatively short-lived transactions are accessing a shared database (online transaction processing). This led to the emergence of the ACID transaction model [G 81, HR 83, BHG 87] that is based on the fundamental principles of atomicity, consistency, isolation, and durability of transactions. The model uses read/write serializability as a natural correctness criterion for the concurrent execution of transactions.

The success of transaction concepts in online transaction processing (OLTP) led to efforts to apply it to other application domains, which require more flexibility or a high degree of concurrency. The early work in extending the conventional transaction model kept the basic ACID principles while adding nesting of transactions [M 82, M 87, HR 87, BBG 89] to provide for fine-grained recovery and intra-transaction parallelism. Other approaches exploited commutativity properties of database operations [Kor 83, Wei 88, Her90, BR 92] to enhance concurrency.

The main characteristic of design applications (like cooperative authoring and CASE) is *user interaction*. In OLTP, programmers prepare transactions and users submit them for execution, whereas in interactive transactions users provide input while the transaction is running and even interactively control the transaction execution. Thus, transactions in these environments are of *long, uncertain duration*. As a result waits imposed by concurrency control are long-duration waits and aborts undo a large amount of work.

The shift from machine-oriented to human-oriented transaction concepts becomes even more important with the emergence and growing acceptance of workflow and groupware systems and mobile computing [Kor 95]. Transaction models in such environments have to support interactive activities of long duration where the classical paradigm of *competition* for resources is replaced by the need to *cooperate*. The emphasis, therefore, is not on preventing access to resources, but rather on the interoperation of concurrent activities of multiple cooperating users by the *semantically correct sharing and exchange of information*.

Obviously, conventional ACID transaction models are not appropriate for cooperative applications. However, for most of these applications, DBMS support is still needed to provide controlled access to persistent data shared among cooperating users. A cooperative transaction model has to allow multiple users to work cooperatively on persistent data but still has to provide transactional execution guarantees for the work of single users as well as for the overall cooperative effort.

In this paper, we investigate transaction models that target on improved support for cooperative applications. To that extent we analyze typical cooperative applications and derive from that analysis basic requirements for consistent access to shared databases in cooperative applications. Among different approaches to support cooperative applications a number of advanced transaction models have been proposed that can satisfy certain of the requirements we identify. By means of a running example we introduce these models and discuss their main properties. A substantial part of this paper is devoted to the cooperative transaction model that has been developed within the TRANSCOOP project[1].

The goal of TRANSCOOP has been the development of a cooperative transaction model and a corresponding specification language that are applicable to a wide spectrum of cooperative applications [AKT+96, AEF+97]. The TRANSCOOP specification language CoCoA allows the declarative specification of workflow-like cooperative scenarios [FEB 96, FEdBA 97]. The TRANSCOOP cooperative transaction model CoAct [RKT+95, WK96, Waes96a, KTW96b] provides the basic transactional support to ensure consistent management of shared data in cooperative applications.

We describe the fundamentals of the TRANSCOOP cooperative transaction model in detail, including our assumptions about the structure of cooperative applications. The CoAct model supports alternating periods of individual and joint work, and allows to exchange and share information consistently. To provide this flexibly, we take an operation-oriented view: the consistency of shared work results is determined, based on the semantics of the operations performed to obtain these results. CoAct builds the core of the TRANSCOOP runtime environment for cooperative applications which has been implemented as an extension of the object-oriented DBMS VODAK [GI 95] developed at GMD-IPSI.

2. Transactional Support for Cooperative Applications

In general, the objective of cooperative applications is to support the work of a group of people engaged in a common task or goal. The term cooperative application refers generally to any cooperation between users where computer systems are used for interactions between users and for sharing and exchanging information among the users [EGR91].

---

[1] This work was partially done in the ESPRIT III LTR project TRANSCOOP (EP8012) which is partially funded by the Commission of the European Communities. The partners in the TRANSCOOP project are GMD (Germany), University of Twente (The Netherlands), and VTT (Finland).

2.1 Characteristics of Cooperative Applications

In the following, we discuss three typical types of cooperative applications with respect to requirements for a cooperative transaction model, namely *Cooperative Hypermedia Document Authoring, Design for Manufacturing*, and *Workflow applications* [TVL+ 97, TV 95, VT95].

Cooperative Hypermedia Document Authoring [TW 95]. Cooperative Hypermedia Document Authoring (CDA) is characterized by multiple authors working interactively on shared, persistent hypermedia documents. Hypermedia document authoring can be considered as a design problem solving process [HF86], mainly characterized by the decomposition of the design problem into smaller subproblems and their solution by interacting activities. An important characteristics of these processes is that the documents to be produced can be described only vaguely in advance. Authoring activities require a high degree of *flexibility* in choosing subsequent actions in order to end up with the final document. An example of CDA is the cooperative hypermedia authoring system SEPIA [SHT89, SHH+ 92, WA 97] which offers different interacting authoring spaces for dedicated authoring activities without constraining the authors in their creative processes. SEPIA's concepts can also be applied to systems engineering and software development processes [BWAH96, BLW 96].

Design for Manufacturing [VFSE 95]. Design for Manufacturing (DfM) can be seen as a variant of Concurrent Engineering. The scope of DfM is the engineering process of discrete complex industrial artifacts, usually separated into upstream processes (product design) and downstream processes (production realization, including engineering, planning, and manufacturing) [SRN 93]. The essential part of DfM is the early involvement of specialists from downstream processes in the upstream design process. Thus, the strengthening of the design process by *overlapping* design phases requires extensive cooperation and coordination facilities. In comparison to cooperative authoring, more detailed knowledge about the engineering processes in different phases and about the sequence of processing is available.

Workflow applications [J+ 96]. Workflows are used to define complicated business processes, e.g., to accomplish the production of goods or services. A workflow consists of a collection of activities (also called tasks or steps) that are partially ordered by control and data flow dependencies. Activities are the basic units of work that are processed by one responsible actor. Thus, workflows focus mainly on the *coordination* of activities. Workflows may involve both automatized/machine-based tasks, where a DBMS or other information systems are involved, and human-based tasks, where human beings are required to intervene and influence the flow of control, and thus the cooperation.

The three application scenarios can be classified as *DBMS-based, asynchronous* cooperative applications, emphasizing different aspects of the communication, collaboration and coordination properties of CSCW systems [EGR91]. Asynchronous cooperative applications do not require that all co-workers are present at the same time. They support an incremental style of working where each co-worker can work at arbitrary time and places on (parts of) the common documents. One can identify the following common charac-teristics (for details, we refer to [TVL+ 97, TV 95, VT95, TW 95, VFSE 95, J+ 96]):

- Multiple concurrent users are involved in multiple activities to satisfy a common goal or to produce a common product or artifact.
- Activities are processed interactively by humans and are usually of long, uncertain duration.
- Cooperative work is characterized by alternating periods of individual and joint work.
- Not all co-workers may be simultaneously present in the cooperative work process.
- Exchange and sharing of persistent data among different users performing several activities is a basic feature.
- There is a need to ensure consistency both for the work of a single user as well as for the cooperative effort.
- Between activities there may exist control flow dependencies that are de-rived from the application domain.
- It is likely that co-workers are geographically distributed and only partially connected, due to the increasing mobility of co-workers.

The relevance of these characteristics varies for the three application do-mains. For example, in workflow scenarios, control flow dependencies are of higher importance than in the cooperative authoring domain. We can iden-tify a spectrum, ranging from cooperative document authoring to workflow applications, where the solutions become more fixed and prescribed, allowing the problem-solving process and termination conditions to be more determin-istically described.

2.2 Motivating Example

Throughout this article, we use an example from the software engineering domain to illustrate the concepts of transactional support for cooperative applications. The example is based on the one presented in [WK96] and sim-ilar to the examples used in [BK91, Kai 95, RC 97]. We have chosen this example because it is more intuitive than CDA, DfM, and workflows and most of the readers are familiar with software development. With respect to the spectrum of cooperative applications presented in the previous section, software development can be classified as a semi-structured design process (like DfM) with a more or less predefined structure at the top-level and some known consistency constraints. Possible steps are specification, implementation, and debugging which may be overlapping and iterative. At the lower abstraction levels the process is rather unstructured (like in CDA).

Assume, a group of programmers, including Alice and Bob, is cooperatively working on the development of a Java application program using a distributed DBMS-based software development environment (SDE). The SDE encapsulates Java application programs, Java packages (which are similar to class libraries), and Java classes as database objects. By providing a well-defined interface to these objects, the SDE abstracts from the internal details of the structure and storage of objects. Within the SDE, a program consists of several class objects and packages. A package object consists of several class objects, sub-packages, and programmer's annotations to the package. Finally, class objects consist of the class' source code, the class' bytecode, and again textual annotations. Examples of interface operations provided by the SDE are browsing/modifying the source code of a class, reading/adding/removing annotations of a class, and compiling the class. To give programmers convenient access to the objects managed by the SDE, the objects can be stored internally as interrelated structured objects, like in [BWAH96, BLW 96, WA 97]. There, the objects are visualized using a generic hypermedia desktop.

Assume that during the development of an application program some bugs occur. Alice and Bob are assigned the task to cooperatively fix the bugs. Alice should fix a bug suspected in class X while Bob should fix the bugs in class Y. Both classes use methods of package Z. Alice starts a debug transaction and edits class X while Bob starts a transaction to fix the bugs in Y. During debugging Bob detects that some bugs in class Y are possibly caused by bugs in Z. Therefore, he starts to work on Z. Although Bob's modifications to Y do not affect class X it may be the case that the modification and re-compilation of Z may introduce inconsistencies with class X.

As discussed in [BK91, Kai 95] the usage of concurrency control policies that apply serializability as their correctness criteria prohibits Alice and Bob to cooperatively work on package Z. Even concurrently adding and reading annotations to classes is not possible. The reason is that serializability does not allow that users' transactions are coupled and are able to influence each other in a controlled way.

2.3 Requirements for a Cooperative Transaction Model

A main objective of a cooperative transaction processing system is to provide a cooperative transaction model that supports the key requirements of a broad spectrum of cooperative applications. Based on our running example, we now discuss the basic requirements for a cooperative transaction model [TVL+ 97, AKT+96, TV 95, VT95, TW 95].

A. Relaxed atomicity. The rollback of the whole cooperative work process in the case of failure is generally not acceptable. It is required that a cooperative process should be able to proceed (and eventually succeed) even if other parts of the cooperative process fail. A failure within one user's activity should not imply the rollback of another user's work in their joint effort.

For example, if a failure occurs within Bob's debug transaction, not the whole cooperative debugging session, i.e., Alice's *and* Bob's transaction, should be rolled back – even if Alice has been able to observe Bob's modifications to Z. Moreover, if the failure occurs during Bob's re-compilation of package Z, only the bytecode of Z should be restored to the state before the compilation started. Bob's modifications to the source code of Z need not to be undone because they are not affected by the failure.

B. Retraction of decisions. To support the interactive control of activities, a cooperative transaction model has to provide services that allow to retract decisions taken by the cooperating actors. For this, the model has to capture the relevant dependencies between users' actions. This allows a user to explore several alternatives to solve a problem and to revise erroneous actions.

For instance, if Bob modifies some classes in Z and then recompiles Z (without success) he might detect that his modifications introduced new errors. In this case, he might want to revert some of his changes. Or, after Bob commits his transaction, Alice might detect that Bob has changed a constructor method in class Z that is often used in class X. If she wants to undo Bob's changes, the transaction model should be able to rollback to a consistent system state, i.e., if Bob's modifications to the source code are undone also the bytecode has to be restored automatically to the old version.

C. Support for exchange of work. The sharing of final, as well as of intermediate artifacts among co-workers is a prerequisite for cooperative applications. A cooperative transaction model should provide mechanisms to facilitate the exchange of tentative or partial results, while at the same time guaranteeing that no anomalies are introduced by the exchanges. The transaction model should offer appropriate primitives for the semantically correct exchange of information between co-workers.

For example, Alice might want to browse the source code of Z while Bob's debug transaction is still ongoing (to check if Bob's modifications affect her work). On the other hand, Alice might wish to annotate class X and make her annotation *visible* to Bob while her transaction is still running. Or, assume Alice is allowed to test class X with the bytecode of Z generated by Bob. To guarantee that no anomalies are introduced, the transaction model should give Alice access either to both the source and the bytecode or only to the new source code of Z (because the new bytecode is based on the modified source code).

D. Support for private and shared data. To explore different solutions of the same problem, different co-worker should be able to work at the *same* time on the *same* data. To avoid interference from co-workers, the cooperative transaction model should be able to manage alternative versions of data objects. Upon user's request, it should be possible to exchange versions and to combine them into a commonly accepted version. Moreover, to support distribution and mobility the model should be able to deal with multiple copies of data objects.

For example, Alice should be able to use the old version of Z for her tests while Bob is modifying and recompiling Z if they decide to *temporarily* allow inconsistencies which are resolved at a later time. Even if Alice wants to modify class Z this should be allowed at the price that *some* modifications have to be undone later to produce a consistent version set of X, Y, and Z. In case Alice wants to debug class X while she is on a business trip she has to reserve and copy the whole package Z onto her laptop in order to be able to test X. This should not preclude Bob from working on the stationary copy of Z. Of course, possible conflicts have to be detected automatically during reconciliation of Alice's work. The necessary conflict resolutions should be guided by the cooperative transaction model.

E. Coordination of individual and joint work. In cooperative applications different users work together. To achieve a common goal, facilities are needed to coordinate each user's work. To describe the pre-planned parts of cooperative scenarios and the decomposition of the overall work, a cooperative transaction model should allow the definition of *execution constraints*. Execution constraints should be able to describe the possible structure of a single user's activity as well as the overall cooperative work process. This includes constraints on the occurrence of particular subactivities and user actions and on their execution order within the overall cooperative process.

An example for an execution constraint for the whole cooperative software development activity is to prohibit the modification of the design document while the development process is solely in the testing phase. This does not preclude to activate the design phase again (if allowed by the execution constraints). An example for an execution constraint at the level of a single user's activity is that Bob only can commit his debug transaction if he has successfully recompiled all modified classes.

Of course, further requirements are imposed on cooperative systems. For example, to support the mutual awareness of co-workers notification mechanisms are needed. Additional communication facilities, like e-mail or audio, may be required for direct negotiation of co-workers. Such services are not covered by a cooperative transaction model that aims at synchronizing the cooperative access to persistent data. Nevertheless, a cooperative transaction model satisfying the above requirements can provide an application-independent nucleus to build a wide spectrum of cooperative applications on top of it.

2.4 Approaches to Support Cooperative Work

The issue of synchronization of multiple cooperating users is treated in several fields, including groupware, workflow systems, and advanced transaction models.

Groupware Systems. Most groupware systems [EGR91] synchronize cooperative access to shared data in a more or less *ad-hoc* manner. Concurrency control in most systems is based on mechanisms like explicit user-controlled locking of objects, different lock modes, extended lock semantics, and notifications [WL93, GS 87]. Some systems are using floor passing protocols [GS 87] to synchronize concurrent operations on shared data, thereby limiting the availability of data. Other systems do not provide any concurrency control at all and rely on social protocols [EGR91]. Other approaches in the CSCW area (e.g., [EG89]) are only applicable to real-time groupware systems like shared whiteboards and synchronous group editors. Most of these systems are based on replication of data and use multicast protocols [BSS91] for synchronization purposes. Real-time groupware systems do not address the issues of persistency of data and recovery to ensure fault-tolerant processing.

Workflow Management Systems. Workflow management is gaining popularity, although the current generation of workflow management systems (WFMS) has several limitations [GHS 95, J+ 96]. Many of these deficiencies results from the strong process orientation of WFMS – neglecting data-centric issues. Deficiencies are, for example, the lack of support for correctness and data consistency (in the case of concurrent workflow tasks), and insufficient recovery mechanisms. Most of the commercial WFMS concentrate on relatively static workflows. Current WFMS do not have adequate modeling and execution support for dynamically determined executions of activities, as required for example in CDA.

Advanced Transaction Models. Transaction models in general are guaranteeing fault tolerance and synchronize concurrent access to shared, persistent data. To support cooperative applications, several advanced transaction models have been proposed in the recent years. The next section will give a detailed discussion of some of them that were particularly relevant for developing the TRANSCOOP cooperative transaction model that is discussed in Section 4. For an overview of these models we refer the reader also to [Elm 92, Hsu 93, BK91, Kai 95, RC 97, VWP+97].

3. Towards a Cooperative Transaction Model

3.1 Semantics-Based Approaches

Usually, the semantics of data sharing in cooperative applications is much more complex than the read/write semantics used by conventional database transaction models. As a result concurrency control policies of conventional transaction models are more restrictive than necessary because they do not take into account the semantics of the data objects for cooperative applications.

3.1.1 Semantics-Based Concurrency Control. Semantics-based concurrency control was first proposed in the context of abstract data types [Kor 83, SS 84, Wei 88] and later adopted for object-oriented DBMS. Its main goal is to achieve a higher degree of concurrency than in traditional read/write transaction models. Additionally, the semantics of data objects can be used to provide increased availability of data and more flexible recovery. For an overview of semantics-based concurrency control techniques we refer to [RC 97].

The idea behind semantics-based concurrency control is as follows. By abstracting from the low-level details, i.e., the concrete implementation in the database, and by exploiting the high-level semantics of data objects, certain concurrency conflicts that might occur in the read/write model can be ignored. The most commonly used approach to capture the semantics of data objects is to specify *commutativity* relations among operations defined on data objects. Informally, two operations commute (do not conflict) if their effect on the object state and their return values are the same regardless of their execution order. This ensures that no transaction can observe a difference between the both execution orders. When a transaction requests the execution of an operation, this request can be granted if the operation commutes with all other operations of uncommitted transactions. This policy ensures that concurrent transactions are serializable at a semantic level and the ACID properties of transactions are preserved. Of course, the operations have to be executed atomically, i.e., sequentially in this case.

Example: Consider the following operations to add and remove annotations to a class object: annC(C:Class):AnnID and remA(C:Class,A:AnnID). Two annC(X) operations both modify the class object X in the SDE, and, hence, they conflict on the level of read/write operations. However, by considering the high-level semantics, they commute, because the resulting set of annotations for the class is the same for both execution orders.   □

Weihl [Wei 88, Wei 89] distinguishes between *backward commutativity* and *forward commutativity*. The difference is the underlying execution model. The former is applicable to an update-in-place execution model whereas the latter is applicable to optimistic concurrency control and deferred-update policies. Other (non-symmetric) semantic relations have been proposed in the literature that relax the requirements on the state equivalence of the data objects and enable an even higher degree of concurrency control. In [Her 86, Her90], the *invalidated-by* relationship has been introduced for optimistic concurrency. *Recoverability* [BR 92] allows non-commuting but recoverable operations to be executed concurrently.

Semantics-based concurrency control fulfills none of the requirements stated in Section 2.3 directly, but it achieves a higher degree of concurrency. Thereby, it reduces the probability of long waits or aborts which is important when transactions are of long duration. The commutativity relations are also used in the TRANSCOOP cooperative transaction model described in Section 4.

3.1.2 Open-nested Transactions. The basic goal of multi-level transactions [Wei 91, W 92] and its generalization to open-nested transactions [W 92, MRW+ 93] is to enhance inter-transaction parallelism and to allow for a finer recovery granularity. This is achieved by modeling a transaction as a tree of subtransactions, by exploiting the semantics of database operations, and through recovery by *compensation* (like in SAGAs [GMS 87]) rather than by state-based undo.

A multi-level transaction has an implicit internal structure where the nodes in the transaction *tree* correspond to executions of database operations at particular levels of abstraction in a layered database system. *Multi-level serializability* replaces traditional read/write serializability as correctness criterion while preserving the ACID properties of transactions. The idea is to exploit the semantics of database operations in level-specific conflict relations based on commutativity. Conflicts at a lower level can be ignored if two operations at a higher level commute. This policy allows more concurrency than "flat" semantic serializability. For open-nested transactions, siblings in the tree are allowed to have different nesting depth. Open-nested transactions are well-suited for object-oriented DBMS. The dynamic method invocation hierarchy can be transformed to an open-nested transaction. In open-nested transactions, *semantic serializability* [MRW+ 93] replaces multi-level serializability.

As a consequence of the early visibility of modifications to commuting subtransactions, the abort of a subtransaction can no longer be implemented by restoring the database state directly to the state before the subtransaction. An already committed subtransaction S has to be undone by its compensating subtransaction that semantically undoes the effects of S. Before a subtransaction S can be compensated, all other subtransactions of the same transaction executed after S have to be compensated in inverse order. This is similar to the approach used in SAGAs. The compensating subtransactions are fully embedded in the concurrency control mechanism, i.e., they are executed as regular transactions.

Example: Figure 1 shows an example of open-nested transactions. Alice starts transaction T_1 and annotates class X while Bob starts transaction T_2 and annotates the same class simultaneously. Each annC(X) subtransaction creates a new annotation and inserts it into the set of annotations associated with X. The leafs of the tree consist of atomic disk operations. In contrast to "flat" semantic concurrency control, it is now possible to execute the annC(X) operations concurrently. Clearly, the schedule at the leaf

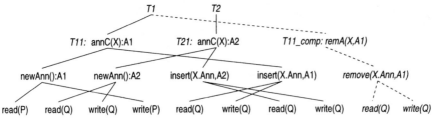

Fig. 1. Example of open-nested transactions

level is not read/write serializable but T_1 and T_2 are semantically serializable. If Alice aborts her transaction later on, the system has to execute the compensating operation for T_{11} to remove her annotation from class X, i.e., T_{11_comp} : remA(X,A1). This is possible without affecting Bob's transaction because T_{21} and T_{11_comp} commute. State-based undo is not possible because Bob's annotation would have been removed from X, too, in this case.
□

Long running transactions are well supported by open-nested transactions because of the high degree of parallelism. In addition, the model provides a finer granularity of recovery (partial rollback). Nevertheless, sharing of tentative data is not possible because the model sticks to serializability as its correctness criteria. User-initiated undo can be implemented by exploiting the commutativity relations and the compensation mechanism (see also Section 4.6.1). In [W 92] some further extensions of open-nested transactions are outlined to adapt them to specific application needs. In general, we can say that requirements A, B of Section 2.3 are partially supported by open-nested transaction.

3.2 Check-out/Check-in, Versioning, and Workspaces

One of the simplest forms of synchronizing the access of a design team to a shared repository is the check-out/check-in model. Data objects have to be explicitly checked-out by a designer, i.e., objects are copied from the shared database to his *private workspace*, where the objects can be manipulated. In the simplest case, checked-out objects are reserved for exclusive access until a later check-in into the shared database. Check-out and check-in have to be atomic. Obviously, this policy restricts the availability of data enormously.

Therefore, the check-out/check-in model appears in most cases in tandem with *versions* and *configurations* [Kat 90], like in version control tools [Tic 85]. A version of an object is simply a "snapshot" of an object's state at a particular point in time. Versions may be mutable or immutable. If an immutable version is checked-out, a new successor version is first derived from the original one and then copied to the workspace. The checked-out version is reserved exclusively, but another user may derive a new version that can be checked out. This results in branches in the object's version history. Of

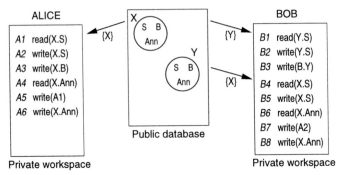

Fig. 2. Check-out/check-in example

course, the parallel versions have to be merged (manually) in order to come up with a single, commonly agreed result of the object. Another problem is to keep track of which versions of different objects form a consistent version set. For example, if there exist several versions of classes X and Y, it is difficult to find out which versions of X and Y can be used to compile executable code. Therefore, versions are grouped into consistent versions sets, called configurations. Dealing with configurations complicates version management and the check-out/check-in process, and might decrease concurrency because always whole configurations have to be reserved.

For software development applications, several extensions of the check-out/check-in model have been developed, taking advantage of automatic software consistency checking in those environments [KF 87, KPS 89, Hon 88]. Due to the fact that such consistency checking mechanisms are not available in all application domains, these approaches are not generally applicable.

Example: An example is shown in Figure 2. Alice checks-out class X, i.e., the source and the bytecode of X and the annotations made to X. Bob checks out class Y. This leads to exclusive locks for X and Y in the public database. Alice edits the source code of X (operations A_1, A_2), compiles the bytecode (A_3), and annotates class X (A_4, A_5, A_6). Bob edits and compiles Y. He recognizes that he needs class X to check if his modifications affect this class. Check-out of X is not possible because it is exclusively reserved by Alice. He can either create a new version of X, that he can check-out, or ask Alice to check-in X. In the former case Bob can not see the modifications of Alice to the source code, not even the annotations Alice made to X. The parallelly developed versions of X have to be manually merged later on. Even if Bob has only annotated class X an automatic merge would not be possible because the check-out/check-in model does not take into account the (semantics of) operations executed in the private workspaces. In the latter case Alice is no longer able to work on X but Bob can observe her modifications. Other problems might occur if Alice is allowed to check-out/check-in only the source code or the bytecode of X. In this case a class is no longer a (implicit) configuration. This would enable a higher degree of cooperation but might violate consistency. For example, if Alice checks-out the source and bytecode of X (now separately) and later checks-in the bytecode, Bob can observe inconsistencies (he might not be aware off) between his version of the source and the bytecode of X. □

Obviously, check-out/check-in models fulfill requirement D (support for private and shared data) stated in Section 2.3. If check-out/check-in models are combined with versioning mechanisms and configurations, they fulfill to some extend also the requirements A, B, and C. Versioning supports the exchange of results among co-workers, if one accepts that versions have to merged later and that version sets may become inconsistent. Retraction of decision and relaxed atomicity is partially supported by versioning, too, because one can "rollback" to immutable versions in the version history.

3.3 Split/Join Transactions and Delegation

The split/join transaction model [PKH 88, KP 92] was developed for open-ended activities characterized by uncertain duration, unpredictable developments, and interactions with other concurrent activities. The model addresses cooperation among users by supporting the *dynamic restructuring* of ongoing transactions. A split command allows to split a running transaction into two transactions, while a join command allows to incorporate two transactions into one transaction. The correctness criteria used is read/write serializability of transactions to be committed. In contrast to other models, there exists no simple relationship between the set of transactions initiated and those that are committed. Serializability is guaranteed by permitting only those restructuring commands that preserve a serializable schedule.

A *split* divides a running transaction T_A into two transactions, T'_A and T_B. Read and write operations that have been executed by T_A are assigned to T'_A or T_B. T'_A and T_B are then responsible for committing or aborting the assigned operations. A split is only allowed to be executed if T'_A and T_B are serializable. Dependent on the assignment of conflicting operations we can distinguish between a serial split where the commit of T_B is dependent on the commit of T'_A and an independent split where T_B and T'_A can commit/abort independently. For interactively executed transactions the serial case is only allowed, if T_A is committed immediately after the split-operation. The *join* command joins a transaction T_A to the target transaction T_B by adding the read and write sets of T_A to T_B. Before the join becomes valid and T_A disappears, T_B has to accept it. Afterwards, T_B can use any resources from T_A and all changes of T_A to the database will become valid at commit of T_B.

A similar concept to split/join can be found in ACTA [CR 90, CR 92]. ACTA is a transaction meta-model that can be used to specify the types of dependencies between transactions. One of its building blocks is the *delegation* primitive [CR 93]. Delegation in ACTA means that the responsibility

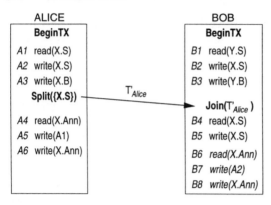

Fig. 3. Split/join example

for committing or aborting operations can be delegated from one transaction to another transaction. In this way, tentative results can be made visible to co-workers.

Example: An example of split/join transactions is shown in Figure 3. Alice and Bob start their own transactions. Bob modifies class Y and recompiles it. Alice does the same for class X. Assume Bob wants to access class X. This is not possible because the source and bytecode of X is locked by Alice (if locking is applied). Therefore, he asks Alice to release the source of X. Alice fulfills his request by splitting her ongoing transaction ($\mathsf{Split}(\{X.S\})$). This results in the creation of a new transaction T'_{Alice} (independent case). The read and write sets of T'_{Alice} consists of the source of X while the read set of the original transaction becomes empty and the write set becomes $\{X.B\}$. Bob joins T'_{Alice} to his running transaction. Now, Bob is able to modify the source of X, but Alice is no longer able to browse or modify the source of X because T'_{Alice} is now under control of Bob. Assume, Alice annotates class X (operations A_4, A_5, A_6 in Figure 3) and Bob tries to annotate X, too. This results in blocking his transactions because B_6 conflicts with A_6 (note that this conflict does not occur if the semantics of operations had been exploited). If Alice splits again her transaction ($\mathsf{Split}(\{X.Ann\})$) and commits the new transaction immediately, Bob can continue because the lock on X.Ann is released now. Note, if Bob now reads the set of annotations he will discover a new annotation but he is not able to read it because it is still under control of Alice.   □

Splitting and joining ongoing transactions enable a cooperative behavior by delegating parts of transactions to a co-worker. Thus, the split/join transaction model fulfills quite well requirement C. Other advantages of the split/join model are adaptive recovery (requirement A) and increased concurrency if the splitted transaction is committed immediately, i.e., the resources are released and made persistent prior to the commit of the original transaction. An open problem is how to ensure that two transactions resulting from a split form again consistent units of work. The requirements A, D, and E (retraction of decisions, private work areas, and coordination of joint work) are not addressed by the model.

3.4 Group-Oriented Approaches and Transactional Workflow

Group-oriented transaction approaches describe the overall working process as a transaction *hierarchy* consisting of group transactions. Individual user transactions form the leaves of the transaction hierarchy. Visibility between transactions is supported by extended lock schemes [KSUW 85, BKK 85, FZ 89, U 92] or by following predefined access patterns that define the application-specific correctness criteria like in [NZ 92, N 90].

In the *cooperative transaction hierarchy* approach [N 90, NZ 92] each group transaction defines a set of rules that specify the way the child transactions can interact and how data objects can be shared among them. Correct histories are specified by *patterns* and *conflicts* [Ska 89] using finite-state automata. Conflicts are comparable to locks in the sense that they specify when certain operations can not be executed. Patterns specify that specific operation sequences have to occur. Cooperation is enabled by allowing non-serializable executions of transactions that belong to the same group. The usability of this model is restricted because significant parts of the cooperative application have to be pre-specified in order to describe whether a particular non-serializable execution is correct or not.

The area of *transactional workflow* approaches [RS 94] usually comprises specification languages to express various *execution constraints* for a set of tasks (assigned to single users). This can be done either by supporting a script language like in the ConTract model [WR 92], by a declarative specification of the execution structure in terms of externally visible execution states [Att 93], or by ECA rules [DHL 90]. Cooperation is characterized in these models by passing results between workflow tasks in a predefined manner. Flexible but controlled sharing of data objects among tasks or among co-workers participating in the same task is not supported by these models. This is essential in non-workflow scenarios like CDA, DfM, and software development.

4. The TRANSCOOP Approach

As described in Section 2.1, cooperative work has several dimensions, and the requirements for a cooperative system largely vary depending on the application. In the TRANSCOOP project, it was the aim to satisfy these requirements by introducing a set of complementary mechanisms, which can be used by the application designer to tailor the system for specific needs [AKT+96, AEF+97, dBKV 97].

For this, a cooperative transaction model and a corresponding specification language have been developed, that are applicable to a wide spectrum of cooperative scenarios. We distinguish between *organizational* and *transactional* aspects of a cooperative activity. The former is mainly concerned with the workflow-like coordination of users within a joint effort. The latter is mainly concerned with consistency of data sharing and exchange.

The specification language CoCoA [FEdB 96, FEdBA 97, EFdBP96] allows the description of both organizational and transactional aspects of a cooperative activity by using declarative language constructs that extend a given database schema [FEdBA 97]. The underlying cooperative transaction model CoAct [RKT+95, Waes96a, WK96, KTW96b, KTWK97] provides the basic transactional support to ensure consistent management of shared, persistent data in cooperative applications.

In this section we describe the building blocks of the TransCoop cooperative transaction model, its formal foundation, and its implementation within the TransCoop demonstrator system. We discuss its relationship to the requirements stated in Section 2.3 and to the advanced transaction models discussed in the previous section.

4.1 Overview of the COACT Transaction Model

The *Cooperative Activity Model* [RKT+95, WK96, KTW96b, KTWK97] (CoAct) starts from the observation stated in Section 2.1, that cooperative work is characterized by alternating periods of individual and joint work [TV 95, TW 95, Kai 95, TVL+ 97]. During individual work periods users explore alternative problem solutions while co-workers may work simultaneously on the same subject. Access to and use of shared data should neither block other users, nor should it affect co-workers un-intendedly. During joint work co-workers should be able to exchange information and to share final as well as intermediate results. Moreover, dynamic subgrouping of co-workers should be possible.

In CoAct we assign a *private workspace* to every user who takes part in a *cooperative activity*. By default, the private workspaces of the co-workers are isolated from each other. Additionally, there is also a *common workspace* for each cooperative activity. This workspace is isolated from the private workspaces; it is not assigned to any single user in the cooperative activity. The common workspace contains the data objects available when a cooperative activity is *started*, and it will contain the results of the cooperative activity when the activity is *committed*. Figure 4 gives an illustration of these constituents of the CoAct model.

To achieve isolation of workspaces we (conceptually) copy the data objects initially contained in the common workspace to all private workspaces. From these copies the users can create their own private versions of data items, which can be independently manipulated. Hence, the modifications to data objects done by different co-workers do not interfere. For each workspace a log of the modifications is kept in a *workspace history*. In CoAct each cooperative activity is described by:

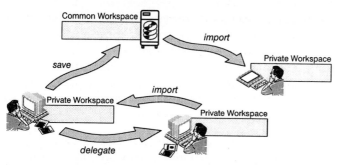

Fig. 4. Workspaces and exchange facilities in CoAct

1. A set of *operation types* $\mathcal{OT}$ that can be invoked by a user in his private workspace. For each operation a *compensating operation* is specified (by a compensation function *comp*) which semantically undoes the effects of the original operation.
2. A set of type-specific merging relations that exploit the semantics of operations. These relations are based on *commutativity* and guide the process of information exchange (*history merging* [WK96, KTW96b].

We assume an environment where the sequence of operations executed in a workspace is composed interactively by the user at runtime (like in SEPIA [SHH+ 92, WA 97]). A user selects the next operation from the predefined operation set $\mathcal{OT}$ and provides the actual input parameter values to the operation. Each user interaction is modeled as a single operation in CoAct. Operations are the smallest units of work within a cooperative activity. An operation is considered to be atomic and to transfer a consistent workspace state to another consistent state. The executed operations are logged in the workspace history together with their input and output parameter values.

Information exchange among workspaces in CoAct is based on the *exchange of operations* instead of data objects. This is an explicit act that is initiated by an actor by invoking one of CoAct's *exchange meta-operations* that are generic meta-operations of the CoAct model (like starting, aborting, or committing of a cooperative activity). All of them are all based on the paradigm of merging workspace histories. The CoAct model provides two different options for exchanging information:

1. Co-workers can directly exchange operation sequences between their private workspaces by means of the *import* and *delegate* meta-operations. Import is used by a co-worker to incorporate a sequence of operations executed in the scope of another workspace into the local workspace. The importing user is responsible for resolving conflicts that may occur during the merge. The delegate meta-operation is used to pass on a set of data operations to a co-worker who is then responsible for merging them into the destination workspace.

2. Co-workers can exchange operations through the common workspace by means of *save* and *import* meta operations. A user can invoke the save meta-operation to incorporate data operations of the user's private workspace into the common workspace, thus making (partial) results public to all co-workers. The user who invokes the save command is responsible for the resolution of conflicts. Other co-workers can then retrieve the saved information using the import meta-operation described above.

The CoAct history merge mechanism ensures that only consistent parts of workspaces are exchanged. *Consistent units of work* are identified by examining the *backward commutativity* relation [Wei 88, LMWF94] between operations contained in a workspace history. The incorporation of operations into a workspace is then realized by the *re-execution* of the operations in the destination workspace. In this way, the effects of these operations are reflected in the private versions of the data objects in the destination workspace.

The semantic correctness of the exchange of operations is guaranteed by ensuring that the re-execution of an operation has an equivalent "view" on the history, in both the destination workspace and the source workspace. Hence, the behavior of a re-executed operation in terms of output results is indistinguishable from its initial execution. We use the *forward commutativity* relation [Wei 88, LMWF94] to check this. If the merge process can not be performed without violating the semantical correctness, the merge algorithm identifies different consistent sets of operations; one of these operation sets can then be used in the merge instead. Merging may result in retracting previous decisions, i.e, undoing operation sequences. This is done by *compensation* in CoAct. To facilitate the merge process for the user, the task of selecting an operation set for the merge can be supported by a software component (without requiring user interactions). In this case, certain merge policies can be specified providing different conflict resolution strategies. The degree of cooperation is scalable depending on the exchange frequency.

If an operation has been successfully incorporated into another workspace, it is conceptually the *identical* operation present in *more than one* workspace. The presence of identical operations in several workspaces allows to achieve a close cooperation between co-workers, because conflicts with identical operations that are present in both workspace histories can be ignored. Conceptually, the co-workers owning the workspaces have already agreed on the results of these "shared" operations.

Those parts of a cooperative activity that are reflected in the common workspace after its completion (commit) are considered as its final result. It is assumed that all users integrate their relevant contributions into the common workspace to produce a single result of the cooperative activity.

4.2 Formalization of the COACT Transaction Model

In the following, we define the basic building blocks of the CoAct model that allow us to derive our notion of correctness in the remainder of this section.

4.2.1 States. Let D be the set of all data objects that can occur in a workspace. Let $dom(d)$ denote for each data object $d \in D$ its domain. Then, a state S is a mapping that assigns to each $d \in D$ a corresponding value from $dom(d) \cup \{\bot\}$. If S denotes the state of a workspace ws, we define $d \in ws :\Leftrightarrow S(d) \neq \bot$. With $S_\bot$ we denote the empty state, i.e., $\forall d \in D : S(e) = \bot$. With $\mathcal{S}$ we denote the set of all possible states.

4.2.2 Operation types. Operation types are deterministic functions that transform a consistent workspace state to another consistent workspace state. Formally, an operation type ot with input parameters $in_1, \ldots, in_n$ and output parameters $out_1, \ldots, out_m$ can be described as a function $ot : \mathcal{S} \times \mathcal{I} \to \mathcal{S} \times \mathcal{O}$ with $\mathcal{I} = dom(in_1) \times \ldots \times dom(in_n)$, $\mathcal{O} = dom(out_1) \times \ldots \times dom(out_m)$.

4.2.3 Operations. With operations we denote atomic instantiations of operation types. We model an operation as a tuple $(id, ot, \mathbf{in}, \mathbf{out})$ consisting of a unique identifier id, the corresponding operation type op, the list of input parameters values $\mathbf{in}$, and the list of output parameters values $\mathbf{out}$. With Ω we denote the (not necessarily finite) set of all operations.

An operation models not only an operation invocation event but also its corresponding response event [Wei 88]. Therefore, we define next whether invocation and response event match for a certain state.

Definition 4.1 (legal operation). An operation $(id, ot, \mathbf{in}, \mathbf{out})$ is *legal* in a state S iff $op(S, \mathbf{in})$ yields output values $\mathbf{out}$.

4.2.4 Histories. A history $H = (O, <_O)$ is a finite set $O \subseteq \Omega$ of operations together with a total order $<_O$ over O reflecting the execution order. We write also $H = [o_1, \ldots, o_n]$ to denote histories. With $H \bullet H'$ we denote the concatenation of two histories H, H'. A history $H' = (O', <_{O'})$ is called a *subhistory* of $H = (O, <_O)$ iff $O' \subseteq O \land \forall o, p \in O' : o <_O p \Leftrightarrow o <_{O'} p$.

Next, we extend the notion of legal operations to legal histories by applying Definition 4.1 to finite operation sequences.

Definition 4.2 (legal history). A history $H = [o_1, \ldots, o_n]$ is *legal* for a state S iff there is a sequence of states $S_0, \ldots, S_{n-1}$ with $S = S_0$, o_i legal in S_{i-1}, and S_i results from the execution of o_i in state S_{i-1} for $i = 1, \ldots, n$. We say a history is legal if it is legal for state $S_\bot$.

With $S_n = [o_1, \ldots, o_n](S_0)$ we refer to the state S_n resulting from the execution of the sequence $[o_1, \ldots, o_n]$ in state S_0. The notion of legal histories allows us to define the equivalence of states. Two states are equivalent if they are not distinguishable for all subsequent operations.

Definition 4.3 (equivalent state, equivalent histories). Two states S' and S'' are *equivalent* ($S' \equiv S''$) iff for all histories H : $H(S')$ legal $\Leftrightarrow$ $H(S'')$ legal. With $H' \equiv H''$ we refer to $H'(S_\perp) \equiv H''(S_\perp)$.

4.2.5 Dependencies within a single history. In this subsection, we introduce the central concept of a *consistent unit of work*. An operation in a history might depend on previously executed operations, i.e., its behavior is influenced by preceding operations. By identifying all relevant predecessors of a given operation, we are able to identify consistent units of work that can be subject of an information exchange.

Since we are interested here in determining dependencies within single workspaces, we need a dependency relation that is based on update-in-place policy. Therefore, we apply the backward commutativity relation bc [Wei 89]. Note that the relation bc is symmetric but not transitive.

Definition 4.4 (backward commutativity relation).
The *backward commutativity* relation $bc \subseteq \Omega \times \Omega$ is defined as follows: $\forall\ o, p \in \Omega$: $(o, p) \in bc :\Leftrightarrow$ forall histories H : $(H \bullet [o] \bullet [p]$ legal $\Leftrightarrow H \bullet [p] \bullet [o]$ legal $) \wedge (H \bullet [o] \bullet [p] \equiv H \bullet [p] \bullet [o])$.

Definition 4.5 (closed subhistory). A subhistory $H' = (O', <_{O'})$ of $H = (O, <_O)$ is *closed* iff $\forall\ o \in O, p \in O', o <_O p : (o, p) \notin bc \Rightarrow o \in O'$.

A closed subhistory contains for each operation every preceding operation it depends on. We consider a closed subhistory as a consistent unit of work.

Theorem 4.1. Each closed subhistory of a legal history is legal.

Proof sketch: By a simple induction we can show that each operation that is not part of the closed subhistory can be removed with the resulting history remaining legal. The induction step is as follows: Consider the last operation that is not part of the closed subhistory. By definition of a closed subhistory, we know that it commutes backward with all subsequent operation. Hence, we can move it to the end of the history and, thus, it can be omitted.   □

The relation bc allows us to define certain other useful properties of histories. A closed subhistory $H' = (O', <_{O'})$ of $H = (O, <_O)$ is *minimally closed* under $Q \subseteq O$ iff $\forall\ o \in O' : (o \in Q) \vee (\exists\ p \in O' : o <_{O'} p \wedge (o, p) \notin bc)$. Two subhistories $H' = (O', <_{O'}), H'' = (O'', <_{O''})$ of history H are called *independent* iff $O' \cap O'' = \emptyset \wedge \forall\ o' \in O', o'' \in O'' : (o', o'') \in bc$. Two closed subhistories that are independent correspond to consistent units of work that can be exchanged among workspaces independently.

4.2.6 Workspace histories. A *cooperative activity* CA is modeled as a set of histories representing the workspaces with an identical initial workspace state S_{init}, i.e., $CA = (S_{init}, \{H_0, H_1, \ldots, H_n\})$. H_0 denotes the common workspace of the cooperative activity whereas $H_i, i > 0$ denote the private workspaces of users. In practice, the number of workspaces can change dynamically as participants may join or leave the cooperative activity.

Conceptually, the state S_{init} is copied to each workspace to achieve isolation of operation executions in different workspaces. Hence, operations can be executed independently in different workspaces. To ensure that subsequent definitions are independent of S_{init}, we require that there exists a history H with $H(S_\perp) = S_{init}$.

4.2.7 Merging of histories. The bc relation allows us to identify consistent units of work that can be subject to an information exchange. If such a unit of work represented by a (minimally) closed subhistory is incorporated into another workspace history, we have to ensure that the exchanged operations behave in the destination history as in the source history.

Since we are in this case interested in determining dependencies between different workspaces, we need a dependency relation that is based on deferred update policy. Therefore, we apply the forward commutativity relation fc [Wei 89]. Note that the relation is symmetric but not transitive.

Definition 4.6 (forward commutativity relation). The *forward commutativity* relation $fc \subseteq \Omega \times \Omega$ is defined as follows: $\forall\, o, p \in \Omega : (o, p) \in fc :\Leftrightarrow \forall$ histories $H : (H \bullet [o]$ legal $\land\ H \bullet [p]$ legal$) \Rightarrow (H \bullet [o] \bullet [p]$ legal $\land\ H \bullet [p] \bullet [o]$ legal $\land\ H \bullet [o] \bullet [p] \equiv H \bullet [p] \bullet [o])$.

We call two histories H', H'' *mergeable* iff both histories are legal and are based on the same initial workspace state. A *merged history* $H_M = (M, <_M)$ is constructed out of two mergeable histories $H' = (O', <_{O'})$ and $H'' = (O'', <_{O''})$, i.e., $M \subseteq O' \cup O''$.

In the following definition, we use $H = (O, <_O)$ to refer to one of the two histories H' or H'' to avoid symmetric conditions.

Definition 4.7 (correctly merged history). We call $H_M = (M, <_M)$ a *correctly merged* history iff

1. $M \subseteq O' \cup O''$
2. $\forall\, o, p \in O : (p \in M\ \land\ o <_O p\ \land\ (o, p) \notin bc) \Rightarrow o \in M$
3. $\forall\, o, p \in O : (o <_O p\ \land\ (o, p) \notin bc\ \land\ o, p \in M) \Rightarrow o <_M p$
4. $\forall\, o' \in (O' \setminus O''), \forall\, o'' \in (O'' \setminus O') : (o', o'') \notin fc \Rightarrow o' \notin M\ \lor\ o'' \notin M$

First, we state that the merged history can only be constructed from operations of the two input histories H' and H''. Second, it is expressed that all relevant predecessor operations of any operation that is part of the merged history have to be included in the merge, too. Third, we require that a relevant ordering of operations in a source history is preserved in the merged history. Fourth, if two operations o' and o'' are not contained in both original histories and do not commute forward, then only one of them can be part of the merged history.

Theorem 4.2. A correctly merged history is legal.

Proof sketch: From properties 2 and 3 we can deduce that the subhistory of M consisting of operations of O is equivalent to a closed subhistory of H in the sense that it differs only in the order of operations that commute backward. Hence, by Theorem 4.1 it is legal. Property 4 guarantees that the history remains legal if operations from both histories interleave. The fact, that property 1 ensures that there cannot be any further operations, completes the proof of the theorem.   □

4.2.8 Compensation. Before we describe an algorithm for merging subhistories of one history into another history, we introduce the notion of *compensation*. Compensation allows us to undo operations in the destination history, which may be required in case of merge conflicts (caused by property 4 in Definition 4.7). Additionally, compensation allows for the interactive exploration of different problem solutions carried out within the private workspaces, because operations can be selectively undone (and redone) by a user.

Definition 4.8 (compensation). The compensation function *comp* given in the specification of a cooperative activity (cf. Section 4.1) is defined as follows: $\forall\, o, o^{comp} \in \Omega : comp(o) = o^{comp} :\Leftrightarrow \forall\, \text{histories}\, H : H \bullet [o]$ is legal $\Rightarrow$ $H \bullet [o] \bullet [o^{comp}]$ is legal $\wedge H \equiv H \bullet [o] \bullet [o^{comp}]$.

Definition 4.8 states that the execution of o^{comp} immediately after o is simply the logical undo of o. This means that no subsequent operation can observe, that the sequence $[o, o^{comp}]$ is part of the history. It is sufficient for the resulting state to be *equivalent* to the state that would have been reached, if the compensated-for operation would never have been executed, i.e., the states need not be identical [KLS 90].

Compensation becomes more difficult if we want to compensate an operation o in case further operations have been performed. These subsequent operations might be dependent on the results of o such that o cannot be compensated without affecting its successors. In this case, we have to compensate all operations p with $o <_O p$ and $(o,p) \notin bc$ to correctly compensate o.

Definition 4.9 (minimal unit of compensation). Let $H = (O, <_O)$ be a history. A subhistory $H' = (O', <_{O'})$ of H is a *unit of compensation* iff $\forall\, o \in O, p \in O', p <_O o : (p,o) \notin bc \Rightarrow o \in O'$. The history H' is a *minimal unit of compensation* for $Q \subseteq O$ iff it is a unit of compensation for H and $\forall\, o \in O' : (o \in Q) \vee (\exists\, p \in O' : p <_{O'} o \wedge (p,o) \notin bc)$.

Definition 4.10 (compensation sequence). Let $H' = (O', <_{O'})$ be the minimal unit of compensation for a set of operations $Q \subseteq O$. Then, the *compensation sequence* C for Q is defined as $[o_n^{comp}, \ldots, o_1^{comp}]$ with $o_i \in O'$, $comp(o_i) = o_i^{comp}$, and $o_j^{comp} < o_i^{comp} \Leftrightarrow o_i <_{O'} o_j$.

Theorem 4.3. Let $H' = (O', <_{O'})$ the minimal unit of compensation for a set of operations $Q \subseteq O$. Let C be the compensation sequence for Q. Let $H'' = (O'', <_{O''})$ be the subhistory of H with $O'' = O \setminus O'$. Then, the following holds: H'' and $H \bullet C$ are legal, and $H'' \equiv H \bullet C$.

Proof sketch: By applying Definition 4.9 and Definition 4.5, one can prove that H'' is a closed subhistory of H. Using Theorem 4.1, it follows that H'' is legal. By applying successively Definition 4.4, it can be proved that $H \equiv H'' \bullet H'$. The repeated application of Definition 4.8 proves that $H \bullet C$ is legal and that $H'' \equiv H \bullet C$.   □

4.2.9 Merge Algorithm. In the following we describe an algorithm to incorporate operations from workspace history $H' = (O', <_{O'})$ into workspace history $H = (O, <_O)$. The merge process is performed in four steps:

1. Select operations $I \subseteq O'$ from the source history H'.
2. Compute the minimally closed subhistory P of H under I.
3. Partition P into the maximal number k of independent closed subhistories.
4. Merge the resulting partitions $P_i = (O_i, <_{O_i}), i = 1, \ldots, k$ into destination history H:

IF $(\forall\, o \in (O \setminus O_i), p \in (O_i \setminus O) : (o,p) \in fc)$
THEN $P_i' = (O_i', <_{O_i'}) :=$ subhistory of P_i with $O_i' = O_i \setminus O$;
        $H := H \bullet P_i'$;

ELSEIF "Decision is to incorporate P_i into H"
THEN $D := \{o \in (O \setminus O_i) \mid \exists\, p \in (O_i \setminus O) : (o,p) \notin fc\}$;
        $C :=$ compensation sequence for D;
        $P_i' = (O_i', <_{O_i'}) :=$ subhistory of P_i with $O_i' = O_i \setminus O$;
        $H := H \bullet C \bullet P_i'$;

First, the set $I \subseteq O'$ of operations to be merged into H is selected. The operations in I do not necessarily comprise a consistent unit of work. To satisfy property 2 of Definition 4.7, we construct the minimally closed subhistory P under I (step 2). The subhistory P (exchange history) is the part of H' to be merged into H.

During the merge, conflicts may occur between operations of H and P. If we allow only an atomic merge of P into H, i.e., to include all or none operations of P, the mechanism would be rather inflexible. In case of a conflict we either have to discard a large portion of H or we cannot include any operation of P at all. Therefore, we allow for a *partial* merge, i.e., to include only parts of P into H. Hence, we partition P into independent closed subhistories $P_1, \ldots, P_k$. Each $P_i = (O_i, <_{O_i})$ can be merged separately into H. Note, that each O_i contains at least one $o \in I$. How an even finer merge granularity can be achieved is described in [KTW96b].

The condition in step 4 ensures that an operation can only be appended to H if it commutes forward with all operations in O that are not already included in O_i. Since we deduced this condition straightforwardly from Definition 4.7, the algorithm obviously constructs a correct merged history and thus $H \bullet P_i'$ is legal. If the condition in step 4 is not fulfilled there are two possibilities how to proceed. First, the user (or the controlling software module)

bc / fc	editC(C1)	compC(C1):B1	annC(C1):A1	readA(C1,A1)	...
editC(C2)	C1 != C2	C1 != C2	True	True	
compC(C2):B2	C1 != C2	True	True	True	
annC(C2):A2	True	True	A1 != A2	A1 != A2	
readA(C2,A2)	True	True	A1 != A2	True	

OT = { editC(C: Class),
    compC(C: Class):Bugs,
    annC(C: Class):AnnID,
    readA(C: Class,A: AnnID),
    ...}

Fig. 5. Sample operations types and commutativity relations of the cooperative activity debug_program

can decide to abandon the incorporation of P_i into H. Second, the operations in O that do not commute forward with those in O_i can be compensated first. In this case it is possible to incorporate all the operations of P_i into H. Theorem 4.3 states that $H'' \equiv H \bullet C$ is legal. With a similar argumentation as above, it is easy to see that $H'' \bullet P_i'$ is a correctly merged history and, hence, legal.

After computing the new histories, we can construct the new workspace state for H by re-executing all operations in P_i that were not already included in H. When all partitions P_i are processed by the merger, the algorithm terminates. Note, that this does not imply that all $o \in I$ have been incorporated into H, since the controlling instance (the user or the software component) might have decided during the merge process to leave out some partitions P_i. To further optimize the merge process, we can utilize the concepts of *masking* and of *transparent* operations[MRKN 92, WK96]. Operations that are masked by other operations may not need to be compensated whereas transparent operations need not to be compensated and re-executed [WK96].

4.3 Example of History Merging

Assume, we have specified a cooperative activity debug_program for the SDE. Sample operation types $ot \in \mathcal{OT}$ and the corresponding bc and fc relations are shown in Figure 5. Users are able to edit the source code of a class object (editC(C:Class)), to compile the class object (compileC(C:Class):Bugs), to annotate a class object (annC(C:Class):AnnID), and to read an annotation of a class (readC(C:Class,AnnID)). Additionally, the compensating operation types are specified with the cooperative activity. For instance, the compensating operation of annC(C):A is removing the annotation, i.e., remA(C,A).

Alice creates an instance of the cooperative activity debug_program. This results in the creation of her private workspace. Alice asks Bob to help her and Bob decides to join the cooperative activity. This results in the creation of Bob's private workspace. After that Alice modifies and annotates class X. In the meantime Bob edits class X, compiles it (successfully), modifies X, and annotates X. The resulting histories (including the dependencies induced by the bc relation) are shown in Figure 6(A). Obviously, Bob's and Alice's

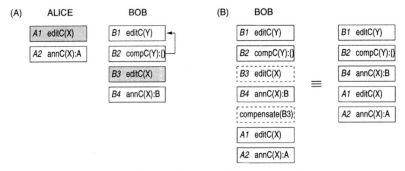

Fig. 6. Example of history merging

editC(X) operations are in conflict, but simultaneous editing is still possible because Alice and Bob work on different copies of class X.

Because Alice is leaving for a business trip, she delegates her work, i.e., her history, to Bob. The operations A_1 and A_2 can be merged separately into Bob's history because both constitute independent closed subhistories. A_1 can be easily integrated because it commutes forward with every operation in Bob's history. A_2 can not simply be integrated because operation A_1 does not commute forward with B_3 (the conflicting operations are grey shaded in Figure 6). Bob decides to take A_1. Therefore, the transaction manager has to compensate B_3 first. This is possible by simply executing the compensating operation of B_3 because B_4 commutes backward with B_3 and, thus, the outcome of B_4 is not affected by the compensation. After the compensation, A_1 and A_2 can be re-executed in Bob's workspace. The resulting history for Bob is shown in Figure 6(B). Note that in this particular case it is not necessary to really execute the compensating operation of B_1 first because B_1 is masked by the re-execution of A_1.

Afterwards, Bob reads Alice's annotation. He recognizes where the problem is, and fixes the bug in class X. The resulting history for Bob is shown in Figure 7(A). When Alice is back, she decides to import Bob's work to get the most recent state of the debugging session. The operations A_1 and A_2 are already included in Alice's history and, hence, we do not have to re-execute them. The only two operations that do not commute forward are A_1 and B_6, but in this case it is possible to incorporate the edit operation B_6 without compensating A_1. The reason is that B_6 is already "based" on A_1 and, thus, we can ignore this conflict (cf. property 4 in Definition 4.7). This concept of identical operations (recognized by equal operation identifiers) enables a close cooperation among the co-workers. It is obvious, that the more histories are already synchronized, i.e., the more operations are contained in *both* histories, the better the cooperation works, i.e., the less operations have to be discarded during a merge. After the transaction manager has re-executed Bob's operations in Alice's workspace, her history looks like the one in Fig-

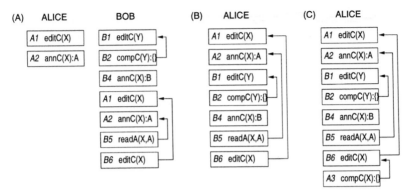

Fig. 7. Example of history merging (continued)

ure 7(B). Note that the histories of Alice and Bob are not identical, but the state of the two workspaces and the corresponding histories are *equivalent*.

Figure 7(C) shows Alice's history after she has successfully compiled class X. The resulting workspace history of Alice is not serializable with respect to Alice's and Bob's operations because there exists a cycle in the dependency graph induced by bc ($A_1 \leftarrow B_6 \leftarrow A_3$). This example shows that the history merging mechanism is able to produce also *non-serializable*, but still consistent, i.e., legal, histories. Thus, the isolation property of transactions is relaxed while ensuring always consistency in the workspaces.

4.4 Organizing the Work Process

The merge mechanism of CoAct enables the participants in a cooperative activity to work concurrently on the same data items without blocking each other, while at the same time ensuring the consistency of their results. This is a basic requirement for all cooperative applications and may even be sufficient for the support of creative work that is performed in a more or less ad hoc fashion, such as cooperative document authoring.

Facilities to define data operations, exchange meta-operations, and the forward and backward commutativity relations required by the CoAct transaction model are available in the CoCoA specification language [FEdB 96, FEdBA 97, FdBE97]. Moreover, CoCoA allows the specification of queries over workspace histories to select operations for exchange. In addition to that, CoCoA allows to define constraints (in so-called *cooperative scenarios*) to describe the coordination of the work process within a cooperative activity Such coordination mechanisms are available within the TransCoop model at two levels: at the workspace level, and at the cooperative scenario level.

With regard to single workspaces the application designer can specify a set of *execution rules*. These rules pose workflow-like restrictions on the order and existence of operations in a workspace history, and define termination states. Execution rules have to be enforced for each private workspace and the common workspace separately [RKT+95]. This allows the enforcement of execution rules even for those applications, where the workspaces are not permanently connected, e.g., in mobile environments [KTW97b, KTW97a]. In CoCoA, a language-based specification mechanism for the execution rules is used. The application designer specifies certain grammars, and the allowed sequences of operations are equal to the words in the generated language. To specify this language multiple grammars can be used. Their combination results in the desired restrictions on sequences of operations that are allowed in the cooperative scenario. In contrast to [Ska 89, NZ 92], our mechanism avoids dead ends caused by interdependencies of different grammars. For details see [KTW+96c, FEdB 96].

To structure the overall work process, and to specify restrictions, that must be obeyed across all workspaces, CoCoA provides a *step* definition mechanism [FEdB 96]. The step mechanism controls whether a user is allowed to execute an operation at a particular point in the scenario. This is performed by explicitly *enabling* the allowed operations. The set of operations that are controlled by the step mechanism include data operations and exchange meta-operations, as well as *communication meta-operations* to initiate sub-steps, step transitions, and/or to terminate a step.

A step governs the operation enabling in multiple workspaces, but it is up to the users to decide whether they want to execute the enabled operations, and in what order. In contrast to execution rules, there are no restrictions on the order or existence of operations executed *within* a step, but step transitions can be made conditional on query expressions on workspace histories. The enabling mechanism is complemented by the possibility to specify *user roles*. Hence, the permission to execute an operation can be restricted to users filling a certain role. Steps can be combined in various ways to form the organizational structure of the work process. The constructs to group steps range from sequential and repetitive execution of steps to nested and parallel steps. For more details on the step mechanism see [FEdB 96, FEdBA 97, FdBE97].

4.5 Prototype Implementation

To prove the applicability of our approach, we built a demonstrator system [dBLP+ 96, Waes96b, KE97]. The TransCoop reference architecture [dBLP+ 95, LdBTW 97] separates between the specification environment providing means for the specification and verification of cooperative scenarios and the runtime environment offering support for the execution of cooperative scenarios.

4.5.1 The Specification Environment.
The components of the specification environment are intended to help the designer of a cooperative application to work with the CoCoA language in the early (conceptual), as well as the late (testing) phases of the application design [EFdBP96]. The specification environment includes a graphical specification editor, a static

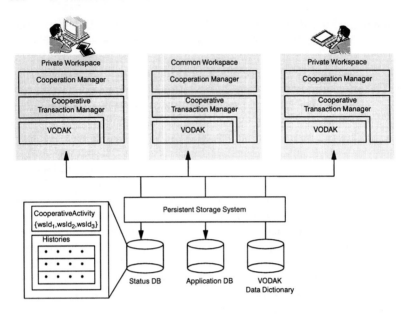

Fig. 8. Runtime architecture of the TRANSCOOP demonstrator system

analysis tool, a dynamic analysis tool, and compilers to the run-time environment. The static analysis tool includes a parser/type-checker, which also performs well-formedness checks on the steps and transitions. The dynamic analysis tool offers simulation and visualization of the organizational aspects of the cooperative scenario. The compilers generate the input for the cooperation manager and the cooperative transaction manager of the run-time environment.

4.5.2 The Runtime Environment. The runtime environment offers support for the execution of cooperative scenarios and forms an application-independent nucleus to build cooperative applications on top of it. It is implemented as an extension of the object-oriented DBMS VODAK developed at GMD-IPSI [GI 95], i.e., all cooperation facilities are supported as DBMS services. The design of the TRANSCOOP runtime environment required an extension of the centralized VODAK architecture in order to meet the architectural and conceptual requirements posed by the COACT cooperative transaction model. Figure 8 illustrates the runtime architecture of the TRANSCOOP demonstrator system.

VODAK database schemata are enriched by a cooperative scenario specification compiled from the COCOA scenario description. In particular, this captures (1) information about which database schema methods are available at the application interface (i.e., the operation types $\mathcal{OT}$), (2) the structure of the overall scenario execution (i.e., the steps, etc.), (3) information about how certain method executions can be compensated (i.e., the compensating function *comp*), and (4) predicates describing how to evaluate the backward and forward commutativity relations (*bc*, *fc*) at runtime. All this additional information is stored in the enhanced VODAK data dictionary.

The private workspace as well as the common workspaces are realized by a modified VODAK instance together with a cooperative transaction manager instance (containing the merge functionality), and a cooperation manager instance (governing the execution of steps, etc.). We apply a dynamic replication scheme to isolate the data in the private workspaces. Durability of workspaces is achieved by traditional database recovery concepts. Before an operation is executed the corresponding history entry is written to the persistent Status-DB (write-ahead logging). In case of a failure the workspace state can be recovered by re-executing the logged operations. This process can be optimized by periodically checkpointing the workspace.

The Status-DB maintains the workspace histories of the participating users and the runtime structure of the step specification; it also provides general administrative information about the state of the scenario, such as the current participants in the scenario, the currently active steps, and the operations enabled by the current steps.

The *cooperative transaction manager* [KTW96a, KE97] ensures the correctness of histories and offers functions to preview the progress of co-workers by means of querying their histories in the Status-DB. Moreover, it provides functions for both the calculation of possible merge alternatives and the enforcement of a specific merge. Conflicts that may occur are semi-automatically resolved within the merge procedure by offering different consistent alternatives in case of a conflict. The controlling user then selects one of the offered solutions using a graphical user interface [KE97]. The execution rule enforcement mechanism has not been implemented.

The *cooperation managers* [Waes96b, KE97] coordinate the execution of a cooperative scenario, i.e., the enabling of data operations, exchange meta operations, communication meta-operations, execution of step transitions, and the mapping of user roles to participants in the cooperative activity. Additionally, they provide information about the current participants and their work progress to establish group awareness. For example, when a delegation is performed, the delegatee is notified in order to control the integration of the respective piece of work into his/her workspace. Further notifications are caused when co-authors join or leave the cooperative activity.

4.6 Discussion and Relationship to Other Transaction Models

In this section, we discuss how the TRANSCOOP cooperative transaction model fulfills the requirements of cooperative applications described in Section 2.3. Afterwards, we compare the model to the advanced transaction models presented in Section 3.

4.6.1 Requirements Revisited. Support for private and shared data (requirement D) is addressed by introducing a common workspace and a private workspace for each participant in a cooperative activity. Each private workspace contains private versions of data objects and constitutes a consistent configuration of the data. Workspaces are realized by a dynamic replication scheme. How our model can support mobility is described in [KTW97b, KTW97a].

Support for the exchange of (tentative) results (requirement D) is realized by the history merging mechanism. By exploiting the backward commutativity relation we make sure that always consistent units of work are exchanged among workspaces. By exploiting the forward commutativity relation we ensure that no inconsistencies are introduced, when operations are re-executed in another workspace. The concept of identical operations enables us to establish a close cooperation among co-workers, because certain conflicts in the cooperation can be ignored. We have shown that the correct merged histories remain legal, i.e., workspaces are always consistent, although we allow non-serializable histories. Cooperation primitives are realized by means of the import, export, and save meta-operations.

Requirement A (relaxed atomicity) is addressed in our model by providing persistence of workspaces (cf. Section 4.5). If a failure occurs in the private workspace, its most recent state can be reconstructed using the workspace history (forward recovery). A failure within a private workspace never affects other workspaces. With respect to the step mechanism, the Status-DB enables forward recovery of the state of the cooperative activity.

To support requirement B (retraction of decisions) we have implemented an undo mechanism. By exploiting the dependencies between operations induced by the backward commutativity relation in a workspace history, it is possible to selectively undo, i.e., compensate, operations. The transaction manager computes the compensation sequence for the selected operations in the history and then executes the compensation sequence in the workspace.

Coordination of individual and joint work (requirement E) is supported at two levels in the TRANSCOOP model. At the workspace level the scenario designer can specify a set of execution rules. To structure the overall work process in a workflow-like manner and to specify restrictions that must be obeyed across all workspaces, we provide a step definition mechanism that is used for operation enabling. The enabling mechanism is complemented by the possibility to specify user roles.

4.6.2 Related Transaction Models. As the reader might have already noticed, the COACT cooperative transaction model shares some ideas with the advanced transaction models described in Section 3. Figure 9 illustrates these relationships.

Like in semantic concurrency control, we exploit the semantics of operations defined on data objects. We use the backward commutativity relation to determine dependencies between operations in single workspace histories.

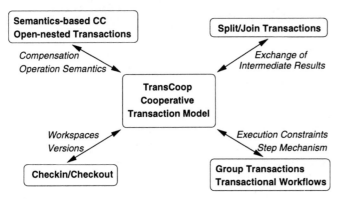

Fig. 9. Relationship of the TRANSCOOP cooperative transaction model to other advanced transaction models

Unlike conventional transaction models, this allows us to dynamically determine operations sequences, that can be considered as consistent units of work, i.e., transactions, and that can be exchanged among workspaces.

To check if the exchange of operation sequences among different workspaces maintains data consistency, we apply the forward commutativity relation. In this respect, our approach is similar to semantics-based optimistic concurrency control [Her 86, Her90] with the difference that we work on multiple copies of data objects in different workspaces. In contrast to conventional transaction models, we do not assume that different histories (of transactions) are disjoint. Thus, more histories are legal in our model. We have illustrated that the larger the intersection of two histories is the better the merge process works.

In [KTW96b], we have investigated the usage of weaker semantic relationships than commutativity for our model, namely recoverability [BR 92] and invalidated-by [Her 86, Her90]. It turned out that these relations suffer from certain anomalies because they are not symmetric.

To handle conflicts that might occur during history merging, we apply the concept of compensation. This is similar to the open-nested transaction model where (partial) rollback is implemented by executing compensating subtransactions for all subtransactions executed after the one to be compensated. Our approach to compensation is more flexible. We use the backward commutativity relation to determine minimal units of compensation and compensation sequences. This ensures that only operations are compensated that are dependent on the one to be compensated, thus minimizing loss of work.

With respect to the workspace concept our approach is close to check-out/check-in models. In the basic check-out/check-in model, checked-out objects are reserved for exclusive access until a later check-in. This may result in blocking of objects over long periods of time. In COACT, we avoid this behavior by providing each user with his own (implicit) consistent configuration in his private workspace. Approaches which combine the check-out mechanism with versioning go into a similar direction but they suffer from the fact that their support for the required merging of different versions is only limited. Most merge mechanisms provided by versioning schemes force the user to choose among one of the generated versions and drop the others. Otherwise, the user has to perform the cumbersome task of integrating the different versions manually. In contrast to this, CoAct is able to merge the work of different users automatically by using the provided operation semantics. Only in cases where users have done irreconcilable work, interference is necessary. Even in this case, our merge algorithm can propose the user different alternatives, which minimize the amount of lost work. Another drawback of check-out approaches is that all objects and subobjects have to be checked-out explicitly whereas in CoAct this is transparent for the users.

Like in the split/join transaction model, we support the explicit exchange of operations among transactions. The split/join model is in contrast to CoAct restricted to serializable executions. This limits the possibility to exchange data operations between transactions by means of the provided split and join primitives. Since the model supports only single data copies, the access to these data items has to be synchronized, e.g., by a locking protocol which limits the availability of data. In addition to this, by splitting or joining a transaction the former owner of the operations looses control over these operations. In contrast to this, in CoAct both users can continue their work based on the exchanged results. Another limitation of the split/join model is the lack of higher level operation semantics. The basic split/join transaction model considers only read and write operations. Hence, it can be extended by using our merge criteria to be more powerful and flexible in splitting and joining, e.g., merging ongoing transactions by utilizing the semantics of operations and thus enabling a closer cooperation between transactions.

Group-oriented transaction approaches structure the overall working process by means of a transaction hierarchy and defining application-specific correctness criteria. The cooperative transaction hierarchy approach [N 90, NZ 92] uses grammars (patterns and conflicts) to define which concurrent executions of sibling transactions are correct from an application's viewpoint. In our model one can specify a set of execution rules for a cooperative activity. These rules pose workflow-like restrictions on the order and existence of operations in a workspace history and define termination states. As opposed to [N 90, NZ 92] we apply these rules only to enforce application-specific correctness of operation sequences within a single workspace and not to define cooperative behavior among workspaces. Moreover, in contrast to [Ska 89, NZ 92], our mechanism avoids dead ends caused by interdependencies of different grammars.

Cooperation in transactional workflow approaches is characterized by passing results between workflow tasks in a predefined manner. There is no opportunity for flexibly passing results back and forth between co-workers.

This is essential in non-workflow scenarios, e.g., cooperative authoring and software development processes. In the TRANSCOOP model, we distinguish between organizational and transactional aspects of a cooperative activity. The former is mainly concerned with the workflow-like coordination of users within a joint effort. The latter is mainly concerned with consistency of data sharing and exchange. The specification language CoCoA deals with both organizational and transactional aspects in a single language without tightly coupling them like in transactional workflows which assign transactional properties to single steps in a workflow. This approach enables more flexible forms of cooperation.

5. Conclusions

Today's workflow systems do not support scenarios with spontaneous cooperation requirements that cannot be prescribed a priori in a specification. In contrast, current groupware approaches support an ad-hoc working style, but give, from a database perspective, no satisfying execution guarantees. The TRANSCOOP cooperative transaction model addresses both criteria: the growing need for models supporting highly dynamic forms of cooperative work, as well as the need for transactional correctness criteria.

CoCoA allows the description of both organizational and transactional aspects of cooperative activities. The underlying CoAct model provides the basic transactional support to ensure consistent management of shared, persistent data in cooperative applications. The nucleus of the exchange facilities in CoAct is the history merging approach. The flexibility of the approach is mainly achieved by its ability to determine consistent units of work dynamically, in terms of performed operations, and its consideration of operation semantics for resolving conflicts.

The TRANSCOOP cooperative transaction model is applicable to a wide spectrum of cooperative applications ranging from creative design applications to structured workflow-like applications. Moreover, the history merging mechanism provides directions for solving open research problems in related fields like mobile wireless computing [KTW97b, KTW97a], database replication, or in supporting semi-automatic merging in versioning approaches.

A question that requires further attention is the specification of commutativity. Specification tools that compute or prove commutativity information automatically from a formal specification of operations will improve practical applicability of the approach. Commutativity analysis tools that are investigated in the framework of TRANSCOOP are a first step in this direction [AEF+97].

Acknowledgements

The authors would like to thank the other TRANSCOOP members at GMD-IPSI, Justus Klingemann and Thomas Tesch, who contributed to this work and the COACT model substantially. Furthermore, we thank all members of the TRANSCOOP teams in Enschede and Helsinki for many inspiring discussions.

The COCOA language was developed by the University of Twente. The TRANSCOOP specification environment was implemented by the University of Twente and partially by VTT. The cooperation manager in the TRANSCOOP runtime environment was implemented by VTT.

Migrating Workflows

Andrzej Cichocki, Marek Rusinkiewicz

Department of Computer Science
University of Houston
4800 Calhoun Rd
Houston, Texas 77004
USA
email: {andrzej,marek}@cs.uh.edu

Abstract. In this paper we present the concept of migrating workflows, and the considerations related to the implementation of this concept. Migrating workflows are a computational metaphor for the way most people conduct their daily business: they visit a place, use a service (perhaps after some negotiation), and move on to the next place. A migrating workflow behaves similarly: it transfers its code (specification) and its execution state to a site, negotiates a service to be executed on its behalf, receives the results, and moves on. Dialog between the workflow and individual sites may influence the workflow's migration. Thus the actual workflow instance is defined during run-time, as an effect of merging the static workflow specification and the local site rules and policies.

1. Introduction

The static workflows used to automate business processes today are difficult to specify correctly, since many employees may be involved in key tasks, but only very few (often none) understand the entire process. Workflows are also difficult to maintain; a small change in the company organization or in business needs may require rewriting of many workflows. These difficulties prevent today's companies from achieving the full benefits of automated business process management.

The remedy to this problem, proposed in this paper, is the concept of *Migrating Workflows*. Migrating workflows implement the computational metaphor that is similar to the way most people conduct their daily business: they visit a place, use a service (perhaps after some negotiation), and move on to the next place. The migrating workflow behaves similarly: it transfers its code (specification) and its execution state to a site, negotiates a service to be executed on its behalf, receives the results, and moves on. The next place visited by the workflow, and the next service requested, is determined by both the goal of the process, and the results of the current requests. Results of a request can be influenced by the site and/or the site's user. Thus the actual workflow instance is defined during the run-time, as an effect of merging the static workflow specification, the local rules and policies, and the decisions made by the user.

The advantages of a migrating workflow approach are numerous. Since most workflow specifications are small compared to the data and partial results on which they operate, the migration provides efficiency by reducing network traffic. The asynchronous nature of migrating workflows makes them ideal for disconnected operations; a task description can be loaded into a portable machine when it is connected to the network, and executed later when it is disconnected. However, the property we consider the most important is that the migrating workflow specification can be *incomplete*. An instance of a workflow, interacting with a succession of local systems and users, will discover missing tasks and data items, and augment itself to achieve its goals.

The migrating workflow concept emerged from the intelligent software agents and distributed transactions fields. Many concepts and solutions presented in the context of mobile agents [Whi 96, GHN+ 97] are applicable or easily adaptable to migrating workflows. This paper is also influenced by the concept of Information Carriers presented in [BMR 94].

The rest of this paper is organized as follows: in Section 2. we introduce the model for migrating workflows. Section 3. presents an example of such a workflow. In Section 4. we discuss an environment in which migrating workflows can be executed, and in Section 5. we consider problems related to process modeling and migrating workflow administration. A short discussion of strengths and weaknesses of the presented approach concludes the paper.

2. Migrating Workflow Model

In this section we present a model for migrating workflows. The main assumption of this model is that an instance of a workflow will *migrate*, i.e., it will transfer the workflow code (its specification) and the whole execution state, including all data gathered during execution, between sites participating in workflow's execution. The workflow will submit its requests for services to local sites. These requests will be handled by the sites according to their local rules and policies.

Let us examine each element of the migrating workflow model in more detail.

Migrating workflow.. A migrating workflow contains a specification of a business process. This specification is a set of requests for local services, and their partial order. Each request has a site associated with it, and the workflow migrates when the desired site is different than the current one. The set of requests, and the associated sites, can be dynamically modified for each instance during run-time. An instance of a migrating workflow carries its data (modified by the interactions with the sites), and a log of its activities (sites visited, requests submitted, etc.). Although the actual specification language of migrating workflows is dependent on implementation, for this paper we assume that a migrating workflow is specified using event-condition-action rules [DHL 90].

To implement necessary control flow conditions, each request should have a state associated with it. The minimal set of states will include "not submitted," "submitted," "done-ok," "notok." These states, in conjunction with the values of the data carried with the workflow, the results of the requests and values of the external variables (e.g. time) will be used to compose the firing conditions for the rules. A rule, if fired, will submit a request to the current site. Depending on the results of the requests, other rules could be fired (and additional requests submitted), or the workflow could migrate to the next site and continue its execution there.

Sites.. Sites offer services to the workflows that visit them. Every service is a representation of a single task that can be handled by this site. The tasks can be either automated (e.g., a database transaction), it may involve user interaction (e.g., a form that is filled out by the user), or both. Each site may provide one or more service. The services are advertised to special "directory service" sites, which, upon request, will provide a list of sites that provide desired services.

The sites have their own policies and rules for incoming workflows and their requests. A site's processing strategies can be specified using a variety of programming paradigms. We assume that the local processing also uses event-condition-action rules. In this case, the event is the submission of a request. The conditions involve a variety of factors, e.g., the data submitted with the request, variables such as time, or the state of the local data sources. The action involve invoking a task application or interaction with the user, and may result in additional rules being fired.

The results of the request will be passed back to the workflow instance. There are many possible results, some very traditional: an error message, a set of data items, or confirmation of an update. However, in the migrating workflow environment, there are other possibilities as well. The site can ask for additional data, in which case the workflow may return to its original user to ask for that additional information. The site may direct the migrating workflow to another site where its request can be fulfilled (redirection), or the site can advise the workflow to execute a new set of requests at a new set of sites (sub-workflow). The workflow instance may act upon such advice, but it may also treat it as an exception. We envision the redirections and sub-workflow as the normal mode of operation that enables the flexibility and versatility of the migrating workflow metaphor.

Logs.. The workflow's activity log is critical to system integrity. Therefore, even though technically the log is a part of both the workflow instance and the site, we present it here as a separate entity. The activity log contains information about all workflow activities and is necessary, for example, to facilitate recovery from logical failures (for example, the workflow needs to know *what* has been done in order to undo it), to enable accountability, to allow process analysis. The workflow must write the log (possibly containing the workflow specification and execution state) to a stable storage at the site to enable crash recovery and workflow reinstantiation. We will discuss the logs (or *trails*) in more detail in the latter parts of the paper.

In general, service requests are not the only possible interactions between a migrating workflow instance and a site. The workflow may, for example,

- execute arbitrary code,
- execute only permitted (or "safe") code ,
- merge its code (rules) with the local code (rules) and execute the resulting program,
- clone itself, so that both workflows continue independent, concurrent execution,
- request that the site deliver to it a notification of an interesting event such as another incoming workflow, or a change in the value of a local data item.

One way to incorporate these possibilities into the migrating workflow model presented here is, for example, that a site could provide "task execution service". The service would enable the workflows to submit arbitrary procedures for execution. This, and other possibilities are left for future investigation.

3. Migrating Workflow – An Example

In this section we present an example of a migrating workflow which illustrates the major features of the model. In particular, we would like to show the migration of the workflow, the dynamic nature of the workflow instance, and the capability for disconnected operations.

Consider a workflow designer that has to automate the process of obtaining an authorization for business travel. According to his notion of the process, the designer specifies the workflow as follows:

1. ask the User where and when he wants to go
2. obtain the address (name) of the travel agency and of the manager from the directory service
3. go to the travel agency
4. obtain a possible itinerary and the cost of the ticket
5. go to the Manager
6. ask for approval
7. go back to the User's site
8. present the results of the execution

Such a workflow would be coded in an appropriate language, and instantiated. The instance of the workflow submits to the user's site a request for the input, interacts with the directory service, and migrates to the travel agency site. It is possible that the process of obtaining a possible itinerary involves several rules and multiple requests (e.g., the workflow needs to make several requests to get the cheapest fare, to reserve the plane, hotel and car, etc.). If the workflow is executed from the user's host, each of these requests would need to be transferred over the network, increasing the network traffic and decreasing the performance. In a migrating environment, all those requests are done locally, at the travel agency site.

Next, the workflow migrates to the manager's site and requests the approval. But unknown to the workflow designer, the company has a new travel authorization process. So the workflow designer's travel authorization specification differs from the actual business process. The manager that approves the trip knows about the new requirement which says that he can approve only those trips that cost less than $1,000; all others must be approved by the company's CFO. So, the manager will insert a *local* rule at his site to enforce this policy. The manager's new site rule states that if the cost of the trip is less than $1,000, the approval request is added to the manager's worklist. For travel expense over $1,000 the workflow is directed to the CFO's site for approval. This rule is executed every time a workflow requests an approval, effectively modifying the workflow specification. This allows for great flexibility of migrating workflows. Next time a policy changes (e.g., managers may approve travel up to $2,000) no workflow will need to be changed. Only a local update of the local rules will be needed.

A travel approval is a simple task for a manager. Usually the tasks required from managers are more complicated. Let's imagine that the workflow contains an additional task. Now the manager will be asked to proof-read the presentation that the user will give on his trip. The execution scenario now has an additional step. The migrating workflow, after migrating to the manager's site, will display an editing window in which the presentation can be reviewed and corrected. Let's imagine further that the manager himself is very mobile, traveling from town to town, meeting customers, spending a lot of time on planes and in hotel rooms. His site (i.e., his laptop) is frequently disconnected from the fixed network, and frequently connected again. Since the migrating workflow moves its code and data to the manager's laptop, it can continue working regardless of the network status. The manager can edit the presentation while flying. When the laptop is reconnected, the workflow will automatically resume its execution. It will migrate to the user's site and present the results of the manager's review.

4. Enactment Mechanisms for the Migrating Workflows

This section discusses issues related to correct and efficient execution of migrating workflows, including the infrastructure necessary for an implementation of a migrating workflow system.

4.1 Execution System Guarantees

Every workflow enactment system, regardless of the paradigm used for execution, should provide certain guarantees for all workflows executed under its control. There are many kinds of such guarantees, and below we discuss some of the most important.

4.1.1 Execution correctness of a single workflow instance. This property guarantees that the final states of processing stations (sites), and the results of the workflow are "correct." For traditional workflows, a correctly executing workflow means simply that all tasks of this workflow will be executed exactly once. Sometimes more elaborate criteria are used, such as a definition of a set of acceptable final states, sets of consistency predicates defined on the data, etc. [RCN 95]. For migrating workflows the problem is much more complex, since the set of tasks executed is determined dynamically. Correctness needs to be defined rather in terms of goal predicate satisfaction, or in terms of obtaining all required data items. For example, the workflow execution is only completed successfully when the data item named "Manager's approval" obtains a definite value, regardless what tasks were or were not executed.

4.1.2 Transactional properties. Transactional properties, such as failure atomicity, or concurrency control, are important properties for certain classes of workflows. Migrating workflows, if they are to be useful, need to provide at least some of these properties. However, we should keep in mind that the intended environment for migrating workflows is office process automation, where the main focus should be on flexibility and robustness, rather than stringent multidatabase serializability.

Failure atomicity.. A workflow should execute entirely, or not at all. The best example for failure atomicity is a "buying a book" workflow, which has two tasks: paying for the book and delivering the book. In general we would like either both of these tasks successfully finished, or neither executed. There should be no partial results left in the workflow system after an unsuccessful workflow.

Migrating workflows use some of the popular techniques for achieving atomicity: forward recoverability and compensation. By far, the most desirable is forward recoverability. As we mentioned earlier, the log (trail) left by a workflow at a site allows us to reconstruct the state of the process after a failure, and continue with its execution. However, in some cases the workflow needs to undo its previous work (mostly in case of a logical failure of the process rather than physical failure of the system). In this case, the only truly usable technique for migrating workflows is compensation [K+ 96]. Since it is natural that each interaction of a workflow with a site is treated as a separate "transaction," it is unreasonable to do the backward recovery by installing before-images.

In many environments where migrating workflows could be used, a request for manual assistance is one of the possible natural and effective failure recovery techniques. In the case of an unexpected fault (e.g., a site responds with an error for every request), the workflow will gather as much information about the failure and its effects as possible and then migrate either back to the originating user or to a predefined operator's site and ask for help. The human operator will then provide the workflow with a next step (or a sub-workflow script) and the workflow will be able to resume its execution, perhaps for long enough to undo some of the undesired effects of its earlier phase of execution. The manual assistance process could evolve over time, as local rules designed for handling commonly occurring requests are installed at the operator's site.

Problems related to recoverability are both technical and administrative. For example, in office work (especially in banking and government offices) there are legal requirements that do not allow "undo" or "rollback" of activities in the database sense, i.e., such that there is no perceptible effect left. Instead, an additional document must be prepared that invalidates the previous results. This is congruous with migrating workflows, that, in order to undo a task, it is necessary to re-visit a site and make a new request. This request will be treated the same way as any other; it will create log records both in the site's log and in the workflow's log.

The ability of the migrating workflows to react dynamically to adverse situations is one of the principal factors enabling robust and reliable systems in highly distributed environment[HCS 97].

Data consistency.. It is well known that uncontrolled interleaving of concurrent operations on data can, and usually does, lead to the introduction of errors in the database. However, access control (concurrency control) may provide various degrees of isolation among the operations (or, in this case, the workflow's tasks). It should be noted that the level of isolation depends on the specific application, and it is not possible to find one criterion that satisfies all requirements. There are tasks that require perfectly consistent data even though this means significant loss of performance, and there are tasks that can accept approximate responses to queries. The ability to provide the required level of data consistency to particular workflow instances is one of the major characteristics of a successful workflow management system.

In the migrating workflow model, data consistency is considered on two levels: local and global. Local consistency is the responsibility of the local site; it accepts requests and uses its own criteria and methods to make sure that the data it controls remains consistent. The global consistency problem is more difficult. Since migrating workflows are dynamic, they may not know where they will go or what they will request. Therefore the only feasible global concurrency control is based on optimistic (validation) techniques rather than on locking schemas. We can imagine a concurrency control method in which every workflow that needs globally serializable access to the data will obtain a global timestamp, and in its wandering will present this timestamp to the sites controlling the data. The site will compare the timestamp with timestamps of other workflows accessing the same data, and make sure that the accesses are serialized in a predefined order (e.g., older workflows preceding younger ones). This way, while some requests could be rejected spuriously, global serializability can be achieved without a need for communication among all the sites.

There is an additional problem with global correctness criteria such as serializability. If a workflow does not request global serializability, it will be granted out-of-timestamp order access to the data. If such a workflow in fact updates data at two or more places, it may introduce inconsistency into workflows that required global serializability. There are some "administrative" solutions to this problem, for example we can deny updates to any non-serializable workflow, or we can partition the data so that it will never create a problem for the serializable ones. However, a more general solution to this problem is necessary.

4.1.3 Deadlines. Most workflow management systems can be considered "real-time" systems, because tasks often have deadlines, both in the form of absolute time ("task should be finished before 5p.m.") and relative time ("task should be finished within 1 hour"). Also, time-based dependencies among tasks are often necessary (e.g., "task should be executed no later than 1 hour after another tasks finishes"). The migrating workflows have three strategies of coping with these deadlines:

- Hard deadlines. The requests are handled on time, or they are aborted, and the workflow initializes the rollback (compensation) procedure.
- Soft deadlines. The system adheres to the "best effort" principle, and tries to execute the tasks to minimize the degree of deadline violation.
- Contingency. When the workflow realizes the deadline can be missed, a contingency task is invoked.

In all cases, a note is written to the log about missing the deadline. Also, an alert can be issued in case the deadline is missed, sending, for example, a message to the user's supervisor.

The real problem with deadlines in migrating workflow environments is that a workflow will have to rely on the local clock in its computations. It is well known that local clocks are truly unreliable, even in the absence of malicious users that will purposely set the clocks on their systems to confuse workflow execution. The only feasible solution to this problem includes post-execution analysis of the deadline violations and administrative pressure on the users, rather that run-time deadline control.

4.2 Architectural Considerations

The architecture of the execution system for migrating workflows is, by definition, completely distributed, i.e., there is no central "execution scheduler", not even a distributed one. The workflow instance itself is the locus of control, and it moves from machine to machine as the execution progresses.

4.2.1 Scalability and performance. Scalability and performance are often cited as the most important characteristics of workflow management systems. There are various aspects to this problem. One is the size and complexity of a single workflow. Although most office process workflows will not consist of more than a few dozen tasks, the production workflows may consist of thousands of tasks with intricate dependencies among them. Another performance and scalability problem is the number of workflow instances executed concurrently. Again, in many cases (e.g. the telecommunication industry) there may be a need for executing thousands of workflow instances per minute. In this case, any centralized system will soon become unusable. Finally, there may be a problem with the size of data accessed and transferred between tasks. Especially in widely distributed and mobile systems, where the data has to be transferred through WAN or wireless links, this problem may prove difficult. Migrating workflows are particularly suitable to handle the last two situations. The completely distributed nature of migrating workflows provides great scalability, and the fact that it is the workflow that moves to the data, and not data that moves to the task, renders the last point moot.

Most companies using workflow products are expecting to grow. Therefore it is necessary for the workflow management systems to allow for the incremental growth. It should be possible to add new entities to the system: users, roles, applications, etc. Again, migrating workflows provide for both graceful upgrades and graceful degradation. It is enough to install a new machine in the system and provide a single rule in a single place (e.g., the one providing directory services) to include this new site in the workflow execution system.

4.2.2 Reliability. Reliability of workflow management systems (i.e., the ability to provide service 24 hours a day, 7 days a week) is, for most users, the most important feature. Thus the architecture of the migrating workflow system must be designed with this characteristics as one of the primary goals.

Due to the completely distributed environment of the migrating workflow system there is no single point of failure that could stop the execution of all workflows. Of course, if a site providing a certain service fails, all the workflows trying to get to that site will be delayed, and all the workflows that are currently at that site will need to be reinstantiated and recovered, but no other workflows will be affected. To minimize the effects of such failures, critical services must be replicated, and the workflows should include a contingency rule stating that in case a particular site is not available, it should go to the other. With workflows that are being executed at the failing site, the situation is more complicated. Time-critical migrating workflows should have *watchers* (sentinels, rear guards), i.e., stationary processes residing on separate machines. A watcher should raise an alarm when the workflow instances it is watching fail to report in a given period of time.

The orthogonal problem to hardware and software system failures are logical failures of workflow instances. An instance may fail due to such circumstances as lack of resources, contention, and others. The flexibility of migrating workflows, and its ability to modify its execution plan on the fly make them ideal to handle such situations.

4.2.3 Flexibility. Flexibility of the workflow enactment system entails a variety of concepts. The system should be easily upgradable with new equipment, and with new software. Also, the system configuration should be flexible enough to follow changes in company organizational structure. However, the main aspect of the flexibility is that the workflow specification itself should be flexible enough to accommodate unpredictable changes in the execution environment. This is one of the main strengths of the migrating workflow model. Change of business policies no longer require rewriting all the workflows, but just a simple change of local rule in a single execution site. A user handling a certain class of task can go on vacation, leaving a simple redirection rule at his site, and all workflows will automatically go there. The fact that the actual instance of a migrating workflow is emerging as its execution progresses, the ability to incorporate local rules into the execution plan, provide the flexibility required in today's fast changing business world.

4.3 Security Considerations

To the traditional problems of computer security (usually seen as a malicious user or program attacking the computer site), migrating workflows add the problem of protection of the workflow itself (i.e., a malicious site attacking the program). Here we will only identify some of the problems and suggest possible solutions. However, we do not present a comprehensive security model here.

- Authentication and authorization among autonomous components of the workflow system (workflow instances and the sites), so that the sites do not execute tasks requested by a malicious user, and users do not accept results from unknown/malicious places.
- Authentication and authorization of the human operator.
- Permissions and authentication for raising events (e.g., time interrupts) that can influence the execution of a workflow.
- Responsibility and delegations of responsibility for the execution of a workflow or tasks (especially when a task involves a human operator). This also requires authenticated logs (history) of execution, no-repudiation techniques, etc.
- Protection of sensitive information in transit between stations. This may require encryption of information.
- Protection of the workflow so that its code, data, and log are not changed by malicious sites/users. Also, arbitrary sites should not be able to gain unauthorized information from the workflow.

- Making sure that no malicious site can "kill" a workflow (imagine a workflow migrating to user's laptop that gets switched off).
- Preventing runaway workflows that jump from place to place consuming resources, potentially depriving other workflows from their chance to be executed.

Some techniques that could be used here include cryptography for protecting the privacy of the data, for electronic signatures, and for authentication[MRS 96]; kerberos-style tickets for resource allocation (the "authority" carried as a unique, yet recognizable token); an expiration date for workflows; and others.

An additional problem in workflow management systems is that in many cases there is a need for relaxing the security to some extent. Consider an emergency situation in a hospital where access to a patient's data is protected by a security system. If the doctor authorized to access this information is for some reason not available, there is a need for "overriding" the security and accessing the data by someone else. However, strict accountability is necessary in this case, and the logs showing exactly who, when and why overrode the access restrictions are of utmost importance.

4.4 User Interfaces

Since in most cases a workflow instance needs to interact with the user, the problem of providing appropriate user interfaces arises. This problem is common for all workflow execution systems, therefore let us consider additional features and restrictions introduced by the migrating workflow environment.

A workflow instance requests a service from a site. This service could be directed to a user. In this case, the site will invoke an application, with its own interface, to interact with the user. This situation has the advantage of the user's familiarity with the interface, and allows the workflow specification to remain small and site-independent. However, in special cases, the workflow may carry its own interface definition and if need be, a specialized form or window could be presented to the user. Here, for the cost of the size of workflow specification, we gain the flexibility of custom interfaces. Of course, both approaches could be combined in a single workflow instance.

Besides the interfaces necessary for workflow instances, there are other situations where a human needs to interact with the workflow system. The local administrator should have an interface to modify local rules and policies, to implement new services and make them available. There should be an interface for the workflow designer to build the workflow. There should be an interface for a user to start the workflow; an interface for the administrator that will need to monitor workflow execution; and others. However, most of these interfaces are the same, or similar to those in traditional workflow systems, and are discussed elsewhere.

4.5 Networking Infrastructure

Migrating workflows need an existing communication infrastructure to move their code and data from site to site. Also, migrating workflows may need to send a message to other workflows or programs, for example to the watcher at a secure site. This communication uses existing computer networks, which can be relatively static (e.g., a slowly changing set of workstations at a company office), or highly dynamic, (e.g., a set of laptops communicating with fixed hosts and with each other using wireless modems). Migrating workflows could operate in both environments. However, the natural ability of performing disconnected operations makes migrating workflows particularly suitable for dynamic and mobile networks.

The transport protocol of the migrating workflow system depends on a particular implementation. However, instead of directly using such low-level protocols as TCP/IP, SMTP, or HTTP, we suggest to base the migrating workflow implementation on one of the existing and emerging mobile agent systems. These systems already provide mechanisms for transporting arbitrary code and data between hosts. Some mobile agent systems also have security models built in, and are capable of utilizing various transport protocols.

Here we would like to present some Mobile Agent systems currently considered to be state-of-the art.

- Java (Sun Microsystems [GM 95]). Java is an interpreted, object-oriented language (with associated libraries) capable of being executed on heterogeneous platforms. The main feature of Java programs is their inherent capability of being transported over the network (most often over the HTTP protocol) and being executed at the remote system. The Java language also includes a comprehensive (although not perfect) security system. Java is not an agent system in itself. However, the two features mentioned above make Java particularly suitable for the development of such. Currently, the most serious drawback of Java is its mediocre performance.
- Telescript (General Magic [Whi 96]). This is one of the most influential, and the least successful of the projects presented here. Telescript is an object-oriented mobile agent language. The main feature of Telescript is its go instruction that moves the code, data and the execution state of the agent to another machine. The agents written in Telescript can interact with each other and with their environment via services located at the server hosts (*places*). Telescript has a quite sophisticated security model involving authority, identity, and permits that are granted for each resource separately. Telescript did not succeed on the market mostly due to the complexity of the language, the use of proprietary hardware and software necessary to run Telescript agents, and the cost of the system.
- Agent TCL (Dartmouth College [G 96]). Agent TCL is a simple platform-independent mobile agent system based on the popular Tcl/Tk [O 94]

scripting language. The agent is simply a Tcl script, that, when executing an `agent_jump` command, is transported (including its execution state) to a new place. Agent TCL's simplicity and availability make it suitable for experiments with mobile agents, but its lack of sophistication, lack of security model (there are plans to include PGP and Safe-Tcl into Agent TCL), and lack of support services such as navigation make it not particularly convenient for any real system.

- ARA (University of Kaiserslautern [PS 97]). ARA is another platform for the mobile agents. The ARA system provides an agent transport and security system core, used by several language interpreters executing mobile agent code. In this way ARA strives to provide an infrastructure in which programs in C, Java and Tcl can be executed as mobile agents in secure environment.
- TACOMA (University of Tromso and Cornell University [JRS 95]). This project focuses on operating system support for mobile agents. It is only a research prototype, based on the Tcl language. Agents are implemented as Tcl procedures carrying "folders," or data and code repositories. An important aspect of this project is the investigation of supporting services for mobile agents such as scheduling, load balancing, and access control.
- Aglets (IBM [CL 96]). Aglets are Java objects that can move from one host to another carrying their state along. The execution context of the Aglets is not preserved, and therefore, after the move, the execution of the object's methods must always start from the beginning. Despite this limitation, Aglets seem to be quite powerful. The system leverages many Java capabilities but also adds such important features as a global naming scheme, automatic failure handling, white board mechanisms, and others.

It is apparent that mobile agent systems are still in their infancy, making the transition from research prototypes to practical implementations. However, we believe the advances in mobile agent technology will make them truly useful for migrating workflows.

5. Workflow Administration Issues

Workflow management systems encompass much more than just workflow execution. There are also issues of business process modeling, workflow specification and analysis, administration, monitoring, and so on. In this section we discuss some of these problems from the perspective of migrating workflows.

5.1 Process Modeling

The basic building blocks of any process model are:

- Goals and completion criteria. This is an invariant in the migrating work-flow model. The workflow makes dynamic decisions about how to execute itself so that its goal can be achieved. The goal (such as "approval for a trip") remains constant, however, the sub-goals (tasks, or requests) can change during execution (e.g., from "get a signature of the manager" to "get a signature of the CFO") depending on the results of interactions with local systems.
- Participants. The workflow designer may assign specific performer roles to the migrating workflow tasks that are known in advance. The workflow execution system resolves (via a special directory service) the roles and then direct the workflow to a particular user's site. The individual assigned to a task will then be held responsible for its completion. For the tasks that were not specified a priori, but discovered during execution of a workflow instance, the participants must be discovered in the same fashion. Thus, the set of participants (even if we consider roles, and not actual individuals) is also dynamic, constructed during the lifetime of the migrating workflow.
- Conditions for task execution (i.e., when the tasks are performed). This is a dynamic decision, made by the workflow instance and by the site handling its requests. It is the responsibility of the local system to decide when the task corresponding to a request is executed. However, workflows themselves may have conditions and deadlines. If they are not met, the workflow may perform some additional tasks: submit another request, send a message to the watcher process, or migrate to an alternative site. Analogously, when a workflow instance wants to migrate to a certain site, it should be able to detect unnecessary delays and undertake an emergency or alternative action.
- Constraints, or invariants. These items represent policies and consistency criteria for business processes. The policies are generally represented by the local rules at the participating sites, the consistency criteria must be encoded both at the sites, and in the workflow specifications.
- Inputs. Input data needed by the workflow can be "discovered" by the workflow exactly the same way as new tasks and sites are discovered. Imagine a workflow instance requesting a plane ticket reservation from a site, and the site responding with a request for an additional data item (e.g., a credit card number). The workflow goes back to the originating user, obtains this additional piece of information, and returns to the travel site, where it submits the corrected request.
- Outputs. Handling of the output data does not differ from the traditional workflow execution systems.
- Metrics (i.e., measurements to be collected for monitoring). Each of the workflows need to carry with it the log of all activities performed during its lifetime, including identifications of the sites, services, users, requests, timestamps, etc. These logs are crucial for all aspects of monitoring, in-cluding the accountability of the participants, performance analysis and

re-engineering. Special attention should be given to security issues. The logs must be protected from tampering, and unauthorized sites should be prevented from reading the data contained in them.

5.2 Workflow Specification

The main strength of migrating workflows is their intuitive specification, based on partial information of actual business processes. The workflow designer does not need to be aware of some of the sites, some services offered by these sites, or some steps or rules involved in the business process. The model of processes can be approximate, since they will be augmented during the execution of workflow instances (of course, the models should be more precise than the three-step plan "start;solve problem;stop"). Creation of such models will still involve analysis of the actual processes in the organization, interviews with the users, etc., but it does not to be as detailed as in the traditional workflows case.

Part of the process modeling and workflow specification task takes the form of providing local rules at workflow execution sites. These rules implement local ways of handling incoming requests (local policies) and will help in augmenting the instances of migrating workflows. Specification of the local rules that depend on a single individual or application, is a much easier task than discovering and specifying business processes, often spanning numerous sites and users.

Care needs to be exercised in specifying default rules that determine what to do if no other rule is applicable in a given situation. Usually such rules will ask a user to resolve the problem, send the workflow back and ask the originating user to resolve the problem, or send the workflow to a supervisor. The firing of the default rules should be very carefully monitored, so that we can discover the most frequent problems and implement rules that can handle them.

The second problem in specifying local rules is that they may interact in an unpredictable ways with local rules at other sites. Thus, it is easy to create sets of local rules that will be inconsistent with each other (and create, for example, an artificial "Catch 22" situation). Since imposing arbitrary restrictions on local rules is infeasible, it seems that the migrating workflow needs to examine periodically its own logs, and react when it sees no progress of its goals while being constantly busy.

Finally, various local tasks need to be implemented. These tasks will be invoked by the site in response to the request submitted by incoming workflows. These tasks will then interact with human users or with automated applications. One of the advantages of migrating workflows is their ability to carry with themselves a description of a task to be executed (e.g., Tcl/Tk script). The task can be then submitted for execution by the site. This method has the advantage of being much more flexible, but it multiplies the system security problems.

5.3 Administration of Migrating Workflows

Administration of the system in which migrating workflows are designed and executed is, due to its inherently distributed nature, a very difficult task. Only the administration of workflow specification is similar for migrating workflows and traditional workflows. In both cases specifications need to be organized in workflow repositories (libraries) with reasonable version control in place, and with proper tools for adding, deleting and modifying them. Tasks that are different in the migrating workflow systems include mostly those related to the administration of the local rules. There are three possibilities: the local rules will be administered by a central authority, the local rules will be administered by local users, or there will be a mix of central and local administration.

All three solutions have advantages and disadvantages. Local rules could be administered from a central site to guarantee that the global policies are implemented correctly at every site. This will also decrease the need for a qualified personnel to handle workflow administration. If the local rules are administered locally, the need for qualified system administrators increases, but the increased autonomy of local sites with respect to implementing their local policies may be worth it. The mixed solution may provide a workable system for moderate cost; however, there inconsistencies may arise in the rules imposed by the central administrator and the local user. Consider the global policy stating that a manager handles the approval of all trips costing no more than $1000, while the local rule made by the manager redirects all requests to the CFO. There is a need for resolution of such conflicts, either by imposing rule precedence, or by consistency checks for each rule added to the system.

Finally, the administration of workflow execution (i.e., execution monitoring, troubleshooting, etc.) is much more difficult in the case of migrating workflows. Since the site on which the workflow instance will be executing is not known to the administrator, the monitoring system must rely on the workflow to report its state. Otherwise only post-completion analysis of workflow's log and the trail left at the sites will be possible. However, since such a trail is distributed over many sites, the reconstruction of the actual execution trace can be quite difficult.

6. Discussion and Summary

In this paper we present the concept of migrating workflows and considerations related to implementation of this concept. Migrating workflows are a natural way to express inherently distributed processes similar to the way people conduct daily business: arriving at a site, using a service, and moving to the next place. Although the migrating workflows can execute concurrent tasks (e.g., by cloning themselves), they are most suitable for sequential processes.

The strength of migrating workflows lies in their ability to react dynamically to an ever-changing environment. A change in company policy will no longer require rewriting all affected workflows. A simple modification of a local rule at a single site will suffice to implement such a change. The flexibility of migrating workflows allows for more robust handling of failures and exceptions, and consequently, for more reliable workflow execution systems. The migration of workflows provide a graceful way of handling disconnected operations in mobile computing environment. Finally, in cases where a workflow needs to process large sets of data, migrating workflows improve system performance by transferring a short workflow specification to sites where huge datasets reside, rather then moving the data.

The disadvantages of migrating workflow systems lie in the difficulties of providing proper security for both the sites executing the workflow instances and the workflows themselves. Also the administration and monitoring of migrating workflows seem to be difficult problems. Despite these issues, migrating workflows are a promising paradigm for the office process automation.

Technology and Tools for Comprehensive Business Process Lifecycle Management

Dimitrios Georgakopoulos[1] and Aphrodite Tsalgatidou[2]

[1]GTE Laboratories Incorporated,
40 Sylvan Road, Waltham, MA 02254, USA
E-mail: dimitris@gte.com

[2]University of Athens, Department of Informatics,
TYPA Buildings, Panepistimiopolis, Athens 157 71, Greece,
E-mail: afrodite@di.uoa.gr

Abstract. *Business processes* are collections of one or more linked activities which realize a business objective or policy goal, such as fulfilling a business contract, and/or satisfying a specific customer need. The *lifecycle* of a business process involves everything from capturing the process in a computerized representation to automating the process. This typically includes specific steps for measuring, evaluating, and improving the process. Currently, commercially available *workflow management systems* (WFMSs) and *business process modeling tools* (BPMTs) provide for complementary aspects of business process lifecycle management. Furthermore, new concepts and interoperating tools in these categories are emerging to provide comprehensive support for managing the entire business process lifecycle. In this paper we provide an overview and an evaluation of the process modeling, analysis, automation, and coordination capabilities provided by integrated BPMTs and WFMSs. We also discuss how state of the art WFMSs and BPMTs can interoperate to provide complete support for the entire business process lifecycle. Although we occasionally discuss research issues, we mainly focus on the state of the art in commercially available technology.

1 Introduction

Business processes are market-centered descriptions of an organization's activities. That is, business processes are collections of activities that support critical organizational functions in realizing an objective or policy goal, such as fulfilling a business contract, and/or satisfying a specific customer need. Business processes are typically implemented by designing corresponding information and/or material processes [MWFF 92].

Information processes relate to automated activities (i.e., activities performed by programs) and partially automated activities (i.e., activities performed by humans interacting with computers) that create, process, manage, and provide information. Typically an information process involves distributing and coordinating work activities among human and information system resources. In addition, effective coordination must deal with throughput delays, achieve efficient human and system resource allocation, provide reliability and consistency, and improve the quality of the resulting products (whether information service or matter).

Material processes are related to the assembly of physical components and the delivery of physical products. That is, material processes relate human activities that are rooted in the physical world. Such activities include, moving, storing, transforming, measuring, and assembling physical objects.

Capturing business processes allows reasoning about the efficiency of an organization's activities. Implementing and automating business processes (by designing and implementing corresponding information and material processes) provides for the actual coordination of the organization's activities.

Business process reengineering (BPR) is the activity of capturing business processes starting from a blank sheet of paper, a blank computerized model, document, or repository. Once an organization captures its business in terms of business processes, it can measure each process to improve it or adapt it to changing requirements. *Continuous (business) process improvement* (CPI) involves explicit measurements, reconsideration, and redesign of the business process.

Reasons cited for business process redesign include increasing customer satisfaction, improving efficiency of business operations, increasing quality of products, reducing cost, and meeting new business challenges and opportunities by changing existing services or introducing new ones. BPR is performed before information systems and computers are used for automating a process. CPI may be performed after BPR and before information systems and computers are used for automating a process. However, typically CPI occurs after a process has been automated. Furthermore, CPI takes into account measurements of the process automation effectiveness.

Information process reengineering and *continuous information process improvement* are complementary activities of BPR and CPI, respectively. They involve determining how to use legacy and new information systems to automate the business processes produced by BPR and CPI. These activities can be performed iteratively to provide mutual feedback. While business process redesign can explicitly address the issues of customer satisfaction, information process reengineering can address the issues of information system efficiency and cost, and take advantage of advancements in technology.

In many organizations the term *workflow* is used to refer to a specific category of automated business processes. The main characteristic of such processes is that they are specified and/or implemented in two tiers. The top tier consists of a single process, which we refer to as the *workflow process*, and it is implemented by a corresponding (workflow) application. The workflow application automates the coordination, control, and communication of the basic process activities. These activities and the information systems or humans that perform them comprise the lower tier. During the workflow process enactment information or tasks are passed from one participating human or system to another for action, according to a set of procedural rules that implement and automate the business rules defined by the workflow process. Workflows are discussed further in Sections 4, 5, and 7.

The *business process lifecycle* involves everything from capturing a business process in a computerized representation to automating the business process (e.g., by implementing a workflow process). These typically include explicit process measurement, analysis, and improvement activities as required by BPR and CPI. The need to manage the business process lifecycle effectively, i.e., to perform *business process management*, has led to the development of new concepts and interoperating tools that support complementary aspects of business process management. Currently, commercially available products that support business process management can be characterized as *workflow management systems* (WFMSs) and *business process modeling tools* (BPMTs)[1]. Both WFMSs and BPMTs support business process definition or specification. However, while the scope of process definition in BPMTs is to provide for process understanding and analysis that can lead to process improvement, the scope of process definition in WFMSs is to support process automation. Therefore, the capabilities and the level of detail of the process definition typically captured by the WFMSs and BPMTs may vary, as needed to support respective automation or analysis purposes. More specifically, WFMSs manage the enactment of processes through the use of software that directly interprets the process definition and coordinates human and system participants that perform process related activities. On the other hand, BPMTs facilitate process evaluation and improvement by analyzing process definitions, simulating process enactment, and analyzing simulation measurements. Although BPMTs may be also capable of analyzing process measurements that are collected while the process is enacted by a WFMS, BPMTs usually lack functional capabilities and process definition detail needed for support process enactment. Therefore, to provide for the entire business process lifecycle, BPMTs and WFMSs must interoperate.

This paper provides an overview and an evaluation of the process modeling, analysis, and coordination capabilities of BPMTs and WFMSs. It also discusses how interoperability between WFMSs and BPMTs can provide complete support for the management of the entire business process lifecycle. More specifically, the rest of paper is organized as follows: Section 2 provides a characterization of business processes. Section 3 describes the business process lifecycle and its management, while Section 4 discusses commercially available BPMT and WFMS technology for supporting the business process lifecycle. The impact of using BPMTs and WFMSs on the business process lifecycle, as well as an evaluation of current BPMT and WFMS technology are then discussed respectively in Sections 5, 6 and 7. One of the major issues in using BPMTs and

---

[1] BPMTs are often referred to as BPR tools.

WFMSs is their integration. This is described in Section 8. Finally, we conclude this paper by discussing critical factors for the success of using BPMTs and WFMSs in supporting BPR, CPI and process implementation. Although we occasionally discuss research issues, we mainly focus on the state of the art in commercially available BPMTs and WFMSs.

2   Characterizing Business Processes

As yet, there is no commonly agreed way to characterize business processes. However, the workflow literature often distinguishes between four kinds of processes (e.g., such a characterization is given by [McC 92]): ad hoc, administrative, collaborative, and production. The basic dimensions along which these kinds of processes are characterized include:
- repetitiveness and predictability of the process and its activities
- mission criticality and value for the organization

A*d hoc* and *collaborative* processes have no set pattern for coordinating activities and for moving information among (typically human) process participants [Kor 94, Bla 94]. Ad hoc and collaborative processes typically involve small teams of professionals performing both synchronous and asynchronous activities. Examples include many office processes, such as business tax returns, product documentation, and sales proposals. In such processes, the ordering of activities is controlled and coordinated by humans [SZ 91]. Furthermore, the ordering and coordination decisions are made while the process is performed. The basic difference between ad hoc and collaborative processes is their relative value for the organization that uses them. In particular, collaborative processes are mission critical and have high value for the organization, since process imperfection or disruption may result in violation of critical business objectives (e.g., significant loss of revenue or inability to offer critical customer services). On the other hand, ad hoc processes are generally not mission critical, since periodic imperfection and disruption can be tolerated (e.g., by repeating the process until it produces the desired result).

Administrative and *production processes* are repetitive and predictable. Therefore, the ordering and coordination of activities in such processes can be specified before they are performed. Administrative processes, such as routing an expense report or travel request for authorization, are generally not mission critical. On the other hand, typical production processes, such as loan application processing, insurance claim processing, or service order and fulfillment in telecommunications are mission critical. Therefore, unlike administrative processes, production processes have high business value.

Currently only administrative and production processes may be effectively supported by commercial BPMTs and WFMSs. Ad hoc and collaborative processes currently receive limited support from *groupware* technology and tools. However, groupware tools lack theoretical foundation, explicit process modeling, and corresponding infrastructure. In addition, they do not interoperate with WFMSs and BPMTs. Due to these problems, in the rest of this paper we focus mainly on administrative and production processes.

To discuss a more specific example of a production process, consider the processes depicted in Figure 1.

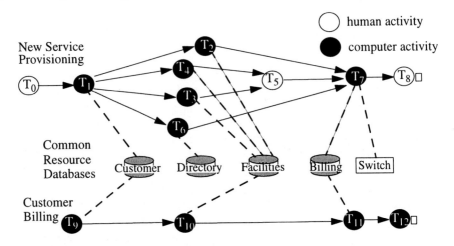

Figure 1. Examples of production processes in telecommunications.

The New Service Provisioning process captures the activities of telephone service provisioning for a new customer. The process takes place when a telephone company customer requests telephone service installation. Activity T_0 involves an operator collecting information from the customer. When sufficient customer data are collected, activity T_1 is performed to:

1. verify that the information provided by the customer is accurate, and
2. create a corresponding service order record.

On completion of T_1, activities T_2, T_3, and T_4 are initiated to perform three circuit provisioning activities. The objective of a provisioning activity is to construct a circuit from a customer location to the appropriate telephone switch and allocate equipment to connect the circuit. Only one of these provisioning activities should be allowed to complete, as all will result in a completed circuit, i.e., a set of lines and equipment that connects the customer to a telephone network (this requirement is not depicted in Figure 1). T_2 attempts to provide a connection by using existing facilities such as lines and slots in switches. If T_2 succeeds, the cost of provisioning is minimal, i.e., the requested connection can be established by allocating existing resources. However, a successful completion of this activity may not be possible if the facilities are not available. T_3 and T_4 achieve the same objectives as T_2 but involve different paths for physical installations of new facilities. T_5 requires manual work for facility installation. The human activity T_5 is initiated by providing installation instructions to the engineers (e.g., via mobile computers) and is completed when the human engineers provide the necessary work completion data. Activity T_6 involves changes in the telephone directory, while T_7 updates the telephone switch to activate service and then generates a bill. Finally, activity T_8 involves a human operator who calls the customer to inform him of the establishment of the requested service and verify that the provided service meets the customer needs.

In addition to the activities involved, the process defines the following activity ordering and dataflow between activities:

1. T_1 waits for data from T_0,
2. T_2, T_3, T_4, and T_6, wait for data from T_1 but do not exchange data, i.e., they can be performed concurrently after activity T_1 is completed,
3. T_5 needs data from T_3 and T_4,
4. T_7 waits from data from T_2, T_5, and T_6, and
5. T_8 needs completion data from T_7.

These dependencies are depicted as arcs in Figure 1. The other process depicted in Figure 1 has explanation similar to that of the New Service Provisioning process.

The relationship of ad hoc, collaborative administrative, and production processes is illustrated in Figure 2 using process value and mission criticality versus process repetitiveness and predictability.

In the following sections we describe the business process lifecycle and discuss its management by contrasting traditional approaches with novel approaches using state of the art BPMTs and WFMSs.

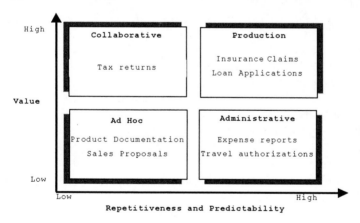

Figure 2. Characterization of Processes

3   Traditional Business Process Lifecycle Management

The business process management approach started in the 1980's when companies began several initiatives to improve performance with an emphasis on quality. This led to the realization that all work activities are business processes (i.e., related decisions and activities required to manage and administer resources of the business). Then, quality objectives were introduced to improve the effectiveness and efficiency of cross functional business processes. In particular, the process lifecycle includes the following:

- Capturing Process Definition
- Reengineering a Process
- Implementing a Process
- Performing Continuous Process Improvement

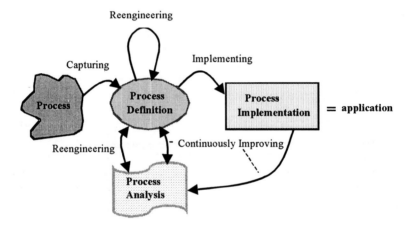

Figure 3. The business process lifecycle.

The process lifecycle elements are illustrated in Figure 3 and they are discussed further in the following sections.

3.1   Capturing Process Definition

In order to capture a process, we need to understand it. This usually involves interviewing people with expert knowledge about the process. Interview methodologies such as those used for expert system design are appropriate for conducting such interviews. When enough knowledge about the process is obtained, the process is captured in process definition.

A process definition is a process abstraction. The process abstraction level in a definition depends on the intended use of the definition. For example, a definition may describe a process at the highest conceptual level necessary for understanding, evaluating, and redesigning the process. On the other hand, another definition may describe the same process at a lower-level of detail required for performing process implementation.

Performing process definition requires a process model. A model typically includes a set of concepts that are useful to describe processes, their activities, the coordination of the activities, and the required *roles* (i.e., skills of the individuals or information systems) that can perform the specified activities. These concepts are embodied in a process definition language.

Validation of the process definition is necessary to determine if the process definition actually represents the intended process. This can be accomplished through behavioral simulation (showing what "happens next?") and/or static analysis (which can be used to answer such questions as: is a certain activity on all paths through this process?), assuming that the process model is rich enough to support this.

3.2   Reengineering a Process

Process reengineering involves design of a new process which is intensive, revolutionary, top down, supported by system solutions and results in dramatic improvements. Process reengineering should be guided by clearly stated business objectives, such as increasing customer satisfaction, reducing the cost of doing business, reducing the time for producing new products and services. Reengineering methodologies are currently an art. Process definition provides a high-level description of a process that facilitates high-level reasoning about business process efficiency; this reasoning may be supported through process simulation and analysis.

3.3   Implementing a Process

Implementation involves realizing a process using computers, software, and information systems. (This does not require that all activities in the process be automated, since there may be some performed by people with no computer support). No implementation or automation is required when the only reason for process definition is to capture business processes and reason about their efficiency. Otherwise, process definitions are used to implement and automate the processes.

Process implementation has traditionally been accomplished indirectly by embedding parts of the process in software systems and relying on human actions to provide adherence to the rest of the process. In this case, the process definition serves as a design for system functions and human behavior. The IT staff typically do the implementation, which often happens without discussions with the business staff specifically about the process.

Implementing a process (new or improved) traditionally includes suitable training and carefully thought-out work instructions to guide the process performers in their intended roles.

3.4   Performing Continuous Process Improvement

Improving a process involves making small course corrections rather than engaging in radical redesign. Measurement of the process execution is the basis for improving the process (and its definition). Measurements can show how often certain paths are taken, what elapsed cycle times are, what costs have been incurred, and similar results. Analysis of this data can lead to ideas for process improvement based on actual process results. In contrast, improvements made after a process is defined but before it is implemented are based on human intuition and possibly simulation with estimated data.

Traditionally, measurement is accomplished by adding instrumentation to software systems and devising ways to measure human activity. Typically, such data must be gathered from multiple sources.

4   Technology and Tools for Business Process Lifecycle Management

In this section we discuss commercially available technology and software systems/tools that has been specifically developed to support aspects of the business process lifecycle. In particular, we focus on the technology and capabilities of commercial BPMTs and WFMSs. Furthermore, we show how BPMTs and WFMSs may together provide comprehensive support for the management of the business process lifecycle. BPMTs are introduced in Section 4.1. An introductory discussion of WFMSs is provided in Section 4.2. Levels of integration between BPMTs and WFMSs are described in Section 4.3. The roles of BPMTs and WFMSs in the business process lifecycle are discussed in Section 5.

4.1   Business Process Modeling Technology and Tools

As we mentioned earlier, BPMTs provide for capturing, understanding, evaluating, and improving (redesigning) business processes. Typical BPMT objectives include [Hol 97]:
1. Ease of use for the business end-user.
2. Well-defined process model objects for accurate measurements.
3. Simulation and analysis techniques.

4. Automated reports to expedite production of high quality outputs.
5. Integration capabilities with WFMSs.

To support these objectives, BPMTs provide the following tools:

- Business process definition tools to produce visual business process models by using one, or more, process modeling methodologies
- Analysis tools to measure long term performance, and facilitate process reengineering or improvement efforts
- Simulation tools to determine the short term impact of a model, and address practical concerns such as "bottlenecks"
- Integration tools to export, translate or share process definitions with WFMSs

Typical BPMT capabilities and data are depicted in Figure 4.

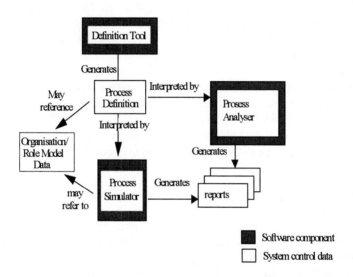

Figure 4. BPMT capabilities and data.

Business process definition/specification is the single most important founding principle of a BPMT. All analysis and subsequent benefits are based on the existence of "good" business process models. For example, if a process is not accurately modeled in a BPMT, no analysis tool can serve any useful purpose. Additionally, a BPMT without sufficient modeling depth can be counter-productive, since conclusions will be reached based on incomplete or inaccurate information.

"Good" process models and corresponding specifications must have the following properties [Hol 97]:

1. Models must show how objects are transferred and where they are going.
2. A process is chronological.
3. Conditions select one of many possible paths when interpreting the specifications of a process.
4. Alternate paths in a process must be separated for measurement.

Business process analysis and simulation measure possible business process outcomes. In particular, since business processes can often have multiple variations (or process cases), a BPMT must measure each possible outcome with a probability of occurrence. The resources required for each possible case can be aggregated and factored by their probabilities to obtain data that are essential for accounting and resource allocation. State of the art BPMTs include predefined reports geared to this purpose.

Another BPMT capability is process simulation. By varying rates of input, a BPMT can simulate activities and assess short-term performance issues, such as "bottlenecks" in a process. Procedures can be developed based on these simulations to successfully plan for and manage uncontrollable variations of input.

BPMTs do not provide business process automation. Instead, BPMTs rely on WFMSs for this purpose. We introduce WFMSs next. In Section 4.3, we discuss the integration of BPMTs with WFMSs. The role of BPMTs in the business process lifecycle is discussed further in Section 5. The capabilities and limitations of commercial BPMTs are discussed in Section 6.

4.2   Workflow Management Technology and Systems

In many organizations the term *workflow* is used to refer to an automated business process, which means that the coordination, control and communication of activities is automated, but the activities themselves can be either automated by information systems or performed by people. *Human activities* include interacting with computers closely (e.g., providing input commands) or loosely (e.g., using computers only to indicate activity progress). Examples of activities include updating a file or database, generating or mailing a bill, and laying a cable. Therefore, workflows are *loosely coupled* (i.e., they are built by linking together human and system activities).

As mentioned above, a business process definition is a process abstraction that depends on the intended use of the definition. In the rest of this paper, when a process definition is intended for process implementation and automation we will call it a *workflow process definition*. When such a definition is intended for business process analysis, improvement, reengineering, we will call it a *business process definition*. This terminology differs slightly from the Workflow Management Coalition's (WfMC) terms [WfM 97], which do not make this distinction.

Figure 5, depicts typical capabilities and data in a WFMS as they are defined by the Workflow Management Coalition (WfMC).

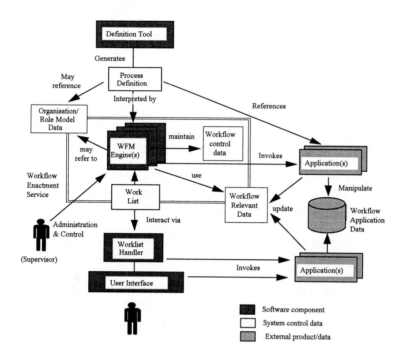

Figure 5. WFMS capabilities and data as defined by theWfMC Reference Model

Definition of workflow processes involves the specification of the *control flow* and *dataflow* dependencies between activities. These dependencies are implemented by a *workflow engine*, which is controlled by a computerized representation of the workflow processes and the corresponding dataflow and control flow dependencies. Each execution instance of a process is called a *workflow process instance*. From the perspective of a workflow processes definition, users play organizational *roles*. Each workflow activity the *resources* it requires, i.e., the application(s) or the organizational role(s) of the users that can perform it. Whenever the workflow engine initiates such an activity, it dynamically selects a specific user form those supporting the role(s) specified in the activity. Users communicate with workflow engines by means of *workflow clients*, programs that provide an integrated user interface to all workflows supported by the WFMS. To request work from a user, the engine places an item in the *worklist* of this user. Workflow clients allow participating users to pick up worklist items and indicate the completion status of the work specified by each work item they have picked.

The role of WFMSs in the business process lifecycle is discussed further in Section 5. The capabilities and limitations of commercial WFMSs are described in Section 7. Next, we discuss the integration of BPMTs and WFMSs.

4.3   Interoperability Between BPMTs and WFMSs

To provide for implementation and automation of business processes, state of the art BPMTs may export, translate, or share process definitions with WFMSs. For example, consider a situation where the business process model used by a BPMT is different than the workflow process model utilized by a WFMS. Their integration involves filtering business process model objects, translating them into appropriate workflow process model objects, validating the resulting workflow process model, and placing it in the representation used by the WFMS engine. Once this is accomplished, the translation process can be automated. In general, the level of integration between BPMT and WFMS can be characterized as follows:

- Level 0: Includes BPMTs that export business process definitions using a proprietary BPMT model and/or representation. WFMSs (or related software) must translate such heterogeneous process models and process representations into the native workflow process and the corresponding process definitions, and import them to the WFMS.
- Level 1: Includes BPMTs that export business process definitions using a workflow process model and representation that can be directly used by a WFMS. BPMTs in this category must translate their business process definitions into the workflow process definitions supported by a target WFMS.
- Level 2: Includes BPMTs and WFMSs that share process models and definitions. BPMTs (WFMSs) in this category must automatically export (import) such definitions or share a common process model repository.

In this paper we consider only BPMTs in Levels 1 and 2. However, it should be noted that even BPMTs and WFMSs at Level 2 may not interoperate fully. For instance, this may occur if the process definition in a BMPT does not contain sufficient level of detail for automation (e.g., it may not specify which application implements each automated activity and how to invoke it).

The role of BPMT and WFMS integration in the business process lifecycle is discussed further next. Issues related to the integration of commercial BPMTs with WFMSs are discussed in Section 8.

5   Role of BPMT and WFMS Technology in the Business Process Lifecycle

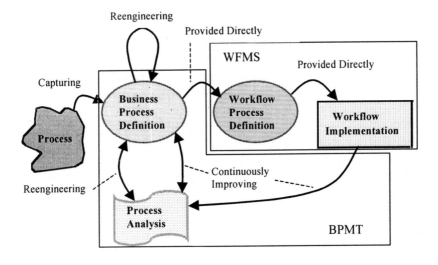

Figure 6. Process Lifecycle with BPMT and WFMS Technology.

In this section we discuss the impact of using BPMT and WFMS technology on the process lifecycle. The changes from the traditional lifecycle management in Section 3 are illustrated in Figure 6.

The specific impact of BPMT and WFMS technology on the elements of the business process lifecycle is discussed further in the following sections.

5.1   Capturing Process Definition

In Sections 3 and 4, we discussed that a process definition is a process abstraction that depends on the intended use of the definition. Furthermore, we noted that both BPMTs and WFMSs provide models and technology for capturing business processes. Therefore, the value of these technologies in capturing a process depends on how well they support the intended use of the process definition. More specifically, BPMTs provide better support than WFMSs in situations where the process definition is intended for business process understanding, reengineering, and improvement. On the other hand, if the objective of process definition is process implementation and automation, a WFMS should be used instead of a BPMT. Thus, business process definition involves the capturing of a process by using a BPMT, while workflow process definition requires use of a WFMS.

To provide comprehensive support for the entire business process lifecycle, we must develop an approach for allowing an organization to transition between its business process definitions in a BPMT and its workflow process definitions in the model of a WFMS product. This is a more complicated issue than it might appear for the following reasons:

- The business process model may not provide sufficient detail so that the process implementation can be based directly on the process definition.
- The workflow process model (and the definition language provided by the WFMS) may be heterogeneous with the business process model (and corresponding definition language) used by the BPMT.

In any of these holds, the business process definition and the workflow process definition are two different entities, as depicted in Figure 6. This category includes commercial BPMTs and WFMSs offered by different vendors that currently interoperate at Level 1.

In an ideal situation, the business process definition used for general business process reengineering and improvement purposes will be exactly what is needed as a workflow process definition for workflow implementation. However, even in this situation business process definitions may differ from workflow process definitions for the following reasons:

- Business process reengineering and improvement neither require that the business process definition be at a working level of detail, nor they require exact correspondence of automated activities with the interfaces of legacy and new systems needed to support the process. Achieving this requires IT knowledge, in addition to business knowledge, and may not simply be a matter of adding detail to the business process definition.
- The models used by WFMSs are in general more comprehensive, requiring information and design decisions that are best made by IT personnel with knowledge of legacy systems and how to achieve workflow throughput, scalability, monitoring, etc.
- Some business process definition languages are best suited for human, not machine, understanding; for example, it may be obvious to humans based on activity titles that two activities are alternatives to each other, but this cannot be detected by a automated algorithm.
- Sometimes process reengineering is focused primarily on the "normal" path through a process. Thus, the business process definition may lack detail on exceptional conditions, error handling, and other details that must be present in a workflow process definition.

Despite these problems, working with a single process definition (whether for understanding, reengineering, improvement, or implementation) is clearly the desirable case. To provide for this, some vendors have begun offering toolkits that include Level 2 integration between the provided BPMTs and WFMSs.

5.2   Reengineering a Process

Reengineering is not affected by introducing WFMS technology. BPMTs provide process models and analysis tools that can support one or more BPR methodologies. These are discussed further in Section 6.

5.3   Implementing a Process

Implementation is not affected by introducing BPMT technology. However, this is where the many advantages of WFMS technology are achieved. WFMSs provide for direct process implementation, driving process automation through the workflow process definition. Here, the process definition is actually part of the implementation. We believe that workflow process implementation will still be a collaboration between business staff and IT staff, with communication between them centered on the process definition. The IT staff will design the optimal implementation.

5.4   Performing Continuous Process Improvement

When BPMT and WFMS technologies are utilized, improving a business process involves making changes to:
- The business process definition, based on process measurements performed when the business process was analyzed by the BPMT.
- The workflow process definition, based on changes in the corresponding business process definition (assuming that the business and workflow process definitions are different).
- The business process definition, based on measurements made when the workflow process definition is enacted by the WFMS.

Logging functions are provided within a WFMS to record activity starts and stops. Thus, BPMTs can introduce monitoring applications to collect measurements from process enactment in WFMSs.

6   Evaluation of Current Business Process Modeling Technology

Commercial BPMTs currently support business process modeling and evaluation for improvement and reengineering purposes. Evaluation is performed by means of analysis, simulation, and report generation techniques. In the following sections, we discuss related BPMT capabilities and limitations.

6.1   Business Process Models and Methodologies

From the perspective of BMPT technology, the modeling of an existing or a proposed process involves the selection and use of:

- a *business process model* (and a BPMT that provides/supports it)
- a *methodology* (that promotes the specific process reengineering and/or improvement goals)

A business process model is a set of business process model objects, we refer to as *core business process objects*, and their relationships [TJ 95]. These encapsulate the most important pieces of information that must be captured by the process definition.

A business process modeling methodology provides a set of rules and techniques for the creation of a process definition and its evaluation. The methodologies we consider here include various BPR (e.g. [Dav 93, HC 93]), CPI, and object-oriented methodologies (e.g. [JEJ 95]). From the perspective of business process modeling and evaluation, the purpose of such a methodology is to provide a set of guidelines and techniques for accomplishing specific process design, reengineering, or improvement goals.

Currently, commercial BPMTs provide process models that can be classified as goal-oriented, activity-oriented, or hybrid.

Goal-oriented models provide core business objects that explicitly support goal-based work. Models in this category are needed to ensure that a process achieves one or more organizational goals. However, goal-oriented models do not necessarily capture how to coordinate all the activities in the process.

Activity-oriented models provide core business objects that capture how to coordinate the process activities, but offer no explicit support for modeling anything else beyond this.

Hybrid models are both goal-oriented and activity-oriented.

Figure 7 depicts the relationship between models in these categories, and examples of goals such models may support.

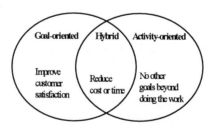

Figure 7. Classification of process models with respect to support for process goals.

Typical examples of goal-oriented models are conversation-based models (and corresponding methodologies) that stem from the Winograd/Flores Conversation for Action Model [MWFF 92]. A conversation-based model assumes that the objective of a business process is to improve customer satisfaction. It reduces every action in a process to four phases based on the communication between a customer and a performer:

- *preparation* - a customer requests an action to be performed or a performer offers to do some action
- *negotiation* - both customer and performer agree on the action to be performed and define the terms of satisfaction
- *performance* - the action is performed according to the terms established
- *acceptance* - the customer reports satisfaction (or dissatisfaction) with the action

The four phases in the loop, their actions, the loops they form, and the customer and performer roles are the core business objects this model provides. Processes are modeled by defining such loops between a customer and performer, and joining each loop with other workflow loops to complete the business process. The performer in one loop can be a customer in another loop.

Examples of BPMTs that support this model include, the ActionWorkflow Analyst tool [MWFF 92] from Action Technologies [Act 97] and the Business Transformation Management tool from Business Transaction Design [Mar 94].

Activity-oriented process models focus on modeling the work instead of modeling the rules and human commitments for achieving specific goals. Activity-oriented process models typically support the following core business objects for process modeling:

- *activity*: a logical step, or unit of work that an individual, a machine, or a group can perform
- *control flow*: the execution order of activities
- *resource*: an object necessary for the execution of an activity, e.g., a document, a data item, an application, a role, a fax machine, a phone, etc.
- *resource flow*: the path of resources between activities, i.e., the source and target activities of each resource and the method of transfer
- *role*: a placeholder for a person or organizational unit assigned to a particular activity.
- *organizational structure*: organizational units, roles, people competence, etc.

As an example of an activity based-model consider the telecommunications process in Figure 1. Although there are some BPMTs that support pure goal-oriented or activity-oriented models, most state of the art BPMTs typically provide hybrid models. Figure 8 depicts a classification of the process models offered by five hybrid BPMTs.

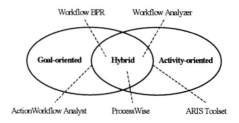

Figure 8. A classification of sample hybrid BPMTs.

More specifically, the ActionWorkflow Analyst tool from Action Technologies lies in the line between goal-oriented and hybrid BPMTs. This is because ActionWorkflow provides a conversation-based model for the higher levels of (abstraction in) the process definition. An activity-based model is used only at the lowest level of the process (e.g., to define the actions in each phase in a loop).

The ARIS Toolset [Ids 97] lies at the opposite end of the spectrum, i.e., on the dividing line between activity-oriented and hybrid process models. In ARIS, business processes are defined top-down or bottom-up using Event-driven Process Chains (EPCs) [KNS 92]. Process Chains are based on an activity-oriented model, referred to as the control view in the ARIS documentation. In addition, each Process Chain may have a goal associated with it. ARIS provide no functionality to validate, evaluate, or enforce goals. Goals specifications are basically text annotations on activity-based (sub) process specifications.

In addition to the control view, ARIS supports the construction of complementary functional, data, and organizational views/models (according to the integrated information systems approach [Sch 92]). Furthermore, it allows the sharing of modeled objects between these views and ensures their consistency. The control view integrates parts of the other views, since it models business processes using information from the functional, data, and organizational views. For the description of the functional, data, and organizational views, established models can be used, e.g. the ER-model can be used for data modeling.

Mainstream hybrid BPMTs include those that provide activity-oriented models that capture addition core business objects. These typically include activity execution time, elapsed time, and cost. By capturing these in combination with their activity-based models, these BPMTs can support a variety of methodologies that aim to improve process efficiency, e.g., by reducing process cost, improving resource utilization cost and/or time, minimizing process execution and elapsed time, etc.. The modeling of such information is important, since the evaluation of a business process often depends heavily on combining such information to reason about its efficiency.

More specifically, the WorkflowBPR by Holosofx [Hol 97] uses Activity Decision Flow (ADF) diagrams for process modeling. ADF diagrams can be nested to support top-down process definition. ADF diagrams provide an activity-oriented model that incorporates attributes for modeling activity cost, execution time, and elapsed time.

The Workflow Analyzer toolset by Metasoftware [Met 97] offers the Workflow Modeler tool (formerly Design/IDEF) which supports the IDEF0 methodology and the IDEF modeling standard IDEF1X [Bru 92]. IDEF (Integrated DEFinition method) is a model used to describe information systems. IDEF0 is very similar to SADT (Structured Analysis and Design Technique) [MG 88, MG 91] which was developed by SofTech Corporation in the 1970's. IDEF is used here to describe complex business processes in sufficient detail. This top-down model is basically a hierarchical activity-oriented model that provides process cost and duration attributes. Just like in WorkflowBPR, these attributes can be used for process analysis and simulation.

ProcessWise Workbench by ICL & Fujitsu [IF 97] provides a default set of core process objects (which are represented by pictures or images) for defining business processes. In addition to being activity-oriented, the process model provided by ProcessWise is object-oriented and hierarchical (so that different levels of details can be specified). Process evaluation information, such as cost, time or volume can be added as attributes to core objects of the model. These can be subsequently used for process analysis and simulation.

6.2   Business Process Analysis

Analysis of the modeled process is performed to identify the process strengths and weaknesses, and determine if the process should be redesigned or proceed to its implementation. Analytical tools used by the various BPMTs include:

- *Case analysis:* measures and analyzes only a specific process path, as directed by the process designer/evaluator. Case analysis typically estimates process cost and/or time attributes. The analysis calculations use probabilities and parameters assigned to the process conditions and activities. These are assigned by the process designer/evaluator.
- *Weighted average analysis*: calculates mean cost and cycle time using data taken from case analysis. It takes into account all potential execution paths and their relevant probabilities of execution, and gives higher weights to paths with the higher execution probabilities.
- *Critical path analysis*: identifies the critical path in a process. The critical path is the series of activities on which the overall completion schedule of the process depends. Any delay in the completion of any activity in the critical path will cause process delays.
- *Throughput analysis*: identifies the process throughput that can be achieved, assuming that all necessary or a specified level of resources is available.

- *Resource utilization*: given a specific workload, assesses the degree of resource utilization a process can achieve.
- *Value chain analysis*: identifies which activities in a process are critical for providing value to the customer, i.e., achieving a process goal.
- *Activity based costing*: allows the process designer/evaluator to associate cost information to the process definition objects, and then performs financial analysis.
- *Process simulation analysis*: this very important analysis technique is discussed further in the following section.

The WorkflowBPR by Holosofx supports three types of analysis: case analysis, weighted average analysis and process simulation analysis. Case analysis is supported by the use of Gantt Charts, Communication Diagrams, Activity Cost Graphs, and Resource Cost Charts.

The Workflow Analyzer by Metasoftware supports activity based costing analysis. To provide this, Workflow Analyzer integrates a financial analysis tool (the EasyABC Plus) where cost and process information is exported for more detailed analysis.

ProcessWise WorkBench provides no specific support for process analysis.

The ARIS Toolset supports case analysis, critical path, and value chain analysis. Also, the ARIS Promt component (fully integrated into ARIS Toolset) enables the evaluation and monitoring of business process costs by supporting activity based costing. Various cost management requirements are supported, including process cost controlling, optimization, benchmarking, and resource management.

6.3   Business Process Simulation

Simulation is very important for evaluating a business process (either new or redesigned) before implementing it. Many BPMTs provide for simulation of business processes and assess performance issues by varying rates of simulation input. For example, these include a wide variety of statistical distribution types ranging from 'normal' (bell shaped curves), trinomial (most, least, average), exponential to pre-assigned volumes at different times of day. BPMTs typically provide statistics on resource utilization, and support for animation so that the user can visualize how work moves through the model. In addition, BPMTs often provide facilities to identify blockages or bottlenecks in the process definition. These occur at activities or conditions where work consistently builds up awaiting for resources or other activities to complete. Finally, some BPMTs, provide facilities for pausing the process simulation during a run, handle concurrent processes (i.e., several processes running simultaneously competing for resources), and maintain queue load statistics for assessing the overall number of worklist items and resources that may build up in process queues maintained by the BPMT.

The simulation component of WorkflowBPR supports discrete simulation and provides for most of the above mentioned aspects. Calendars providing the availability of resources are used during simulation, so the simulation output is based on real schedules. The simulation analysis information can also be exported to other analysis tools, such as Microsoft's Excel.

The Workflow Analyzer of Metasoftware incorporates the Workflow Simulator which automatically translates the process model to a dynamic analysis model. This approach provides a smooth transition from modeling to simulation. Simulation results are displayed graphically and allow the visual assessment of key factors such as bottlenecks, idle resources and operating costs. A variety of graphic formats, from pie charts to bar charts and spreadsheets are provided. Costing statistics can also be produced using the resource costs specified in the process model. Another feature of Workflow Analyzer is that the process model can be exported in a form that is readable by the Design/CPN Simulator [PS 90]. This provides powerful simulation capabilities using information that has been inserted as annotations to the process definition. Design/CPN is based on hierarchical colored Petri nets.

The ProcessWise WorkBench supports both time based and event based discrete simulation. It also provides for arrival rate distribution, animation, queuing statistics, and concurrent processes.

ARIS Promt (the integrated simulation component of the ARIS Toolset mentioned before) allows the simulation of ARIS process models. It provides various simulation scenarios, capacity-oriented evaluation of business processes, discovery of performance gaps, identification of resource bottlenecks, evaluation of process using according to time and cost criteria.

6.4   Business Process Evaluation Reports and Documentation

BPMTs can typically generate reports for analysis data. In particular, process designers/evaluators can compose ad-hoc, user-defined analysis reports, as needed. In addition, BPMTs provide a set of pre-defined, pre-formatted analysis reports. Both types of reports typically include charts and diagrams.

WorkflowBPR offers a variety of reporting options, providing flexibility in reviewing analysis data from different perspectives. For example, a process designer/evaluator can generate reports to evaluate a process from an enterprise perspective, a resource flow perspective, or an activity perspective that includes scheduling and costing information. Also, 'as is' process and 'to be' process reports can be generated. These provide analysis information on resource utilization and costs associated with resources. Various charts and diagrams, e.g., Gantt charts for viewing scheduling information or resource requirement charts, can be generated. An interesting feature of this tool is the automatic generation of a Process Improvement Document. This uses real data from modeling and analysis activities and assembles them into a Microsoft Word document. Such a document is very useful for justifying BPR and CPI initiatives.

ProcessWise provides similar user-defined and pre-defined reporting.

The ARIS Toolset provides for entire documentation of business processes. The ARIS documentation can be used for other purposes too, like management presentations, user training or ISO 9000 certification.

7   Evaluation of Current Workflow Management Technology

In the following sections we discuss the features and capabilities currently supported by WFMSs. These include commercially available products and home-built applications currently in use in various organizations. However, although a combination of BPMT and WFMS technology currently provides the most comprehensive support to the business process lifecycle, commercial WFMSs are sometimes not the only (and in some cases not the best) infrastructure technology that can be used to implement and automate business processes. Therefore before we describe any specific WFMS capabilities, we first discuss the perspective of commercial WFMSs and their vendors. In particular, in the following paragraph we characterize WFMSs from the perspective of process implementation and automation requirements. In addition, we discuss the relationship of WFMS technology to other infrastructure technologies that can support process implementation and automation.

Seen from the process implementation and automation perspective, process requirements can be characterized by considering the degree to which a process depends on humans or software for performing and coordinating activities. Such a characterization is depicted in Figure 9. On the one extreme, human-oriented processes requires humans collaborating in performing activities and coordinating activities. The requirements for process implementation in this environment are to support the coordination and collaboration of humans and to improve human throughput. Humans, however, must ensure the consistency of process objects and results.

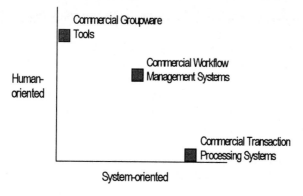

Figure 9. Processes with respect to software and human supported activities

On the other extreme, system-oriented processes require computer systems that perform computation-intensive operations and automated activities. In addition to being highly automated, system-oriented processes access heterogeneous, autonomous, and/or distributed (HAD) information systems. While human-oriented process implementations often control and coordinate human activities, system-oriented process implementations control and coordinate automated activities (typically with little or no human intervention). Consequently, system-oriented process implementations must include software for various concurrency control and recovery techniques to ensure consistency and reliability.

In human-oriented process, the main issues to address include:
- human-computer interaction matching human skills to activity requirements
- changing office culture, i.e., how people need or prefer to work

In systems-oriented process, the issues to address include:
- matching business process requirements to functionality and data provided by existing information system and/or their applications
- interoperability among HAD systems
- finding appropriate software activities to perform process activities
- determining new software required to automate business processes
- ensuring correct and reliable system execution

Issues such as exception handling, user overrides, prioritization, and deadline may appear in different forms in both types of process, and need to be addressed. Also depicted in Figure 9 are points indicating process characteristics and issues that are addressed by:
- groupware systems,
- commercial WFMSs, and

- commercial transaction processing (TP) systems (e.g., distributed DBMSs, TP monitors).

Groupware systems are typically used to support the implementation of processes involving predominantly human activities. Commercial TP systems are used to provide for the implementations of system-oriented processes involving activities submitted as DBMS or TP monitor transactions. Although, WFMSs overlap with groupware and TP monitors, most commercial WFMSs are designed to address the requirements of processes in the center of the process space depicted in Figure 9.

Having provided this general perspective, in the following sections we discuss the workflow process models, tools, and infrastructure provided by commercial WFMSs. We use examples from actual WFMS products, as needed.

7.1 Workflow Model

Workflow management systems typically support activity-oriented models. Some toolkits that provide tightly integrated BPMTs and WFMSs (i.e., Level 2 integration), also provide hybrid process models through the BPMT model. Examples of toolkits in this category include the ARIS toolkit, the ProcessWise toolkit, and the ActionWorkflow Process Builder – Analyst and Developer editions [Act 97].

Activity-oriented workflow and business process models typically support similar core process objects. In particular, activity-oriented workflow models typically support the following:

- *activity*
- *control flow*
- *workflow resource*: a workflow data object, an application, and/or a role necessary for the execution of an activity
- *workflow data*: e.g., a scanned or electronic document, a spreadsheet, a graphics image, a voice message, a fax, an email, etc.
- *dataflow*: the path of workflow data between activities
- *organizational structure and roles*
- *participant/performer*: person, group or application that fills roles and interacts while performing activities in a particular workflow instance.

There are two basic differences between core process objects in workflow and business process models. The first is the scope of resources which in workflow process models is limited to computerized resources (i.e., data, applications, and human roles) and resource flow is basically dataflow. The second difference is the notion of participant that implies assignment of "real" human resources and applications for performing each workflow instance. This is not required for business process modeling, since process evaluation either does not depend on participants or they can be probabilistically simulated.

To provide different levels of abstraction, activity-oriented models (and the WFMSs that provide them) typically support the nesting of workflow processes.

Higher levels of abstraction help in capturing the business process as it relates to the operations and the organization (sub)units that participate in carrying out the process. Modeling at these higher levels is typically devoid of implementation, technology or software. These levels can be imported from a BPMTs. The lower levels of abstraction are required to capture a variety of details about the actual information systems and applications required to support the implementation of workflow activities.

Examples of commercial WFMSs that provide activity-oriented workflow models include IBM's FlowMark [Ibm 97], FileNet's Ensemble and Visual Worklow [Fil 97], InConcert [InC 97] and EASTMAN SOFTWARE Workflow [Eas 97] (the latter originated from Wang's Open/Workflow).

In the following paragraphs we describe the core process objects in the Workflow Process Definition Language (WPDL) defined by the WfMC [WfM 97]. Although WPDL is currently incomplete, it is an attempt for defining industry standard scripting language for representing workflow processes. We discuss WPDL because it supports a set of specific core process objects that provide the workflow engine with the details of the process to be executed. Furthermore, this is a specific example of a process representation that can be use to communicate process definitions between a BPMT (or a workflow process definition tool) and a WFMS. WPDL provides the following core process objects:

Workflow Process Definition: describes the process itself, i.e. name and/or ID of process, etc.. The workflow process definition optionally contains a reference to an external organizational model.

Workflow Process Activities: each activity is defined through four dimensions, the who, the what, the how and the when:

1. The activity is assigned to one or more workflow participants, who are permitted to play the role in this activity.
2. The activity is assigned to an application, which will be invoked during runtime.
3. Activities are related to one another via transition conditions. Transition conditions are usually based on workflow data.
4. Optionally an activity depends on a time frame (earliest begin, deadline, etc.).

Workflow Participant Definition: describes the performer of an activity in terms of a reference to an (external) organizational model. The definition of such a performer does not necessarily refer to a single person, but also to a function or any other organizational entity.

Transition Information: describes the navigation between different process activities, which may involve sequential or parallel operations. Thus activities are connected to each other by transition information.

Workflow Application Definition: defines one to n applications that are assigned to an activity. These applications will be invoked during run time by the WFMS. The workflow application definition reflects the interface between the workflow engine and the application.

Workflow Process Relevant Data: data used by a WFMS to determine particular transition conditions and may affect the choice of the next activity to be executed. Such data is potentially accessible to workflow applications for operations on the data and thus may need to be transferred between activities.

Organizational/Role Model Data: (possibly external) data that may be referenced by the   process definition data to describe the identify and relationships of human and automated resources associated with workflow activities. The organizational/role model data may contain information about the identity of human and automated resources, organizational structure of resources, role information identifying the function that resources can perform.

Workflow Control Data: internal control data maintained by the workflow engine. They are used to identify the state of individual process or activity instances. These data may not be accessible or interchangeable outside of the workflow engine but some of the information content may be provided in response to specific commands (e.g. query process status, give performance metrics, etc.).

7.2   Dataflow

Some WFMSs (e.g., HP's AdminFlow [Hew 97]) support the flow of only process relevant data. Others (e.g., IBM's FlowMark [Ibm 97]) support the flow of any data specified in the workflow process definition (i.e., independently of whether such data is referenced in a transition condition). In practice, the ability to pass data among the participants is what determines the effectiveness of a WFMS. For example, during the processing of an international patent, each patent application involves a significant number of documents referencing other information sources and patents. Each existing patent is also a large collection of documents. Additional attached information such as articles and scientific papers are smaller in size but can be numerous. To the application itself, related patents and relevant articles are included as part of the documentation. Hence, transferring the case from the initial stages to the evaluation stages involves moving a great deal of information around (often from country to country as is the case with the European Patent Office).

The typical support provided for data flow is to ensure the existence of all information objects before an activity is started, and to locate and retrieve these objects. This typically requires no specific action on the part of the user, who will experience that all activities on the worklist come with all documents and information needed to do the work. Current WFMSs achieve this by allowing the process designer to specify whether the WFMS should provide dataflow by moving data references rather than the data itself. Some WFMSs rely on specialized external systems to perform dataflow. For example, the EASTMAN SOFTWARE Workflow [Eas 97] relies on Microsoft Exchange and an imaging system for storing and routing data involved in dataflow, including scanned or faxed images, spreadsheets, graphics, voice, email, and multimedia objects. HP's

AdminFlow [Hew 97] uses a CORBA Object Request Broker (ORB) [OMG 97] to perform dataflow by moving object references. Other WFMSs, such as FlowMark [Ibm 97] and InConcert [InC 97], integrate imaging systems with the workflow engine to handle the movement of scanned documents. However, such integration is often poor and the engine has minimal control over the flow of data, complicating dataflow synchronization with control flow.

7.3   Workflow Process Definition Tools

Most WFMSs provide tools for graphical specification of workflow processes. The available tools for workflow process design typically support the iconic representation of activities. Definition of control flow between activities is accomplished by:

1. connecting the activity icons with specialized lines/arrows which specify the activity precedence order, and
2. composing the transition conditions which must hold before the workflow execution moves from one activity to another.

Dataflow between activities is typically defined by filling up dialog boxes that specify the input and output data to and from each activity. In some WFMSs, such as FlowMark, dataflow definition involves using specialized lines/arrows to draw dataflow paths between activities.

Assuming that BPMTs are used to model business processes and that BPMTs and WFMSs interoperate, the role of workflow process definition tools is limited, since either the entire workflow process definition or a significant part of it is usually performed at the BMPT.

7.4   Analysis, Simulation, and Animation Tools

Most workflow products provide workflow process animation tools, but depend on external BPMTs for simulation and analysis. Therefore, the sophistication of analysis and simulation provided by BPMTs, as well as the degree of integration and interoperability between BPMTs and WFMSs have a direct impact on the ability to validate and evaluate workflow processes.

7.5   Workflow Monitoring and Tracking Tools

Workflow monitoring tools can present different views of workflow process execution. They illustrate which activity or activities are currently active, by whom they are performed, the priorities, deadlines, duration, and dependencies. Administrators can use such monitoring tools to compute statistics such as activity completion times, workloads, and user performance, as well as to generate reports and provide periodic summary of workflow process executions.

In Section 5, we discussed that workflow execution data and statistics may be fed back to a BPMT to facilitate process evaluation and improvement.

7.6   Basic WFMS Infrastructure: Architecture, GUIs, and APIs

Many commercial WFMSs have loosely-coupled, client-server architectures that divide and distribute the WFMS functionality in components similar to those illustrated in Figure 5. Examples of WFMSs having such architectures include FlowMark, FileNet's Visual Workflow, and EASTMAN SOFTWARE Workflow. In such WFMSs, the WFMS engine is typically the central component, and it is often referred to as the WFMS server. Process Definition data, workflow control data, workflow relevant data, and organization/role data are usually kept in a centralized database (or a set of such databases) under the control of the WFMS engine, its (client) tools, and/or the external applications invoked by the workflow process. Most WFMS engines and tools take advantage of the data manipulation capabilities of a commercial database management system (DBMS), such as ORACLE, Informix, Sybase, and ObjectStore.

WFMSs typically offer proprietary GUIs and (client) tools for graphical process specification, process monitoring, process invocation, and interaction with human participants. However, the advent of the Web has made many workflow product designers consider Web browsers and GUIs for WFMS (client) tools. Using the Web as a front-end platform allows for workflow processes that are geographically spread out. Since many users already use Web-browsers, there is no need to distribute client software, thus enabling a wider class of WFMS applications. Many WFMSs currently support web-enabled tools for starting and monitoring workflow process instances, including among others FileNet's Ensemble and Visual Workflow, IBM's FlowMark, UES' KI Shell [Ues 97], and ActionWorkflow's Metro [Act 97]. Web-enabled client tools are becoming a de facto standard in current WFMS.

Many state-of-the-art WFMSs, including FlowMark and InConcert, have complete application programming interfaces (APIs). This allows everything that can be done through the user interface also to be done via an API. In addition, the API can be used to introduce specialized user interfaces and tools designed to meet specific application requirements.

7.7   Advanced WFMS Infrastructure: Distribution, Scalability, and Component Redundancy

Commercial WFMS currently may not support more than several hundred workflow instances per day if they are used directly off the shelf (i.e., all the clients and server components provided by the vendor are utilized, and the default settings and configurations are used). However, there are processes, such as the one illustrated in Figure 1, that require handling of a larger number of workflow instances. In addition, the use of more powerful computers may not necessarily yield corresponding improvements in WFMS throughput. These problems are due to limited (or lack of) engine and worklist handler scalability, distribution and component redundancy for dealing with load balancing and engines failures.

Workflow vendors have realized some of these limitations in earlier versions of their products, and they are currently introducing improvements to address them. In particular, the latest WFMSs versions from several vendors (including FlowMark, InConcert, and Plexus) allow the use of multiple WFMS engines for supporting distributed workflow process execution. In addition, vendors (such as IBM) currently provide capacity planning tools that can estimate the number of WFMS engines required to support the execution requirements of a given process. However, in WFMSs like FlowMark distributed workflow process execution requires manual replication of the process definition in all engines that may be involved in the process execution. This approach suffers form potential configuration problems. For example, consider the process in Figure 1. Suppose that a capacity planning tool has estimated that several dozens of engines needed to support a realistic version of this process. In the event of a process update, all engines must have consistent process definitions before the process can be executed. However, currently WFMSs do not provide process configuration management and do not ensure the consistency of process definition in different engines.

Another serious limitation in the current approaches for distributed workflow execution is the lack of automatic load balancing. In the following paragraphs we discuss server (engine) scalability and component redundancy issues, and describe approaches for addressing these problems.

Just like any other client-server system, the architecture of a WFMS typically corresponds one of the client-server architectures shown in Figure 10 through Figure 13 [GE 95]. Figure 10 shows an architecture in which there is a server process for each client. Suppose that each of the X clients uses Y applications and that each application opens Z files. Such an architecture does not scale well because of the large number ($X*Y*Z$) of connections in the system and also the large number ($X*Y$) of server process running on the server machine.

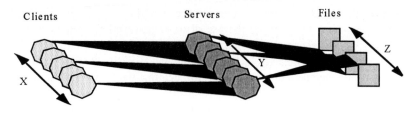

Figure 10. Server-Process-per-Client (X*Y*Z connections)

Figure 11 shows a process per server architecture in which the functionality of the Y applications is provided by one multi-threaded server process. In this case the server process becomes a bottleneck and in the absence of Operating System provided threads, it cannot use multiprocessors effectively. Furthermore, the server program packed with several applications becomes hard to maintain as faults cannot be easily isolated.

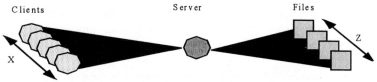

Figure 11. Process-per-Server (X+Z connections)

Figure 12 shows an architecture in which the server functionality and data are partitioned and there is a server process for each partition. As long as the partitioning of the functionality balances the load on the server processes, this architecture addresses the scalability problem to a large extent. However, each client has to be aware of the application partition and any change in the partitioning requires considerable reorganization. Moreover, it is difficult to achieve a proper partitioning of functionality or data.

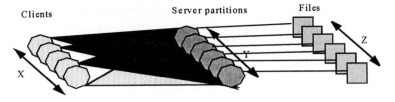

Figure 12. Process-per-Application-per-Server Partition (X+1 connections per server)

Figure 13 shows a "three-ball" architecture where a router between the client and server processes is used to manage a pool of servers. The router automatically balances the load among the servers for each application, spawns new server processes to handle heavy load, and restarts failed server processes. This system can be scaled up further by replicating the router process. In many modern systems, the router is provided by a TP monitor.

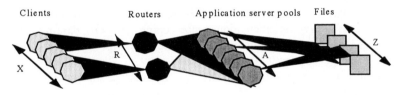

Figure 13. Three-Ball (X+A connections per router).

Out of the box, workflow products can be categorized into one of the "two-ball" architectures Figure 9 through Figure 12. Therefore, they have limited scalability. Consequently, a workflow application's scalability needs should be carefully matched with the scalability provided by the product. To this end, assistance from vendor, preferably in the form of a capacity planning tools, should be sought. In some cases workarounds for the scalability problem will need to be devised.

In many cases a simple partitioning of the instances on geographical basis may be sufficient to scale up. For example, a process for handling visits to customer premises in a particular state can be implemented using several workflow servers – one for each state.

In other cases, e.g., a process for handling service calls from customers all over the country, such a partitioning of instances among workflow servers may not be possible. In such situations WFMS users will have to develop additional complementary software components, e.g., the third ball of the "three-ball" architecture of Figure 13. This software would have to implement the functionality attributed to the router of Figure 13.

In still other situations, the scalability of a deployment can be improved by replacing certain heavy-weight components of the product. For example, a general purpose, but inefficient, worklist handler provided by a product can be replaced with a custom light-weight worklist handler built using the API provided by the vendor.

7.8   Interoperability Among WFMSs and Heterogeneous Applications

For workflow processes that access heterogeneous information systems, interoperability among heterogeneous systems and WFMSs is important for the following reasons:

- generic code allows access to heterogeneous information systems without recording when these systems change,
- the absence of code for routing and other types of coordination enables fast development of applications with fewer errors, as opposed to applications that are developed using more conventional methods such as 4GL programming, and
- changes in participating information systems require minimal workflow re-implementation, since coping with this requires no code changes in workflow implementations except re-specification of heterogeneous system interfaces.

Currently, interoperability means that various interface standards on different levels are available, such as protocol standards (e.g., e-mail, TCP/IP), platform standards (e.g., MS-Windows, UNIX, Windows NT), and object interface standards (e.g., OLE, CORBA). However, interoperability at the workflow level requires additional technology and standards that exploit and extend current technology industry solutions for interoperability, such as those developed by the Object Management Group and the World Wide Web Consortium. Because many types of errors could arise in a distributed heterogeneous computing environment in which the workflow is executed or enacted, error handling is generally considered to be a difficult problem. The difficulty is enhanced by the inherent complexity of business processes. Error prevention and handling is one problem area where new breakthroughs are needed in order to deliver genuinely robust workflow processes.

7.9   Concurrency Control, Recovery, and Advanced Transactions

Issues of concurrency control are well-understood issues in database and transaction processing products. State-of-the-art WFMSs take different approaches to concurrency control as compared to database and transaction processing products, depending on perceived workflow process requirements.

Current approaches (e.g., check-in/check-out, pass-by-reference/pass-by-value, etc.) are primitive when compared to how DBMS support concurrency. Some WFMSs allow multiple users/applications to retrieve the same data object concurrently. However, if each user decides to update that data object, new versions of the data item are created to be reconciled (merged) by human intervention. The rationale for this approach is the assumption that data object updates are rare. Thus, consistency can be handled by humans who review the data object versions and decide which version to keep.

To support limited forward recovery, contemporary WFMSs utilize transaction mechanisms that are provided by the DBMSs that maintain the process relevant data. In particular, such WFMSs issue database transactions to record workflow process state changes in these DBMSs. In the event of a failure and restart, the WFMS accesses the DBMS(s) to determine the state of each interrupted workflow instance, and attempts to continue executing workflow processes from the point they have been interrupted by a failure. However, such forward recovery is limited to the internal components of the WFMS.

State-of-the-art WFMSs currently offer virtually no support for automatic undoing of incomplete workflow instances. Workflow designers may specify the withdrawal of a specific instance from the system while it is running, possibly at various locations, for which an undo operation is needed at the process level (as opposed to the transaction level). When some business processes fail they can be compensated rather than rolled back. For example consider a workflow for purchasing a house. If the sale of a house is canceled halfway, compensation payments must be made. Recovering from such failures requires that much of the recovery is designed specifically for this workflow application. Also, erroneous execution typically requires some form of human intervention. These issues illustrate that error detection, handling, and recovery are more complicated in the context of business process than they are the database transaction context.

The workflow vendors and the research community are debating whether it is possible to use database management system technology and transaction processing monitor technology, or the extended/relaxed transaction models [GHM 96] that have been developed to deal with the limitations of database transactions.

8   Evaluation of Current BPMTs and WFMSs Integration

In Section 4, we discussed that major BPMT objectives include: (i) to function as universal process definition and monitoring tools for WFMSs, and (ii) to provide for implementation and automation of business processes through integration with WFMS. To achieve these objectives, BPMTs must export (and possibly translate) their process definitions to WFMSs, or share process models and definitions with WFMSs. In the following sections we describe approaches current BPMTs use to provide these, and discuss related requirements and technology.

8.1   Loose Integration

The category of loosely integrated BPMTs and WFMSs includes several BPMTs providing Level 1 interoperability (as defined in Section 4.3). That is, typical BPMTs in this category provide direct and unmediated input of process definitions into WFMS engines from different vendors. Such BPMTs must export their business process definitions using the workflow process model and representation expected by the WFMS(s). Therefore, BPMTs in this category translate their business process definitions into the workflow process model definitions supported by one or more target WFMSs.

Integration with each workflow vendor involves filtering business process model data for appropriate components, translating it into WFMS engine terminology, validating it, and placing it in readable format. Once this is accomplished, systems can be interfaced to save time, minimize redundancy, and insure proper process validation.

Products in this category include Holosofx's WorkflowBPR and Meta's Workflow Analyzer. WorkflowBPR provides direct support for three specific export environments, FileNet's Visual WorkFlo, IBM's FlowMark and the standard WPDL format defined by WfMC. Workflow Analyzer provides specific support for FileNet. Such products offer solutions designed specifically for each target WFMS. The WPDL interface offered by Workflow BPR and some other BPR tools deserves additional discussion.

As we discussed in Section 7.1, WPDL is currently under development by the WfMC, the only workflow standards body. The WfMC is developing interface specifications that will enable interoperability between WFMSs, as well as between WFMS and BPMTs (since from the perspective of WFMS, a BPMT may be thought as an external process definition tool).

The WfMC has developed a standard Workflow Reference model (Figure 5) and identified a set of interfaces to enable products to interoperate at a variety of levels. The diagram of Figure 14 provides a pictorial description of the WfMC workflow reference model interfaces. Details concerning the definitions and specification of the components and interfaces of the reference model as well as other documents relating to the standards can be found in [WfM 97].

WPDL is part of the WfMC interface 1, designed for process definition import and export. Translation (perhaps only partially automated) from a business process definition to the workflow process definition may be possible through this representation. Unfortunately, Interface 1 is defined in draft format and is incompletely specified. In addition to BPMTs, some WFMSs also have import/export capabilities that are versions of this interface.

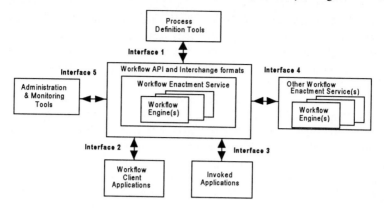

Figure 14. Workflow Reference Model - Interfaces

8.2   Tight Integration

This category typically includes toolkits that provide tightly integrated BPMTs and WFMSs having Level 2 interoperability (as defined in Section 4.3). That is, BPMTs and WFMSs in this category use the same process model and share process definitions. The latter is typically accomplished if the BPMT and the WFMS share a common process definition repository, or the BPMT provides direct and unmediated input of process definitions into the WFMS engine. Currently commercial products in this category include toolkits, such as the ARIS and ProcessWise. Such toolkits are typically offered by BPMT vendors attempting to enter the WFMS market.

8.3   Reverse Integration

In this case, a WFMS is used to define the process. The objective of reverse integration is to be able to import the process in a BPMT. This allows the BPMT to provide the following:

- real time monitoring of workflow processes
- evaluation and improvement of legacy processes designed using a WFMS
- definition of *legacy application-aware* business process, i.e., processes that take into account the existing functionality of legacy systems as basic activity elements in the process design.

Although no BPMT currently provides reverse integration, some vendors (e.g., Holosofx) are currently extending their products to provide reverse integration facilities with WFMSs. Clearly, this will allow BPMTs to define, monitor, and evaluate existing processes designed and implemented using a WFMS. In the following sections we focus on the issue of legacy application-aware processes which we consider as one of the most important limitations in current BPMT and WFMS technology.

Process modeling methodologies and technology provided by BPMTs and WFMSs, have not addressed the problem of workflow implementation involving legacy information systems. For organizations that rely on legacy information systems, business and workflow process specification for performing workflow implementation requires mapping workflow process specifications to legacy system functionality and data. If this is not done, BPR and CPI may produce process specifications that cannot be supported by the legacy information systems.

Today, many processes are embedded within legacy systems to manage the initiation, sequencing, scheduling and monitoring of associated system functions, such as displaying a screen to a user, or initiate transactions to validate a service address or assign a telephone number. The embedded processes may control the sequence of such functions. However, in these legacy systems, functions and process are not separated within the modules of the system. As shown at the top of Figure 15, the functions and processes are intimately intertwined.

Legacy systems provide a limited number of API's through which their functions can be invoked, we refer to such functions as API-provided functions. The API-provided functions are often at a very high level of granularity including a substantial amount of process-relevant code. For example, a legacy system might provide an API for establishing new telephone service and for canceling telephone service, but no APIs for finer grained services such as assigning a new telephone number or adding a new customer into the customer database. The goal of BPMT and WFMS technology is to *accommodate* this legacy situation, and ultimately *rework* legacy systems to:

1.   separate functions from process (to some useful degree),
2.   express the process explicitly, and
3.   invoke the functions from the process.

This is illustrated in the lower part of Figure 15.

Accommodating Legacy Systems: WFMSs and reverse integration of BPMTs and WFMSs can accommodate legacy systems in two ways. First, a BPMT and a WFMS can used to design and implement the activities or subprocesses corresponding to existing API-provided functions. The existing legacy system API's can be used as the implementation of an activity or subprocess. In the example in Figure 1, wherever the business process calls for establishing telephone service for a new customer, the existing legacy system API would be called. Second, the workflow process can be adapted to exploit the existing functions of the legacy system. So, in the case where a business

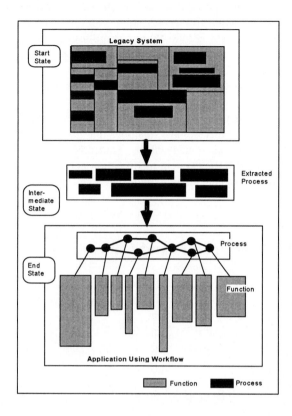

Figure 15. Process Extraction from a Legacy System

process needs to assign a telephone number, the business process could include steps for creating a dummy new customer telephone service order, and later canceling that telephone service order, in order to get at the legacy system function that assigns a telephone number. In both these cases of accommodation, the legacy system does not have to be modified.

Reworking Legacy Systems: In the longer term, there is the option to "break up" (in whole or in part) certain existing legacy systems to make its processes and functions reusable in one or more business processes. Certain systems function can be separated out of the existing API-provided functions, each independently invoked. Once these finer grain functions become available, they can be reused from one business process to another. In the example in Figure 1, this would allow telephone number assignment and service address validation, both subfunctions in the original API-provided function for establishing a new customer, to become new separate functions.

In addition, there is the option that certain embedded processes may be separated out of the legacy applications and into a workflow process definition. In those cases where the process is unlikely to change in the future, the cost is probably not justified. But, if the process is likely to change, there can be a definite benefit. In this case, the (re)use of these functions by other processes will require exportation of related workflow subprocesses and activities from the WFMS to a BPMT.

In cases where any legacy system modification is contemplated, analysis is needed to identify embedded processes and functions that have potential for reuse and that can be extracted with reasonable effort. Tradeoffs will have to be made between the cost and risk of legacy system modification and both the short term cost/benefit of workflow implementation and the long term cost/benefit as processes change.

9   Critical Success Factors and Conclusion

In the paper we described BPMT and WFMS technologies and tools. In addition, we proposed that the combination of these can provide support for comprehensive process lifecycle management.

However, even given the ideal BPMT and WFMS technology there are other critical factors that are necessary to ensure the success of BPMTs and WFMSs in supporting BPR, CPI, and process implementation. We believe that the most important among these critical success factors are:

- the organization must be process-centered and the executive commitment to process management must be strong
- the division of responsibilities between process and participating applications must be at the appropriate level

Since both BPMT and WFMS technologies focus on the explicit support of business processes, its deployment requires that the organization be process-centered. That is, there must be a commitment to all aspects of managing the business by process, including explicit process definition, process reengineering, process measurement and evaluation, continuous process improvement, and efficient and rapid process implementation. Executive commitment to process management is also crucial to the successful use of BPMTs and WFMSs. Time and resources must be allocated to define processes correctly and at a working level of detail that includes exception handling and process recovery from failures. Since the primary functions of BPMTs and WFMSs are to evaluate, implement, and enact a process as defined, a substantial risk is poorly defined processes being evaluated and implemented through BPMTs and WFMSs.

Another critical issue is selecting the granularity of workflow activities to be implemented by (new or legacy) applications. Since this divides the process management responsibility between the WFMS-supported process and participating applications (i.e., between the WFMS and the applications supporting the workflow implementation), this determines how well the process can be managed by the WFMS and how easily the process can be adapted as business requirements change. If the level of granularity of activities is too high, the process will be hard to change because the right building blocks are not there. In addition, the management of the process may not contain enough detail to provide insights into current process performance or future performance improvements. If the level of granularity of activities is too low, the process will take longer to develop, the extra effort will not provide any benefit, and the BPMTs and WFMSs will manage unnecessary process detail. In general, frequently changing (sub)processes are best handled by the WFMS, while stable processes can remain in code.

If these critical success factors are met, we envision that the business process management lifecycle will be managed as follows. The business staff responsible for defining the business vision, deciding related business goals, and determining how to meet them, uses BPMT technology to define and evaluate business processes. With the help of IT, they decide which processes are candidates for WFMS implementation and define those processes at a working level of detail, i.e., the level of detail at which processes can be managed WFMS technology. These are accomplished by using a combination of integrated BPMTs and WFMSs, as discussed in this paper. IT staff completes the workflow implementation and assist with its operation using WFMS technology. The business staff monitors the process execution, using tools provided by WFMSs (or BPMTs when there are products supporting reverse integration). These tools provide complete visibility into the state of the process. This visibility gives the business staff great power to manage the process while it is being executed. For example, if a part of the process becomes 'stuck' because an unanticipated situation arises such that the process cannot continue, this will become visible and steps can be taken by the business staff to remedy the problem and continue the process.

We believe that such a unified approach to the utilization of integrated BPMT and WFMS technology provides the most benefits throughout any process-centered organization.

Acknowledgements

K. Huff and H. Sinha contributed in earlier versions of Sections 3, 7.7, and 8.3. The members of the GTE GISP Workflow Strategy team influenced many aspects of the discussion in this paper.

Recent Trends in Workflow Management Products, Standards and Research

C. Mohan

IBM Almaden Research Center
650 Harry Road, K01/B1
San Jose, CA 95120, USA
mohan@almaden.ibm.com
http://www.almaden.ibm.com/u/mohan/

Abstract. In the last few years, workflow management (WFM) has been the focus of intense activity in terms of products, standards and research work worldwide. Work in many areas of computer science impacts workflow management. Many workflow companies and research groups are in existence now. Several conferences and workshops are being held regularly. In this paper, I briefly summarize the recent trends in WFM products, standards and research. I address technical as well as business trends.

1. Introduction

While workflow management (WFM) as a concept has existed for many years, it is only in the last few years that it has become very popular in the commercial as well as research world. Several workflow companies and research groups are currently in existence, especially in Europe and North America. Numerous products with varying functionalities have been released in the last few years. Many conferences and workshops are being held frequently. Some of the trade magazines and industry conferences regularly give excellence awards in recognition of leading/innovative products and implemented novel/important workflow applications. Efforts on standardizing workflow concepts and interfaces are in progress under the auspices of the Workflow Management Coalition (WFMC) and the Object Management Group (OMG).

Historically, workflow had its origins in office automation. Initially, manual routing of folders with routing slips was replaced by imaging-based, document-centric systems. Later, general-purpose, graphical workflow management systems (WFMSs) were developed.

Over the years, various definitions have been proposed for concepts relating to WFM. For example, Giga Group (http://www.gigaweb.com/) once gave the following definition: *"we call the operational aspects of a business process - the sequence of tasks and who performs them, the information flow to support the tasks, and the tracking and reporting mechanisms that measure and control them - the workflow"*. It should be noted that the aim of WFM is not to automate necessarily all the tasks of a workflow process. Some tasks (also called activities) might continue to involve humans and even for automated tasks the determination of when to initiate them and/or determining whether such automated tasks have successfully completed might be left to humans. The emphasis is much more on automating the tracking of the states of the tasks of a workflow, and allowing specification of preconditions to decide when tasks are ready to be executed (intertask dependencies) and of information flow between tasks. Giga also defined the associated management software as follows:

"workflow software is designed to improve business processes by providing the technology enabler for automating these aspects of the workflow: routing work in the proper sequence, providing access to the data and documents required by the individual work performers, and tracking all aspects of the process execution". One of the chief goals of WFM is to separate process logic from task logic which is embedded in individual user applications. This separation allows the two to be independently modified and the same task logic to be reused in different processes, thereby promoting software reuse, and the integration of heterogeneous and isolated applications. This is similar to the distinctions which have been made in the software engineering community between programming in the large versus programming in the small. Such modular programming concepts were popularized during the 1970s. They have been revived now in the context of object-oriented programming.

The focus in the last few years on business process reengineering by enterprises as a cost saving and service improvement measure has contributed significantly to the recent popularity of WFMSs. WFMSs have been widely deployed in the following types of businesses/organizations: banking, accounting, manufacturing, brokerage, insurance, healthcare, government departments, telecommunications, university administration and customer service. Some of the novel applications being considered for WFMSs are: system monitoring and exception handling, and systems administration. A point to note is that WFM is not intended to deal with only *business* processes. Attempts are being made to embed workflow functionality in the operating system so that the OS can exploit it for allowing specification of administration policies for a variety of routine and exceptional situations. Some organizations have found the high-level process definition capabilities of WFMS products to be a useful functionality by itself. These organizations use the WFMSs as process documentation tools for the purposes of, for example, ISO9000 certification. This is a first step towards the subsequent full-blown *operational* exploitation of WFMSs.

Traditionally, WFMSs and workflow applications have been divided into four broad categories: *production, administrative, collaborative* and *ad hoc.* While this is not a very strict categorization, it helps to distinguish the design points of different products somewhat reasonably. Over the years, vendors have tried to reposition/redesign their products to cover more of this spectrum of applications.

2. Market Trends and Business Considerations

The WFM market has grown steadily in the last few years, although the rate of growth has slowed down a bit in the recent past. A market research report, dated August 1997, from the workflow industry watcher Delphi Group (http://www.delphigroup.com/) estimated that the overall workflow market for the calendar year 1996, including software and vendor services, rose 14.3% to US$933 million (from US$816 million in 1995). Delphi has projected that the market will grow 12.4% to US$1.05 billion in 1997. The Delphi report did not include revenues from groupware products like Lotus Notes/Domino (http://www.lotus.com/). Depending on the definition of what constitutes workflow software, different market analysis firms come up with different numbers for the size of the market. But, there is general agreement that commercially workflow is a very significant market with a lot more potential in store.

FileNet (http://www.filenet.com/) is widely believed to be the current market leader, although the company has suffered losses in the recent past and has been forced to restructure its operations. According to Delphi, Staffware (http://www.staffware.com/) had the greatest revenue growth in 1996 (134% to $18 million). In keeping with the trends in the PC arena, some of the workflow vendors have recently reduced their products' per seat prices dramatically. This is the case especially for products which operate with Microsoft's messaging product Exchange (http://www.microsoft.com/exchange/). After the purchase of Lotus by IBM, the price for a Lotus Notes client was also reduced. The increase in the popularity of the web has also contributed to the downward trend in prices.

Unlike in the case of some other products, WFMSs involve a longer sales cycle, since their adoption requires executive approval and end user commitment. Adopting a WFMS necessitates a cultural change in the way an organization does its business. It requires group consensus and retraining. Typically, implementing a workflow solution involves the hiring of consultants for advice. VARs (Value-Added Resellers), tool vendors and consultants stand to benefit economically from the complexities involved in implementing WFM applications. Considering the difficulties that users face in customizing a general-purpose WFMS product for specific applications, In-Concert (http://www.inconcertsw.com/) has recently decided to concentrate on producing vertical market-specific (e.g., engineering, manufacturing and telecommunications) products.

The WFM market has been undergoing a great deal of consolidation in the last couple of years. There have been many mergers and partnerships involving companies that produce workflow and related products (document management, imaging, text search, e-mail, forms management and groupware). Some of the significant events were: purchase of Lotus (developer of the groupware product Notes/Domino) by IBM (producer of the workflow product FlowMark and imaging/document management product ImagePlus

VisualInfo); acquisition of Odesta Systems (LiveLink workflow product) by the text search company OpenText (http://www.opentext.com/); acquisition of the imaging product company WaterMark and document management company Saros, and a partnership with Novell by FileNet; purchase of the imaging/workflow company Sigma by Wang and the subsequent sale of Wang Software to Kodak (resulting in the formation of Eastman Software); Eastman Software's partnership with text search technology company Verity (http://www.verity.com/); partnership between workflow vendor Action Technology (http://www.actiontech.com/) and document management company PC DOCS (http://www.pcdocs.com/); purchase of Delrina by Jet-Form (http://www.jetform.com/); acquisition of workflow vendor CSE Systems (http://www.csesys.co.at/english/english.htm) by document and filing systems vendor Louis Leitz Enterprises; formation of Mosaix from the merger of ViewStar with Digital Systems International.

Some of the planned mergers did not come to fruition - e.g., the one involving Staffware and CSE Systems, and another one relating to ViewStar and Caere. It is anticipated that in the next few years there will be a shakeout in the market and some of the smaller companies will disappear due to inadequate revenues and their inability to keep up with the competition. All the same, new players are still entering the market: application development tools vendor Forte recently introduced its Conductor workflow product (http://www.forte.com/Product/conductor/index.htm) and Oracle has included workflow functionality in its InterOffice product (http://www.oracle.com/products/interoffice/html/features.html).

One of the major consequences of the above partnerships/acquisitions is that several product suites, where each suite consists of many related products, have been released. This has resulted in improvements in the interoperability amongst the products within a suite. More synergy has been brought about amongst imaging, document/forms management, and workflow products. Example suites are FileNet's Discovery Suite (http://www.filenet.com/prods/edm/suite.html), IBM's EDMSuite (http://www.software.ibm.com/data/edmsuite/) and Open Text's Livelink Intranet.

Users have demanded better tools to help them in using WFMSs effectively. They have also asked for better synergy between related products produced by different vendors. In response, companies that have specialized in business process and data modelling have begun to work with workflow vendors to better integrate their products.

Several information sources on WFM exist on the internet. Workflow And Reengineering International Association (WARIA) is a non-profit organization whose mission is to make sense of what's happening at the intersection of business process reengineering (BPR), workflow and electronic commerce, and reach clarity through sharing experiences, product evaluations, networking between users and vendors, education and training. The

WARIA web site (http://www.waria.com/) has a listing of BPR, group-ware, and workflow vendors and consultants. The Concordium web site (http://www.concordium.co.uk/) also includes a list of WFMS products.

In addition to Delphi and Giga Group, a number of other market research firms also track the workflow area. They are Creative Networks (http://www.cnilive.com/), Dataquest (http://www.dataquest.com/), Gartner (http://www.gartner.com/), International Data Corporation (http://www.idc.com/), Meta Group (http://www.metagroup.com/), Patricia Seybold Group (http://www.psgroup.com/) and Sodan (http://www.sodan.co.uk/). Sodan publishes a newsletter called Workflow World ten times each year.

3. Workflow Standards

The Workflow Management Coalition (WFMC) is the main organization that is involved in workflow management standardization efforts (http://www.aiai.ed.ac. uk/project/wfmc/). It was formed in 1993 and it currently has about 200 members (vendors, users, analysts, systems integrators, universities, ...). WFMC defined a reference model for a WFMS's architecture. Version 1.1 of the document (WFMC-TC-1003) describing the model was published in November 1994. This model has 5 interfaces and application program interfaces (APIs) relating to those interfaces are intended to be standardized. The interfaces/APIs are: (1) Process definition model and interchange APIs, (2) Client APIs, (3) Application invocation interface, (4) Workflow interoperability, and (5) Administration and monitoring.

As WFMC releases its specifications for the various interfaces, vendors have been releasing new versions of their products to support those standards (http://www.aiai.ed.ac.uk/project/wfmc/validation.html). The workflow API (interface 2, WAPI) specification (WFMC-TC-1009) was initially released in November 1995 and the latest version (1.2) was released in October 1996. In October 1996, an interoperability abstract specification (interface 4) which is designed to ensure that businesses can exchange and process work from two or more workflow engines was published (WFMC-TC-1012). A specific binding for the requests and responses of the abstract specification was also released at the same time (WFMC-TC-1018). This binding uses internet mail for transport, and MIME (Multipurpose Internet Mail Extension) and CGI (Common Gateway Interface) for content encoding. In November 1996, an audit data specification (interface 5) was unveiled (WFMC-TC-1015). WFMC published "Workflow Handbook 1997" in January 1997.

While users find it very convenient to define process models using graphical tools, different products provide the graphical support differently. As a result, WFMC decided that it would be too difficult to arrive at a graphical standard for process definitions. Consequently, a language based standard is being worked on for this purpose. Products like FlowMark already support such a language (FlowMark Definition Language, FDL) to allow the convenient export and import of process definitions between different workflow installations.

WFMC and OMG are trying to coordinate their activities to marry workflow and CORBA object technologies. In July 1997, OMG released a call for proposals for a workflow management facility within OMG's object management architecture (http://www.omg.org/library/schedule/CF_RFP9.htm). The plan is to define the interfaces and semantics required for manipulating and executing interoperable workflow objects and metadata.

4. Technical Trends

From a technical perspective, WFM is very interesting since it brings together principles, methodologies and technologies from various areas of computer science and management science: database management, client server computing, programming languages, heterogeneous distributed computing, mobile computing, graphical user interfaces, application (new and legacy) and subsystem (e.g., CICS and MQSeries) integration, messaging, document management, simulation, and business practices and reengineering. Integrating different concepts from these areas poses many challenges. Factors like scalability, high availability, manageability, usability and security also further aggravate the demands on the designs of WFMSs.

Functionality Evolution. At the beginning, many of the WFMS products were designed for imaging-based applications. Of late, imaging is being made an optional component of WFMSs, thereby broadening the utility of such systems for a wider set of applications. This is also a consequence of more and more information being digitally captured via online data entry rather than such information having to be extracted from paper documents via imaging technologies like optical character recognition (OCR).

There are a number of similarities between WFMSs and transaction processing monitors (TPMs) since both manage a collection of applications with a significant number of similar requirements in terms of performance, industrial-strength features, interoperability, etc. While, for this reason, WFMSs can be thought of as the next stage in the evolution of TPMs, as a matter of fact none of the existing WFMS products that I know of came about as a result of enhancing any TPM!

Embedded Workflow. In the last few years, many general purpose business application packages have been developed for managing human resources, manufacturing, sales, accounting, etc. by companies like Baan, Oracle, PeopleSoft and SAP. The market for such products has grown tremendously as customer organizations try to avoid producing homegrown solutions. Vendors' generic application packages can be tailored to take into account the special needs of a particular enterprise. Developers of such packages - like SAP (http://www.sap.com/workflow/wrkflow.htm) and PeopleSoft (http://www.peoplesoft.com/) - have incorporated work-flow functionality into their products. This allows different functionalities of those products to be conveniently invoked in a well-defined order to implement some specific application requirements. Baan V, to be released in 1Q 1998, will also include workflow functionality (http://www.baan.com/3_Solutions/Concepts/work/default.htm).

Web-based Workflow. With the widespread and rapid popularity of the worldwide web, very quickly many WFMS products have been adapted to work in the context of the web. The degree of sophistication of web support varies from product to product. Some products permit workflows to be initiated or controlled from a browser. Worklist handling via the web is another form of support that is provided by a few products. In summary, it is the client side WFMS functionality that has been made available through a web browser. The advantage of web support is that no specialized WFMS-specific client software needs to be installed to invoke workflow functionality at a workflow server. In the future, more sophisticated support can be anticipated which would allow the execution of inter-enterprise workflows spanning the internet and involving multiple web/workflow servers. Some of the products with basic web support are: Action Technology's ActionWorks Metro 3.0, JetForm's InTempo (http://www.jetform.com/p&s/intempo.html), Mosaix's ViewStar Process@Work (http://www2.mosaix.com/ProcessAutomation/DataSheets/DataSheet6.html), CSE Systems' CSE/WorkFlow NoLimits, Open Text's Livelink Intranet, SAP Business Workflow 3.1, Staffware's Staffware Global (http://www.staffware.com/aboutsta/97_oview.htm), and Ultimus's Ultimus CyberFlow (http://www.ultimus1.com/). Process@Work requires the web server Microsoft Internet Information Server 2.0. Staffware Global includes a new client written in Java which can be invoked via a web browser by a user to receive, track and process work. Netscape is bundling Open Text's Livelink Intranet with its SuiteSpot server software family, thereby making available Livelink's workflow functionality via Netscape Communicator client software. ActionWorks Metro 3.0 comes with over 20 ready-to-run administrative applications that support key human resources, sales/marketing and support processes.

Distributed Workflows. WFMS architectures have evolved from supporting mostly single workgroup type environments to providing enterprise-wide (and even inter-enterprise level) functionality. With such enhancements, a single workflow is allowed to span servers and clients across wide area networks. This provides additional scalability, availability and manageability since more servers can be involved in a single workflow and the impact of server failures can be minimized. Eastman Software's OPEN/workflow 3.1 (http://www.eastmansoftware.com/) and IBM's Flow-Mark 2.3 (http://www.software.ibm.com/ad/flowmark/) provide support for distributed workflows involving multiple servers. The former product also allows work queues to be replicated for improved availability.

Ad Hoc Workflows. Production WFMSs are being enhanced to provide support for ad hoc workflows with different levels of flexibility. Also, new products which are specifically intended for ad hoc workflows have been introduced recently. Novell released Groupwise Workflow (http://www.novell.com/groupwise/) which is based on messaging. It uses as its core workflow engine FileNet's Ensemble (http://www.filenet.com/prods/ensemble.html). Several e-mail based WFMS products have been developed recently on top of Microsoft's Exchange messaging product. Products in this category include Staffware for Microsoft Exchange, Keyfile's Keyflow 2.0 (http://www.keyfile.com/), JetForm's FormFlow (http://www.jetform.com/p&s/formflowov.html), Reach Software's WorkMan 2.1 (http://www.worksoft.com/) and Ultimus. Some systems like InConcert 3.6 (http://www.inconcertsw.com/prodinfo/welcome.htm) and TeamWARE Flow (http://www.teamware.us.com/) allow executing workflow instances to be dynamically modified. This functionality permits a workflow process to be instantiated without the entire process being completely defined at first and the process design to be inferred by tracking the dynamic modifications that are performed. Once the process is completely defined based on the observance of how the former evolved, the template so generated can be used for instantiating future process instances of that kind.

Process Modeling. Business process and data modelling companies like HOLOSOFX (http://www.holosofx.com/) and IDS-Scheer (http://www.ids-scheer.de/english/index.htm) are enhancing their respective products Workflow-BPR and ARIS Toolset to generate workflow schema definitions (e.g., FlowMark Description Language versions of workflow definitions for use with FlowMark). This is analogous to, in the relational DBMS world, 4GLs being used to generate SQL programs rather than forcing users to hand code SQL. HOLOSOFX's Workflow-BPR and FileNet's Visual WorkFlo (http://www.filenet.com/prods/vwtext.html) have been integrated so that the former's output (e.g., process definitions) can be fed into the latter. Also, feedback information from the latter can be fed to the former to refine assumptions made during process analysis. IBM's Business Process Modeler (http://www.software.ibm.com/ad/promodel/) can also produce input for FlowMark in the form of FDL schema definitions. Users have been demanding tools for enterprise modelling, analysis and simulation of workflows. InConcert has been integrated with CACI Product Company's SIMPRO-CESS (http://www.caciasl.cm/simprocess.html). Adaptive Information Systems' Work Modeler (http://www.ais-hitachi.com/) supports simulation of workflows. It is part of the company's AdaptFile/VisiFLOW software suite. ViewStar's Process Architect visual workflow builder provides an animated simulation feature to perform "what if" analyses of throughput and to help identify bottlenecks. FlowMark provides an animation tool to step through the execution of a process (even partially specified) for the purpose of *debugging* the process's definition.

Metamodel. The features of the metamodel supported by the different WFMS products are similar to the ones found in parallel programming languages. Some of them are: block structuring, iteration, recursion, conditional and unconditional branching, and parallel branches. Some systems like Flow-Mark distinguish the types of connections between activities: data and control. Data flow may be modeled with input and output data containers being associated with activities or via the descriptions of documents that flow through activities. Conditions may be associated with the control flow connections to decide under what conditions control will flow through those connections.

Groupware. The groupware product Lotus Notes has been around for many years. Recently, the Notes server has been renamed to be Domino and the name Notes is now associated with the client. Domino provides some basic workflow functionality and permits building workflow applications with both database-based and mail-based architectures. Recent releases of Domino provide support for advanced concepts such as agents, field-level replication, integrated web access, web serving, etc. Domino has been ported to run even on the IBM mainframe operating system Posix-compliant OS/390. Other vendors have built products which provide high-level process definition capabilities on top of Domino/Notes. Some of these products are Action Technology's Action Workflow, Pavone's GroupFlow (http://www.pavone.de/wpub_pav/21de.htm) and ONEstone Information Technologies' ProZessware (http://www.onestone.de/). FlowMark 2.3 supports runtime clients based on Lotus Notes, thereby allowing users to take advantage of the replication and disconnected operation features of Notes. With such a client, worklist items and process definitions are made available as Notes documents.

OO Architecture. Some of the WFMSs (e.g., FlowMark) are built using an object-oriented language like C++. Not all such systems expose the object-oriented architecture of the system for users to tailor the system's functionality. InConcert is an exception in this regard. Objects representing workflow processes and tasks are manifested externally via APIs. Such API functions appear to applications as object classes which are tailorable.

WFMS State Repository. Most WFMSs' servers use a relational DBMS as the repository for keeping track of workflow process definitions, organization structure, runtime information on process and activity instances, workflow data, etc. Typically, installations are allowed to choose a DBMS from a variety of different RDBMS products. As described before, some products use Lotus Notes/Domino as the repository. FlowMark currently uses ODI's ObjectStore OODBMS as the repository but work is in progress to make DB2 available as a repository in Release 3.0. The usage characteristic of a DBMS by a WFMS is very different from the usual assumptions made about most database accesses being read-only. As a matter of fact, most accesses made by a workflow server to its repository will be in the form of update transactions. This is because most of the time the server accesses the repository to perform state transitions in the workflow process graph at the time of activity/process instance completions/initiations. Such actions have to be recorded persistently. The update transactions executed by the workflow servers tend to be of short duration. The locking granularity that the DBMS supports can have a significant impact on the number of workflow clients that can be supported. High availability features in the repository DBMS are crucial since any failure of the DBMS would make the WFMS's operations come to a standstill since the workflow server needs access to it to do its process navigation on an activity completion.

Transaction Concepts. While much research has been done in the area of advanced transaction models, none of the current WFMS products supports the transaction concept in any explicit fashion. Typically, the products do not even guarantee that if an activity's execution is an ACID transaction that the execution of that activity and the recording of that activity's completion in the workflow server's repository will be done atomically. The consequence is that the activity may complete successfully but the client node where the activity executed may crash before the activity completion notification is sent to the server and then the server will continue to think that the activity is still in progress. Human intervention will be needed to resolve this situation. This scenario becomes especially difficult to handle where the activity program is a legacy application which was written without its usage in a workflow context in mind.

Worklist Handling. When an activity becomes ready to execute, the manner in which information about the ready activity is propagated to the worklists of the users capable of executing that activity differs from system to system. In some systems if such a user is currently logged on his/her worklist is updated immediately and asynchronously at the user's client machine to include the new activity. In other systems, the update happens only when the user explicitly requests a refresh of the worklist. Yet another approach is to give each user the option of specifying whether the refresh should be performed immediately or on demand. Each approach has its tradeoffs with respect to scalability, performance, ease of use, responsiveness, etc. Once a user finishes executing an activity, how the next activity to be performed by the user is chosen also varies from system to system. In *push* systems, the user is given the specific next activity to perform. That is, the user is not given a choice and the sytem decides on work scheduling. Typically, this approach is adopted in production (clerical worker) environments. In *pull* systems, the user looks at the worklist which contains a list of ready activities and chooses which one to process next. That is, the user does self scheduling. Typically, this approach is adopted in knowledge worker environments.

Telephony Integration. ViewStar 5.0 integrates workflow management with telephony, thereby allowing companies to manage phone calls and the actions they trigger as part of a coherent business process. The intent is to integrate front-office (customer care, help desk, ...) and back-office (underwriting, inventory control, loan applications, billing, accounts payable and receivable, ...) processing.

Application Development. A number of vendors have added support for Microsoft's Object Linking and Embedding (OLE) technology. This allows OLE-enabled applications to be very easily invoked by a WFMS as a consequence of starting executions of activities. Activity implementations become much easier to code since passing of data from the workflow engine to the invoked applications is automated. Support for OMG's CORBA has not been forthcoming as much as for OLE in WFMS products.

Document Handling. Different WFMSs provide different degrees of support for handling documents. Some WFMSs have built-in document management. Examples of such systems are Eastman Software's OPEN/workflow 3.1 and Keyfile's Keyfile. Certain WFMSs have tight coupling with external document management products. Products built on top of Lotus Notes/Domino, for example, belong to this category. Some products (like FlowMark) have a loose coupling with a document management system (e.g., ImagePlus VisualInfo (http://www.software.ibm.com/is/image/vi21.html)).

Intercomponent Communication. Some products like FlowMark currently use their own home-grown messaging mechanisms for communication between their components. In the case of FlowMark, work is in progress to replace the special purpose messaging scheme with IBM's MQSeries (http://www.hursley.ibm.com/mqseries/) which provides persistent messages and transaction support across a wide variety of platforms. As mentioned before, products based on Exchange and Groupwise use the mail system for almost all their communications needs. WFMS products based on Lotus Notes/Domino use that groupware product's native support for messaging. As far as I know, CORBA is not yet supported by WFMS products for this purpose.

5. Research Projects

Overall, the workflow research community has not had enough impact on workflow products. There are a few exceptions, of course. Action Technology's Action Workflow originated from research done at Stanford University. InConcert's InConcert grew out of office automation research performed at the Computer Corporation of America. Pavone's GroupFlow came out of research work carried out at the University of Paderborn in Germany. Some of the ideas from the Intelligent Control Nets project at Xerox PARC were commercialized in the now-defunct FlowPath product of Bull which was sold to Wang.

Much of the research work on workflow management has concentrated on workflow specification (e.g., intertask dependencies) and verification, transactional workflows (e.g., advanced transaction models) and extensions of ideas from active database management to workflow management. There are only a few workflow research groups which are engaged in seriously prototyping their research results using either home-grown WFMSs or commercially available WFMS products. At least some of the prototypes replicate functionality that is already widely available in one or more products.

A number of issues deserve serious attention from researchers: modeling of external events, exception handling (combining production and ad hoc workflows), interoperability, process schema inference, supporting object-oriented views of workflow definitions (e.g., inheritance), fault tolerance, benchmarks, load balancing, ...

In the following, I describe very briefly some of the systems-oriented workflow projects.

Exotica (http://www.almaden.ibm.com/cs/exotica/) was a research project that was in existence for a few years (until early 1997) at the IBM Almaden Research Center in San Jose, USA. That project explored issues like scalability, availability, distributed workflows via transactional messaging, disconnected workflow client operations, mapping advanced transaction models on top of WFMSs, alternate workflow repositories, OLE support, and ad hoc workflows. This work was done in the context of IBM's workflow product FlowMark, groupware product Lotus Notes and messaging product MQSeries. Prototyping work was done to support disconnected/mobile clients in FlowMark. A number of papers were written which describe possible enhancements to FlowMark to address the previously mentioned issues.

MENTOR (http://www-dbs.cs.uni-sb.de/) was a joint research project of the Union Bank of Switzerland and the University of Saarland at Saarbrucken, Germany. This project concentrated on the specification, verification and distributed execution of workflows based on state and activity charts.

METEOR (http://lsdis.cs.uga.edu/workflow/) is a research project at the University of Georgia at Athens, USA. Their ORBWork prototype exploits CORBA for intercomponent communications. It is a fully distributed implementation of the workflow server functionality. It is realized using Iona Technologies' Orbix object request broker and associated products. Some of the METEOR work was done in the context of healthcare applications.

METUFlow (http://www.srdc.metu.edu.tr/metuflow/) is a research project at the Middle East Technical University in Ankara, Turkey. The METUFlow prototype also uses CORBA as its communication infrastructure, thereby resulting in a totally distributed implementation of the workflow server functionality.

MOBILE (http://www6.informatik.uni-erlangen.de/) is a research project at the University of Erlangen, Germany. The project advocates the idea of building a WFMS in a modular fashion so that the resulting system is easy to extend.

OpenPM (http://www.hp.com/hpj/oct96/oc96a8.htm) is a research project at Hewlett-Packard Laboratories in Palo Alto, USA. The OpenPM prototype formed the basis for the HP product AdminFlow (http://www.hp.com/csopress/97apr7b.html). OpenPM uses CORBA-based communications infrastructure and supports OpenView-based systems management environment. It also allows specification of compensation scopes and actions.

Panta Rhei (http://www.ifi.uni-klu.ac.at/~herb/workflow.html) is a research project at the University of Klagenfurt, Austria. Their prototype explores support for the internet and advanced transaction concepts. Its architecture is based on web technologies. It is implemented in Java.

WASA is a research project at the University of Muenster, Germany (http://wwwmath.uni-muenster.de/~dbis/Weske/Common/wasa.html).
It concentrates on scientific applications such as geoprocessing, molecular biology or laboratory environments where the requirement to dynamically modify running workflows is considered to be higher than in more traditional workflow applications. A prototype has been implemented in Java with Oracle being used as the repository.

WIDE (http://dis.sema.es/projects/WIDE/) is an European Esprit project involving Politechnic of Milan (Italy), Sema Group (Spain), ING Bank, Manresa Hospital and University of Twente (Holland). The goal of the project is to extend distributed and active database technologies to the workflow arena. The results of WIDE will be implemented in Sema's WFMS product FORO.

6. Conclusions

As I briefly outlined in this short paper, workflow management is a very active field with numerous products and research groups. Technically it is an exciting field since it amalgamates technologies, principles and methodologies from numerous areas of computer science. The product landscape is being transformed significantly due to the absorption of emerging technologies like the worldwide web, and due to mergers and partnerships involving numerous companies which produce complementary products. With the emergence of support for workflow management in process modeling and application development tools, WFMSs are becoming a little easier to use. There is a significant amount of hope riding on the work of the Workflow Management Coalition in order to achieve interoperability across different vendors' products and to make inter-enterprise workflows a reality. Workflow management has a very significant role to play in disparate organizations' drive to improve their efficiency and customer service.

A more comprehensive tutorial presentation on which this paper is based is available at http://www.almaden.ibm.com/u/mohan/nato97.eps

Kerem – Reasoning About the Design of Partially Cooperative Systems

Opher Etzion

Information Systems Engineering Group
Faculty of Industrial Engineering and Management
Technion - Institute of Technology
Haifa, 32000, Israel
e-mail: ieretzn@ie.technion.ac.il
fax: 972-4-8235194

Abstract. Inter dependencies among information systems is required by a growing number of applications. Partial cooperation occurs when a collection of independent systems have some forms of inter dependencies. These inter dependencies may take a diversity of forms, and various levels of complexity. This paper introduces the **Kerem** model which serves as a modeling and reasoning tool for partially cooperative systems. The paper presents the two main features of Kerem: the modeling tool for expressing the specification of a cooperative system, and a static analysis reasoning tool, capable of reasoning about validation diagnosis, change management, and issue ad-hoc queries about the cooperative system's behavior.

1. Introduction and Motivation

1.1 Partially Cooperative Systems

Workflow models represent the behavioral aspect of work processes and interaction among different components. In this paper we concentrate upon modeling partially cooperative systems. A partially cooperative multi-system is a collection of information systems that co-exist concurrently and independently, however there may be some inter dependencies among various systems. A System is a set of related activities, whose dynamics can be roughly modeled by a state-transition model. There are several types of Inter-dependencies among systems that are discussed in this paper:

- **Resource Sharing:** The interaction between the systems is materialized in the sharing of some critical resources. Consequently, the systems should obey a protocol of concurrency control to guarantee orderly utilization of that resource.
- **Message Passing:** A system may send a direct message to another system. The receiving system reacts to the message according to its internal logic.
- **Events Subscription:** A system may subscribe to be notified when events occur. An event can be either reported by other systems or be an external event.
- **Status Inquiry:** A system may inquire about the status of other systems.

 – **Enforce Change:** A system may be authorized to enforce change (i.e.
abort) the actions of other systems.

As an example consider the following setting: In a bank there are six servers
$s_1, \ldots, s_6$. s_1, s_2, s_3 are tellers that serve clients in a routine way, using a
well-defined process. Each teller has pre-assigned clients. s_4 is a clerk that
acts as an exception handler, i.e. receives messages from other servers, and
makes decisions about exceptional situations. s_5 is a controller, that controls
$s_1, \ldots, s_4$, is authorized to abort their current functions, and allocate ad-hoc
tasks to the server. All servers are required to report certain events to all other
servers who may be interested in the event. s_6 handles loans and investments
in a procedure independent of the other servers, and is not connected with
either s_4 or s_5. In this example there are different modes of cooperation:

 – There is a single copy machine in the bank. In the work process of all
servers there may be a need to use photostatic copies of documents, thus
a queue may be formed around this single resource.
 – The servers s_1, s_2, s_3 can send messages to the server s_4, assigning an exceptional case, for example, a client requesting an outstanding overdraft.
 – A server may send an event to all interested servers, for example, a notification that a new order to check books have arrived, and each teller can
retrieve the checkbooks ordered by his or her clients.
 – s_5 can order any other server (except s_6) to suspend the service, and prepare an urgent aggregate report.

Our aim is twofold:

 – to provide a modeling tool, able to express complex cooperative settings.
This tool should be a specification language that can be translated into
executable code. The modeling capability should capture both intra-system
and inter-system connections.
 – to provide a reasoning tool about a design expressed by the model.

1.2 The Need for Reasoning

One of the obstacles in the implementation of a multi-system that is combined
of many systems, with various complex relationships among them, is the
difficulty in the design and maintenance of such a setting. The problems
stems from the added complexity, and the possible mutual influences among
systems. We propose to ease the task by the utilization of a tool that will
provide the following functionalities:

Design Diagnostics: In the debug and validation phase, a tool is required
to accept a design as an input, and issue diagnostics about suspected
problems. Types of problems that are dealt with are: scenarios that may
lead to a non consistent reaction to a single message or event, scenarios
that may lead to non converge of operations, indications for incomplete

design, example: Event with no subscribers, messages that are never retrieved.

Change Management: In the maintenance phase, it is often required to
make changes either in the internal logic of a system, or in the cooperative protocols among different systems. The problem is to locate all
the possible consequences of this change. The change management tool
should assist in this task.

Ad-Hoc Queries: In the development phase as well as in the maintenance
phase there may be a need to ask ad-hoc queries that may be of interest
to the system designer. Question are of the type: *what are all the entities
of a system shared with other systems?, who are all the subscribers to an
event? what are all the entities that are possibly updated as a result of a
given message?*

1.3 Outline

This paper concentrates on these two topics. Section 2 describes the modeling
tool and its capabilities, Section 3 deals with all aspects of the reasoning part,
Section 4 concludes the paper and refers to related work.

2. The Modeling Tool

This section presents the basic primitives of the modeling tool, the relationships between each primitives and the other primitives are discussed next and
a complete example demonstrates the primitives and their inter-connections.

2.1 The Basic Primitives

The basic primitives are: *event, task, entity, actor, system* and *system state*
A partially cooperative system is composed of a collection of individual systems. The primitives are utilized in the specification of an individual system's
behavior as well as its relationships with other systems within the cooperative
environment.

An **event** denotes an occurrence in the domain of discourse, having possible implications upon other components. An event can either be detected
by a sensor, or signaled by a component. Events are classified according to
their locality and their complexity.

A *local event* is an event that is relevant within the context of a single
system. This type of event is identified by a system level event detector that
exists for each system.

A *global event* is an event that is relevant within the context of the entire cooperative system. A *global event* should be reported to a global event
detector that exists in the cooperative system's level.

The complexity partition of event separates simple events from composite events that are composed of simple or other composite events and logical or temporal relationships among them (such as: e1 = e2 or e3, e1 = e2 occurs before e3 etc.). An example of a composite event language is SNOOP [CK 94].

Events are the means for reactive cooperation. The system that detects (or creates) the event signals it to all other systems that are both authorized and interested to use it. It is not aimed necessarily at a specific system, and is independent of other system's state. Its effect on the interested systems is determined by these systems and may be hidden from the detecting system. Reaction to an event may create more events, thus an event may indirectly and conditionally trigger more reactions.

A **task** is a basic unit of work that is performed by a system. At any point during the activespan of a system, the system may perform one or more tasks. The flow of control in the system is determined by a set of tasks and by the relationships among tasks. Each activated task can be described by a series of task states and transition.

An **entity** is an information item that is being consumed or produced by a system. An entity can have different location modes:

– Internal to a single task.
– Shared among different tasks within a single system.
– Shared among different systems within a cooperative system.

An **actor** is an agent of any type that can interact with or controls the various system.

A **system state** is an abstraction that denotes the status of the system. Each state is mapped to a set of histories of task activations and tasks states. All the histories that a single state s maps to, are considered to be *state equivalent*. If a system is at system state s_1, it is possible to require to alter its state to s_2, this is done by calculating a path of states from s_1 and s_2 and complete the history gap among them (if possible).

Next we describe the relationships among the different primitives.

2.2   The Event Perspective

2.2.1 Event to event relationship. An event is related to another event in a **composition relationship**. A composite event is composed of events and operators on these events, thus the detection of an event may also imply the detection of a composite event. The composition relationship creates a partially ordered set of events

2.2.2 Event to task relationship. An event may have three different relationships with a task.

triggering relationship: Detection of an event may (conditionally) trigger the execution of a task. The condition may depend upon the system state, the values of entities, the history of the events or any combination of those.

enforces change relationship: Detection of an event may (conditionally) enforce a change in a task's state, i.e. abort the task.

notification relationship: Detection of an event may send a message to notify a task about the event. This relationship denotes that the task does not change its state, but refers to the event notification as an entity that may be utilized by the task.

2.2.3 Event to entity relationship. An event has a **reference relationship** to an entity. It means that when the event is reported it contains a reference to one or more entities, which are accessible by the event detector, the control manager, and tasks and actors that are related to the event.

2.2.4 Event to actor relationship. An event has **notification relationship** to an actor, sending a message to an actor about the event.

2.2.5 Event to system state relationship. An event may be related to a system state by the **enforce change** relationship, according to which, an event may (conditionally) enforce the change of a system state. This is contingent on the authorization of the event to do so, and the feasibility of changing from the current state to the desired state. This high-level operation is decomposed to **trigger** and **enforce change** in a task level.

2.3 The Task Perspective

2.3.1 Task to event relationship. A task may have three different relationships to an event.

signal relationship: A task may signal an event to the local (or global) event detector.

subscription relationship: A task may subscribe as being interested to be notified about the event. This creates the **notification relationships** between the same event and task.

event history relationship: A task may access (if authorized) the event history, and issue queries about it.

2.3.2 Task to task relationship. A task may have four different relationship to other tasks:

notification relationship: A task sends a message to notify a specific task about a change in state in this task.

activation relationship: A task may activate another task.

enforce change relationship: A task, if authorized, may change the state of another task.

task history relationship: A task, if authorized, may query other task about its current state, and the history of its states.

2.3.3 Task to entity relationship. There are two types of relationships between a task and an entity. **reference relationship** that denotes that a task consumes the state of an entity, and **update relationship** that denotes that the task either creates or changes the state of an entity.

2.3.4 Task to actor relationship. There are two types of relationships between a task and an actor. **notification relationships** according to which the task sends a message to an actor, and **prompt relationships** according to which a tasks sends a question to an actor, and waits for the actor's response.

2.3.5 Task to system state relationship. A task may **enforce change** or **inquire** about a system's state. These relationships can be applied to the system which owns the task, or to any other system, contingent upon authorization.

2.4 The Entity Perspective

2.4.1 Entity to event relationship. An entity may **signal** an event. This denotes an entity-driven event. The event occurs when an entity of a given type is being modified, regardless of the task which has performed the actual modification.

2.4.2 Entity to task relationship. A task activation may also be an entity-driven activity. In a similar fashion to the entity-event relationship, a modification in an entity of a certain type may creates **activation relationship** that activates a task.

2.4.3 Entity to entity relationship. A modification in an entity can activate a hidden task that modifies another entity. Although this relationship can be modeled as a task activation, we supply an option to model it as an hidden task. This relationship is called **derivation relationship**

2.4.4 Entity to actor relationship. A modification of an entity may trigger **notification relationship** to an actor, directly by the entity.

2.4.5 Entity to system status relationship. A modification of an entity may **enforce change** in a system status.

2.5 The Actor Perspective

2.5.1 Actor to event relationship. An actor may **signal** events. This is a complimentary way to the event detection and signaling mechanism.

2.5.2 Actor to task relationship. An actor may have several types of relationships with a task.

- **notification relationship:** An actor sends a message to a task.
- **activation relationship:** An actor may activate a task.
- **enforce change relationship:** An actor may enforce a task to change its internal state.
- **history query relationship:** An actor may query a task about its state history.

2.5.3 Actor to entity relationship. Like a task an actor can either have **reference relationship** or **update relationship** with an entity. These operations are carried out by hidden tasks.

2.5.4 Actor to system state relationship. An actor, if authorized, can either **query history** or **enforce change** in a system's state.

2.6 An Example

The following example is a demonstration of the modeling system.

- There are three systems t1, t2, t3.
- The system s1 consists of the tasks t11,t12,t13,t14,t15,t16.
- The system s2 consists of the tasks s21,s22,s23.
- The system s3 consists of the task s31,s32.
- There are four inter-system events e1,e2,e3,e4.
- There are entities of two different types et1,et2.
- There is one actor a1.

The behavioral description of the system is designated by the following relationships:

- The system s1 performs a cycle, starting at t11, and then concurrently execute t12,t13. After the execution of both either t14 or t15 is executed depending on the combination of final states of t12,t13. After the execution of each of them t11 is executed again. t16 is being executed only if the event e1 is detected, when it is detected the cycle aborts, t16 is executed and then t11 is activated again.
- The system s2 invoked and executes t21 and then a cyclic activation of t22. t23 is being activated as a result of the occurrence of the event e3 within 5 seconds of the occurrence of the event e2(composite event e11). It executes concurrently with t22 and when it ends signals the event e1.
- The system s3 is activated by the event e4. The task t31 is activated if the event e1 occurred at least once between the two last occurrences of the event e4 (composite event e12), the task t32 is activated otherwise(composite events e13). Depending of the finite state of the task t31, either the system terminates, or the task is activated again. After the termination of the task t32 event e1 is signaled and the system terminates.

- Entities of the type et1 are consumed by the tasks t11,t12,t22,t32 and are updated only by the task te22.
- Entities of the type et2 are both consumed and updated by the tasks t11,t12,t13,t14,t15,t16,t21,t22,t31.
- Event e2 is signaled when any new entity of the type et2 is inserted.
- Events e3,e4 are signaled only by the actor a1.
- The task s16, if arrives at a certain state, is authorized to change the state of the system s3, to abort, thus making it inactive.

The relationships of the different primitives is shown in the following tables. Table 2.1. shows the connections between events and other primitives, Table 2.2. shows the connections between tasks and other primitives, Table 2.3. shows the connections between entities and other primitives, and Table 2.4. shows the connections between actors and other primitives. For simplicity we eliminated the system state discussion in this example, and also information about the type of relationship in all cases in which the type is obvious.

Table 1. The Event Relationships Table

event-id	events relationships	tasks relationships	entity relationships
e1	e12, e13	t16	
e2	e11		et2
e3	e11		
e4	e12, e13		
e11		s23	
e12		s31	
e13		s32	

3. Reasoning About a Design Model

The relationship tables model is translated into a directed graph, whose nodes are the primitives, and whose edges are the relationships among primitives. The graph, as a whole, contains many details, even for a modest system, thus its full presentation may not be useful. However, sub-graphs that answer certain queries may be useful as a form of retrieval. This graph is the basis to the reasoning process. The reasoning process is contains several components: static analysis, and dynamic (simulation-based analysis). In this Section we describe both the requirements and the implementation of the static analysis reasoning system. A simulation based system is not described in this paper. The discussion is partitioned into three parts: the diagnosis sub-system that

Table 2. The Task Relationship Table

task-id	events relationships	tasks relationships	entity relationships
t11		t12 and t13	et1 (c), et2(u)
t12		t14 (cond)	et1 (c), et2(u)
t13		t14 (cond)	et2(u)
t14		t11	et2(u)
t15		t11	et2(u)
t16		t11	et2(u)
t21		t22	et2(u)
t22		t22	et1(u),et2(u)
t23	e1		
t31			et2(u)
t32	e1		

Table 3. The Entity Type Relationship Table

entity-id	events relationships	tasks relationships	entity relationships
et1			
et2	e2		

Table 4. The Actor Relationship Table

actor-id	events relationships	tasks relationships	entity relationships
a1	e3,e4		

provides the system designer with diagnostic observation about the design of the cooperative system, a change management sub-system that provides information about the (direct and indirect) consequences of such changes. The query system enables the system designer to query any aspect of the design.

3.1 Diagnostics

The complexity of a design makes the task of validate the reasonblessness of a design very difficult to achieve without a computerized tool. Referential integrity diagnostics are excluded from this discussion. The diagnosis process can be applied on an entire design, a specific type of primitive (e.g. task) or a specific instances of primitives (e.g. tasks t11, t12). For each diagnosis a diagnostic message is provided, accompanied by a sketch of the appropriate sub-graph that demonstrates it. The following requirements are checked by the diagnosis process:

3.1.1 Events Diagnostics. The events diagnostics verify the following properties:

1. *Each event has a signalling source.* This is easily identified by the presence of each event in the event relationship of any primitive.
2. *Each event is consumed either by a composite event, or by other primitive.* This is easily identified by looking at the event's own entry.
3. *Each event does not inflict contradictory states in a system.* This is identified by looking at the state changes in the transitive closure of the event, i.e. all the states that are changed as a result of either the event, any composite event that is directly or indirectly triggered by the event, or each task that is directly or indirectly triggered by the event. Let ss1 and ss2 be two states of the same system that are enforced by this transitive closure of an event e. The event e satisfies the diagnostics condition (i.e. is diagnosed as problematic) if ss1 and ss2 are contradictory states, i.e. a system cannot be in both states simultaneously.
4. *Each event does not trigger different tasks that update the same entity.* An event e satisfies the diagnostics conditions if there are two tasks t1 and t2 that belongs to e's transitive closure, as defined above, and there exists an entity type et for which both tasks t1 and t2 update. This diagnostics points out a possible problem of confluence [AWH 92], different order of activations may yield different results, thus the system may not be deterministic.

3.1.2 Tasks Diagnostics.

1. *Each task is being invoked.* This diagnostics involves checking that each task is referred to either by an event or by other task with a trigger relationship.

2. *Each task does not inflict contradictory states in a system.* The event's check is applicable to this case.
3. *Each task does not trigger different tasks that update the same entity.* The event's check is applicable to this case.
4. *Each task does not signal contradicting events.*
   Events e1,e2 are considered to be contradictory if none of them is diagnosed by the contradiction diagnosis (contradicting state, same entity update) yet the union of the transitive closure of an hypothetical composite event "e1 and e2" is diagnosed by one of these contradictory diagnoses. A Task t satisfies the diagnosis condition if it directly (or indirectly) signals two events e1 and e2 that are contradictory.

3.1.3 Entity diagnostics.

1. *Each entity is updated* either by a task, or by a derivation relationship to other entity.
2. *Each entity is consumed* by a task, or another entity related by a derivation relationship, or an event.
3. *An entity does not derive itself.* The diagnosis condition is satisfied, for an entity et if either et derives (directly or indirectly) itself, or if a modification in et signals event whose transitive closure results in the update of et. This is a diagnosis of a possible infinite loop in the design.

3.2 Change Evaluation

Change evaluation is the process of checking the implication of adding, modifying or deleting any primitive or relationship in the cooperative system. The addition of new instances of primitives do not imply any change, but the change of their relationship to others in the system does. For each such modification, the implications can be reported as: **all implications**, or specific types of implications. This is reported by a listing accompanied by a sketch of the appropriate sub-graph. Note that not all modifications in relationships create a behavioral change. The following changes are reported:

3.2.1 Events relationships changes.

1. *composition relationship insertion:* If an event e1 is added to be a component in the composite event e11, the specify all the tasks that are triggered directly or indirectly by e11 and have been previously triggered by e1. Specify all the entities that are consumed (updated) by e11 and that have not been previously consumed (updated) by e1.
2. *composition relationship deletion:* If an event e1 is deleted as a component in the composite event e1, specify the same tasks and entities as in the insertion case, with the appropriate heading.
3. *triggering relationship insertion:* If an event e is added to trigger the task t, then report the transitive closure of t, w.r.t. to tasks and entities.

4. *triggering relationship deletion:* If an event e triggering relationship with the task t is deleted, then report the transitive closure of t, as not becoming not effective.

5. *enforce change insertion:* If an event e enforces a change in a system state, then report on the transitive closure of all possible paths between other states and the changed state.

6. *enforce change deletion:* In a symmetric way, report the same as the insertion case, with the appropriate heading.

3.2.2 Tasks relationships changes:

1. *signal relationship insertion and deletion:* If a signal relationship from a task t to an event e is inserted or deleted, then report on the transitive closure of e.

2. *activation relationship insertion and deletion:* if an activation relationship from a task t1 to a task t2 is inserted or deleted, then report on the transitive closure of t2.

3. *enforce change relationship insertion and deletion:* The change relationship of a task, behaves in a similar fashion to the *enforce change* relationship in an event.

4. *update relationship insertion and deletion:* If an update relationship from a task t to an entity type et is inserted or deleted, then report on the transitive closure of et, i.e. all the entities that are directly or indirectly derived from et, and the transitive closure of all the events triggered by it.

3.2.3 Entities relationship changes:

1. *signal relationship insertion and deletion:* The same as the signal relationships of a task.

2. *activation relationship insertion and deletion:* The same as the activation relationships of a task.

3. *derivation relationship insertion and deletion:* The same as the update relationship of a task.

3.3 Query System

The query system answers queries of three types:

1. *What are all the consequences of a primitive instance α?* This is answered as the transitive closure of the primitive. If α is an event, it lists all the events directly or indirectly composed of it, all the tasks directly or indirectly activated by it, all the state changes and possible paths enforced by it, and all the entity types consumed or updated by it. In a similar way the transitive closure of other primitives is also composed. This query may be reduced to consequences of a single type.

2. *What are all the direct consequences of a primitive instance α?*. In this case, the previous query is applied, but is restricted to neighboring nodes in the graph.

3. *Is it possible to get from an instance α to an instance β*. The answer is either no, or a specification of all possible paths in the graph.

4. Conclusion

4.1 Related Work

There workflow area models business processes. One of its functionalities is to model the behavior of different components. A recent survey of workflow models can be found in [JB 96]. Most of the workflow models are simple and cannot model complex interactions.

An infrastructure to model complex interactions exist in languages and models such as ACTA [CR 90].

The reasoning part is a continuation of a work done on active databases [Etz 95]. This is a more general case than active databases, but it shares some of the basic primitives as well as some of the basic problems that should be detected such as: confluence and termination [AWH 92],[BCW 93].

Debuggers for rule based systems are presented in [Beh 94] that describes a simulation based system. and in other recent works such as: [B+ 96], [BGB 95],[JUD 96].

[W 97] describes a static and two types of dynamic analysis algorithms for rule based systems.

4.2 Concluding Remarks

The **Kerem** model presented in this paper is a partially cooperative model aimed at the modeling and reasoning about complex interactions among systems. It can be used to model *extranets* scenarios, or any type of complex interactions among systems. The static analysis part has been fully designed, and a prototype implementation is under development. The dynamic reasoning algorithms based on simulation are currently under design. Another direction of future work will deal with looking upon evolution of workflows, using temporal database techniques.

Workflow Technologies Meet the Internet

Umeshwar Dayal, Qiming Chen, Tak W. Yan

Hewlett-Packard Laboratories
Palo Alto, CA 94304, USA
{dayal, qchen, tyan}@hpl.hp.com

Abstract. Workflow systems are increasingly used in large enterprises for automating complex business processes, where demands are placed on high performance, continuous availability, and end-user mobility. Furthermore, the ubiquitous Internet and Intranets are rapidly becoming the distributed infrastructure over which enterprises want to deploy such services. In this paper, we discuss the opportunities provided by Internet/Intranet technologies to enhance the capabilities of a workflow system. The use of Web browser-based *open clients* allows users to interact with a workflow system from virtually any computer. Advanced features such as applets allow the end user to dynamically acquire workflow applications and tools. In contrast to existing workflow systems, which have monolithic "workflow engines" and system specific server/client connections, we propose an architecture consisting of distributed, dynamically configurable server components, interacting with one other through messages. Redundant workflow servers can be easily added to meet load demand and to provide high availability. Finally, for inter-enterprise processes (such as those arising in electronic commerce), we describe techniques that facilitate cooperation and synchronization across process boundaries without compromising security or autonomy.

1. Introduction

Business processes often involve multilevel, long-duration, collaborative and transactional activities; and require the coordination of many database systems, applications, and agents. *Workflow* is an emerging technology for business process automation, monitoring, integrity enforcement, and recovery [N 90] [DHL 91] [MS 93] [C 86] [LR 94] [KS 94]. Increasingly, workflow systems are being deployed in large enterprises, such as financial institutions and telecommunication companies, to automate business-critical, large-scale processes involving participants throughout the enterprise. Thus, issues such as distribution, high performance, scalability, continuous availability, extensibility, and end-user mobility that were previously not addressed now become critical to the success of workflow technology.

The architecture of most workflow systems is based on the reference model defined by the Workflow Management Coalition [WfMC 95], a group of vendors and users working to develop standards for open workflow system architecture and application programming interfaces (APIs). At the core of a workflow system in the reference model is the workflow engine, responsible for orchestrating the control and information flows within a business process.

We very briefly summarize some key workflow terminology, excerpted from the Workflow Management Coalition glossary [WfMC 94b].

A *process* is a "coordinated (parallel and/or serial) set of process activities that are connected in order to achieve a common goal." A *process activity*, manual or automated, is a "logical step or description of a piece of work that contributes toward the accomplishment of a process." "A computerized representation or model of a process that defines both the manual process and the automatable workflow process" is called a *process definition*.

A *workflow participant* (or *agent*) is a resource (e.g., a human, an external application program, or a combination of both) that "performs partial or in full the work represented by a workflow process activity instance." A *process role* is a "synergistic collection of workflow process activities that can be assumed and performed by a workflow participant for the purpose of achieving process objectives." A *work item* is a "representation of work to be processed in the context of a workflow process activity in a workflow process instance." A *worklist* is a list of work items.

In early workflow systems, the workflow engine was monolithic and centralized, and task execution was also typically centralized. Current workflow systems permit distributed task execution, often using a distributed object infrastructure such as CORBA for invoking remote applications and resource managers; however, they still have monolithic and centralized workflow engines.

Today, the public Internet and corporate Intranets have become the ubiquitous communication infrastructure for developing and deploying distributed services on top of heterogeneous computing platforms.

The Internet provides opportunities for enhancing workflow technologies and vastly increasing their adoption in critical business processes. In this paper, we explore three areas of opportunity: (a) open clients, (b) component-based servers, and (c) inter-enterprise processes.

In a large enterprise, mobile users need to access a workflow system on the road, say from a laptop computer in a hotel or from a desktop computer in a guest office. In the Workflow Management Coalition reference model, a human workflow participant interacts with a workflow system in three ways: defining workflow processes, performing administrative and monitoring tasks, and accessing work-list tools. Currently, existing client applications (e.g., process-definition tools) are typically customized and hardware platform-specific, and a user must have access to such client software to be able to communicate with the workflow system. If he happens to have access to a computer and tries to contact his workflow system, he is still out of luck if the client software is not installed. Furthermore, it is very difficult to upgrade the functionality of the server. For example, if a workflow server provides a new API function to allow users to get a survey report about certain types of business processes, a user at a workflow client cannot directly invoke the function without upgrading the client software. It is even impossible for a client to retool itself dynamically by acquiring server provided software on the fly.

In this paper, we propose support for *open workflow clients*, clients that have no workflow specific functionalities built-in, but that are based on generic World Wide Web browsers. The phenomenal development of the World Wide Web has meant that Web browsers have now become the universal client interface for remote interactive access; virtually every computer in an enterprise will have Web browser software installed. It is thus compelling to develop workflow tools on this platform. Equipped with such tools, the end user can interact with a workflow system from virtually any computer connected to the enterprise network using a generic Web browser. This supports mobility – the user can access the workflow system from anywhere he needs to. Another important advantage is that, with new Web technologies such as network-transportable applets (written in Java or Javascript), the end user can acquire workflow tools from the workflow engine over the network. It is not necessary to have the software pre-installed on the user machine. This promotes further user mobility, as well as easy maintainence of software – tools can be upgraded transparently on the server side.

The second impact of the Internet is that it enables the decomposition of a workflow engine into a collection of distributed, interoperating *workflow component servers*. These component servers work together in a cooperative manner to comprise a distributed workflow engine. By componentization, we can (1) enhance performance – multiple component servers performing the same functionality can be selectively added to meet the demand for a particular service; (2) improve availability – redundant component servers can run on separate, perhaps geographically distributed, machines; (3) facilitate co-operation among workflow systems – components from different engines can easily work together to support distributed process/subprocess execution; (4) maintain or upgrade engine functionality incrementally – a component of the engine can be maintained or upgraded incrementally, without affecting the other parts of the engine. Further, the component servers can themselves be moved over the Internet, allowing us to dynamically configure workflow services for highly dynamic applications. In particular, by making the component servers lightweight applets, an inexpensive workflow engine can be quickly configured for simple processes (e.g., order management for a small website such as a bookstore) that do not require the full workflow machinery necessary for enterprise-scale processes.

Finally, enterprises are looking to use the public Internet as the basis for *inter-enterprise processes* such as electronic commerce transactions or supply-chain management. Many technical issues still have to be resolved before such processes can be implemented: security and privacy; payment mechanisms; information interchange protocols; and negotiation, bidding, and brokering protocols. Because of autonomy and security requirements, an inter-enterprise business process is best modelled as a collection of cooperating business processes. This necessitates the development of transactional models for cooperating business processes that support data and control flow, and failure and exception handling across process boundaries.

In the next three sections of this paper, we address, respectively, the issues of open workflow clients, component workflow servers, and a transactional model of cooperating business processes.

2. Open Workflow Clients

The World Wide Web is rapidly becoming a commodity, ubiquitous intra-enterprise communication and application platform. It is desirable to take advantage of this emerging platform to develop support for open workflow clients based on Web browsers. First, Web browsers are widely available, thus allowing mobile users to connect to a workflow system virtually at any time and from anywhere. Secondly, using Web browsers as open workflow clients implies a migration from workflow system-specific client-server connections to open client connections. Consequently a user can access multiple, heterogeneous workflow systems through a single interface (the Web browser). Many existing workflow products now provide end user access from a Web browser.

We first very briefly summarize the key concepts associated with the World Wide Web. The Web provides a global client-server architecture. A Web client (browser) and a Web server communicate via the *HyperText Transport Protocol (HTTP)*. A client sends a request containing a *Universal Resource Locator (URL)* to a server. The URL may refer to the name of a static remote file (e.g., a plain text document, a *HyperText Markup Language (HTML)* document, an image, or an audio/video file), or it can encode information that specifies a server-side application program, together with the application parameter values supplied by the user. In the former case, the server retrieves the object from the file system, and sends it back to the client. In the latter case, the server invokes the application program, which takes the input parameter values and generates results that are shipped back to the client. This capability allows the Web server to act as a *gateway* to other systems, such as database systems or legacy systems.

To extend this approach to access workflow systems, one or more workflow gateways are implemented. These are responsible for handling end user communication to and from a workflow domain. An open client talks to the gateway via HTTP, requesting URLs. The gateway receives the URL request, invokes applications that access the workflow servers. It then packages the response into an HTML document, and ships it back to the client.

Security is critical to the feasibility of open workflow clients. The server and the client must authenticate each other before transmitting any confidential information, and messages between the two parties must be encrypted. Existing Web protocols such as *Secure HTTP* and *Secure Socket Layer* support these requirements. *Applets* are platform-neutral programs, written in languages such as Java and JavaScript, that can be transported across networks. They run in an interpretive run-time environment that can guarantee the security of the local host executing remote applets.

Through an open Web client, a user can retrieve work-items, query process-related information, acquire workflow applications dynamically, and report back activity results. In figure 1, we show an open workflow client interacting with a workflow engine through three gateways that provide this functionality. Many commercial workflow products now provide some of these capabilities.

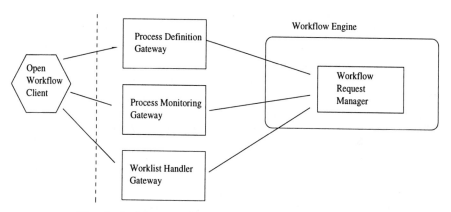

Fig. 1. Architecture Supporting Open Workflow Clients

Consider a user visiting another office in his company. From his temporary office, he has access to a computer connected to the enterprise Intranet. He opens up the generic Web browser on the computer and connects to a workflow gateway (he knows in advance the URL of the gateway in his workflow system) via HTTP. The gateway receives the HTTP request, displays an authentication form for the user to sign in. After successful authentication, the gateway retrieves the user's worklist from a Workflow Request Manager (WRM). The user can then view the work-items. He can select a work-item to work on, and interactively retrieve process-relevant data through the gateway, which in turn queries the appropriate workflow servers for him. The data is then displayed on the browser.

Suppose that the user now needs a spreadsheet application to do some analysis on his data and he finds that no spreadsheet software is installed on his computer. Fortunately, he can download a simple spreadsheet program from his gateway, and continue his work. Finally, when he is finished with the analysis, he reports back his results to the gateway, and the gateway relays the results to the workflow engine.

Holding worklists on a WRM not only allows mobile users to access their worklists from a well-known place, but also enables multiple users who can perform the same tasks to share their workload. It also relieves the workflow system from the job of figuring out how to reach the users and send out their work-items. Triggers may be set in the WRM to detect that a work-item for a user has not been acted upon in a certain timeout period, and to then place the work-item on an alternative worklist (if one exists) or to take some other corrective action.

Another important interface to a workflow engine is the administration and monitoring interface. A user should be able to start a process instance from a Web browser, monitor the status of ongoing or finished processes, and also perform administrative tasks, such as monitoring server load.

For example, a user can access the status of a particular business process from a Web browser through the following steps: he connects to his gateway, which shows him a form to select the process he wishes to check on. His request is processed by a gateway program, which accesses the workflow engine to retrieve the process status. The status is then displayed on the Web browser.

The monitoring can range from a simple status query, such as in the example above, to sophisticated statistical analysis. In the latter case, the user may download analytical tools from the server to help him analyze the data.

A privileged user may also download process definition tools, implemented as applets, from the gateway. Using these tools, the user can define processes on the client machine. When he is finished, the definition is shipped back to the workflow system. To support very complicated graphical interfaces for defining processes, scripting languages may not be sufficient. In that case, plug-ins that can be used with browsers may have to be implemented. However, as plug-ins may not be preinstalled or even available on every browser, this option compromises the openness of the client and should be used only as a last resort.

3. Workflow Component Servers

A workflow engine provides a number of different services for business process definition, execution, monitoring, request handling, task dispatching, and worklist management, as well as databases for storing process related data.

For instance, a coordination service is responsible for executing ("enacting") a process instance according to the process definition. It checks process-related conditions, and drives the transition from one workflow process activity to the next. The transitions are durably logged and can be undone or redone.

An organization service is used to resolve agent activity assignments and to locate resources. It maps activity requirements into roles suitable for carrying out the activity, and then selects participants to fill the roles.

A transport service is responsible for actively pushing work/data out to external systems/ workflow participants. Examples include sending a message to workflow participants via some messaging system (e.g., electronic mail, Lotus Notes), or invoking external applications (e.g., via CORBA).

Process-related data is maintained in databases as workflow objects. These include the templates (definitions) and instances of processes and activities, as well as worklist objects. A database service interfaces with the underlying database systems. Application data other than that specified as attributes of activities, is stored in various external databases.

Typically, existing workflow systems have a single monolithic workflow engine that provides all of these services. In a component-based system, however, a service can be provided by one or more component servers, which are standalone, loosely coupled, distributed, and possibly replicated for high availability. The component servers cooperate in a plug-and-play manner via message passing (Figure 2).

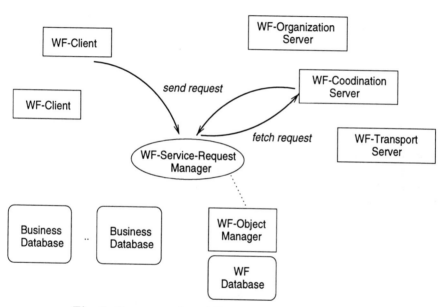

Fig. 2. Component-based Workflow Server Architecture

For maximum flexibility, all component servers are derivable from the same interface class, and are provided with the same basic capabilities for communication, resource management and so on. Their behaviors differ either due to the service methods they implement statically or that they download dynamically. Logical server names and addresses are used to indicate the flow of messages, and these are bound to physical addresses at run-time. By implementing the servers as Java programs, they can be made light-weight and portable to any platform; also, since Java programs are interpreted, the "workflow system" can be dynamically configured out of some collection of these component servers (Figure 3).

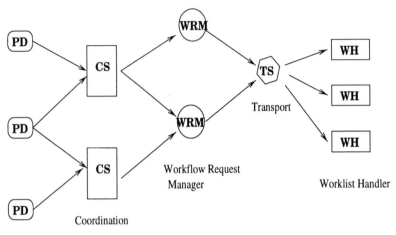

Prcocess Definition

Fig. 3. Redundant Open Servers

An essential ingredient of such an architecture is the active flow of information in messages. This includes the flow of application data, process meta-data, task meta-data, as well as Java classes representing programs, among workflow servers, agents and clients, over the Internet. Examples include sending a subprocess from one server to another for remote execution, sending a request from one component server to another for processing, sending a task to the worklist handler, or loading a Java class to a component server or to a web client. To support active information flow, tasks, processes and data packets all have to be "linearized", for example by representing them as nested NamedValues. A message then is an object constructed from a vector of nested NamedValues plus some envelope information.

Workflow component servers collaborate through sending and fetching requests. A request is an event associated with an operation, target process and activity objects, zero or more parameters, and an optional request context. The requests for each type of service are kept in a designated worklist as work-items, and a worklist is accessible through some *Workflow Request Manager (WRM)*. The worklists are physically stored in a database or in a persistent recoverable queue.

A workflow service requester is isolated from the service provider and can asynchronously make requests for services. It sends its request to a WRM. For example, a coordination server can make a request to store certain process relevant data by sending a database request to a WRM. The WRM locates the appropriate worklist to append the request to. For example, on receiving the database request, it places the request on the database service worklist. A server polls its assigned worklists to find and pick up work-items suitable for it to work on, and the WRM may also poke those servers if a certain work-item is marked urgent or if no response is received after a given period of time.

This communication mechanism provides decoupled interconnection among multiple cooperative system components. Redundant component servers (e.g., coordination or organization servers), running on multiple machines, can be easily added to enhance system performance and availability. When there are redundant servers of the same type, load among them is automatically balanced, as each server picks up work-items at its own pace. Also, we can upgrade a component or perform maintainance work on it one redundant server at a time, without disrupting workflow services. For performance and availability of workflow request management, we may have multiple WRMs.

For management purposes, workflow component servers may be grouped together based on spatial distribution, organizational boundaries, and resource availability. We refer to a group of system components necessary for providing workflow services as a *workflow domain*. This also indicates the scope where workflow objects such as processes, activities, and their instances can be identified without ambiguity. As a basic unit of process management, typically a workflow domain has workflow servers and other system resources centered around a common application environment and often in the same geographic area, although geography does not necessarily determine the domain boundaries. At a minimum, a workflow-domain configuration includes multiple workflow servers for providing coordination, transport, organization, and database services with a designated database; and a local WRM for managing local work-lists, one for each type of participating workflow server. Cross-domain requests are handled by a global WRM. Other servers such as those for handling domain directory and security, can also be added.

This feature allows a logically integrated process to have nested subprocesses physically handled in *decentralized* and *cooperative* workflow domains. By decentralized we mean that both flow control and data control are distributed without a dominant site; by cooperative we mean that the process is enacted by the combined efforts made in multiple workflow systems, when no single system has sufficient resources or the authority to handle the entire process. Such process management offers the promise of speed, reliability and extensibility. Also, in the case of inter-enterprise processes, each enterprise has its own workflow domains separate from those of other enterprises, for reasons of autonomy, security, and manageability. Such processes are also modelled naturally as consisting of cooperative subprocesses.

Determining the workflow-domain for a process to run in, for a workflow server to bind to, or for a request to be sent to or fetched from, is generally called workflow-domain resolution, and can be summarized as follows.

– Domain resolution for processes
  The workflow-domain for running a process or a subprocess can be pre-specified statically or modified at run time, and all activities of that process inherit this binding. Thus, for example, a travel arrangements process can be defined without statically binding the process to a particular travel reservation workflow system.
– Domain resolution for workflow servers
  A workflow server is domain-specific. It is bound to a single workflow-domain at a time; such a binding is static but modifiable. A workflow server communicates with a local WRM for handling in-domain requests, and with a global WRM for handling cross-domain requests.
– Domain resolution for workflow users
  A user as a workflow client is domain-free and can be involved in processes executed in multiple workflow-domains (e.g. a travel agent may arrange trips as part of many travel arrangements processes). Generally, the client sends a request with the envelope information specifying the domain to which it belongs.

Multiple distributed workflow-domains provide a cooperation environment for the enactment of complex business processes. The workflow objects containing process metadata (such as activity definitions and instances) must be accessible to all the workflow-domains cooperating to enact a process. This can be accomplished by putting the metadata in a shared, centralized, but remotely accessible, database or repository. However, the shared repository frequently becomes a bottleneck of concurrency and reliability. Using logically centralized, but physically distributed, databases may be expensive since these databases have to be synchronized.

An alternative is to package and send metadata in requests between workflow domains. When it is necessary to send a subprocess template, together with other process information, to a foreign workflow-domain for execution, the workflow objects bearing the necessary process information are *exported* to the database of that foreign workflow-domain. When the subprocess is completed, the exported workflow objects are sent back for reconciliation.

Exporting a workflow object means making a value copy of it in the destination database as a new workflow object. A copy may itself be copied, as a subprocess may export its own subprocesses. A copy is subject to session semantics, namely, the updates on it are made visible to other workflow-domains only after the session involving these update operations is successfully terminated. Typically, a session spans the execution of a subprocess. Accordingly, a copy has a session-based lifetime in the foreign database.

4. A Transactional Model for Cooperative Business Processes

In Internet workflows, not only the execution of activities, but also their control, may be distributed. For example, a business process may be initiated in one workflow domain but its subprocesses may be enacted in other workflow domains, possibly connected to different databases. In fact, for reasons of autonomy and security, the details of a subprocess may be hidden from the domains in which the process or other subprocesses are executed.

Many extended transactional models have been developed for defining the data sharing and failure recovery semantics of potentially distributed business processes [N 90] [M 89] [C 92] [B 93] [KS 94] [GHKM 94] [Hsu 93] [BMR 94] [DHL 90] [B 92]. Organizing a transactional business process hierarchically allows its effects on data objects to be controlled level by level with well understood semantics. However, many existing workflow systems only support a "flat" specification of business processes based on flow graphs [LR 94] [MS 93]. For flexibility, it is useful to allow the modeling of a business process as a hierarchy (e.g., of subprocesses), with flat structured transactions at each level. In [CD 97], we introduced such a transactional process model.

A transaction T may *represent* a block of subtransactions. Since a subtransaction can represent another inner block, multilevel block nesting (and hence a transaction hierarchy) can be formed through the coupling of transactions and blocks. A business process is a top-level block that may contain multilevel nested blocks representing either subprocesses or nested process modules [A+ 95] [CD 96]. Transactions contained in a block are linked via control flow and data flow, using flow control constructs such as conditional branching, parallel splitting and joining, and looping.

It is important to separate the *specification model* and the *execution model* of a business process. The former provides a template that describes the structure and control flow of the process. The latter is dynamically constructed at run time to express the actual progress of the process instance by recording the history of its execution, and thus can be used not only for animation, but also for failure recovery, of the process instance. Transactions forming conditional branches or even loops in the process specification are described linearly according to their actual execution.

For failure handling, a transaction at any level may be paired with a contingency transaction $\tilde{T}$. A transaction T may also be paired with a compensation transaction $\bar{T}$ that can logically eliminate its effects. A compensation or contingency transaction can be flat or hierarchical, and may be structured differently from the original transaction. A contingency transaction may in turn have its own contingency transaction.

Requiring that every failure of a step cause the entire business process to fail is expensive, because rolling back a process could potentially erase a lot of work. A combination of *backward failure recovery* and *forward failure recovery* allows a process to partially roll back to a semantically accepted restart point, then continue to "roll forward", making further progress.

Rolling back involves two steps: determining the failure affected scope, and undoing the transactions in that scope based on well-understood semantics. In general, transactions with results internal to that scope should be aborted, and those with results externalized beyond that scope should be compensated for. A transaction T may be recoverable inside the block in which it occurs, meaning that there exists a recovery-plan within its block; the block execution can roll back to a transaction called the *rollback-point* of T, and then restart from that transaction, possibly through an alternative path (by executing contingency transactions, if these have been specified) [A$^+$ 94]. Rolling back transactions in a block may undo several transactions, which in turn might require having to undo several transaction hierarchies if those transactions represent inner blocks.

In a multilevel transaction hierarchy, if the failure of a transaction T is not recoverable inside its block, it will cause the whole block to fail, that is, cause the transaction representing the block to fail. Moreover, the failure can be further propagated along the transaction hierarchy until such an ancestor transaction of T is reached that is recoverable inside its own block. For instance, if that ancestor is non-critical to its block or is provided with a contingency transaction, then its abortion does not cause its block to fail. In this way, block nesting can avoid aborting the whole business process since the failure may be recoverable at a certain level, and the "abort-up" chain terminates at that level.

The hierarchical transaction/block coupling allows a process to be handled at different abstract levels, and offers significant flexibility in hierarchical control. For example, compensating the collective effects of a block of transactions at a higher level can avoid defining compensation transactions for each of them, since the latter is sometimes impossible (e.g. *arrange-travel* may be compensated for directly by *cancel-travel*, or indirectly by canceling each step of the process).

In the case of inter-enterprise workflows, multiple *in-progress* processes often need to *synchronize* and *cooperate* for accomplishing joint work. For example, in managing a supply chain, an activity *order parts* in one process depends on activity *supply parts* in another to succeed. THis means that a failure occurring in one process may lead to the failure of the other process. Cooperation also means that activities in multiple processes may need to share *partial, un-externalized intermediate results*. The activities *order parts* and *supply parts* may need to share *purchase contract* data.

The traditional hierarchical transactional models do not support such cooperation. In-progress *atomic transactions* cannot cooperate since they are isolated and unable to exchange intermediate results. *Closed nesting* [GR 93] [M 85] allows intermediate levels of control but still ensures atomicity of the whole transaction hierarchy: every subtransaction commits to its parent upon termination, and in this way the intermediate results of a closed transaction hierarchy are kept internal to the transaction until it is completely finished ("commits thorugh the top").

Open nesting allows a subtransaction to commit to the database independently of its parent, making its results visible to public [W 92] [B 92]. In this way, in-progress open nested transactions may cooperate by exchanging persistent partial results by accessing the shared database. However, process level atomicity and protection are sacrificed as the partial results committed to the database are also accessible to other, irrelevant, processes.

In [C 95], we described an approach to the above problem, based on *contract transactions* that allow interaction between transaction hierarchies representing different business processes. The results of a contract transaction that should be visible to all the participating processes are committed to a *contract-top* transaction, which serves as the common root and object pool [U 92] over the transaction hierarchies of these processes. The data held by the contract-top transaction is accessible to these processes but inaccessible to public until all of the participating processes are completed.

Let us consider the cooperation between two processes P_A and P_B through a *contract transaction* (which links one subtransaction, T_A, of P_A and another, T_B, of P_B) and a *contract-top* transaction, C_{top}.

- The above contract transaction may be treated either as the parent or as the child of T_A and T_B; accordingly, it is called their *contract-parent* or their *contract-child* transaction, respectively.

  When the contract transaction is the contract-parent of T_A and T_B (as C_{parent} in Figure 4(a)), it controls T_A and T_B in terms of application specific protocols and provides an *object pool* for them. T_A and T_B can be sequential, concurrent, or even conversational [U 92] [H$^+$ 92] [N 90] subtransactions of C_{parent}. For example, given two independent software design processes, one for a graphic tool and another for an application, to allow the application design to view or to copy the specification of the tool design, a contract-parent can be established between proper subtransactions of these two processes.

  When the contract transaction is the *contract-child* of T_A and T_B (as C_{child} in Figure 4(b)), it can *inherit data* from T_A and T_B and *perform operations* on this data. For example, a *broker* transaction can be treated as the contract-child of transactions *buyer* and *seller*, which gets a request from *buyer* and a product list from *seller* to make a purchase agreement.

- As the common root of processes P_A and P_B, C_{top} can be logically viewed as an object pool, or an internal data container for *all* the contract-parent and contract-child transactions between P_A and P_B. Data held in C_{top} (such as the above purchase agreement) is accessible to both P_A and P_B, but not externalized until their completion. However, this data cannot be modified by any transaction in a single process, as contract related data should not be changed by a single party. P_A and P_B are treated as *open subtransactions* of C_{top} and able to commit independently.

- The contract-parent transaction C_{parent} commits to C_{top} only. The results of *contract-child* transaction C_{child} may be divided into three parts: those committed to C_{top} which are accessible to both P_A and P_B (e.g. the above purchase agreement), those committed to T_A which are private to P_A (e.g. information reported to *buyer*), and those committed to T_B which are private to P_B (e.g. information reported to *seller*).

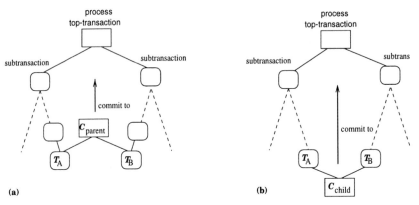

(a)   (b)

Fig. 4. Contract Transactions

When a transaction is *vital* to its parent, its failure causes its parent to fail, otherwise its failure can be ignored, and the parent transaction can continue [DHL 91] [B 92]. In the presence of contract transactions, a contract-child (such as C_{child} in Figure 4(b)) or a child of a contract-parent (such as T_A in Figure 4(a)) has two parents, and may have different levels of "vitalness" to these parents.

In addition to the vitalness of a child to a parent, we introduce the *vitalness of a parent to a child*, such that when a transaction is *non-vital* to a child, its failure can be ignored by that child. By default, a parent transaction is *vital* to its children. However, if necessary,

- a contract-top transaction can be non-vital to a particular process's top-transaction, which allows the process to survive its failure, and more significantly, to survive the failure of another cooperative process;
- a contract-parent transaction can be non-vital to a particular child transaction, which allows the failure of a contract to be ignored (e.g. inability to reach an agreement may not be fatal to a design transaction).

Cross-process transaction dependencies may be introduced as a result of introducing *contract transactions* to link the transaction hierarchies of these processes. As an example, suppose we require that the subtransaction of T_B

in Figure 4(b), can succeed only when the subtransaction T_A succeeds; one can specify

$$vital(T_A, C_{parent}) \wedge vital(C_{parent}, T_B).$$

meaning that the failure of T_A causes T_B to fail, and hence an abort/ compensation dependency between them is created.

In some other cases, failing to make a contract may not be fatal to cooperative processes. The above *vitalness* properties allow us to provide a variety of failure semantics appropriate for different situations.

When a transaction, say T_y, in one business process has a fail dependency on a transaction, say T_x, in another business process (either via a contract transaction or not), the need for failure handling across transaction hierarchies arises (Figure 5).

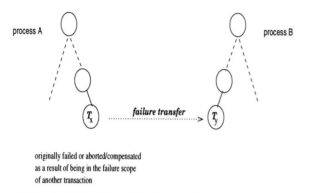

originally failed or aborted/compensated
as a result of being in the failure scope
of another transaction

Fig. 5. Failure Transfer Across Transaction Hierarchies

Failure handling in a transaction hierarchy where the failure *occurs originally*, and in a transaction hierarchy where the failure is *transferred* from another transaction hierarchy, are different, and this difference affects both the failure scope determination and the failure recovery process. This is because, in the former case, the block and (direct) ancestors of the originally failed transaction, up to its closest ancestor that is *in-block-recoverable*, are still *in-progress*, since a transaction may not terminate until all the transactions in the block it represents terminate. However, in the latter case, the transaction, say T_B, to which the failure is transferred in, plus its ancestors, may already have been committed. In [CD 97], we describe an approach to locate such an ancestor of T_B that is *in-block-recoverable* and also *in-progress*; then start top-down recovery from this ancestor's block.

5. Conclusions

Enterprise-wide process management essentially involves heterogeneous information and decentralized, cooperative activities, managed by one or more workflow engines. Increasingly, enterprises are looking to implement such processes on the ubiquitous Internet and Intranets. In this paper, we have discussed three areas in which the adoption of Internet/Intranet technologies enhances the capabilities of a workflow system.

The use of Workflow Request Managers and Web browser-based *open clients* allows users to interact with a workflow system from virtually any computer, to retrieve dynamic information created by programs on the fly, to enable workflow operations, and to automatically acquire server provided workflow tools.

In contrast to existing workflow systems, which have monolithic "workflow engines" and system specific server/client connections, we described an architecture consisting of distributed, *dynamically configurable server components* interacting with each other through messages. Redundant workflow servers can be easily added for enhancing system availability and reliability. Multiple distributed workflow domains are supported for management purposes.

Cross workflow-domain or inter-enterprise processes require extensions to the strictly hierarchical transactional models that have been proposed so far for expressing the semantics of business processes. In particular, we described contract transactions as a way of enabling cooperation among processes (through the controlled sharing of partial results) amd we described failure handling across hierarchical processes.

Many of the capabilities described in this paper have been implemented in a prototype at Hewlett-Packard Laboratories.

Workflow Reuse and Semantic Interoperation Issues

Leonid Kalinichenko

Institute for Problems of Informatics
Russian Academy of Sciences
Vavilova 30/6, Moscow, V-334, 117900
leonidk@synth.ipi.ac.ru

Abstract. Workflow specification is a complex construct highly integrated (corre-lated) with specifications of other types. Designing a workflow we should consider semantics of workflow objects and objects related to them in an integrated way.

Reusable components are treated semantically interoperable in context of a specific application. For components and for specification of requirements canonical object model semantics and ontological semantics are considered jointly to provide complete specifications

In frame of complete specifications, a notion of the most common reduct for a pair of type specifications is introduced as the basis for detection of reusable frag-ments. This notion is based on a refinement technique. An approach for component-based design with reuse is outlined.

The multiactivity (workflow) canonical specification framework is defined. The notion of workflow refinement is based on systematic analysis of functional and concurrent workflow specification properties merging conventional well grounded specification refinement technique with determining of process bisimulation equiv-alence.

A simple example showing a uniform representation of heterogeneous workflow specifications in the canonical model is introduced. The example is used to show how common workflow reducts can be identified and composed in process of the information system development.

1. Introduction

Recently emphasis in object technologies has moved to development of com-mon models and architectures which efficiently provide for a capability of joint usage of heterogeneous, pre-existing, distributed software and informa-tion sources for application problem-solving. Such collaboration of heteroge-neous components (called 'interoperability') allows for composition of systems from pre-existing heterogeneous and distributed components. This develop-ment paradigm of interoperable open systems technology is unprecedented in scale.

Currently WWW, CORBA 2.0 and Java provide a truly portable platform for building and deploying large-scale, distributed client/server applications across both public and private networks.

---

[*] This work is partially supported by the Russian Foundation for Basic Research grant 97-07-90369 and by the INTAS project 94-1817

In spite of enormous potential of the new middleware architectures and accompanied technologies, real progress of their deployment is not so impressive. To exploit efficiently such component-ware technologies, many issues still deserve better understanding and further investigation. The problem of components is that they do not have sufficient clean semantic specifications to rely on for their reuse.

The gap between the existing Object Analysis and Design (OAD) methods applying mostly top-down technique and the demand of the middleware architectures and methodologies for the development based on a composition of interoperating components remains to be large. Current OMG Request for Proposals (RFP) [OMG 96c] for Object Analysis and Design do not even try to close the gap: design with reuse is beyond the scope of the RFP.

A number of various computational, data and knowledge models based on an object paradigm is continuosly increasing. These models are used for development of software and data services, information systems and their subsystems that technically can easily become components of the middleware. Such heterogeneity and lack of well-defined semantics of the respective models creates a big obstacle for their interoperability. Current submissions to OMG according to Meta Object Facility RFP, Business Object Facility RFP and Object Analysis and Design RFP [MF 96, BO 96, OMG 96c] clearly reflect this diversity and a lack of sound foundations.

But probably the largest obstacle for the interoperability of components consists in the application semantics of components technically interrelated through the middleware. Reconciliation of their application concept base that is an obvious prerequisite for their interoperation constitutes a problem.

In the SYNTHESIS project that is under development at the Russian Academy of Sciences we look for the approaches to fill in the gaps mentioned. The project is aimed at the component-based information systems development using semantic interoperability as a kernel idea. We believe that information resources (components) can meaningfully interoperate only in the interests of solving of a specific application problem. We focus on the issues of semantics of the specifications we get on different phases of the information system development. We strictly distinguish between application semantics and object model semantics.

The latter we represent in frame of a "canonical" object model used for uniform representations of various object and data model specifications in one paradigm. The canonical model remains to be a semi-formal one reflecting a lot of semantics freely explained in natural language. This is what we observe in the real world of components that might be connected to the middleware.

To give the canonical model exact meaning, we construct a mapping of this object model into the Abstract Machine Notation of the B-Technology [AB 96] providing precise meaning for the language. Thus, we get the semi-formal object model and its formal counterpart that we can use together as a common paradigm for:

1. different models used on the phases of requirement planning, analysis and design of the information systems;
2. uniform specification of pre-existing components.

Such canonical model provides capabilities of consistency check of specifications on different phases of the information system development. But what is more important is that the concept of *refinement* of the specifications relying on the pre-existing components becomes inherent for the model. This property is fruitfully used on various phases of the process of the system development.

Specifying components developed in different object models, we should preserve information and operations of their types while mapping them into the canonical types. The required state-based and behavioural properties of the mappings lead to a proof that a source type model is a refinement of its mapping into the canonical type model.

Thus specifications of components of existing software or legacy system descriptions can be extracted and transformed into a collection of homogeneous and equivalent specifications for further reuse at the design phase.

Application semantics of specifications we consider separately in frame of the ontological approach. Ontological definitions provide a conceptual framework for talking about an application domain and an implementation framework for problem solving. Ontological specification is treated as a well organised collection of *concept definitions.* Concepts are composite descriptions of individuals or types defining their attributes, concept interrelationships and concept "micro-theories" including rules (constraints) and functions. Semiformal and formal (model-based) specifications for concepts are provided. We base the ontological model we introduce on the canonical object model.

For each of the component specification suspected to be relevant to the application the reconciliation of its ontological context with the application domain ontological context should be made.

A process of the component-based information system development arranged around the middleware concept is elaborated here as a CASE-like activity. The requirement planning and analysis phases of the conventional system development process are augmented with ontological specifications and complete specifications of type invariants and operations defined in the canonical model. The design phase is completely reconsidered: this is the design with reuse of the pre-existing components homogeneously specified in the canonical model.

The component-based design in the interoperable environment imposes a strict demand on *semantic interoperability* of components as the basis for such compositions. To cope with such severe demands, we should provide complete specifications in a notation suitable for their manageable and justifiable transformations.

To discover component types (classes) and their fragments relevant for the concretization of an analysis model type (class) we undertake an associative search of the component constituents ontologically relevant to the the respective application constituents. As the result we get sets of specifications of probably relevant component types and classes.

Further we should select among probably relevant constituents those that really may be used for the concretization of an application domain type (class). For reuse a model of composite object integrating data and behaviour from various sources is applied.

Type specifications and their reducts are chosen as the basic units of specification manipulation. For their manipulation, the algebra of type specifications is introduced. The operations of the algebra are used to produce the specifications of the respective compositions of their operands.

Taking a type reduct is a basic operation of manipulation and transformation of type specifications. Reducts of the component type specifications can be used as minimal fragments potentially reusable for the respective reducts of the analysis model types. The identification of the fact of type reducts reusability is the main concern of the design. Reusable type specifications should be *conformant* to an analysis model type.

The heuristic procedure for the *most common reduct* construction for a pair of ontologically relevant type specifications is the basic one for reuse. The process of design is based on this procedure driven by ontologically relevant pairs of types. The common reducts discovered by the procedure are used in type algebra expressions and object calculus formulae to define new types that should be constructed at the design phase.

In design phase, specifications of concretization types (classes) are constructed as the mediating definitions above the reusable reducts of the component types involved. Correctness of the results of design can be verified using formal facilities of the canonical model.

All the considerations above are applied first to nonconcurrent type components and then to workflow specifications.

Workflow specification can be considered like a megaprogram defined above various components of an information system (including workflows themselves). Workflow specification is a complex construct highly integrated (correlated) with specifications of other types. Designing a workflow we should consider semantics of workflow objects and objects related to them in an integrated way.

We introduce a canonical model for specification of a workflow-like dynamic behaviour and show how industrially supported workflows can be homogeneously defined. The model can be equally applied for specification of multiactivities, declarative interresource constraints and multiresource applications. An orthogonal set of the canonical workflow model facilities includes: 1) high level Petri net- and script-based specifications making possible definition of concurrent execution, data and control flow between the execution components (such as activities or heterogeneous information resources); 2) function (object calculus-based) specification facilities introduced to define activities and assertions over heterogeneous information resources; 3) type specification facilities providing a relevant information resource model.

Notions of types, functions and predicates defined in object calculus are basic constituents of the canonic model for the workflow definition. A process of identification of common reducts for workflow-like type definitions is illustrated. The reducts are used as minimal reusable fragments providing a basis for creating their compositions applied as concretizations of specifications of requirements.

We identify reusable workflow reducts considering behavioural abstractions of scripts in frame of process algebras. Process algebras are algebraic theories being intensively developed as an instrument to define and study process behaviour [BW 90, BE 94, FZ 94]. Using the notion of bisimulation developed there we can identify common workflow reduct. Complete axiomatization of process algebras makes possible to recognize that different workflow reducts are bisimulation equivalent. Complete justification of workflow reducts reusability is based on the notion of their refinement relation.

The paper is structured as follows. We start with discussing of component-based information system development life cycle. Then semantic interoperation reasoning is introduced as a specific culture of the information systems design with reuse. Specification refinement is defined as a fundamental notion for component-based development. Most common reduct of types is introduced as a reusable fragment suitable for further compositions in course of the component-based development. The notions of loose and tight ontological relevance of specifications are provided. A uniform, canonical workflow specification framework is defined. An overview of the capabilities of the canonical model is given. An approach for workflow design with reuse is introduced. A notion of workflow specification refinement is provided. A simple example showing a uniform representation of heterogeneous workflow specifications in the canonical model is introduced. The example is used to show how common workflow reducts can be identified and composed in process of the information system development.

2. Related Research and Technological Developments

Focusing on semantic interoperability, reuse and workflows, we mention here several works selected among numerous works in the related directions to illustrate the state of the art and the demand of the emerging technologies.

In [LE 96] an issue of integrating of information coming from disparate contexts is studied. Semantic interoperability is defined as "an exchange information in a meaningful manner" between sources and receivers.

The shared ontology is required to specify a common domain knowledge described in a shared language. The shared ontology is defined as a set of propositions and deductive relationships between them. Propositions describe things, attributes and states in the first order predicate language. Deductive rules define admissible conversions between propositions (including generalization and aggregation-based rules, unit and scale conversion rules, time and space hierarchy conversion rules).

Context definition rules also should be established associating source propositions to the shared ontology proposition and the shared ontology propositions to propositions in receivers thus reconciliating propositions of receivers and sources through the shared "ontological" propositions.

Context mediation according to this approach is equivalent to transforming propositions from a source, through deduction, to propositions that satisfy the requirements of the receiver's context. These ideas are illustrated by Prolog programs defining how the mediated answers returned in response to queries to satisfy the context requirements of the receiver.

The approach [LE 96] is elaborated in a very restrictive context of a flat relational model without functions. Thus semantic interoperability is considered on a signature level. More deep semantics of types that is required in object models of interoperation middlewares is not taken into account. Ontological definitions are accompanied schema definitions expressed in a Prolog-like manner. Well established hierarchical concept definitions are not attempted.

The goal of the InfoSleuth Project [BO 97] is to develop technology that will expedite the process of searching for pertinent information in a geographically distributed and constantly growing network of information resources. In this type of environment, there can be no centralized database administrators or systems analysts to document database semantics or to write application programs that smooth over differences in access languages and database structures. InfoSleuth must be able to efficiently sift through the multitudes of potentially relevant information sources and discover the information that is pertinent to an individual or organization.

InfoSleuth is comprised of a network of cooperating agents communicating by means of KQML [GK 94] used to carry semantic messages expressed in the Knowledge Interchange Format [GF 92]. KIF provides a common communication mechanism for the interchange of knowledge between widely disparate programs with different internal knowledge representation schemes.

Each resource agent advertises its capabilities to some broker agent. The capabilities are specified in terms of one or more of the ontologies. Semantic brokering enables requests to be specified in terms of the concepts in an ontology and matches those semantic concepts to the resources that are currently best suited to handle those specific requests. The broker agent utilizes a representation of the ontology exported by the resource agent in LDL. KIF statements resulted from the user queries formulated in terms of the common ontology are mapped into LDL queries and then are sent to deductive DB to perform rule-based matching of advertisement to user requests. The deductive mechanisms of LDL help determine the consistency of the constraints in the user query and those exported by the resource agent. Thus the relevance of the information managed by resource agent will be recognized.

The basic rule for data relevance: if the conjunction of all the user constraints is satisfiable with all the resource constraints then the resource contains data relevant to the user request. Common vocabulary enables the dynamic matching of requests to applicable resources.

The resource agent translates queries expressed in a common query language (KQML/KIF) into language understood by the underlying system (mapping between ontology concepts and terms and the local data concepts and terms). Then a query is executed and the results are mapped back into the format understood by the requesting agent.

Applying cooperation agent technology, InfoSleuth is a beakthrough into the dynamic mediated interoperation of data over information network. Another foundations (beyond deductive capabilities of LDL) are required to identify arbitrary servers around network providing not only data but also behavioural (computational) capabilities.

According to OMG or ODP Trading Function [OT97] *a trader* is a third party object that enables clients to find suitable servers in a distributed system:

- A trader accepts service offers from exporters of services when exporters wish to advertise service offers. A service offer contains the characteristics of a service that a service provider is willing to offer and the location of an interface at which the service is available. Service offers are stored by the trader in a centralised or a distributed database.
- A trader accepts service requests from importers of services when importers require knowledge about appropriate service providers. A service request is an expression of service requirements made by an importer.
- A trader searches its service offer database to match the importer's service request. And, if required, a trader can also select the most preferred service offer(s) (if one exists) that satisfies the importer's service request. The list of matched service offers, or the selected service offers, is returned to the importer.

Every service is an instance of a service type that is offered at an interface. Associated with each service type is at least an interface signature type which determines the computational signature at the service interface. A set of relationships for the signature types is maintained. The relationships include equivalence relationship, and super/subtype relationships.

The approaches mentioned so far reflect reached state of technologies for search for data or computation services around the network relevant for some application. What is specific for the Workflow interoperation and reuse.

The Workflow Management Coalition (WfMC) [WfM 96] mission is to promote the use of workflow through the establishment of standards for software terminology, interoperability and connectivity between workflow products. The Coalition has proposed a framework for the establishment of work-flow standards. We mention here only one category of standards – the Work-flow Interoperability interface (4) - Definition of a variety of interoperability models and the standards applicable to each. Workflow interoperability is defined as the ability of two or more workflow engines to communicate and interoperate in order to coordinate and execute workflow process instances across those engines.

According to WfMC, interoperability can work at a number of levels rang-ing from gateways for specific workflow systems and Workflow API (including limited or complete operation set), to a shared format for process definitions and protocol compatibility including standardization of the transmission of definitions, workflow transactions and recovery.

For the upper layers WfMC is defining a process definition language (WPDL) to identify a generic set of functionality. The potential offered by this approach is not only that a single process definition can be enacted upon a variety of workflow engines, but also that parts of a suitably modular pro-cess definition can be enacted on different workflow engines (as resources become available).

Interface (4) defines the IDL specifications intended as an abstract rep-resentation of the operations required to effect interoperability between two (or more) workflow engines. The message specifications are intended as ab-stract representations of the information that needs to be passed between two workflow engines in order to effect the operations described.

Among other interoperability models identified by WfMC we distinguish the nested sub-process model assuming that a process instance enacted on a workflow engine causes the creation and enactment of a sub-process instance on a second engine and then waits for its termination before carrying on with its own enactment.

The OMG Workflow Facility [WF 97] is intended to define interfaces and their semantics required to manipulate and execute interoperable workflow objects and their metadata. The Workflow Facility will serve as a high-level integrating platform for building flexible workflow management applications incorporating objects and existing applications. Among others, the following capabilities of the Workflow Facility are emphasized:

1. *integration* defined as a utilization of workflow- unaware applications and/or objects within the workflow context.
2. *interoperability* among different Workflow Facility implementations.
3. *support of reuse of workflow schemas.*

3. Conventional Versus Component-Based Information Systems Development Life Cycles

We focus on systems development in objects due to the fact that the interoperation technologies are inherently object-oriented.

Component-based systems development is outside the scope of the conventional object analysis and design framework. Modeling facilities currently used [OMG 94] are of no concern of pre-existing components, their interoperability and reuse.

Conventional object analysis and design methods are characterized by using noncomplete specifications, applying object metamodels with vague semantics, ignoring well-defined facilities for a problem domain semantics specification, providing no specific methods for adequate specifications of pre-existing components.

In particular, conventional life cycle models have significant problems supporting components reuse: (i) component reuse is not the top-down process, it possesses features of a bottom-up, component-driven development; (ii) reuse perspective involves looking beyond the development of a single project or a system; (iii) reuse should be based on much higher component abstraction besides that simply captured in code.

Component-based information systems construction needs a component-oriented view of development, it is biased towards production of components to be used in constructing many different applications belonging to various application domains. We intend to build information systems from existing components primarily by assembling, replacing, wrapping and adapting the interoperable parts. Components in their turn may have similar structure. This is why the components approach is called sometimes 'fractal' - that is scale invariant.

The range of possible component-oriented life cycle models can be characterized by two extremes with respect to structuring of the pre-existing components in heterogeneous interoperable information resource environment (HIRE):

1. *loose* or no subject *structuring* over information resources in HIRE;
2. *strict* superimposition of subject *structure* over HIRE to control development, registration and proper placement of new components into the structure.

Applying a *loose structuring,* we assume a work in a dynamically changing world, where there is no formal control and a specific structure over the information resources under development. Good analogy to that might be Internet and WWW. Each information resource (component) may be freely produced and published in a certain application context independently of the others.

Applying a *strict structuring,* we assume that formal (standardized) structure of application domains over HIRE is established. Each structuring of a specific domain is named as a *framework*. Thus each information resource pretending to become a component, should compete for a proper placement in a framework (frameworks) and can be included there after proper certification.

Component development and component use in new information systems (these two different kinds of life cycles) are going concurrently.

We see that there is an essential difference between a component-based information systems life cycle and a conventional one: two different concurrent life cycles – component building and information systems development – are separated into parallel life cycles. We shall see also that the information systems component-based development process is also significantly different of the conventional one.

Further we assume that no pre-determined subject structuring over information resources in HIRE is established. That is, we assume that components can be freely and autonomously developed and published in a net similarly to publishing of home pages in the WWW. We assume work in a world without any preliminary control over development of new components.

We do not preclude a possibility of further classification (a *subject spacing*) to be built-in onto the infrastructure in the form of independently functioning subject repositories and subject agents working for their formation in different *subject spaces*. Once an information resource has been advertised, it can be discovered by an agent acting on behalf of a subject spacer. Such agents carry out continuous searches to collect into a common repository the information resource descriptions that might be useful for the information system developers.

We can imagine different forms of development scenarios in HIRE (e.g., centralized development and implicit or explicit subject spacing, cooperative development, development with active participation of components, etc.).

4. Semantic Interoperation Reasoning Approach

Semantic interoperability means interoperability of components intended for support of a specific application. Semantic interoperability takes into account ontological, structural, behavioural specifications of components. These specifications are interpreted in the context of a possibly different application domain.

Semantic interoperability implies that the information resources (components) can meaningfully interoperate only in the interests of solving of a specific application problem. In another words, it means that correct compositions of information resources can be semantically interoperable in the context of a specific application (in particular, this requirement signifies that the application contexts of the information resources involved should be coherent and their composition should be consistent within the context of the intended application).

Semantic interoperation reasoning (SIR) is a specific culture of the information systems development in HIRE. Fundamental issues of SIR include: reaching of coherence of the ontological contexts of resources and of the application; searching for resources and their subcomponents that could serve as concretizations of the application specification of requirements; creation of compositions of resources (or their subcomponents) that could serve as a consistent, coherent concretization of the application; checking (proving) that constructed specification is truly a concretization of the application requirements.

The following requirements are included into the basic prerequisites of the SIR framework [KE 94]:

1. Completeness of specifications of the available components and of the information system requirements
   By completeness we mean that the specifications should be sufficient to reason that a component is applicable to a given application problem (perhaps, after some contextual, functional, extensional, etc. reconciliation). Specifically it means that we are able to decompose the application specification and locate its fragment for which the component (or its fragment) could be considered a concretization. Or it means that the specifications should be sufficient to reason that a collection of components is composable into a consistent, coherent entity reusable for a given problem (or its fragment) as a whole.
2. Provision of homogeneous ("canonical") equivalent specifications for heterogeneous components
3. Uniformity of a modelling paradigm for different layers of the information system development
4. Provision of sound foundations to support justifiable concretization of requirements applying coherent composition of pre-existing components
   We need mathematically based techniques for specification model against which a description can be verified. We assume here transitional computer-assisted strategy of incorporation of formal methods into the development process [FR 94]. 'Transitional' means that we introduce a semi-formal canonical model and its interpretation in the formal notation. Semi-formal specifications provide a useful bridge between users and requirements engineers on one side and formally biased system developers on the other.
5. Provision of megaprogramming as the basic programming paradigm for information systems development in HIRE
   We consider interoperability to be the universal paradigm for megaprogramming. Interoperability implies composition of behaviours. In a non-distributed homogeneous system such composition can be formed by a collection of objects interoperating through an internal message passing mechanism. In a distributed heterogeneous system such composition is again formed by objects representing components in the global object

space and interoperating through a broker. At the same time we emphasize semantic megaprogramming implying that the components can meaningfully interoperate only in the interests of solving of a specific application problem.

6. SIR facilities should be based on the core interoperation technologies (for instance, CORBA - compliant)

4.1 The SIR Framework Models

We assume the following macro layers and respective specification models of the architecture supporting the SIR framework:

- Ontological specification layer
- Specification of Requirements / Analysis layer
- Design layer
- Implementation layer
- Component specification layer

We assume that the semantics behind any of these models is provided by one and the same descriptive canonical object model treated in a semi-formal style and a having a formal interpretation.

A general picture showing logical functioning of the SIR framework is presented on the Fig.1 Here we emphasize that for the forward development phase (the flow at the left side of the picture) as well as for the backward development phase (the flow at the right side of the picture) we should have in mind an application domain that subsumes application semantics for a specification of requirements or for a specification of a pre-existing component (an information resource). We can meaningfully interpret pre-existing components in context of some application. Therefore, we should establish a coherence of the respective application contexts. Ontological specifications for both phases should be introduced for that.

4.2 Design with Reuse

Design is the component-based process of concretization of a specification obtained on an analysis phase by an interoperable composition of pre-existing information resources from HIRE.

The design specification is a refinement of the analysis specification adapting it to the actual heterogeneous interoperable information resource environment. The object types and classes defined at the analysis phase are refined during the design.

The concretization of the analysis specification and its constituents follows the steps (techniques):

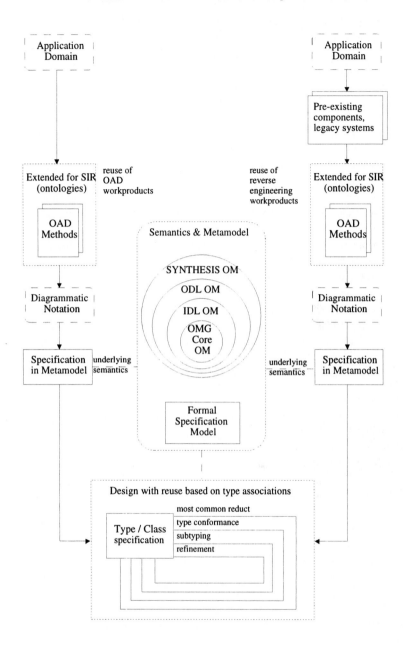

Fig. 1. SIR Framework

1. Ontological Contexts Integration.

   For each specification of an information resource suspected to be relevant for the application the integration of its ontological context with the application domain ontological context should be provided. Technically it means construction of the extended ontological specifications establishing the resource/application ontological concepts relationship.

2. Searching for ontologically relevant components

   To discover information resource types (classes) and their fragments relevant for the concretization of an application specifications an associative search of the pre-existing components names based on their ontological correlation with the application specification constituents names is undertaken. Then we take into account interconcept associations interpreted as subtyping relationships between metaclasses defining the respective concepts. As the result, for each constituent of an application specification we get a collection of specifications of probably relevant information resource constituents.

   We can compare the way of reasoning here with a metaphoric thinking. The essence of metaphor is understanding and experiencing one thing in terms of another. The human conceptual systems is metaphorically structured. We rely on similarities between ontological concept definitions to infer metaphoric structure of the concept relevant entities (types). Our objective is establishing of suitable relationships between fragments of types to benefit of this for the types partial reuse.

3. Preliminary identification of reusable fragments

   This step consists in selecting among probably relevant resource types (classes) those that really may be used for the concretization of the application domain type (classes). For reuse a model of composite object integrating data and behaviour from various sources is applied. The data and/or behaviour residing at each source is regarding as a fragment of composite object. Reducts (projections of object types) are considered as patterns of reuse and composition.

   Two different cases are considered.

   Software service reuse. The functional reducts of ontologically relevant component types are discovered justifying that they are the refinements of reducts of the specification types.

   Data service reuse. For ontologically relevant component classes the relevant state (data) reducts are discovered. Instances of the relevant data reducts can be reused as fragments of the instances of the specification class. Relying on unique keys, the data fragments taken from different sources can be joined into required instances.

   For both cases after preliminary identification of possibly relevant reducts the refinement condition can be verified.

4. Concretization type (view) construction

The specification of the concretization types is constructed as a composition type definition above the reducts of the component types involved. We try to cover the required type with the minimal number of conformant component types (reducts) to be involved into a composition. For classes views constructed above the identified relevant mergeable data reducts are specified.

5. Verification of the concretizations

For each constructed concretization of the application type (class) their transformation into the formal notation can be undertaken to verify the refinement conditions. For the verification necessary proof obligations can be automatically generated and proved.

After that the concretization types and views can be integrated into the application specification hierarchy as proper subtypes (subclasses) of the designed types (classes).

We define the design phase to be neutral to the possible object analysis and design methods as well as to the possible reverse engineering methods.

5. Specification Refinement

For the purpose of design with reuse we need a formal basis to reason that pre-existing component or its part can serve as an implementation of a fragment of a specification of requirements. We focus on *model-based specifications* [S 89, AB 96] making possible to represent the statics and dynamics of information systems. The *static aspects* include the states a system can occupy and the invariant relationships (constraints) that should be preserved as the system moves from state to state. The *dynamic aspects* include possible operations and changes of state that happen. Specification of an operation (function) consists of a definition of properties and relationships that state transitions caused by the operation should satisfy. For that predicates relating values of state variables before and after operation are defined.

The notion of execution of a model-based specification consists of the proof of the initial consistency of the model and the preservation of the invariants by the operations. There exist also a provable way of development of programs from specifications by proper *concretization* of abstract data types and operations of the specification by concrete data types and programs satisfying strict concretization conditions.

In the SYNTHESIS project we focus on the Abstract Machine Notation (AMN) and B-technology [AB 96] and on the mapping of the canonical object model specifications into AMN.

AMN is a notation for expressing specifications. Each construct of the notation receives a precise mathematical definition. A central feature of the notation is that of an *abstract machine*. This is a modularization concept related to such notions as *class* in SIMULA, *abstract data type* in CLU, *package* in ADA, etc. Abstract machine allows to organize large specifications as independent fragments having well-defined interfaces.

Process of design according to the B-technology is based on a step-wise transformation of more abstract specifications into more concrete ones. This activity is called a *refinement*.

Algorithmic refinement consists in removing of non-determinism by being more and more precise about the way our operations are to be eventually made concrete through sequencing and loop. At the same time we should relax pre-conditions.

Data refinement consists in removing completely all variables whose types are too complicated to be implemented as such and in replacing them by simpler variables whose types correspond to those found in programming notations: that is, essentially, natural numbers taken in certain intervals (scalar types) and functions from scalar types to themselves (array types). Data refinement also includes some algorithmic refinement at the same time.

Now, the refinement of the abstract machines is defined as follows: a machine N is said to refine a machine M if a user can use N instead of M without noticing it. Both machines must have the same operation names (each with same input and output parameters respectively). Both machines are said to have the same operational signature.

Sufficient condition for N to refine M is the requirement that each operation of N data refines the corresponding operation of M. Of course, we must have at our disposal a certain abstraction relation linking two variable spaces of our machines.

The transitional approach of incorporation of AMN into component-based information systems development consists in mapping of canonical type (class) specifications into AMN to reach justifiable reasoning on specification reuse and composition in process of the information systems design. The refinement is the fundamental relationship used in this process.

6. Type Specification Reuse and Compositions

6.1 Most Common Reduct

Information system development is a process of construction and refinement of type specifications. Considering development with reuse, we need operations on type specifications leading to transformation of their specifications - decomposition and composition.

The basic operation of a type specification decomposition — getting of a *type reduct*.

An **algebraic system** is an object $U = < S, O_u, P_u >$, consisting of an S-sorted family of non-empty carrier sets $\{A_s\}_{s \in S}$ (also denoted by A), a set of operations $O_u = \{O_u^1, ..., O_u^n\}$ defined on A, a set of predicates $P_u =$

$\{P_u^1, ..., P_u^m\}$ defined on A. Arguments of operations and predicates take their values from carrier sets of the algebraic system.

A signature Σ_u of an algebraic system U includes carrier sets, a set of operation symbols indicating operations argument and result types and a set of predicate symbols indicating predicate argument types.

Establishing a correspondence of type specification with the notion of the algebraic system U, we notice the following. An extension A_T of a type T elements of which denote "proxies" of instances of the type is one of the carriers of the respective algebraic system U. Other carriers can be defined using the complex sort constructors like cartesian product ($\times$), powerset ($\wp$), set comprehension ($\{x | x \in s \wedge P\}$), etc. Operations and invariants of the type specification T correspond to operations and predicates of the respective algebraic system U.

Among operations we shall distinguish state attributes $Att_T \subseteq O_T$. Each state attribute is modelled as a function $A_T \to A_s$ where the sort A_s denotes a type of the attribute.

Definition 6.1. Type reduct *A reduct R_T of a type T, or a reduct of the respective algebraic system U is defined as a subsignature Σ'_u of Σ_u that includes an S'-sorted family of non-empty carrier sets $\{A_s\}_{s \in S'}$ ($S' \subseteq S$, a carrier A_T is included into S'), a set of operations $O'_u \subseteq O_u$, a set of predicates $P'_u \subseteq P_u$ defined on A'.*

We immediately extend this definition from the signature level to the specification level so that a type reduct R_T can be considered a *subspecification* (with a signature Σ'_u) of a specification of a type T. The specification of R_T should be formed so that R_T becomes a supertype of T.

Decomposing a type specification, we can get its different reducts on the basis of various type specification subsignatures. Reducts create a basis for their further compositions.

Definition 6.2. *A **common reduct** for types T_1, T_2 is such reduct R_{T_1} of T_1 that there exists a reduct R_{T_2} of T_2 such that R_{T_2} is a refinement of R_{T_1}. Further we refer to R_{T_2} as to a* conjugate *of the common reduct.*

Operations of the type T_1 are suspected to belong to its common reduct with T_2 if operations with the equal signatures can be found in T_2 up to the parameter type relationship (contravariant for the argument types and covariant for the result types).

A specification of an operation of T_1 to be included into the resulting reduct is chosen among such pre-selected pairs of operations of operand types if the operations in a pair are in a refinement order (for the common reduct (resulting supertype) more abstract operation should be chosen). If the pre-selected operations are not in a proper refinement order then they are considered to be different operations and will not be included into the common reduct.

Definition 6.3. *A most common reduct* $R_{MC}(T_1, T_2)$ *for types* T_1, T_2 *is a reduct* R_{T_1} *of* T_1 *such that there exists a reduct* R_{T_2} *of* T_2 *that refines* R_{T_1} *and there can be no other reduct* $R_{T_1}^i$ *such that* $R_{MC}(T_1, T_2)$ *is a reduct of* $R_{T_1}^i$, $R_{T_1}^i$ *is not equal to* $R_{MC}(T_1, T_2)$ *and there exists a reduct* $R_{T_2}^j$ *of* T_2 *that refines* $R_{T_1}^i$.

The notion of a type reduct is fundamental for the component-based design: it constitutes a basis for determining reusable fragments. An approach for searching for such fragments and most common reduct formation will be shortly considered further.

Other operations providing for creation of composition of reusable specification fragments are join, meet and product operations applied to complete type specifications. The operations are based on a concept of a common type reduct and a refinement condition.

6.2 Process of Common Reduct Detection

For each pair of type specifications Ts and Tr (each Tr should be ontologically relevant Ts) we try to construct their common reduct. We start with identification of their *common signature reduct*. This procedure takes into account only signatures of types ignoring their complete specifications. After that most common reducts are constructed. This makes possible to identify the common reduct of Ts, Tr and the respective concretizing reduct of Tr that can be imagined as a conjugate of a common reduct that incorporates necessary conflict reconciliation with Ts specifications. Finally, if required, we can justify the concretizations constructed so far by formal proofs.

Our objective is to find for each pair of ontologically relevant types Ts, Tr a maximal collection A of pairs of attributes (a_{Ts}^i, a_{Tr}^j) that are also ontologically relevant and satisfy the type constraints so that a_{Tr}^j could be reused as a_{Ts}^i.

General approach to form A for the pair of ontologically relevant types Ts and Tr is the following:

1. All ontologically relevant pairs of immediate state attributes (a_{Ts}^i, a_{Tr}^j) of the types belong to A if type of a_{Tr}^j is a subtype of type of a_{Ts}^i. This requirement can be completely checked for built-in attribute types. For the user defined types a pair of ontologically relevant attributes is conditionally included into A: final check is postponed until user defined attribute types relationship will be clarified.

2. All ontologically relevant pairs of immediate functional attributes (a_{Ts}^i, a_{Tr}^j) of the types belong to A if signatures of functions a_{Ts}^i and a_{Tr}^j satisfy the following requirements:

   a) they have equal numbers of input parameters and of output parameters pairwise ontologically relevant;

  b) for each ontologically relevant pair of input parameters their types
     should be in a contravariance relationship;
  c) for each ontologically relevant pair of output parameters their types
     should be in a covariance relationship.
3. A pair of immediate attribute a^i_{Ts} of type Ts and of immediate attribute
   $a^j_{Tr'}$ of a component type Tr belongs to A if they do not satisfy conditions
   1) or 2) above but $Ts, Tr, a^i_{Ts}, a^j_{Tr'}$ are included into reusable structures
   (paths) suggested by the reusable path detecting rules.

On analysis of attribute pairs we recognize and resolve the various conflicts
between the application and component types.

Specific attention deserves structural conflicts that are resolved in a process of reusable path detecting process. This process resembles the processes
developed for the database schema integration approaches [KF 95].

6.3 Construction of Concretizing Types and Views

The main goal of this step is to create views and concretizing types for each
application class and type. Also the additional, auxilary views and concretizing types may be created.

Briefly, the process of creating the concretizing type for an arbitrary application type is the following.

We start with constructing of a concretizing type over all or several concretizing reducts. Then we can construct the concretizing type over the concretizing types we have obtained and other concretizing reducts. And so on,
until eventually we construct the concretizing types refining analysis model
types.

The process of creating the view for arbitrary application class is the
following.

For types of instances of the application class and relevant component
classes, we construct reducts, concretizing reducts and concretizing types as
said above. Then we can construct views over the component classes with
type instances corresponding to the concretizing reducts and/or concretizing
types. We also can construct views over the views we get while we construct
view for the considered application class over all relevant component classes.

The result of this step is a set of created reducts, concretizing reducts,
concretizing types and views which will be used during the implementation
phase.

7. Ontological Relevance of Specifications

7.1 Tight Ontological Relevance

Definition 7.1. Ontological specification *is a set of definitions of
domain-specific knowledge representation primitives (concepts) for describing*

of domain vocabulary (names of individuals, functions, predicates, classes) in a form that is both human and machine readable. The specification contains also a set of rules (axioms) associated with the vocabulary or with particular terms. Ontological specifications provide a conceptual framework for talking about an application domain and an implementation framework for problem solving. Ontological specifications play the role of a coupling interfaces among components providing the basis for them to interoperate.

An ontological specification allows a specifications of requirements and a set of resources to agree on the meaning of the basic terms from which an infinite number of assertions and queries may be formulated. We treat ontological specification as a well organized colection of *concept definitions*. Concepts are composite descriptions of individuals or types defining their attributes, concept interrelationships and concept "microtheories" including constraints and functions. Types generally are used to judge as valid those expressions where a function is applied only to values in a specific domain. For the current work we apply the SYNTHESIS object model for ontological specifications. Basic decision made for such specifications is that a concept definition is modelled by a type specification. Basic interconcept specification relationships are the same as for the types, that is: subtyping and classification.

The distinguishing feature of current approach is that we emphasize domain specific ontologies (lexicons) instead of global ontologies and that we treat concepts as (meta)types (in object model) to be based on their subtyping and refinement relationships instead of stating their equivalence through articulation axioms or coordinating them through subsumption in "description logic". We provide semi-formal and formal (model-based) specifications for concepts. Treating concepts as types we can apply well established formal models, notations and tools to justify properties of individual concept specifications (e.g., consistency) and their interrelationships (based on refinement).

For portability reasons, a mapping of the SYNTHESIS ontological specifications into Ontolingua [GR92] (and back) can be provided.

Multilayer classification works well in the model: individuals, corresponding to a concept are instances of a type, concepts of the first layer are instances of the concepts (metatypes) of the next higher layer, etc. Other relationships can be based on the associated concept extents related to the real world.

The framework we use combines uniformity (one and the same set of facilities for ontological and conventional specifications) with the sound foundations.

Definition 7.2. Tight ontological relevance of specifications. *A constituent I_r of a resource specification is tightly ontologically relevant to a constituent I_s of a specification of requirements of the same kind (type, class, function, attribute, etc.) if (i) I_r is loosely ontologically relevant to I_s and (ii) I_r is an instance of at least one ontological class (metatype) C_r^o that is* *a specialization of an ontological class (metatype) C_s^o containing I_s as an instance (for such specialization C_r^o instance type should be a subtype of the C_s^o instance type) or I_s and I_r belong to one and the same ontological class (metatype).*

7.2 Loose Ontological Relevance

We emphasize also *verbal* definitions of concepts and their constituents: these are natural language definitions of terms involved into a concept definition. Such definitions are used as the primary semantic representations of the terms for further references. For instance, verbal definition provides for preliminary concept matching and establishing a similarity associations between concepts in course of the context integration. Natural language descriptions of terms reflect possible spectrum of their meaning allowing to treat them as verbally-defined notions. Based on such linguistic descriptions the associations relating terms are provided to form the primary semantic net. We assume that preparation and analysis of term descriptions is provided by experts (experienced in a particular application domain) and generally is not formal.

We assume that ontological definitions are provided for specification of requirements (collected in Application Ontology Modules – AOM), for specification of information resources (collected in Resource Ontology Modules – ROM) and for common domain-specific ontology (collected in Common Ontology Modules – COM). A collection of ontological modules of a particular level (specification of requirements or component) constitutes a definition of a context of that level. We assume that each ontology module consists of the respective concept specifications. We assume also that with each named constituent of an ontological specification or a specification itself a verbal definition of the respective constituent is associated.

In the sequel we use words "name" and "co-name" in the following meaning. Usually we use the "name" notion to denote entities (concept specifications and their constituents) appeared in the AOM or ROM (such as types, classes, metaclasses, attributes, functions, assertions). On the other hand, "co-name" is used to denote concepts constituting COMs – the common lexicon of an application domain. Such collection of co-names is considered to be application and component independent. We consider co-names of the concepts of the common lexicon for a certain application domain.

A rough scenario of ROM/AOM ontology formation is the following. First, verbal-based name associations at the specification of requirements level should be formed. All names of each AOM of the application description (including names used in the linguistic definitions of concepts) should be mapped to the co-names of the common lexicon. As the result of this mapping, a name correlation can be advised. After that proper AOM name interrelationships will be defined by the expert, new co-names may be added to the COM. Similarly verbal name associations for component specifications by the analogous mapping of the ROM names to common lexicon should be formed. Finally as the result of the expert decisions establishing correspondence between the application and information component contexts, the interrelationship of ROM to AOM names will be provided.

Thus our basic decisions concerning verbal-based concepts associations are the following:

- Each name used in the component definition or in the specification of requirements should be defined by the natural language phrase including one or more terms. In such phrases entity names or names of properties possessed by an entity or any other term characterizing the name may be used. Each co-name of COM should be also introduced linguistically to represent its real world meaning;
- Similarity functions are introduced to establish the positive associations between terms (positively linked terms are synonyms in some context, terms which are typically used in the same context, etc.). Calculation of similarity functions between terms is based on an interpretation of a verbal definition of a term by a vector of co-names. Similarity is equal to cosinus of an angle between such vectors [1];
- Name interrelationships are established as the result of expert decisions that may be based on the estimation of name/co-name correlations.

Definition 7.3. Loose ontological relevance of specifications. *A constituent I_r of a component specification is loosely ontologically relevant to a constituent I_s of a specification of requirements of the same kind (type, class, function, attribute, etc.) if I_r name has a positive association to I_s name or if I_r name is a hyponym of I_s name.*

A prototype of component-based information systems design method according to the approach sketched in sections 4 - 7 is under development now.

8. A Uniform Script–Based Multiactivity Framework

A workflow is a collection of activities (assigned to human or automated actors) that are automatically managed by a workflow management system. Workflows can be related to parts of a business process or other organizational procedures. A workflow consists of segments (sub-workflows) that can be decomposed further.

Introducing a script-based workflow specification framework, we prefer to use term 'multiactivity' (instead of workflow) focusing on language and modeling facilities for representation of internal view of workflows: their external appearance (graphical representations, human participant-oriented tools, etc.) will not be our concern here. We consider long-lived, collaborated multiactivities as multilevel collections of interrelated activities. An activity is a

---

[1] Basic ideas of these calculations belong to G.Salton.

description of a piece of work that forms one logical step within a process. An activity may be a manual activity, which does not support computer automation, or an automated activity.

A multiactivity is seen as a pattern of actions with their temporal ordering, control and data flow relationships. We present here the script-based multiactivity framework as it is incorporated into the SYNTHESIS language [KA 95].

8.1 An Overview of the Relevant SYNTHESIS Language Features

Here only a few SYNTHESIS language features are briefly presented that are necessary to make further examples readable. The declaration of any entity (including the entities of the language itself, such as types, classes, functions, assertions) is given in the SYNTHESIS language by means of a *frame*. Generally frame may be considered as a structured symbolic model of some entity or of some concept used to represent such individuals. Syntactically a frame is always represented in brackets { and }. The slot names and their values are separated by a colon. The values of a slot are separated by commas. Atomic value, frame, collection of formulae of object calculus, set of values may be used as slot values. Different slots in a frame are separated by semicolons.

Each frame may be declared to belong to some class. After such declaration the frame becomes an object (an instance of the class (classes) mentioned). Such class membership is given by a slot in :< class name list > .

Syntactically each functional attribute of a type is defined by declaration of a function:

< function declaration >::= {< function identifier >;
            in : function; [params : {< formal parameter list >};]
            [< specification >]}
< formal parameter identifier >::=< parameter sort symbol >< typed variable >
::= −| + | < empty >
< typed variable >::=< variable > [/ < type qualifier >]
< type qualifier >::=< type name > | < class name > | < attribute name >

The meaning of a parameter sort symbol:

+ input parameter; - output parameter; < empty > input & output parameter.

8.2 Script Types

Here we concentrate on the basic facilities for the definition of concurrent and asynchronous behaviour of HIRE as a dynamic system. *Scripts* are used for description of long-running multiactivities (workflows, transactions) in terms of sequences of activities and dataflows leading to changes of states of the information resources included into HIRE. Our script model is based on high level Petri nets [JE 91]. Scripts are defined as types that may be organized into the subtyping hierarchy. Each instance of a script type corresponds to a particular activation of a multiactivity (transaction) defined by a script type. As an object, such instance is characterized by an object identifier and a collection of script attributes.

< script type specification >::=
        {< type identifier >; in : script;
        [params : {< formal parameter list >};]
        [supertype :< supertype name list >;]
        instance_section : {[< attribute specification list >;]
        [initial :< initial marking >;]
        states :< state section >;
        [gates :< state section >;]
        [transitions :< transition section >;]}}

Mechanisms of scripts are quite different from behavioural model of objects based on the message passing and method call. Like a Petri net, a script models the dynamic system behaviour in terms of states (or places) and transitions. As usual, a net is represented by a bipartite directed graph arcs of which connect nodes taken from two sets: a set of states and a set of transitions. In the desription of a transition arcs are defined by the lists of input (from) and output (to) state names of the transition. Script dynamics are modelled by *tokens* that are produced in the initial states of a script on its creation, in the output states of transitions or are coming to the external states of a script from the outside. In one script instance a number of tokens of different types can coexist. The states are places where collections of tokens can be accumulated to wait for appropriate conditions to enter transitions. The tokens are typed (as in the coloured Petri nets [JE 91]). Token type for a state is given by the phrase token or may be assumed by default. Token identifier can be used in the script assertions and conditions.

< transition section >::=< transition specification > |
        < transition specification >, < transition section >
< transition specification >::=
        {[< transition name >;]
        from :< list of input state names >; [bind_from :< binding list >;]
        to :< list of output state names >; [bind_to :< binding list >;]
        [conditions :< assertion list >;]
        activity :< function declaration >}

A state (place) description of a script can include a definition of assertions that should be satisfied in order that a token which is placed into the state could be activated.

< state section >::=< state specification > |
        < state specification >, < state section >
< state specification >::=

```
{< state name >;
[token : {< identifier >:< type >; }]
[assertions : {< assertion list >}]}
```

A description of each transition may include a list of transition conditions that should be simultaneously satisfied in order that a transition could be fired and a description of activities that should be taken on such firing. Syntactically transition activities are prescribed by function declarations given inside of the transition specification in the activity slot. In particular, an activity may lead to the call of a transaction (a multiactivity) that may conform to various transaction (multiactivity) models. Types of input tokens that may be moved into a transition from its input states is determined by input parameters of the function prescribing the transition activity. The output parameters of the function determine output tokens that will be moved out of a transition after the activity execution. Transition activities can create sets (of tokens) defined on the types of output parameters of activities. Actions may have no parameters. In such cases tokens (input and/or output) have type Tnone. Type of ingoing to a state tokens should coincide or should be a subtype of the token type defined for the state. Types of input tokens of a transition should coincide or be the subtypes of the types of the corresponding input parameters of the transition activity.

On definition of a transition the rules for binding its input and output may be given.

```
< element of binding list >::=
            {< state identifier > [, < input/output parameter name >
            [, < factor >][, < condition >]}
< factor >::=< variable > | < integer >
```

Input (output) binding rules provide for establishing of the correspondence of tokens ingoing from (outgoing to) the defined states to input (output) parameters of the transition activity. Binding rules make possible to declare logical conditions that tokens ingoing from (outgoing to) the defined states should satisfy and (or) to declare a number of tokens that should be consumed (produced) on the input (output) of the transition. On default this number is equal to one.

In each of the input states of a transition tokens can be accumulated and are considered in FIFO (or priority-based) order. A collection of active tokens taken from all of the input states (selected in the given order in quantity established for each input state) should be considered together to fire the transition. If the transition fires, all tokens of this collection are removed from the input states. If several transitions are conflicting for consuming of the same tokens for the transitions to be fired, nondeterministic choice of the transition is made.

The actions on transition firing consist in a call for a transition activity with actual parameters defined by the tokens entering the transition according to the input binding rules. As the result, the tokens with the types determined by the output parameters of the activity will be produced. If an activity has no output parameters, an empty token will be formed. The tokens satisfying output binding rules produced in the defined quantities will be directed to each state given by the list of the output states **to** of the transition.

In assertions declared for a state the variables referring to the token attributes may also be used together with variables denoting arbitrary information resources and script attributes.

In a script external states can be specified to place tokens directed from other scripts or from objects. External *incoming* and *outgoing* states of a script are declared differently. For declaration of an *external incoming state* functional attribute of a script should be defined. Names of these functions should coincide with names of states considered due to such definition to be external. Input parameter of these function define a type of an external token (or a message) that could be directed to this state from another script or from an object. For that in a **to** list of a transition references to external states of another scripts (through **gates**) are allowed. Such names may be qualified by a script class name. Placing of a token (message) into an external incoming state is a result of a corresponding method call that will be associated with a script as an object. External outgoing states are declared in a state section as **gates**. For external outgoing states assertions should not be given. In transitions names of external outgoing states may be qualified by variables referencing proper instance of a script containing respective ingoing states.

Using **initial** it is possible to define initial marking of a script by declaring constants (denoting tokens) that should be placed in the defined states on a script creation.

< element of initial marking list >::=
$\qquad$ {< state identifier > [, < factor >][, < constant >]}

Hierarchical scripts in which a transition may be substituted by the whole (child) script can be defined. The parameters of the child script may include input and output states of the transition that should be substituted as actual states. In the activity of a transition to be substituted instead of the function declaration the child script can be referred as follows.

< child script >::= {< script identifier >;
$\qquad$ in : script; [params : {< formal parameter list >};]

Type **state** may be used for typing of formal parameters of a transition and of a child script. An example of a hierarchical script definition follows.

{*trscript;*
in: script;
states:

```
        {s1; ...}; {s2; ...};
transitions:
        {A;
          from: s2; to: s1;
          activity: {subscript1; in:script; params: {s2, s1 } }
        },
        {B;
          from: s1; to: s2;
          activity: ...
        };
};
{subscript1;
in: script;
params: {sp1/state, sp2/state};
states: {ss1; ...}, {ss2; ...}, {ss3; ...};
transitions:
        {P;
          from: ss2; to: ss1;
          activity: ...
        },
        {Q;
          from: ss1; to: ss3, sp2;
          activity: {subscript2; in: script; params: {ss1, ss3, sp2 }}
        },
        {R;
          from: ss3, sp1; to: ss2;
          activity: ...
        }
};
{subscript2;
in: script;
params: {ps1/state, ps2/state, ps3/state };
states: {sss1; ...};
transitions:
        {U;
          from: ps1; to: sss1, ps2;
          activity: ...
        },
        {V;
          from: sss1; to: ps3;
          activity: ...
        }
}
```

Specification of the script components as a coloured Petri net is given in Appendix A.. How to get to multiactivity (multitransaction) specificatons, declarative multi-resource constraint specifications and multi-resource inter-operation programming using scripts is analyzed in [KD 93, K 93].

8.3 Capabilities of the Canonical Model

In this subsection we refer to important capabilities of the canonical model that were experimentally checked.

8.3.1 Capturing of structural aspects of multiactivity modeling.

The hierarchical script technique appeared to be useful for specification of various kinds of multiactivities (multitransactions) emphasizing their specific types of activity dependencies. *Multiactivity modeling* considering long-running application processes (*workflows*) with complex patterns of temporal, sequential, causal and other interactivity interdependencies were discussed elsewhere [DHL 91, Elm 92, LI 92]. Most often hierarchically - structured multitransactions (multiactivities) could be specified with various relationships between a parent and different child constituents. Child constituents may have different dependencies with their parents if the transaction model supports various spawning or coupling models.

First-order logic based formalism declaratively specifying component transaction and related objects dependencies that should be preserved was experienced in [CR 91]. Thus intercomponent structural dependencies were declaratively specified. In [NZ 92] *operation machines* were introduced as the user definable synchronization mechanisms for specifying patterns and conflicts reflecting cooperative transaction structural dependencies. An operation machine is presented as the finite state automata. To cope with the proper procedural control of the structural dependencies, dependency finite states automata were introduced [Att 93]. Transaction Specification and Management Environment (TSME) [GHKM 94] is proposed as a facility to support the definition and construction of specific extended transaction models corresponding to application requirements.

In [KH 94] we showed how to use the canonical script model for capturing of structural aspects of the multiactivity modeling. The idea consisted in localization of structural interactivity dependencies of multiactivities (such as introduced in [CR 91]) in the concept of Generic Intercomponent Control Modules (GICM) capturing semantics of the related multiactivity (multi-transaction) models. GICM accumulates facilities for proper interpretation of significant events establishing *interactivity dependencies* for a specific multi-activity model. An activity is conveniently represented by hierarchical scripts [KA 95] where the specific structuring features of a particular multiactivity are reflected in the child scripts generated from the generic GICM script once designed for each specific multiactivity model. Such generic localization leads to the possibility of specification and generation of multiactivities (multitransactions) possessing necessary application (implementation) structural properties. Application of this approach to the sequential SAGA model and to the closed nested transaction model was shown in [KH 94] where examples of generic GICM scripts for such models were constructed.

GICM were incorporated as junctions between process "chunks" into a *chunk* multiactivity model [KH 94]. *Chunk* is a code of a piece of an activity between "significant events" (such as termination of the current activity, spawning of another (child or the same level) activity or chunk, aborting of the current or a child activity). On such call/return events (controlled by *chunk junction*) specific control depending on the multiactivity model may be applied. We assume that the definition of the chunk interface and dynamic chunk call are available. So, component multiactivity is abstracted as a sequence of chunks with significant events in between. Compensating chunk (*cochunk*) having a specific role of providing of compensating activity for the corresponding chunk that might have commited before committing of the whole multiactivity or of the parent chunk was also introduced.

Thus common features of the multiactivity (multitransaction) model and activity dependencies can be explicitly and generically intro- duced using the hierarchical script facility including such dependen- cies as commit-dependency, abort-dependency, weak-abort-dependency, termination-dependency, exclusion-dependency, compensation-dependency, begin-dependency, serial-dependency [CR 91], etc.

The variety of activity relationships in the multiactivity model expressed by the generic junction script may include also execution order, executional conflicts, causal dependencies, mutual exclusion, etc. Specific interactivity de- pendencies (e.g., serial dependency, termination dependency, exclusive depen- dency, conflicting dependency, causal dependency, etc.) may be introduced using script-based facilities.

Analogously the correctness properties of different multiactivity models are expressible in terms of such types of constraints as: 1) an activity A can occur only after another activity B; 2) an activity A can occur only if certain condition is satisfied (a necessary condition for the activity); 3) reaching of a condition requires the occurence of an activity A (a sufficient condition for the activity).

A library of various generic junction scripts (GICMs) corresponding to different multiactivity (multitransaction) models may constitute the core of the generator of specific multiactivities (multitransactions) belonging to con- crete models.

Chunk model provides also for decomposition of the multiactivity con- cretization problem into subproblems for which the conventional refinement methodology could become applicable. Such decomposition is based on the following principles:

– isolation of the pure functional kind behaviour of the concurrent kind;
– structural localization of concurrency control in GICM (junctions);

– multiactivity specification abstraction of particular concurrency model. The specification can be made free of unnecessary concurrency details (imposed by efficiency, reliability and implementation constraints).

Application of these principles leads to the following general framework suitable for the multiactivity concretization:

1. treatment of chunks as pure functional behaviour refining them using conventional refinement technique. In particular, this leads to a possibility of reuse of the pre-existing (atomic) transactions as chunks;
2. aggregation of chunks linked by junctions having no specific concurrency requirements;
3. treating separately stepwise concretization of junctions with a specific concurrency requirement.

8.3.2 Homogenizing specification of a dynamic behaviour in HIRE. One and the same set of a canonical script model features appeared to be sufficient for (i) the declarative specification of multitransaction (multiactivity), (ii) interresource constraints support as well as (iii) for the support of an executable level of heterogeneous multi-resource interoperation [KD 93]. Related researches for such specifications include areas of active databases, declarative specification of interdatabase constraints [SR 92], multiactivity and multitransaction models [DHL 91, Elm 92], flexible transaction specification and execution, multi-resource execution environment [RO 90], workflow management systems [MSKW 96].

Multiactivity (multitransaction) specification. Capabilities of the canonical model were demonstrated specifying the termination dependency in a multitransaction. Most transaction models use commitment protocols to assure that all subtransactions constituting a top transaction are either committed or aborted. Typically they assume the existence of a prepared to commit state. A subtransaction which finished all its operations can wait in this state for a commit or abort signal from global transaction manager. However, some DBMSs do not offer a visible prepare to commit state. Execution of noncompensable subtransaction in such a DBMS can violate the consistency of the system. In such cases we can execute compensable subtransactions with the understanding that they will be compensated when a top transaction aborts. Specifications of both cases were experienced.

Declarative information resource constraint specifications. For concreteness a specification of *polytransaction* model has been experienced. Polytransaction model [SR 92] was introduced for maintaining consistency among interdependent data stored in multiple database systems. An important feature of the model is that the declarative definitions of mutual consistency requirement can be used to generate a set of related transactions that manage interdependent data. The constraints are separated from the application programs to facilitate the maintenance of data consistency requirements and flexibility of their implementation.

Multi-resource interoperation programming. There are several options of interfacing with autonomous systems representing the information resources in HIRE. Such systems may be encapsulated preserving their functionality, transformed to the canonical, homogeneous model of the HIRE (defined in our case by the SYNTHESIS language) or allowed to be used directly according to their predefined native interfaces. The HIRE architecture should be flexible enough to support different variants that may be chosen to gain efficiency or convenience of attaching of new systems. Here we shall focus on the form of the executable interoperation expressions that may be considered as an object code produced by the query, constraint or function (transaction) compilers. This form should include the definition of tasks for autonomous software systems involved (in their native languages, if required), definition of data and control flow between such tasks, definiton of the higher level operations making proper merging or combining of the partial autonomous results to express the semantics of a particular query (assertion) or to support the execution of a function, a multitransaction or its part. Any software system may be incorporated into HIRE as a *service* by providing it with a specially written local agent preserving the autonomy of the software system. Such agent may have a form of an encapsulator, of a transformer, or of an interface preserving commands of the system. Scripts are convenient to specify multiactivities associated with a distributed application over autonomous software systems, the sequence of activities, the execution status dependencies, data paths reaching the maximum allowed degree of concurrency.

8.4 An Example of a Funding Agency Multiactivity Specification

For a specific example we take an application dealing with the management of research funding. We imagine a centralized Agency managing funds dedicated to research and development projects. A research consortium submits a proposal to the Agency to get a grant. Here we focus on an Agency activity related to decision making concerning proposals acceptance/rejection. First, we provide a specification of the required Agency activity using scripts. We assume that developing the workflow, pre-existing information systems dealing with proposal selection activities will be taken into consideration in an attempt of reusing their implementations.

   To improve readability, we provide a picture (Fig. 2) of the following script specifying the required Agency workflow. On the picture the names of the script transition activities are shown.

   In the script specification the application semantics of transitions are provided by comments included after each transition definition. Comments are represented also by frames starting with a key word 'comment'.

```
{agency_workflow;
in: script;
instance_section:
```

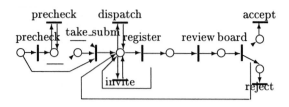

Fig. 2. Agency workflow net

{

states:

{new_prop; token: {npt: Proposal}},
{next_check; token: {nct: Proposal}},
{checked; token: {cht: Proposal}},
{assign_experts; token: {aet: Review}},
{pre_rev; token: {prt: Review}},
{post_rev; token: {art: Review}},
{for_accept; token:{fat: Review}},
{for_reject: {frt: Review}};

{comment; We assume that the mutable types **Proposal** and **Review** are defined elsewhere. The type **Review** is a subtype of the **Proposal** type. Note, please, that tokens used by the script obtain the **Proposal** or the **Review** type. }

transitions:

{

   from: new_prop;
   bind_from:
    {new_prop, Proposal.leader.works_for <> 'Academy' };
   to: next_check, checked;
   bind_to:
    {next_check, Proposal.checked = F},
    {checked, Proposal.checked = T };
   activity: {precheck; in: script;
    params: {sb/Proposal }}

},

{comment; The precheck activity assures that a submitted proposal contains all formally required information. This activity assumes a correction iteration with the authors (if required). Proposal.checked reflects whether a preliminary check (precheck) for a proposal had been completed. If after the iteration the check is positive, Proposal.checked is set to T otherwise to F. Proposals coming from the Institutes of the Academy of Sciences do not need prechecks.

```
}
{
            from: next_check;
            bind_from:
                {next_check, Proposal.checked = F };
            to: next_check;
            activity: {precheck; in: script;
                params: {sb/Proposal}}
},
```

{comment; Here a "loop" of prechecks is planned to make a proposal formally clean. }

```
{
            from: new_prop, next_check, checked;
            bind_from:
                {new_prop, Proposal.leader.works_for = 'Academy' },
                {next_check, Proposal.checked = T };
            to: assign_experts;
            activity: {take_subm; in: script;
                params: {+sb/Proposal, -rev/Review }}
},
```

{ comment; The Review type as a subtype of the Proposal type adds to the Proposal type an attribute defined as an array of expertises nominated to different experts. Preparation of expertises includes nomination of experts (the process of nomination is reflected by marking in the expertise data the current experts' reachability (Review.Expertise[i].reach) and their agreement to take responsibility for an expertise (Review.Expertise[i].taken). The take_subm activity forms an instance of the Review type. On creation of the instance, values of the mentioned attributes are set to Null. Review.expnumb contains actual number of experts nominated for reviewing of a proposal. On creation of a Review instance, this value is set to 0). }

```
{
            from: assign_experts;
            bind_from:
                {assign_expert, Review.expnumb = 0 or
                Review.Expertise[Review.expnumb].reach = F or
                (Review.Expertise[Review.expnumb].reach = T &
                Review.Expertise[Review.expnumb].taken = F)
    };
            to: assign_experts;
            activity: {dispatch; in: script;
            params:{rev/Review}}
},
```

{comment;   The   dispatch   activity   tries   to   nominate   next   expert
candidate   and   checks   whether   he/she   is   reachable.   Returns   Re-
view.Expertise[Review.expnumb]. reach = F if the expert is not reachable. If
an expert is a "staff" expert he need not be invited and can be nominated by
dispatch. In this case Review.Expertise[Review.expnumb].taken gets T value. }

{
          from: assign_experts;
          bind_from:
              {assign_expert, Review.expnumb <> 0 &
              (Review.Expertise[Review.expnumb].reach = T &
              Review.Expertise[Review.expnumb].taken = Null) };
          to: assign_experts;
          activity: {invite; in: script;
          params:{rev/Review}}
},

{comment; The invite activity communicates with the next expert candidate
and checks whether he/she agrees to provide an expertise for this particular
proposal. The activity finally sets Review.Expertise[Review.expnumb].taken =
F or T depending on the expert's decision. }

{
          from: assign_experts;
          bind_from:
              {assign_expert, Review.expnumb <> 0 &
              (Review.Expertise[Review.expnumb].reach = T &
              Review.Expertise[Review.expnumb].taken = T) };
          to: assign_experts, pre_rev;
          bind_to:
              {assign_expert, Review.expnumb < K },
              {pre_rev, Review.expnumb = K };
          activity: {register; in: function;
              params: {rev/Review}}
},

{comment; The register activity finalizes registering of the next expert for
the proposal. }

{
          from: pre_rev;
          to: post_rev;
          activity: {review; in: script;
              params:{rev/Review}}
},

{comment; The review activity provides reviewing of a proposal by the nominated experts. }

```
{
            from: post_rev;
            to: for_accept, for_reject, assign_experts;
            bind_to:
                  {assign_experts, return = 'additional_expertize' },
                  {for_accept, return = 'accept' },
                  {for_reject, return = 'reject' };
            activity: {board; in: script;
                  params:{rev/Review, -return/string }}
}
```

{comment; The Agency board makes a decision concerning acceptance or rejection of a proposal, or in complicated cases, assigns a new reviewing process. }

```
{
            from: for_accept;
            to: :
            activity: {accept; in: function;
                  params:{rev/Review }}
},
{
            from: for_reject;
            to: :
            activity: {reject; in: function;
                  params:{rev/Review }}
}
```

{comment; The accept and reject activities provide the required notification of the authors. }

```
}};
```

The definition of the script above provides a specification of the required Agency workflow.

8.5 Pre-existing Workflow Specifications

We assume that there exists already an information system developed for the Industrial Labs providing an expertise for their projects. We assume that two different workflow management systems – FlowMark and Staffware [IBM 94, SWare 95] are used to manage (i) collecting submissions and reviewers nomination and (ii) reviewing process and submission acceptance decision respectively. These two workflows may interoperate if during the acceptance procedure an additional expertize is required.

To simplify an example we assume that names of activities and variables in conditions in FlowMark and Staffware diagrams coincide with the names of analogous activities of the Agency workflow specification. In reality such

474   Leonid Kalinichenko

name correlation appears as the result of ontological analysis and reconciliation.

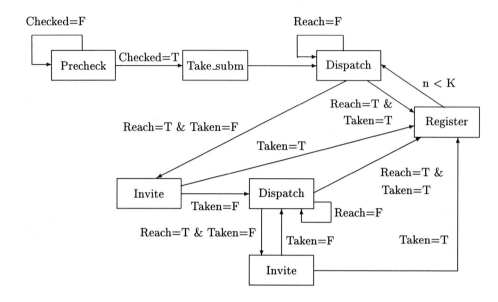

Fig. 3. FlowMark process diagram

On Fig. 3 we show a control flow in the FlowMark process specification (preliminary details on FlowMark can be found in Appendix C.). We represent a FlowMark activity by a rectangle. We show only control connectors assuming that data go the same routes. In this example we assume that start condition of each activity evaluates to true if at least one of the incoming connectors evaluates to true.

Applying mapping of the FlowMark diagram into the canonical workflow model according to the rules defined in Appendix C. and making obvious glueing of states, we get a script definition the "skeleton" of which looks as follows (Fig. 4).

On Fig. 5 we show a control flow in the Staffware procedure specification (preliminary details on Staffware can be found in Appendix B.). We represent a Staffware step by a rectangle. We use only normal and automatic steps here and horizontal lines connecting them. New activity names (**patrev** and **econrev**) mean patent and economy expertize.

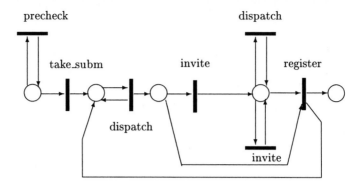

Fig. 4. Canonical FlowMark process representation

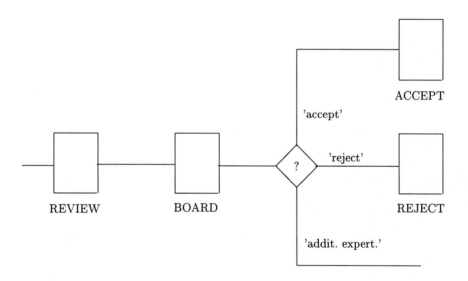

Fig. 5. Staffware procedure diagram

Applying mapping of the Staffware diagram into the canonical workflow model according to the rules defined in Appendix B., we get a script definition the "skeleton" of which looks as follows (Fig. 6).

To save space we do not include a specification of the complete scripts defining the Industrial Labs workflows.

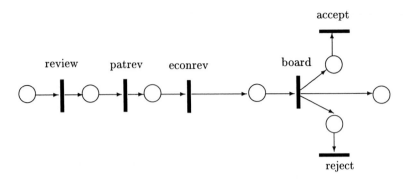

Fig. 6. Canonical Staffware procedure representation

Further part of the paper shows how we can decide that the Industrial Labs script can be reused to implement the Agency script.

9. Workflow Design with Reuse

It has been already noted that in the SYNTHESIS framework scripts are used for specification of multiactivities of the designed information system and of the pre-existing resources. The objectives of the specifications include: concretization of multiactivities by pre-existing resource dynamics, checking of consistency of specifications (such as deadlocks and reachability of a certain state), multiactivity specification with certain dynamic interdependencies between activities, checking of the multiactivity consistency constraints and correctness dependencies. These specimens of the design procedures demonstrate the level of semantic interoperation reasoning necessary to deal with the information system dynamics. Here we continue to focus on the issues of the multiactivity specification refinement, specifically how to decide whether the pre-existing dynamics (expressed by scripts) can be reused for a certain specification of a workflow under design.

It is clear that scripts are too complicated constructs to analyse them as a whole. Here we present an approach of getting a behavioural abstraction of a script as patterns of actions that are implied by its specification (a Petri net). Our intention is to treat such patterns as processes in a particular process algebra. First we introduce a specific process algebra that we shall use further in our analysis.

9.1 An Introduction into the Basic Process Algebra with Iteration

The process algebra [BW 90] is an algebraic theory for the description of process behaviour. This algebraic theory is given by a signature defining the processes and a set of equations (axioms) defining the equality relations on these processes. The notion of a process applying the operational semantics is based on the notion of a *transition system* that can be defined as a tuple $< S, L, T, s >$ where

  S is a set of states,
  L is a set of labels,
  $T \subseteq (S \times L \times S)$ is a transition relation,
  $s \in S$ is the initial state.

The signature Σ of a process algebra specifies the constants and function symbols that may be used in describing processes. Also variables from a set V may be used to define a process.

Let Σ be a signature and V a set of variables. Terms over signature Σ are defined as:

  $v \in V$ is a term,
  if $c \in \Sigma$ is a constant symbol, then c is a term,
  if $f \in \Sigma$ is an n-ary function symbol and $t_1, \ldots, t_n$ are terms then $f(t_1, \ldots, t_n)$ is a term.

The set of all terms over a signature Σ is denoted by $\Upsilon(\Sigma, V)$. The set of all ground terms (terms not containing variables) is denoted by $\Upsilon(\Sigma)$. For constants of the process algebra we will use a finite set A of atomic activities $a, b, \ldots$ and specific constants such as ε denoting an *empty activity* (or *skip*) and $\sqrt{}$ (pronounce as 'tick') denoting successful termination of a process. The atomic activities are taken as labels in the definition of a transition system above.

Let Ω denotes a process algebra axiom system. We denote by $\Psi(\Omega)$ a class of processes evolving over Ω and containing A as elementary processes. For the set S of states in the definition of a transition system we use $\Psi(Omega)$. Then for $a \in A$ a transition $p \overset{a}{\longrightarrow} p'$ expresses that by executing a the process p evolves into p'. p' represents the remainder of p to be executed. The transition $p \overset{a}{\longrightarrow} \sqrt{}$ expresses that the process p can terminate successfully after executing a. The transition relation T can be defined by rules that should be admissible in frame of Ω. Functional terms in Σ are constructed using operators of a particular algebra. Processes can be specified using algebraic expressions over Σ and V.

To reason of a possibility of reusing one process specification for another, they are compared on the basis of *bisimulation equivalence* [PA 81].

Definition 9.1. *Two process terms are* bisimilar *if they have the same branching structure.*

More formally, two processes $p, q \in \Psi(\Omega)$ are bisimilar (this fact is denoted by $p \leftrightarrow q$) if there exists a binary, symmetric relation R between processes such that:

1. $R(p, q)$
2. *if $R(p', q')$ and $p' \xrightarrow{a} p''$ then there is a transition $q' \xrightarrow{a} q''$ such that $R(p'', q'')$*
3. *if $R(p', q')$ and $p' \xrightarrow{a} \sqrt{}$, then $q' \xrightarrow{a} \sqrt{}$*

Bisimulation equivalence is a congruence relation with respect to all operators of a process algebra defined. Axiomatization of an algebra should be sound with respect to bisimulation equivalence. It means that equality of process terms in an axiom $(p = q)$ implies $p \leftrightarrow q$. In well-defined algebras Ω is a complete axiomatization with respect to bisimulation equivalence, i.e., if $p \leftrightarrow q$ then $p = q$.

For our purpose we fix here a basic process algebra with iteration as it is defined in [FZ 94]. BPA^* contains the following binary operators. The binary operators $+$ and $\cdot$ are called the alternative and sequential composition. The alternative composition of the processes p and q is the process that either executes process p or process q but not both. The sequential composition of the processes p and q is the process that first executes process p and upon completion thereof starts with the execution of process q.

For the iteration the binary Kleene operator x^*y is used that is understood as $y + x(x^*y)$ [KL 56]. In expressions $\cdot$ will often be omitted, so pq denotes the same as $p \cdot q$. As binding conventions, $*$ binds stronger than $\cdot$, which in turn binds stronger than $+$.

Table 1 contains complete axiomatization for BPA^* [FZ 94]. We shall use the terms equality defined by the axioms to deduce terms bisimulation and therefore to deduce that we can substitute a term (actually, a script) instead of another term or a script.

Table 1. The axiom systems BPA^*

(A1)	$x + y$	$=$	$y + x$
(A2)	$x + (y + z)$	$=$	$(x + y) + z$
(A3)	$x + x$	$=$	x
(A4)	$(x + y)z$	$=$	$xz + yz$
(A5)	$(xy)z$	$=$	$x(yz)$
(A6)	$x \cdot (x^*) + y$	$=$	x^*y
(A7)	$x^*(y \cdot z)$	$=$	$(x^*y) \cdot z$
(A8)	$x^*(y \cdot ((x + y)^*) + z)$	$=$	$(x + y)^*z$
(A9)	$x \cdot \varepsilon$	$=$	x
(A10)	$\varepsilon \cdot x$	$=$	x

9.2 Script Processes

We restrict ourselves here with the consideration of deterministic processes [H 85] such that the behaviour of a process on its first $n+1$ steps is determined by the behaviour of the process on its first n steps only. Another restriction comes out of a class of script behaviour patterns representable by the terms of BPA^*.

In BPA^* a script type will be abstracted as a pair $< \alpha, t >$ where:

- α is the set of the atomic activities which are relevant for a script type;
- e is a process algebra expression composed of algebraic operators and atomic activities to abstract the script type behaviour (denoting all legal script firing sequences).

For a set of atomic activities of a script type (constants of a process algebra) we shall use a set of names of activities defined in transitions of a script assuming that such names are unique. We say that this set (α) forms an *alphabet* of a script type.

A *script language* Λ is formed by the set of all firing sequences (denoted by sequences of a script alphabet tokens). We abstract Λ as a class of processes $\Psi(\Omega)$ evolving over an axiom system of BPA^*.

Selectors for a script type $N = < \alpha, e >$ include:

- $S_a(N) = \alpha$ (a set of activity types);
- $S_e(N) = e$ (a process algebra expression over α and Ω).

Projection of a process algebra expression e to a script alphabet B is defined as $e \backslash B$ that is equal to e with replacing of all activity types in e not belonging to alphabet B by ε (an empty activity).

9.3 Refinement of Scripts

Script Q refines script N iff (we refer here to the definition of the script type given in Appendix A.):

1. $S_a(N) \subseteq S_a(Q)$;
2. $S_e(N) = S_e(Q) \setminus S_a(N)$ that is process algebra abstractions of N and of a reduction of Q to N are bisimulation equivalent;
3. Each transition t_Q whose activity is included into the projection $S_e(Q) \setminus S_a(N)$ should be in one-to-one correspondence with a transition t_N in N. Each such pair (t_Q, t_N) should satisfy the following condition. Input places of t_Q should be in one-to-one correspondence with the input places of t_N. For output places of the pair (t_Q, t_N) it is required that to each output place of t_N an output place of t_Q should correspond. Corresponding places (p_N, p_Q) should be such that a type of a token $C(p_Q)$ should be a subtype of $C(p_N)$ and $Ap(p_Q)$ should logically imply $Ap(p_N)$. $F(t_Q)$

should be a refinement of $F(t_N)$ and $G(t_N)$ should logically imply $G(t_Q)$ for each pair of corresponding transitions (t_N, t_Q).

All places of Q corresponding to input and output places of N should be declared as respective ports in Q (incoming places or outgoing places (gates) respectively). For each pair of input places a token type of Q place should be a supertype of a token type of the corresponding N place. For each pair of output places a token type of Q place should be a subtype of a token type of the corresponding N place. For each pair of places an initialization of a place in Q should be a refinement of the initialization of the respective place in N.

4. For corresponding pairs of transitions their ingoing and outgoing correlated arcs (a_N, a_Q) (their relationship is established by the correlation of input and output places of the transition pair) should satisfy the condition that $E(a_Q)$ should be a refinement of $E(a_N)$. It means that $E(a_Q).Par$ type should be a subtype of $E(a_N).Par$, $E(a_Q).Oce$ should logically imply $E(a_N).Oce$ and $E(a_N).Z = E(a_Q).Z$.

5. Initial marking M_Q of Q should refine an initial marking M_N of N so that for the corresponding pairs of places (p_N, p_Q), $M_Q(p_Q)$ should be a refinement of $M_N(p_N)$.

Definition 9.2. *Script type Q is a subtype of script type N iff Q refines N.[2].*

9.4 Script Type Reducts

We define a basic operation of a script type specification decomposition — getting of a *script type reduct*.

We define a script type reduct analogously to type reduct assuming that ingoing places may stand for 'operations' of a script. Again, an extension A_V of a script type V elements of which denote "proxies" of instances of the script type is one of the carriers of the respective algebraic system U.

Definition 9.3. Script type reduct *A reduct R_V of a script type V is defined as a subspecification of V such that V is a script subtype of R_V. Set of all incoming and outgoing places of R_V should be included into the set of all incoming and outgoing places of V.*

Decomposing a script specification, we can get its different reducts on the basis of various script specification subsignatures. Script reducts create a basis for their further compositions.

Definition 9.4. *A common script reduct for script types V_1, V_2 is such script reduct R_{V_1} of V_1 that there exists a script reduct R_{V_2} of V_2 such that R_{V_2} is a*

---

[2] Note, that if it is required that an entity should refine another entity, it means that we should apply for them the refining procedure – conventional (for functions and types) or that of the above for scripts.

refinement of R_{V_1}. *Further we refer to* R_{V_2} *as to a* conjugate *of the common script reduct.*

Definition 9.5. *A* most common script reduct $R_{MC}(V_1, V_2)$ *for script types* V_1, V_2 *is a script reduct* R_{V_1} *of* V_1 *such that there exists a script reduct* R_{V_2} *of* V_2 *that refines* R_{V_1} *and there can be no other script reduct* $R_{V_1}^i$ *such that* $R_{MC}(V_1, V_2)$ *is a script reduct of* $R_{V_1}^i$, $R_{V_1}^i$ *is not equal to* $R_{MC}(V_1, V_2)$ *and there exists a script reduct* $R_{V_2}^i$ *of* V_2 *that refines* $R_{V_1}^i$.

The notion of a script reduct is fundamental for the component-based workflow design: it constitutes a basis for determining reusable fragments. The process of searching for such fragments and most common script reduct formation will be considered further.

9.5 Process of a Script Design with Reuse

Definition 9.6. *A* conformance association *between script types* V_1, V_2 *holds (we say "V_2 conforms to V_1") iff there exists a common script reduct of* V_1 *and* V_2.

For a collection of script types T we define a *conformance of a script type* V as a sub-collection of types $S = \{t_1, t_2, ..., t_n\}$ in T such that any script type t_i in t conforms to S.

The conformance of V characterizes a reuse perspective for a script type V. Alongside with such reduct-based conformances that are not easy to detect, we provide also a notion of *ontological conformance of a script type* V as a sub-collection of script types $S = \{t_1, t_2, ..., t_n\}$ in T such that any type t_i in S is ontologically relevant to V. Loose and tight ontological conformances of types are distinguished. We can speak also of ontological conformances of constituents of script type specifications (such as places, transitions, gates etc.).

Thus we rely on a range of conformances starting with a loose ontological conformance and ending with a conformance based on the most common reduct of script types.

In a script design phase we distinguish between the following basic steps:

1. Establishing ontological conformances for each constituent of the analysis model
   On this step for each constituent Con_s of the analysis model we get a collection $Scon_r$ of constituents of the component specifications of the same kind that are ontologically relevant to Con_s. Loose and/or tight ontological relevance is established.
2. Common reducts identification and construction
   For each pair of script type specifications t_s and t_r (each t_r should belong to ontological conformance of t_s) we try to construct their common reduct. We start with identification of their *common signature reduct*.

This procedure takes into account only signatures of script types ignoring their complete specifications. After that most common reducts are constructed. This makes possible to identify the maximal reduct of t_s and the respective concretization reduct of t_r.

3. Construction of hierarchical compositions of scripts

We focus first on the most common reducts identification for type t_s and its ontologically conformant type t_r.

Our objective is to find for each pair of ontologically conformant script types t_s, t_r a maximal collection A of pairs of constituents $(at_s{}^i, at_r{}^j)$ that are also ontologically relevant and satisfy preliminary constraints such that $at_r{}^j$ could be reused as $at_s{}^i$.

General approach to form A for the pair of ontologically relevant types t_s and t_r is the following:

1. All ontologically relevant pairs of places $(at_s{}^i, at_r{}^j)$ of the script types belong to A if type of $at_r{}^j$ is a supertype of type of $at_s{}^i$. We should check also that an activity predicate function of $at_s{}^i$ should logically imply an activation predicate function of $at_r{}^j$.

2. For all ontologically relevant pairs of transitions their activity declarations $(at_s{}^i, at_r{}^j)$ belong to A if signatures of functions $at_s{}^i$ and $at_r{}^j$ satisfy the requirements established for a pair of ontologically relevant pair of functional attribute of types to be included into a common reduct of a type.

   After that we should check that $at_r{}^j$ is a refinement of $at_s{}^i$ and that the guarding function of an application script transition should imply the guarding function of the pre-existing script transition.

In this process establishing mediating functions reconciliating possible type and value conflicts is assumed.

Now, we can construct a candidate common script type reduct out of the constituents in A. After constructing of a candidate common reduct N and its conjugate Q, we take their subexpressions $S_e(N)$ and $S_e(Q) \setminus S_a(N)$ and apply equivalent transformations to $S_e(N)$ based on the process algebra axiom system trying to reduce $S_e(N)$ to $S_e(Q) \setminus S_a(N)$. We repeat this procedure for different subscripts N and Q until we get satisfying subexpressions of $S_e(R)$ and $S_e(P)$ or fail.

Thus we are looking for potentially reusable patterns of pre-existing behaviours and transforming corresponding subexpressions $S_e(N)$ to such patterns. Finally we obtain bisimilar processes identifying common reducts.

For a script type t_s we repeat the process for all script types t_r conformant to t_s. Among successful discoveries of most common reducts, we choose those disjoint common reducts that gives the best cover of t_s. Each common reduct in t_s is transformed to a transition that is to be hierarchically substituted by conjugate of a common reduct (a pre-existing script reduct) with the respective assignment of places relating input and output places of the t_s reduct with the external incoming and outgoing places of the t_r reduct. Implementation of such strategy is in a good accordance with the nested sub-process model identified by WfMC.

The uncovered remainder of t_s identifies those part of the script type that is to be implemented from scratch.

9.6 Example of the Most Common Reduct Identification

Now, we apply (partially) the workflow design procedure to our example. Looking for common script reducts we shall take into account only bisimulation equivalence condition. The idea of the design is to reuse pre-existing workflows as reducts of the Agency workflow specification. The reducts are easily identifiable.

For the Agency workflow specification (Fig. 2) a process algebra expression for the workflow reduct responsible for submissions collection and expert nomination appears as:

$Agency\_coll\_nom$ =
(precheck · precheck*take_subm + take_subm) · ((dispatch + invite)*register)

An expression for the workflow reduct responsible for submissions review and acceptance looks as:

$Agency\_rev\_acc$ = review · board(accept + reject + add_expertise)

For the pre-existing FlowMark workflow specification (Fig. 4) we get:

$IndLab\_FM$ =
precheck*take_subm · (dispatch*(invite((dispatch + invite)*register) + register))

For the pre-existing Staffware workflow specification (Fig.6) we get:

$IndLab\_SW$ =
review · patrev · econrev · board(accept + reject + add_expertise)

Projecting the last expression onto the alphabet of the Agency workflow script we get:

$IndLab\_SW'$ = review · ε · ε · board(accept + reject + add_expertise)

Taking into account that according to the axiom A9:

review · ε · ε = review

we see that $IndLab\_SW'$ is bisimulation equivalent to $Agency\_rev\_acc$.

Now, we apply equivalent transformations to $Agency\_coll\_nom$ to reduce it to $IndLab\_FM$:

According to the axiom A6 of the algebra axiom system, we get:

(precheck · precheck*take_subm + take_subm) = precheck*take_subm

According to the axiom A8, we get:

(dispatch + invite)*register = dispatch*(invite((dispatch + invite)*register)+ register)

Applying these transformations, we obtain equivalent expressions thus justifying that the processes abstracted from the Agency script reduct and from the FlowMark to script mapping are bisimilar. After that we should check other refinement conditions to be sure that pre-existing workflows refine the reducts we have identified. If required, a conventional specification refinement technique [AB 96, MO 94] should be applied.

10. Conclusion

To exploit efficiently component-ware technologies, the components should have sufficient clean semantic specifications for their reuse. Reusable components are treated semantically interoperable in context of a specific application.

Uniform descriptions of heterogeneous components are provided in frame of canonical object model having formal, model-theoretic semantics. Concept of refinement of specifications is inherent for the model.

Application semantics of specifications are considered separately in frame of the ontological approach. Concept specifications are assumed to be provided in frame of the canonical object model.

An approach for component-based design with reuse is based on the ontological contexts integration, associative search of the component constituents ontologically relevant to the the respective application constituents, identification of reusable fragments, construction of compositions of components concretizing specifications of requirements. The notion of common type reduct constitutes a basis for determining reusable fragments. Process of common reducts detection is specified.

The script-based multiactivity (workflow) specification framework is defined. For the workflow refinement we consider a behavioural abstraction of scripts as patterns of activities (firing sequences) corresponding to their specifications.

Complete justification of existence of common reduct (reusable fragment) for a pair of workflow specifications is based on the notion of workflow refinement.

The refinement is based on systematic analysis of functional and concurrent workflow specification properties merging conventional well grounded specification refinement technique with detecting of process bisimulation equivalence. For the latter admissible patterns of activities of a script are modelled as process algebra expressions implied by a script model. Complete axiomatization of process algebras provides for equivalent transformation of such expressions and their partial ordering making possible to reason that a behaviour given by a pre-existing workflow fragment can be considered a refinement of the required multiactivity behaviour.

Further research is required to develop more uniform modeling facilities for adequate justification of reusable workflow fragments selection and composition.

A. Definition of a Script Type

Scripts are based on the SYNTHESIS type system, object calculus and functions. Places are annotated with types and object calculus formulas, transitions - with object calculus formulas and functions. A binding is a term substitution replacing variables in formulas and input (output) parameters in transition functions with constants represented as tokens of the predetermined types. In a binding a type of a token should be in a subtyping relation with a type of the corresponding variable or parameter.

Script type may be abstracted as a variant of coloured Petri nets:

- $(P,T,A;N)$ is a *net structure* (directed bipartite graph) with finite set of places P, finite set of transitions T, finite sets of arcs A and a node function N from A into $PxT \cup TxP$;
- $C : P \rightarrow$ Type is a *type function* mapping places into SYNTHESIS types (basically, abstract data types having mutable or immutable values). Each token belonging to a place must have a value of the given type or of its subtypes.
- $Ap : P \rightarrow Oce^*$ is an *activation predicate function* mapping places into object calculus expressions defining formulas that should be satisfied for a token of the place to become active (only active tokens could be used in firing of the transitions);
- $G : T \rightarrow$ Oce is a *guard function* mapping each transition into an object calculus expression defining a predicate that should be satisfied for a transition to fire;
- $F : T \rightarrow$ Funct is an *activity function* mapping each transition into a function definition determining a function to be applied on firing of a transaction; binding of input and output parameters of the function is given by an arc expression function;
- $E : A \rightarrow (Par \times Oce \times Z)^*$ is an *arc expression function* mapping each arc into an object calculus expression defining a subset of transition input (output) sets of tokens that might be bind to some input (output) parameter of a transition function. This subset may be forwarded from (into) the place on transition firing. Additionally an integer may be added stating a number of tokens that might be consumed (produced) on transition firing in this particular binding;
- $H : T- > \sum$ is a *labelling function* mapping transitions into an alphabet that includes also an empty sequence;

– I : P– > (V x Z)* is an *initialization function* mapping each place into an expressions giving values of the token type defined for the place and a number of those values that should be created initially in the places.

Script dynamics is defined as follows. A token distribution in a script is a function M defined on P such that $M(p)$ is an element of the powerset of the type $C(p)$ values. A binding distribution is a function Y defined on T such that $Y(t)$ is an element of all bindings for t (a binding is a proper substitution for variables and parameters for a transition).

A marking in a script is a token distribution and a step is a binding distribution. The set of all markings for a given script s is denoted by M_s and the set of all steps - by Y_s. M_0 is an initial marking.

When a step is enabled it transforms M into a directly reachable marking removing (adding) tokens from (to) places by concurrently enabled transitions included into a step. The direct reachability of M_2 from M_1 is denoted as $M_1[Y > M_2$.

A finite firing sequence of a script is a sequence of markings and steps:
$$M_1[Y_1 > M_2[Y_2 > ...M_n[Y_n > M_{n+1}$$
where M_1 is a start marking and M_{n+1} is an end marking.

B. Interpretation of Staffware in the Canonical Workflow Model

B.1 Staffware Features

Staffware is intended for automating administrative and production tasks with well-defined rules. It is a client-server based product. Staffware stores data in its proprietary flat file database.

Scenario definition. In Staffware a scenario definition is a procedure and its instantiations are cases. It consists of activities called steps that have an addressee (name of the actor assigned to the step). Staffware usually has a form attached to each step. All data are defined by creating different types of (case) variables and forms that are stored in a database.

A Staffware graphical procedure definition consists of icons that are connected to each other with the control flow. Icons represent different kinds of steps and control structures. A question mark icon symbolises conditional routing and an hour glass icon symbolises a wait statement (here activities to be waited for are connected by a dashed connector). Document icons are activities with forms attached. If a document icon has a clock sign a deadline is attached to it.

There are three kinds of steps in Staffware:

1. A (normal) step is the most common step type to which always a form is attached.

2. An automatic step executes an external program without user interaction.
3. Events are activities that can be used for controlling an already running case, altering the data related to it.

Each step consists of four possible parts: (i) an addressee, (ii) a form that the addressee receives (in case of a normal step), (iii) activity that takes place after the release of the step, (iv) a deadline (optional) of the step completion.

Staffware offers typical routing features (sequentiality, forks, joins, loops and conditional routing). Routing from one step to another is specified by activities defined in the steps. An activity is simply the name of the the next step to be processed after the current one. Conditional routing can be accomplished by defining conditional activities. It is possible to synchronise re-joining control flow branches.

The optional deadline section in the step definition provides a mechanism for imposing a restriction on the period of time for a step to be released.

Scenario management. A case is started with the first step from the procedure definition. Then the form belonging to the step is sent to the addressee or automatic step is executed.

The step is locked until the addressee has finished and released it. After releasing the step it is deleted from the work queue and the control flow goes to the step that was defined as an activity of the released step. A form related to the next step is sent to corresponding addressee. The flow proceeds this way until the terminating stop-activity is reached.

B.2 Mapping of the Staffware Workflow Model into the Canonical Model

Mapping of a Staffware workflow specification into the canonical one can be accomplished using the following rules:

1. Each step S is mapped into a transition T_S with the activity specified corresponding to the program (manual) activity of the step.
2. To each horizontal line connecting symbols of step $S1$ and step $S2$ and positioning to the right of $S1$ and to the left of $S2$ generally two arcs and a state P of a script correspond. One arc leads from T_{S1} to P. Another arc leads from this state to T_{S1}. A line connecting $S1$ and $S2$ is equivalent to referring $S2$ as an activity in the step $S1$. If this is a conditional activity then additionally the condition is mapped into a condition of an element of the output binding list of T_{S1} related to P.
   A type of a token in P correponds to a form that should be attached to $S2$.
3. An activity A start condition is mapped into a guard of T_A interpreted by an assertion included into a **conditions**: list of T_A or into into conditions

of elements of the input binding list of T_A or into both depending on the start condition.

An activity A exit condition is mapped into assertions included into all states listed in the to: list of output state names of T_A.

4. If a deadline constraint is imposed on a step $S1$ then additional line goes down from this step to another step $S3$ denoting an activity that should start in course of a deadline violation. Additionally to the mapping rule 2 above, in this case a state $P1$ and a transition T_{S3} is generated. One additional arc leads from T_{S1} to $P1$. Another arc leads from this state to T_{S3}. A type of token ingoing into $S1$ is appended with an attribute t that takes as a value the start time of T_{S1} activity.

A condition $current - t \leq T$ is set as an element of the output binding list of T_{S1} related to P. A condition $current - t > T$ is set as an element of the output binding list of T_{S1} related to $P1$. Here T is an established period of deadline, $current$ is equal to current time.

5. Applying rules 1, 2 and 3 above to a Staffware procedure we get a specification of a script that models this procedure incuding Staffware routing features (sequentiality, forks, joins, loops and conditional routing).

6. To start the procedure, a token should be placed into the input state of the first step of the procedure. This will establish an initial marking of the script.

C. Interpretation of IBM FlowMark in the Canonical Workflow Model

C.1 FlowMark Features

FlowMark is a robust workflow management system intended to automate production workflows. A distinguishing feature of the product is separating control and data flow. It allows hierarchical modelling and re-usability.

Scenario Definition. A process in FlowMark is presented as a weighted, coloured, directed graph of activities where both control and data flows occur as different kinds of edges. Activities represent a piece of work that the assigned actor can complete.

A program activity has an executable program assigned to it. The programs must be implemented as external programs called via provided APIs. Other processes can be reused as activities. Such activities are called process activities.

In the FlowMark process model there can be two kinds of connectors linking activities:

1. A control connector which can have a transition condition associated to it allowing the control flow through it only when the condition evaluates

to true. By defining multiple connectors starting from one activity (and having transition conditions evaluated to true) it is possible to define parallel control flows.

2. A data connector specifies the data flow between the data containers of the activities. There can also be multiple data connectors leaving from or incoming to one activity. The data are written into and read from the data containers by the programs associated to the activities via APIs.

Each activity and process has a private input container and output container for the parameter storage and exchange between the activities. Each data container is defined by a data structure that consists of data structure members. It is possible to set start conditions and exit conditions for the activities to determine when the activity may start or end. The evaluation of the transition conditions as well as the exit conditions uses the values in the data containers.

The start condition enables to synchronise the re-joining control flows since it is possible to choose the start condition to evaluate to true either if at least one of the incoming connectors evaluates to true or only if all incoming connectors evaluate to true. A deadline definition in FlowMark is possible for notifying the specified person when the process or activity is not completed in the time allowed.

Scenario management. Once a new process instance has to execute, a copy of the related process template is made and used for steering it. When a process instance is started the process execution component of the FlowMark server executes the process template in the following way:

1. First, it finds the start activities and distributes them to the appropriate actors. Control connectors that have a transition condition evaluated to true are selected.
2. For the non-start activities the start control is checked after one or all (depending how re-joining control flows have synchronised) transition conditions of the incoming connectors have been evaluated to true or marked to come from a dead path.
3. When no further control connectors with a transition condition evaluated to true are found, the process is finished.

C.2 Mapping of the FlowMark Workflow Model into the Canonical Model

Mapping of a FlowMark workflow specification into the canonical one can be accomplished using the following rules:

1. Each activity A is mapped into a transition T_A with the activity specified corresponding to the program (manual) activity. If this is a process activity, a nested script will be created.

2. To a connector linking an activity A and activity B two arcs and a state P of a script correspond. One arc leads from T_A to P. Another arc leads from this state to T_B.

   A type of a token corresponds to a type of data in the output data container of A associated to this connector. We assume that to a control connector such data type also corresponds containing data required for routing. If there is a transition condition associated to a connector then it is mapped into a condition of an element of the output binding list of T_A related to P.

3. An activity A start condition is mapped into a guard of T_A interpreted by an assertion included into a conditions: list of T_A or into into conditions of elements of the input binding list of T_A or into both depending on the start condition.

   An activity A exit condition is mapped into assertions included into all states listed in the to: list of output state names of T_A.

4. Applying rules 1, 2 and 3 to a FlowMark process we get a specification of a script that models this process incuding multiple ingoing and outgoing connectors, synchronization and re-joining of control flows, parallel data and control flows, etc.

5. To start the process, transitions corresponding to starting activities of a workflow should be identified and tokens should be placed into the input states of these transitions. This will establish an initial marking of the script.

References

[AAFZ 95] S. Acharya, R. Alonso, M. Franklin, and S. Zdonik. Broadcast disks: Data management for asymmetric communications environments. Proc. ACM SIGMOD Intl. Conf. on Management of Data, San Jose, CA, May 1995.

[AAEM 97] G. Alonso, D. Agrawal, A. El Abbadi, and C. Mohan. Functionality and limitations of current workflow management systems. IEEE Expert 12(5), 1997.

[A+ 94] G. Alonso, M. Kamath, D. Agrawal, A. El Abbadi, R. Gunthor, and C. Mohan. Failure handling in large scale workflow management systems. Research Report, RJ 9913, IBM Almaden Research Center, 1994.

[A+ 95] G. Alonso, D. Agrawal, A. El Abbadi, C. Mohan, R. Gunthor, and M. Kamath. Exotica/FMQM: a persistent message-based architecture for distributed workflow management. Proc. IFIP WG8.1 Working Conference on Information System Development for Decentralised Organizations, 1995.

[A+ 96] G. Alonso, R. Guntor, M. Kamath, D. Agrawal, A. El Abbadi, and C. Mohan. Exotica/FMDC: a workflow management system for mobile and disconnected clients. Distributed and Parallel Databases 4(3), 1996.

[A 97] B. Arpinar. Concurrency control and transaction management in workflow management systems. PhD thesis, in preparation, Dept. of Computer Engineering, Middle East Technical University, 1997.

[Arp 97] S. Arpinar. Recovery and compensation in workflow management systems. PhD thesis, in preparation, Dept. of Computer Engineering, Middle East Technical University, 1997.

[A+ 97] Alonso, G., Agrawal, D., El Abbadi, A., and Mohan, C. Functionalities and limitations of current workflow management systems. IEEE Expert (Special Issue on Cooperative Information Systems) 12(5), 1997.

[AAE 96] G. Alonso, D. Agrawal, and A. El Abbadi. Process Synchronization in Workflow Management Systems. 8th IEEE Symposium on Parallel and Distributed Processing (SPDS'97). New Orleans, October 1996.

[AAHD 97] I. B. Arpinar, S. Arpinar, U. Halici, and A. Dogac, Correctness of workflows in the presence of concurrency. Third Intl. Workshop on Next Generation Information Technologies and Systems (NGITS), Neve Ilan, July 1997.

[AB 96] J.-R.Abrial. The B-Book. Cambridge University Press, 1996.

[ABFS 97] G. Alonso, S. Blott, A. Fessler, and H.-J. Schek. Correctness and parallelism of composite systems. Proc. 16th ACM Symposium on Principles of Database Systems, Tucson, AZ, May 1997.

[Act 95] Action Technologies. Metro tour. Technical report, http://www.-actiontech.com/., Action Technologies, 1995.

[Act 96] Action Technologies. Action workflow enterprise series 3.0: process builder user's guide. Action Technologies, 1996.

[Act 97]   Action   Technologies: Action   workflow   and   metro.
             http://www.actiontech.com, 1997.
[AE 94]   G. Alonso, and A. El Abbadi. Cooperative modeling in applied ge-
             ographic research.   Intl. J. Intelligent and Cooperative Information
             Systems, 3(1) May 1994.
[Aea91]   A. Elmagarmid et al. The pegasus heterogeneous multidatabase sys-
             tem. IEEE Computer 24(12), 1991.
[AEF⁺97]   K. Aberer, S. Even, F. Faase, Kaijanranta H, J. Klingemann,
             A. Lehtola, O. Pihlajamaa, T. Tesch, J. Wäsch, P. Apers, and E. J.
             Neuhold. Transaction support for cooperative work: an overview of
             the TRANSCOOP project. Technical report, The TRANSCOOP Consor-
             tium, 1997. Document distributed at the Workshop on Extending Data
             Management for Cooperative Work, Darmstadt, June 1997.
[AFZ 97]   S. Acharya, M. Franklin, and S. Zdonik. Balancing push and pull for
             data broadcast. Proc. ACM SIGMOD Intl. Conf. on Management of
             Data, Tucson, Arizona, May 1997.
[AG 95a]   P. Antunes and N. Guimaraes. Beyond formal processes: augmenting
             workflow with group interaction techniques, Proc. of ACM COOCS95,
             Milpitas, CA, August 1995.
[AG 95b]   P. Antunes, and N. Guimaraes. Structuring elements for group inter-
             action, Second Conference on Concurrent Engineering, Research and
             Applications (CE95), Washington, DC, August 1995. Concurrent Tech-
             nologies Corporation.
[AGM 88]   R. Abbott and H. Garcia-Molina. Scheduling real-time transactions:
             a performance evaluation. Proc. 14th Intl. Conf. on Very Large Data
             Bases, pp 1–12, Los Angeles, CA, 1988.
[AH 97]   G. Alonso and C. Hagen. Geo-Opera: Workflow concepts for spatial
             processes. Proc. Fifth Intl. Symposium on Spatial Databases, Berlin,
             Germany, July 1997.
[AIL 96]   V. Anjur, Y. Ioannidis, and M. Livny. FROG and TURTLE: Visual
             bridges between files and object-oriented data. Proc. 8th Intl. Conf.
             on Scientific and Statistical Database Management, Sweden 1996, pp.
             76–85, IEEE Computer Society Press, Los Alamitos, CA.
[AKT⁺96]   K. Aberer, J. Klingemann, T. Tesch, J. Wäsch, and E. J. Neuhold.
             Transaction models supporting cooperative work – the TRANSCOOP
             experiences. Proc. Intl. Symposium on Cooperative Database Systems
             for Advanced Applications (CODAS '96), Kyoto, Japan, December
             1996.
[Alo 96]   Alonso, G., Agrawal, D., El Abbadi, A., Kamath, M., Gunthor, R., and
             Mohan, C. Advanced transaction models in workflow contexts. Proc.
             18th IEEE Intl. Conf. on Data Engineering, New Orleans, LA, 1996.
[AM 97]   G. Alonso, C. Mohan, S. Jajodia and L. Kerschberg (eds.). Work-
             flow management: the next generation of distributed processing tools.
             Advanced Transaction Models and Architectures. Kluwer Academic
             Publishers, 1997.
[ANRS 92]   M. Ansari, L. Ness, M. Rusinkiewicz, and A. Sheth. Using flexible
             transactions to support multi-system telecommunication applications.
             Proc. 18th VLDB Conference, August 1992.
[App 96]   H.-J. Appelrath, H. Behrends, H. Jasper, and O. Zukunft. Case stud-
             ies on active database applications: lessons Learned. Intl. Conf. on
             Database and Expert Systems Applications, Zurich, 1996
[Arax 97]   Araxsys (1996): the araxsys solution. http://www.araxsys.com, 1997.
[Ari 97]   Ariba: introducing ariba ORMS^{TM}. http://www.ariba.com, 1997.

[ARM 97]   Alonso, G., Reinwald, B., and Mohan, C. Distributed data manage-
            ment in workflow environments. RIDE 1997.
[Arm 88]   M.P. Armstrong.   Temporality in spatial databases.   Proceedings
            GIS/LIS, pp. 880–889, November 1988.
[AS 96]   G. Alonso and H.-J. Schek. Database technology in workflow envi-
            ronments. Informatik/Informatique (J. of the Swiss Computer Science
            Society), April 1996.
[AS 96b]   G. Alonso and H.J. Schek. Research issues in large workflow manage-
            ment systems. In [She 96], Athens, GA, May 1996.
[Att 93]   P.A. Attie, M.P. Singh, A. Sheth, and M. Rusinkiewicz, Specifying and
            enforcing intertask dependencies. Proc. 19th Intl. Conf. on Very Large
            Data Bases, September 1993.
[AVA⁺ 94]   G. Alonso, R. Vingralek, D. Agrawal, Y. Breitbart, A. El Abbadi, H.-J.
            Schek, and G. Weikum. Unifying concurrency control and recovery of
            transactions. 19(1):101–115, January 1994.
[AWH 92]   A. Aiken, J. Widom, and J.M. Hellerstein. Behavior of database pro-
            duction rules: Termination, confluence and observable determinism.
            Proc. ACM SIGMOD, pp. 59–68, June 1992.
[B 91]   R.Butler. Designing organizations. Routledge, 1991.
[B 92]   A. Buchmann, M. Ozsu, M. Hornick, D. Georgakopoulos, and F.A.
            Manola. A transaction model for active distributed object systems.
            In Transaction Models for Advanced Database Applications, A. Elma-
            garmid (ed.), Morgan-Kaufmann, 1992.
[B 93]   O. Bukhres, J. Chen, A. Elmagarmid, X. Liu, and G. Mullen. Interbase:
            A multidatabase prototype system. Proc. ACM-SIGMOD'93, 1993.
[B⁺ 93]   Breitbart, Y., Deacon, A., Schek, H., Sheth, A., and Weikum, G.
            Merging application-centric and data-centric approaches to support
            transaction-oriented multi-system workflows. ACM SIGMOD Record
            22(3), 1993.
[B⁺ 96]   E. Baralis et al. Support environment for active rule design. J. of
            Intelligent Information Systems 7(2):129–150, 1996.
[BBa 97]   R. Bayardo, W. Bohrer, and R. Brice et al. Semantic integration of
            information in open and dynamic environments. SIGMOD'97, 1997.
[BBG 89]   C. Beeri, P.A. Bernstein, and N. Goodman. A model for concurrency
            control in nested transaction systems. J. of the ACM 36(2):230–269,
            1989.
[BCW 93]   E. Baralis, S. Ceri, and J. Widom. Better termination analysis for ac-
            tive databases. Proc. 1st Intl. Workshop on Rules in Database Systems,
            pp. 163–179, August 1993.
[BDG⁺ 94]   A. Biliris, S. Dar, N. Gehani, H.V. Jagadish, and K. Ramamritham.
            ASSET: A system for supporting extended transactions. Proc. 1994
            SIGMOD Intl. Conf. on Management of Data, pp. 44–54, May 1994.
[BDHS 96]   P. Buneman, S.B. Davidson, G.G. Hillebrand, and D. Suciu. A query
            language and optimization techniques for unstructured data. In SIG-
            MOD 96, pp. 505–516, 1996.
[BE 94]   J. Bergstra, I. Bethke, and A. Ponse. Process algebra with iteration
            and nesting. Computer Journal 37(4), 1994.
[Beh 94]   H. Behrends. Simulation-based debugging of active databases. Pro-
            ceedings of the 4th Intl. workshop on Research Issues in Data Engi-
            neering, pp. 172–180, 1994.
[Bern 95]   P. A. Bernstein, C. Dellarocas, T. W. Malone, and J. Quimby. Software
            tools for a process handbook. In [Hsu 95]

494   References

[Bet 94]   Mark Betz. Interoperable objects: laying the foundation for distributed object computing. Dr. Dobb's Journal: Software Tools for Professional Programmer, October 1994.

[BGB 95]   E. Benazet, H. Guhel, and M. Bouzeghoub. Vital: a visual tool for analysis of rules behavior in active databases. Proc. Intl. Workshop Rids'95. Lecture Notes in Computer Science 985, pp. 182–196, Springer-Verlag, 1995.

[BHG 87]   P.A. Bernstein, V. Hadzilacos, and N. Goodman. Concurrency Control and Recovery in Database Systems. Addison-Wesley, 1987.

[BJ 94]   C. Bussler, and S. Jablonski. Implementing agent coordination for workflow management systems using active database systems. Intl. Workshop on Active Database Systems, Houston TX, 1994.

[Bjo 73]   L.A. Bjork. Recovery scenarios for a DB/DC system. Proc. 28th ACM Annual Conference, pp. 142–146, Atlanta, GA, 1973.

[Bjo 94]   D. Bjorner. Prospects for a viable software industry. Computers as our better partners. Proc. Intl. IISF/ACM Symposium Tokyo, World Scientific, 1994.

[BK91]   N. S. Barghouti and G. E. Kaiser. Concurrency control in advanced database applications. ACM Computing Surveys 23(3), 1991.

[BKK 85]   F. Bancilhon, W. Kim, and H. Korth. A model of CAD transactions. Proc. 11th Intl. Conf. on Very Large Databases, pp. 25–33, Stockholm, Sweden, August 1985.

[Bla 94]   D. Black. Workflow Software: A Layman's Handbook, Part I. INFORM, April 1994.

[BLW 96]   A. Bapat, M. Löhr, and J. Wäsch. Hypermedia support for the integrated systems engineering environment MUSE. Proc. Fifth Intl. Conf. on Data and Knowledge Systems in Manufacturing and Engineering (DKSME '96), pp. 123–140, Phoenix, AZ, October 1996.

[BJS 96]   C. Bussler, S. Jablonski, and H. Schuster. A new generation of workflow management systems: beyond taylorism with MOBILE. ACM SIGOIS Bulletin 17(1):17–20, 1996.

[BK 94]   I.Z. Ben-Shaul, and G.E. Kaiser. A paradigm for decentralized process modeling and its realization in the oz environment. Proc. 16th Intl. Conf. on Software Engineering, Sorrento, Italy, 1994.

[BLC 95]   T. Berners-Lee and D. Connolly. Hypertext Markup Language 2.0. http://www.w3.org/hypertext/WWW/MarkUp/html-spec/html-spec-toc.html, June 1995. RFC 1866.

[BLFF 95]   T. Berners-Lee, R. Fielding, and H. Frystyk. Hypertext transfer protocol - HTTP/1.0. http://www.w3.org/WWW/Protocols, August 1995. RFC 1945.

[BMR 94]   D. Barbara, S. Mehrota, and M. Rusinkiewicz. INCAS: A Computation Model for Dynamic Workflows in Autonomous Distributed Environments. Technical report, Matsushita Information Technology Laboratory, April 1994.

[BMR 96]   D. Barbara, S. Mehrota, and M. Rusinkiewicz. INCAs: Managing dynamic workflows in distributed environments. J. of Database Management 7(1), 1996.

[BN 97]   P.A. Bernstein, and E. Newcomer. Principles of transaction processing for the systems professional. Morgan Kaufmann, 1997.

[BO 96]   Common Business Objects and Business Object Facility, RFP, OMG, cf/96-01-04.

[BO 97]   B. Bohrer et al. InfoSleuth: Semantic integration of information in open and dynamic environment. Proc. ACM SIGMOD Conference, May 1997.

[BR 92]   B. R. Badrinath, and K. Ramamritham. Semantic–based concurrency control: Beyond commutativity. ACM Transactions on Database Systems 17(1):163–199, 1992.

[BR 95]   G. Booch, Rumbaugh. Unified method for object-oriented development- documentation set. Version 0.8, http://www.rational.com, 1995.

[Br 92]   M.L. Brodie. The Promise of Distributed Computing and the Challenges of Legacy Systems. In Advanced Database Systems: Proc. 10th British National Conference on Databases, P.M.D. Gray and R.J. Lucas (eds.), Springer-Verlag, 1992.

[Bru 92]   T. Bruce. Designing quality databases with IDEFIX information models. Dorset House Publishing, 1992.

[BRS 96]   Stephen Blott, Lukas Relly, and Hans-Jörg Schek. An open abstract-object storage system. Proc. ACM SIGMOD Intl. Conf. Management of Data, Montreal, Canada, June 1996.

[BSR 96]   A. Bonner, A. Shrufi, and S. Rozen. LabFlow-1: A database benchmark for high throughput workflow management. Proc. Fifth Intl. Conf. on Extending Database Technology (EDBT96), Avignon, France, March 1996.

[BSS91]   K.P. Birman, A. Schiper, and P. Stephenson. Leightweight causal and atomic group multicast. ACM Transactions on Computer Systems 9(3):272–314, 1991.

[BW 90]   J. Baeten, W. Weijland, Process Algebra, Cambridge University Press, Cambridge, UK, 1990.

[BW 96]   A. Brayner, and M. Weske. Using FlowMark^{TM} in Molecular Biology (in German). EMISA Forum 2/1996, 14–21.

[BWAH96]   A. Bapat, J. Wäsch, K. Aberer, and J. Haake. HyperStorM: An extensible object-oriented hypermedia engine. Proc. Seventh ACM Conference on Hypertext (HYPERTEXT '96), pp. 203–214, Washington, DC, March 1996.

[C 86]   Q. Chen. A rule-based object/task modelling approach. Proc. ACM-SIGMOD'86, SIGMOD Rec. 15(2), 1986.

[C 92]   Q. Chen and Y. Kambayashi. Coordination of data and knowledge base systems in distributed environment. Proc. IFIP TC2/WG2.6 Conf. on Semantics of Interoperatable Database Systems, DS-5, 1992.

[C 95]   Q. Chen and U. Dayal. Contracting transaction hierarchies (extended abstract). Proc. RIDE'96, 1995.

[C 97]   Catapult. Microsoft Outlook'97 - Step by Step, Microsoft Press, 1997.

[Cas 96]   F. Casati, S. Ceri, B. Pernici, and G. Pozzi. Semantic workflow interoperability. Intl. Conf. Extending Database Technology, Avignon, 1996.

[Cat 94]   R.G.G. Cattell (ed.). The object database standard: ODMG-93 (Release 1.2). Morgan Kaufmann, 1994.

[CCPP 96b] Casati, F., Ceri, S., Pernice, B., and Pozzi, G. Workflow Evolution. ER, 1996.

[CD 96]   Q. Chen and U. Dayal. A transactional nested process management system. Proc. 12th Intl. Conf. on Data Engineering, New Orleans, LA, February 1996.

[CD 97]   Chen, Q., and Dayal, U. Failure handling for transaction hierarchies. Proc. Intl. Conf. on Data Engineering, 1997.

[CG 97]   L. Carriço, and N.Guimarães. Facilitating Analysis and Diagnosis in Organizations. Proc. CAiSE97, Barcelona, June 1997.

[CGS 97]   Ceri, S., Grefen, P., and Sanchez, G. WIDE: A distributed architecture for workflow management. RIDE 1997.

[CHS91]   C. Collet, M. Huhns, and W. Shen. Resource integration using a large knowledge base in Carnot. IEEE Computer 24(12):55–62, December 1991.

[Cin 97]   I. Cingil. Verification of workflow specification. PhD thesis, in preperation, Dept. of Computer Engineering, Middle East Technical University, 1997.

[CJ 90]   W. Cellary, and G. Jomier. Consistency of versions in object-oriented databases. Proc. 16th Intl. Conf. on Very Large Data Bases, pp. 432–441, 1990.

[CK 94]   S. Chakravarthy and S.-K. Kim. Resolution of time concepts in temporal databases. Information Sciences 80(1-2):43–89, 1994.

[CKO 92]   B. Curtis, M. Kellner, and J. Over. Process Modeling. Comm. ACM 35(35), 1992.

[CL 96]   D. Chang, and D. Lange. Mobile agents: A new paradigm for distributed object computing on the WWW. Proc. OOPSLA'96 Workshop, 1996.

[Cla 86]   E. M. Clarke, E. A. Emerson, and A. P. Sistla. Automatic verification of finite state concurrent systems using temporal logic specifications; A practical approach. ACM Transactions on Programming Languages and Systems 8(2), 1986.

[Clat]   R. McClatchey, N. Baker, W. Harris, J.-M. Le Goff, Z. Kovacs, F. Estrella, A. Bazan, and T. Le Flour. Version management in a distributed workflow application. Proc. 8th Intl. Workshop on Database and Expert Systems Applications 1997, Toulouse, IEEE Computer Society Press, 10–15.

[CM 94]   Sharma Chakravarthy and Deepak Mishra. Snoop: An expressive event specification language for active database. Data and Knowledge Engineering, November 1994.

[CM 95]   N. Craven, and D. Mahling. A task basis for projects and workflows. Proc. Conf. on Organizational Computing Systems (COOCS), pp. 237–248, Milpitas, CA, 1995.

[CMS95]   CMS Technical proposal. The CMS Collaboration, January 1995. Available from ftp://cmsdoc.cern.ch/TPref/TP.html.

[COR 95a] CORBA: The Common Object Request Broker Architecture, Revision 2.0. The Object Management Group, July 1995.

[Cor 95b] Transarc Corporation. RQS System Administrator's Guide and Reference. Transarc Corporation, 1995. ENC-D4003-02.

[Cor 95c] Transarc Corporation. Writing Encina Applications. Transarc Corporation, 1995. ENC-D5012-00.

[CR 90]   P.K. Chrysanthis, and K. Ramamritham. Acta: a framework for specifying and reasoning about transaction structure and behavior. Proc. ACM SIGMOD, pp. 194-203, 1990.

[CR 91]   P.K. Chrysanthis, and K. Ramamritham. A Formalism For Extended Transaction Models. Proc. 17th Conference on Very Large Databases (VLDB), pp. 103–112, Barcelona, Spain, September 1991.

[CR 92]   P. K. Chrysanthis and K. Ramamritham, ACTA: The SAGA continues. In Database Transaction Models for Advanced Applications, A. K. Elmagarmid (ed.), Morgan Kaufmann 1992.

[CR 93]   P. K. Chrysanthis, and K. Ramamritham. Delegation in ACTA to control sharing in extended transactions. IEEE Data Engineering Bulletin 16(2):16–19, June 1993.

[CR 97]   A. Cichocki and M. Rusinkiewicz. Migrating workflows. In this volume.

[CVJ 94]   W. Cellary, G. Vossen, and G. Jomier. Multiversion object constellations: A new approach to support a designer's database work. Engineering with Computers 10:230–244, 1994.

[D+ 93]   Dayal, U., Garcia-Molina, H., Hsu, M., Kao, B., and Shan, M. Third generation TP monitors: A database challenge. SIGMOD, Washington, DC, 1993.

[D+ 97]   Das, S., Kochut, K., Miller, J., Sheth, A., and Worah, D. ORBWork: A Reliable Distributed CORBA-based Workflow Enactment System for METEOR$_2$, The University of Georgia, UGA-CS-TR-97-001.

[Dav 73]   C.T. Davies. Recovery semantics for a DB/DC system. Proc. 28th ACM Annual Conference, pp. 136–141, Atlanta, GA, 1973.

[Dav 93]   T. Davenport. Process innovation. Cambridge, MA:Harvard Press, 1993.

[dBKV 97]   R. de By, W. Klas, and J. Veijaleinen (eds.). Transaction management support for cooperative applications. Kluwer Academic Publishers, 1997.

[dBLP+ 95]   R. de By, A. Lehtola, O. Pihlajamaa, J. Veijalainen, and J. Wäsch. A reference architecture for cooperative transaction processing systems. VTT Research Notes 1694, VTT Technical Research Centre of Finland, 1995.

[dBLP+ 96]   R. de By, A. Lehtola, O. Pihlajamaa, J. Veijalainen, and J. Wäsch. Specification of the TRANSCOOP Demonstrator System. Report DIII.2, Esprit-III LTR Project TRANSCOOP (P8012), April 1996.

[DDO96]   A. Dogac, C. Dengi, and M.T. Ozsu. Building interoperable databases on distributed object management platforms. Comm. ACM, 1998.

[DDS 95]   Davis, J., Du, W., Shan, M. OpenPM: An enterprise process management system. IEEE Data Engineering Bulletin, 1995.

[DDS 97]   Du, W., Davis, J., Shan, M. Flexible specification of workflow compensation scopes. Proc. Int. Conf. on Groupware, Pheonix, AZ, 1997.

[DDSD 97]   Du, W., Davis, J., Shan, M., and Dayal, U. Flexible compensation of workflow processes. Hewlett-Packard Laboratories Technical Report, HPL-96-72, 1997.

[Delphi 97a] Delphi Consulting Group. Workflow - 1996 in perspective. Delphi Insight Series Report, Boston, MA, 1997.

[Delphi 97b] Delphi Consulting Group (1997): Wide Area Workflow, The Delphi Seminars & Institutes, 1997.

[DES 97]   Du, W., Eddy, G., and Shan, M. Distributed resource management in workflow environments. Proc. 5th Conf. on Database Systems Advanced Applications, Melbourne, Australia, 1997.

[DG 94]   W. Deiters, and V. Gruhn. The Funsoft Net Approach to Software Process Management, Intl. J. Software Engineering and Knowledge Engineering 4(2), 1994.

[DHL 90]   U. Dayal, M. Hsu, and R. Ladin. Organizing long running activities with triggers and transactions. Proc. ACM-SIGMOD Conference, pp. 204–214, Atlantic City, NJ, June 1990.

[DHL 91]   U. Dayal, M. Hsu, and R. Ladin. A transaction model for long-running activities. Proc. 17th Intl. Conf. on Very Large Databases, pp. 113–122, September 1991.

[DPS 95]   Du, W., Peterson, S., and Shan, M. Enterprise workflow architecture. Data Engineering, Taipei, Taiwan, 1995.

[DS 93]   Dayal, U., and Shan, M. Issues in operation flow management for long-running activities. Data Engineering Bulletin 16(2), 1993.

[DSE 97]   Du, W., Shan, M., and Elmagarmid, A. Consistent execution of work-flow processes. HPL Technical Report, HPL-97-71, 1997.

[DSW 94]   A. Deacon, H.J. Schek, and G. Weikum. Semantics-based multilevel transaction management in federated systems. Proc. 10th Intl. Conf. of Data Engineering, Houston, TX, February 1994.

[DWS 96]   Du, W., Whitney, C., and Shan, M. SONET configuration management with OpenPM. Proc. 12th Intl. Conf. on Data Engineering, New Orleans, LA, February 1996.

[Eas 97]   EASTMANSOFTWARE, http://www.eastmansoftware.com, December, 1997.

[EDNO 96]   C. Evrendilek, A. Dogac, S. Nural, and F. Ozcan. Query optimization in multidatabase systems. J. of Distributed and Parallel Databases 5:77–114, 1996.

[EFdBP96]   S. J. Even, F. J. Faase, R. A. de By, and O. Pihlajamaa. The TRANSCOOP specification environment. Report DIV.4, Esprit-III LTR Project TRANSCOOP (P8012), 1996.

[EG89]   C. A. Ellis and S. J. Gibbs. Concurrency control in groupware systems. Proc. ACM SIGMOD Conference on Management of Data, pp. 399–407. MCC, Austin, TX, May 1989.

[EGR91]   C. A. Ellis, S. J. Gibbs, and G. L. Rein. Groupware: Some issues and experiences. Comm. ACM 34(1):38–58, January 1991.

[Egi 97]   K. Egilmez. Flow Nets. Production control of manufacturing systems laboratory, Boston University. http://cad.bu.edu/pcms/kaan/flownets.html

[EGN 94]   J. Eder, H. Groiss, and H. Nekvasil. A workflow system based on active databases. Proc. Connectivity 94, R. Oldenburg Verlag, Vienna, pp. 249–265, 1994.

[EL 95]   Eder, J., and Liebhart, W. The workflow activity model WAMO. Proc. 3rd Intl. Conference on Cooperative Information Systems, CoopIS, Vienna, May 1995.

[EL 96]   J. Eder and W. Liebhart Workflow recovery. Proc. 1st Intl. Conf. on Cooperative Information Systems (CoopIS96), Brussels, Belgium, June 1996.

[EL 97]   J. Eder, and W. Liebhart. Workflow transactions. In Workflow Handbook, P. Lawrence (ed.), Wiley, 1997.

[ELLR 90]   A.K. Elmagarmid, Y. Leu, W. Litwin, and M.E. Rusinkiewicz. A multidatabase transaction model for interbase. Proc. 16th VLDB Conference, August 1990.

[Elm 92]   A.K. Elmagarmid (ed.). Transaction models for advanced database applications. Morgan Kaufmann, 1992.

[ELP 97]   J. Eder, W. Liebhart and H. Pozewaunig. Time issues of workflow management systems. May 1997.

[Eme 90]   E.A. Emerson. Temporal and Modal Logic. In Handbook of Theoretical Computer Science, J. van Leeuwen (ed.), Elsevier, 1990.

[EN 93]   C. A. Ellis, and G. J. Nutt. Modeling and enactment of workflow systems, Invited Paper, 14th Intl. Conf. on Application and Theory of Petri Nets, 1993.

[ER 95]   C. Ellis, K. Keddara, and G. Rozenberg. Dynamic change within workflow systems. Proc. Conf. on Organizational Computing Systems (COOCS), Milpitas, CA 1995, 10-22.

[ES 88]   E. A. Emerson, and J. Srinivasan. Branching temporal logic. In Lecture Notes in Computer Science 354, deBakker, J.W., de Roever, W.-P., Rozenberg, G. (eds.), Springer-Verlag, 1988.

[ESA 91]   ESA PSS-05-02, ESA Board for Software Standardisation and Control, 1991.

[Etz 95]   O. Etzion. Reasoning about the behavior of active database applications. Proc. Intl. Workshop Rids'95, Lecture Notes in Computer Science 985, pp. 86–100, Springer-Verlag, 1995.

[EW 94]   C. Ellis, and J. Wainer. Goal-based models of collaboration. Collaborative Computing, 1:61-86, 1994.

[F 91]   K.A. Frenkel. The human genome project and informatics. Comm. ACM 34(11):41–51, November 1991.

[F 95]   L. Fischer. The workflow paradigm - The impact of information technology on business process reengineering. Future Strategies, Inc., Alameda, CA, 2nd edn., 1995.

[F 97]   S. N. Foley and J. L. Jacob. Specifying security for computer supported collaborative working. J. of Computer Security 3(4), 1994-1995.

[FC 96]   B. Farshchain and H. Carlsen. Workflow modeling in the norwegian BEST pilots. Orchestra Esprit Project 8746, D 5.4.3, Taskon, 1996.

[FEB 96]   F. J. Faase, S. J. Even, R. A. de By. Language Features for Cooperation in an Object-oriented Database Environment. Intl. J. of Cooperative Information Systems, 1996.

[FEdB 96]   F. J. Faase, S. J. Even, and R. A. de By. An introduction to CoCoA. Report DIV.3, Esprit-III LTR Project TRANSCOOP (P8012), 1996.

[FEdBA 97] Frans J. Faase, Susan J. Even, Rolf A. de By, and Peter M. G. Apers. Integrating organisational and transactional aspects of cooperative activities. Proc. Workshop on Database Programming Languages (DBPL), 1997.

[FdBE97]   F. Faase, R. de By, and S. Even. The TRANSCOOP specification environment, chapter 6. In [dBKV 97].

[Fil 97]   FileNet: Ensemble and visual workflow. http://www.filenet.com, December, 1997.

[FR 94]   M.D. Fraser, K. Kumar, and V.K. Vaishnavi. Strategies for incorporating formal specifications in software development. Comm. ACM 37(10), 1994.

[FZ 89]   M. F. Fernandez and S. B. Zdonik. Transaction groups: A model for controlling cooperative transactions. Proc. Int. Workshop on Persistent Object Systems, pp. 341–350, January 1989. Newcastle, New South Wales.

[FZ 94]   W. Fokkink, and H. Zantema. Basic process algebra with iteration: Completeness of its equational axioms. Computer Journal 37(4), 1994.

[FZ 96]   M. Franklin and S. Zdonik. Dissemination-based information systems. IEEE Bulletin of the Technical Committee on Data Engineering, 19(3):20–30, 1996.

[G 81]   Gray, J. The transaction concept: virtues and limitations, VLDB 1981.

[G 94]   N. Goodman. An object-oriented DBMS war story: developing a genome mapping database in C++. In Modern Database Systems— The Object Model, Interoperability, and Beyond, W. Kim (ed.), pp. 216–237, Addison-Wesley 1995.

[G 96]   R. S. Gray. Agent Tcl: A flexible and secure mobile-agent system. Proc. Fourth Annual Usenix Tcl/Tk Workshop, 1996.

[G 97]   N. Guimarães (ed). Organizational change, evolution, structuring and awareness. ESPRIT Project 8749, Orchestra, Research Reports, Springer-Verlag, 1997.

[G$^+$ 97]   E. Gokkoca, M. Altinel, I. Cingil, N. Tatbul, P. Koksal, and A. Dogac. Design and implementation of a distributed workflow enactment service. Proc. Conf. on Cooperative Information Systems (CoopIS '97), Charleston, SC, June 1997.

[GAP 97]   N. Guimaraes, P. Antunes, and A. Pereira. The Integration of workflow systems and collaboration tools. In this volume.

[GE 95]   H. Groiss and J. Eder. Interoperability with world wide workflow. 1st World Conf. on Integrated Design and Process Technology, Austin, TX, December 1995.

[GE 96]   H. Groiss and J. Eder. Integrating workflow systems and the world wide web. Workflow Handbook 1997, P. Lawrence (ed.), Wiley, 1996.

[Gen 86]   H. J. Genrich. Predicate/Transition Nets. In: Advances in Petri Nets. Lecture Notes in Computer Science 254, Springer-Verlag, 1986.

[Gok 97]   E. Gokkoca. Design and implementation of guard handler for a distributed workflow enactment service. MSc thesis, Dept. of Computer Engineering, Middle East Technical University, 1997.

[GF 92]   M.Genesereth, and R.E.Fikes et al. Knowledge interchange format reference manual. Stanford University Logic Group, 1992.

[GG 89]   M. Goodchild and S. Gopal. Accuracy of spatial databases. Taylor and Francis, 1989.

[GH 94]   Georgakopoulos, D., and Hornick, M. A framework for enforceable specification of extended transaction models and transactional workflow. J. of Intelligent and Cooperative Information Systems 3(3), 1994.

[GHKM 94]   D. Georgakopoulos, M. Hornick, P. Krychniak, and F. Malona. Specification and management of extended transactions in a programmable transaction environment. Proc. Data Enginering'94, 1994.

[GHM 96]   D. Georgakopoulos, M. Hornick, and F. Manola. Customizing transaction models and mechanisms in a programmable environment supporting reliable workflow automation. IEEE Transactions on Knowledge and Data Engineering 8(4), 1996.

[GHN$^+$ 97] S. Green, L. Hurst, B. Nangle, P. Cunningham, F. Somers, and R. Evans. Software agents: A review. http://www.cs.tcd.ie/-Brenda.Nangle/iag.html, May 1997.

[GHS 95]   D. Georgakopoulos, M. Hornick, and A. Sheth. An overview of workflow management: from process modeling to workflow automation infrastructure. J. of Distributed and Parallel Database Systems 3(2):119–153, April 1995.

[GI 95]   GMD-IPSI. VODAK V4.0 User Manual. Arbeitspapiere der GMD 910, Technical Report, GMD, April 1995.

[GK 94]   M. Genesereth, and S. Ketchpel. Software agents. Comm. ACM 37(7), 1994.

[GKT 95]   A. Geppert, M. Kradolfer, and D. Tombros. Realization of cooperative agents using an active object-Oriented database system. Intl. Workshop on Rules in Database Systems, Athens, 1995.

[GM 95]   Gosling and McMilton. The Java language environment: A white paper. http://javasoft.sun.com.

[GMS 87]   Garcia-Molina, H., and Salem, K. Sagas. SIGMOD 1987.

[GP 96]   N. Guimarães and A.P. Pereira. Workflow modeling, automation and augmentation. Proc. NSF Workshop on Workflow and Process Automation in Information Systems: State of the art and future directions, Athens, GA, May 1996.

[GR92]   T.R. Gruber. Ontolingua: A mechanism to support portable ontologies. Stanford university, June 1992.

[GR 93]   J. Gray and A. Reuter. Transaction Processing: Concepts and Techniques. Morgan Kaufmann, 1993.

[Gra 95]   J. Gray. Parallel Database Systems 101. Tutorial presented at the 15th ACM SIG Intl. Conf. on Management of Data (SIGMOD'95). San Jose, CA, May 1995.

[GRS 94]   D. Georgakopoulos, M. Rusinkiewicz, and A.P. Sheth. Using tickets to enforce the serializability of multidatabase transactions. IEEE Transactions on Knowledge and Data Engineering 6(1), 1994.

[GS 87]   I. Greif and S. Sarin. Data sharing in group work. ACM Transactions on Office Information Systems 5(2):187–211, 1987.

[Gue 93]   R. Guenthoer. Extended transaction processing based on dependency rules. 2nd Intl. Workshop on Interoperability in Multidatabase Systems, Vienna, 1993.

[H 85]   C.A.R. Hoare. Communicating sequential processes. Prentice-Hall International, 1985.

[H 93]   G.L. Hammonds. Confidentiality, integrity, assured service: tying security all together. ACM SIGSAC New Security Paradigms Workshop, 1993.

[H 95]   T. Hermann. Workflow management systems: ensuring organizational flexibility by possibilities of adaptation and negotiation. Proc. Conf. on Organizational Computing Systems (COOCS'95), 1995.

[H 97]   Y. Han. HOON A formalism supporting adaptive workflows. Technical Report No. UGA-CS-TR-97-005, Dept. of Computer Science, University of Georgia, October 1997.

[H$^+$ 92]   S. Heiler, S Haradhvala, S. Zdonik, B. Blaustein, and A. Rosenthal. A flexible framework for transaction management in engineering environments. In Transaction Models for Advanced Database Applications, A. Elmagarmid (ed.), Morgan Kaufmann, 1992.

[HA 97]   C. Hagen and G. Alonso. Flexible exception handling in the OPERA process support system. 1997.

[HAD 97]   U. Halici, B. Arpinar, and A. Dogac. Serializability of nested transactions in multidatabases. Intl. Conf. on Database Theory (ICDT '97), Greece, January 1997.

[Har 87]   D. Harel. State charts: a visual formalism for complex systems. Science of Computer Programming 8:231-274, 1987.

[Har 87a]   D. Harel, A. Pnueli, J. P. Schmidt, and R. Sherman. On the formal semantics of state charts. Symposium on Logic in Computer Science, Ithaca, New York, 1987.

[Har 88]   D. Harel. On visual formalisms. Comm. ACM 31(5), 1988.

[Har 90]   D. Harel et al. Statemate: a working environment for the development of complex reactive systems. IEEE Transactions on Software Engineering 16(4), 1990.

[Has 96]   H. Hasse. Einheitliche theorie für korrekte parallele und fehlertolerante Ausführung von Datenbanktransaktionen. Technical Report 11569, ETH Zürich, Department Informatik, 1996.

[HC 93]   M. Hammer, J. Champy. Reengineering the Cooperation, A Manifesto for Business Revolution, HarperBusiness, New York, 1993.

[HCS 97]   L. Hurst, P. Cunningham, and F. Sommers. Mobile agents - smart messages. Proc. First Intl. Workshop on Mobile Agents, Berlin, Germany, April 1997.

[Her 86]   M.P. Herlihy. Optimistic concurrency control for abstract data types. Proc. fifth ACM Symposium on Principles of Distributed Computing, 1986.

[Her90]   M. Herlihy. Apologizing versus asking permission: Optimistic concurrency control for abstract data types. ACM Transactions on Database Systems 15(1):96–124, 1990.

[Hew 97]   Hewlett Packard: AdminFlow. http://www.ice.hp.com/, 1997.

[HF86]   J.R. Hayes and L. Flowers. Writing research and the writer. American Psychologist 41(10):1106–1113, 1986.

[HGM 93]   N.I. Hachem, M.A. Gennert, and M.O. Ward. The gaea system: A spatio-temporal database system for global change studies. In AAAS Workshop on Advances in Data Management for the Scientist and Engineer, Boston, MA, pp. 84–89, February 1993.

[HHSW 96]   Y. Han, J. Himminghofer, T. Schaaf, and D. Wikarski. Management of workflow resources to support runtime adaptability and system evaluation. Proc. PAKM'96, Intl. Conf. on Knowledge Engineering, Basel, Switzerland, October 1996.

[HK 94]   J. Helbig, P. Kelb. An OBDD-Representation of state charts. Proc. European Design and Test Conference, 1994.

[HK 96]   P.C.K. Hung and K. Karlapalem. Task oriented modeling of document security in CapBasED-AMS. In IPIC'96: Intl. Working Conf. on Integration of Enterprise Information and Processes, Cambridge, Massachusetts, November 1996.

[HK 97a]   P.C.K. Hung and K. Karlapalem. A paradigm for security enforcement in CapBasED-AMS. Proc. Second IFCIS Intl. Conf. on Cooperative Information Systems, CoopIS'97, pp. 79–88, 1997.

[HK 97b]   P.C.K. Hung and K. Karlapalem. A logical framework for security enforcement in CapBasED-AMS. Intl. J. of Cooperative Information Systems, December 1997.

[HL 87]   C. Hwang and M. Lin. Group decision making under multiple criteria: methods and applications. Springer-Verlag, 1987.

[HN 95]   D. Harel, A. Naamad. The STATEMATE semantics of state charts. Technical Report, i-Logix Inc., October 1995.

[Hol 95]   D. Hollingsworth. The workflow reference model. Draft 1.1 TC00-1003, Workflow Management Coalition, July 1995.

[Hol 96]   D. Hollingsworth. The workflow reference model. Technical Report TC00-1003, Workflow Management Coalition, http://www.aiai.ed.-ac.uk/WfMC/, December 1996.

[Hol 97]   Holosofx: Workflow Analyzer. http://www.holosofx.com, December 1997.

[Hon 88]   M. Honda. Support for parallel development in the Sun network software environment. Proc. second Int. Workshop on Computer-Aided Software Engineering, pp. 5–7, Cambridge, MA, July 1988.

[HP 94]   HP workManager programming reference. Part No. B2999-90040, April 1994.

[HR 83]   T. Härder and A. Reuter. Principles of transaction-oriented database recovery. ACM Computing Surveys 15(4):287–317, 1983.

[HR 87]   T. Haerder and K. Rothermel. Concepts for transaction recovery in nested transactions. Proc. ACM SIGMOD Conference on Management of Data, 1987.

[HSTR 89]   J. Huang, J.A. Stankovic, D. Towsley, and K. Ramamritham. Experimental evaluation of real-time transaction processing. Proc. 10th Real-Time Systems Symposium, December 1989.

[Hsu 93]   M. Hsu. Special issue on workflow and extended transaction systems. Bulletin of the Technical Committee on Data Engineering 16(2), 1993.

[Hsu 95]   M. Hsu. Special issue on workflow systems. Bulletin of the Technical Committee on Data Engineering, IEEE 18(1), 1995.

[Hu 95]   Patrick Hung. A capability-based activity specification and decomposition for an activity management system. MSc. thesis, The Hong Kong University of Science and Technology, 1995.

[I 93]   Y. Ioannidis (ed.). Special issue on scientific databases. Data Engineering Bulletin 16(1), 1993.

[IBM 94]   IBM FlowMark, Modeling Workflow. IBM Corporation, September 1994.

[IBM 95]   IBM. FlowMark - Managing Your Workflow, Version 2.1. IBM, March 1995. Document No. SH19-8243-00.

[IBM 96]   IBM. IBM FlowMark: Modeling Workflow, Version 2 Release 2. Publ. No SH-19-8241-01, 1996.

[Ibm 97]   IBM: FlowMark. http://www.software.ibm.com, 1997.

[IF 97]   ICL and Fujitsu: ProcessWise. http://www.process.icl.net.co.uk, 1997.

[Ids 97]   IDS-Scheer: Aris Toolset. http://www.ids-scheer.de, 1997.

[ILGP 96]   Y. Ioannidis, M. Livny, S. Gupta, and N. Ponnekanti. ZOO: A desktop experiment management environment. Proc. 22nd Intl. Conf. on Very Large Data Bases, pp. 274–285, 1996.

[InConcert] InConcert. Technical product overview. XSoft, a division of Xerox. 3400 Hillview Avenue, Palo Alto, CA 94304. http://www.xsoft.com.

[InC 97]   InConcert. http://www.inconcertsw.com. 1997.

[Iona 96]   Orbix Reference Guide, Iona Technologies Ltd., 1996.

[Iona 97]   Iona Technologies Ltd, Dublin. See http://www.iona.com/

[J 94]   S. Jablonski. MOBILE: A Modular Workflow Model and Architecture. Proc. 4th Intl. Working Conf. on Dynamic Modeling and Information Systems, The Netherlands 1994.

[J+ 96]   Juopperi, J., Lehtola, A., Pihlajamaa, O., Sladek, A., Veijalainen, J. Usability of Some Workflow Products in an Inter-organizational Setting. IFIP WG8.1 Working Conference on Information Systems for Decentralized Organization, Norway, 1996.

[JAD+94]   S. Joosten, G. Aussems, M. Duitshof, R. Huffmeijer, and E. Mulder. WA-12: An Empirical Study about the Practice of Workflow Management. University of Twente, Enschede, The Netherlands, July 1994.

[Java 97]   http://www.javasoft.com/

[JB 96]   S. Jablonski and C. Bussler. Workflow Management: Modelling Concepts, Architecture, and Implementation. Intl. Thompson Computer Press, 1996.

[JE 91]   K. Jensen. Coloured petri nets: a high level language for system design and analysis. High level Petri Nets Theory and Application, Springer Verlag, 1991.

[JEJ 95]   I. Jacobson, M. Ericsson, and A. Jacobson. The object advantage, business process reengineering with object technology. ACM Press, Addison-Wesley, 1995.

[JK 97]   S. Jajodia and L. Kerschberg (eds.). Advanced Transaction Models and Architectures. Kluwer Academic Publishers, 1997.

504   References

[JNRS 93]   W. Jin, L. Ness, M. Rusinkiewicz, and A. Sheth. Concurrency control and recovery of multidatabase work flows in telecommunication applications. Proc. ACM SIGMOD Conference, May 1993.

[JRS 95]   D. Johansen, R. van Renesse, and F. B. Schneider. An introduction to the TACOMA distributed system. Technical Report 95-23, University of Tromso, Norway, 1995.

[JST97]   S. Jablonski, K. Stein, and M. Teschke. Experiences in Workflow Management for Scientific Computing. Proc. Workshop on Workflow Management in Scientific and Engineering Applications (at DEXA97), Toulouse, France, September 1997.

[JUD 96]   A. Jahne, S.D. Urban, and S.W. Dietrich. A prototype environment for active rule debugging. J. of Intelligent Information Systems 7(2):111–128, 1996.

[JZ 96]   H. Jasper and O. Zukunft. Zeitaspekte bei der Modellierung und Ausfuhrung von Workflows. In Geschaftsprozessmodellierung und Workflowsysteme, S. Jablonski, H. Groiss, R. Kaschek and W. Liebhart (eds.), Proc. Reihe der Informatik '96 2, pp. 109-119, Oldenburg, 1996.

[K 93]   L.A. Kalinichenko. Specification and implementation of dynamic behaviour in the interoperable environment of information resources. Russian Academy of Sciences, IPIAN, Technical Report, October 1993.

[K 95]   L.A. Kalinichenko. Structural and behavioral abstractions of the multiactivities intended for their concretizations by the pre-existing behaviors. Second Intl. East-West Database Workshop, Klagenfurt, Springer-Verlag, 1995.

[K+ 96]   P. Krychniak, M. Rusinkiewicz, A. Sheth, G. Thomas, and A. Cichocki. Bounding the effects of compensation under relaxed multi-level serializability. Intl. J. of Parallel and Distributed Databases 4:355–374, 1996.

[K 98]   P. Karagoz. Design and implementation of task handler for a distributed workflow enactment service. MSc. thesis, Dept. of Computer Engineering, Middle East Technical University, 1998.

[KA 95]   L.A. Kalinichenko. SYNTHESIS: a language for description, design and programming of interoperable information resource environment. Institute for Problems of Informatics of the Russian Academy of Sciences, September 1995.

[KAGM 96]   M. Kamath, G. Alonso, R. Günthör, and C. Mohan. Providing high availability in very large workflow management systems. Proc. Fifth Intl. Conf. on Extending Database Technology (EDBT'96), Avignon, France, March 1996. Also available as IBM Research Report RJ9967, IBM Almaden Research Center, July 1995.

[Kai 95]   G.E. Kaiser. Cooperative transactions for multiuser environments. In [Kim 95], chapter 20, pp. 409–433.

[Kap 95]   G. Kappel, P. Lang, S. Rausch-Schott, and W. Retschitzegger. Workflow Management Based on Objects, Rules, and Roles. In: [Hsu 95]

[Kar 97]   G. Karjoth. A Security Model for AGLETS. IEEE Internet Computing 1(4), 1997.

[Kat 90]   R.H. Katz. Towards a unified framework for version modelling in engineering databases. ACM Computing Surveys 22(4), 1990.

[KD 93]   L.A. Kalinichenko. A declarative framework for capturing dynamic behavior in heterogeneous interoperable information resource environment. Proc. RIDE -IMS'93, Vienna, April 1993.

[KE 94]   L.A. Kalinichenko. Emerging semantic-based interoperable informa-
            tion system technology. Computers as our better partners. Proc. Intl.
            IISF/ACM Symposium, Tokyo, World Scientific, 1994.

[KE97]   J. Klingemann and S. Even. The TRANSCOOP demonstrator system,
            chapter 8. In [dBKV 97], 1997.

[Kea93]   W. Kim et al. On resolving semantic heterogeneity in multidatabase
            systems. Distributed and Parallel Databases 1(3), 1993.

[KF 87]   G.E. Kaiser and P.H. Feiler. Intelligent assistance without artificial
            intelligence. Proc. 32th IEEE Computer Society Intl. Conference, pp.
            236–241, San Francisco, CA, February 1987.

[KF 95]   W. Klas, P. Fankhauser et al. Database integration using the open
            object-oriented database system VODAK. In Object Oriented Multid-
            abase Systems: A Solution for Advanced Application, Omran Bukhres,
            Ahmed K. Elmagarmid (eds.), Chapter 14. Prentice Hall, Englewood
            Cliffs, N.J., 1995.

[KGH 98]   K. Karlapalem, J. Gray III, and P. C. K Hung. Issues in document
            security enforcement for activity execution in CApBasED-AMS. Proc.
            12nd Intl. Conf. on Information Networking ICOIN-12, Tokyo, Japan,
            January 1998.

[KGM 93a]   B. Kao and H. Garcia-Molina. Deadline assignment in a distributed
            soft real-time system. Proc. 13th Intl. Conf. on Distributed Computing
            Systems, pp. 428–437, 1993.

[KGM 93b]   B. Kao and H. Garcia-Molina. Subtask deadline assignment for com-
            plex distributed soft real-time tasks. Technical Report 93-1491, Stan-
            ford University, 1993.

[KH 94]   L.A. Kalinichenko. Homogeneous localization of structural interactiv-
            ity dependencies in megaprograms using scripts. Proc. Intl. Work-
            shop on Advances in Databases and Information Systems (ADBIS'94),
            Moscow, May 1994.

[Kim 95]   W. Kim (ed.). Modern database systems: the object model, interoper-
            ability, and beyond. Addison-Wesley, 1995.

[KL 56]   S.C. Kleene. Representation of events in nerve nets and finite au-
            tomata. Automata Studies, Princeton University Press, Princeton,
            1956.

[Kle 91]   J. Klein. Advanced rule driven transaction management. Proc. 36th
            IEEE Computer Society Intl. Conf. CompCon Spring 1991, pp. 562–
            567, San Francisco, CA, March 1991.

[KLS 90]   H.F. Korth, E. Levy, and A. Silberschatz. A formal approach to recov-
            ery by compensating transactions. Proc. 16th VLDB Conf., Brisbane,
            Australia, 1990.

[KNS 92]   G. Keller, M. Nuttgens, and A.W. Scheer. Semantische prozessmod-
            ellierung auf der grundlage ereignisgesteuerter prozessketten (EPK).
            In Veroeffentlichungen des Instituts fur Wirtschanftsinformatik, A.W.
            Scheer (ed.), No. 89, Saarbruecken, 1992.

[Kok 97]   P. Koksal, S. Arpinar, and A. Dogac. Workflow history management.
            ACM SIGMOD Record, 27(1):67–75, March 1998.

[Kor 83]   H.F. Korth. Locking primitives in a database system. J. of the ACM,
            30(1):55–79, 1983.

[Kor 94]   P. Korzeniowski. Workflow software automates processes. Software
            Magazine, February 1993.

[Kor 95]   H.F. Korth. The double life of the transaction abstraction: fundamen-
            tal principle and evolving system concept. Proc. 21st Intl. Conf. on

Very Large Databases (VLDB), pp. 2–6, Zurich, Switzerland, September 1995.

[KP 92]   G.E. Kaiser and C. Pu. Dynamic restructuring of transactions. In [Elm 92], Chapter 8, pp. 265–295.

[KPS 89]   G.E. Kaiser, D.E. Perry, and W.M. Schell. Infuse: fusing integration test management with change management. Proc. 13th IEEE Computer Software and Applications Conf., pp. 552–558, Orlando, FL, September 1989.

[KR 96]   M. Kamath and K. Ramamritham. Correctness issues in workflow management. Distributed System Engineering 3(4), 1996.

[KR 96b]   M. Kamath and K. Ramamritham. Bridging the gap between transaction Management and workflow management. In [She 96].

[KS 94]   N. Krishnakumar and A. Sheth. Specification of workflow with heterogeneous tasks in Meteor. VLDB 1994.

[KS 95]   N. Krishnakumar and A. Sheth. Managing heterogeneous multi-system tasks to support enterprise-wide operations. Distributed and Parallel Databases 3(2):1–33, 1995.

[KS 96]   H. Kaufmann and H.-J. Schek. Extending TP-Monitors for intra-transaction parallelism. Proc. 4th Intl. Conf. on Parallel and Distributed Information Systems (PDIS'96), Miami Beach, FL, December 1996.

[KSK 93]   N. Kamel, T. Song, and M. Kamel. *An approach for building an integrated environment for molecular biology databases.* Distributed and Parallel Databases 1, 303–327, 1993.

[KSM 97]   K. Kochut, A. Sheth, and J. Miller. ORBWork: a dynamic workflow enactment service for METEOR$_2$, 1997.

[KSUW 85]   P. Klahold, G. Schlageter, R. Unland, and W. Wilkes. A transaction model supporting complex applications in integrated information systems. Proc. ACM SIGMOD Conf. on Management of Data, pp. 388–401, Austin, TX, May 1985.

[KTW96a]   J. Klingemann, T. Tesch, and J. Wäsch. Design of the TRANSCOOP cooperative transaction manager. Report DV.3, Esprit-III LTR Project TRANSCOOP (P8012), May 1996.

[KTW96b]   J. Klingemann, T. Tesch, and J. Wäsch. Semantics-based transaction management for cooperative applications. Proc. Intl. Workshop on Advanced Transaction Models and Architectures (ATMA), pp. 234–252, Goa, India, August – September 1996.

[KTW+96c]   J. Klingemann, T. Tesch, J. Wäsch, J. Puustjärvi, and J. Veijalainen. Definition of the TRANSCOOP cooperative transaction model. Report DV.2, Esprit-III LTR Project TRANSCOOP (P8012), April 1996.

[KTW97a]   J. Klingemann, T. Tesch, and J. Wäsch. Cooperative data management and its application to mobile computing. Intl. J. on Cooperative Information Systems, 1997.

[KTW97b]   J. Klingemann, T. Tesch, and J. Wäsch. Enabling cooperation among disconnected mobile users. Proc. 2nd IFCIS Intl. Conf. on Cooperative Information Systems (CoopIS), June 1997.

[KTWK97]   J. Klingemann, T. Tesch, J. Wäsch, and W. Klas. The TRANSCOOP transaction model. In [dBKV 97], Chapter 7.

[KYH 95]   K. Karlapalem, H.P. Yeung, and P.C.K. Hung. CapBasED-AMS: a framework for capability-based and event-driven activity management system. Proc. 3rd Intl. Conf. on Cooperative Information Systems, 1995.

[LA 94]   F. Leymann and W. Alterhuber. Managing business processes as an information resource. IBM Systems J. 33, 326–347, 1994.

[Lam 77]   L. Lamport. Proving the correctness of multiprocess programs. IEEE Transactions on Software Engineering 3(2), 1977.

[Lan 88]   G. Langram. Temporal GIS design tradeoffs. Proc. GIS/LIS, pp. 890–899, November 1988.

[Law 97]   P. Lawrence (ed.). Workflow handbook 1997. Wiley, 1997.

[LdBTW 97] A. Lehtola, R. de By, H. Tirri, and J. Wäsch. The TRANSCOOP architecture. In [dBKV 97], Chapter 5, 1997.

[LE 96]   J.L. Lee. Integrating information from disparate contexts: a theory of semantic interoperability, PhD thesis, MIT, June 1996.

[Le 97]   J. Lyon and K. Evans, and J. Klein. Transaction Internet Protocol (TIP). Technical Report draft-lyon-tip-nodes.02.txt, Tandem and Microsoft, February 1997.

[LeG96]   J-M Le Goff et al. CRISTAL: cooperating repositories and an information system for tracking assembly lifecycles. CMS NOTE 1996/003.

[Ley 95]   F. Leymann. Supporting business transactions via partial backward recovery in workflow management systems. GI-Fachtagung Datebanken in Buro, Technik und Wissenchaft (BTW), Dresden, Germany, Springer-Verlag, 1995.

[Ley 96]   F. Leymann. Transaction concepts for workflow management systems (in German). In [VB 96].

[LHC93]   The Large Hadron Collider Accelerator Project, CERN AC93-03 1993.

[LI 92]   L. Liu and R. Meersman. Activity model: a declarative approach for capturing communication behavior in object-oriented databases. Proc. 18th Intl. Conf. on Very Large Data Bases, Vancouver, August 1992.

[Lin97]   C. Lin. A graphical workflow designer for the METEOR$_2$ workflow management system. MSc thesis, in preparation, University of Georgia, Athens, GA, 1997.

[LL 73]   C.L. Lin and J. Layland. Scheduling algorithms for multiprogramming in hard real-time environments. J. of the ACM 20(1):46–61, 1973.

[LM 96]   L. Liu and R. Meersman. The building blocks for specifying communication behavior of complex objects: an activity-driven approach. ACM Transactions on Database Systems 21(2), 1996.

[LMWF94]   N. Lynch, M. Merrit, W. Weihl, and A. Fekete. Atomic transactions. Morgan-Kaufmann, 1994.

[Lotus 96a] Lotus Corporation. Lotus white paper: notes release 4 application development primer. http://www.lotus.com/ntsdoc96/22de.htm.

[Lotus 96b] Bolin and Ordonez. Lotus Notes: the complete reference. McGraw-Hill, 1996.

[LP 97]   L. Liu and C. Pu. An adaptive object-oriented approach to integration and access of heterogeneous information sources. Distributed and Parallel Databases 5(2), 1997.

[LPBZ 96]   L. Liu, C. Pu, R. Barga, and T. Zhou. Differential evaluation of continual queries. IEEE Proc. 16th Intl. Conf. on Distributed Computing Systems, Hong Kong, May 1996.

[LPL 96]   L. Liu, C. Pu, and Y. Lee. An adaptive approach to query mediation across heterogeneous databases. Proc. Intl. Conf. on Coopertive Information Systems, Brussels, June 1996.

[LR 94]   F. Leymann and D. Roller. Business process management with Flowmark. Proc. 39th IEEE Computer Society Intl. Conf., pp. 230–233, San Francisco, CA, February 1994, http://www.software.ibm.com/-workgroup.

[LSV96]   F. Leymann, H.-J. Schek, and G. Vossen. Transactional workflows, 1996. Dagstuhl Seminar 9629.

[LV 90]   D.P. Lanter and H. Veregin. A lineage meta-database program for propagating error in Geographic Information Systems. Proc. GIS/LIS, pp. 144–153, November 1990.

[LV97]   R. Laddaga and J. Veitch (guest eds.). Dynamic object technology. Comm. ACM 40(5):37–69, 1997.

[M 78]   D. Malone. Strategic planning: applications of ISM and related techniques. Proc. Intl. Conf. on Cybernetics and Society, 1978.

[M 79]   H. Mintzberg. The structuring of organizations. Prentice-Hall, 1979.

[M 81]   J.E.B. Moss. Nested transactions: an approach to reliable computing. MIT Report mit-lcs-tr-260, April 1981.

[M 82]   J.E.B. Moss. Nested transactions and reliable distributed computing. Proc. IEEE Symposium on Reliability in Distributed Software and Database Systems, 1982.

[M 85]   E. Moss. Nested transactions. MIT Press, 1985.

[M 87]   J.E.B. Moss. Log-based recovery for nested transactions. Proc. 13th Intl. Conf. on Very Large Databases, 1987.

[M 89]   D. McCarthy and U. Dayal. The architecture of an active database system. Proc. ACM-SIGMOD'89, 1989.

[M 93]   H. Mintzberg. Structure in fives: designing effective organizations. Prentice-Hall, 1993.

[M 95]   N. Muller. Focus on OpenView. CBM Books, 1995.

[M⁺ 96]   E. Mesrobian, R. Muntz, E. Shek, S. Nittel, M. LaRouche, and M. Kriguer. OASIS: An Open Architecture Scientific Information Systems. Proc. 6th Intl. Workshop on Research Issues in Data Engineering 1996, 107–116.

[MAGK 95]   C. Mohan, G. Alonso, R. Gunthor, M. Kamath. Exotica: a research perspective of workflow management systems. Data Engineering Bulletin 18(1), 1995.

[Man92]   F. Manola et al. Distributed object management. Intl. J. of Intelligent and Cooperative Information Systems 1(1), March 1992.

[Mar 94]   R. Marshak. Software to support BPR: the value of capturing process definitions. Workgroup Computing Report, Patricia Seybold Group, 17(7), July 1994.

[McC 92]   S. McCready. There is more than one kind of workflow software. Computerworld, November 1992.

[MB 91]   D. McCarthy, M. Bluestein. Workflow's progress. The Computing Strategy Report, 8(12), Forrester Research, Inc., 1991.

[MC 96]   R. Medina-Mora and K. Cartron. Action workflow in use: Clark County Department of Business License. Proc. 12nd Intl. Conf. on Data Engineering, New Orleans, LA, February 1996.

[McM 93]   K.L. McMillan. Symbolic model checking. Kluwer Academic Publishers, 1993.

[Met 97]   MetaSoftware. http://www.metasoftware.com, 1997.

[MF 96]   Meta-Object Facility. RFP, OMG, cf/96-05-02.

[MG 88]   D. Marca and C.L. McGowan. SADT, McGraw-Hill, 1988.

[MG 91]   D. Marca and C.L. McGowan. IDEF0/SADT business process and enterprise modeling. Eclectic Solutions, 1991.

[MH 94]   C. Mohan and D. Haderle. Algorithms for flexible space management in transaction systems supporting fine granularity locks. Proc. EDBT'94 Conf., Cambridge, UK, pp. 131–144, March 1994.

[MHR 96]   B. Mitschang, T. Haerder, and N. Ritter. Design management in CON-CORD: combining transaction management, workflow management, and cooperative control. RIDE, New Orleans, 1996.

[MHS 95]   G. Mark, J. Haake, and N. Streitz. The use of hypermedia in group problem solving: an evaluation of the DOLPHIN electronic meeting room environment. European Conf. on Computer Supported Cooperative Work, ECSCW'95, Stockholm, Sweden, September 1995.

[Mil 89]   R. Milner. Communication and concurrency. Prentice-Hall, 1989.

[ML 87]   T. Mitchell and J. Larson Jr. People in organizations. McGraw-Hill, 1987.

[MLB+ 97]   R. McClatchey, J.-M. Le Geoff, N. Baker, W. Harris, and Z. Kovacs. A distributed workflow and product data management application for the construction of large scale scientific apparatus. In this volume.

[MLK 96]   R. McClatchey, J.-M. Le Goff, and Z. Kovacs. An application of workflow management and product data management conventions in a distributed scientific environment. Manuscript, 1996.

[MN 95]   M. Marazakis and C. Nikolaou. Towards adaptive scheduling of tasks in transactional workflows. In Winter Simulation Conf., Washington DC, 1995.

[MO 94]   C. Morgan. Programming from specifications. Prentice-Hall, 1994.

[Moh 96]   C. Mohan. State of the art in workflow management research and products. Tutorial Notes, SIGMOD, Montreal, Canada, 1996.

[MP 92]   Z. Manna and A. Pnueli. The temporal logic of reactive and concurrent systems: specification. Springer-Verlag, 1992.

[MPSK 97]   J. Miller, D. Palaniswami, A. Sheth, and K. Kochut. WebWork: Meteor$_2$'s web-based workflow management system. University of Georgia, UGA-CS-97-002, 1997.

[MRKN 92]   P. Muth, T.C. Rakow, W. Klas, and E.J. Neuhold. A transaction model for an open publication environment. In [Elm 92], Chapter 6, pp. 159–218.

[MRS 96]   Y. Minsky, R. van Renesse, and F.B. Schneider. Cryptographic support for fault-tolerant distributed computing. Proc. 7th ACM SIGOPS European Workshop on Systems Support for Worldwide Applications, Connemara, Ireland, September 1996.

[MRW+ 93]   P. Muth, T.C. Rakow, G. Weikum, P. Brössler, and C. Hasse. Semantic concurrency control in object-oriented database systems. Proc. 9th IEEE Intl. Conf. on Data Engineering, pp. 233–242, Vienna, Austria, April 1993.

[MS 93]   D. McCarthy and S. Sarin. Workflow and transactions in Inconcert. Bulletin of the Technical Committee on Data Engineering, IEEE Computer Society, 16(2), 1993.

[MSKW 96]   J.A. Miller, A. Sheth, K.J. Kochut, and X. Wang. Corba-based runtime architectures for workflow management systems. J. of Database Management, Special Issue on Multidatabases, Vol. 7, 1996.

[Mut 97]   P. Muth, D. Wodtke, J. Weissenfels, A.K. Dittrich, and G. Weikum. From centralized workflow specification to distributed workflow execution, 1997.

[MV+ 96]   C.B. Medeiros, G. Vossen, and M. Weske. GEO-WASA: supporting geoprocessing applications using workflow management. Proc. 7th Israeli Conf. on Computer Systems and Software Engineering, Herzliya, Israel 1996, 129–139, IEEE Computer Society Press, Los Alamitos, CA.

510   References

[MVW 96]   J. Meidanis, G. Vossen, and M. Weske. Using workflow management
             in DNA sequencing. Proc. 1st Intl. Conf. on Cooperative Information
             Systems (CoopIS96), Brussels, Belgium, June 1996.
[MWFF 92]   R. Medina-Mora, T. Winograd, R. Flores, and F. Flores. The action
             workflow approach to workflow management technology. Proc. ACM
             Conf. on Computer Supported Cooperative Work (CSCW'92), ACM
             Press, Toronto, Ontario, pp. 281–288, 1992.
[N 90]   M. Nodine and S. Zdonik. Cooperative transaction hierarchy: a trans-
             action model to support design applications. Proc. of VLDB'90, 1990.
[N⁺ 91]   J. Nunamaker, A. Dennis, J. Valacich, D. Vogel, and J. George. Elec-
             tronic meeting systems to support group work. Comm. ACM 34(7),
             1991.
[NSSW 94]   M.C. Norrie, W. Schaad, H.-J. Schek, and M. Wunderli. Exploiting
             multidatabase technology for CIM. Technical report, Computer Sci-
             ence Department, Database Research Group, ETH Zürich, July 1994.
[NZ 92]   M.H. Nodine, S.B. Zdonik. Cooperative transaction hierarchies: trans-
             action support for design applications. VLDB Journal 1, pp. 41 – 80,
             1992.
[O 94]   J. Ousterhout. Tcl and the Tk Toolkit. Addison-Wesley, 1994.
[Obe 94]   R. Obermack. Special issue on TP monitors and distributed trans-
             action management. Bulletin of the Technical Committee on Data
             Engineering, IEEE, 17(1), March 1994.
[Obe 96]   A. Oberweis. Modeling and execution of workflows with Petrinets (in
             German). Teubner, 1996.
[OD 95]   R. Ortiz and P. Dadam. Towards the boundary of concurrency. Proc.
             2nd Intl. Conf. on Concurrent Engineering Research and Applications,
             1995.
[ODV 93]   T. Ozsu, U. Dayal, and P. Valduriez. Distributed object management.
             Morgan-Kaufmann, 1993.
[OHE 96]   R. Orfali, D. Harkey, J. Edwards. The essential distributed objects
             survival guide. Wiley, 1996.
[Old 91]   E.-R. Olderog. Nets, terms, and formulas: three views of concurrent
             processes and their relationship. Cambridge University Press, 1991.
[OMG 91]   Object Management Group and X/Open. The Common Object Re-
             quest Broker: architecture and specification. OMG Document 91-12-1,
             1991.
[OMG 92]   The Object Management Architecture guide, version 2.1. OMG Pubs,
             1992. The Common Object Request Broker: architecture and specifi-
             cations. OMG Pubs, 1992.
[OMG 94]   Object analysis and design: analysis of methods, OMG. Wiley, 1994.
[OMG 95]   CORBA services: Common Object Services Specification. Transaction
             Service:V 1.0, OMG Document, March 1995.
[OMG 96a]   Object Management Group Publications, Common Facilities RFP-5
             (Meta-Object Facility) TC Document cf/96-02-01 R2, 5/13/96.
[OMG 96b]   Object Management Group Publications, Product Data Management
             Enablers RFP, Manufacturing Domain Task Force Document mfg/96-
             08-01.
[OMG 96c]   Object analysis and design facility RFP-1, OMG, ad/96-05-01.
[OMG 97]   Object Management Group, http://www.omg.org, 1997.
[ONK⁺ 96]   F. Ozcan, S. Nural, P. Koksal, C. Evrendilek, and A. Dogac. Dy-
             namic query optimization on a distributed object management plat-
             form. Proc. 5th Intl. Conf. on Information and Knowledge Manage-
             ment (CIKM), MD, 1996.

[OSS 94]   A. Oberweis, G. Scherrer, and W. Stucky. INCOME/STAR: methodology and tools for the development of distributed information systems. Information Systems, 19(8), 1994.

[OT97]   ODP Trading Function - Part 1: specification. ISO/IEC IS 13235-1, ITU/T Draft Rec X950 - 1, 1997.

[P 87]   J. Porras, Stream analysis: a powerful way to diagnose and manage organizational change. Addison-Wesley, 1987.

[P 92a]   G. Pernul. Canonical security modeling for federated databases. Proc. IFIP TC2/WG2.6 Conf. on Semantics of Interoperable Database Systems, 1992.

[P 92b]   G. Pernul. Security constraint processing during multilevel secure database design. Proc. IEEE Computer Security Applications Conf., 1992.

[PA 81]   D. Park. Concurrency and automata on infinite sequences. LNCS 104, Springer-Verlag, 1981.

[PAGM 96]   Y. Papakonstantinou, S. Abiteboul, and H. Garcia-Molina. Object fusion in mediator systems. Proc. VLDB 96, Bombay, India, September 1996.

[PBE 95]   E. Pitoura, O. Bukhres, and A. Elmagarmid. Object orientation in multidatabase systems. ACM Computing Surveys 27(3), June 1995.

[PEL 97]   H. Pozewaunig, J. Eder, and W. Liebhart. ePERT: Extending PERT for workflow management systems. Proc. 1st East-European Symposium on Advances in Database and Information Systems ADBIS '97, St. Petersburg, Russia, September 1997.

[Pet77]   J.L. Peterson. Petri-Nets. Computing Surveys 9(3), 1977.

[PGGU 95]   Y. Papakonstantinou, A. Gupta, H. Garcia-Molina, and J. Ullman. A query translation scheme for rapid implementation of wrappers. Proc. Intl. Conf. on Deductive and Object-Oriented Databases, 1995.

[PGMU 96]   Y. Papakonstantinou, H. Garcia-Molina, and J. Ullman. Medmaker: a mediation system based on declarative specifications. Proc. ICDE 96, pp. 132–141, New Orleans, February 1996.

[PGMW 95]   Y. Papakonstantinou, H. Garcia-Molina, and J. Widom. Object exchange across heterogeneous information sources. Proc. ICDE 95, pp. 251–260, Taipei, Taiwan, March 1995.

[PGP 89]   B. Patton, K. Giffin, and E.Patton. Decision-making group interaction. HarperCollins, 1989.

[PKH 88]   C. Pu, G.E. Kaiser, and N. Hutchinson. Split-transactions for open-ended activities. Proc. 14th Intl. Conf. on Very Large Databases (VLDB), pp. 26–37, Los Angeles, CA, August 1988.

[PO94]   J. Peters, M.T. Ozsu. Reflection in a uniform behavioural object model. In Lecture Notes in Computer Science 823, R.A. Elmasri, V. Kouramajian, B. Thalheim (eds.), pp. 34–45, Springer-Verlag, 1994.

[PR 96]   E. Panagos and M. Rabinovich. Escalations in workflow management systems. Proc. DART Workshop, Rockville, MD, November 1996.

[PR 97]   E. Panagos and M. Rabinovich. Predictive workflow management. Proc. 3rd Intl. Workshop on Next Generation Information Technologies and Systems, Neve Ilan, Israel, June 1997.

[Pri 94]   F. Primastava. TUXEDO: An open approach to OLTP. Prentice-Hall, 1994.

[PS 90]   V.O. Pince and R.M. Shapiro. An integrated software development methodology based on hierarchical colored Petri nets. In Advances in Petri Nets, G. Rozenberg (ed.), Springer-Verlag, 1990.

[PS 97]   H. Peine and T. Stolpmann. The architecture of the Ara platform for mobile agents. Lecture Notes in Computer Science, 1219. Springer-Verlag, 1997.

[R 55]   J. Ross. Elections and electors. Eyre and Spottiswoode, London, 1955.

[R 89]   M. Rusinkiewcizh et al. OMNIBASE: design and implementation of a multidatabase system. Proc. 1st Annual Symposium in Parallel and Distributed Processing, pp. 162–169, Dallas, May 1989.

[R 91]   S. Ram. Special issue on heterogeneous distributed database systems. IEEE Computer Magazine 24(12), 1991.

[R 92]   S. Robbins. Essentials of organizational behavior. Prentice-Hall, 1992.

[R 97]   M. Reichert and P. Dadam. A framework for dynamic changes in workflow management systems. Proc. 8th Intl. Workshop on Database and Expert Systems Applications 1997, Toulouse, IEEE Computer Society Press, 42–48.

[Rad 86]   E. Radeke. Extending ODMG for federated database systems. Proc. 7th Intl. Conf. on Database and Expert Systems Applications, Zurich, Switzerland, September 1986.

[Rad 91]   F.J. Radermacher. The importance of metaknowledge for environmental information systems. Proc. 2nd Symposium on the Design and Implementation of Large Spatial Databases, Vol. 1, pp. 35–44, August 1991.

[RC 97]   K. Ramamritham and P. K. Chrysanthis. Advances in concurrency control and transaction processing. IEEE Computer Society Executive Briefing, IEEE Computer Society Press, 1997.

[RCN 95]   M. Rusinkiewicz, A. Cichocki, and L. Ness. Towards a transactional model for workflows. Proc. 3rd Intl. Symposium on Applied Corporate Computing, pp. 29–38, Monterrey, Mexico, October 1995.

[RD 94]   B. Rieche and K. Dittrich. A federated DBMS-based integrated environment for molecular biology. Proc. 7th Intl. Working Conf. on Scientific and Statistical Database Management 1994, 118–127.

[Rei 85]   W. Reisig. Petri Nets: an introduction, Springer-Verlag, 1985.

[RKT+95]   M. Rusinkiewicz, W. Klas, T. Tesch, J. Wäsch, and P. Muth. Towards a cooperative transaction model: the cooperative activity model. Proc. 21st Intl. Conf. on Very Large Databases (VLDB), pp. 194–205, Zurich, Switzerland, September 1995.

[RNS 96]   M. Rys, M.C. Norrie, and H.-J. Schek. Intra-transaction parallelism in the mapping of an object model to a relational multi-processor system. Proc. 22nd VLDB Conf., Mumbai (Bombay), India, September 1996.

[RO 90]   M. Rusinkiewicz, S. Osterman, A. Elmagarmid, and K. Loa. The distributed operational language for specifying multisystem application. Proc. 1st Intl. Conf. on Systems Integration, April 1990.

[RS 94]   M. Rusinkiewicz and A. Sheth. Specification and execution of transactional workflows. In Modern Database Systems: The Object Model, Interoperability, and Beyond, W. Kim (ed.), Addison-Wesley, 1994.

[RS 95]   A. Reuter and F. Schwenkreis. ConTracts: a low-level mechanism for building general-purpose workflow management systems. In [Hsu 95].

[RSW 97]   F. Ranno, S. Shrivastava, and S. Wheater. A system for specifying and coordinating the execution of reliable distributed applications. Technical Report, University of Newcastle upon Tyne, England, 1997.

[RVW 97]   T. Reuss, G. Vossen, and M. Weske. Modeling samples processing in laboratory environments as scientific workflows. Proc. 8th Intl. Workshop on Database and Expert Systems Applications 1997, Toulouse, IEEE Computer Society Press, pp. 49–55.

[RWL 96]   T. Reenskaug, P. Wold, and A. Lehne. Working with objects: the Ooram software engineering method. Manning Publications, 1996.

[S 83]   D. Sink. Using the nominal group technique effectively. National Productivity Review, pp. 82–93, Spring 1983.

[S 87]   L. Suchman. Plans and situated actions. Cambridge University Press, 1987

[S 89]   J.M. Spivey. The Z notation. A reference manual, Prentice-Hall, 1989.

[S 91]   A. Sheth. Special issue in multidatabase systems. ACM SIGMOD Record 20(4), December 1991.

[S 95]   M. Silver. The BIS guide to workflow software: a visual comparison of today's leading products. Technical report, BIS Strategic Decisions, Norwell, MA, 1995.

[S 96a]   M. Singh. Synthesizing distributed constrained events from transactional workflow specifications. Proc. 12nd Intl. Conf. on Data Engineering (ICDE'96), New Orleans, February 1996.

[S 96b]   M. Singh. Distributed scheduling of workflow computations. Technical Report, Department of Computer Science, North Carolina State University, 1996.

[S97]   A. Sheth. From contemporary workflow process automation to adaptive and dynamic work activity coordination and collaboration(keynote talk). Proc. Workshop on Workflow Management in Scientific and Engineering Applications at DEXA97, Toulouse, France, September 1997.

[S$^+$ 96]   A. Sheth, D. Georgakopoulos, S. Joosten, M. Rusinkiewicz, W. Scacchi, J. Wileden, and A. Wolf. Report from the NSF workshop on workflow and process automation in information systems. SIGMOD Record 25(4):55–67, December 1996.

[Sch 92]   A.W. Scheer. Architecture of integrated information systems. Springer-Verlag, 1992.

[Sch 96]   H.-J. Schek. Improving the role of future database systems. ACM Computing Surveys 28(4), December 1996.

[SDDC 96]   M. Shan, J. Davis, W. Du, and Q. Chen. Business process flow management and its application in the telecommunication management network. Hewlett-Packard Journal 47(5), 1996.

[SGHH 94]   N. Streitz, J. Geissler, J. Haake, and J. Hol. DOLPHIN: integrated meeting support across local and remote desktop environments and liveboards. Proc. ACM 1994 Conf. on Computer Supported Cooperative Work CSCW '94, Chapel Hill, NC, October 1994.

[Shan 96]   S. Shan. OpenPM: an enterprise business process flow management system. SIGMOD, Montreal, Canada, 1996.

[She 96]   A. Sheth (ed.). Proc. NSF workshop on workflow and process automation in information systems. University of Georgia, May 1996, http://LSDIS.cs.uga.edu/activities/NSF-workflow.

[SHH$^+$ 92]   N. Streitz, J. Haake, J. Hannemann, A. Lemke, W. Schuler, H. Schütt, and M. Thüring. SEPIA: a cooperative hypermedia authoring environment. Proc. 4th ACM Conf. on Hypertext, pp. 11–22, Milan, Italy, Nov. – Dec., 1992.

[SHLL 95]   H. Stark and L. Lachal. OVUM evaluates workflow. OVUM Ltd., UK, 1995.

[SHT89]   N.A. Streitz, J. Hannemann, and M. Thüring. From ideas and arguments to hyperdocuments: travelling through activity spaces. Proc. 2nd ACM Conf. on Hypertext (Hypertext '89), pp. 343–364, Pittsburgh, PA, November 1989.

[SI 95]   K.D. Swenson and K. Irwin. Workflow technology: tradeoffs for business process re-engineering. Proc. COOCS'95, pp. 22–29, Milpitas, CA, 1995.

[Si⁺ 96]   R.M. Sivasankaran, J.A. Stankovic, B. Purimetla, D. Towsley, and K. Ramamritham. Priority assignment in real-time active databases. VLDB Journal 5(1):19–34, 1996.

[Sie96]   . Siegel (ed.). CORBA fundamentals and programming. Wiley, New York, 1996.

[SJ 96]   A.-W. Scheer and W. Jost. Business process modelling within business organizations (in German). In [VB 96].

[SJo 96]   A. Sheth and S. Joosten. Workshop on workflow management: research, technology, products, applications and experiences, August 1996.

[SK 95]   E. Simon and A.K. Dittrich. Promises and realities of active database systems. Proc. Intl. Conf. on Very Large Data Bases, Zurich, 1995.

[SK⁺ 96]   A. Sheth, K. Kochut, J. Miller, D. Worah, S. Das, and C. Lin. Supporting state-wide immunization tracking using multi-paradigm workflow technology. Proc. 22nd Intl. Conf. on Very Large Data Bases, Bombay, India, September 1996. A demo version of this application is at http://lsdis.cs.uga.edu/demos.

[Ska 89]   A.H. Skarra. Concurrency control for cooperating transactions in an object-oriented database. ACM SIGPLAN Notices 24(4):145–147, April 1989.

[SL 90]   A. Sheth and J.A. Larson. Federated database systems for managing distributed, heterogeneous, and autonomous databases. ACM Computing Surveys 22(3):183-236, 1990.

[SR 92]   A. Sheth, M. Rusinkiewicz, and G. Karabatis. Using polytransactions to manage interdependent data. In [Elm 92], Chapter 14.

[SR 93]   A. Sheth and M. Rusinkiewicz. On transactional workflow. IEEE Data Engineering Bulletin, 1993.

[SRG 94]   L. Stein, S. Rozen, and N. Goodman. Managing laboratory workflow with LabBase. Proc. 1994 Conf. on Computers in Medicine.

[SRH 97]   N. Streitz, P. Rexroth, and T. Holmer. Does roomware matter? Investigating the role of personal and public information devices and their combination in meeting room collaboration. Proc. European Conf. on Computer Supported Cooperative Work, ECSCW'97, Lancaster, UK, September 1997.

[SRN 93]   A. Storr, U. Rembold, and B.O. Nnaji. Computer integrated manufacturing and engineering. Addison-Wesley, 1993.

[SS 84]   P. M. Schwarz and A. Z. Spector. Synchronizing shared abstract data types. ACM Transactions on Computer Systems 2(3):223–250, 1984.

[SS 95]   R.M. Soley (ed.) and C.M. Stone. Object Management Architecture guide. 3rd edn., Wiley, 1995.

[SSAE 93]   T.R. Smith, J. Su, D. Agrawal, and A. El Abbadi. Database and modeling systems for the earth sciences. IEEE Bulletin of the Technical Committee on Data Engineering 16(1):33–37, March 1993.

[SSE⁺ 95]   T. Smith, J. Su, A. El Abbadi, D. Agrawal, G. Alonso, and A. Saran. Computational modeling systems. Information Systems 20(2), 1995.

[SSW 95]   W. Schaad, H.-J. Schek, and G. Weikum. Implementation and performance of multi-level transaction management in a multidatabase environment. Proc. 5th Intl. Workshop on Research Issues on Data Engineering, Distributed Object Management, Taipei, Taiwan, 1995.

[ST 96]   B. Salzberg and D. Tombroff. DSDT: durable scripts containing
             database transactions. Proc. 12th Intl. Conf. on Data Engineering,
             New Orleans, LA, February 1996.
[Sun 95]   Sun Microsystems. The Java language specification. Sun Microsys-
             tems, 1995. http://java.sun.com/doc/language_specification.html.
[SW 93]   H.-J. Schek and A. Wolf. From extensible databases to interoperabil-
             ity between multiple databases and GIS applications. Proc. 3rd Intl.
             Symposium on Large Spatial Databases, Singapore, June 1993.
[SW 95]   H. Saastamoinen and G. White, On handling exceptions. Proc. of ACM
             COOCS95, Milpitas, CA, August 1995.
[SWare 95]   Staffware for Windows graphical workflow definer. Staffware plc., 1995.
[SWY 93]   H.-J. Schek, G. Weikum, and H. Ye. Towards a unified theory of con-
             currency control and recovery. Proc. ACM SIGACT/SIGMOD Sym-
             posium on Principles of Database Systems, pp. 300–311, June 1993.
[SZ 91]   T. Schael and B. Zeller, Design principles for cooperative office support
             systems in distributed process management. In Support functionality
             in the office environment, A. Verrijn-Stuart (ed.), North-Holland, 1991.
[SZ 96]   A. Silberschatz and S. Zdonik. Database systems, breaking out of the
             box. http://www.cs.brown.edu/people/sbz/cra/paper.ps, September
             1996.
[T 91]   M. Turoff. Computer-mediated communication requirements for group
             support. J. of Organizational Computing 1(1):85–113, 1991.
[T 98]   N. Tatbul. Guard generation for a distributed workflow enactment ser-
             vice, MSc thesis, Dept. of Computer Engineering, Middle East Tech-
             nical University, January 1998.
[Ta 97]   R. Taylor. Endeavors: useful workflow meets powerful process. Proc.
             Information and Computer Science Research Symposium, University of
             California at Irvine, February 1997, http://www.ics.uci.edu/endeavors.
[Tea 97]   TeamWare. http://www.teamw.com, December 1997.
[TF 95]   B. Thuraisingham and W. Ford. Security constraint processing in
             a multilevel secure distributed database management system. Proc.
             IEEE Transactions on Knowledge and Engineering 7(2), 1995.
[ThS 94]   R.K. Thomas and R.S. Sandhu. Conceptual foundations for a model
             of task-based authorizations. Proc. Computer Security Foundations
             Workshop VII, CSFW 7, 1994.
[Tic 85]   W.F. Tichy. Rcs: a system for version control. Software Practice and
             Experience 15(7):637–654, 1985.
[TJ 95]   A. Tsalgatidou and S. Junginger, Modeling in the reengineering pro-
             cess. SIGOIS Bulletin, ACM 16(1):17-24, August 1995.
[TKP 94]   A.Z. Tong, G.E. Kaiser, and S.S. Popovich. A flexible rule-chaining
             engine for process-based software engineering. Proc. 9th Knowledge-
             Based Software Engineering Conf., Monterey, CA, 1994.
[Tre 96]   M. Tresch. Principles of distributed object database languages. Tech-
             nical Report 248, ETH Zürich, Dept. of Computer Science, July 1996.
[TRV 96]   A. Tomasic, L. Raschid, and P. Valduriez. Scaling heterogeneous
             databases and the design of Disco. Proc. Intl. Conf. on Distributed
             Computer Systems, 1996.
[TRV 97]   A. Tomasic, L. Raschid, and P. Valduriez. A data model and query
             processing techniques for scaling access to distributed heterogeneous
             databases in Disco. IEEE Transactions on Computers, special issue on
             Distributed Computing Systems, 1997.

516   References

[TS 93]   R.K. Thomas and R.S. Sandhu. Towards a task-based paradigm for flexible and adaptable access control in distributed applications. ACM SIGSAC New Security Paradigms Workshop, 1993.

[TS 94]   M. Tresch and M.H. Scholl. A classification of multi-database languages. Proc. 3rd Intl. Conf. on Parallel and Distributed Information Systems (PDIS), Austin, TX, IEEE Computer Society Press, September 1994.

[Tux 94]   TUXEDO System 5. System Documentation, Novell, 1994.

[TV 95]   T. Tesch and P. Verkoulen (ed.). Requirements for the TRANSCOOP transaction model. Report DII.2, Esprit-III LTR Project TRANSCOOP (P8012), January 1995.

[TV 95a]   J. Tang and J. Veijalainen. Transaction-oriented workflow concepts in inter-organization environments. Intl. Conf. on Information and Knowledge Management, Baltimore, 1995.

[TV 95b]   J. Tang and J. Veijalainen. Enforcing inter-task dependencies in transactional workflows. CoopIS 1995.

[TVL⁺ 97]   T. Tesch, P. Verkoulen, A. Lehtola, J. Veijaleinen, O. Pihlajamaa, and A. Sladek. Application requirements, Chapter 4. In [dBKV 97], 1997.

[TW 95]   T. Tesch and J. Wäsch. Transaction support for cooperative hypermedia document authoring: a study on requirements. Proc. 8th ERCIM Database Research Group Workshop on Database Issues and Infrastructure in Cooperative Information Systems, pp. 31–42, Trondheim, Norway, August 1995.

[TWF]   TeamWare Flow. Collaborative workflow system for the way people work. P.O. Box 780, FIN-00101, Helsinki, Finland.

[U 92]   R. Unland and G. Schlageter. A transaction manager development facility for non-standard database systems. In Transaction Models for Advanced Database Applications, A. Elmagarmid (ed.), Morgan-Kaufmann, 1992.

[Ues 97]   UES: KI Shell. http://www.ues.com, December 1997.

[VB 96]   G. Vossen and J. Becker (eds.) Business process modeling and workflow management: models, methods, tools (in German). Intl. Thomson Publishing, Bonn, Germany, 1996.

[VFSE 95]   P.A.C. Verkoulen, F.J. Faase, A.W. Selders, and P.J.J. Oude Egberink. Requirements for an advanced database transaction model to support design for manufacturing. Proc. Flexible Automation and Intelligent Manufacturing Conf., pp. 102–113, Begell House, Inc., Stuttgart, Germany, June 1995.

[VJ 88]   V. Vroom and A. Jago, The new leadership, managing participation in organizations. Prentice-Hall, 1988.

[VLP 95]   J. Veijalainen, A. Lehtola, and O. Pihlajamaa. Research issues in workflow systems. ERCIM Database Research Group Workshop on Database Issues and Infrastructure in Cooperative Information System, Norway, 1995.

[VT95]   P. Verkoulen and T. Tesch (eds.). Requirements for the TRANSCOOP specification language. Report DII.1, Esprit-III LTR Project TRANSCOOP (P8012), January 1995.

[VWP⁺97]   J. Veijaleinen, J. Wäsch, J. Puustjärvi, H. Tirri, and O. Pihlajamaa. Transaction models in cooperative work: an overview. In [dBKV 97], Chapter 3, 1997.

[VWW96]   G. Vossen, M. Weske, and G. Wittkowski. Dynamic workflow management on the web. Fachbericht Angewandte Mathematik und Informatik 24/96-I, University of Müenster, 1996.

[VWW 97]   G. Vossen, M. Weske, and G. Wittkowski. Towards flexible workflow management for scientific applications. Manuscript, University of
Müenster, 1997.

[W 92]   G. Weikum and H.-J Schek. Concepts and applications of multi-
level transactions and open nested transactions. In Transaction Models
for Advanced Database Applications, A. Elmagarmid (ed.), Morgan-
Kaufmann, 1992.

[W 95]   X. Wang. Implementation and performance evaluation of CORBA-
based centralized workflow schedulers. MSc thesis, University of Georgia, August 1995.

[W 96]   G. Wittkowski. Design and implementation of a workflow system in
Java (in German). Diploma thesis, University of Münster, 1996.

[W 97]   M. Weske. Flexible modeling and execution of workflow activities.
Proc. 31st Hawaii Intl. Conf. on System Sciences (HICSS-31), 1998.

[W 97]   E. Weissman. Reasoning about the behavior of an active database.
MSc thesis, Technion-Israel Institute of Technology, July 1997.

[WA 95]   J. Wäsch and K. Aberer. Flexible design and efficient implementation of a hypermedia document database system by tailoring semantic
relationships. Proc. 6th IFIP Conf. on Database Semantics (DS-6),
Atlanta, GA, May – June 1995.

[WA 97]   J. Wäsch and K. Aberer. Flexible design and efficient implementation
of a hypermedia document database system by tailoring semantic relationships. In Database Applications Semantics, R. Meersman and
L. Mark (eds.), Chapman & Hall, 1997. Revised version of [WA 95].

[Waes96a]   J. Wäsch. History merging as a mechanism for information exchange
in cooperative and mobile environments. Datenbank-Rundbrief, Mit-
teilungsblatt der GI-Fachgruppe Datenbanken, Ausgabe 17, May 1996.

[Waes96b]   J. Wäsch (ed.). Design of the TRANSCOOP demonstrator system. Report DVII.1, Esprit-III LTR Project TRANSCOOP (P8012), October
1996.

[WCD 95]   J. Widom, S. Ceri, and U. Dayal (eds). Active database systems.
Morgan-Kaufmann, 1995.

[WCH$^+$93]   D. Woelk, P. Cannata, M. Huhns, W. Shen, and C. Tomlinson. Using
carnot for enterprise information integration. Proc. 2nd Intl. Conf. on
Parallel and Distributed Information Systems, pp. 133–136, January
1993.

[Wei 88]   W. E. Weihl. Commutativity-based concurrency control for abstract
data types. IEEE Transactions on Computers 37(12):1488–1505, 1988.

[Wei 89]   W. E. Weihl. The impact of recovery on concurrency control. Proc.
8th ACM SIGACT-SIGMOD Symposium on Principles of Database
Systems, pp. 259–269, 1989.

[Wei 91]   G. Weikum. Principles and realization strategies of multilevel transaction management. ACM Transactions on Database Systems 16(1),
March 1991.

[Wei 93]   G. Weikum. Extending transaction management to capture more consistency with better performance. Invited Paper. Proc. 9th French
Database Conf., Toulouse, 1993.

[Wei 96]   J. Weissenfels, D. Wodtke, G. Weikum, and A.K. Dittrich. The MEN-
TOR architecture for enterprise-wide workflow management. Proc.
NSF Workshop on Workflow and Process Automation in Information
Systems, Athens, GA, May 1996.

[WF 86]   T. Winograd and F. Flores. Understanding computers and cognition,
Addison-Wesley, 1986.

[WF 97]   Workflow facility draft. RFP. OMG, cf/97-03-14.

[WfMC 94a]   The Workflow Management Coalition Group. A workflow manage-
             ment coalition specification. Technical report, The Workflow Manage-
             ment Coalition, November 1994. http://www.aiai.ed.ac.uk/WfMC/.

[WfMC 94b]   Workflow Management Coalition. Glossary: a workflow management
             coalition specification. Workflow Management Coalition Standard,
             WfMC-TC-1011, 1994.

[WfMC 94c]   Workflow Management Coalition. Workflow reference model. Work-
             flow Management Coalition Standard, WfMC-TC-1003, 1994.

[WfMC 95]   Workgroup1A The Workflow Management Coalition. The workflow
             reference model. Workflow Management Coalition Document, 1995.

[WfM 96]   Workflow   Management   Coalition.   http://www.aiai.ed.ac.uk:80
             /WfMC, 1996.

[WFMC 96]   Workflow Management Coalition glossary and terminology. Document
             Number WFMC-TC-1011, June 1996. http://www.aiai.ed.ac.uk:80/-
             WfMC.

[WfM 97]   Workflow Management Coalition.
             http://www.aiai.ed.ac.uk/WfMC/index.htm, 1997.

[WH 93]   G. Weikum and C. Hasse. Multi-level transaction management for
             complex objects: implementation, performance, parallelism. VLDB
             Journal 2(4), 1993.

[Whi 96]   J. White. Telescript technology: mobile agents. White Paper of General
             Magic, 1996.

[WI 92]   G. Wiederhold, P. Wegner, and S. Ceri. Toward megaprogramming.
             CACM, 35(11), November 1992.

[Wie 92]   Gio Wiederhold. Mediators in the architecture of future information
             systems. IEEE Computer, pp. 38–49, March 1992.

[Wie 95]   Gio Wiederhold. I3 glossary. Draft 7, March 1995.

[WK96]   J. Wäsch and W. Klas.   History merging as a mechanism for
             concurrency control in cooperative environments.   Proc. RIDE-
             Interoperability of Nontraditional Database Systems, pp. 76–85, New
             Orleans, LA, February 1996.

[WL93]   U.K. Wiil and J.J. Leggett. Concurrency control in collaborative hy-
             pertext systems. Proc. 5th ACM Conf. on Hypertext, pp. 14–18, Seat-
             tle, November 1993.

[Wod 96]   D. Wodtke. Modeling and architecture of distributed workflow man-
             agement systems (in German). Dissertation thesis, University of the
             Saarland, 1996.

[Wod 96a]   D. Wodtke, J. Weissenfels, G. Weikum, and K.A. Dittrich. The Mentor
             project: steps towards enterprise-wide workflow management. Proc.
             12nd IEEE Intl. Conf. on Data Engineering (1996), pp. 556–565.

[Wod 97]   D. Wodtke, J. Weissenfels, G. Weikum, A.K. Dittrich, and P. Muth.
             The MENTOR workbench for enterprise-wide workflow management.
             ACM SIGMOD Conf., Demo Program, 1997.

[Wor 97]   D. Worah. Error handling and recovery for the ORBWork workflow
             enactment service in METEOR. MSc thesis, LSDIS Lab, Computer
             Science Department, University of Georgia, May 1997.

[WR 92]   H. Waechter and A. Reuter. The ConTract model. In Database
             Transaction Models for Advanced Applications, A. Elmagarmid (ed.),
             Morgan-Kaufmann, 1992.

[WS 96]   D. Worah and A. Sheth. What do advanced transaction models have
             to offer for workflows? Proc. Intl. Workshop on Advanced Transaction
             Models and Architectures, Goa, India, 1996.

[WS 97]   D. Worah and A. Sheth. Transactions in transactional workflows. In Advanced Transaction Models and Architectures, S. Jajodia and L. Kerschberg (eds.), Kluwer Academic Publisher, 1997.

[WVM 96]   M. Weske, G. Vossen, and C.B. Medeiros. Scientific workflow management: WASA architecture and applications. Fachbericht Angewandte Mathematik und Informatik 03/96-I, University of Münster, 1996. http://wwwmath.uni-muenster.de/ dbis/Weske/Common/wasa.html.

[WW 97]   D. Wodtke and G. Weikum. A formal foundation for distributed workflow management based on state charts. Proc. 6th Intl. Conf. on Database Theory, Delphi, Greece, January 1997.

[Y 95]   H. Yeung. An event-driven activity execution for an activity management system. MSc thesis, The Hong Kong University of Science and Technology, 1995.

[YOL97]   L.L. Yan, T. Ozsu, and L. Liu. Accessing heterogeneous data through homogenization and integration mediators. Proc. 2nd IFCIS Conf. on Cooperative Information Systems (CoopIS-97), Charleston, SC, June 1997.

[Zhe97]   K. Zheng. Designing workflow processes in METEOR$_2$ workflow management system. MSc thesis, LSDIS Lab, Computer Science Department, University of Georgia, June 1997.

Index

NATO ASI Series F

NATO ASI Series F

Including Special Programmes on Sensory Systems for Robotic Control (ROB) and on Advanced Educational Technology (AET)